11/04

Encyclopedia of
the Crusades

Encyclopedia of
the Crusades

Alfred J. Andrea

Greenwood Press
Westport, Connecticut • London

Library of Congress Cataloging-in-Publication Data

Andrea, Alfred J., 1941–
  Encyclopedia of the crusades / by Alfred J. Andrea.
      p. cm.
  Includes bibliographical references and index.
  ISBN 0–313–31659–7 (alk. paper)
  1. Crusades—Encyclopedias. 2. Europe—History, Military—Encyclopedias.
3. Europe—Church history—600–1500—Encyclopedias. 4. Islamic Empire—
History, Military—Encyclopedias. I. Title.
D155.A6   2003
909.07—dc21   2003048544

British Library Cataloguing in Publication Data is available.

Library of Congress Catalog Card Number: 2003048544
ISBN: 0–313–31659–7

First published in 2003

Greenwood Press, 88 Post Road West, Westport, CT 06881
An imprint of Greenwood Publishing Group, Inc.
www.greenwood.com

Printed in the United States of America

The paper used in this book complies with the
Permanent Paper Standard issued by the National
Information Standards Organization (Z39.48–1984).

10 9 8 7 6 5 4 3 2 1

This book is dedicated with love to my son and daughter:
Peter Damian and Kristina Ladas Andrea

Contents

Preface	xiii
Acknowledgments	xv
Introduction	xvii
Abbasids	1
Acre	1
Adhémar of Monteil	3
Al-Adil	4
Adrianople	4
Agnes of Courtenay	5
Aimery of Lusignan	5
Albigensian Crusade	6
Aleppo	10
Alexius I Comnenus	10
Alice of Antioch	12
Alice of Champagne	12
Almohads	13
Almoravids	14
Amalric	14
Anatolia	16
Al-Andalus	16
Anna Comnena	16
Antioch	17
Apocalypse and the Crusades	19
Armenia	21
Armor	22
Ascalon	26
Assassins	27
Ayn Jalut, Battle of	29
Ayyubids	29

Bailli	31
Baldwin I (of Boulogne)	31
Baldwin II (of Le Bourcq)	33
Baldwin III	33
Baldwin IV	34
Baldwin V	35
Baldwin IX of Flanders and I of Constantinople	35
Balian II of Ibelin	36
Baltic Crusades	38
Baybars	39
Bernard of Clairvaux	41
Bohemond I of Taranto	42
Bohemond II	44
Bull, Papal	44
Byzantine Empire	45
Cairo	49
Calixtus II, Pope	50
Cannibalism	51
Capetians	52
Carmelites	55
Castles, Crusader	55
Cathars	59
Cavalry	60
Charles of Anjou	61
Children's Crusade	63
Chivalry	64
Christians, Eastern	65
Chronicles	68
Cid, El	68
Cîteaux, Order of	70
Clermont, Council of	72
Conrad of Montferrat	73
Constance of Antioch	74
Constantinople	75
Constantinople, Latin Empire of	77
Councils and Synods	79
Criticism of the Crusades	80
Cross, Crusader's	81
Cross, True	83
Crusade of 1122–1126	83
Crusade of 1239–1241	84
Crusader States	86
Cyprus	89
Damascus	93
Damascus Crusade	93

Damietta   94
Deus Vult (God Wills It)   95
Disease   95
Dominicans   96
Dorylaeum, Battle of   96
Edessa   99
Edward I   100
Eighth Crusade   101
Eleanor of Aquitaine   102
Eugenius III, Pope   103
Eustace III of Boulogne   104
Fatimids   105
Feudalism   105
Field of Blood, Battle of the   107
Fifth Crusade   108
Financing the Crusades   113
First Crusade   116
Fourth Crusade   122
Francis of Assisi   128
Frankish Greece (Latin Greece)   130
Franks   132
Friars, Mendicant   132
Fulcher of Chartres   133
Fulk of Anjou   133
Fulk of Neuilly   134
German Crusade   137
Gesta Francorum (The Deeds of the Franks)   138
Godfrey of Bouillon   139
Great German Pilgrimage of 1064–1065   140
Greeks   141
Gregory VII, Pope   141
Gregory IX, Pope   142
Gregory X, Pope   142
Guy of Lusignan   143
Hattin, Battle of   147
Henry of Champagne   148
Heretics   149
High Court (Haute Cour)   150
Historians and Chroniclers, Islamic   151
Historians and Chroniclers, Latin   152
Hohenstaufens   155
Holy Land   158
Holy Sepulcher, Church of the   159
Holy War/Just War   160
Honorius III, Pope   161

Hospitalers   163
Hugh of Vermandois   164
Indulgence, Crusade   165
Infantry   166
Infidel   167
Innocent III, Pope   167
Investiture Controversy   169
Isaac II Angelus   170
Isabella I   171
Isabella (Yolanda) II   172
Islam   172
Islamic Peoples   174
Jaffa   177
James of Vitry   178
Jerusalem, City of   178
Jerusalem, Kingdom of   182
Jerusalem, Latin Patriarchate of   184
Jews and the Crusades   185
Jihad   188
John of Brienne   189
Al-Kamil Muhammad, Nasir ad-Din   191
Kerbogha (Karbuqa; Kerbuqa)   192
Khorezmians (Khwarazmians; Khwarismians)   193
Kilij Arslan I   194
La Forbie, Battle of   195
Lance, Holy   195
Languedoc   197
Las Navas de Tolosa, Battle of   197
Latin East   198
Latins   198
Lazarus, Order of Saint   198
Legates, Papal   199
Levant   199
Louis IX   200
Mamluks (Mameluks)   203
Manuel I Comnenus   206
Manzikert, Battle of   207
Margaret of Provence   208
Maria of Montferrat   208
Massacres   209
Melisende   210
Mercenaries   211
Middle East   213
Military Orders   213
Military Orders of Iberia   215

Military Orders of the Baltic   216
Missionaries   216
Mongols   218
Montferrat, Family of   221
Montjoie   222
Moors   222
Mosul   222
Noncombatants   225
Normans   226
Nur ad-Din Mahmud (Nur ed-Din; Nur al-Din)   227
Oliver of Paderborn   229
Ottomans   230
Outremer   231
Papacy, Roman   233
Paschal II, Pope   234
Peace and Truce of God   235
Pelagius   235
Peter the Hermit   236
Philip IV   238
Pilgrimage   239
Pillage and Plunder   241
Political Crusades   243
Poulain   245
Preaching   246
Prester John   247
Prisoners   248
Privileges, Crusader   250
Raymond IV of Saint-Gilles   253
Reconquista   255
Recruitment   261
Relics   261
Reynald of Châtillon   263
Ribauds   265
Richard I the Lionheart   265
Robert II of Flanders   268
Robert II of Normandy   269
Roger of Salerno   271
Saints, Warrior   273
Saladin (al-Malik al-Nasir Salah ad-Din Yusuf Ibn Ayyub)   274
Santiago de Compostela   277
Saracens   278
Second Crusade   278
Seljuks (Selchüks, Seljukids, Selchükids)   283
Sergeant   284
Settlement and Colonization   285

Seventh Crusade   289
Shepherds' Crusade (Crusade of the Pastoureaux of 1251)   292
Shia   293
Sibylla (Sibyl; Sybil)   294
Siege Warfare   295
Sixth Crusade   300
Slavery   303
Song of Roland, The   304
Stephen of Blois and Chartres   305
Sunnism   307
Syria-Palestine   307
Tafurs   309
Tancred   309
Templars   311
Teutonic Knights   314
Third Crusade   315
Transjordan   320
Tripoli   320
Turcopoles   322
Turks   322
Tyre   322
Urban II, Pope   325
Vow, Crusader's   327
Walter Sansavoir   329
Weapons, Hand   329
William of Tyre   331
Women   332
Zangi (Zengi), Imad ad-Din   335
Zangids   335
Important Crusade Dates and Events   337
A Basic Crusade Library   341
Index   345

Preface

The crusades are a publishing growth industry. A recent search on amazon.com under the subject heading *crusade* resulted in a list of 465 book titles. To be sure, many of the books, such as *Stone Crusade: A Historical Guide to Bouldering in America* (1994), have absolutely nothing whatsoever to do with Western Europe's medieval crusades. Still, when the search was narrowed to *crusades, medieval,* the inquiring browser was left with a list of 187 titles, and most had been published within the last ten years. Now, that is impressive. Indeed, it is almost overwhelming. Of course, in light of the nine-hundredth anniversary of the crusaders' capture of Jerusalem that was reached on July 15, 1999, the current troubles in the Middle East, and the terrible events of September 11, 2001, this fascination with the crusades is understandable.

The books in that long list fall into three categories: the good, the bad, and the downright ugly. Some of the good are very good, indeed. The work of recognized scholars in the field, they are listed in the pages of this encyclopedia where appropriate. The bad and the ugly tend to be works of romantic history often written by persons with agendas, either hidden or transparent. A number of individuals, issues, phenomena, and movements associated with the crusades tend to attract popularizers and romancers of every sort. These magnets for crusade mythmaking include, but are not limited to, Saladin, Richard the Lionheart, the Templars, the Fourth Crusade, and the Children's Crusade. More bad history and nonsense has been written on these and similar topics than good history.

The *Encyclopedia of the Crusades* presents the most up-to-date scholarship on the crusades to a general audience in a way that is readable and enjoyable. Convinced that bare-bones, just-the-facts encyclopedia articles are deadly dull, the author has attempted to tell stories, whenever possible, and to illustrate points by quoting liberally from the medieval records themselves.

To assist you, the reader, in gaining the most from this book, the author has included several aids. First, there are cross-references. Entry titles are highlighted in **bold** each time they are initially mentioned in another entry. Think of these highlighted terms as links. Sure, you cannot click on them; you have to turn pages. But by turning to these links you will get a fuller picture of whatever you are researching. If a particular entry title is not mentioned by name in an article but is relevant to the issue under consideration, it is listed at the end of the article under **Related Entries.** In addition, the encyclopedia has a detailed index, which will assist you in tracking down broad issues and hidden items. For example, there are no specific entries on *tolerance* and *intolerance,* but a number of entries relate directly to these issues. Likewise, there is no specific entry for the Templar castle of *Saphet,* but it appears prominently in two entries.

To assist you in exploring in greater depth a particular crusade, person, or phenomenon, most entries are followed by a list of suggested books for further study. Several criteria govern the choice of this literature. First, with only one exception, they must be books, not articles. Second, they must be in English because the *Encyclopedia* is aimed at a general, English-speaking readership. Third, the works must be either translated *primary sources* (recorded evidence contemporaneous with the Age of the Crusades, such as the accounts of Western and Islamic historians and chroniclers) or historical studies written by acknowledged modern experts in the field. As already noted, a good deal of nonsense has been written on the crusades. The author of this encyclopedia has endeavored to shield you from misinformation and garbled history simply by not listing such books.

Immediately following the *Encyclopedia's* last entry, "Important Crusade Dates and Events," provides a handy chronological overview of the main events and characters of the classic Age of Crusades (1095–1291). That is followed by an annotated list of general books on the crusades, "A Basic Crusade Library," which supplements the sources and more specialized studies that appear with many of the entires.

Thirty-six years of university teaching have also convinced the author of the value of maps and illustrations. The eye is an almost indispensable medium for learning. Some illustrations are photos he has taken; others are artwork taken from medieval manuscripts. Altogether, they and the maps are intended to help you visualize the crusades and all that surrounded them.

One final point: the purpose behind this encyclopedia. Knowing about the medieval crusades will not help anyone forecast what will happen tomorrow or next year or ten years from now in the Middle East. History does not repeat itself, and if there are any laws of history, they have so far eluded this author. He is convinced, however, that a thorough understanding of the crusades, in all of their complexity, will enable a person to better understand and place into a fuller context many of the problems and issues that confront our world today. With such an understanding, we can make informed decisions as we exercise our responsibilities as citizens of our nation and our world.

A. J. Andrea
Burlington, Vermont

Acknowledgments

First, I must acknowledge Professor Thomas F. Madden of Saint Louis University, who suggested me to Greenwood Publishing for this project and commented on my original table of contents. Several editors at Greenwood have provided encouragement and assistance at various stages of the book's preparation. They include Barbara A. Rader, Kevin Ohe, Elizabeth Kinkaid, and especially John Wagner. Special thanks go to Kate Lau, Photographic Services Coordinator at the Walters Art Museum, Baltimore, Maryland, for her help in securing photos of various medieval manuscript illuminations that appear on some of these pages. Frank Martini, the cartographer who prepared the maps for this book, deserves sympathy for putting up with my almost incessant e-mails, as well as praise for a job well done.

Introduction

The term *crusade* conjures up many images in the modern mind. Some are positive to the point of gross historical misrepresentation. Such notions are usually based on romantic visions of medieval **chivalry** that became widespread in the nineteenth century and that continue, even today, to insinuate themselves into popular books, especially works of fiction. The engraving of **King Louis IX** by Gustave Doré (1832–1883) that appears on the next page, produced as an illustration for an 1877 edition of Joseph François Michaud's *Histoire des croisades,* depicts many of the attributes that are often ascribed to crusaders: idealism, piety, self-sacrifice, steadfastness of purpose, courage in the face of cruel and evil foes, purity of heart, and a sure conviction that their cause was just and holy.

This idealized view of the crusades and those who participated in them has long been part of the cultural heritage of the West and has resulted in the word becoming an everyday term applied to any enterprise undertaken for a righteous cause. Thus, an annual fund-raising drive in Louisville, Kentucky, bears the title Crusade for Children, and the Reverend Billy Graham has conducted over 400 Crusades for Christ during the past half century. And what American politician does not yearn to be praised for possessing a crusading spirit? Is not the same true of investigative crusading journalists? At the same time, the word retains a darker, yet still-positive connotation—that of a terribly costly, life-and-death struggle against evil. Thus, Dwight D. Eisenhower entitled his memoirs of World War II *Crusade in Europe,* and President George W. Bush initially called for a "crusade against evil-doers" as the United States embarked on a war on terrorism.

Of course, as President Bush quickly learned, *crusade* is a double-edged term. For many it represents everything that is presumably wrong with Western civilization. A BBC film production, *The Crusades* (1995), starring Terry Jones, formerly of the Monty Python troupe, portrays the crusades as a series of vicious wars waged by intolerant and barbaric Christian Europeans against their sophisticated and civilized neighbors, primarily **Muslims,** but also **Eastern Christians**

St. Louis a prisoner in Egypt. King Louis IX, brave, noble, and holy (note the halo) in the midst of tormenting captors is compared with Jesus crowned with thorns and mocked. Before departing on the Seventh Crusade, King Louis purchased the putative Crown of Thorns and other relics of the Passion (suffering) of Jesus from the emperor of Constantinople and deposited them in Sainte Chapelle, which he specially built for the relics between 1239 and 1248. Doré assumed his viewer would make that connection. Dover Pictorial Archives.

and **Jews.** Although this four-part film series is replete with egregious errors that rise to the level of howlers and despite its tendency to sacrifice balanced interpretation for simplistic commentary, the cheap joke, or an artsy effect, it has its admirers and has enjoyed a long run on television and in the schools. Likewise, the book *Holy War: The Crusades and Their Impact on Today's World* (1998), by the English theologian Karen Armstrong, has garnered much attention and many devotees. Armstrong admits she is not a trained historian, and the factual errors that abound in her work are testimony to that, but to her credit she attempts with some success to provide her reader with a triple vision: the crusades and similar **holy wars** as perceived from the perspectives of Christians, Muslims, and Jews. Her desire to present a balanced picture does not, however, preclude her judging the crusades to be a terrible tragedy in which the aggressive soul of the West was forged and the foundation laid for today's troubles in the **Middle East.** A third work that has recently appeared is James Reston Jr.'s *Warriors of God* (2001). Focusing on **Richard the Lionheart, Saladin,** and the **Third Crusade,** Reston has produced a work of popular history that attempts to present the epic clash between these two champions of holy war in a way that does justice to each side. Nevertheless, Reston boldly states: "[T]here is nothing in Islamic history that rivals the terror of the Crusades or the Christian fanaticism of the twelfth century" (p. xix). Clearly he did not explore the long and variegated history of **Islam** in sufficient depth. Neither did he study his sources for the Third Crusade critically or carefully. The book is well written, but the author's putative facts and facile judgments should not be accepted as authoritative.

If Jones, Armstrong, and Reston view the crusades negatively, imagine how these wars are perceived in the Islamic World. There the word *crusade* is generally a synonym for evil aggression and Western imperialism. Mehmet Ali Agca, who shot Pope John Paul II in 1981, justified his action by referring to his victim as "the supreme commander of the crusades." More recently, the attacks on the United States of September 11, 2001, were viewed by those who perpetrated and supported them as part of what Osama bin Laden characterized as a holy war against "Jews and American crusaders." Indeed, many Muslims in the Middle East perceive the state of Israel as simply a modern variation of the medieval **crusader states,** and many Muslim leaders of the region, from Egypt's Gamal Abdel Nasser in the 1950s to Iraq's Saddam Hussein, have wrapped themselves in the mantles of the twelfth- and thirteenth-century leaders of the Islamic counter crusades. Their argument is: History is on our side as we battle these latter-day crusaders, the Zionists and their American puppet-masters. It took our forebearers 200 years to drive the original crusaders into the sea; our current struggle is only a half-century old.

Clearly the crusades, as viewed on the street and in the popular media, are interpreted in a variety of conflicting ways, and the varying perspectives are very much the products of culture and politics. But what about professional historians who have dedicated their lives to studying these holy wars and their associated institutions? How do they see them?

The answer is: Despite a fair amount of consensus on numerous issues, historians happily debate the meaning and matter of the crusades and are as divided among themselves over them as they are over every other era and phenomenon in the human past. Quite simply, the raw evidence for the crusades—our primary sources—while plentiful, is fragmentary, flawed, and open to many interpretations. But this is true of all historical records and artifacts. We have more questions than answers, even as we uncover new evidence and look at old evidence with new eyes, and almost all of our answers are provisional at best. This does not mean that we do not know a lot about the crusades or that all interpretations of the evidence are equally valid. It simply means that the crusades, taken as a whole and divided into their many parts, are as provocative for historians as they are for nonhistorians. Led by scholars in Great Britain, the United States, France, and Germany, crusade scholarship is alive and flourishing as historians continue to delve into these holy wars.

On one level all historical study is a dialogue between the present and the past, as each generation asks questions of the past that have particular relevance or interest to it. Several of the most fruitful forms of recent crusade research have been a focus on crusading families and other types of networks that drew individuals into the crusades and the classification of crusaders by social rank, sex, region of origin, and similar characteristics. A number of the entries in this encyclopedia reflect that research, and the substantial number of entries on crusader **women** owes much to current emphasis on gender studies. Another important area of contemporary interest is what French historians refer to as the history of mentalities—that is, study of the beliefs, values, imaginative landscapes, and worldviews of the people who either participated in or resisted the crusades. Concern with getting into the minds and motivations of crusaders and those who supported them has resulted in a recent flurry of scholarship in such areas as crusade **preaching** and **recruitment,** the cult of **relics,** and European Christendom's **apocalyptic** fears and hopes.

As the foregoing suggests, crusade history is much more than just military or political history. Battles, **weapons,** strategy, tactics, and political institutions are valid areas of crusade study, and a number of entries deal with such items, but they are in the minority. Increasingly historians have come to view the crusades through cultural and social prisms, and this encyclopedia reflects that tendency—a tendency made all the sharper because its author specializes in the study of religious history. To his mind, medieval **Latin** Christianity and the crusades were inextricably intertwined.

Another important area of inquiry that has blossomed over the past half century is study of the impact of the crusades on the East and the manner in which various **Levantine** peoples reacted to these invasions from the West. In this encyclopedia **Byzantines,** Muslims, and others affected by the crusades are not treated as victims but rather as full-fledged actors in the high drama of the crusades.

Then there are the continuing debates among crusade historians over the exact definition of *crusade* and the crusades' chronological and geographical parameters.

Defining a crusade is not as easy as it might initially seem because the crusade as an idea and an institution took a century to develop into full form—from its inception in 1095–1096 to the pontificate of Pope **Innocent III** (r. 1198–1216). And even after it had achieved this level of coherence, it continued to respond to new stimuli and challenges. In effect, the crusade was a constant work in progress.

Consider, for example, that although the **First Crusade** got under way in 1096, it is not until the mid-1190s that words that we can translate as *crusade* and *crusader* finally appear. Both of these modern English words have distant origins in the Old Spanish *cruzada,* which means "an act or undertaking marked with a **cross.**" The word and similar variations, such as the Old French *croiserie* (crusade) and *croisé* (crusader), appeared toward the very end of the twelfth century as vernacular derivations of the Latin term *crucesignatus* (someone signed or marked with a cross), which only became fashionable in the mid-1190s. During the preceding century what we call crusades were referred to by a variety of other terms: *the business of the cross* or *the business of Jesus Christ; relief for the Holy Land* or *the journey to Jerusalem; the expedition of the cross* or *the way of the Holy Sepulcher; the journey of the most holy pilgrimage* and even *the universal passage.* Before terms such as *croisés* began to emerge just before 1200, crusaders were normally called *peregrini* (**pilgrims**), and the term continued to be applied to them right through the thirteenth century and beyond. They were pilgrims, of course, because the focal point of the crusades, at least as first articulated, was **Jerusalem.**

The fact that it took the Christian West a century to name, define, and impose an institutional uniformity on the crusade has led one historian, Christopher Tyerman, to argue in a provocative book, *The Invention of the Crusades* (1998), that the so-called crusades of the eleventh and twelfth centuries became crusades only after the fact, when Christian Europe created a fully articulated notion of crusade after the Islamic recovery of Jerusalem in 1187 and during the reign of Pope Innocent III that soon followed. Before then, "what we call crusades in fact covered a fragmented series of military and religious activities that lacked coherence" (p. 9). As stimulating as his arguments are, Tyerman has failed to convince most crusade historians that there were no true crusades or notions of crusading prior to the creation of the crusade as a fully formed institution around 1200. While recognizing the slow evolution of the crusade as an idea and an institution, most historians of the crusades would simply say that although twelfth-century Western Christians could not necessarily define a crusade, they knew one when they saw it. All of this leads us to ask four basic questions: What was a crusade? Where were they fought? When did the crusades take place? How many were there?

In his short but important book *What Were the Crusades?,* 3rd ed. (2002), Jonathan Riley-Smith writes:

To contemporaries a crusade was an expedition authorized by the pope on Christ's behalf, the leading participants in which took **vows** and consequently enjoyed the **privileges** of protection at home and the **indulgence,** which, when the campaign was not destined for the East, was equated with that granted to crusaders to the **Holy Land** (p. 5, bold added).

This sums up most but not all of the important features of a crusade. As Riley-Smith notes further, the crusade was also a penitential exercise that enabled its participants to make themselves right with God. Because they were penitents and because the liberation and defense of Jerusalem always served as either the goal or the model for all crusades, even those that did not go to the Holy Land, these warrior-penitents were viewed and treated as pilgrims. Of course, they were a special breed of pilgrims because they waged holy war. But not only was their war holy, it was also seen as a **just war** fought in defense of Christendom. They saw themselves not as aggressors but as servants of God who were reclaiming what was rightfully God's and that of God's Chosen People—the faithful Christians of the Roman Church.

Three questions remain: Where and when were these just and holy wars fought, and how many of them were there? These questions stand at the center of a debate that divides crusade historians into two major camps: they who favor a narrow definition and narrow limits and they who argue for broad ones.

The first group has been termed the "traditionalists." So-called traditionalists focus exclusively on Jerusalem and the Holy Land and restrict the crusades to those holy wars waged in the East between 1096, when the First Crusade got under way, and 1291, when the last crusader strongholds in **Syria-Palestine** were captured by the **Mamluks.** The second group, known as "pluralists," has a much broader view and counts as crusades the Spanish **Reconquista,** crusades in the **Baltic,** and crusades against perceived enemies of the Church in Europe, such as **heretics** and the papacy's **political** enemies. Moreover, pluralists do not see 1291 as the terminal point of the crusades. Rather, they have discovered a vibrant crusading tradition that extended far into early modern times, some would say as late as the seventeenth or even eighteenth centuries. The pluralists, who are ascendant in contemporary crusade scholarship, have contributed a number of important new studies of the so-called Later Crusades, such as Norman Housley's *The Later Crusades, 1274–1580: From Lyons to Alcazar* (1992).

The author of this encyclopedia is an avowed pluralist, and its entries reflect that. They not only cover crusades in the Holy Land and the crusader states that existed there for almost 200 years, but also deal with crusades in Spain, North Africa, the Baltic, the Balkans, and at home in Western Europe. At the same time, space precludes the encyclopedia's doing justice to the Later Crusades, that is, those of the fourteenth century and following. Consequently, although a few entries deal with phenomena that occurred before the First Crusade and even fewer touch on matters that took place after 1291, this encyclopedia largely limits its scope to events and people relevant to the classic Age of the Crusades, 1095/1096–1291.

To make the crusading movement comprehensible, the author has bestowed numbers on eight major crusades: the First Crusade (1096–1102); the **Second Crusade** (1147–1149); the **Third Crusade** (1188–1192); the **Fourth Crusade** (1202–1204); the **Fifth Crusade** (1217–1221); the **Sixth Crusade** (1227–1229); the **Seventh Crusade** (1248–1254); and the **Eighth Crusade** (1270–1272). All eight were large, papally blessed expeditions whose purpose was to engage Islamic enemies in and around the Holy Land, and crusade historians generally agree on the distinctive numbers accorded the first five of these crusades. Nevertheless, the author's numbering system is arbitrary and even misleading on three levels. First, medieval Westerners did not number their crusades. It is a practice that began with modern historians. Second, crusade historians disagree over how, if at all, to number the major crusades that took place after 1221. Third, there were hundreds, even thousands, of small and medium-sized crusades that went overseas during the classic Age of the Crusades. To single out only eight of them with distinguishing numbers distorts this reality. Nevertheless, there they are. For the purposes of easy categorization, we have eight major and a number of minor crusades to **Outremer** described in these pages, as well as crusades closer to home, such as the **Albigensian Crusade** and the Reconquista.

Several unofficial, or popular, crusades also find their way into these pages, the so-called **Children's Crusade** and two **Shepherds' Crusades.** Arguably they were not crusades because they were not set in motion by the **Roman papacy** and their participants were not accorded crusader status, which included the crusade indulgence and other privileges. To exclude them, however, is unthinkable because they were driven by many of the same impulses and forces that moved hundreds of thousands, indeed millions, of Western Christians to embark on official crusades. Research of the past fifty years has demonstrated that to overlook the spiritual, religious, and other psychological factors that motivated crusaders is to fail to understand the inner spirit of this centuries-long mass movement.

A

Abbasids

The dynasty that produced **Islam**'s **Sunni** caliphs from 750 to 1258.

From 762 to 1258 the Abbasid Caliphs resided in Baghdad. With the **Mongols'** destruction of the city and execution of Caliph al-Mustasim, both in 1258, the Abbasid dynasty effectively ended, although the **Mamluk** sultans supported a shadow Abbasid caliph in **Cairo** from 1261 to 1517. After 1517 the **Ottoman** rulers of **Constantinople** claimed the caliphate.

A caliph is the presumed successor of the Prophet Muhammad. Not a prophet himself, the caliph is the visible head of the *Umma,* or community, of Islam. The first Abbasid caliphs claimed the authority to overthrow the Umayyad dynasty of caliphs (r. 661–750) and to restore piety, order, and justice to the Islamic community by virtue of their descent from the family of the Prophet Muhammad through his paternal uncle al-Abbas. The Umayyads could make no such blood-relationship claims.

For their first century and a half the Abbasid caliphs were vigorous and effective, although they were never able to assert their authority over Spain, which remained loyal to the Umayyads, and western North Africa, which went its own way. Early in the tenth century the Abbasids experienced a major diminution of their authority. Rival independent powers arose within the family of Islam, most serious of which were the **Fatimids** and the Buyids. Even more serious was the emergence of powers behind the throne that transformed the Abbasid caliphs into figureheads. In 945 the leader of the Buyid family of Iran occupied Baghdad and forced the caliph to recognize him as supreme *emir,* or commander. In 1055 Buyid power ended when the **Seljuk** warrior Tughrul Beg entered Baghdad and forced the caliph to bestow on him the title *sultan* (holder of power) in recognition of the fact that he was the effective political and military power within the state. The Abbasid caliphs retained only moral, religious, and symbolic authority. **Related Entries:** Almohads; Almoravids; Islamic Peoples; Reconquista; Shia.

Acre

Known as St. Jean d'Acre in the Age of the Crusades, Acre was the chief port of the **Latin kingdom of Jerusalem** and served as its capital from 1191 to 1291. It was also the headquarters of the **Templars,** the **Hospitalers,** and the **Teutonic Knights,** as well as two minor **military orders,** Saint Thomas of Acre and **Saint Lazarus.**

The Venetian Quarter, Acre.

Situated on the Bay of Haifa in northern **Palestine,** Acre occupies a spit of land that forms a protected but shallow harbor. In the age of the crusades the city was well known for its mixed population of **Latins, Eastern Christians,** and **Muslims** and was notorious for its hustlers, dangers, filth, overwhelming stench, and periodic epidemics. Its European population contained a large percentage of criminals because of the European practice of commuting court sentences to settlement in the **Holy Land** and the fact that many criminal-colonists went no farther than Acre. Around the year 1200 the small, densely packed port city held about 5,600 residents, not counting transients. During the thirteenth century the population rose substantially as refugees from areas recaptured by the Muslims gravitated toward the kingdom's new capital, thereby necessitating an expansion of Acre's walls and suburbs.

Initially captured by Arab forces in 638, Acre passed back into Christian hands when King **Baldwin I** took the city in 1104. The city soon became a magnet for the maritime powers of the West, especially Italians, who established self-governing quarters within the city to serve their commercial needs. In addition to expanding and protecting their interests at Acre, Venetians, Genoese, Pisans, Provençals, and Catalans also focused their crusade efforts on this port, which they used to funnel soldiers and supplies into the Holy Land.

Saladin captured Acre on July 9, 1187. Two years later, in August 1189, King **Guy of Lusignan** laid **siege** to the city, while a Pisan naval squadron blockaded the harbor. Over the next year and a half, contingents from England, France, the Low Countries, Denmark, and Germany reinforced King Guy's small army, while fleets from Genoa and Venice joined Pisa in providing naval support.

King **Philip II** of France arrived with his army in late April 1191, followed by King **Richard I** of England and his forces in early June. Finally giving into exhaustion, the Muslim defenders of Acre surrendered on July 12.

For the next century, less sixty-one days, Acre remained in Christian hands and served as the capital of the revivified but truncated Latin kingdom of Jerusalem and the crusader states' major lifeline with Europe, until it succumbed to **Mamluk** attack. Following a forty-four-day siege, the city fell on May 18, 1291, except for a handful of Templars who fought on from their surrounded castle headquarters until May 28, when the whole edifice collapsed, killing them all. Most of Acre's inhabitants were **massacred,** the few survivors were sold into **slavery,** and the city was destroyed. With this conquest, the sultan of Egypt was assured victory over the few remaining crusader strongholds in the Holy Land. The last was evacuated on August 14, 1291. **Related Entries:** Jaffa; James of Vitry; Louis IX; Montjoie; Settlement and Colonization; Third Crusade; Tyre.

Suggested Reading

Bernard Dichter, *The Orders and Churches of Crusader Acre* (1979).

Adhémar of Monteil

Bishop of Le Puy and **papal legate** to the **First Crusade.**

On his way to the **council** of **Clermont,** Pope **Urban II** visited his friend Adhémar at Le Puy in southern France on August 15, 1095, and probably discussed his plans for launching a **holy war.** Three months later Bishop Adhémar was at Clermont. There, immediately following the pope's sermon, Adhémar was the first to come forward seeking permission take up the **crusader's cross.** In turn, the pope publicly appointed him papal representative to and clerical leader of

the army. Apparently Urban and Adhémar had planned this piece of theater.

What specific role the pope envisioned for Adhémar is not fully clear. The bishop had military experience and, according to one tradition, had already journeyed as a **pilgrim** to **Jerusalem.** Possibly Urban intended him to serve as overall commander-in-chief of the various armies. If so, it was not to be, but the bishop did play a minor military role in the crusade and exercised a tremendous amount of spiritual and moral authority over the crusaders as long as he lived.

As a fighting bishop, Adhémar led his own band of soldiers but joined himself and his retinue to the much larger army of Count **Raymond of Saint-Gilles.** While in the Balkans, the bishop was mistakenly wounded by **mercenary** soldiers of the **Byzantine** emperor but recovered and apparently bore no ill feelings over the incident.

Once in **Anatolia,** Adhémar played a role in the victory at the **Battle of Dorylaeum.** At a pivotal moment in the battle, the bishop's troops, with him at their head, came over a hill at the enemy's rear, causing panic and flight.

More significant than his military contributions were Adhémar's priestly ministrations and diplomatic skills. His sermons and overall spiritual guidance helped at times to raise the morale of an all-too-often despairing army. His abilities to communicate with tact and to project an aura of reason charmed both Byzantines and fractious crusader lords alike. Symeon, the Greek Orthodox patriarch of Jerusalem, who resided in exile on **Cyprus,** counted Adhémar as an ally and friend, despite Symeon's distaste for some of the ways of the **Latin** Church. As a result, Symeon sent generous gifts of food to the famine-ridden army at the **siege** of **Antioch.**

When Adhémar died of **disease** at Antioch on August 1, 1098, the army lost a valuable leader, a unifying force, and a friend. Or had it? Even in death, Adhémar continued to have an impact on the army. On July 6, 1099, it seemed as though the crusade would end in disaster before the walls of **Jerusalem.** The city appeared impregnable, and news of the imminent arrival of an Egyptian relief force circulated through the ranks. Just then a priest named Peter Desiderius announced that the sainted bishop of Le Puy had appeared to him in a dream. The bishop had deplored the selfish bickering of the crusade leaders and ordered all crusaders to fast and walk barefoot as penitents around the city's walls. If they did so and were truly contrite, the city would fall to them in nine days. Wanting to believe in miracles, the pilgrims acted accordingly. Jerusalem fell to them on July 15. **Related Entries:** Lance, Holy; Visions.

Al-Adil

Al-Adil Abu Bakr Sayf ad-Din, known to the **Latins** as **Saphadin,** brother of **Saladin,** ruler of Upper Mesopotamia (r. 1193–1198), ruler of **Damascus** (r. 1198–1200), and sultan of Egypt and **Syria** (r. 1200–1218).

Al-Adil served his brother faithfully, but, following Saladin's death in 1193, he involved himself in a series of shifting alliances and intrigues aimed at dispossessing his three nephews of their lands and power. Finally, al-Adil was able to gain hegemony over the **Ayyubid** empire in 1200 when he wrested the sultanate of Egypt and Syria from Saladin's grandson, al-Mansur. The only region of Saladin's empire that remained semi-independent was **Aleppo,** which Saladin's son, al-Zahir Ghazi, retained by virtue of recognizing al-Adil's supremacy. As sultan of Egypt, al-Adil bore the initial onslaught of the **Fifth Crusade;** on his death in 1218, the sultanate of Egypt passed

to his son, **al-Kamil,** who brought the war against the crusaders in the Nile Delta to a successful conclusion. Like his brother before him, al-Adil divided his lands among his four sons, but by 1218 al-Kamil had gained hegemony over his fellow Ayyubid rulers. **Related Entries:** Chivalry; Third Crusade.

Adrianople

A key **Byzantine** city northwest of **Constantinople,** which served as a point of transit, resupply, and conflict for various crusader armies marching overland from Europe.

The first crusaders to reach the city were the forces led by **Peter the Hermit,** who arrived on July 22, 1096, to a warm reception. **Godfrey of Bouillon**'s contingent was the only element of the second wave of the **First Crusade** to travel through Adrianople, which it left without incident on December 8, 1097. During the **Second Crusade** the German emperor **Conrad III** marched through Adrianople without stopping, in hope of avoiding conflict. It was not to be. Troops from his army went back to the city and set fire to a monastery to avenge a murder. During the **Third Crusade** the army of Emperor **Frederick I Barbarossa** (who forty-two years earlier had led the soldiers who torched the monastery) became the largest crusader force to encamp at Adrianople. As Frederick's troops marched toward Constantinople, they frequently clashed with the imperial troops of **Isaac II,** and in the midst of that bloody passage the German emperor decided to winter at Adrianople, which his main army entered on November 22, 1189. The Germans found the city abandoned and proceeded to **pillage** it. Meanwhile, a vociferous war party within the German army was calling for a direct assault on

Constantinople in the coming spring. On January 21, 1190, however, Byzantine envoys arrived at Adrianople expressing Isaac's desire for peace. Several German plenipotentiaries were dispatched to Constantinople to work out the details. They returned to Adrianople on February 14 with a treaty of peace that guaranteed Frederick's army safe passage across the Dardanelles and prevented any crusader attack on Constantinople—at least so far as the Third Crusade was concerned.

The army and navy of the **Fourth Crusade** did attack and capture Constantinople in 1203 and again in 1204. The result of the second capture was the establishment of the **Latin empire of Constantinople,** and Adrianople played a role in the early history of that short-lived empire inasmuch as it provided the setting for the clash of two Catholic Christian armies in the spring of 1205—the forces of the **Latin** Emperor **Baldwin I** and the troops of Kalojan, head of the Vlacho-Bulgarian kingdom.

The conflict was largely a manifestation of power politics played by two states that vied to control the region known as Thrace. Adrianople had successfully revolted against its new Venetian overlords, who apparently had mistreated the inhabitants. When Emperor Baldwin marched north to **besiege** the city, Kalojan rushed to support it. In the ensuing battle the Latin forces were cut to pieces; Baldwin was captured and died soon thereafter under suspicious circumstances.

Baldwin's brother and successor, Emperor Henry I, managed to regain Adrianople, but the city continued to change hands until it was retaken by the Byzantine empire-in-exile at Nicaea around 1247. A century later, sometime around 1369, the **Ottoman Turks** captured the city. Located in modern European Turkey, today it is known as Edirne. **Related Entries:** Christians, Eastern; Hohenstaufens.

Agnes of Courtenay

Wife of King **Amalric,** mother of **Baldwin IV** and **Sibylla.**

Agnes, the widowed daughter of the count of **Edessa,** married the future King Amalric in 1157, but before he succeeded his brother **Baldwin III** as king in 1163, the **High Court** of **Jerusalem** forced him to end his marriage to her as a prerequisite to assuming the crown. The official reason was that they were third cousins, and their marriage was within the prohibited degree of blood relationship. The deeper reason might have been that the barons feared that, like Queen **Melisende,** she would take an active role in state affairs. If so, the fear was well founded, as the reign of her son showed. Agnes was never crowned queen of Jerusalem, but between 1176, when Baldwin IV came of age, and her death in late 1184 or early 1185, Agnes was the power behind the throne. She was quite capable in that role, but her forceful personality earned her the enmity of several **historians,** such as **William of Tyre,** who characterized her as a "grasping woman, utterly detestable to God." The fact that she blocked his election to the **patriarchate of Jerusalem** probably influenced his judgment. **Related Entries:** Crusader States; Women.

Aimery of Lusignan

Constable of **Jerusalem** (1181–1194), count of **Jaffa** (r. 1193–1194), lord of **Cyprus** (r. 1194–1197), king of Cyprus (r. 1197–1205), and king of Jerusalem (r. 1197–1205).

Aimery came to the **Levant** with his older brother **Guy of Lusignan** after being expelled from Poitou in France by their **feudal** lord, **Richard the Lionheart.** Both brothers rose rapidly in the ranks of the nobility of the kingdom of Jerusalem by virtue of their birth, relationships, luck, and marriages. When Guy died in 1194, Aimery succeeded him as lord of Cyprus and three years later received a crown and royal title from Emperor **Henry VI,** who claimed Cyprus as an imperial **fief.** Later that year the barons of Jerusalem chose Aimery to marry Queen **Isabella I,** the recently widowed heiress of the kingdom, thereby selecting him to become king. Aimery's selection was largely due to pressure from the Germans, and it initiated a period of profound **Hohenstaufen** involvement in the affairs of the **Latin East.** Following his coronation as king of Jerusalem, Aimery concentrated his full energies on **Syria-Palestine** and neglected Cyprus. He campaigned with the forces of the **German Crusade of 1197** that captured Beirut. Although Aimery intended to rule as a strong monarch, baronial power and opposition grew during his reign and substantially limited his authority.

After he died on April 1, 1205, Isabella ruled in her own name until her death shortly thereafter. With Aimery's death the crowns of Cyprus and Jerusalem were separated. The former was inherited by his son by a previous marriage, Hugh, whereas the latter passed to **Maria of Montferrat,** Isabella's daughter from a former marriage. **Related Entries:** Amalric I; Conrad of Montferrat; John of Brienne; Women.

Albigensians

See Cathars.

Albigensian Crusade (1209–1229)

A series of campaigns against the **Cathars** of **Languedoc,** the Albigensian Crusade is best understood when viewed in six segments: 1209, 1210–1214, 1214–1215, 1216–1218, 1219–1225, and 1226–1229. Additionally, the crusade had an eleven-year

gathering storm and a fifty-year post-conflict period of radical reconstruction. From start to finish the war was fought with extreme brutality, and each side was guilty of atrocities. It was a typical civil war in which two cultures within a single polity fought viciously in defense of their visions of right and righteousness.

Steps toward the Crusade

By the end of the twelfth century, the Cathar Church had become so deeply rooted in southern France, especially among **women** in the ranks of the lower nobility, that the Roman Church considered these **heretics** a major challenge to the spiritual well-being of Christendom. The belief was that unless the Church could get its own house in order and extirpate the blasphemy of heresy, it would never be worthy of liberating **Jerusalem.**

Upon his accession in 1198, Pope **Innocent III** began dispatching a series of **Cistercian** emissaries and **legates** to reform and reinvigorate the clergy of Languedoc to counter Catharism. The Cistercians' results were meager, and the pope began to entertain the idea that secular force was needed. In May 1204 Innocent called upon King **Philip II** to do his duty in suppressing heresy in the south and offered an **indulgence** in return, but he stopped short of calling for a **holy war** or an armed invasion of Languedoc. Philip turned a deaf ear, as he did to a similar plea from the pope in February 1205. In November 1207 the pope went two steps farther when he dispatched a letter not only to the king but throughout France, calling Philip and his followers to "root out this harmful filth," which flourished throughout Toulouse. In return, he offered not only an indulgence equal to that of crusaders, but papal protection of their families, lands, and goods. Although Innocent called for the suppression of heresy and confiscation of the heretics' possessions, he stopped short of summoning Christendom to an all-out holy war. That was to come early the next year.

Toulouse was the epicenter of Catharism. The count of Toulouse, Raymond VI of Saint-Gilles, the great-grandson of one of the heroes of the **First Crusade** and the grandson of a crusader who had died on the **Second Crusade,** was noted for his easygoing ways, and Catharism flourished under his relaxed rule. In April 1207 Innocent's legate to Toulouse, the Cistercian monk Peter of Castelnau, excommunicated Count Raymond for his alleged protection of heretics. On January 14, 1208, Peter was murdered by a soldier in the service of the count. Innocent was convinced that Count Raymond was behind the assassination, and on March 10, 1208, he issued a **crusade bull** against Count Raymond and all heretics, whom he characterized as "more evil than the **Saracens.**" He further authorized his crusaders to seize and occupy the heretics' lands. With this incentive added to normal **crusade privileges, recruits** were sure to enlist.

The general response was enthusiastic, although King Philip was not happy at this papal intrusion into the affairs of his kingdom and refused to take part or assist the crusade. In March 1208 the pope named Arnold Amalric, the abbot of **Cîteaux,** as chief papal legate to the crusade, and in the year that followed momentum for the crusade built. The army was scheduled to muster at Lyons on June 24, 1209. Realizing his impossible situation, Count Raymond made a humiliating submission to papal authority six days before the scheduled time of assembly, and on June 22 he assumed the **crusader's cross** against his own people. With these two acts, Count Raymond deflected the crusade away from himself and onto his nephew, Raymond Roger Trencavel, the viscount of Béziers.

The Campaign of 1209: The Emergence of a Crusade Leader

An army of maybe 20,000, of whom about half were camp followers, assembled at Lyons. Many of the **knights** who joined came as **feudal vassals,** which meant that they were obligated to serve only forty days in the field—the traditional period of military service owed each year by a vassal. If the army was to achieve anything, it would have to move fast.

The army, largely composed of northern French, set out in early July, with Arnold Amalric at its head. When Raymond Roger tried to avert disaster by pleading innocence and asking mercy before the abbot, the legate summarily dismissed him. On July 22 the army captured the city of Béziers in a bloodbath in which Cathars and Catholics, men, women, and children alike, were indiscriminately slaughtered and the city put to the torch. Reportedly, 20,000 died that day, but the true numbers will never be known. On August 15, Carcassone, the key fortress-city of Toulouse, surrendered after a wearing **siege,** and Raymond Roger was led off in chains. A few days later the barons elected Simon of Montfort, a minor noble from the region of Paris, the new viscount. Simon, a veteran of the **Fourth Crusade,** who had refused to participate in the attack on Zara and who left the army after that incident to make his separate way to **Syria-Palestine,** combined in his person religious fervor, a sense of mission, bravery, ruthlessness, and ambition—a dangerous combination. On November 10, Raymond Roger died in prison at the age of twenty-four. Although relieved of this impediment, Simon of Montfort faced the problem of governing his new holdings. The crusade army melted away after the capture of Carcassone, and Simon was left with a small force to control a large and devastated region and to root out heresy. His expedient was to build up his own army by giving out **feudal fiefs** to knights from northern France. The process of bringing Languedoc under the political and cultural domination of the North had begun.

More crusade campaigns would be needed to expand upon these initial military successes and to destroy the heretics' infrastructure. Because each subsequent campaign would be essentially a summer expedition, it was left to Simon to serve as the crusade's year-to-year leader, and he did so for nearly nine years.

The Campaigns of 1210–1213: Montfort's Mounting Successes

During the summers of 1210 and 1211 Simon and his seasonal crusaders picked off a number of castles and towns of the former lord of Trencavel, forcing King Peter II of Aragon, the feudal overlord of the Trencavel lands, to acknowledge Simon as the new viscount. In addition, in February 1211 Count Raymond VI was again excommunicated for tepidity in eradicating heresy, and Simon took the opportunity to begin offensive operations against Toulouse in 1211, which he continued with mounting success in 1212, capturing a number of key towns and castles. In addition to relying on his own vassals and seasonal forty-day crusaders, Simon found himself increasingly forced to hire **mercenaries,** even though church law forbade their use against Christians and within Christian lands.

As Simon's successes mounted, King Peter II of Aragon became deeply concerned and intervened, first diplomatically and then militarily. Peter, the crusader-hero of the **Battle of Las Navas de Tolosa** of July 16, 1212, marched into Toulouse with a massive army to defend his vassal, Count Raymond VI, against the crusader-hero, Simon. The two armies met at Muret on September 12, 1213. Although greatly outnumbered, maybe by as much as three or four to one, Simon

won a resounding victory, and King Peter was killed, along with large numbers of the Aragonese. After Muret, it seemed as though Simon would soon conquer all of Toulouse.

The Campaigns of 1214–1215: Apparent Victory

In April 1214 Count Raymond, seeking to cut his losses, begged forgiveness and had the ban of excommunication lifted. Regardless, Simon continued his military advances and successes. Meanwhile, Louis, the son of Philip II and the future King **Louis VIII,** joined the crusade in 1215, but because Simon already controlled most of Toulouse, Louis's expedition was largely a parade. On November 30, 1215, the Fourth Lateran Council found Raymond VI guilty of harboring heretics and deprived him of his lands but awarded him an annual pension for life. It further declared that all lands conquered from heretics or supporters of heretics were to go to Simon. However, Count Raymond's remaining lands, largely the marquisate of Provence, were to be held in trust by the Church for the count's underage heir, the future Raymond VII. Early the next year King Philip confirmed Simon as count of Toulouse.

The Campaigns of 1216–1218: The Turning Tide

Simon was now at the height of his powers, but the two Raymonds and their supporters launched a counteroffensive. Many devout Catholics, including King James I of Aragon, joined the cause of the "rebels," who increasingly saw themselves as fighting for Southern independence from Northern aggression.

Because the papacy and Western Europe were now involved in all-out support of the **Fifth Crusade,** Simon saw his supply of seasonal crusaders dwindling, and he had to rely increasingly on mercenaries to defend his new possessions. The war see-sawed, and then took a positive turn for the family of Saint-Gilles when Simon was killed at the **siege** of the city of Toulouse on June 25, 1218, and leadership passed to Simon's son, Amalric. One month to the day of Simon's death the crusaders raised the siege and departed from Toulouse.

1219–1225: Apparent Reconquest

The year 1219 began inauspiciously for Amalric when a crusader detachment was destroyed in what proved to be the war's last pitched battle in an open field. Amalric's forces were dwindling, despite Pope **Honorius III**'s best efforts to raise enthusiasm and money for the crusaders. Prince Louis of France arrived on his second crusade into Languedoc in June but proved ineffective. After besieging Toulouse for forty-five days, he burned his siege machines, released his **prisoners,** and departed.

The next several years witnessed continuing retreat on Amalric's part, due largely to the small size of his forces. In June 1221 Pope Honorius even gave formal approval to the creation of a new **military order,** the Knighthood of the Faith of Jesus Christ, to provide the crusade with a standing army, but nothing came of it.

In 1222 Raymond VI died, but the war of reconquest went on under Raymond VII. In January 1224 he was able to force the outmanned and impecunious Amalric to surrender Carcassone, which had served as crusade headquarters since 1209. With this coup he was able to return the viscounties of Béziers and Carcassone to the family of the late Raymond Roger Trencavel. It now seemed that the crusade had been defeated.

1226–1229: Royal Intervention and Reconciliation

Amalric had one more card to play, King Louis VIII, who had succeeded to the throne of France in 1223. In January 1226 Amalric

unconditionally handed over his rights to Toulouse to King Louis, who then took the crusader's cross. In June the king left Lyons with a large crusading army, and on September 9, he captured Avignon. But two months later, on November 8, he died, probably of **disease.** Despite the king's death, the crusade went on, with his overwhelming forces devastating the countryside.

The momentum had shifted dramatically and irrevocably back to the crusaders, and their final victory was a foregone conclusion, now that the full weight of the monarchy supported the war. Faced with certain defeat, Raymond sued for peace. Happily for him, the regent of France, Blanche of Castile, found the price of continuing the crusade too costly, and the new pope, **Gregory IX,** was also ready to negotiate a peace. The result was the Peace of Paris of April 12, 1229. Raymond VII made his peace with the Church and the Crown, offering submission to both under terms that contemporaries considered harsh and humiliating. The young count retained a good portion of his ancestral lands, but clauses in the treaty guaranteed that all of the lands of Saint-Gilles would ultimately pass under **Capetian** control after his death.

The Inquisition

The crusade was over, but Catharism still was alive in Languedoc. The Church now began to seek and root out heretics. In March 1233 Pope Gregory IX ordered a general inquisition for all of southern France and entrusted that work to the **Dominicans,** who proved zealous in the task. Backed by the force of secular authorities, Dominicans (and some Franciscans) conducted tribunals throughout Languedoc, examining and judging suspected heretics wherever they found them. The object was to gain confessions and to impose penances upon contrite sinners, but unrepentant heretics who refused to recant and accept the imposed penances faced death by burning. In 1279 the Inquisition of Toulouse formally suspended its activities, but by then Catharism had largely been eradicated (or driven deep underground). Probably 5,000 or fewer hard-core Cathars were executed during the fifty years following the Peace of Paris, but their example of martyrdom was enough to impel most Cathars to assume at least the external signs of fidelity to the Church of Rome. **Related Entries:** Friars, Mendicant; Massacres; Missionaries; Raymond IV of Saint-Gilles; *Ribauds*.

Suggested Reading

Primary Sources

Edward Peters, ed., *Christian Society and the Crusades, 1198–1229* (1971); Peter of les Vaux-de-Cernay, *The History of the Albigensian Crusade,* trans. by W. A. and M. D. Sibly (1998); William of Puylaurens, *The Chronicle of William of Puylaurens: The Albigension Crusade and Its Aftermath,* trans. by W. A. and M. D. Sibly (2003); William of Tudèle, *The Song of the Cathar Wars: A History of the Albigensian Crusade,* trans. and ed. by Janet Shirley (1996).

Historical Studies

James B. Given, *Inquisition and Medieval Society: Power, Discipline, and Resistance in Languedoc* (1997); Bernard Hamilton, *The Medieval Inquisition* (1981); Brenda Stalcup, ed., *The Inquisition* (2001); Joseph R. Strayer, *The Albigensian Crusades* (1971 and 1992); Jonathan Sumption, *The Albigensian Crusade* (1978).

Alcántara, Order of

See Military Orders of Iberia.

Aleppo

A city in northern **Syria** that served as an **Islamic** stronghold and center of interregional trade during the age of the crusades.

Aleppo was initially captured by Islamic forces in 636. In 969 it was recaptured by the **Byzantines,** but in 1015 it passed into the hands of the **Fatimids** of Egypt. In 1085 the **Seljuk Turks** annexed it. Until 1129 it was governed by various independent Turkish leaders; in that year, **Zangi,** governor of **Mosul,** conquered and occupied the city.

From 1129 to 1260 Aleppo flourished as a center of Islamic military power, commercial prosperity based on vigorous international trade, and religious scholarship. All of this was destroyed when the **Mongols** sacked the city in 1260, and Aleppo did not recover for centuries thereafter. Its new **Mamluk** rulers only began rebuilding the city in 1300, but even that modest recovery was interrupted by the Black Death of 1348. For the rest of the fourteenth and most of the fifteenth century, Aleppo remained a minor provincial town.

Late in the fifteenth century, with the destruction of Genoa's Black Sea commercial bases and the consolidation of the empire of its new masters, the **Ottoman** Turks, Aleppo witnessed a dramatic turnaround, as major trade routes were once again directed through the city.

Today its vast citadel, originally constructed in the twelfth century and later restored by a Mamluk sultan, stands as a reminder of the city's importance in the Crusade Era. **Related Entries:** Ayyubids; Damascus; Nur ad-Din Mahmud; Saladin; Zangids.

Suggested Reading

Yasser Tabbaa, *Constructions of Power and Piety in Medieval Aleppo* (1997).

Alexius I Comnenus (r. 1081–1118)

Emperor of **Constantinople** during the **First Crusade.**

Alexius Comnenus seized the **Byzantine** throne at a time of crisis. Discontentment and rebellions threatened to tear the empire apart from within, and external foes threatened to rip it apart by conquest. Pechenegs, a **Turkic** people, had conquered and settled the northeastern Balkans; following the disaster at **Manzikert** in 1071, **Anatolia** was now largely a land ruled by **Seljuk** Turkish lords; and the **Normans,** having conquered Byzantine southern Italy, were preparing to invade the Albanian provinces of the empire. Of all of these threats, Alexius considered the Norman invasion led by Robert Guiscard and his son **Bohemond** the most dangerous.

Despite many setbacks and military defeats, Alexius's doggedness, his judicious use of diplomacy and **mercenary** troops (including large numbers of Turks and Westerners), and a fair measure of good luck combined to enable him to meet and defeat the Pecheneg and Norman threats in the Balkans and to suppress his domestic enemies. By 1095 Alexius was ready to turn to Anatolia and the Seljuks, just as word reached him of the arrival of **Latin** armies on their way to fight the Turks and liberate **Jerusalem.**

The irony was that these armies were largely a consequence of Alexius's repeated overtures to the West for mercenaries to enlist in his struggles against his Seljuk enemies, but the emperor never envisioned or wanted masses of independent Western warriors and assorted hangers-on marching through his empire, especially when some of them were the same Normans whom he had recently fought in the Balkans. However, despite some early confrontations and clashes, the **First Crusade** did not start out too badly for Alexius or Byzantium. Although armies of the crusade's first wave, the so-called **People's Crusade** of 1096, clashed with Byzantine forces in the Balkans

and raided the countryside around Constantinople, they were fairly well received by the emperor but quickly transported across the Bosporus to Anatolia. When the great **Frankish** lords of the second wave arrived with their forces Alexius insisted on their swearing to return to him all former imperial lands that they might conquer and on their rendering him **feudal** homage and fealty, thereby acknowledging his overlordship. Several lords balked at these demands, and there was even some brief but bitter fighting in Constantinople's suburbs before the holdouts among the Frankish lords acceded to the emperor's demand.

Following settlement of this affair, the Franks were ferried across the straits and, in the company of imperial troops, marched toward Nicaea, the capital of the Seljuk sultanate of Rum. Nicaea surrendered to the imperial army on June 19, 1097. Alexius then detached a cavalry squadron under one of his best generals (a Turkish force commanded by a Turk!) to accompany the crusaders to **Antioch** and beyond, while the emperor secured western Anatolia, which was strategically more important to Byzantium.

Antioch, which had been under Byzantine control as recently as 1085, fell to the crusaders on June 3, 1098, after a long and bitter **siege.** Prior to its capture the emperor's representative left the army (apparently for supplies and reinforcements) and never returned. Alexius failed to push through to Antioch to provide the army with much-needed support as it faced a Turkish counterattack, and he failed to answer in a timely manner a crusader offer to take over leadership of the crusade after the crusaders had repulsed a Turkish siege of crusader-held Antioch. Using this perceived imperial treachery and ineptitude as an excuse, Bohemond of Taranto (Alexius's former Norman enemy) successfully claimed the city as his own, and Antioch became the wedge dividing the crusaders from the man who had provided the inspiration for Pope **Urban II**'s crusade appeal. From Antioch the crusaders marched to Jerusalem without Byzantine support.

Although Alexius managed in 1108 to force Bohemond to acknowledge imperial overlordship, the victory was empty. **Tancred,** Bohemond's successor, refused to accept imperial direction. In his exasperation, Alexius actually proposed in 1111 an alliance against the crusaders with the Seljuk sultan at Baghdad. In the end, Alexius's preoccupation with Antioch defeated his attempts to wrest more than the western regions of Anatolia from the Seljuks and enabled the Turks to consolidate their hold over most of the peninsula. **Related Entries:** Anna Comnena; Clermont, Council of; Godfrey of Bouillon; Raymond of Saint-Gilles; Stephen of Blois.

Suggested Reading

Primary Source

The Alexiad of the Princess Anna Comnena Being the History of the Reign of Her Father, Alexius I, trans. by Elizabeth A. S. Dawes (1967).

Alice of Antioch

Regent of the principality of **Antioch** (r. 1130 and 1135–1136).

Alice was born around 1106 as the second daughter of **Baldwin II of Le Bourcq,** count of **Edessa,** and the **Armenian** noblewoman, Morfia. In 1126 she married **Bohemond II** of Antioch and two years later gave birth to a daughter, **Constance.** When Bohemond died in 1130, Alice immediately began governing the principality without waiting for her father, who was now king of **Jerusalem,** to appoint a regent for the two-year-old princess. Alice had visions of ruling as sovereign, and when she heard that her father was on his way to Antioch to assume for himself

the burden of regency there, she secretly sent word to **Zangi,** offering to place herself under his authority if he would confirm her as Antioch's ruler. King Baldwin, however, intercepted Alice's messenger and ordered him hanged. He then took possession of Antioch, removed Alice from power, and ordered her banished into comfortable exile.

The following year Baldwin II died, and Alice reasserted her claim to power. She allied with the counts of **Tripoli** and Edessa, who also wanted to throw off the overlordship of the king of Jerusalem, and revolted against King **Fulk,** her brother-in-law. In 1132 King Fulk was forced to sail to Antioch, suppress the rebellion, and assume the regency himself. Despite the unsuccessful uprising, Alice remained in comfortable exile.

In 1135 Alice successfully appealed to her sister, **Melisende,** Fulk's wife, to arrange her return to Antioch. Although King Fulk retained the title of regent, Alice now seized power, which she initially shared with the **Latin** patriarch of Antioch, a disreputable cleric named Radulph. Soon, however, she put him aside.

Alice next offered to marry her nine-year-old daughter to the son and heir of Emperor **Manuel I Comnenus,** hoping to gain the **Byzantine** emperor as an ally against Fulk. When Fulk heard of this plan from the angry Patriarch Radulph, he moved quickly, choosing Raymond of Poitiers as Constance's husband. He further arranged the child's abduction and a quick marriage ceremony performed by Radulph. Once Constance was married, Alice lost all claim to power and retired permanently into exile. **Related Entries:** Bailli; Women.

Alice of Champagne

Queen of **Cyprus** (r. 1208–1218); regent of Cyprus (r. 1218–1232); regent of **Jerusalem** (r. 1243–1246).

Alice, daughter of **Henry of Champagne** and Queen **Isabella I** of Jerusalem, married the thirteen-year-old King Hugh I of Cyprus in 1208, and assumed the regency for her eight-month-year-old son Henry I, when Hugh died in 1218. In 1223 she left Cyprus for **Syria,** having unsuccessfully quarreled with her uncles, who exercised administrative oversight. In 1229 Alice advanced a claim to the throne of Jerusalem, urged on by an anti-**Hohenstaufen** faction that resisted the claim of **Conrad,** the one-year-old son of **Frederick II** and **Isabella II.** Nothing came of Alice's claim immediately, but when Conrad, who was still in Europe, reached his majority in 1243, the barons of the kingdom chose Alice to act as Conrad's regent, or **bailli,** until he arrived to take possession of the crown. For the next three years Alice ruled the kingdom, with the title "lady of Jerusalem." When she died in 1246, her son Henry I succeeded her, adding to the title king of Cyprus that of lord of Jerusalem. **Related Entry:** Women.

Almohads

A Berber sect and dynasty from western North Africa that in the twelfth century united all of North Africa (except Egypt) and southern Spain into a caliphate that rivaled the claims of the **Abbasids** of Baghdad.

The Almohads (from the Arabic *al-Muwahhid,* which means "they who affirm God's unity"), began as a religious reform movement that waged **jihad** against the **Almoravids,** conquering their last Moroccan outposts in 1147. By 1163 the Almohads' North African possessions reached from the western borders of **Fatimid** Egypt to the Atlantic. In 1146 they invaded southern Spain and overran what remained of **Islamic al-Andalus** by 1172.

In 1195 the caliph's forces routed the army of Alfonso VIII of Castile at the Battle

The **Koutoubia Mosque** of **Marrakesh,** constructed by the **Almohads** in the twelfth century to replace an eleventh-century Almoravid mosque. The brick pilings of the earlier mosque are in the foreground. In destroying and then rebuilding the mosque, the Almohads underscored their divinely mandated authority to replace the "heretical" Almoravids. The square minaret, which rises 230 feet and is visible from eighteen miles away, is considered a jewel of Islamic architecture and served as the model for the minaret of Seville's Grand Mosque.

of Alarcos, but on July 16, 1212, a combined Christian army of Spaniards and French crushed the Almohads at **Las Navas de Tolosa** in an epic turning point of the **Reconquista.** A dozen years later **Muslim** Iberia was ravaged by civil war, and in 1228, Caliph Idris I lost his Spanish lands. The dynasty limped along in North Africa until the death of its last caliph in 1269. **Related Entries:** Cid, El; Islam; Islamic Peoples; Moors.

Almoravids

A sect and dynasty of **Sunni Muslims** noted for its strict observance of **Islam** that arose among the Berber tribes of western North Africa during the mid–eleventh century.

After conquering Morocco and portions of Algeria, the Almoravids were called into **al-Andalus** in 1086 to stem the collapse of Islamic power there and to roll back the Christian advance. They took over and ruled the southern regions of the Iberian Peninsula until displaced in the twelfth century by a second wave of North African religious reformers and defenders of Islam, the **Almohads. Related Entries:** Cid, El; Islamic Peoples; Moors; Reconquista.

Amalric

Fifth **Latin** king of **Jerusalem** (r. 1163–1174).

The reign of Amalric, one of the kingdom's most energetic monarchs, witnessed the high-water mark of royal power and the kingdom's last period of significant offensive operations. By 1169, with its resources overextended and a new enemy arising in the person of **Saladin,** the kingdom found itself on the defensive, a position that would be a constant reality until the kingdom's collapse in 1291.

At the age of twenty-seven, Amalric succeeded his childless brother, **Baldwin III,** as king. The price he had to pay for winning over certain barons was to put aside his wife, **Agnes of Courtenay.** He did so, but only after securing acknowledgment that his two children by that marriage, **Sibylla** and **Baldwin (IV),** were legitimate and in line to succeed him. He later married the **Byzantine** princess, Maria Comnena, and by her had another daughter, **Isabella (I).**

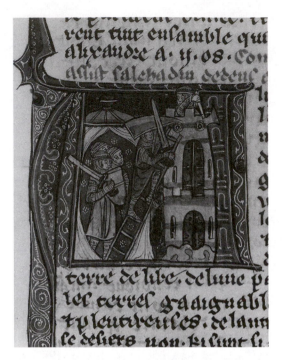

King Amalric's forces unsuccessfully besiege the Egyptian port city of Alexandria in 1167. While one Frank assaults the city by ladder, three others remain behind in a tent. From a manuscript copy of the *Estoire d'Eracles,* a continuation of William of Tyre's history to 1229. Late thirteenth century (1295?), Paris or northern France. The Walters Art Museum, Baltimore.

Amalric was a first-rate legislator, who defended and extended royal prerogatives, and a tough-minded judge. He was particularly concerned with controlling the **military orders** and limiting their ability to act independently of royal policies. In the 1160s he decreed that all **feudal** rear **vassals** (the vassals of the king's tenants-in-chief and other great lords) had to recognize the king as their liege lord and render an oath of loyalty to him. By this act he made all vassals, no matter how great or small, peers who shared the right to sit in the **High Court** and have their grievances heard there. It also established the principle that every **knight** in the kingdom owed the king his immediate loyalty and support. In the short term the law strengthened royal power, but during the thirteenth century it enabled the kingdom's fief-holders to present a solid front of opposition to various royal initiatives. Amalric could not have foreseen this.

In the area of foreign affairs, Amalric is most noted for his attempt to conquer Egypt, a policy that his brother Baldwin III had initiated but left unrealized at his death. Baldwin III had opened the offensive with the capture of **Ascalon** in 1153, the key to any attempt to invade Egypt. Significantly, Amalric had been count of **Jaffa** and Ascalon prior to his accession to the throne.

King Amalric made brief incursions into Egypt in 1163 and again in 1164, but it was only in 1167 that he undertook a concerted effort to dominate this rich land to the southwest. Although he withdrew after a successful campaign in support of his **Muslim** ally, the vizier Shawar, he brokered a good deal, whereby he received an annual subsidy of 100,000 *dinars* from his ally, and a **Frankish** garrison was stationed in **Cairo.** In effect, Egypt was a protectorate of the kingdom of Jerusalem—at least for the moment.

In August 1167, soon after returning from Egypt, Amalric married Maria Comnena, Emperor **Manuel**'s grandniece. A little over a year later, he concluded a treaty with the emperor that called for a combined **Latin-Greek** invasion and partition of Egypt in 1169. Circumstances, however, forced Amalric's hand, and he felt compelled to set off on his fourth expedition into Egypt in the autumn of 1168 without Byzantine support. The Frankish army launched a surprise attack and drove all the way to Cairo but was forced to retreat and returned home in January 1169. On October 27, 1169, a combined Franco-Byzantine force arrived before

Damietta, where it met spirited resistance led by Saladin. On December 13 the Christian allies agreed to an armistice with the Muslim enemy and raised the **siege.** On its homeward journey the Byzantine fleet was wracked by a series of storms that destroyed many of its 200 vessels.

These setbacks at the beginning and end of 1169 only served to strengthen Saladin's hand in Egypt and paved the way for his successful coup in 1171, whereby he stripped the **Fatimids** of all authority. In a real sense, Amalric's aggressive foreign policy had helped to generate the kingdom of Jerusalem's most formidable foe.

In December 1170 Saladin launched a counterattack into Gaza, but Amalric's vigorous defense forced a retreat. More significant, an Egyptian fleet recaptured the port of Eilat, thus denying the kingdom direct access to the Red Sea. It was now clear that Amalric's Egyptian strategy was in shambles, and a new and more dangerous enemy had arisen to his south. Added to that was the fact that **Nur ad-Din** was still a constant menace in the north.

Mindful of these problems, Amalric traveled to **Constantinople** in the spring of 1171, where he convinced Emperor Manuel to renew the Franco-Byzantine alliance aimed at conquering Egypt. Although a diplomatic victory, it proved to be an empty pact with no consequences. Events elsewhere, especially along the kingdom's Syrian frontier, absorbed Amalric's attention.

Upon hearing of Nur ad-Din's death on May 15, 1174, Amalric tried to take advantage of the situation by launching a new campaign in the north. Forced to break off his incursion, he was on his way home when suddenly he took ill. He died on July 11, 1174, at the age of thirty-eight, without realizing that the death of Nur ad-Din, which had seemed a heaven-sent opportunity for the Latins, would prove to be the opening that Saladin needed to unify Egypt and Syria. With that unification, the kingdom of Jerusalem would be fighting for its life. **Related Entries:** Fulk of Anjou; William of Tyre.

Anatolia

Known to medieval Europeans as *Romania* (the land of the Romans, or **Byzantines**), Anatolia is the peninsula that lies south of the Black Sea and comprises modern Asiatic Turkey. Separated from Europe by two narrow straits, the Dardanelles and the Bosporus, and the intervening Sea of Marmara, Anatolia was the heartland of the Byzantine empire until its conquest by the **Turks,** a long process that began in the eleventh century. Armies of the first three crusades marched through Anatolia on their way to **Syria-Palestine. Related Entries:** Armenia; Edessa; Ottomans; Seljuks.

Al-Andalus

An Arabic term of indeterminate origin and meaning that refers to the regions of the Iberian Peninsula ruled by various **Muslim** powers between 711 and 1492. Because of shifting political-military realities, the area that encompassed al-Andalus was not constant during these more than seven centuries. Today the most spectacular remains of the rich **Moorish** culture that flourished in al-Andalus may be seen in the architecture of southern Spain, especially in the cities of Granada, Seville, and Córdoba. Significantly, this area of modern Spain is called *Andalusia.* **Related Entries:** Almohads; Almoravids; Cid, El; Las Navas de Tolosa, Battle of; Reconquista.

Suggested Reading

Primary Source

Abd Allah, *The Tibyan: Memoirs of Abd Allah b. Buluggin, Last Zirid Amir of Granada,* trans., by A. T. Tibi (1986).

Historical Studies

Richard A. Fletcher, *Moorish Spain* (1992); Hugh Kennedy, *Muslim Spain and Portugal: A Political History of al-Andalus* (1996).

Anna Comnena (1083–after 1148)

Daughter of **Alexius I** and **historian** of her father's reign.

Anna Comnena's fame rests on the *Alexiad,* a lengthy history of her father's life and achievements. Composed in the 1140s during the reign of Emperor **Manuel I Comnenus,** whom Anna seems to have despised because of his pro-Western policies, the *Alexiad,* by way of contrast, presents Emperor Alexius as the epitome of Homeric heroism and Christian piety. Alexius appears as the embodiment of the valor of Achilles and the cunning of Odysseus, but at the same time he is the "thirteenth apostle" and ever zealous to defend Orthodox Christianity.

In stark contrast to Alexius are the Westerners (or Kelts, as she terms them), especially the **Normans,** whom Anna characterizes as rascally barbarians, although she acknowledges their courage and fighting skills. **Bohemond of Taranto** comes in for special treatment, and Anna's portrait of him exhibits both contempt and grudging admiration. She claims he went on crusade not to worship at the **Holy Sepulcher** but to fulfill his father's ambition of seizing the Roman (**Byzantine**) empire. At the same time, Anna admires Bohemond's physical beauty and military prowess. The only crusader lord whom she treats with unreserved generosity is **Raymond of Saint-Gilles,** count of Toulouse, who enjoyed good relations with her father.

Although it is a highly eccentric piece of partisan history and was composed well after the events of the **First Crusade,** Anna Comnena's *Alexiad* provides valuable testimony for anyone interested in the Byzantine view of the First Crusade and its aftermath.

Suggested Reading

Primary Sources

Anna Comnena, *The Alexiad,* trans. by Elizabeth A. S. Dawes (1967); Anna Comnena, *The Alexiad,* trans. by E. R. A. Sewter (1969).

Historical Studies

Georgina Buckler, *Anna Comnena: A Study* (1929); Thalia Gouma-Peterson, ed., *Anna Komnene and Her Times* (2000).

Antioch

A city of northern **Syria** that became the nucleus of the principality of Antioch (1098–1268). Italo-**Norman** crusaders carved out and settled the principality, but they gave way to colonists from the heartland of France after the disastrous **Battle of the Field of Blood** of 1119.

Antioch was one of the great commercial cities of the ancient Mediterranean and the site of one of the five most important patriarchal seats in the imperial Church (Rome, Constantinople, Alexandria, and Jerusalem being the other four). Arab **Muslims** captured the city in 638, and **Byzantine** forces retook it in 969. In 1084, it fell to the **Seljuk Turks,** who held it until the arrival of the armies of the second wave of the **First Crusade.**

The crusaders, about 40,000 strong counting **noncombatants,** reached Antioch on October 21, 1097, accompanied by a small Byzantine **cavalry** detachment under

High on Mount Silpius lie the remains of the citadel of Antioch. The citadel held out long after the city fell to the crusaders on June 3, 1098, and on June 28 its Turkish garrison raised the red flag to signal Kerbogha that a crusader break-out against the besieging Turkish relief force was imminent. Shortly after Kerbogha's defeat, the garrison surrendered to Bohemond.

the command of a Turkish general named Taticius. Facing them was a well fortified city, whose predominantly Christian population was kept in check by a Turkish garrison of around 5,000. The combined crusader and Byzantine forces proceeded to lay **siege** to Antioch, with the assistance of a Genoese resupply fleet that arrived in mid-November at the nearby port of Saint Symeon.

Given its size and location, on the Orontes River and backed up to a mountain, Antioch could not be fully encircled. This allowed the city to be reinforced and resupplied on occasion. Any siege would be as hard on the besiegers as the besieged. Despite the arrival of supplies from the West and from Byzantine **Cyprus,** the army's major problem was feeding itself, as it settled down for a long and brutal siege. As they exhausted nearby sources of food, the army's foragers had to range farther and farther away from their camps, and the crusaders increasingly suffered a high mortality rate due to famine and **disease.** The crusaders also suffered numerous battle casualties, as Antioch's Turkish defenders sallied out of the city at will, attacked the widely scattered crusader camps, and ambushed isolated crusaders.

Over the winter, the siege became quite bitter for both sides, but especially for the starving crusaders. On December 31, 1097, the crusaders met and defeated, at great cost, a relief force from **Damascus,** and on February 9 the crusaders defeated a second relief force from **Aleppo,** again at great cost. Both victories enabled the crusaders to tighten the noose around the city, but from the crusaders' perspective, they themselves were nearly finished. Adding to their problems was the fact that sometime in February the Byzantine commander left, promising to return with supplies, but he never did. This only deepened the crusaders' sense of desperation and abandonment by Emperor **Alexius I.**

Sometime around February the army's leaders named **Stephen of Blois** as overall commander. Ironically, Stephen would abandon the siege and the army on June 2, 1098, one day before the city fell into crusader hands. The fall of Antioch was due to a bargain struck up between **Bohemond of Taranto** and a traitorous commander of a portion of the city walls. A small band of crusaders secretly entered the city on the night of June 2–3 and opened a gate, allowing the army to pour in. A terrible **massacre** of the weakened surviving defenders and citizens of Antioch ensued, with many **Eastern Christians** numbered among the victims.

The crusaders captured Antioch in the nick of time because the vanguard of a third and massive Turkish relief force arrived the next day, June 4. The former besiegers were now the besieged, and the crusaders' situation was more desperate than ever before.

It was in this context that Peter Bartholomew had his famous **vision** of the **Holy Lance.** Discovery of the putative lance so raised the spirits of an army that was falling to pieces that the crusaders sallied forth and counterattacked the Turkish force on June 28. The attack was audacious, and it succeeded. The anonymous ***Gesta Francorum*** records that as they marched out to battle, the crusaders saw a countless host of warriors bearing white banners and riding white horses coming down from the mountains. At first confused, the crusaders then realized that this was a heavenly host, led by Saints George, Mercurius, and Demetrius, coming to their aid.

Antioch was now securely in crusader hands, but a crucial issue remained: Who would take charge of the city? Bohemond claimed the city by right of conquest. Despite Emperor Alexius' legitimate claim to the city, the crusade leaders' oaths to the emperor, and **Raymond of Saint Gilles**'s opposition to Bohemond's claim, Bohemond became prince of Antioch. Over the next several years he and his nephew **Tancred** built up a strong principality, despite the efforts of Alexius I to reclaim the city and its surrounding territory. For close to two centuries, this economically prosperous and culturally diverse principality served as a bulwark of crusader power in the north. Not even **Saladin** could take the city during his victorious march through **Syria-Palestine** in 1187–1188.

On two occasions, in 1108 and 1137, the princes of Antioch were forced to acknowledge the nominal overlordship of the Byzantine emperor, and between 1216 and 1219, the king of Cilician **Armenia** controlled the principality through his great-nephew. Despite these momentary setbacks, the princes of Antioch were essentially independent of all external authority until 1268, when **Baybars,** sultan of Egypt and Syria, captured and destroyed the city, thereby ending the 170-year life of the principality.

Related Entries: Adhémar of Monteil; Cannibalism; Constance; Crusader States; Jerusalem, Kingdom of; Kerbogha; Mamluks; Reynald of Châtillon; Robert II of Normandy; Settlement and Colonization; Saints, Warrior.

Suggested Reading

Primary Sources

The "Canso d'Antioca": An Occitan Epic Chronicle of the First Crusade, trans. by Carol Sweetenham and Linda M. Patterson (2003); Fulcher of Chartres, A History of the Expedition to Jerusalem, 1095–1127, trans. by Frances Rita Ryan (1969); Walter the Chancellor's "The Antiochene Wars": A Translation and Commentary, trans. by Thomas S. Asbridge and Susan B. Edgington (1999).

Historical Study

Thomas S. Asbridge, The Creation of the Principality of Antioch, 1098–1130 (2000).

Apocalypse and the Crusades

The notion that the struggle to liberate **Jerusalem** from the **Muslims** was somehow tied to the battle with the Antichrist, the Second Coming of Jesus, the Last Judgment, and the end of the world—all of which were foretold in the Bible's New Testament.

The final book of the Christian New Testament, known as *The Apocalypse of John,* is a strange, not easily interpreted account of what claims to be a revelation (apocalypse means "revelation") given to John the Apostle regarding the Last Days. One of the book's most vivid images is of a seven-headed, ten-horned Beast from the Abyss that Christians identify as the evil Antichrist, a false messiah who will imitate Christ, deceive people with Satan-inspired wonders, claim divine honors, and reign on Earth. In the end, however, Jesus, the True Messiah, will destroy the Antichrist and his minions, and a new Jerusalem will come down from Heaven. The world of the past will be over, replaced by this new holy city where God resides with His faithful ones.

By the ninth century, Christians in Spain were associating **Islam** with the Antichrist, and in 850 fifty or more were put to death in **Muslim** Córdoba for claiming that Muhammad was a false Christ. Because Christians viewed Islam as a pernicious parody of the Gospel message and because Jerusalem, the site of the promised new holy city, had been in Muslim hands since 638, it was not a major leap for some crusaders and **preachers** of the crusade to view this undertaking as a necessary step in ushering in the Final Days and God's total victory over evil.

There is no good reason to think that Pope **Urban II** employed Antichrist imagery or an apocalyptic message in his sermon at **Clermont.** It is interesting, however, that Guibert of Nogent, who composed a highly

The Last Judgment, **Notre Dame Cathedral, Paris, 1220–1230, restored in the nineteenth century. The saved are on Christ's right in the bottom level and the damned on the left, being led off to Hell. Note the devils in the middle foreground trying to cheat by tipping the scales of justice against the soul being weighed. Beneath Christ's feet is the Heavenly City of Jerusalem. The two angels flanking him display the instruments of his Passion (suffering): the cross and nails. The fear of damnation and belief in the imminence of the Last Judgment drove many to take up the crusader's cross.**

theological **history** of the **First Crusade** in the period 1106–1109, put apocalyptic promises into the mouth of Urban in his version of the pope's crusade sermon. According to Guibert, who was not at Clermont in November 1095, the pope claimed that it was necessary to recapture Jerusalem so that there would be Christians in the **Holy Land** to resist the Antichrist, whose time of appearance was close at hand. In other words, the crusaders were God's agents who would, in accordance with the prophecies of *The Apocalypse of John,* prepare the way for the Final Battle with Evil and the Second Coming of Christ. All evidence suggests that this notion was Guibert's and not Urban's,

but Guibert was not alone in placing the crusade into an apocalyptic context. Although the theme was a minor thread in the ideology of the crusades, it sprang up from time to time.

In 1204 and agin in 1205 Pope **Innocent III** welcomed the recent capture of **Constantinople** by the army of the **Fourth Crusade** by noting in two separate letters that this miraculous event would ultimately result in the recovery of Jerusalem and the conversion of the children of Israel—two events that were necessary preludes to the Final Days. In a **papal bull** of 1213 in which this same pope sought to rouse Christendom to one final, great effort to liberate Jerusalem, he offered a brief history of Islam and a prophecy of its imminent collapse. Noting that Muhammad had "seduced many from the truth" in the early seventh century, Innocent noted: "We have confidence . . . that the end of this beast approaches. Its number, according to *The Apocalypse of John,* is enclosed within 666, of which almost 600 years have been completed."

During the **Fifth Crusade,** the very crusade that Innocent was promoting in 1213, a number of prophetic books circulated throughout the crusader camp. One of these, *The Prophecy of the Sons of Agap,* predicted a series of imminent Christian victories over Islam, including the conquest of Mecca. This, in turn, would presage the arrival of the Antichrist, who would be named *Mexadeigan.* The prophecy did not say when he would appear or when or how he would be ultimately defeated. This and similar apocalyptic prophecies apparently played a major role in convincing the **papal legate,** Cardinal **Pelagius,** to embrace an aggressive strategy that led to disaster.

Apocalyptic imagery was a two-edged sword and was used to explain crusade reverses, as well as to pump up expectations of victory. **Bernard of Clairvaux,** in response to the disastrous failures of **Louis VII** and **Conrad III** on the **Second Crusade,** predicted the imminent coming of the Antichrist. If Bernard thought the crusaders' failure to take **Damascus** was a sign that the Antichrist was on his way, two German commentators, Gerhoh of Reichersberg and an anonymous **chronicler** from Würzburg, were convinced that the failed crusade was proof that the Antichrist was actively working in their midst. The Würzburg chronicler portrayed the Second Crusade's preachers (and presumably Bernard of Clairvaux was at the head of the list) as pseudo-prophets and "witnesses of the Antichrist." In his treatise "An Inquiry into the Antichrist," Gerhoh concluded that because the sin of avarice

(one of the beasts of the Apocalypse) pervaded Christian society in both the **Latin East** and the West, God willed that false preachers and false miracles should deceive many to take the **crusader's cross** and, thereby, to die miserable deaths in the East. **Related Entries:** Children's Crusade; Criticism of the Crusades; Great German Pilgrimage of 1064–1065; Political Crusades; Shepherds' Crusade.

Suggested Reading

Bernard McGinn, *Antichrist: Two Thousand Years of the Human Fascination with Evil* (1994); Gary West, *Religious Enthusiasm in the Medieval West: Revivals, Crusades, Saints* (2000).

Armaments

See Armor; Siege Warfare; Weapons, Hand.

Armenia

A Christian culture centered largely in two areas: Greater Armenia, roughly located between the Euphrates River in the west and the Caspian Sea in the east; and Lesser, or Cilician, Armenia in southeast **Anatolia,** formed in the second half of the eleventh century by migrants from Greater Armenia.

Around 314 the ancient kingdom of Armenia became the first state to adopt Christianity as its official religion. In the mid–fifth century it broke with the Church of the Roman empire over doctrinal issues and was ever after considered a **heretical** branch of Christendom by the **Byzantine** Orthodox Church of **Constantinople.** Because of the Armenians' anti-Byzantine sentiments, crusaders often found Armenian Christians to be willing allies, especially during the **First Crusade.**

As early as 1097, the crusaders encountered a number of petty Armenian principalities, including Greater Armenia's **Edessa,** which became a **crusader state** in February 1098. Between about 1196 and 1375 an independent Armenian kingdom flourished in Cilicia, and its monarchs were players in the game of power politics and shifting alliances that characterized the crusader states and their neighbors.

Although the king of Cilician Armenia agreed to communion with the **Roman papacy** late in the twelfth century, a union that lasted down to 1361, most Armenians remained separated by doctrine, language, ritual, and organization from the Churches of Rome and Constantinople. **Related Entries:** Baldwin I of Boulogne; Castles, Crusader; Christians, Eastern; Tancred.

Suggested Reading

Primary Source

Matthew of Edessa, *Armenia and the Crusades: Tenth to Twelfth Centuries: The Chronicle of Matthew of Edessa,* trans. by Ara E. Dostourian (1993).

Historical Studies

Thomas S. R. Boase, ed., *The Cilician Kingdom of Armenia* (1978); George A. Bournoutian, *A Concise History of the Armenian People* (2002); Jacob G. Ghazarian, *The Armenian Kingdom in Cilicia during the Crusades* (2000); Robert H. Hewson, *Armenia: A Historical Atlas* (2001); Sirarpie Der Nersessian, *The Armenians* (1970).

Armor

Body armor afforded some protection from the dangers of combat when even superficial wounds could become septic and cause agonizing death. While every soldier sought to protect his body from enemy **weapons,** the armor that crusade-era combatants wore varied widely. Culture, class, personal finances,

Ruins of the harbor castle at Korykos in Cilician Armenia constructed during the reign of Alexius I to protect the strategically important port. Here we see the remains of an Armenian chapel.

Saint Mauritius, a warrior saint, carved in northern Bavaria around 1250, wears a conical helmet and carries a large, kite-shaped shield—armor typical of 150 years earlier.

and military function determined to a great extent the quality, quantity, and type of one's armor. Another factor affecting variation was technological evolution over time in the areas of metallurgy and armaments.

Frankish Crusaders

The massive suits of plate armor that dominate modern museum rooms dedicated to medieval armaments date mainly from the fifteenth century and beyond, and certainly not from the classic Age of the Crusades. **Frankish** crusader **knights** wore a protective, knee-length coat known as a *hauberk,* which was fashioned either from chain mail (linked circles of iron) or small "fish-scale" metal plates. Weighing about twenty-five pounds, it covered the upper arms, as well as the torso and upper legs, was slit front and back to facilitate mounting and riding and was cushioned by a padded undergarment. Originally *helms,* or helmets, were conical and had a rectangular piece of iron, known as a *nasal,* that extended down to protect the nose. A leather strap secured the helm to the head. Underneath the helm the knight wore a *coif,* or hood, made of chain mail or, less commonly, fabric or leather. Under the coif, especially when worn without a helm, there was a padded cap to absorb shock. The late twelfth/early thirteenth century witnessed the development of the *great helm,* a flat-topped, cylindrical, "soup-can" helmet that covered the entire head and face, with slits for visibility and ventilation. While affording more protection, the great helm also impaired sight, breathing, and mobility. Consequently, many thirteenth-century knights chose to fight wearing only a chain coif to protect the head, neck, and cheeks. During the latter half of the twelfth century the lower arms and hands, lower legs, and feet gained protection from mail mittens and *chausses* (mail leggings that extended down to cover the feet). For fashion and identity, a fabric *surcoat* bearing a knight's distinctive emblem was now worn over the hauberk. By 1200 metal plates were sometimes fastened under the surcoat, and this additional layer of protection became more common as the century wore on. In the mid–thirteenth century shaped leather and iron-plate devices to protect the elbows, knees, and shins also became the norm.

During the **First Crusade,** and for many years thereafter, knights carried on the left arm a huge kite-shaped shield with an arched top that covered the vulnerable left side of the body from shoulder to knee. The right side of the body was protected by a sword or lance. During the late twelfth cen-

Franks and Muslims in early thirteenth-century armor. The battle between Roland and Farragut from *The Charlemagne Window,* **Chartres Cathedral, France. Note the circular Saracen shield and the triangular crusader shield and "soup-can-style" great helm. In the lower right-hand corner, Muslim warriors wear the** *baida,* **or egg-shaped helmet.**

tury the shield became smaller and triangular in shape, enabling the knight to see better. Pictorial evidence from the late thirteenth-century **kingdom of Jerusalem** shows that some Frankish knights had adopted the two types of even smaller shields favored by **Islamic** mounted warriors—round and oval. As body armor became heavier and more effective, some knights apparently thought that a small shield allowed them to fight with greater speed and agility and afforded even better visibility.

Contrary to Hollywood's depiction of medieval warriors, when not faced with the imminent threat of battle, knights did not normally travel about in their armor. It made no sense to do so. Beyond the issues of com-

fort and muscle fatigue, there were the dangers of heat stroke and dehydration.

A good war horse was expensive and scarce in **Outremer,** but knights considered such horses essential if they were to maintain their military functions and social status. Moreover, a knight unhorsed in battle was fairly easy prey. Consequently, some knights, certainly not all, provided their horses with armor. Possibly due to Islamic influences, from the mid–twelfth century onward some knights fit mail, fabric, or leather armor under the *caparisons,* or horse-coverings, of their steeds. By the mid–thirteenth century some horses went into battle wearing chain-mail caparisons known as *bards.* A full bard included a hood-like device of chain mail that protected head, neck, and throat.

Knights were members of the **feudal** hierarchy and not only could afford such expensive armor (and the armor became increasingly expensive as it evolved) but also were expected by reason of their status and presumed military importance to wear it—no matter the cost. Rank always has its burdens. Crusaders lower on the scale, those in the rank and file, were less well protected.

Infantry soldiers wore what they could afford or scavenge, and this included armor of mail, quilted fabric, or leather. Cloth armor might not seem to be effective protection, but a **Muslim chronicler,** describing a battle of 1191, notes that some Christian foot soldiers had ten arrows stuck harmlessly in their quilted body armor.

The standard infantryman's iron cap evolved in early thirteenth-century **Normandy** from the early conical cap to the *chapel-de-fer,* or "iron hat." Also known as a kettle-hat, because it resembled an upturned kettle, it was rounded with a broad brim. The brim replaced the nose guard, or nasal, by providing some protection from sword blows to the face delivered from above by an enemy horseman. The crusader who had such protection probably felt fortunate.

As was the case with their Muslim counterparts, Frankish foot soldiers secured whatever type of shield they could—wood, metal, or leather, old or new, Eastern or Western.

Muslim Warriors

Common foot soldiers in the armies of Islam normally went without expensive mail armor, unless they could **plunder** it from the enemy or pick it up among the debris of the battlefield. They might, however, afford fabric or leather armor. Some infantrymen, especially **Turks,** wore a Central Asian type of splint armor, which was made of overlapping, fairly large, rectangular plates, or scales, of metal or wood. Those who were fortunate enough also secured an egg-shaped metal cap (the *baida,* or "egg"). Some of these had nasals, or nose guards, but most did not. The cap might also have an *aventail,* a piece of chain mail that hung from the rear and protected the back and sides of the neck, but in all probability this extra protection was available only to richer members of the army. Because the baida was a mark of prestige, not too many foot soldiers had one.

A shield normally completed the protective gear of the average Muslim soldier on foot. Islamic infantry shields came in a variety of shapes and sizes. Some were quite large and kite-shaped and constructed to be held on the ground to create a defensive wall. Most shields, however, were fairly small and either round or oval. Whatever its size, shape, or composition, the shield was a necessary piece of equipment. For a fair percentage of the poorest foot soldiers, a shield might be their only protection against enemy missiles and thrusts.

Not all Muslim mounted warriors were rich, but all of the richer members of the army were mounted. Those members of the **cavalry** who did not belong to the elite stratum of society probably were still better off than the average foot soldier and could afford better armor. Cavalrymen who fought in the Turkish style with primary reliance on their compound bows were, on average, not the richest members of the army, but they took great pride in their appearance. Their reliance on speed and mobility and their moderate wealth resulted in their wearing padded, brightly colored topcoats of brocade or silk and turbans or fur-trimmed hats. The somewhat slower but richer horse soldiers who fought in the Arab, or **Syrian,** style with sword and lance had only the best metal armor for themselves and their horses.

The practice of providing horses with armor probably began with well-to-do Muslim cavalrymen, although the chain armor they gave their horses was light and flexible, so as not to limit too much speed and mobility. Likewise, Islamic metal body armor was lighter and more flexible than its Frankish counterpart. Somewhat like the Western hauberk, the *zardiya* was a riveted chain-mail coat that reached to the knees or even the ankles. A shorter metal tunic, made of chain mail or metal scales or small metal brads attached to felt and known as a *kazaghand,* was also popular (and far more comfortable). Verses from the Koran often were incised into the body army and inscribed onto the shirts worn under the armor in the belief that they afforded the wearer divine protection. A baida with aventail and a round shield, each of which might have its own Koranic verses, completed the well-dressed Arab-style horse soldier's defensive attire. A less well-dressed comrade might wear only a cloth turban on his head, but turbans had been known to deflect sword blows.

Despite changing styles and technical breakthroughs in armor manufacture, metal armor was so costly that it tended to be passed down through the generations. It was not unusual to see a Frankish warrior in 1200 wearing his great-great-grandfather's helm and hauberk from the First Crusade, and it was not unusual for a Muslim warrior in the army of **Saladin** to be wearing a chain-mail hauberk that some ancestor had taken off a fallen crusader nearly a century earlier. **Related Entries:** Castles, Crusader; Sergeant; Siege Warfare.

Suggested Reading

Robert Elgood, *Islamic Arms and Armour* (1979); David Nicolle, *Arms and Armour of the Crusading Era, 1050–1350: Western Europe and the Crusader States* (1999).

Artillery

See Siege Warfare.

Ascalon

A strategic port city along the southern **Palestinian** coast that seesawed between **Frankish** and **Muslim** occupation from 1153 to 1247.

Ascalon first came into the consciousness of the crusaders when, not far from the city, they won a resounding victory over **Fatimid** forces on August 12, 1099. The victory brought with it tremendous booty and secured the crusaders' hold on **Jerusalem,** which they had captured less than a month earlier. Despite the crusader victory, Ascalon remained in Muslim hands until it fell to the army of King **Baldwin III** on August 22, 1153, after a prolonged **siege.** Prior to its capture, Ascalon served as a forward base for numerous Egyptian invasions. With its capture, the Franks secured their southern frontier and also completed their conquest of the entire Palestinian coast.

Thirty-four years later, on September 5, 1187, Ascalon surrendered peacefully to **Saladin** in return for his promise to release King **Guy of Lusignan** and the master of the **Order of the Temple,** both of whom had been captured at **Hattin.** Saladin then proceeded to destroy Ascalon's fortifications.

King **Richard I** reoccupied Ascalon in January 1192 and for the next seven months worked on refortifying the city. All of this labor was nullified in September, when a demilitarized Ascalon, stripped again of its walls, was handed back to Saladin as part of a truce arrangement.

Two of the few positive accomplishments of the **Crusade of 1239–1241** were recovery of Ascalon in late 1239 and subsequent refortification of the city. Less than eight years later, on October 14, 1247, **Ayyubid** forces from Egypt recaptured stones and timbers sunk into Ascalon's harbor, rendering it useless as a port. **Related Entries:** First Crusade; Third Crusade.

Assassins

A **Shia** sect, more correctly known as the *Nizari Ismailis,* noted for its use of murder to eliminate rivals.

Today the term *assassin* means someone who kills a public figure by stealth or treachery, and it had this meaning as early as the thirteenth century in Europe, thanks to tales that filtered back from the **crusader states** regarding a radical Shia element that murdered **Muslim** and Christian princes alike. The name originates from the Arabic

Crusaders (wearing late thirteenth-century armor) besiege Antioch during the First Crusade. Manuscript copy of the *Estoire d'Eracles,* a continuation of William of Tyre's history to 1261. Produced in Paris around 1300. The Walters Art Museum, Baltimore.

Count Henry of Champagne and his escorts are welcomed by the Assassins' Old Man of the Mountain. To demonstrate their loyalty to their master, two Assassins leap to their death from the tower of the castle of *al-Kahf.* Manuscript copy of the *Estoire d'Eracles,* a continuation of William of Tyre's history to 1261. Produced in Paris around 1300. The Walters Art Museum, Baltimore.

Ascalon, and it remained in Muslim hands for the rest of the Age of the Crusades.

In 1270, as part of a strategy of making **Syria-Palestine** a place that could not support future crusades, **Baybars** ordered *hashishin,* which means "users of hashish," a mind-altering drug, and it was applied only to the **Syrian** branch of the Nizari Ismailis. Contemporary Western reports imputed the use of hashish to the Assassins, but reliable Islamic sources were silent on the issue. If the Assassins used the drug, it was not to incite themselves to murderous fanaticism because hashish does not normally induce that state. Possibly some used it as a means of anticipating the delights of Paradise that awaits Islamic martyrs. It is just as likely that many non-Assassin contemporaries applied the term simply as an expression of contempt or fear for the exotic beliefs and perceived wild behavior of these Ismailis.

The Order of Assassins began as a militant splinter group of Ismailis in the mountains of northern Iran under the leadership Hasan-i Sabbah, who offered a messianic brand of Shia that he termed "New Preaching." In 1090 Hasan and a handful of followers seized the fortress of *Alamut* to use as a base in their revolt against the **Seljuk Turks.** In the eyes of these Persian Shias, not only were the Seljuks oppressive alien overlords, they were false Muslims by virtue of their **Sunnism.**

Four years later, as Hasan-i Sabbah was consolidating his position within Iran, a major schism developed within Ismaili Shia when the presumptive heir to the **Fatimid** caliphate, a man named Nizar, was passed over in favor of his younger brother in 1094. Nizar's revolt, defeat, and death inspired Hasan and the vast majority of Persian Ismailis to break off all relations with their Egyptian coreligionists. Hasan now became the undisputed leader of a new Islamic religious-political entity—Nizari Ismailism—that found itself at war with both the Seljuks and the Fatimids.

Always greatly outnumbered by their enemies, Hasan's followers resorted to the strategy of selective assassination of high-ranking foes. The first of what became a long series of calculated killings had already taken place in 1092 with the murder of the Egyptian vizier Nizam al-Mulk. To their victims, the killers were criminal terrorists at war with true religion and civilization; to Nizaris, the assassin was an honored and pious executioner. If he died in the act, as many did, he was a holy martyr.

Early in the twelfth century, Nizarite preachers moved into northern Syria, which was also under Seljuk domination, spreading their message there among receptive Ismailis and establishing a branch of their movement that the crusaders would call the Assassins and whose leader would be known in European lore as the *Old Man of the Mountain.*

Whether in Iran or Syria, the Nizari Ismailis comprised a small, closed society with secret oaths and rites, closely guarded esoteric doctrines, and hierarchical ranks. Knowledge about them was and is fragmentary and confused, and a number of unfounded legends arose in both Muslim and Christian literature about this sect. An often-repeated story in medieval Europe is the death-leap legend in which Assassin fanatics leap to their deaths from high towers or walls at the command of the Old Man of the Mountain to demonstrate their loyalty and allow him to intimidate some potential enemy whom he is hosting. Supposedly **Henry of Champagne** witnessed such a performance in 1194. There is no credible evidence to substantiate this or similar stories.

The truth regarding Nizari activities was fantastic enough. Despite their small numbers, they struck terror among Muslims and Christians alike wherever they operated. Under their greatest leader in Syria, Sinan ibn Salman, they made two unsuccessful attempts on the life of **Saladin.** Apparently the two attempted assassinations of Saladin convinced this champion of Islamic unity and Sunni orthodoxy to adopt a policy of tolerance toward the Nizaris.

Some groups refused to be intimidated by the Assassins. They included the **Templars** and the **Hospitalers,** both of which not only fought the Assassins, but at times allied with them, sometimes even against common Christian enemies. In addition, both **military orders** forced the Assassins to pay them annual tribute. The **Mongols** and **Mamluks** were also unintimidated and combined to destroy the Nizaris as an effective political force. When Mongol forces invaded Iran in 1256 their first objective was neutralizing Ismaili strongholds. *Alamut,* the first and greatest of the Nizari **castles,** fell that year; the last Ismaili fortification in Iran succumbed in 1258. In Syria the story was similar. **Baybars,** the Mamluk defender of Islam against the Christians and the Mongols, could not tolerate the continued existence of these supposed **heretics** and terrorists. In 1273 the Mamluks occupied the last Assassin stronghold in Syria; shortly before then they had deported the last Old Man of the Mountain to Egypt. **Related Entries:** Conrad of Montferrat; Edward I; Islamic Peoples.

Suggested Reading

Farhad Daftary, *The Assassin Legends: Myths of the Isma'ilis* (1994); M. G. S. Hodgson, *The Order of the Assassins* (1955); Bernard Lewis, *The Assassins: A Radical Sect in Islam* (1968).

Ayn Jalut, Battle of

The high-water mark of the **Mongol** advance into **Syria-Palestine** and a decisive setback for them that led to the **Mamluks'** gaining possession of Syria and joining it to Egypt to create a new **Middle Eastern** empire.

Following their **pillage** of **Aleppo** in January 1260 and occupation of **Damascus** in March, Mongol forces under the command of Kitbogha (a member of a Central Asian branch of Christianity known as *Nestorianism*) penetrated into northern Palestine with the intention of pushing all the way to Egypt. Because the **Franks** at **Acre** felt equally threatened by the Mongol advance, they spurned an alliance with the Mongols and granted safe passage through their lands to Qutuz, Mamluk sultan of Egypt. On September 3, 1260, the sultan's army defeated the Mongols at Ayn Jalut (The Spring of Goliath) not far from Nazareth.

Following this victory, occupied Islamic cities in Syria rose in rebellion against their Mongol captors and welcomed in the Mamluks. The immediate consequence of Ayn Jalut was that the Mongols were driven from Syria, but at the time the setback probably did not seem to the Mongols that significant because they had committed only a small portion of their forces to this theater of operation.

Not deterred, the Mongols continued to dream of conquering Egypt, and they continued to invade Syrian lands into the early fourteenth century. They even momentarily drove the Mamluks out of Syria in 1300. Nevertheless, Syria-Palestine was now beyond their grasp. Indeed, arguably Syria-Palestine was never a land the Mongols could conquer because it lacked the proper grasslands to sustain their **cavalry** forces. Whatever the case, the Mongol il-khans of Persia would and did have to try different tactics, which included proposing alliances with the Christians of the West against the Mamluks. **Related Entries:** Ayyubids; Missionaries.

Ayyubids

The Kurdish family of Najm ad-Din Ayyub, father of **Saladin** and **Saphadin,** that ruled Egypt from 1174 to 1250 and **Syria** from 1176 to 1260.

The Ayyubids reached the height of their powers under the leadership of Saladin, who united Syria and Egypt in 1176. Saladin held his empire together by apportioning out parts of it to close relatives, who ruled in his name and under his overall command. Following Saladin's death in 1193, Ayyubid unity disappeared, as kinsmen became competitors. The three chief centers of power and competition were: (1) **Cairo,** from which Egypt was governed; (2) **Damascus,** which controlled southern Syria; and (3) **Aleppo,** the capital of northern Syria.

During the early years of this competition, Saladin's brother **al-Adil** (Saphadin) managed to outmaneuver Saladin's sons and a grandson to gain hegemony for himself and his own four sons, who succeeded him as sultans in Egypt and Damascus. Of these four sons, the most notable was **al-Kamil,** who ruled in Egypt until 1238. Aleppo remained in the hands of the family of Saladin.

The Egyptian branch of the Ayyubids came to an end with a coup that began with the murder of Sultan Turan Shah in 1250 by a faction of his **Mamluk** soldiers. The two Syrian branches managed to hang on for another decade but were swept away in the wake of the **Mongols'** destruction of Aleppo and capture of Damascus in 1260. By 1263 the Syrian Ayyubids had lost out to the new champions of Islam in the Middle East, the Mamluk sultans of Egypt, who led the successful counteroffensive against the Mongols in **Syria-Palestine** and joined Syria with Egypt to form a powerful empire bent on the full destruction of the **crusader states. Related Entries:** Baybars; Islamic Peoples.

Suggested Reading

Primary Source

Ahmad ibn Ali Maqrizi, *A History of the Ayyubid Sultans of Egypt,* trans. by Ronald J. C. Broadhurst (1980).

Historical Study

R. Stephen Humphreys, *From Saladin to the Mongols: The Ayyubids of Damascus, 1193–1260* (1977).

B

Babylon

See Cairo.

Background to the Crusades

See Christians, Eastern; Clermont, Council of; Great German Pilgrimage of 1064–1065; Gregory VII, Pope; Investiture Controversy; Manzikert, Battle of; Reconquista; Urban II, Pope.

Bailli

The regent for an underage or incapacitated king or queen of **Jerusalem.**

From the reign of the infant **Baldwin V,** it was clearly established that relatives had first claim to the *baillage,* and of these, parents had the strongest claim. In the absence of a surviving parent, the office of regent would pass to the next closest relative, male or female, from the royal branch of the family. To be eligible, the claimant had to appear before the **High Court,** which examined and ruled on the would-be *bailli*'s degree of relationship with the monarch. During the period in which absentee **Hohenstaufen** kings resided in Europe (1229–1268), they resorted to appointing administrative *baillis,* who served as their

deputies in the **Holy Land. Related Entries:** Alice of Champagne; Baldwin IV; Isabella (Yolanda) II; John of Brienne; Maria of Montferrat; Sibylla.

Baldwin I (of Boulogne)

Count of **Edessa** (r. 1098–1100) and first **Latin** king of **Jerusalem** (r. 1100–1118).

Baldwin of Boulogne traveled on the **First Crusade** in the retinue of his older brother, **Godfrey of Bouillon,** duke of Lower Lorraine. Left out of the division of family lands, Baldwin was one of a handful of landless younger sons in search of a principality—a cohort whose numbers and impact on the crusade many modern historians have exaggerated.

When Duke Godfrey sought permission for his army to cross Hungary on its way to Constantinople, King Coloman demanded that Baldwin, his wife Godvere, and their children serve as hostages to guarantee that there would be no **pillaging.** Consequently, Godfrey's army passed through Hungary without incident.

As the army passed though **Anatolia,** Baldwin and **Tancred** broke off from the main force in early September 1097. With their respective followers, the two young commanders set off on separate routes southward into Cilicia, a region inhabited by **Armenian** Christians but under **Turkish** domination. Undoubtedly both men wished to acquire land and riches, but the primary impetus behind the expeditions seems to have been the army's leaders' desire to secure their right flank, to create a base of supplies for their advance into northern Syria, and to liberate fellow Christians. Despite some nasty confrontations between Baldwin and Tancred, the operation was a success.

Around this time Baldwin's wife died, and with her died his hopes of an inheritance from his father-in-law. That might have been a factor in his decision to undertake a second Armenian adventure. After consulting with his brothers, Baldwin marched east with a small force, liberating Armenian towns along the way. Meanwhile, the main crusader force marched south toward **Antioch.**

As Baldwin moved east, he received an invitation from Thoros, lord of Edessa, to help him secure his hold on the city and surrounding territory. Baldwin accepted and reached the city in February 1098. The aged and unpopular Thoros adopted Baldwin as his son and heir, but this might have been a fatal error. On March 9 there was an uprising, in which Thoros and his wife were killed. Most historians suspect Baldwin helped engineer the riot. Whatever the truth, the Edessans accepted Baldwin as their new lord, and he married an Armenian princess to cement the relationship.

Baldwin then proceeded to carve out the first significant **crusader state,** the county of Edessa, which would serve as a northeastern buffer, protecting crusader lands to the south until its capture by **Zangi** in 1144. But Baldwin served as count of Edessa for only a little more than two years.

On July 18, 1100, his brother Godfrey, the prince of Jerusalem and defender of its churches, died. Both **Bohemond** of Antioch and Baldwin had adherents who pushed forward their names as successors to Godfrey, but Bohemond had the misfortune of being captured by **Muslim** forces in July or August. Still, not leaving anything to chance, Baldwin acted quickly and decisively. Placing Edessa into the capable hands of his cousin, **Baldwin of Le Bourcq,** Count Baldwin marched south to Jerusalem, which he reached on November 9. Four days later he was declared king of Jerusalem. Secure in his new position, he delayed his coronation until December 25, 1100, when he was crowned at the Church of the Nativity in Bethlehem. The symbolism of the date and site could not have been more obvious. A new era had dawned with the creation of the crusader kingdom of Jerusalem.

As king of Jerusalem, Baldwin I succeeded in engineering the deposition of Daimbert from the **patriarchate of Jerusalem.** Daimbert, a distinguished church reformer whom **Urban II** had dispatched to the East to replace the deceased **Adhémar of Monteil** as **papal legate,** appears to have envisioned turning Jerusalem into a vassal-state of the Church or, at least, creating an independent church that would serve as the moral voice of authority in the kingdom. Whatever his goal, Daimbert picked the wrong opponent. Baldwin, who had trained for the priesthood as a youth, had absolutely no sympathy for church reformers who supported the extreme papal position advocated by **Gregory VII** and Urban II. As a result of Baldwin's decisive actions, the kingdom of Jerusalem was firmly established as a secular, **feudal** monarchy.

Baldwin also demonstrated strong abilities in two other crucial areas. He proved willing and able to settle disputes among the fractious great lords of the East, thereby greatly enhancing the prestige and authority of his office. He was also an active campaigner and conqueror. By the end of 1110 he had conquered almost the entire Palestinian coast, with **Acre** his most important conquest. He also extended his kingdom southward, all the way to the Red Sea, and halted Egyptian and **Seljuk** attacks on his lands.

When Baldwin I died on April 2, 1118, while withdrawing his army from Egypt, he left behind a true kingdom in which the king served as undisputed overlord of all the **Frankish** lords of **Outremer. Related Entries:** Eustace III of Boulogne; Fulcher of Chartres; Investiture Controversy.

Baldwin II (of Le Bourcq)

A second-level leader of the **First Crusade,** count of **Edessa** (r. 1100–1118), and king of **Jerusalem** (r. 1118–1131).

Baldwin left home in August 1096 with the forces of his cousin, **Godfrey of Bouillon.** He distinguished himself at the **Battle of Dorylaeum** and soon thereafter joined his cousin **Baldwin of Boulogne** in journeying to Edessa and establishing there the first **crusader state.** He later rejoined the army as it closed on Jerusalem, accompanied **Tancred** in the capture of Bethlehem, and partook in the **siege** and capture of Jerusalem in July 1099. He joined **Bohemond of Taranto** in **Antioch** at some unknown time, but in the summer of 1100 traveled back to Edessa to accept rule over the county from Baldwin of Boulogne, who was on his way to Jerusalem to become its first **Latin** king.

King Baldwin I died on April 2, 1118, and five days later Baldwin of Le Bourcq arrived in Jerusalem unannounced, having heard of his cousin's death as he traveled south to spend Easter in the Holy City. The barons met and elected Baldwin king, and he was duly crowned on Easter Sunday, April 14. The following year Baldwin II handed over Edessa to his cousin, Joscelin of Courtney.

Baldwin II proved to be a strong and competent monarch who continued his predecessor's policies of expanding the territories of the kingdom, extending royal authority, and strengthening the kingdom's military infrastructure. Following the disaster at the **Battle of the Field of Blood** of June 28, 1119, Baldwin rushed north, stabilized the situation, rewon some key strongholds, and took charge of the principality of Antioch, which he ruled for four years. By this act alone he underscored the king of Jerusalem's ultimate responsibility for and authority over the other crusader states. His request for another crusade to aid the embattled **Latin East** resulted in Pope **Calixtus II**'s **Crusade of 1122–1126,** which captured **Tyre** in July 1124. Ironically, Baldwin was a captive at the time, having been captured in April 1123 and not released until August 1124. He and Baldwin I had established such a stable state that the kingdom managed to function without its king for more than fifteen months. King Baldwin also was a patron of the emerging **Order of the Knights Templar** and gave them the royal palace in the so-called Temple of Solomon as their headquarters.

Because he and his wife, Queen Morfia, had only daughters, he summoned **Fulk V of Anjou** from France to marry his eldest daughter **Melisende,** thereby becoming next in line to assume the duties of kingship. When Baldwin II died on August 21, 1131, he passed on to Fulk and Melisende a strong monarchy and a stable state. With him died, however, the last of the old breed of First Crusade veterans who remained in the East. **Related Entries:** Alice of Antioch; Eustace III of Boulogne.

Baldwin III

The first native-born king of **Jerusalem** (r. 1143–1163), Baldwin continued the work of his three predecessors in building up the power and authority of the royal establishment.

Baldwin was only thirteen when his father, King **Fulk of Anjou,** died on November 10, 1143, and **Melisende,** Baldwin's mother, was crowned co-monarch alongside her underage son in the **Church of the Holy Sepulcher** on Christmas Day. In 1145 Baldwin came of legal age but Melisende was not willing to part with her share of royal power. Even as he matured into a seasoned warrior who enjoyed the respect of the lords of his kingdom, Baldwin felt himself being pushed increasingly aside by his mother. Finally, in the spring of 1152 Baldwin moved decisively to assert his sole claim to the crown, resorting to an attack on the citadel of Jerusalem, where his mother took refuge. Melisende was forced to capitulate and retire to her dowry lands around Nablus, which she continued to rule until her death.

Both before and after his coup, the young king's reign was eventful: **Edessa** fell to **Zangi** in 1144; the **Second Crusade,** in which Baldwin participated, attacked **Damascus** and utterly failed; **Nur ad-Din** arose as the new champion of **jihad;** from 1152 onward Baldwin frequently found it necessary to intervene in the affairs of **Tripoli** and **Antioch,** thereby strengthening royal claims to authority over the other **crusader states; Ascalon,** the last Palestinian port still in **Muslim** hands, fell to Baldwin's forces in 1153; he fought an intermittent war with Damascus in 1157–1160; and he entered into an alliance with **Manuel Comnenus** in 1158 when he married the emperor's niece, Theodora. Baldwin died at the age of thirty-three on February 10, 1163, before he could realize his grand plan of uniting all the Christian powers of the East in a grand alliance aimed at the conquest of Egypt. In death, he was eulogized as a great king. If we can believe **William of Tyre,** even large numbers of local Muslims lamented his passing, and Nur ad-Din refused to attack the kingdom during its period of mourning out of respect for the memory of a great prince. **Related Entry:** Amalric.

Baldwin IV

The "leper king" of **Jerusalem** (r. 1174–1185).

The coronation of Baldwin IV by Amaury, Latin patriarch of Jerusalem. A manuscript copy of the *Estoire d'Eracles*, a continuation of William of Tyre's history to 1229. Late thirteenth century (1295?), Paris or northern France. The Walters Art Museum, Baltimore.

The son of King **Amalric,** Baldwin IV, like his uncle **Baldwin III,** was only thirteen when he succeeded to the throne. Also like his uncle, he was noted for his learning, keen intelligence, sense of **chivalry,** and qualities as a warrior. Because he contracted the most deadly form of leprosy, his reign was short and interrupted by medical crises that necessitated frequent regencies, but throughout he conducted himself with fortitude and a good measure of success in foreign and domestic affairs.

Baldwin's leprosy, which began to manifest itself around 1171, was the determining factor throughout his life and reign. When King Amalric died on July 11, 1174, he left behind a fifteen-year-old daughter, **Sibylla,** and Baldwin. Although Baldwin had not yet officially been diagnosed as a leper, it was obvious he was ill. Nevertheless, the **High Court** chose to recognize him as king in hope that, if he proved to have leprosy, a suitable husband would be found for Sibylla during the next two years, when the king was still a legal minor. He could then abdicate before assuming his royal powers, and Sibylla and her husband could rule as co-monarchs. It did not work out that way.

Baldwin IV came of age on July 15, 1176, and by then it was obvious that he had leprosy, but he was resolved to fight the **disease** and do his duty as king. Despite his desire to abdicate as his disease progressed, he discovered that it was necessary for him to remain on the throne to hold the kingdom's factions in check and to provide a modicum of stability in his realm. At the same time, he would spend most of the rest of his life searching for a suitable successor because his disease precluded his marrying and fathering children.

When Sibylla married William of **Montferrat** in November, Baldwin thought William would be a worthy deputy and heir. William, however, died in June, leaving behind a pregnant wife, who gave birth to a son, **Baldwin (V).** In 1180 King Baldwin gave permission for Sibylla to marry **Guy of Lusignan,** and in the summer of 1183 his health had so degenerated that he appointed Guy, who was his heir apparent, **bailli** (regent). Guy proved incompetent and was removed from office after a few months. In November 1183 King Baldwin had his five-year-old nephew, Baldwin, crowned co-king.

Baldwin IV died in 1185, sometime before May 16. He was not quite twenty-four. **Related Entries:** Agnes of Courtenay; Lazarus, Order of Saint.

Suggested Reading

Bernard Hamilton, *The Leper King and His Heirs: Baldwin IV and the Crusader Kingdom of Jerusalem* (2000).

Baldwin V

The "boy king" of **Jerusalem** (r. 1185–1186).

Baldwin, the son of **Sibylla** and William of **Montferrat,** was crowned co-king by his dying uncle, **Baldwin IV,** on November 20, 1183, with provision for the five-year-old boy's guardianship and regency upon Baldwin IV's death. When his uncle died in early 1185, the boy became sole king, but he died in **Acre** the following year. He was buried, alongside his six royal predecessors, in the **Church of the Holy Sepulcher**'s chapel of Mount Cavalry. **Related Entries:** Bailli; Guy of Lusignan.

Baldwin IX of Flanders and I of Constantinople

Count of Flanders and Hainaut, a leader of the **Fourth Crusade,** and the first **Latin** emperor of **Constantinople** (r. 1204–1205).

Count Baldwin IX of Flanders (r. 1194–1205) assumed the **crusader's cross** on Ash Wednesday, February 23, 1200, in the city of Bruges. Joining him were his wife, Marie, two brothers, a nephew, and other Flemish nobles. The twenty-eight-year-old count was the most powerful and probably richest **feudal** vassal of France and had a well deserved reputation for piety and justice. With the death on May 24, 1201, of his brother-in-law, Count Thibaut III of Champagne, who had sworn the cross on November 28, 1199, Baldwin became the unchallenged second-highest-ranking leader of the army of the Fourth Crusade—second only to Marquis Boniface of **Montferrat.**

Because of his rank, Baldwin played a key role in all the strategic decisions made in the course of the crusade. His unquestioned courage in battle before the walls of Constantinople only added to his authority.

Following the crusaders' second capture of the city in April 1204, only two credible candidates emerged in the contest for the office of Latin emperor: Baldwin and Boniface. With the aid of the Venetian electors, who found Boniface unacceptable, Baldwin was elected emperor and was duly enthroned on May 16 as Baldwin I.

Countess Marie, who had remained in Flanders until the birth of their daughter, Margaret, arrived in **Acre** just as news reached the city of Baldwin's election as emperor. The new empress never had a chance to rejoin her husband because she took ill and died soon after landing at Acre, a city noted for its **diseases.**

A year plus one day after the Latin capture of Constantinople, on April 14, 1205, Emperor Baldwin was captured in battle at **Adrianople** by the forces of the Vlacho-Bulgarian king, Kalojan. Baldwin died under mysterious circumstances while in captivity and probably before the year was over. **Related Entries:** Constantinople, Latin Empire of; Cross, True; Frankish Greece.

Balian II of Ibelin

Lord of Nablus, defender of **Jerusalem** in 1187, and supporter of **Conrad of Montferrat**'s claim to the crown of the **kingdom of Jerusalem.**

So great was his fame and reputation that the Arab **historian** Ibn al-Athir referred to him as "Balian ibn Barzan [Balian, the son of Barzan], ruler of Ramla, who was almost equal in rank to the king." It is not clear if Balian ever held Ramla, following the exile in 1186 of his elder brother Baldwin, the lord of Ramla. What is clear is that in the autumn of 1187 Balian was the *de facto* king of the holy city while King **Guy** was a **prisoner** of **Saladin.** Several years later he became a would-be king maker.

Much of what we know or think we know about Balian comes from the partisan *Chronicle of Ernoul,* which probably was composed by Balian's squire, Ernoul. Because of Ernoul's desire to paint his lord as a hero, we cannot accept his stories as unvarnished truth. Regardless, other sources, both **Latin** and Arabic, also show that Balian played a heroic role in the disasters of 1187 and continued to be a major figure in the politics and life of the **Latin East** for several years thereafter.

Balian was among the few **knights** who managed to break through the encircling enemy force at the **Battle of Hattin** and reach the safety of **Tyre.** When Saladin set **siege** to the city, Balian sent word to the sultan, with whom he was already acquainted, requesting a guarantee of safe conduct so that he could travel to Jerusalem to rescue his wife, Maria Comnena, the widow of King **Amalric I,** and their children. Saladin agreed, with the stipulation that Balian swear to spend only one night in the city and not take up arms against him. Balian agreed.

When Balian arrived, he found Jerusalem overrun with refugees, stripped of most of its soldiers, in turmoil, and leaderless. Heraclius, the **patriarch of Jerusalem,** convinced Balian that he was needed in the city and did not need to honor his oath to an **infidel.** Balian then took charge of Jerusalem's defenses, after having extracted oaths of loyalty from the city's defenders. To bolster his small force, he knighted all boys of noble lineage who were fifteen or older and also knighted thirty non-noble Latin citizens of the city.

When Saladin's army arrived and laid siege to the city, Balian led the defenders in a spirited resistance, which cost the besieging army many casualties. Early in the siege, Balian, who still enjoyed good relations with Saladin, convinced the sultan that circumstances had prevented his honoring his oath. He further convinced Saladin to provide an escort for Maria, the children, and several other people of rank to the safety of **Tripoli,** which was still in crusader hands.

Most residents of Jerusalem could not begin to hope for such a **chivalric** gesture. Despite the defenders' bravery and limited successes, the situation grew bleaker every day and seemed hopeless, especially once the sultan's army managed to undermine a portion of the city's walls. **Massacre** seemed imminent. Saladin had originally offered the city generous terms of surrender, but when it refused his offer and resisted, the sultan openly declared his intention of visiting upon the Christians of the city the same sort of bloodshed that the crusaders had inflicted on the city's **Muslims** in 1099.

To avoid such a fate, Balian resorted to negotiation. He requested a meeting with Saladin and convinced him that, faced with certain death, the defenders were prepared to destroy the city, including all of its Muslim sanctuaries, and to kill every Muslim **prisoner** in it before they went down fighting. The threat worked, and Saladin offered new terms of surrender, by which he allowed the Latin inhabi-

tants to ransom themselves from captivity once they surrendered the city, at the rate of ten golden *byzants* for each man, five for a **woman,** and two for a child. All the indigent could be ransomed by a single payment of 100,000 *byzants.* Balian accepted, and arranged for the immediate release of 7,000 poor (two women or ten children were computed as the equivalent of one man for purposes of ransom) with a payment of 30,000 *byzants.* Balian tried his best to raise additional money for the release of more of the city's poor and failed. He also appealed with only partial success to Saladin's well-known sense of charity. Despite several acts of spontaneous generosity by Saladin and his brother **al-Adil,** by which they freely released several thousand captives, a large number of Jerusalem's poorest inhabitants were **enslaved**—anywhere from 11,000 to 16,000.

After the city capitulated on October 2, Balian took charge of one-third of the many thousands who were allowed to leave. The **Templars** and **Hospitalers** each took charge of a third, as well. Escorted by Muslim troops who acted as a security force, the three contingents made their way to Tripoli. There Balian was reunited with his wife and children.

Although all of his lands were overrun by Saladin's army, Balian did not give up. By November 1189 he was at the siege of **Acre.** When Queen **Sibylla** and her two small daughters died there in the summer of 1190, Balian saw an opportunity to reverse his fortunes. King Guy's claim to the throne rested on his marriage to Sibylla, and with her death the heiress to the throne became Balian's stepdaughter, **Isabella,** the daughter of King Amalric and Maria Comnena. For this reason, Balian supported the marriage of Conrad of Montferrat and Isabella and Conrad's claim to the throne.

Conrad's untimely death did not destroy Balian's hopes because Isabella then married **Henry of Champagne,** thereby making Henry king, and for a short while Balian enjoyed a special place of authority within the kingdom. During the summer of 1192 he also served in the **Third Crusade**'s final military operations and was employed as a negotiator for the truce with Saladin that was concluded in September 1192. Through this peace settlement, he also managed to gain the estate of Caymont from Saladin. Sometime during the following year, 1193, he died, but not before he had reestablished his family's fortune and power. **Related Entries:** Crusader States; Historians and Chroniclers, Islamic; Historians and Chroniclers, Latin; Settlement and Colonization.

Baltic Crusades (1147–1525)

Crusades of conquest, colonization, and conversion waged against various pagan and Christian peoples along Europe's northeastern frontier that were carried on by Germans and Scandinavians from 1147 to 1525.

Unlike the crusades in the **Middle East,** the Baltic Crusades contained an overt **missionary** purpose. Also, unlike the crusades in the **Levant** and the **Reconquista,** the Baltic Crusades were not fought to recover land previously held by Christians. They were wars of conquest and expansion, although they were often justified as defensive reactions to cross-border incursions. Unlike the **crusader states** of the **Latin East,** lands conquered along the Baltic were systematically settled and culturally transformed, at least to the point that their indigenous peoples were converted to **Latin** Christianity.

The Baltic Crusades began inauspiciously in 1147 during the **Second Crusade** as a series of almost comic-opera, papally sanctioned campaigns against the Wends, a pagan Slavic people. After 1147, Germans

and Danes intermittently continued to fight the Wends down to 1185, but they no longer had papal authorization or any **crusade privileges** and, so, were not technically crusaders. The wars resulted in the conquest of Pomerania in 1185. Although it initially passed under the authority of the Danish King Canute VI, Pomerania eventually was transformed into northeastern Germany (today it is northwestern Poland). During the Wendish Wars the **Cistercians** played a key role by establishing monasteries along the ever-expanding border, which served as **missionary** bases.

Pope Alexander III authorized a crusade against Baltic peoples far to the east of Pomerania as early as 1171 or 1172, but the conquest and settlement of eastern Baltic lands only began when Popes Celestine III and **Innocent III** respectively authorized a crusade in Livonia (modern Latvia) in 1193 and 1199.

During the thirteenth century the Baltic World was transformed by crusaders from Denmark, Sweden, and especially Germany. With papal support, crusades were launched by Scandinavian kings, German bishops, and various **military orders,** especially the **Teutonic Knights,** who in the 1230s became the Latin West's chief force in its expansion eastward. First the Livs, Letts, and Estonians, and then the Prussians and the Finns, underwent conquest, dispossession, colonization, and conversion. Out of these conquests four new political entities emerged: the dominions of Latvia and Prussia and the duchies of Estonia and Finland. Each was firmly anchored to Latin Christendom and opened to the influx of Western settlers, trade, and culture.

Of course, there was much resistance, revolts were frequent, and not every land or people was conquered or culturally transformed. In 1240 a crusade against the Russian principality of Novgorod got under way with the full authorization of Pope **Gregory IX,** who desired the conversion, by force if necessary, of a people who followed the religious traditions of **Constantinople.** Spearheading the invasion were the Teutonic Knights. Their advance was stopped cold on April 5, 1242, when Prince Alexander Nevsky defeated them at the Battle of Lake Peipus. Russia remained firmly wedded to its **Byzantine** Christian culture.

By 1300 the Baltic was a Latin Christian sea, but this did not mean that all native cultures were lost. German settlers, participating in what is known as the *Drang nach Osten* (Push to the East), densely colonized Pomerania and western Prussia and made them German. Farther east, however, the German presence was less overwhelming to the point that native languages and cultures survived.

In 1309 the Teutonic Knights established their headquarters at Marienburg in Prussia, a land that they had established as a sovereign state between 1226 and 1234. Now, with no holdings or responsibilities left to them in **Syria-Palestine,** they concentrated their full energies on the Baltic. In 1245 they had received the rare privilege from the **papacy** of being able to call crusades on their own, without prior papal approval. Anyone enlisting in these crusades would enjoy all crusade privileges, including the **indulgence.** In essence, the Teutonic Order was allowed to wage a perpetual crusade, which it did against pagan and Christian foes alike with increasing vigor.

During the fourteenth century the order prospered due to its rich agricultural holdings, its involvement in Baltic commerce, and its crusading victories. Its very success, however, in defeating and converting the pagan Lithuanians proved its undoing when the recently converted Lithuanians allied with the Catholic Poles against the order. During the early fifteenth century the

Knights' crusading momentum came to a virtual halt, especially after their crushing defeat at Tannenberg on July 15, 1410, at the hands of Polish and Lithuanian forces. After that, there was a century of decline. The conversion to Lutheranism of the order's grand master in 1525 and his installation as the secular duke of Prussia marked the anticlimactic end of the Baltic Crusades. **Related Entries:** Bernard of Clairvaux; Military Orders of the Baltic.

Suggested Reading

Primary Source

Henry of Livonia, *The Chronicle of Henry of Livonia,* trans. by James A. Brundage (1961; revision due in 2004).

Historical Studies

Eric Christiansen, *The Northern Crusades,* 2nd. ed. (1997); Alan V. Murray, ed., *Crusade and Conversion on the Baltic Frontier, 1150–1500* (2001); William Urban, *The Baltic Crusade,* 2nd. ed. (1994) and *The Prussian Crusade,* 2nd. ed. (2002).

Barons' Crusade

See Crusade of 1239–1241.

Baybars

A Kipchak **Turk** who became the fourth **Mamluk** sultan of Egypt and **Syria** (r. 1260–1277).

Baybars is often termed "the second **Saladin,**" and the two leaders did share some common features. Both were outsiders, one a Kurd, the other a Turkish *mamluk,* or slave-soldier, but each presented himself as the legitimate leader of **jihad** against all **infidel** enemies. Both ruled over a united Egyptian-Syrian empire from which they launched a series of successful campaigns against the **crusader states.** Both came close but did not quite succeed in throwing the **Franks** into the sea.

Their differences are equally striking. Whereas Saladin came from an established family that had been integrated for a long while into the Arabo-Persian culture of **Islam** and the political-military structure of the **Middle East,** Baybars was a former slave and convert to the faith and remained a Turkish warrior chieftain. Saladin had a reputation for loyalty and generosity, to the point of even treating some **Frankish prisoners** with a mercy that transcended the norms of his day; Baybars orchestrated the assassinations of two previous sultans and usually **massacred** his Frankish captives. Saladin faced some opposition from various **Muslim** quarters, including the **Assassins,** but had no significant external enemies, other than the Franks and the armies of the **Third Crusade;** in addition to the Franks, Baybars faced the greatest external enemy that Islam ever confronted—the **Mongols.** The fact that he held his own against the Mongols and advanced against the Franks suggests that Baybars was a better strategist and field commander than Saladin.

Baybars ascended to the Mamluk throne through the murder of Sultan Qutuz on October 24, 1260. To give himself greater legitimacy, on June 13, 1261, Baybars installed as the new caliph of Islam, but now resident in **Cairo,** an **Abbasid** prince who had escaped the massacre in Baghdad. In turn, the caliph invested Baybars with rule not only over Egypt and Syria, which Baybars actually controlled, but also over portions of Iraq that were in Mongol hands and western Arabia, the spiritual homeland of Islam. The caliph was a puppet and the caliphate an empty office, but this fiction allowed Baybars to style himself "servant of the two Holy Places." This title, which Saladin had used, signified that Baybars was the sultan of sultans, the defender of the holy cities of Mecca and Medina and, by extension, all of Islam.

The Mongols remained a constant threat to Syria and even Egypt, and for that reason Baybars considered them a greater menace to his lands and to Islam than the crusader states. Nevertheless, whenever the situation allowed, Baybars turned his attention to destroying Frankish power, especially between 1265 and 1271 when he waged major campaigns against the fortified positions of the princes and **military orders.** The weakness of the Frankish states at this time, especially of the **Latin kingdom of Jerusalem,** which had no resident king between 1229 and 1269, and the constant squabbling among the Franks greatly aided Baybars's advance. His crowning achievement was the capture of **Antioch** in May 1268, which was accompanied by a wholesale slaughter of the city's inhabitants that shocked even Muslim **chroniclers.**

Concern over his Syrian frontier and the Mongol menace forced Baybars to agree to a ten-year, ten-month, ten-day, ten-hour truce with the kingdom of Jerusalem in 1272, and death intervened in 1277 before he could resume his jihad.

Before death claimed him, Baybars had succeeded in crippling the two powers that posed the greatest threat to Islam in the Middle East: the Mongols and the Franks. Nine campaigns against the Mongols had done much to check their aggressiveness, although they remained a threat to Syria until the early years of the fourteenth century. Twenty-one victories over the Franks meant that they were now confined to a narrow strip of coast. Indeed, Baybars's successes against the Franks assured his successors of eventual total victory—a victory that came in 1291. **Related Entries:** Ayn Jalut; Castles, Crusader; Edward I; Siege Warfare.

Suggested Reading

Abdul-Aziz Khowaiter, *Baibars the First: His Endeavours and Achievements* (1978); Peter Thorav, *The Lion of Egypt: Sultan Baybars I and the Near East in the Thirteenth Century*, trans. by Peter M. Holt (1996).

Bernard of Clairvaux (1090–1153)

A **Cistercian** monk and the leading European churchman of the first half of the twelfth century, Bernard promoted the cause of the **Templars, preached** the **Second Crusade,** inspired crusading in the **Baltic,** and played a major role in shaping Western Christendom's vision of **holy war.**

Bernard of Clairvaux preaches the Second Crusade. A manuscript copy of the *Estoire d'Eracles*, a continuation of William of Tyre's history to 1229. Late thirteenth century (1295?), Paris or northern France. The Walters Art Museum, Baltimore.

Bernard entered the monastery of **Cîteaux** in 1112. His piety and leadership were apparent to all; three years after his entry he was dispatched to establish a monastery at nearby Clairvaux. Bernard immediately became its abbot, or religious head, and retained that office until his death thirty-eight years later. Bernard was a monk who sincerely longed for a life of solitude and quiet prayer. It was not to be. His high energy, intense religious fervor, and the demands of those who called upon him for help constantly pulled him out of his monastery and involved him in the major moral, theological, and ecclesiastical issues of his day, including the crusades.

Bernard's first foray into crusade matters was in support of the new Order of the Temple. In 1129 the abbot participated in the **Council** of Troyes in Champagne, which accepted a modified version of the Templars' original rule. Some of the modifications crafted at Troyes, which made the order's way of life more monastic, were due to Bernard's influence. Sometime thereafter Bernard composed the treatise *In Praise of the New Knighthood*. In it he contrasted the new **knights** of Christ, who successfully struggled for salvation by selflessly fighting evil, with worldly knights, who selfishly and fruitlessly battled for the riches of the world, thereby damning themselves to Hell. What is more, he claimed the Templars were free of all guilt when they took the lives of their enemies because they committed acts of *malicide* (the killing of evil) rather than homicide.

On March 1, 1146, Pope **Eugenius III,** a former monk of Clairvaux, authorized his former abbot to preach what would become the Second Crusade. Thirty days later

Bernard invested King **Louis VII** of France with the **crusader's cross** at Vézelay in Burgundy. Bernard's letters and sermons supporting the upcoming crusade struck a new note that engendered tremendous enthusiasm among those who heard the message. According to Bernard, the crusade was a unique gift from a loving God, who did not really need the crusaders' help but chose to offer them this opportunity for repentance and salvation.

While Bernard was inciting the French to undertake the crusade, to the east an unauthorized crusade preacher, a Cistercian monk named Ralph, found highly receptive audiences in the German cities and towns of the Rhine. Ralph's message contained strong anti-Jewish overtones, and he aroused many of his listeners to furies of violence against their Jewish neighbors. When the abbot of Clairvaux heard of these outrages, he quickly moved to stop Ralph by dispatching letters that made it clear that the **Jews** were not to be attacked or forcibly converted. He also sent Ralph packing back to his monastery.

At the same time Bernard seized the opportunity opened up by Ralph's successful preaching to move into Germany, where he convinced Emperor **Conrad III** to accept the call to crusade, thereby adding a large German force to the contingents that Louis of France would lead. While in Germany, Bernard also gave his blessing to a group of barons from northeastern Germany to meet their crusade obligations by campaigning against the pagan Wends, a Slavic people who dwelled east of the Elbe River. In supporting this northern crusade, Bernard called on Christians "to utterly annihilate or surely convert" the pagan enemy, fighting them "until, with God's help, either their religion or their tribe is wiped out." With this proclamation, which Pope Eugenius echoed in his official authorization of the Wendish Crusade, Bernard gave the Baltic Crusade a special mission—conversion of the unbeliever. What is more, by tying **missionary** work with crusade warfare in the North, Bernard contributed to a growing sentiment in the West that conversion of the **Muslim** unbelievers was also a valid goal of the crusades in **Outremer.**

The Second Crusade neither conquered nor converted the Muslims of **Syria-Palestine.** Louis and Conrad's efforts ended in dismal failure, and much of the subsequent **criticism** fell on Bernard, who was perceived as the author of the failed crusade. Bernard's response was that God had judged the crusaders sinful and lacking in faith, and Divine Justice, which is perfectly just, had deemed them unworthy of success. **Related Entries:** Apocalypse and the Crusades; Bull, Papal.

Suggested Reading

Primary Sources

"In Praise of the New Knighthood," in *The Works of Bernard of Clairvaux,* Vol. 7, trans. by Conrad Greenia (1977), pp. 115–167; Bernard of Clairvaux, *Letters,* trans. by Bruno Scott James, 2nd. ed. (1998).

Bohemond I of Taranto (1050s–1111)

Leader of the Italo-**Norman** contingent of the **First Crusade** and prince of **Antioch** (r. 1099–1111).

Bohemond, eldest son of the Norman adventurer Robert Guiscard, had been involved in eastern affairs long before the First Crusade. In March 1081 Guiscard, with Bohemond as second in command, invaded the Balkan lands of the **Byzantine Empire,** thereby coming into conflict with Emperor **Alexius I,** whom Bohemond would later come to know during the First Crusade. When his father returned to Italy in 1082,

Bohemond assumed command of the invading forces. Despite some initial successes, Bohemond was forced to abandon operations and return to Italy in late 1083 or early 1084. A second invasion of the Balkans by Guiscard and his sons that got under way in the fall of 1084 ended ingloriously with Guiscard's death on July 17, 1085.

What made the situation worse for Bohemond was the fact that his father had not provided for his eldest son's inheritance. A younger half-brother secured Guiscard's southern Italian and Sicilian duchies, and Bohemond was left landless. Two wars against his half-brother won for Bohemond the Italian port of Bari, as well as other lands in the south of Italy. In 1089 Pope **Urban II** visited Bari at Bohemond's invitation. Six years later Urban's call for a crusade would have a profound effect on his former host's fortunes and life.

Apparently Bohemond only began to think about crusading when he noted numerous **pilgrim**-crusaders embarking from the ports of southern Italy in 1096. Unable to secure a major principality for himself in Italy, Bohemond probably saw the expedition to the East as an opportunity he could not let slip away. In August 1096 he placed the **crusader's cross** on his shoulder and convinced large numbers of Norman **knights** to follow his example and leadership.

In the autumn of that year Bohemond's army crossed the Adriatic, landed on the shores of the Balkans, and marched to **Constantinople,** which it reached in April 1097. Despite their mutual distrust, Emperor Alexius treated Bohemond generously, and Bohemond reciprocated by taking an oath of allegiance to the emperor.

Notwithstanding that oath, Bohemond seized Antioch for himself the following year. After a seven-and-a-half-month **siege** of the city by the combined crusader armies,

Bohemond negotiated Antioch's betrayal by a disenchanted officer of the defending forces. Before revealing his plan to his colleagues, Bohemond demanded their promises that he would be awarded Antioch if his troops were the first to enter it and if the emperor did not come to reclaim the former Byzantine city in person. All of the leaders, except **Raymond of Saint-Gilles,** agreed. Just before sunrise on June 3, 1098, the traitor allowed almost sixty of Bohemond's knights to scale the walls and capture three towers. They then opened a key gate to the onrushing crusaders, and the city was captured in a bloodbath.

For the rest of the campaign at Antioch, Bohemond served as commander of the crusader forces and led the counterattack that threw back the **Turkish** army of **Kerbogha** that had arrived too late to catch the crusaders outside of Antioch's walls. When the emperor failed to arrive at Antioch and with Bohemond's rival Raymond of Saint-Gilles marching south toward **Jerusalem,** the Norman forcibly ejected Raymond's Provençal troops from the strongholds in the city that they occupied and declared himself prince of Antioch in early 1099.

Rather than join the march to Jerusalem, Bohemond consolidated his position in and around Antioch, even though Alexius still claimed the city. As he sought to extend his dominion, Bohemond was captured by **Muslim** forces in July or August 1100 while campaigning in northern **Syria.** Two Western sources claim Emperor Alexius vainly offered Bohemond's captor large sums of gold in return for his handing Bohemond over, presumably so that the emperor could bend Bohemond to his will. Released in an amiable **prisoner** exchange in the summer of 1103, Bohemond returned to Antioch and picked up his offensive operations in northern Syria, especially against **Aleppo.** His efforts proved unsuccessful.

Threatened by both Turks and Byzantines, Antioch was in a perilous situation. The situation was desperate enough to impel Bohemond to undertake a hazardous winter voyage to Europe, where he hoped to secure help. Leaving his nephew **Tancred** as regent of the principality, Bohemond left in late autumn 1104 and arrived in Italy in January 1105.

During 1105–1106 Bohemond traveled through Italy and France, where he was hailed as a hero. With the blessing of Pope **Paschal II,** Bohemond used this opportunity to stir up hostility toward Alexius I, whom Westerners already blamed for the difficulties encountered by the armies of the First Crusade, and to raise an army for the purpose of attacking the Byzantines.

In the fall of 1107 Bohemond launched a crusade on the Albanian coast, but Alexius was ready and cut off the Norman's forces by land and sea. Bohemond was forced to sue for peace in September 1108. By terms of the treaty, Bohemond swore an oath of **feudal** vassalage to Alexius and acknowledged that he held Antioch as an imperial fief. Bohemond returned to southern Italy, where he died in March 1111 in the midst of efforts to raise a new army to lead to the East. **Related Entries:** Anna Comnena; Baldwin I of Boulogne; *Gesta Francorum;* Lance, Holy.

Bohemond II

Son of **Bohemond I of Taranto** and prince of **Antioch** (r. 1126–1130).

Born in southern Italy around 1109, the young Bohemond arrived in the **Holy Land** in late 1126 to secure his patrimony—the principality of Antioch. Following his arrival, he married **Alice,** daughter of King **Baldwin II** of **Jerusalem.**

Bohemond II's reign was short and inglorious. While Bohemond was campaigning against **Turkish** enemies, Joscelin I of Courtenay, count of **Edessa,** invaded the principality and compelled the Antiochenes to acknowledge momentarily his rule. Joscelin and Bohemond reconciled, thanks to the intervention of Baldwin II, but Bohemond's problems were not over. In February 1130 Bohemond was killed while fighting **Turkish** forces in **Anatolia,** leaving behind a widow, Alice, and infant daughter, **Constance.**

Bull, Papal

An official papal proclamation distinguished by the leaden seal, or *bulla,* bearing the pope's name that is attached to it.

By the time of the **Second Crusade,** for a crusade to be an official crusade that carried with it the full range of **privileges** accorded crusaders, it had to be called by a pope, who from the mid–twelfth century onward did so by issuing a formal bull in the form of an *encyclical,* a letter sent out in copies to all relevant archbishops in the West. The archbishops, in turn, would circulate word of the bull to their subordinate bishops and other high-ranking clerics, usually by convening a provincial **council.** These churchmen would then guarantee that word reached all of the faithful within their areas of authority and responsibility. Additionally, the **papacy** commissioned **legates** and other clerics to **preach** the crusade in specially designated areas throughout Europe. In theory and practice, word of the pope's intention as set out in his crusade bull reached every level of Western Christendom.

Papal bulls were written in **Latin,** the official language of the Roman Church, and were known by the first several words of text, such as *Audita tremendi* (Upon hearing of the terrible), which Gregory VIII issued in 1187 when he called for the **Third Crusade.**

Each crusade bull was an exercise in forceful rhetoric designed to rouse Christendom to a new effort. Each also set the crusade into a clear theological and spiritual context. In the case of *Audita tremendi,* Pope Gregory VIII explained that the defeat at **Hattin** was a call to repentance and reformation that a merciful and loving God sent his people who had brought the disaster upon themselves through their sins. Therefore, before setting off, they should first amend their lives and should undertake the crusade for the right reasons, as a means of penance and out of love for God and their fellow Christians.

The papacy had a long institutional memory, and later crusade bulls tended to echo and build upon earlier ones. It became the tradition, for example, to enumerate the **privileges** offered each crusader, especially the plenary **indulgence.** At the same time, certain bulls set precedents and served as milestones in the evolution of the crusade as an institution.

Although there were earlier papal letters authorizing **holy war,** *Quantum praedecessores* (How greatly our predecessors), which Pope **Eugenius III** issued in 1145 for the Second Crusade, became a model for all subsequent crusade bulls by virtue of its careful delineation of crusade privileges. **Innocent III**'s crusade bulls of 1198 and 1199, which set in motion the **Fourth Crusade,** established new ways of raising revenues to support crusade efforts in the East, which became standard practice thereafter.

By the thirteenth century, the crusade had evolved into a clearly delineated legal institution that received its legitimacy from the **Roman papacy.** For that reason, because popular movements such as the so-called **Children's Crusade** of 1212 and the **Shepherds' Crusade** of 1251 lacked formal papal authorization, they were not considered official crusades, and church lawyers did not consider the **vows** their participants took to be binding. Early in the twelfth century, however, it was not that clear. The **Damascus Crusade** of 1129 apparently lacked formal papal authorization, but its participants regarded themselves as crusaders and were seen as such by their contemporaries. **Related Entries:** Crusade of 1122–1126; Fifth Crusade; Financing the Crusades.

Byzantine Empire

The **Greek**-speaking, eastern Mediterranean empire centered on **Constantinople,** a city whose original Greek name was *Byzantion* (*Byzantium* in **Latin**).

Byzantine is a modern term that historians use to differentiate, from the cultures that preceded it, the civilization that took shape during the sixth century and flourished down to the mid–fifteenth century. Byzantine civilization resulted from the fusion of three key elements: (1) the traditions of the late Roman empire; (2) Eastern Orthodox Christian traditions; and (3) the cultural heritage of Hellenistic antiquity, itself a fusion of Greek, western Asiatic, and Egyptian elements.

The boundaries of the Byzantine empire were constantly shifting. As early as the seventh century the empire lost the lands of **Syria-Palestine,** Egypt, and North Africa to **Islam,** but at its height of power in the age of Emperor Basil II (r. 976–1025), the empire reached from southern Italy in the West to the lands surrounding the Black Sea in the East. For most of its history, the heart of the empire was **Anatolia,** which provided the bulk of Byzantium's resources. A victory by the **Seljuk** Turks at **Manzikert** in 1071, however, occasioned the collapse of the Byzantine empire's eastern borders and the rapid loss of most of Anatolia. After dealing with a series of crises in the Balkans, Emperor **Alexius I** turned to the recovery of

Mosaic portraits in the Church of Hagia Sophia of Emperor John II Comnenus (r. 1118–1143), son of Alexius I, brother of Anna Comnena, and father of Manuel I, and his Hungarian wife, Empress Irene. They flank the Virgin Mary and Christ. Although overshadowed by his father and son, Emperor John was an exceedingly able ruler, diplomat, and soldier, especially in his relations with his Turkish and Frankish neighbors.

Anatolia, and to that end he appealed to the West for **mercenaries** to serve in his army. One of his appeals struck a chord in Pope **Urban II,** who was inspired by it to set in motion a movement that became the **First Crusade.**

Ultimately, misunderstanding, grief, and tragedy were the results of this meeting between Eastern and Western Christendom. Confrontations between Westerners and Byzantines began as early as the First Crusade and sharpened over the course of the twelfth century, especially during the **Second** and **Third Crusades.** By the time of the **Fourth Crusade,** it was quite easy for many crusaders to believe that Byzantines were traitors to Christianity and false friends. In that atmosphere, justifying the capture and sack of Constantinople in April 1204 was not difficult. With that conquest and the estab-

lishment of the **Latin empire of Constantinople** and the carving out of various principalities in **Frankish Greece,** the Byzantine and Roman Catholic churches entered into a state of bitter schism, which has lasted to today.

Following the Byzantine recapture of Constantinople in 1261, several emperors, as a diplomatic ploy, offered the Western Church the promise of ecclesiastical reunion, which would entail the Byzantine Church's submission to the authority of the **Roman papacy.** In 1274 Emperor Michael VIII forestalled an attack on his empire by **Charles I of Anjou** by concluding a formal reunion with Rome at the Second **Council** of Lyons. In 1439 Emperor John VIII traveled to Florence to submit the Byzantine Church to Rome's authority in a vain attempt to gain crusader help against the advancing

Ottoman Turks. Both proclamations of reunion were empty letters, repudiated by the vast majority of Byzantine Christians, who hated and feared Western Christians more than Muslims. On its part, the West was unable to provide Byzantium with any effective military help.

With all of its lands in Ottoman hands, except for the capital city of Constantinople, Byzantium grimly held on until the city finally succumbed to the cannons and overwhelming forces of Sultan Mehmed II on May 29, 1453. The Byzantine empire was now only a memory. **Related Entries:** Anatolia; Anna Comnena; Christians, Eastern; Cyprus; Isaac II Angelus; Manuel I Comnenus; Manzikert, Battle of.

Suggested Reading

Michael Angold, *The Byzantine Empire, 1025–1204* (1984); Charles M. Brand, *Byzantium Confronts the West, 1180–1204* (1968); Jonathan Harris, *Byzantium and the Crusades* (2002); Ralph-Johannes Lilie, *Byzantium and the Crusader States: 1096–1204,* trans. by J. C. Morris and Jean E. Ridings (1993); Paul Magdalino, *The Byzantine Background to the First Crusade* (1996); Cyril Mango, ed., *The Oxford History of Byzantium* (2002); Geoffrey Regan, *First Crusader: Byzantium's Holy Wars* (2003).

C

Cairo

Built in northern Egypt during the tenth century by the **Fatimids** as their administrative and military center, it successively served as the capital of the **Ayyubid** and **Mamluk** empires. Throughout the Age of the Crusades, it was a major center of commerce and **Islamic** learning.

Cairo, whose Arabic name is *al-Qahirah* (the Victorious), arose in 969 as a military-palace complex just outside of the city of Fustat. As the Fatimids prospered, Cairo flourished, as did Fustat. The collapse of Fatimid fortunes, however, brought a sudden and dramatic end to Fustat but inaugurated a grand new era for Cairo. In November 1168, during the last days of the Fatimid empire as war raged in Egypt, a **Turkish** commander ordered the burning of unfortified Fustat to deny it to the **Frankish** army of his sometime ally, King **Amalric** of **Jerusalem,** and Fustat's large population sought refuge within Cairo's walls. Although Fustat was later partially rebuilt, most of the refugees remained in Cairo, thereby transforming what had been a low-density suburb for a ruling elite into a high-density metropolis, which reached a population of about a half million at the height of its medieval growth before the epidemic of the Black Death severely reduced its inhabitants in the mid–fourteenth century.

From 1169 to about 1260, under the rule of **Saladin** and his successors, Cairo continued to grow, becoming the most prosperous and important city in the Islamic World. Much of Cairo's prosperity was due to a strategic location that enabled it to serve as the fulcrum for trade between the Red Sea–Indian Ocean region and the Mediterranean, but beyond that, much of Cairo's importance was due to the preeminence of its many famous mosques and academies.

The crusading West was quite aware of the primacy of Cairo—a city that Westerners called *Babylon* (not to be confused with ancient Babylon in Iraq). For that reason the leaders of the **Fourth Crusade** planned to capture the city by way of a seaborne assault on the Egyptian port of Alexandria. Circumstances, however, took the army of that crusade to **Constantinople** rather than to Egypt. The forces of the **Fifth Crusade** did reach Egypt and managed to capture the city of **Damietta** in what proved to be a disastrous bid to march on Cairo. In 1250, twenty-nine years after the inglorious end of the Fifth Crusade's attempt to take the city, the army of **Louis IX** of France met a similar defeat as it threatened Cairo during the **Seventh Crusade.**

Cairo's Gate of Victory. Charles W. Wilson, *Picturesque Palestine, Sinai and Egypt*, 2 vols. (New York: D. Appleton & Co., 1881), 2:370.

Cairo was a primary objective of the **Mongols** during the last half of the thirteenth century, but they got no closer than northern **Palestine,** where they were turned back in 1260 by the Mamluks, whose leader had seized the sultanate of Egypt the previous year. Mamluk sultans ruled from Cairo until 1517, when the conquering army of the **Ottoman** Turks marched into the city. **Related Entries:** Ayn Jalut, Battle of; Baybars.

Suggested Reading

André Reaymond, *Cairo,* trans. Willard Wood (2000).

Calatrava, Order of

See Military Orders of Iberia.

Calixtus II, Pope

Roman pope (r. 1119–1124) whose letters calling for crusade in the East and Spain launched the two-front **Crusade of 1122–1126** and added to the West's growing notion of what a crusade was.

In response to overtures from King **Baldwin II** of **Jerusalem,** in late 1120 or early 1121, Calixtus sent letters to Venice and most likely to France and Germany summoning Western Christians to take up the **crusader's cross** in defense of the **Latin East.** By this action, the pope set in motion the Venetian portion of the Crusade of 1122–1126 that resulted in destruction of an Egyptian fleet off the shore of **Ascalon** in May 1123 and the capture of **Tyre** on July 7, 1124.

Between March 18 and April 6, 1123, Pope Calixtus presided over the First Lateran Council. On April 2, 1123, four days before the end of the **council,** Calixtus dispatched a letter to all the faithful in which he granted the same **crusade indulgence** to persons fighting **Muslims** in Spain as to those fighting in the East. King Alfonso I (the Battler) of Aragon had captured Saragossa in 1118, and apparently Calixtus hoped to keep the pressure on the **Moors.** In addition to this call for crusaders, Calixtus threatened excommunication to all who did not make an honest effort to fulfill their **crusade vows** to go to either the East or Spain before Easter 1124.

As a consequence of the pope's appeal for crusading in Spain, King Alfonso raided southern Spain during the winter of 1125–1126.

In a letter composed between January 1096 and July 29, 1099, **Urban II** had extended the crusade indulgence to warriors fighting the Moors in Iberia. A few years later, Pope **Paschal II** urged the soldiers of Castile who had vowed to participate in the so-called **Crusade of 1101** to do their penance by fighting Muslims at home. Calixtus took this double precedent, reiterated it, and expanded it. Whereas Urban and Paschal had tried to dissuade Spaniards from leaving Iberia to go to the aid of **Eastern Christians,** Calixtus invited all the faithful to wage crusade in Spain in support of the Christian advance.

By his calls for crusade in both the East and Iberia Calixtus underscored two principles that became an integral part of crusade ideology: **Holy war** against **Islam** was to be fought on multiple fronts; and the **Reconquista** was a full-fledged crusade. **Related Entries:** Bull, Papal; Eugenius III of Boulogne; Second Crusade.

Cannibalism

Cannibalism was rare during the crusades, but there is solid evidence that some members of the army of the **First Crusade** consumed human flesh as they campaigned in **Syria** in 1098.

Cannibalism is taboo in most cultures, and when members of such cultures engage in it, they do so only under extraordinary circumstances and even duress. Such circumstances include hunger to the point of starvation and the blood lust of combat, where it becomes a form of mutilation of an enemy's body. In either instance, cannibalism can serve as a deliberate means of terrorizing an enemy.

Cannibalism is more often rumored about than practiced, and this was true for the era of the crusades. Stories circulated in the West regarding alleged acts of cannibalism by the **Mongol** armies that swept out of Inner Asia in the thirteenth century, but there is no credible evidence to support these reports. Indeed, unwarranted charges of cannibalism are often laid against an alien culture as a means of placing its people in the ranks of the uncivilized.

Within the **Turkish** epic tradition that took shape during the Crusade Era, the **Franks** appear as barbaric eaters of human flesh. While much of this characterization is the stuff of poetic exaggeration and arises out of a need to transform enemies into demons of mythic proportions, there is evidence that some crusaders were guilty of cannibalism in the course of the First Crusade. How many persons were involved and how frequent were these acts is impossible to say. It is clear, however, that crusader cannibals consumed Turkish bodies at **Antioch** and Ma'arra in 1098.

One of our best sources for cannibalism at Antioch is the *Chanson d'Antioche (The Song of Antioch),* a late twelfth-century French epic whose poet claimed that he reworked an earlier *chanson* composed by a crusade participant known as Richard the Pilgrim. According to the poem, the besieging crusaders were so overcome by hunger that members of the army's humblest classes, known as **Tafurs,** sought the advice of **Peter the Hermit,** who advised them to eat the bodies of fallen Turks, which littered the ground nearby. They did so, roasting the meat within sight of the anguished defenders of the city. Later the Tafurs surpassed this outrage by exhuming bodies from local Turkish cemeteries for another grisly feast.

As the crusade leaders debated their next action following their capture and successful defense of Antioch, the troops were kept occupied by a foray against the fortified town of Ma'arra (Ma'arrat an-Nu'man). Following a two-week **siege,** the crusaders entered the city on December 12, 1098, and proceeded to butcher most of the inhabitants. Several contemporary **Latin historians and chroniclers** agree that following the city's capture, some of the crusaders proceeded to eat their enemies. According to the **Norman** chronicler Ralph of Caen, the troops boiled adults in cooking pots and impaled and roasted children on spits.

After the incident at Ma'arra, there is no solid evidence of further crusader acts of cannibalism in this or subsequent crusades. The rumors persisted, however, in song and story. Given the ferocity of crusade warfare and the privations suffered by all sides, it is not difficult to imagine that there were other isolated cases of cannibalism by both crusaders and **Muslims. Related Entry:** Massacres.

Capetians

The French royal family, which played a key role during the classical Age of the Crusades, a role that mirrors the triumphs and tragedies, dreams and disillusionments, ideals and realities of two centuries of crusading.

Every **Latin** Christian culture in Europe, from Iceland to Poland from Sicily to Nor-

way, participated in the crusades, but of all the peoples involved, the French were preeminent. In many respects, the crusades would not have begun nor could they have lasted for as long as they did without French support, and that included all levels of French society. In an age when monarchs were looked to as God-anointed leaders, it was expected that the French royal house of Capet would lead the people of "Sweet France" in these **holy wars.** Indeed, according to a myth enshrined in **The Song of Roland,** French monarchs had led Christendom's struggle against **Islam** since the days of Emperor Charlemagne.

No Western monarch went on the **First Crusade.** Even though the First Crusade was summoned by a French **pope** and its armies had a disproportionately large French presence, there was no way that King Philip I (r. 1060–1108) was going to take up the **crusader's cross.** He was enormously fat, lethargic, out of fighting shape, and excommunicated because of marital irregularities. In fact, Pope **Urban II** confirmed Philip's excommunication at the same **Council of Clermont** where he summoned Western Christians to wage holy war against the **Turks.** Despite Philip's absence, the royal family was represented on crusade by his brother, **Hugh, count of Vermandois,** who took part in the second and third waves of the crusade and died of a battle wound in October 1101.

The first Capetian monarch to campaign on crusade was Louis VII (r. 1137–1180), who led French troops across the Balkans and **Anatolia** to **Jerusalem** and then on an ill-conceived attack on **Damascus** in 1147–1148. The **Second Crusade** failed in all of its Eastern objectives, and widespread disillusionment followed in its wake. Louis seems to have blamed himself for the disaster, and in the search for scapegoats some European writers also faulted him. By and large, however, despite the setback to crusading fervor in the West that followed this crusade, Louis's participation appears, on balance, to have raised his and his dynasty's prestige throughout France. At the same time, none other than the pope himself, Hadrian IV, counseled King Louis in 1159 against undertaking a new crusade, this time against the **Moors** in Spain, by reminding him of how Christendom had been weakened by the king's earlier crusade.

Louis's son and successor, Philip II (r. 1180–1223), participated in the **Third Crusade** and played an instrumental role in the recapture of **Acre** in 1191. Although his crusade activities were overshadowed by his nominal **feudal** vassal, **Richard I the Lionheart,** Philip's crusading only added to the growing tradition of Capetian crusade leadership.

Philip's son Louis, while still a prince and heir apparent, twice swore the cross and in 1215 and 1219 led armies against the **Cathars** of **Languedoc** during the **Albigensian Crusade.** In January 1226, less than three years into his reign as King Louis VIII (r. 1223–1226), he undertook his third and last crusade against the Cathars, dying of natural causes on November 8 while on campaign. This royal intervention came at a critical juncture in the twenty-year-long crusade and swung momentum away from Count Raymond VII of Toulouse. Without King Louis's campaign and the follow-up by his lieutenants, the Peace of Paris of 1229, which ended crusade hostilities, would not have been such a resounding victory for the **papacy** and the Crown of France.

Louis VIII was succeeded by a son twelve years of age, **Louis IX,** the thirteenth century's greatest crusader-king. Louis IX's crusade in the East between 1248 and 1254, the **Seventh Crusade,** established him as Europe's crusader hero without peer. Although he was captured in April 1250,

along with most of his surviving soldiers, his defeat did little to injure his reputation. Rather, his courage and constancy in battle and captivity won him praise. Serving alongside him were his brothers Alphonse of Poitiers, **Charles of Anjou,** and Robert of Artois. Of these, Robert was killed in combat.

Following payment of half his ransom, Louis was released and traveled to Acre in May 1250. Later that year, his brothers Alphonse and Charles returned home, along with a number of other prominent French **knights** and lords. The king, however, decided to stay in the **Holy Land.** As far as Louis was concerned, his crusade was not over, as long as most of his surviving crusaders, maybe as many as 12,000 men, **women,** and children, remained **prisoners** in Egypt and as long as the **kingdom of Jerusalem** was threatened by the **Ayyubids** of **Syria.** For the next four years Louis effectively ruled the kingdom by virtue of his prestige and resources. He rebuilt key fortifications, negotiated with the **Assassins** and **Mongols,** generally stabilized the **crusader states,** and bought back the freedom of all available Christian captives and **slaves** in Egypt, even those who had not been part of his crusade force. In April 1254 he departed for home, rich in glory and **relics** but burdened by a sense of guilt and failure. He was determined to return on crusade.

Between 1254 and 1270 Louis maintained contact with the Holy Land, assisting it with soldiers and funds. As **Frankish** fortunes declined in the East in the face of **Mamluk** attacks, he took up the crusader's cross again in March 1267. His brothers Alphonse and Charles, sons Philip, John, and Peter, a nephew, and a son-in-law likewise assumed the cross. It was truly a family affair.

The crusade sailed to Tunis, where Louis took ill and died on August 25, 1270; three days earlier Alphonse had died on his way to Genoa for reinforcements. In many respects, Louis's death marked the end of the classical Age of the Crusades, although the crusader states still had twenty-one more years of life ahead of them.

Because of his piety, sense of Christian **chivalry,** and commitment to the crusade ideal, the papacy recognized Louis as a saint in 1297. In a later era, wherever French colonists and explorers traveled in the Americas, they carried with them the cult of Saint Louis, as the name of Saint Louis, Missouri, bears witness.

If Louis was a saint, his brother Charles of Anjou, who participated in both the Seventh and **Eighth Crusades,** was more the sinner. In addition to these two crusades, in 1265 Charles successfully fought as a crusader and papal agent against Manfred of **Hohenstaufen,** claimant to the crown of Sicily, thereby acquiring the kingdom for himself in 1266. In 1277 Charles purchased the crown of Jerusalem and reigned as an absentee king until 1282.

In 1283 Pope Martin IV called a crusade against King Peter III of Aragon in defense of Charles's claim to the island of Sicily. King Philip III (r. 1270–1285), Charles's nephew, collected crusade taxes from the French clergy and recruited an army of more than 8,000 to fight a fellow Christian. The crusade was a fiasco. Philip, who had been sick almost to the point of death in the Tunisian campaign of 1270, took ill again as his defeated army retreated before the victorious forces of King Peter. On October 5, 1285, the king, an ill-fated, two-time crusader, died. Charles had died nine months earlier.

The new king of France, **Philip IV** (r. 1285–1314), was a pragmatic statesman. Seeing that this was the wrong crusade at the wrong time, he made peace with Peter.

King Philip became an active champion of the crusades only upon the accession in 1305 of a French pope who took the name Clement V in memory of Pope Clement IV, a Frenchman, a patron of Charles of Anjou, and a friend of Louis IX. Clement V was also an unrelenting advocate of a crusade to recover the Holy Land and envisioned the Capetian king of France as a natural leader of that enterprise. On his part, as early as December 29, 1305, Philip agreed in principle to undertake a crusade, with the understanding that it would be at a time of his choosing and would involve the conquest of the **Byzantine empire** by his brother Charles of Valois. Like Charles of Anjou before him, King Philip associated a successful crusade with the establishment of French hegemony in the East.

Although plans were formulated, **indulgences** proclaimed, and papal permission to tax the clergy in support of a crusade granted in 1306 and 1312, Pope Clement's crusade never got under way. King Philip finally assumed the crusader's cross in June 1313, but he died in November 1314 with his crusade still a dream. In his will he left behind funds for a crusade, but nothing ever came of it.

Despite all of this late-in-life activity in support of a crusade, evidence suggests that Philip's vision of a crusade differed essentially from that of his sainted grandfather. Philip viewed the crusade as essentially an extension of the authority and prestige of the French state, a state to whose power and autonomy he devoted his entire reign. Unlike King Louis IX, Philip IV placed the interests of the Christian French monarchy, which for him was the state, above the interests of Christendom in general.

Capetian crusade involvement had traveled far in two centuries but so had the crusades, the crusade ideal, and the state of Christendom in both the West and the East. **Related Entries:** Criticism of Crusades; Eleanor of Aquitaine; Financing the Crusades; Margaret of Provence; Military Orders; Montferrat, Family of; Political Crusades; Templars.

Carmelites

Officially the Order of Our Lady of Mount Carmel, the Carmelites were the only **Latin** religious order to originate in the **crusader states** that did not have a military function.

Toward the end of the twelfth century, groups of **Frankish pilgrims** who decided to live as penitent hermits began to congregate on Mount Carmel near Haifa, a mountain sacred to the memory of the Prophet Elijah. Early in the thirteenth century the **Latin patriarch of Jerusalem,** Albert of Vercelli (r. 1206–1214), provided them with a simple rule that recognized their solitary way of life devoted to prayer, contemplation, and self-denial. According to that rule, they were to live in unpopulated areas, cut off from most contact with the rest of the world. During the 1230s groups of these hermits began to migrate west into **Cyprus,** Sicily, Italy, France, and England, where they initially sought out remote areas and established hermitages based on the model of Mount Carmel. Soon, however, younger recruits, who had never been to the East, began advocating change, namely that the order, much like the Franciscans and the **Dominicans,** become actively engaged in evangelical work, especially **preaching.** In 1247 Pope Innocent IV allowed the Carmelites to settle wherever they wished, by implication leaving the way open for them to move near towns and cities, where they could practice an active ministry. Over the next three decades the Carmelites adopted a way of life and a constitution that transformed them into **mendicant friars.** Despite their Eastern origins, the Carmelites of Europe were never nearly as active as the Franciscans and the Dominicans in crusade

work, largely because of their small numbers and the slow process of their transformation from hermits to friars. Meanwhile, back in the East, the hermits of Mount Carmel, who also had a site near **Tyre,** continued to live a precarious existence until their monastic refuges were overrun by the **Mamluks** in the late thirteenth century. With the fall of **Acre** in 1291 they vanished from **Syria-Palestine,** but continued to reside in Cyprus until the island was captured by the **Ottomans** in 1571. **Related Entries:** Francis of Assisi; Military Orders.

Suggested Reading

Andrew Jotischky, *The Perfection of Solitude: Hermits and Monks in the Crusader States* (1995).

Castles, Crusader

The **Franks** were a small minority in the **Holy Land,** and the only way they could control the lands they conquered was by occupying strategically located fortified positions, either castles or towns with defensive walls.

The crusaders who came to the East were already well acquainted with the techniques of constructing fortifications adapted to varying types of terrain. Nevertheless, upon arrival in the East, they also discovered **Byzantine, Armenian, Turkish,** and **Arab** fortifications. Some they could only marvel at, such as the great land walls of **Constantinople;** others they conquered and occupied, such as the Byzantine walled city of **Antioch,** Armenian **Edessa,** and **Jerusalem,** whose walls and citadel bore the imprint of its Arab conquerors. The fortifications the crusaders encountered left an imprint on their own constructions, and this was especially true of the Armenian round tower, which offered a better field of fire than the European square tower and no blind spots. One reason Arme-

Medieval Recycling: A harbor fortification at Korykos, Cilician Armenia. The use of ancient columns to strengthen castle walls was common throughout the Middle East during the Crusade Era. Ironically, this produced weaker walls.

nian models so impressed the crusaders was that Armenian fortresses in Cilicia were largely castles built by independent lords on defensible rock outcroppings. This paralleled the European experience, and it also suited the means the crusaders adopted to control the lands they settled.

Almost as soon as they had carved out their principalities, the crusaders began to build new fortifications, as well as occupying existing castles and fortified cities. Crusader fortresses constructed in the countryside during the twelfth century were of two types: single, freestanding stone towers and enclosed castles. Square stone towers were the most numerous. The sites of seventy-five towers in the **kingdom of Jerusalem** alone are known today, and more remain to be discovered. The stone tower was usually the cen-

ter of power for a **knight** who held a small estate and even for a baron of modest means. Kings and lords of greater means and responsibilities built larger, multiroom enclosed castles situated on hilltops. As **Baldwin I** expanded his kingdom's reach into **Transjordan,** he constructed castles, such as *Montréal,* built in 1115, that allowed him to control a network of trade routes. In the reign of King **Fulk** Transjordan was given out as a **feudal** lordship, and in 1142 the lord of Transjordan, who bore the colorful name Pagan the Butler, built the great castle of *Kerak* as the center of his power. From castles such as *Montréal* and *Kerak* moderately sized garrisons could command fairly large areas.

All of the crusader castles of Transjordan, however, fell to the forces of **Saladin** in 1188, following the battle of **Hattin,** and they were never recovered. In fact, most of the Frankish castles and cities of **Outremer** were lost to Saladin's forces in the wake of the disaster at Hattin, and these losses had a profound effect on how the Franks subsequently constructed and garrisoned their castles.

Even after the **Third Crusade** stabilized their position and rewon significant amounts of territory, the crusader-colonists found themselves almost totally confined to the coastal plain that ran along the Mediterranean. Given a situation that was more precarious than it had been before the rise of Saladin, the **Latin** settlers turned to the major **military orders,** the **Templars, Hospitalers,** and the recently founded **Teutonic Knights,** to build or rebuild and garrison the significantly larger and stronger castles that they now felt they needed.

The Templars and Hospitalers had constructed, purchased, and been given a fair number of enclosed castles and a few towers well before Saladin's victorious sweep through the **crusader states.** Templar fortresses before 1187–1188 served primarily as bases from which they defended **pilgrimage** routes throughout the kingdom of Jerusalem. One such castle was *Le Toron des Chevaliers,* which guarded the southern route from **Jaffa** to Jerusalem. Hospitaler fortified sites dating from this same period were farther away from well-traveled pilgrim pathways, on the Hospitalers' rural estates and in other more remote but equally strategic locations. One of their more impressive castles was *Belvoir,* which commanded the northern Jordan Valley. The dimensions of its outer wall measure roughly 110 yards by more than 140 yards, making it one of the largest enclosed castles of its day. Its size suggests it quartered no more than 500 men and probably far fewer, and of these probably no more than 80 were men-at-arms. Purchased by the Hospitalers in 1168, it was lost thirty years later and never recovered.

Following the Third Crusade, that is, after 1192, castle building and maintenance

Ruins of the Templar castle of *Baghras* in Cilician Armenia. Note how the castle dominates the surrounding countryside.

Belvoir, **a twelfth-century Hospitaler castle that commanded the Jordan Valley. The tourists in the picture are distinguished historians visiting Israel for a crusade conference.**

throughout the crusader states shifted almost totally away from individual lords to the richer, more organized military orders. The military orders soon found themselves awash with castles. These included former castles recovered in the Christian counter-offensive, castles that the Templars and Hospitalers managed to hold onto during Saladin's offensive, castles that the orders constructed to meet their new duties, and castles sold or donated to them by lords who no longer felt capable of defending them. Whether rebuilt, renovated, or constructed for the first time, these castles were larger and stronger than earlier crusader fortifications.

Under the terms of a truce, in 1240 the Templars reacquired the castle at *Saphet,* which **Muslim** forces had held since 1188. Using enslaved Arab **prisoners,** the Templars

rebuilt and expanded the fortress over a period of three years, creating one of the largest and most magnificent castles in Outremer. One thirteenth-century census counted fifty brother knights, thirty Templar **sergeants,** fifty mounted **Turcopoles,** 300 crossbowmen, 820 hired staff and laborers, and 400 **slaves.** Despite its size and numbers of soldiers, the castle fell to **Baybars** in 1266.

The Templars had strongholds scattered throughout the crusader states, whereas the Teutonic Knights assumed defensive responsibilities primarily in the hills of Galilee, slightly north of **Acre.** Around 1227 they began construction of their chief castle, *Montfort,* and by the 1240s it was fully operational. In 1271, however, it fell to Baybars, and today is little more than a heap of rubble.

The finest surviving example of the massive castles of the military orders is *Krak des*

Chevaliers, which can be visited today in that region of the nation of **Syria** that was once the county of **Tripoli.** The Hospitalers built their original castle during the 1160s on a hill that had been fortified since at least the eleventh century. The twelfth-century fortress was sufficiently strong enough to resist successfully Saladin's sweep though the region. During the thirteenth century the Hospitalers added to the castle's defensive works and turned *Krak* into an offensive center that enabled them to exact tribute from neighboring Muslim towns, as well as from the **Assassins.** At the height of its power *Krak* had a garrison of 2,000.

After reaching their high-water mark around 1250, the power of the castles of the military orders ebbed away rapidly, and from the 1260s they were systematically captured and destroyed by the **Mamluks.** On March 3, 1271, the forces of Baybars began a **siege** of *Krak;* by March 29 the outer walls had been breached. On April 8 the surviving Hospitalers were allowed to retire in safety to Tripoli, thereby surrendering *Krak*.

Defeat was the fate of every other castle of the military orders in the crusader states. In 1291, with the fall of Acre, the military orders quit the Holy Land, although the Templars managed to hold onto the castle of *La Roche de Guillaume* in Cilician Armenia until 1299. **Related Entries:** Aleppo; Damietta; Louis IX; Tyre.

Suggested Reading

Robert W. Edwards, *The Fortifications of Armenian Cilicia* (1987); C. N. Johns, *Pilgrims' Castle ('Atlit), David's Tower (Jerusalem) and Qal'at ar-Rabad ('Ajlun): Three Middle Eastern Castles from the Time of the Crusades,* ed. by Denys Pringle (1997); Hugh Kennedy, *Crusader Castles* (1994); Kristian Molin, *Unknown Crusader Castles* (2001); Denys Pringle, *Fortification and Settlement in Crusader Palestine* (2000).

Cathars

A **Greek** word that means "those who are purified," it was the self-descriptive term favored by a sect that became the object of attack and persecution in the **Albigensian Crusade.** Other names that the Cathars were known by included Bogomils, Manichaeans, and Albigensians.

Bogomil was a tenth-century Bulgarian priest whose followers exported their brand of Christianity to the West during the late eleventh century along crusade and trade routes. Manichaeans were members of a faith that arose in Iraq in the third century and held doctrines closely resembling those of the Cathars. Albi was a city in **Languedoc** that was a twelfth- and thirteenth-century hotbed of Catharism.

Cathars were dualists who believed in two antithetical divinities: a god of spirit, light, immortality, and goodness; a god of matter, darkness, corruption, and evil. The former was the god of the New Testament, the latter of the Old Testament. The Cathars, who considered themselves the only true Christians, rejected all matter as evil, and this included things as widely diverse as sexual acts, **relics,** and the sacraments of the Church. They also rejected the doctrines of the Incarnation (God becoming a true human in the person of Jesus), and Jesus' death, Resurrection, and bodily Ascension into Heaven.

The rise of Catharism in Europe apparently had some connection with the crusades, especially the **First Crusade,** inasmuch as the areas in which it initially sprang up—Flanders, Champagne, the Loire Valley, and the Rhineland—were regions that had large numbers of returned crusaders. Apparently some crusaders, especially ill-educated lower clerics and uneducated soldiers from the rank and file, had come into contact with dualist ideas in the Balkans and farther east and transported them back home.

Cathars began to appear in significant numbers in northern Europe before the mid–twelfth century and occasioned a response of repression by the established Church. By the mid-1160s groups of dualists from the North were fleeing to the more hospitable climate of northern Italy and Languedoc, where they merged with local Cathars. In Languedoc, especially, they found a home. There a general atmosphere of tolerance, easygoing church leaders, a deep-seated anticlericalism on the part of the local lower nobility, and weak government at the top combined to allow Catharism to prosper and develop into a rival Church. By the end of the twelfth century Languedoc's Cathar Church presented a challenge to the entire Roman Church that could not be overlooked. **Related Entries:** Christians, Eastern; Heretics; Holy Sepulcher, Church of the.

Suggested Reading

Malcom Barber, *The Cathars: Duelist Heretics in Languedoc in the High Middle Ages* (2000).

Cavalry

Warriors on horseback were effectively used by both **Islamic** and **Frankish** armies but differed in type and function.

Islamic armies in the Age of the Crusades consisted largely of warriors on horseback who fought in two different styles: **Arab** and **Turkish.** The Arab- or Syrian-style cavalryman wore chain-mail **armor** like his Frankish counterpart and fought with a sword and lance or spear. The Turkish-style horse man followed the traditions of the steppes of Central Asia, which meant he was lightly armored and used a compound bow as his primary **weapon.** He might also carry a mace, sword, knife, or light thrusting lance

The defeat of Kilij Arslan at Nicaea as portrayed in a late thirteenth-century French manuscript. Note how the artist portrays the Turks (in the conical helmets) as fighting Western style. The chain mail depicted here is thirteenth century. A manuscript copy of the *Estoire d'Eracles*, a continuation of William of Tyre's history to 1229. The Walters Art Museum, Baltimore.

as a secondary weapon for when he closed with the enemy. Turkish-style horse archers far outnumbered the Arab-style mounted warriors. Whether on offense or defense, Turkish-style cavalry forces employed the tactic of charging, harrying, and retiring but always probing for a weakness that would allow them to concentrate their forces for a decisive attack. When circumstances proved unfavorable, they would retreat, but often retreat was only feigned, designed to lure the enemy into an ambush.

Muslim horse archers vastly outnumbered the foot soldiers in their armies and depended on speed, mobility, terror, guile, and showers of arrows to overwhelm the enemy. To the contrary, Western horse warriors generally constituted no more than twenty percent of the force of any crusade army.

Crusader horsemen fell into two classes: **knights,** who were nobles or near-nobles, and mounted **sergeants,** who were commoners. Whereas knights were armed with sword and lance, wore iron body mail (normally chain or scale armor), and served exclusively as a shock force, mounted sergeants bore an assortment of weapons and armor and served a variety of roles. These included acting as skirmishers and scouts, as well as serving in the ranks alongside the knights.

Knights depended on their heavy weapons and the effect of their massed assaults to carry the day. While awaiting the proper moment to attack or when placed on the defensive, Western knights would find shelter behind an **infantry** screen of bow- and spearmen. Conversely, the cavalry protected the infantry. The tactics of enemy horsemen fighting in the Turkish style made it impossible for crusader foot soldiers to hold off the enemy indefinitely and also prevented them from carrying on unassisted offensive operations. Without the support of their own cavalry, crusader infantry forces would eventually be cut to pieces. Mutual cooperation between horse and foot soldiers was a standard military doctrine of the crusaders and helped their armies to counter the superior maneuverability and firepower of Muslim horse soldiers.

Westerners grew to appreciate the special qualities of horsemen who fought in the Turkish manner and used some of their **Turcopoles** as horse archers. During the twelfth century such auxiliary light cavalry forces became a regular part of the armies of crusader **Syria-Palestine. Related Entries:** Chivalry; Dorylaeum, Battle of; Feudalism; Field of Blood, Battle of the; Hattin, Battle of.

Suggested Reading

John France, *Western Warfare in the Age of the Crusades, 1000–1300* (1999); Ann Hyland, *The Medieval Warhorse: From Byzantium to the Crusades* (1994); Christopher Marshall, *Warfare in the Latin East, 1192–1291* (1992); R. C. Smail, *Crusading Warfare, 1097–1193,* 2nd. ed. (1995).

Charles of Anjou

Brother of King **Louis IX,** crusader and papal champion, king of Sicily (r. 1266–1282), king of Naples (r. 1282–1285), prince of Achaea (r. 1278–1285), and nonresident king of **Jerusalem** (r. 1277–1282). Charles's crusade exploits reflect the ways in which the crusades of the late thirteenth century had deviated from the vision of Pope **Urban II.**

Charles participated in both the **Seventh** and **Eighth Crusades.** In April 1250, while fighting in the Nile Delta, he was captured (along with his brothers Louis and Alphonse), released a month later and shortly thereafter left for home. On Sunday, August 24, 1270, he arrived at the shores of Tunis, just as King Louis expired. Because his nephew, King Philip III, was still recovering from the **disease** that had killed his father, Charles took over command of the army and managed to stabilize the military situation. On October 30 Charles reached an agreement with the emir of Tunis that enabled the crusader army to withdraw honorably. Part of the agreement awarded the crusaders a total of 210,000 ounces of gold as a war indemnity, but really it was a bribe to quit Tunisian soil. One-third of the gold went to Charles. The treaty also ratified all of the traditional commercial privileges in Tunisia of Charles's kingdom of Sicily, and the emir doubled the annual fee paid by Tunisians to trade with Sicily. Additionally, all supporters of Charles's **Hohenstaufen** enemies were to be expelled from Tunisian soil. Charles then returned to Sicily without following up the planned second stage of the crusade—a campaign in either **Syria** or Egypt. Of all the participants of the Eighth Crusade, Charles seems to have been the only one who arrived home richer in the goods of this world than when he left.

In addition to these two crusades, in 1265 Charles assumed the crusader's mantle as a champion of the papacy against Manfred of Hohenstaufen, claimant to the crown of Sicily. Granted full **crusader privileges,** Charles triumphed and was accepted as king of Sicily in 1266, which at the time encompassed the southern half of the Italian peninsula, as well as the island of Sicily. Charles's ambitions did not stop there.

In 1277 Charles purchased the crown of Jerusalem from one of its claimants, Mary of **Antioch,** a transaction approved by the **papacy.** The **Knights of the Temple** and the Venetians also supported Charles's claim on the kingdom. With their help, Charles was able to rule the kingdom for five years through the services of a **bailli,** or residentrepresentative, in **Acre.** In 1282 events in Sicily forced Charles to call his troops and representative home.

Following provisions of a treaty concluded in 1267 through the agency of the papacy, the death in 1278 of the prince of Achaea brought this rich principality into Charles's possession. Achaea, located in the southern Greek peninsula known as the Peloponnese, was one of the major **Frankish** states of the **Latin empire of Constantinople,** which had been carved out in the wake of the **Fourth Crusade.** With this title and land, Charles also inherited a vague claim to the right to restore the fortunes of the Latin empire, which had lost **Constan-**tinople to Emperor Michael VIII Palaeologus in 1261. In the early 1280s, with the support of a French pope, Martin IV, Charles conspired to launch a holy crusade against the restored **Byzantine empire.** The crusade never got under way because of a successful rebellion on the island of Sicily in 1282.

Known as the Sicilian Vespers, it threw Charles's French occupiers out of the island, leaving Charles only with southern Italy, which then became the kingdom of Naples. Following their successful rebellion, the islanders invited King Peter III of Aragon to accept the crown of Sicily.

Pope Martin IV, ever the loyal defender of French royal interests, excommunicated King Peter and declared his kingdom of Aragon forfeit. When it became clear that Peter would not break, Martin called a holy crusade against him, with the crown of Aragon to go to Charles of Valois, the second son of King Philip III of France. King Philip assumed the cross and marched off to holy war in defense of his uncle's and son's political claims. The crusade was a disaster and was in complete retreat by the autumn of 1285.

Charles never lived to see the debacle, having died on January 7. He did live long enough to see his son and heir, Charles the Lame, captured by the Catalan forces of Peter III—a captivity that lasted from 1284 to 1289. With these dual setbacks and his own death, Charles of Anjou's dream of a grand Mediterranean empire, founded on crusades largely launched against fellow Christians, was over. **Related Entries:** Capetians; Criticism of the Crusades; Frankish Greece; Political Crusades.

Suggested Reading

Jean Dunbabin, *Charles I of Anjou: Power, Kingship and State-Making in Thirteenth-Century Europe* (1996).

Children's Crusade

A mass movement that involved largely the rural poor of all ages, it took place briefly in 1212, with focal points in two locations: west-central France and the Rhineland. The question of how, if at all, they were linked, is open and might never be resolved. Many historians also question whether the French participants saw themselves as crusaders.

Just as the first wave of the **First Crusade** has mistakenly been termed the "Peasants' Crusade," so the term "Children's Crusade" presents a false impression of the character and makeup of this crusade. Its leaders were, indeed, young. Stephen, the shepherd-boy leader of the French wave, might have been only twelve. It is likewise true that a large number of young people

Children's Crusade. Gustave Doré's rendering of this event is typical of the manner in which this so-called crusade has been romanticized. Dover Pictorial Archives.

marched with both groups, but many older people also joined, and we have no way of knowing what percentage of the participants were teenagers or younger. What we can say is that society tended to refer to people of low social and economic status as *pueri,* or "children," no matter their age. Serfs, because of their dependent status, were perpetual *pueri.* Nevertheless, it is possible that a majority of the participants were under the age of twenty.

Reliable evidence for the motives that drove the so-called Children's Crusade, as well as for its significant events and their sequence, is hard to come by and harder, still, to piece together. The participants did not leave behind documents, and the churchmen who described the crusade, often on the basis of rumors, had little or no understanding of and often no sympathy for what they described.

It is likely that many who were caught up in this expression of mass religious enthusiasm were driven by **apocalyptic** hopes and fears that sprang from the sermons they heard and the Last Judgment sculptures they saw on the facades of so many churches.

In 1212 crusades were being waged in three corners of Europe: the **Baltic, Spain,** and **Languedoc** (the **Albigensian Crusade**). With so many **holy wars** at hand, crusade **preachers** were crisscrossing Europe enlisting recruits and often setting off bursts of religious hysteria. Two persons caught up in the fervor were a young man from Cologne named Nicholas and a young French shepherd named Stephen. Both young men and their followers claimed a special spiritual strength by virtue of their poverty and low status. Seeing themselves as the meek, who Jesus had promised would inherit the Earth, they claimed that the high and the mighty had failed to recover **Jerusalem** because of their sins of pride and greed, but they, the poor, would succeed.

Beginning around Easter, Nicholas's followers streamed out of the Low Countries and the Rhineland and gathered strength in numbers as they marched south with the intention of sailing to **Outremer.** A large number of them reached Genoa. There some abandoned the trek, apparently disappointed when the waters did not part for them, while others pushed on to other ports. One late story, which is open to doubt, claims that a band of Germans traveled west to Marseilles, where two unscrupulous entrepreneurs offered them free passage aboard seven ships headed to the **Holy Land.** Two of the vessels sank with all passengers; the other five sailed to ports in Tunisia and Egypt, where the crusaders were sold into **slavery.** Some of Nicholas's followers apparently made contact with Pope **Innocent III,** either in Rome or through papal emissaries who intercepted them in northern Italy. According to the story, the pope praised them for their devotion but dispensed them from their **vows** and urged them to return home and await his calling an official crusade. Perhaps it is no coincidence that in April 1213 the pope began to set in motion a new crusade.

Whatever the truth, the movement that seems to have coalesced around Nicholas of Cologne was over by the end of summer. Many of Nicholas's followers never returned home. Some joined the Albigensian Crusade; others settled wherever they found themselves. As little as we know about the Rhineland Children's Crusade, we know even less about the French Children's Crusade.

Stephen, a shepherd from Cloyes, claimed to have received a letter from Jesus in the guise of a **pilgrim.** Letters from Heaven were common in the Age of the Crusades. As the story goes, Stephen was instructed to deliver the letter, which apparently contained instructions for a new crusade, to King **Philip II.** In the course of his trek to Paris, Stephen attracted a large following. Two sources claim 30,000, but most medieval **chroniclers** notoriously exaggerated the numbers of crowds and armies. As they traveled, they chanted, in reference to the **relic** lost twenty-five years earlier at **Hattin:** "Lord God, exalt Christianity! Lord God, restore the **True Cross** to us!" After they delivered the letter to the masters of the University of Paris, who were quite skeptical of its origins and authenticity, the so-called crusade broke up. A number of Stephen's followers, however, took the opportunity to join the Albigensian Crusade. **Related Entries:** Fifth Crusade; Ribauds; Shepherds' Crusade.

Chivalry

A code developed in Western Europe that dictated the ideal conduct of a *chevalier,* or warrior on horseback.

All war is brutal, and medieval warfare was especially brutal. Partly as a response to the Church's attempts to modify the horrors of warfare and partly out of a desire to set themselves apart from the rest of society, Western **feudal** warriors articulated a code of **knightly** conduct that governed their lives, profession, and class. An early form of the code permeates *The Song of Roland.* Roland and his comrades, all *chevalier* **vassals** of Emperor Charlemagne, display the virtues of valor, steadfastness, military prowess, prudence (except for the rash and strong-headed Roland), loyalty to their **feudal** lord to the point of death, respect for and loyalty to one another, and a sense of honor that informs their every thought and action. Without honor there could be no glory.

Such ideals are common among military elites. Warriors who belonged to the upper strata of **Islamic** society had their own codes of behavior and honor. The twelfth-century **Syrian** warrior, poet, and memoirist Usamah ibn Munqidh praised the **Franks** whom he encountered as men of extraordinary courage who valued military prowess above all else but who had no sense of honor, which was especially evident in the manner in which they failed to govern their **women.** This mystified him because, as he noted, "courage as a rule springs only from a sense of honor and a readiness to take offense."

Both crusader and **Muslim** warriors who were capable of the utmost callousness toward their enemies, whom they equally considered to be godless **infidels** and polytheists, could and did on occasion recognize and salute the other's bravery and martial abilities. The story is told by an anonymous English **chronicler** of the **Third Crusade** that at the Battle of **Jaffa** of August 5, 1192, King **Richard I the Lionheart** was in the thick of the fray, "cutting to pieces countless numbers with his flashing sword." Suddenly in the midst of battle he spied a **Turk** riding rapidly toward him leading two magnificent Arabian horses, which **al-Adil (Saphadin)** had dispatched in recognition of the king's abilities as a fighter and because he noticed that Richard seemed to be short of mounts. Richard accepted the horses and later repaid his Muslim foe handsomely for the gesture. In an aside, the chronicler remarked that Saphadin would have been worthy to be ranked with the noblest of men if only he were a Christian.

This story, whether true or not, reflects the highest ideals of chivalry, but chivalry had little application in ideal or reality to the vast majority of common soldiers and civilians who suffered the horrors of war. Chivalric gestures were normally reserved only for the high-born, and even then were often unevenly applied. Following the Battle of **Hattin, Saladin** treated the captured King **Guy** with great courtesy and generosity, but he also ordered the summary decapitation of all captured **Templars** and **Hospitalers,** except for the master of the Temple, who was spared and held for ransom.

Yet, there are always exceptions to general rules. Saladin's nephew, **al-Kamil,** treated all of the crusaders whom he captured in August 1221 at the end of the **Fifth Crusade** with almost unheard-of kindness. The **Latin** churchman **Oliver of Paderborn** was so overcome by the sultan's generosity in feeding and protecting the defeated crusaders that he wrote: "Those whose parents, sons, and daughters, brothers and sisters whom we killed with various tortures, whose possessions we scattered, or whom we cast naked from their homes, refreshed us with their own food as we were dying of hunger, even though we were under their dominion and power." **Related Entries:** Cannibalism; Holy War/Just War; Louis IX; Massacres; Pillage and Plunder; Prisoners; Reynald of Châtillon; Slavery; Peace and Truce of God.

Suggested Reading

Richard Barber, *The Knight and Chivalry* (2000); Maurice H. Keen, *Chivalry* (1984) and *Nobles, Knights and Men-at-Arms in the Middle Ages* (1996).

Christians, Eastern

Christians of Ethiopia, the **Middle East,** Central Asia, India, and beyond.

Christianity began as a religion of the Middle East, drawing heavily from Judaism and a variety of Eastern religions of salvation. During the early centuries of the Christian Era, Christianity in its various forms was strongest and most deeply rooted in the Eastern Mediterranean, and even triumphant **Islam** did not eradicate these ancient Christian cultures. Indeed, the conversion of the Middle East to Islam (as opposed to its

The entrance to the Church of the Nativity in Bethlehem. Reduced in size by the crusaders (note the outline of the Gothic arch), it was further reduced by either the Mamluks or Ottomans—probably to control pilgrim traffic and to emphasize the inferior status of their Christian subjects.

conquest) was a slow process that took many centuries and was never fully completed.

According to one tradition, the first state to accept Christianity as its official religion was **Armenia,** which adopted the faith around 314. A year earlier Constantine the Great had granted freedom of worship to Christians within the Roman empire and began the process of transforming Christianity into an imperial religion. By 325 he thought of himself and acted as a Christian emperor. When he dedicated the new imperial capital, **Constantinople,** in 330, he intended the city to be a bulwark of orthodox Christianity against **heresy** and paganism. A few years later (the traditional date is

333), the king of Ethiopia, in the highlands of northeast Africa, accepted Christianity as the official state religion. The Georgians of the southern Caucasus region also accepted the faith in the fourth century, probably due to Armenian and Eastern Roman influences.

Wherever Christianity found roots—Persia, Egypt, **Anatolia,** India, and the list goes on—converts adapted it to fit their cultures and languages, even as Christianity profoundly altered the cultures in which it found homes. In addition to this normal process of two-way cultural adaptation, there was the additional phenomenon of differing Christian creeds, or forms of belief.

During the fourth and fifth centuries, major Christological controversies wracked the Eastern Roman empire, as factions of Christians argued and fought over differing interpretations of the identity and nature of Jesus Christ. Was he God from all eternity and of the same divine substance as God the Father? Was he God by adoption and, therefore, created? Did he have one nature or two? If one nature, was he true God or true man? If two natures, how were they joined? Did he have one will or two? If two, how did these divine and human wills coexist?

The imperial Church, with its dual centers of authority in Constantinople and Rome, declared a number of the answers that emerged to be heresies. The sole official yardstick for orthodoxy was the faith as defined by imperial church **councils.** As a result of uncompromising conciliar definitions, a number of supposedly heretical Christian Churches were marginalized as far as the Roman Mediterranean World was concerned. The Nestorians, for example, who drew a sharp distinction between Jesus the man and Christ the divine savior, were condemned by the Council of Ephesus in 431, but their doctrine was accepted as the official faith of the Persian Christian Church in 486. With their religious center in Baghdad, Nestorians looked farther east, sending **missionaries** into Central and East Asia from the sixth through the eleventh centuries.

In 1095 Pope **Urban II** launched the **First Crusade,** in part to rescue captive Eastern Christians from presumed **Turkish** oppression. The Eastern Christians whom the pope and his **Latin** contemporaries knew best were **Byzantine,** or **Greek,** Christians who looked to Constantinople for guidance and authority. Large numbers of Byzantine Christians inhabited Sicily and southern Italy, the latter having been part of the Byzantine empire until the late eleventh century. As far as the eleventh-century **Roman papacy** was concerned, Byzantines shared the same faith as Latins but had inexplicably drifted away from papal authority. Well before 1095, the pope had already entered into correspondence with **Alexius I** regarding how they might reestablish full communion between the Churches of Rome and Constantinople. Certainly some of the traditions of the Byzantines, such as marriage of lower clergy, troubled papal reformers, but they saw Constantinople as part of one universal Church as far as doctrine was concerned.

The crusaders who arrived in the East had a wide variety of experiences with Byzantine Christians. Some were positive and led to deeper understanding; many were negative, even hostile, and led to mistrust and misunderstanding. Over the course of the first century of crusading, the sense of belonging to the same Christian family grew weaker, as Greeks and Latins developed many reasons to look upon one another as deviant Christians. One consequence of this growing animosity was the sack of Constantinople in 1204.

In addition to Byzantines, the crusaders discovered a wide and dizzying variety of other Christian groups in the East. Although we do not have demographic data, it seems clear that Christians still were at least a sizeable minority throughout the Middle East and, in various regions, were a majority. Even Egypt had a large Christian population (as it still does today).

Early in the thirteenth century **Oliver of Paderborn,** in his history of the **Fifth Crusade,** described a number of the different Christian communities that he encountered or learned about while on crusade. They included the *Monophysites* of Ethiopia and Nubia, who maintained that Christ had only one nature, and it was divine; the Georgians, who were very close in all matters to the Greeks; the Armenians and the Nestorians, the **Syrians** and the Russians; the Copts of Egypt and the Maronites of Lebanon. His list, although not complete, covers most of the major Eastern Christian congregations that a Western **pilgrim** to the **Holy Land** would encounter in groups both large and small. As Oliver further noted, the Arab Maronites of Lebanon had recently been united with the Church of Rome, as indeed they had in 1182 (and remain so today). The Maronites were the only Eastern Christian church to unite permanently with Rome in the Age of the Crusades, although at times it seemed others would. Certainly, the Western Church tried its best through both papal diplomacy and missionary work, especially by **mendicant friars** in the thirteenth century.

While widening schism was the reality on the level of ecclesiastical hierarchies and structures, on the personal level there was a significant amount of intermarriage among Latin and Eastern Christians of every sort. Human relations often transcend ideology and culture. **Related Entries:** Antioch; Crusader States; Edessa; Fourth Crusade; Gregory X, Pope; *Poulain;* Prester John; Settlement and Colonization; Turcopoles.

Suggested Reading

A. S. Atiya, *A History of Eastern Christianity* (1968); Judith Herrin, *The Formation of*

Christendom (1987); Tia M. Kolbaba, *The Byzantine Lists: Errors of the Latins* (2000); John McManners, ed., *The Oxford Illustrated History of Christianity* (1995).

Chronicles

Narratives that present a sequence of historical phenomena without interpreting what they mean.

A true history, which derives from a **Greek** word that means "learning through inquiry," tells a story but also provides an analysis of what it narrates; a chronicle, which derives from Greek and Latin words that mean "time," reports in chronological fashion a series of events without providing analytical commentary or any attempt to discover or show patterns and meaning.

The crusades provided rich material for both **historians** and chroniclers. Among the Arabs, Ibn al-Athir's *The Perfect History,* which spanned the entire **Islamic** World of his day from the era before Muhammad to 1231, was a true history. Its author attempted to trace causal links and to present his conclusions clearly and convincingly. To the contrary, as the title suggests, Ibn al-Qalanisi's *Continuation of the Chronicle of Damascus* is a series of one event after another. Although he presents highly detailed stories and connects them into a coherent narrative, the reader still winds up with a chronicle whose parts are greater than the whole because there is no overarching interpretation.

Among the **Latins,** crusade histories were more the norm than the exception because Westerners saw these **holy wars** as epochal events within the history of salvation. Nevertheless, some Latin chroniclers told crusade stories simply as items of passing interest and without attempting to place them into any grand context. Roger of Hoveden's *Chronicle,* for example, which primarily focuses on events in England and France from 1172 to 1193, contains his eye-witness, detailed description of the **siege** of **Acre** during the **Third Crusade.**

During the thirteenth century Western chronicles tended to become longer and more complex, and a fair number of important chroniclers emerged whose wide-ranging interests and connections allowed them to incorporate detailed and sometimes well-informed crusade stories into their chronicles. Two such chroniclers were the **Cistercian** monks Ralph of Coggeshall and Alberic of Trois-Fontaines. Neither the English Ralph nor the French Alberic ever went on crusade. Nevertheless, each used the international network provided by the **Order of Cîteaux** to gather information about crusades both recent and long past. At times the stories they relate are more mythic than historical, and often they present garbled versions of reality. But their works are important sources for the modern historian, if for no other reason than they illustrate how the crusades were viewed from the distant perspective of Europe. **Related Entries:** Apocalypse and the Crusades; Historians and Chroniclers, Islamic; Historians and Chroniclers, Latin.

Suggested Reading

Beryl Smalley, *Historians in the Middle Ages* (1975).

Cid, El

Rodrigo Díaz de Vivar (ca. 1043–1099), better known as *El Cid* (from the Arabic *sayyid,* which means "lord"), hero of the Castilian epic *Poema de Mio Cid* (*The Poem of My Lord*).

Rodrigo Díaz was an adventurer, a soldier of supreme skill, a cruel ruler, an opportunist, and a **mercenary** who sold his services to the most generous paymaster, regardless of whether he was Christian or **Muslim.** He was never a crusader, but very much like his French epic counterpart, Roland, Rodrigo Díaz became a legendary symbol of the Christian struggle against **Islam.** In his case, the Spanish **Reconquista.**

The disjunction between the myth of the Cid's waging **holy wars** of reconquest and the historical reality of his deeds and motives is great, but the legend tells us much about the ideology that fueled the later Reconquista, just as the facts of Rodrigo Díaz's life reveal much about the tangled political-military situation in Iberia around the time of the **First Crusade.**

Rodrigo Díaz died in Valencia in July 1099—the same month and year in which the **Franks** captured **Jerusalem.** Had he lived in an earlier era, he probably would not have metamorphosed into a crusader-hero, but it was Don Rodrigo's good fortune to live and die at the right moment. Evidence suggests that the Cid's exploits were already a matter of popular song before the mid–twelfth century, but the epic through which we chiefly know him today was probably composed between 1175 and 1207, when King Alfonso VIII of Castile's wars with the **Almohads** were heating up. Consequently, the poem portrays Rodrigo as a pious Christian warrior who constantly invokes the aid of **Santiago** and fights unceasingly against Muslim enemies. Nowhere is there any mention or allusion to his ever having served as a mercenary in the pay of a Muslim lord. Very much like the **Song of Roland,** the poem has a warrior-bishop who fights alongside the Cid, slays Muslim enemies, and offers an **indulgence** to all who fall in battle against the **Moors.** Also like *The Song of Roland,* the poem celebrates the virtue of **feudal** loyalty and presents Rodrigo, who in life had been supremely self-serving, as a paragon of **knightly** devotion to his lord, King Alfonso VI.

The historical Cid was less than the perfect Christian warrior and **vassal,** and his exploits underline the ambiguous world of shifting alliances that characterized Iberia in the late eleventh century. Rodrigo was a Castilian who entered the service of King Sancho II of Castile and later passed into that of the late Sancho's brother, enemy, and successor to the throne of Castile, Alfonso VI of León-Castile. Rodrigo was exiled in 1081 after incurring Alfonso's ire for attacking the lands of the **Moorish** ruler of Toledo, who at the time was Alfonso's client. For five years the Cid served the Muslim lords of Saragossa against both their Christian and Muslim enemies. The invasion of Spain and defeat on the field of battle of King Alfonso VI by the **Almoravids** in 1086 brought about a reconciliation between Rodrigo and the king, who believed he needed the Cid's services, and Rodrigo was willing to sell them. In 1089 Rodrigo again earned the king's anger for his failure to link up with the royal army in a campaign against the Almoravids. With his lands confiscated by the king, the Cid became a bandit chieftain. In 1092 he invaded Castile as a warning to Alfonso not to besiege Muslim Valencia in southeast Spain, on which he had his own designs. After a brilliant campaign, Rodrigo Díaz conquered the city of Valencia in June 1094 but soon found himself besieged in the city by an Almoravid army. The Cid routed his enemies with a surprise sortie, thereby achieving the first defeat of an Almoravid army in Iberia by any force. The victory assured his fame throughout the peninsula. During the next several years Rodrigo Díaz expanded his territory with a series of successful campaigns against the Almoravids. Throughout this period he seems to have acted as his own man, entirely independent of any connection with Alfonso VI, but the king might have supported him inasmuch as they fought a common Almoravid enemy.

Five years after his conquest of Valencia, the Cid died in bed. His widow, Jimena, who was his equal in courage and determination, was forced, after a heroic defense of the city, to abandon it. With the assistance of Alfonso VI, who saw the city as indefensible, Valencia was set on fire, and Donna Jimena retreated to Castile, bearing with her the body of the Cid. **Related Entries:** Al-Andalus; Chivalry; Women.

Suggested Reading

Primary Sources

Historia Rodrigo (*The History of Rodrigo*) in Simon Barton and Richard Fletcher, trans. and eds., *The World of El Cid: Chronicles of the Spanish Reconquest* (2000), pp. 90–147; *Poem of the Cid: A Modern Translation with Notes,* trans. by Paul Blackburn and George Economou (1998).

Historical Study

Richard Fletcher, *The Quest for El Cid* (1990).

Cistercians

See Cîteaux, Order of.

Cîteaux, Order of

More popularly known as the Cistercians, monks of the Order of Cîteaux played important roles in the **Second, Third, Fourth,** and **Albigensian Crusades.**

The order began in Burgundy in 1098 as a single monastery that attempted to offer its members a purer, more rigorous form of monastic life. Under the charismatic influence of **Bernard of Clairvaux,** Cistercian monasteries sprang up throughout Western Europe, and this rapidly expanding monastic order found itself involved in crusades, especially during the period 1145–1229. It was also a visible presence in the **Latin East** through monasteries established there dur-

ing the twelfth and thirteenth centuries. The rule and ideals of the Order of Cîteaux also served as models for a number of **military orders,** most notably the **Templars.** On the less positive side, the Order of Cîteaux also produced Ralph, the monk who incited anti-**Jewish** riots in the Rhineland while **preaching** the Second Crusade, and Master Jacob, the leader of the **Shepherds' Crusade** of 1251, seems to have been a former Cistercian monk.

The Order of Cîteaux contained within itself the creative tension of contradictory principles: the monastic ideals of solitude and stability (living secluded in one monastery for one's entire religious life) and the dynamism of an ardent reform movement that sought to transform the world. Bernard of Clairvaux, who almost single-handedly launched the Second Crusade, epitomized that tension. He was a mystic who yearned for a life of solitude and prayer, yet he immersed himself in the affairs of Christian society out of a desire to sanctify it. He did not believe it proper for monks to go on crusade but did not hesitate to preach the crusade to the laity, believing that the crusade was God's gift to sinners, whereby they could save their souls through **holy war.** Indeed, for Bernard, for **Eugenius III,** a Cistercian monk who became pope, and for so many other Cistercians involved in the crusades, the crusade was an act of love— the loving service offered a loving God by a contrite sinner.

The Second Crusade marked the order's first venture into crusading. In addition to Pope Eugenius and Bernard, other Cistercians involved in the crusade included Godfrey, bishop of Langres and a former monk of Clairvaux, who traveled with **Louis VII,** and Otto, bishop of Freising, a former abbot (head of a monastery) who accompanied his half-brother, Emperor **Conrad III,** and commanded a portion of the German army.

The general disillusionment that plagued European Christians after the failure of the Second Crusade's campaign in the East put a momentary damper on the order's involvement in crusading and the Latin East. During the entire twelfth century the order established only four monastic houses in **Outremer,** and only one of them, Belmont, founded in 1157 in the **county of Tripoli,** was a success. However, the crisis occasioned by the disaster at **Hattin** in 1187 once again drew the Cistercians into crusade work. In addition to supporting the Third Crusade through their prayers, the order saw several of its more prominent members not only preach the crusade but also enlist and lead troops across the sea. The Cistercian archbishop of Canterbury, Baldwin of Ford, commanded a group of English crusaders and died while on campaign. Henry of Horburg, bishop of Basel and former monk of Cîteaux, also died on this crusade, a victim of **disease.** A third Cistercian to give his life was Archbishop Gerard of Ravenna, who sailed from Venice at the head of a large group of crusaders. He led a mixed force of Italians and Germans to the siege of **Acre,** where he was killed while leading an assault upon the city.

Notwithstanding the actions of these monk-bishops, most Cistercians continued to agree with Bernard of Clairvaux that it was improper for monks to travel on crusade in any capacity. Despite this sentiment, the tradition of direct Cistercian involvement in the crusades continued and peaked in the Fourth Crusade. As early as 1198, **Fulk of Neuilly,** with papal permission, enlisted Cistercians as crusade preachers. Ultimately six Cistercian abbots traveled across the sea on the crusade, and one of them died along the way. One of the returning abbots, Martin of Pairis, came back with a rich trove of **relics** that he had plundered in **Constantinople,** and Abbot Martin's exploits became the nucleus around which one of his monks, Gunther, fashioned his age's most sophisticated **crusade history,** the *Hystoria Constantinopolitana* (*The Constantinopolitan History*).

Cistercian involvement in the crusades and in the lands of Outremer continued well after 1204. Quite a few Cistercians preached the Albigensian Crusade, and several played key roles in the crusade itself, including Arnold Amalric, abbot of Cîteaux, who served as senior **papal legate** to the crusade in its early years. One of the Cistercians involved in the crusade, Peter of Vaux-de-Cernay, composed its most important eyewitness history. In the thirteenth century a few Cistercian monasteries sprang up in the **Latin empire of Constantinople,** in **Frankish Greece,** and in the kingdom of **Cyprus,** as well as in the **crusader states** of **Syria-Palestine.** Despite this activity, it is correct to say that the classic era of Cistercian crusade involvement lasted less than a century. During the early thirteenth century a new element in the Roman Church, the **mendicant friars,** became the **papacy**'s most effective tool in promoting the crusades and carrying out associated activities. **Related Entries:** Carmelites; Criticism of the Crusades; Dominicans; Francis of Assisi; Missionaries; Mongols.

Suggested Reading

Primary Sources

Alfred J. Andrea, ed. and trans., *The Capture of Constantinople: The "Hystoria Constantinopolitana" of Gunther of Pairis* (1997); W. A. Sibly and M. D. Sibly, trans., *The History of the Albigensian Crusade: Peter of les Vaux-de-Cernay's "Historia Albigensis"* (1998).

Historical Studies

Michael Gervers, ed., *The Second Crusade and the Cistercians* (1992); Beverly M. Kienzle, *Cistercians, Heresy, and Crusade in Occitania, 1145–1229: Preaching in the Lord's Vineyard* (2001).

Clermont, Council of (November 18–27, 1095)

The venue at which Pope **Urban II** set in motion the **First Crusade.**

The Council of Clermont was one of a series of convocations presided over by Pope Urban II as a means of demonstrating papal authority and furthering a program of moral and institutional reform throughout the Western Church, while he struggled with Emperor Henry IV in a bitter battle known as the **Investiture Controversy.**

By 1094 Urban's fortunes in this struggle had so improved that he could pick up the pace at which he convened church **councils** aimed at promoting the papal reform program and marshaling support against the imperial party. In early March 1095 he held such a council in the northern Italian city of Piacenza. An embassy from the **Byzantine** emperor, **Alexius I,** arrived at the council, requesting that the pope urge Western warriors to join the emperor's forces in defense of the **Eastern Christian** lands. The pope did just that in a public sermon outside the city, in which he appealed for fighting men to render faithful service to Alexius. Apparently he had some success.

Later in the year Urban crossed the Alps to his native France with the dual intention of fixing the French Church more firmly in his camp of papal reform and appealing for aid for the embattled Eastern Christians. It was at Clermont on November 27, again in an open-air public sermon, that Pope Urban repeated his call for military help against the **Turks,** who were supposedly oppressing the churches and peoples of the Christian East, but the manner in which he framed his appeal differed radically from that made at Piacenza. Those differences provided the ideological basis for the crusades.

Urban's sermon was one of the most important speeches in the history of the West, but no verbatim transcript of it was preserved. There are five early twelfth-century accounts of the pope's speech, four by people who were probably at Clermont, but each account was composed long after the event, with the earliest dating to no earlier than 1101. Not only were the accounts based on memory—always an inexact guide—but each author also composed a version of the pope's sermon that reflected his *interpretation* of what Urban said. These interpretations were colored by each person's knowledge and understanding of the crusade's outcome, by each author's attempt to demonstrate his rhetorical skills, and by each author's worldview. As a consequence, the five sermons that these **historians** set down differ greatly in form, style, and even substance.

Despite the differences, sufficient common elements among them and enough other documentary evidence from the period 1095–1096 point to certain inescapable conclusions. Rather than recruiting **mercenary** soldiers to serve in Emperor Alexius's armies, the pope appealed directly to the many French lords and other fighting men at Clermont to travel east as **pilgrims**—but armed pilgrims—to liberate **Jerusalem** as an integral part of their aiding imperiled fellow Christians. To those who performed this task piously and with a true sense of contrition, he offered a plenary, or full, **indulgence** for all their sins. What was more, this was to be a papal army fighting a **holy war** called in the name of Christ. It is clear that Urban intended the army to follow the spiritual and moral direction of **Adhémar of Monteil,** whom he commissioned as **papal legate.**

All sources report that Urban's sermon received immediate, enthusiastic response at Clermont, and in the months that followed his appeal was broadened to include almost all of Western Christendom, except for Spain, where Christians were already engaged in fighting **Muslims** in the **Reconquista.** The call for an armed pilgrimage to Jerusalem was as successful as it was broad, and because of that success the papal war that Urban articulated at Clermont became something radically new, as the three waves of the First Crusade demonstrated. **Related Entries:** Apocalypse and the Crusades; Cross, Crusader's; *Deus Vult;* Fulcher of Chartres; Noncombatants; Papacy, Roman; Peace and Truce of God; Peter the Hermit; Preaching; Privileges, Crusader; Raymond IV of Saint-Gilles.

Conrad II (IV)

See Hohenstaufens.

Conrad III

See Hohenstaufens; Second Crusade.

Conrad III/Conradin

See Hohenstaufens.

Conrad of Montferrat

Hero of the **siege** of **Tyre,** husband of **Isabella I,** and uncrowned king-elect of **Jerusalem.**

In 1185 Conrad, future marquis of **Montferrat** (r. 1188–1192), traveled to **Constantinople** to wed Theodora, sister of Emperor **Isaac II,** even though he seems to have already had a wife back home in northern Italy. The alliance proved fruitful for Isaac. In 1187 the Byzantine army's most capable general, who had destroyed an invading **Norman**-Sicilian army, rebelled and led his army against Constantinople. This revolt was stemmed at the walls of the city by an army of **mercenaries** led by Conrad of Montferrat. Soon thereafter, however, Conrad, feeling unappreciated at an increasingly anti-Western imperial court, abandoned his wife and slipped away to **Syria,** apparently unaware that the **crusader states** were in imminent danger of being totally overrun by the forces of **Saladin.**

Unable to land at **Acre,** which had fallen to Saladin's forces, Conrad sailed to Tyre. The city's commander had already agreed to terms of capitulation, but Conrad's timely arrival on July 14, 1187, only ten days after the disaster at **Hattin,** gave new heart to the defenders, who turned over leadership to Conrad. It was a wise choice. According to the Arab **historian** Ibn al-Athir, Conrad "was a devil incarnate in his ability to govern and defend a town, and a man of extraordinary courage." Immediately upon assuming control of Tyre, whose population was being swelled almost daily by **Frankish** refugees from lands overrun by Saladin's army, Conrad began a systematic and vigorous program of shoring up the city's defenses in anticipation of the coming assault.

When the siege began in November, Conrad and the city were ready to resist. Several Western sources tell the story of Saladin's bringing before the walls of the city Conrad's father, William the Elder, who had been captured at Hattin. When Saladin threatened to execute his **prisoner** on the spot if Conrad did not surrender the city, Conrad shot a crossbow bolt in the general direction of William to demonstrate his resolve to fight on regardless of what happened to his father. Saladin could only marvel at Conrad's resolve and, according to one source, mutter, "This man is an **infidel** and very cruel."

Between November 13, 1187, and January 1, 1188, when Saladin abandoned the siege, Tyre held on grimly, thanks in large part to Conrad's abilities. Before and during the month-and-a-half-long siege, Conrad also sent appeals to the West for aid, which helped rouse enthusiasm for a new crusade.

In June 1188, King **Guy of Lusignan,** who had been captured at Hattin, was released from captivity and marched to Tyre to take possession of the city. Conrad refused him entry, claiming that he was no longer king of **Jerusalem.** A struggle for power now broke out between the two men. In 1190 King Guy's wife (and Conrad's former sister-in-law), Queen **Sibylla,** sister of the late King **Baldwin IV,** mother of the deceased **Baldwin V** (Conrad's late nephew), and heiress to the kingdom, died. Inasmuch as Guy's claim to the kingship stemmed from his marriage to his co-monarch, Conrad seized the opportunity. The next heiress in line was **Isabella (I),** Sibylla's half-sister. Conrad prevailed upon Isabella's mother, the dowager queen Maria, to convince her daughter to leave her husband, Humphrey, the lord of **Transjordan,** and to marry him. Despite the fact that Conrad still had a wife back in Constantinople (and possibly another in Italy), Isabella agreed. Her marriage was annulled (the reason given was she had only been eight when she was engaged), and she wed Conrad (who had judiciously bribed members of the kingdom's **High Court** who sat in judgment of the case).

Conrad now declared himself king by virtue of his marriage, and when King **Philip II** of France arrived at Acre on April 20, 1190, Conrad had a powerful ally because of his family connections with the **Capetian** royal house. King Guy, however, refused to surrender his claim, knowing that he had a powerful ally in King **Richard I** of England, whose crusade forces were expected to arrive momentarily to assist in the siege of Acre. With this impasse, Isabella and Conrad retired to Tyre, where Isabella gave birth to a daughter, **Maria of Montferrat,** in 1191.

Following the capture of Acre on July 12, 1191, King Richard attempted to settle the controversy with a compromise. Guy was confirmed as king, but Conrad was made his heir. The settlement soon fell through. Conrad held himself aloof from Richard and Guy's crusading activities and carried on his own negotiations with Saladin. To avert a civil war, Richard assembled the great barons and churchmen of the kingdom on April 16, 1192, and asked them who should be king. They chose Conrad, and preparations were made for Conrad's coronation.

Twelve days later, however, two **Assassins** cut Conrad down in Tyre. Clearly the two killers had been sent by Rashid al-Din Sinan, the Old Man of the Mountain, or leader of the Assassins of Syria. His motive in sending them was never established, although theories abounded, including one rumor that implicated King Richard. That rumor is not believable, but another, more believable story that circulated claimed that Saladin had paid the Assassin leader a large sum of money for the deaths of either Richard or Conrad, and Conrad was the easier target. There might be truth in that rumor, but maybe one does not need to look any further than the Old Man of the Mountain himself. Conrad had seized one of the Assassins' richly laden cargo ships and killed its crew. That was motive enough. **Related Entries:** Amalric; Third Crusade.

Constance of Antioch

Daughter of **Bohemond II;** princess and regent of **Antioch** (r. 1149–1153; 1161–1163).

Following Bohemond II's death in 1130, his widow, **Alice,** attempted to seize control of Antioch, thereby disinheriting her two-year-old daughter, Constance. The plot was foiled by Alice's father, King **Baldwin II,** who assumed the regency for himself. As regent, Baldwin would govern Antioch in Constance's name until she married, assuming he lived that long. When King Baldwin II died in 1131, the new king of **Jerusalem,**

Fulk, took over the regency, and in 1136 he arranged a marriage between Constance and Raymond of Poitiers, to frustrate Alice's renewed attempt to seize control of the principality. Raymond served as prince of Antioch until his death in battle in 1149.

Constance, now widowed at age 22 and with at least three children, took control of the government of Antioch. King **Baldwin III** urged her to remarry, but she refused until 1153, when she fell in love with a newcomer from the West, **Reynald of Châtillon,** who assumed the title and duties of prince of Antioch. Reynald, a brave and dashing adventurer, was an unfortunate choice. His intemperate nature proved his downfall. In November 1161 during a **pillaging** expedition into **Muslim** territory, he fell into the hands of **Nur ad-Din** and was held **prisoner** for fifteen years.

Upon Reynald's capture, Constance was determined to hold the principality in her own hands. When her son Bohemond III (r. 1163–1201) reached his eighteenth year in 1162, Constance refused to surrender control of Antioch to him. To gain an ally who could help her secure her position, she arranged the marriage of her daughter Maria with the **Byzantine** emperor, **Manuel I Comnenus,** who claimed Antioch as a **vassal** state of the empire. These actions incensed Antioch's barons and **Latin** patriarch, who conspired with an **Armenian** prince to drive Constance from power. In 1163 she was forced into exile, and her son was installed as prince. When her husband was released from captivity in 1176, Constance was dead. The place, time, and circumstances of her death are unknown. **Related Entries:** Eleanor of Aquitaine; Melisende; Women.

Constantinople

Capital of the **Byzantine empire,** captured by the army of the **Fourth Crusade** on April 12–13, 1204, occupied as the capital city of the **Latin empire of Constantinople** until its liberation on July 25, 1261, and finally captured by the **Ottoman Turks** on May 29, 1453. Today it is known as Istanbul.

Constantinople began its life in the first half of the seventh century B.C.E. as *Byzantion,* a colony of the Greek city-state of Megara. Its location could not have been more advantageous. The city is situated on a triangular peninsula that commands the southern entrance to the Bosporus, a roughly twenty-two-mile strait that connects the Sea of Marmara with the Black Sea. The coastal regions of the Black Sea provided the Ancient Mediterranean World with a large percentage of its grains and access to the steppes and peoples of western Central Asia. The Sea of Marmara is connected to Greece's Aegean Sea by a strait known as the Hellespont, or the Dardanelles. Adding to the site's obvious commercial value was the fact that the Byzantine Peninsula is bordered on the north by a natural harbor, known as the Golden Horn, which stretches for about five miles from the two streams that feed it.

Byzantion was formally incorporated into the Roman empire in 73 C.E., and in the **Latin** language of the Romans, it became known as *Byzantium.* Its prime strategic location moved Constantine I, the first Christian Roman emperor, to transform Byzantium, up to then a fairly small trading city, into Constantinople, the capital of his new Christian empire, in 330. Almost overnight, Constantinople became one of the great cities of the world. By the mid–fifth century, when Emperor Theodosius II completed the massive land walls that still stand today, Constantinople was a major center of government, commerce, industry, and the arts. At the height of its splendor in the early eleventh century, its land and sea walls, which stretched some seventeen miles, enclosed as many as a million people.

Ruins of Constantinople's fifth-century land walls, a complex of three walls separated by dry moats.

Thanks to the water that borders it on three sides and a triple curtain of massive land walls on its fourth side, the city was easily defended. This was a blessing because the city was probably the most besieged and attacked urban center in the world in the period between 330 and 1453. During those 1,123 years, Constantinople's attackers included Ostrogoths, Huns, Persians, Avars, Pechenegs, Arabs, Vikings, Russ', Bulgars, **Seljuk Turks,** crusaders, and Ottoman Turks. Of these, only two groups, Western European crusaders in 1203 and again in 1204 and Ottoman Turks in 1453, succeeded in capturing the city. As a bulwark against attack from Asia and Europe, Constantinople was without peer.

To the crusaders who passed through Constantinople from 1096 onward, the city was almost beyond description. **Fulcher of Chartres,** an **historian** of the **First Cru-sade,** wrote: "Oh, what a noble and beautiful city is Constantinople! . . . It would be quite tedious to enumerate all of the different forms of wealth there: gold, silver, vestments of many different types, and holy **relics.**" Robert of Clari, who left behind his memoir of the Fourth Crusade, was equally awe-stricken. In his words: "I do not think that among the forty richest cities of the world there was as much wealth as was found in Constantinople. For the **Greeks** say that two-thirds of the world's wealth is in Constantinople; the other one-third is scattered throughout the rest of the world."

The wealth of Constantinople and the Byzantines' apparent reluctance to share their goods with crusaders caused a certain amount of envy and friction from the start. The early stages of the First Crusade witnessed inter-mittent skirmishing in Constantinople's suburbs between Byzantine troops and crusaders who were stealing food and other goods. A number of factors, however, including a still strong sense of shared Christian bonds, prevented these clashes from blowing up into full-scale battles or attacks on the city. The same was true of the **Second** and **Third Crusades.** Despite misunderstandings, clashes, and a growing sense of mutual mistrust, a sense of their belonging to the same Christian family prevented crusaders from direct attacks on Constantinople. It was only during the Fourth Crusade, when an unforeseen and complex series of events brought crusaders to the city and into direct conflict with the citizens of Constantinople, that crusaders actually assaulted and captured the city.

The first assault, which took place on July 17, 1203, was repulsed, but it caused Emperor Alexius III to panic and abandon the city, whereupon the crusaders and the young Byzantine prince whose cause they championed were invited into the city. The second assault, which was launched on April 8, 1204, was undertaken to capture the city for themselves. This also was repulsed with heavy losses. Four days later the crusaders were on the attack again, and by the morning of the 13th, the city was theirs. There followed fifty-seven years, three months, and twelve days of occupation, as the crusaders turned Constantinople into the capital of the Latin empire of Constantinople.

The city was liberated from Western control in 1261 by the army of Emperor Michael VIII Palaeologus, whose empire-in-exile had been centered in Nicaea. The city into which Michael VIII rode in triumph on August 15, 1261, was half ruined, due to three fires that had been set by the army of the Fourth Crusade, the sack of the city in April 1204, and general neglect by the Western occupiers. At great expense, Michael and his successors rebuilt and repopulated the city, setting in motion an age of artistic and intellectual renaissance, even though the empire was now a shadow of its former self. In 1282 Constantinople faced the threat of attack by **Charles of Anjou,** king of Sicily, but a revolt on that island forced him to abandon his plans. Constantinople's woes were hardly over, however.

A new **Islamic** menace, the Ottoman Turks, arose in the fourteenth century. By 1402 the Ottomans had conquered almost all of **Anatolia** and most of the eastern and central Balkans, and Constantinople was now surrounded by Ottoman lands. Between 1397 and early 1402, the city itself was under Ottoman **siege,** but the siege was lifted to meet an emergency in eastern Anatolia. When Mehmed II succeeded to the sultanate in 1451, the Byzantine empire consisted of little more than the city and its small population. In the spring of 1453, Mehmet pressed his attack on Constantinople. Thanks to superior cannons, overwhelming numbers of well-trained troops, and brilliant generalship, the Turkish armies breached the land walls of the city. Despite an heroic defense of the city by Constantinople's small army, the city was carried in a bloodbath on May 29. Constantinople's last emperor, Constantine XI, died fighting at the walls. **Related Entries:** Christians, Eastern; Hohenstaufens; Montferrat, Family of.

Suggested Reading

Michael Maclagan, *The City of Constantinople* (1968).

Constantinople, Latin Empire of (1204–1261)

Founded by the predominantly French and Venetian participants of the **Fourth Crusade,** it lasted from the capture of the city on April 13, 1204, to the **Byzantine** recapture of Constantinople on July 25, 1261.

With their conquest of the imperial city, the crusaders claimed authority over the entire Byzantine empire, and a commission of twelve Venetians and twelve **Franks** drew up a treaty of partition. The capital was divided between the Latin emperor, **Baldwin I** (and his successors), and the Venetians, with the former receiving five-eighths of the city and the latter three-eighths. The rest of the empire was divided three ways: imperial domains, Venetian possessions, and **feudal** principalities for the other crusader lords. Most of these lands had yet to be conquered when they were partitioned out, and some never were.

This carved-up empire was a hybrid affair. The various Frankish lords who were awarded principalities owed at least nominal fealty to the Latin emperor, but the Venetians ruled their possessions in and around Constantinople, as well as the island of Crete, independently, even though they were obligated to share in the empire's defense. Other Venetian holdings, especially in the Aegean Islands, were conquered by private Venetians who held their lands as **vassals** of the Latin emperor or some other Frankish lord but whose loyalties tended toward Venice.

Between 1204 and 1261 the Venetians could more or less rightfully claim to hold "one quarter and one-half of a quarter" (three-eighths) of the entire empire, and these possessions gave Venice a position of unassailable commercial hegemony in this region of the **Levant**. Venice's most important possessions in the empire were in the waters around Constantinople, which now, for the first time, gave the Venetians direct access to the markets of the Black Sea. Even after the Byzantines rewon Constantinople, they could no longer exclude Venice and its rival, Genoa, from the Black Sea and markets that traded goods from Central and East Asia.

The **Greek** counterattack on the Latin empire was led by two empires-in-exile that arose in Byzantium's unconquered territories: the despotate of Epirus in the eastern Balkans and the empire of Nicaea in western

The supposed burial spot of Venice's doge, Enrico Dandolo, in Constantinople's Church of Hagia Sophia.

and central **Anatolia.** The latter produced Emperor Michael VIII Palaeologus, who reestablished Byzantine rule in Constantinople in 1261. Even after the recovery of Constantinople, **Latins** continued to govern areas of Greece and the Aegean Islands for centuries to come. Venice, for example, held on to Crete to 1669 and lost its last island strongholds to the **Ottoman Turks** in 1691.

Although the Byzantine empire experienced a cultural renaissance following recovery of its capital, militarily and politically the empire never fully recovered from the dual traumas of the Fourth Crusade and the Latin empire. Certainly Christendom did not recover because Byzantine Christians never forgot or forgave Latin Christians for the Fourth Crusade and their efforts to submit the captive Byzantine Church to the authority of the **Roman papacy. Related Entries:** Charles of Anjou; Crusade of 1239–1241; Frankish Greece; John of Brienne; Latin East; Missionaries.

Suggested Reading

Primary Sources

Crusaders as Conquerors: The Chronicle of Morea, trans. by Harold E. Lurier (1964); Geoffrey of Villehardouin, *The Conquest of Constantinople* in *Memoirs of the Crusades.* trans. by Frank T. Marzials (1965).

Historical Studies

Michael Angold, *The Fall of Constantinople, 1204: Byzantium, the Fourth Crusade and Its Consequences* (2002); Thomas F. Madden, *Enrico Dandolo and the Rise of Venice* (2003); Robert Lee Wolff, *Studies in the Latin Empire of Constantinople* (1976).

Councils and Synods

A formal assembly of church leaders convened to determine correct doctrine and practices and to establish discipline and policies.

Regional councils convened by archbishops or patriarchs are often called synods but may also be called councils. Councils that claim to represent the entire Church are known as General, or Ecumenical, Councils, and they are believed to be infallible whenever they issue authoritative statements regarding the faith. As far as the **Byzantine** Church is concerned, there have been only seven true General Councils of the Church. Held exclusively in the East between the years 325 and 787 and under the authority of the emperor of **Constantinople,** they defined the basic tenets of *orthodox* (right thinking) Christianity. According to the Roman Church, an additional thirteen General Councils have been held in the West, under the authority and presidency of the **papacy,** since 1123. Several of these Western General Councils, as well as several European synods, had important consequences for the crusades.

The most important crusade council was a regional synod convened and presided over by Pope **Urban II**—the **Council of Clermont** of 1095, which launched the **First Crusade.** Another French regional council, that of Troyes of 1129, modified and then gave its blessing to the rule of the **Order of the Temple.**

In 1123 Pope **Calixtus II** gathered together in Rome at least 300 church leaders from all over the West. Held at the Lateran, a complex consisting of the papal palace and the cathedral of Saint John, this council, known as the First Lateran Council, celebrated the end of the **Investiture Controversy,** a struggle that had affirmed the centrality of the Roman papacy within the Church. As far as the pope was concerned, I Lateran was a General Council of the universal Church, even though no representatives from any Eastern Church were present.

The First Lateran Council clearly made the crusade a central element of papal concern and policy. It reaffirmed the **crusade indulgence** for anyone who labored "to overcome the tyranny of the **infidels**" and placed their possessions and families under papal protection. It further threatened excommunication against anyone who had put on the **crusader's cross** with a view to journeying to either **Jerusalem** or **Spain** and then removed it. All **crusade vows** were to be completed before Easter 1124.

The Fourth Lateran Council of 1215 extended the same crusade indulgence and **privileges** to those who fought **heretics** as were given to those who went to aid the **Holy Land.** Even so, the liberation of Jerusalem was Pope **Innocent III**'s primary crusade goal, and the final decree of the council was a lengthy and detailed set of procedures for the convening, **recruiting, financing,** and prosecution of what became the **Fifth Crusade.**

In 1245 the First Council of Lyons, held by **Innocent IV** in France because Rome was barred to him, responded to the recent capture of Jerusalem by calling for a new crusade in a decree modeled upon that of IV Lateran. This summons served as the official sanction for what became the **Seventh Crusade.** Additionally, the council published a formal **bull** deposing Emperor **Frederick II,** and one of the many charges brought against him was that his treaty of 1229 with the sultan of Egypt had allowed the **Muslims** to keep control of the Dome of the Rock sanctuary on the Temple Mount.

The **bull** *Zelus fidei* (Zeal for the faith), issued in July 1274 by Pope **Gregory X**'s Second Council of Lyons, also authorized a crusade in words borrowed from earlier conciliar decrees. To support the crusade, the council imposed the heavy tax of a tenth on all clerical income for six years, declared a general six-year peace throughout Europe, and prohibited all trade with eastern **Saracen** lands for six years. The plan was ambitious; its execution was less so. The crusade

never got under way. Part of the reason was that the pope died a year and a half after the council concluded its business. A more significant factor was that Europe's great lords had more pressing interests at home. Europe's classic Age of the Crusades was over. **Related Entries:** Bernard of Clairvaux; Crusade of 1122–1126; Christians, Eastern; Khorezmians; Louis IX; Political Crusades.

Suggested Reading

Primary Source

Norman P. Tanner, ed., *Decrees of the Ecumenical Councils,* 2 vols. (1990).

Historical Study

Norman P. Tanner, *The Councils of the Church: A Short History* (2001).

Criticism of the Crusades

The voiced opinion that either a particular crusade, or the crusades in general, had failed in one way or another or that the entire enterprise of crusading was wrong or wrongly conducted.

Criticism of crusading by Western Europeans during the Crusade Era was a minority opinion. **Muslims** were vociferous in their unanimous damnation of crusading, and the **Byzantines** were almost as loud and united in their general rejection of their Western coreligionists' approach to **holy war.** Criticism of crusading by Westerners was another matter. From the beginning there were voices in the West raised in protest, and the issues they protested grew in number as the Crusade Era grew older, but the protesters were always a small minority. Western critics of the crusades fell into two groups: A very small group questioned the idea of holy war; a larger group found fault with the way the crusades were conducted.

Medieval Europe did not lack pacifists, but their relative numbers were minute. One notable voice of protest against crusade warfare was Isaac L'Etoile, the twelfth-century abbot of an obscure **Cistercian** monastery in France. Abbot Isaac judged the **Templars,** whom **Bernard of Clairvaux** praised as the New Knighthood, to be a "new monstrosity." He also openly wondered what unbelievers thought of a Christian Church that freely **plundered** and religiously **massacred** them in the name of Christ, rather than showing them Christ's gentleness and patience.

Critics of the ways in which the crusades were carried out arrived at their positions through various paths. Some were discouraged by the failures of massive expeditions that had raised hopes to a high level. In the wake of the failed **Second Crusade,** recriminations, especially against the perceived author of the crusade, Bernard of Clairvaux, were widespread, and King **Louis IX**'s defeat and capture in Egypt in 1250 also produced bitter disappointment. Some critics were disillusioned by their own negative experiences while on crusade. In 1214 the French Cistercian abbot Adam of Perseigne, who had participated in an ill-fated campaign in the **Holy Land** in 1202–1203, wrote to a bishop friend that clerics who abandoned their pastoral duties at home to participate in crusade **pilgrimages** sinned. In his words, "Christ paid the price of his own blood not for the acquisition of the land of **Jerusalem** but rather for the acquisition and salvation of souls."

A large percentage of the critics aimed their barbs at perceived abuses that arose as the crusading movement matured. Complaints regarding royal and papal taxation as means of **financing the crusades** were raised from the late twelfth century onward. Although most Westerners accepted the thirteenth-century **papacy**'s policy of allowing people to redeem their **crusade vows,** the practice had its outspoken critics. Of all the papal crusade practices that came under attack, probably none was more severely criticized than the papacy's use of crusades in Europe against **heretics,** such as the **Albigensian Crusade,** and its political enemies, such as Emperor **Frederick II** and his heirs.

Notwithstanding these criticisms, most Western Christians accepted and supported the concept and the reality of crusading, especially crusades against Muslims and pagans, throughout the period from 1095 through 1492, when the **Reconquista** was crowned with its final victory. What is more, although secular, Protestant, and even some Catholic voices were raised in increasing number and volume against the crusade ideal in the sixteenth century and following, crusading against **Islam** and other perceived enemies of the Faith remained a popular notion in Catholic Europe for several centuries more. Indeed, crusading became so woven into the fabric of Western culture that it was accepted, in altered forms, by Protestants and secularists, as well as Catholics, as a legitimate response to perceived evil. **Related Entries:** Capetians; Children's Crusade; Francis of Assisi; Friars, Mendicant; Hohenstaufens; Innocent III, Pope; Political Crusades; Shepherds' Crusade.

Suggested Reading

Elizabeth Siberry, *Criticism of Crusading 1095–1274* (1985); Palmer A. Throop, *Criticism of the Crusade: A Study of Public Opinion and Crusade Propaganda* (1940).

Cross, Crusader's

The emblem worn by crusaders as a symbol of their commitment.

Pilgrims customarily wore and carried tokens of their special status. For example, in addition to the traditional satchel and staff, pilgrims to **Santiago de Compostela**

wore the scallop shell of Saint James. Because crusaders were pilgrims—armed pilgrims in the service of Jesus Christ—it was considered appropriate that they bear a symbol that brought to mind Jesus' victory over sin. According to Robert the Monk, Pope **Urban II** informed his audience at the **Council of Clermont** that the cross would serve as the badge of those who journeyed to liberate **Jerusalem,** and it remained so throughout the age of the crusades. By the late twelfth century, crusading pilgrims were generally known throughout Europe as *crucesignati*—those signed with the cross.

Initially the assumption of the crusader's cross was an informal event in which crusaders sewed crosses on their clothing with little or no thought as to uniformity of location or color. In the course of the twelfth century this began to change. The shoulder or breast became the normal places on which crosses were placed, and an English source for the **Third Crusade** notes that the king of France and his followers wore red crosses, the king of England and his men white crosses, and the count of Flanders and his contingent green crosses. There is no evidence that this color scheme became a tradition, but what became customary sometime before 1200 was reception of the cross in a church ceremony in which the crusader also took the **crusade vow.** By the end of the twelfth century, formal rites had evolved for the solemn investment of crusaders with their crosses, but the rituals varied widely throughout Europe. **Related Entry:** Cross, True.

Descent from the Cross. **The cult of devotion to the cross and the crucified Christ became widespread in Europe in the years preceding the First Crusade. A late eleventh- or early twelfth-century Romanesque tympanum (the carved triangular space above a church entryway) at the Basilica of San Isidoro, burial place of the Spanish kings of León, many of them crusaders in the Reconquista.**

Cross, True

Wood believed to come from the cross on which Jesus was crucified.

The earliest Christian sources are silent regarding the disposition of the wood on which Jesus died. One pious legend credits Saint Helena, mother of Emperor Constantine I, with discovering the True Cross in 326 in a grotto in **Jerusalem** that later was enclosed by the **Church of the Holy Sepulcher.** Evidence does not support the legend, but legends often have a power that supersedes sober history. By the end of the fourth century a significant number of fragments of wood were revered in Jerusalem, **Constantinople,** Rome, and elsewhere as portions of the True Cross, and many more appeared in subsequent centuries.

Whatever their origin, pieces of wood from the presumed True Cross are some of Christendom's most sacred **relics.** Because "those signed with the cross" were struggling to reclaim the land made holy by Jesus' sacrifice, the True Cross was a crusade relic that only the Holy Sepulcher could match in power and mystique. A few weeks after the crusaders captured Jerusalem in 1099, a Syrian Christian resident of the city led them to a piece of the True Cross that had been hidden for safekeeping. It was this relic that the armies of the Latin **kingdom of Jerusalem** carried as a talisman into battle.

The relic was lost in 1187 when the army of King **Guy of Lusignan** lost it at the **Battle of Hattin** to the forces of **Saladin.** The loss struck Western Christians as equal in magnitude to the destruction of the grand army that had been defeated that day, and they devoted a good deal of labor to negotiating and working toward the cross's recovery. All of their efforts failed, and that particular piece of the True Cross was lost forever.

There were, however, sufficient remaining pieces of the Lord's Wood to satisfy a number of later crusader relic hunters. At least three high-ranking clerics of the army of the **Fourth Crusade** brought home pieces of the True Cross purloined from Constantinople. Another putative portion of the True Cross was carried by an English priest from Constantinople to England. In 1205 **Emperor Baldwin I** of the **Latin empire of Constantinople** rashly rushed off to fight at **Adrianople** without bringing the relic with him—a relic that former **Byzantine** emperors had carried into battle. When Baldwin discovered his error, he dispatched his chaplain to bring back the sacred wood, but it was too late. As the priest headed back to the army with the relic, he received word of the disaster at Adrianople. Being a practical man, he changed direction and took his sacred prize back home to England. There he bequeathed it to the monastery of Bromholm. The relic, which became known as the Holy Rood of Bromholm, gained a reputation for miraculous powers and turned the monastery into a center of **pilgrimage. Related Entries:** Cross, Crusader's; Holy Land; Lance, Holy.

Suggested Reading

Carsten P. Thiede, *The Quest for the True Cross* (2002).

Crusade of 1101

See First Crusade.

Crusade of 1107

See Bohemond I of Taranto.

Crusade of 1122–1126

Not all crusades have been dignified with a number. This little-known crusade, inspired by Pope **Calixtus II,** set several precedents: First, its Venetian crusaders stopped on their way to the East to settle a score with the

Byzantine empire, foreshadowing by eight decades their diversion of the **Fourth Crusade** to Zara; second, the crusade was fought on two fronts, the East and **Spain,** foreshadowing the better-known **Second Crusade;** third, the pope's encyclical letter of 1123 anticipated later **papal crusade bulls.**

The Venetian Crusade

In 1120 or 1121 Calixtus wrote the Venetians (and probably also the French and the Germans) summoning them to a new crusade effort in the **Latin East** in response to an appeal from King **Baldwin II** following the disaster of the **Field of Blood** of June 1119. The Venetians flocked to the cross and dispatched a large fleet on August 8, 1122.

Their crusading fervor did not prevent them from attacking the Byzantine island city of Corfu to settle a score with Emperor John II, who had refused to renew their commercial privileges in the empire, but they abandoned the **siege** when they learned that King Baldwin had fallen into **Muslim** hands. Accompanied by German, French, and Bohemian crusaders, the Venetians reached the shores of **Syria-Palestine** in May 1123. After destroying an Egyptian fleet and making their **pilgrimage** to **Jerusalem** and Bethlehem over the Christmas season, the crusaders sailed to the port city of **Tyre,** which they besieged on February 16, 1124, in alliance with land forces from the **kingdom of Jerusalem.** The city fell on July 7, 1124.

By prior agreement, the Venetians were rewarded with one-third of Tyre and its surrounding land, the right to hold their own courts, a commercial quarter in Jerusalem, total free trade using their own weights and measures, and freedom from all customs taxes throughout the kingdom. These privileges essentially gave Venice extraterritorial sovereignty in its trading quarters and seriously undermined the king's judicial authority over all residents in his kingdom. They

also served as a model for privileges that were soon granted to the other European maritime cities that traded with the kingdom.

With this accomplished, the Venetians sailed home, **pillaging** Byzantine territory in the Aegean as they proceeded west. The action brought its desired end; in August 1126 Emperor John II confirmed Venice's commercial privileges, and later he extended them.

The Spanish Crusade

While all of this was taking place, Calixtus issued a letter on April 2, 1123, to all of Western Christendom in which he extended the **crusade indulgence** to everyone who fought against **Islam** in Spain. The result was dramatic but not decisive.

Over the winter of 1125–1126, King Alfonso I of Aragon raided deep into Muslim-occupied southern Spain and led back to Saragossa, a city he had captured in 1118, a large number of Christians (reportedly 10,000) who chose to leave their homes in **al-Andalus** and migrate to Christian-held lands. He settled these immigrants in Aragon's Ebro River Valley in northeast Spain. **Related Entries:** Councils and Synods; Reconquista.

Crusade of 1239–1241

Also known as the *Barons' Crusade,* it consisted of three related operations on two fronts: the Balkans and **Palestine.**

The Balkan campaign momentarily relieved pressure on the **Latin empire of Constantinople;** the two campaigns in the **Holy Land,** one French and the other English, were noted for their negotiations rather than their combat. By playing **Syria** off against Egypt, the crusaders managed to recover and refortify **Ascalon** and regain a number of other key sites, including **Jerusalem,** which was lost in 1239 and recovered in 1241.

Prologue

The 1229 truce between **Frederick II** and **al-Kamil** was due to end in July 1239. In anticipation, Pope **Gregory IX** began planning for a crusade as early as September 1234. **Preaching** in England and France was so successful that the pope had to caution the bishops of France to stop crusaders from leaving for the East prematurely.

Appeals for help from the Latin empire of Constantinople, which was facing a coalition of Bulgarian and **Byzantine** forces, caused the pope to shift his attention away from the **Latin kingdom of Jerusalem.** During the winter and spring of 1236–1237, Gregory tried to redirect some crusaders away from the Holy Land and toward **Constantinople.**

This caused confusion in France, where crusaders, ready to travel overseas, were now uncertain where they should go. The confusion was multiplied when Gregory was forced to delay official starting times for both expeditions. Finally, the departure date for the campaign in support of Constantinople was set for August 1238, and the campaign in the Holy Land was set for August 1239.

The Campaign in the Balkans

A large army assembled in Italy in 1238 to sail to Constantinople but was held up by **Frederick II,** who had little enthusiasm for the pope's two-front crusade. The army disintegrated; most crusaders went home or sought passage to the Holy Land, and few sailed to Byzantium. In France, meanwhile, the young co-emperor of Constantinople, Baldwin II, was raising funds and gathering troops. One source credits him with enlisting 30,000 crusaders, but this seems an inflated estimate. In fact, only two great barons joined his entourage, Humbert, lord of Beaujeu, a veteran of the **Albigensian Crusade,** and Thomas of Marly. This army

then marched overland to the northern Balkans during the summer of 1239.

The crusaders limited fighting to a few small offensive operations but managed to capture Çorlu in Thrace in 1240. The Latin empire of Constantinople was already tottering and would lose Constantinople back to the Greeks in 1261, but the expedition possibly extended its life a bit.

Humbert of Beaujeu returned home safely but was not satisfied that he had done enough crusading. In 1248 he sailed with King **Louis IX** on the **Seventh Crusade** and served valiantly in the Nile Delta, where he died in 1250.

The French Campaign in Palestine

A number of prominent French lords took the cross, including Thibault IV, count of Champagne (r. 1201–1253) and king of Navarre in northern Spain (r. 1234–1253), and the army received a generous subsidy from King Louis IX, who had also helped underwrite the Balkan expedition. In all, the French managed to **recruit** about 1,500 **knights** and at least four or five times that number of **sergeants** and other soldiers.

Emperor Frederick II had promised, as claimant to the kingship of Jerusalem, to join and lead the expedition. It is not clear how sincere he was in this offer, but his second excommunication, which Gregory IX laid upon him in March 1239, made it a moot issue. Leadership then fell to Thibault, a romantic figure but an inept ruler, an unsuccessful rebel against the authority of King Louis, and an ineffective warrior. He was also very lucky.

The army departed in August 1239, sailing from Marseilles and several subsidiary ports, and reached **Acre** in September, where the crusaders enjoyed the city's pleasures for two months. On November 2 the army set out for Ascalon, reinforced with several thousand knights supplied by local barons and the **military orders.** Along the way, detachments fought two bloody engagements, winning one and losing the other. Upon reaching Ascalon, the army inexplicably turned around and retreated back to Acre, without refortifying it.

While the crusaders enjoyed Acre's urban delights for the second time, the **Muslim** lord of **Transjordan** marched into Jerusalem and in mid-December 1239 captured and destroyed its sole fortification, the citadel, known as the Tower of David. The city was again in **Saracen** hands.

Luckily for the kingdom of Jerusalem and the crusaders, the **Ayyubid** empire was rapidly disintegrating, with **Damascus** and **Cairo** becoming quite hostile toward each other. The sultan of Damascus opened negotiations with Thibault and offered to return a number of key sites to the kingdom in return for the crusaders' aid against Egypt. Thibault accepted, and a combined crusader-Damascene army met at **Jaffa** and advanced on Ascalon. The alliance between Muslims and crusaders soon broke down, due to fierce opposition within both camps to dealing with **infidels,** but before it did, the crusaders reoccupied Ascalon.

Thibault then entered into negotiations with the sultan of Egypt, who was anxious for peace. Soon an accord was reached, despite opposition within the crusader ranks (some even resisted the new treaty because they favored an alliance with Damascus). This second treaty secured the promised return of Jerusalem and a number of southern Palestinian sites, whereas the first treaty, with the Ayyubid sultan of Syria, had regained a number of northern locations.

Even though Jerusalem had not yet been handed over, Thibault was impatient to leave for home and did so in September 1240. Some French stayed behind to work on the refortification of Ascalon, but it would be up to the next wave of crusaders to ensure that Thibault's gains were not lost or squandered.

The English Campaign in Palestine

As the French were sailing home, ships bearing 800 English knights and an unknown number of other soldiers were heading toward Palestine, under the command of Richard, earl of Cornwall. The small army reached Acre on October 8, 1240.

Earl Richard, who had a large treasury, decided that his money and forces could be best employed in rebuilding Ascalon's walls. The work was completed by mid-March 1241. At the same time, he negotiated successfully with the sultan of Egypt for the actual handing over of Jerusalem and the release of captured crusaders. Once both been returned, Richard decided his work was finished, and he departed for home on May 3, 1241.

Neither Thibault nor Richard won any military glory, but through negotiation they managed to swell the kingdom to its greatest territorial extent since the disasters of 1187. Indeed, Earl Richard achieved something that even his hero uncle and namesake, **Richard I the Lionheart,** had failed to do—recover Jerusalem. **Related Entries:** John of Brienne; Hohenstaufens; Khorezmians.

Suggested Reading

Primary Source

Janet Shirley, trans. *Crusader Syria in the Thirteenth Century: The "Rothelin" Continuation of the "History" of William of Tyre with part of the "Eracles" or "Acre" Text* (1999).

Crusader States

Between 1098 and 1109 the armies of the **First Crusade** carved out four major states in **Anatolia** and **Syria-Palestine:** The

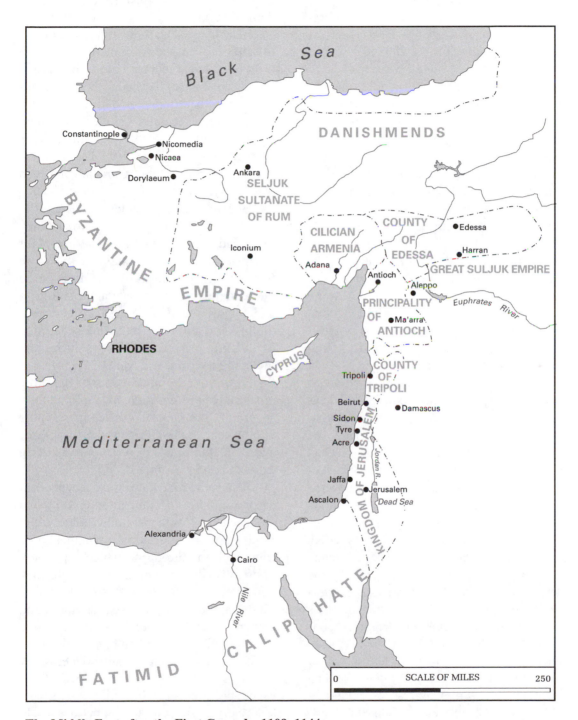

The Middle East after the First Crusade, 1109–1144.

county of **Edessa** (1097–1150); the principality of **Antioch** (1098–1268); the **kingdom of Jerusalem** (1099–1291); and the county of **Tripoli** (1109–1289).

The crusader states were governed according to the **feudal** principles that the settlers had known back home. European feudalism, however, was not a monolithic entity. Significant regional differences existed. Because Italian-**Norman** feudal institutions differed significantly from those of **Languedoc,** the principality of Antioch, established by **Bohemond of Taranto** and his nephew **Tancred,** differed in substance and style from the county of Tripoli, founded by the family of **Raymond of Saint-Gilles.** In like manner, King **Baldwin I,** the true founder of the kingdom of Jerusalem, introduced the customs of Lorraine into his new kingdom. Edessa, which was sparsely settled by Westerners, was the least feudalized of the four crusader states.

Even though the crusader-colonists brought with them various feudal worldviews of how states and societies should be organized, they did not occupy an empty land. The rich multicultural traditions of lands that had been settled and organized since the dawn of agriculture influenced the types of governments and societies carved out by the **Franks** in the **Levant.**

Prior to 1097 Edessa was an **Armenian** semi-independent state, and naturally many Armenian institutions were adopted by the new Western lords. Antioch was still **Byzantine** in population, culture, and institutions in 1098, having been only recently conquered by **Islamic** forces in 1084. Consequently, the governor of the capital city of this crusader principality, the duke, held an office modeled in many respects upon that of the Byzantine *dux,* although his duties differed in some respects. Whereas the *dux* had been primarily a military official, the crusader duke was largely a civil official with

limited military responsibilities. The kingdom of Jerusalem had a few **knights** who were **Eastern Christians** and several lords of villages who had Arab names, although the preponderant majority of its knights and lords were Franks. It was in the kingdom's civil administration that natives played a major role, especially as secretaries and scribes. Deeds and other legal documents were often written in Arabic, which necessitated the employment of Christian and even **Muslim** Arabs.

Because each crusader state was created as an independent entity, they remained throughout their histories four separate and distinct states. At the same time, the king of Jerusalem claimed to be the feudal overlord of the counts of Edessa and Tripoli and also claimed a preeminent dignity and authority that superseded that of all **Latin** princes and lords in the region, including the prince of Antioch. This meant that, although the inhabitants of the three other states did not recognize him as their sovereign, the king of Jerusalem was able to intervene in the affairs of the other three states. In fact, his intervention was often expected and welcomed.

Just as the four states were independent of one another, despite interventions and alliances, they were also independent of all foreign powers. There were no mother countries back in Europe on which they were politically dependent, even though they depended greatly on a steady stream of immigrant settlers, **pilgrims,** crusaders, and resources from the Latin West. It is true that the Byzantine empire had historical claims on the lands that comprised the four crusader states and claimed sovereignty over them, especially over the principality of Antioch, whose prince for several brief periods had to acknowledge imperial overlordship. Nevertheless, the claims of **Constantinople** to authority over Antioch were only theoretical, at best, and they were far less so over the other three crusader states. **Related Entries:** Acre; Alice of Antioch; Baldwin II of Le Bourcq; Baldwin III; Castles, Crusader; *Poulain;* Settlement and Colonization; Transjordan.

Suggested Reading

Jonathan Phillips, *Defenders of the Holy Land: Relations between the Latin East and the West, 1119–1187* (1996); Sylvia Rozenberg, *Knights of the Holy Land* (1999).

Crusades

See Albigensian Crusade; Baltic Crusades; Children's Crusade; Crusade of 1122–1126; Crusade of 1239–1241; Damascus Crusade; German Crusade; Political Crusades; Shepherds' Crusade; and all numbered Crusades, First through Eighth.

Cyprus

The second crusader kingdom established in the **Latin East,** Cyprus was in Western hands from 1191 to 1571. A fertile island not far from the coast of **Palestine,** it served crusaders as an important forward base and resupply station, especially during the **Fifth** and **Seventh Crusades.**

Cyprus had been part of the **Byzantine empire** until the rebel Isaac Comnenus seized the island and set himself up as a rival emperor around 1183. His reign did not last long. King **Richard I the Lionheart** captured Cyprus from Isaac in May 1191 while en route to **Acre** on the **Third Crusade.** Finding himself unable to govern the island, Richard sold it to the **Templars.** They, in turn, faced with a bloody revolt in reaction to their attempts to exploit the island and its people to the hilt, sold it to **Guy of Lusignan** in May 1192. Guy, the former **king of Jerusalem,** now became lord of Cyprus and

established a dynasty, the Lusignans, that ruled the island until 1489. Guy brought with him a number of his **feudal** barons and **knights** from the kingdom of Jerusalem who were searching for new lands to replace those lost to **Saladin.** With these **vassals,** Guy and his successors established a feudal system based on that of the kingdom of Jerusalem. In 1194 Guy was succeeded by his brother **Aimery,** who received a royal title and crown from Emperor **Henry VI** in September 1197. By this act, which was part of Henry's overall strategy to exert his hegemony over the Central and Eastern Mediterranean, the kingdom of Cyprus became an imperial **fief.** It was not until 1247 that the island kingdom was released from this dependency.

The autumn of 1197 proved to be an eventful season for King Aimery because he also was chosen to marry the recently widowed **Isabella I** of Jerusalem and was crowned alongside her in October. He now wore two crowns—Cyprus and Jerusalem—and chose to spend most of his time in **Acre,** the capital-in-exile of the kingdom of Jerusalem. Because his infant son and sole heir died just about the same time as he in 1205, at Aimery's death the two crowns were again separated.

Under King Aimery a Latin Church hierarchy was established on Cyprus and supported by lands and possessions taken from the island's indigenous **Greek** Church and also by tithes extorted from an unwilling Byzantine Christian populace, which was treated as a subservient class. The chief Latin prelate was the archbishop of Nicosia, under whom three bishops and a host of lesser clergy served. Latin monasteries, such as the **Cistercian** house of Our Lady of the Fields, were also introduced, and during the thirteenth century convents of **mendicant friars,** especially of **Dominicans,** sprang up in the island's cities. The two major **military orders,** the Templars and the **Hospitalers,** also established themselves on the island and prospered from their agricultural holdings, especially wine-producing vineyards. Following the fall of Acre in 1291, both orders briefly moved their headquarters to Cyprus.

Alongside this Latin Church, a still-vibrant Byzantine, or Greek, Church, continued to command the faith and obedience of the vast majority of the island's people. In addition, there were **Armenian,** Syrian, and Nestorian Christian minorities that were equally devoted to their religious traditions. The same essentially unbridgeable chasms that separated Western Christian masters and **Eastern Christian** subjects in the **Latin empire of Constantinople** were evident a decade earlier in Cyprus and for almost four centuries thereafter, despite the attempts of several popes, such as **Gregory IX,** to compel the Cypriots to accept the ways of the Roman Church. There was precious little cultural or, for that matter, genetic fusion between Cypriots and **Franks.**

Whatever cultural interchange and inter-marriage did take place occurred largely among the island's commercial and artisan classes. Western merchants, especially Italians, had begun taking up residence on Cyprus well before the Third Crusade, and Guy and his successors were generous in welcoming and bestowing privileges upon bourgeois settlers. The towns and cities of Cyprus, especially the port city of Famagusta, grew in size, population, and wealth during the period of Western occupation. Although many Western urban settlers lived within their own ethnic communities, undoubtedly some took Cypriot spouses and adopted Eastern ways of life.

When **Conrad III (Conradin)** was executed in Naples in 1268, the **Hohenstaufen** line of nonresident kings of **Jerusalem** died

with him, and the crown of Jerusalem passed to King Hugh III of Cyprus (r. 1267–1284). Not since the days of King Aimery had both crowns been united in a single person. Hugh III's sons and successors, John I (r. 1284–1285) and Henry II (r. 1285–1324), had the sad fate of witnessing from afar the final days of the kingdom of Jerusalem.

With Acre's fall in 1291 the crusader states of **Syria-Palestine** were dead, but Frankish crusader institutions, with some modifications, continued to survive on Cyprus for almost another two centuries. The myth of the lost kingdom of Jerusalem also persisted there, and the kings of Cyprus continued to be invested with the crown of Jerusalem.

Lusignan Cyprus reached its apogee of commercial prosperity and military power in the mid–fourteenth century. Under King Peter I (r. 1359–1369) Cyprus became the West's center for aggression against **Islam.** His fleets conducted raids along the coasts of **Anatolia,** Syria-Palestine, and Egypt. His sack of Alexandria in 1365 gained only plunder but sufficiently excited imaginations in Europe that Geoffrey Chaucer identified his idealized Knight of the *Canterbury Tales* as a veteran of that campaign.

After Peter's death, Cyprus's fortunes rapidly declined. In 1426 a **Mamluk** invasion and victory forced King Janus (r. 1398–1432) to acknowledge the overlordship of the sultan of Egypt, who now claimed the right to confirm the kings of Cyprus in their office. In 1489 Venice seized control of Cyprus to deny it to the **Ottomans.** Despite Venice's relative strength, the Italian republic still acknowledged the sultan of Egypt's authority over the island and agreed to pay him an annual tribute of 8,000 gold ducats. The loss of its chance to seize Cyprus was a major blow to the Ottomans, and it was not until 1571 that the Ottomans managed to wrest the island from the Venetians, who formally ceded it in a peace treaty of March 1573. **Related Entries:** Crusader States; Frankish Greece.

Suggested Reading

Primary Source

The Templar of Tyre, *The Deeds of the Cypriots,* trans. by Paul Crawford (2001).

Historical Studies

Nicholas Coureas, *The Latin Church in Cyprus, 1195–1312* (1997); Peter W. Edbury, *The Kingdom of Cyprus and the Crusades, 1191–1374* (1991) and *Kingdoms of the Crusaders: From Jerusalem to Cyprus* (1999).

D

Damascus

A city of southern **Syria** that crusaders unsuccessfully attacked in 1126, 1129, and 1148.

Along with **Aleppo,** Damascus was one of the two most important **Muslim** strongholds in Syria throughout the Age of the Crusades. Additionally, it was one of **Islam**'s major cultural centers, noted especially for its schools of law, and an important center of commerce tied into trade routes extending to China, the Indian Ocean, sub-Saharan Africa, and the West.

From 1076 to 1174 Damascus was dominated by various **Seljuk Turkish** *atabegs* (governors). In 1139 the city entered into an alliance with the **kingdom of Jerusalem** to frustrate the designs of a common enemy, **Zangi,** but the alliance ended with the attack on Damascus by the armies of the **Second Crusade** in 1148. In 1154 **Nur ad-Din** occupied the city, made it his capital and the center of **Islam's** countercrusade, and it remained so until his death in 1174. Between 1174, when it capitulated to **Saladin,** and 1260, it was under the rule of the **Ayyubid** dynasty. Following its partial destruction by the **Mongols** in 1260, the city passed into **Mamluk** hands. Under the Mamluks Damascus experienced a golden age of pros-

perity and cultural efflorescence down to around 1400, despite a second devastation of the city by the Mongols in 1300. **Related Entries:** Crusade of 1122–1126; Damascus Crusade; Historians and Chroniclers, Islamic.

Suggested Reading

Primary Source

H. A. R. Gibb, trans. and ed., *The Damascus Chronicle of the Crusades: Extracted and Translated from the Chronicle of Ibn al-Qalanisi* (1967, reissued 2003).

Damascus Crusade (1129)

An unsuccessful attempt by King **Baldwin II** to capture **Damascus,** the Damascus Crusade is a rare example of a crusade engendered by the **Latin East** and recruited by agents who traveled through Europe on the sole authority of the **king of Jerusalem.**

Because there is no clear evidence of papal support of this expedition, it is debatable whether or not it was a crusade in the strictest sense of the term. At the same time, the crusade as an institution was still in an early stage of evolution, and its participants thought of themselves as warrior-**pilgrims** (the term "crusader" having not yet been coined), swore **crusade vows,** wore the **cru-**

sader's cross, and were accorded the status of crusaders when they arrived in the East.

King Baldwin sent emissaries to the West in 1127 to recruit crusaders for his projected campaign against Damascus. He had raided the city's lands in 1125 and 1126 but realized his army was too small to **besiege** Damascus successfully. Consequently, he needed the help of crusader lords and their retinues.

One lord on whom the king's agents concentrated was Count **Fulk V of Anjou,** who was invited to **settle** in **Outremer** and marry Baldwin's daughter and heiress, **Melisende.** At the urging of Hugh of Payns, founder of the **Order of the Temple,** Count Fulk agreed in May 1128 to participate in the expedition and to consider marriage to Melisende.

On his part, Hugh of Payns took the opportunity that this visit to the West afforded to publicize his order, solicit grants of land to support its work in the East, and invite **knights** to join it. Hugh also attended the **Council** of Troyes in January 1129, where the order received its first official endorsement by any ecclesiastical authority in the West and also acquired its rule.

Records indicate that large numbers of knights and foot soldiers from across northwestern Europe, including England and Scotland, swore the cross in 1128 and early 1129. Count Fulk and a substantial body of men-at-arms reached the **Holy Land** in May 1129, and others followed over the next several months. According to an Arabic source, the army that eventually assembled contained 2,000 knights and numerous foot soldiers.

The campaign got under way in November 1129, and the army advanced to within six miles of Damascus. The ambush and killing of a considerable numbers of **Franks,** followed by a horrendous storm, threw Baldwin's army into confusion. It abandoned its camp and returned home dispirited and in disarray. **Related Entry:** Bull, Papal.

Damietta

An Egyptian port city at the mouth of the Nile that the **Franks** considered to be the key to **Cairo.** On three occasions it was the object of **Latin** attack; twice it was captured by crusaders and twice surrendered back to the Egyptians.

On October 27, 1169, King **Amalric** of **Jerusalem,** in concert with **Byzantine** naval forces, laid **siege** to the city out of fear of **Saladin,** who was on his way to upsetting the balance of power in the **Levant.** According to **William of Tyre,** had the Christians moved decisively upon arrival, they could have taken the city. Instead, they delayed their attack by three days, allowing **Turkish** reinforcements to strengthen the city's defenses. Eventually the city's vigorous defense and famine within the Frankish camp forced the Christians to break off the siege in mid-December. As soon as both sides agreed to a truce that would enable the Christians to retire in peace, the Damiettans threw open their gates and allowed their enemies to enter and freely use the city's markets for three days.

The second time that a Frankish army entered Damietta, in the course of the **Fifth Crusade,** the city was a wasteland that had nothing to offer in its markets. Following a siege that stretched from May 27, 1218, to November 8, 1219, the crusaders entered a city devastated by **disease,** famine, and battle. As many as 50,000 inhabitants out of an estimated population of 60,000 had perished, and most of the survivors were sick, with many dying and all too weak to continue the fight. Damietta remained in crusader hands until August 29, 1221, when they surrendered it back following a crushing defeat in the delta.

The army of the **Seventh Crusade** discovered Damietta abandoned and entered it on June 6, 1249, after only a slight skirmish on the beach the previous day. On May 6, 1250, however, the defeated crusaders were forced to return the city as part of a truce settlement. **Related Entries:** Francis of Assisi; Al-Kamil; Louis IX; Margaret of Provence.

Deus Vult (God Wills It)

The war cry of the **First Crusade.**

According Robert the Monk of Rheims, when **Pope Urban II** finished his appeal at **Clermont** for an armed **pilgrimage** to liberate the **Holy Sepulcher,** the crowd cried out spontaneously and with one voice, "God wills it!" In Robert's **Latin** prose this reads as *Deus vult.* Then, according to Robert, Urban told the crowd that its unanimous spontaneity was a sign that God was present and had inspired them to utter these words, and he instructed them that this should henceforth be their war cry whenever they attacked the enemy.

Robert is the only **historian** to mention this dramatic moment at Clermont, but many other sources clearly show that *Deus vult* or, more likely, the twelfth-century French version *Deus lo volt* was employed to inspire crusaders as they went into combat. Three sources tell us that the crusaders shouted it out as they stormed **Antioch** on June 3, 1098. One historian, **Fulcher of Chartres,** writes: "The Franks shouted out in a loud, single voice, 'God wills it! God wills it!' For this was our signal cry whenever we were about to push forward on any enterprise." **Related Entries:** Apocalypse and the Crusades; Holy War; Saints, Warrior.

Disease

The constant, mysterious enemy and occasional ally of all combatants and **noncombatants** during the Age of the Crusades.

Prior to the rise of modern medicine, more soldiers and camp followers died of disease than of battlefield wounds. In the mid–nineteenth century, the ratio of deaths due to disease as opposed to combat was roughly 2:1 for the Union Army in the Civil War and almost 4:1 for British troops in the Crimean War. Given the unsanitary conditions of military camps and of battlefields littered with corpses, epidemics could and did burn through armies with great frequency. This was especially true of armies that found themselves in static positions, for example during a **siege** or in a long-term encampment. One source for the **Fourth Crusade** notes, with some obvious exaggeration, that the crusaders encamped on Venice's Isle of Saint Nicholas (the Lido) during the summer and early fall of 1202 experienced such a high mortality rate that "the dead could barely be buried by the living."

Armies in strange lands encountered new diseases that could and usually were particularly devastating. In such cases, mortality rates could rise to as high as fifty percent of those exposed, although ten to twenty percent was more the norm. The army of the **Seventh Crusade,** which numbered about 25,000 men-at-arms, including between 2,500 to 2,800 **knights,** camped on **Cyprus** between mid–September 1248 and late May 1249. During that time some 250 knights and uncounted large numbers of rank-and-file crusaders died of disease. In all, probably at least ten percent of the army never left the island.

Even when a disease does not kill, it can debilitate an army. In February 1250 that same army of the Seventh Crusade, which was then bogged down in the Nile Delta, experienced an enervating epidemic of what appears to have been scurvy, most likely brought on by a poor diet of grains and salted meat. In this weakened condition it was no match for the Egyptian forces that surrounded it. **Related Entries:** Baldwin IV; Damietta; Lazarus, Order of Saint; Siege Warfare.

Dominicans

Officially the Order of Preachers, an order of **mendicant friars** founded in the early thirteenth century by Dominic Guzman, a Castilian priest, in response to the need to counter the teachings of the **Cathars** in **Languedoc.**

From the beginning, the Dominicans were conceived as being a congregation of educated clerics who specialized in **preaching** missions. In 1220 the order adopted, perhaps because of Franciscan influences, a policy of total poverty and mendicancy. Dominic began preaching against the Cathars in 1206, and in 1215 he established a base in Toulouse for a number of like-minded clerics who had joined him. In that same year he received Pope **Innocent III's** authorization of his new order. In 1217 he announced that his followers were to embark on a universal preaching mission, and they scattered to cities in Italy, France, England, and Spain. In 1233 Pope **Gregory IX** established a papal Inquisition for Languedoc, to root out the vestiges of **heresy** there, and entrusted it to the Dominicans. The Dominicans became associated with papally licensed Inquisitions in southern France and northern Italy, and in 1254 were joined by the Franciscans as inquisitors in Italy. The Dominicans proved so zealous in their work that a pun was made of their unofficial name, whereby they were called the *Domini Canes* (The Hounds of the Lord).

Along with the Franciscans, Dominicans preached crusades, functioned as papal diplomats to the **Byzantines,** in unsuccessful efforts to secure a reunion of the **Greek** and **Latin** Churches under papal leadership, and served as **missionaries** among a variety of peoples within and beyond the **Latin East.** By 1228 the Dominicans had established convents in **Acre, Constantinople,** and **Cyprus,** and had as many as seven houses scattered through **Frankish Greece. Related Entries:** Carmelites; Cîteaux, Order of; Francis of Assisi.

Dorylaeum, Battle of (July 1, 1097)

The misnamed crusader victory that opened the road to **Antioch** for the army of the **First Crusade.**

Nicaea fell to combined **Byzantine** and crusader forces on June 19, 1097. On June 26, the crusaders, along with a small Byzantine detachment, left the city and headed southeast. After two days of marching, the crusader army divided into two groups, a main force of more than 30,000 and a vanguard of fewer than 20,000.

On the morning of July 1, the army was headed toward Dorylaeum, the key to entry onto the **Anatolian** plain and all roads leading to **Syria.** The crusaders, however, were still two or three days' march away from this ancient fortress, although **Anna Comnena** later mistakenly identified the "plain of Dorylaeum" as the site where a major battle took place that day. When the army's advance element, which was more than three miles ahead of the main body, sighted a large mounted **Turkish** force, it stopped to set up camp to protect its **noncombatants** and baggage. As **infantry** and dismounted **knights** established a defensive perimeter around the camp, a **cavalry** unit rashly charged the Turkish horsemen, only to be driven back.

The Turks counterattacked, carrying the fight into the camp, where bitter fighting ensued throughout the remainder of the morning. In the midst of this desperate battle, camp **women** played a key role by carrying much-needed water to the crusader soldiers. Around noon, after five or six hours of combat had already elapsed, the main crusader force arrived and turned the tide of battle.

Mounted fighting continued until mid-afternoon as the crusaders pursued the routed enemy. When it was over, both armies counted enormous losses. The **historian** Albert of Aachen estimated that some 4,000 crusaders and 3,000 Turks fell that day.

The large number of casualties was a stunning setback for the Turks, whose relatively small population of warriors could not sustain such losses. Hereafter, the crusaders had a fairly unhindered passage across Anatolia, as **Seljuk** forces were reluctant to meet them again in pitched battle. This crusader victory also set the stage for the Byzantine reconquest of western Anatolia. With the myth of Turkish invincibility in battle destroyed, a number of cities rose in rebellion against their Seljuk overlords. **Related Entries:** Adhémar of Monteil; Kilij Arslan I; Tancred.

E

Edessa

An **Armenian** city in **Anatolia** (today the Turkish city of Sanliurfa) that from 1098 to 1144 served as the capitol of the county of Edessa, the first **crusader state.**

During its short history, the county acted as a buffer along the northeastern frontier of the **Latin East** and a salient that cut off the **Seljuks** of the sultanate of Rum from the sultanate of the Great Seljuk. **Baldwin of Boulogne** took possession of Edessa in March 1098. Two years later, when he assumed the title **king of Jerusalem,** he handed over the county to his cousin, **Baldwin of Le Bourcq,** who ruled Edessa from 1100 to 1118. Between 1104 and 1108 first **Tancred** and then Roger of Salerno governed Edessa as regent while Baldwin of Le Bourcq was a **prisoner.** In 1118 Baldwin of Le Bourcq assumed the kingship of Jerusalem, and in 1119 he rewarded Joscelin of Courtenay, a loyal supporter who had been captured fighting alongside him in 1104, with the county. Joscelin I was succeeded in 1131 by Joscelin II, the last count of Edessa.

Joscelin II was on campaign when **Zangi** began his **siege** of Edessa on November 28, 1144. Wishing to move rapidly,

Zangi ordered the undermining of several key towers, which collapsed on December 24. His troops rushed into the city; slaughter and **pillage** ensued, and the city capitulated on December 26. Zangi spared the lives of captured **Eastern Christians** in the city as best he could, but he ordered the systematic **massacre** of all the **Franks** and the destruction of their churches. The fall of Edessa impelled Pope **Eugenius III** to set in motion the **Second Crusade.**

Joscelin II moved his capital to Turbessel as Zangi continued to advance across the county and capture its fortified towns and **castles.** Following Zangi's assassination in September 1146, Joscelin briefly reoccupied Edessa, which welcomed him on October 27, but failed to capture its citadel. A few days later **Nur ad-Din** retook the city amid a terrible slaughter. Joscelin escaped, but thousands died, perhaps as many as 30,000, and about half that number were **enslaved.**

Joscelin managed to hold the line west of Edessa at the Euphrates River and to reign over a truncated county until 1150, when he was captured and imprisoned until his death in 1159. His wife sold the county's remaining strongholds to the **Byzantine empire,** but the empire lost them before 1151 had ended. **Related Entries:** Antioch; Tripoli.

Suggested Reading

Primary Source

Matthew of Edessa, *Armenia and the Crusades: Tenth to Twelfth Centuries: The Chronicle of Matthew of Edessa,* trans. by Ara E. Dostourian (1993).

Historical Studies

Robert L. Nicholson, *Joscelyn I, Prince of Edessa* (1954); Judah B. Segal, *Edessa: The Blessed City,* 2nd. ed. (2001).

Edward I

The last great lord from the West to go on crusade during the Age of the Crusades, Edward left England in 1270 as a prince and returned in 1274 as king (r. 1272–1307).

Lord Edward, eldest son of King Henry III and grandnephew of **Richard I the Lionheart,** took the **crusader's vow** in June 1268 and departed England in August 1270 with a small force of crusaders that fit into thirteen vessels. His plan was to link up with King **Louis IX** in Tunis and there be joined by reinforcements led by his brother, Edmund. Edward arrived in Tunis in November 1270 to discover that King Louis was dead and the crusade army was pulling out of North Africa. Edward reluctantly went to Sicily, where he spent the winter and was reinforced by Edmund's crusaders.

When Edward and Edmund reached **Acre** on May 9, 1271, their combined forces numbered fewer than 1,000—about 200–300 **knights** and around 600 foot soldiers. The size of this army prevented Edward's undertaking any significant operations. After several desultory raids that accomplished nothing, Edward gave his blessing to a truce that the **Frankish** lords concluded in April 1272 with Sultan **Baybars.**

There being no further reason to wage war, Edmund left in May 1272, and Edward probably would have followed soon after, but he was seriously wounded on June 16 when an **Assassin,** disguised as an **Eastern Christian,** attempted to kill him. Recovery was slow, and he was not ready to depart until September 22, 1272. Before sailing away, Edward left behind funds to endow a small garrison at Acre and to build a tower on the city walls.

While in Sicily in December, Edward discovered that his father had died and he was now king. Regardless, he did not rush back to England. In July 1273 he was in Paris, where he did homage to his cousin Philip III for the duchy of Aquitaine, and then went on to Bourdeaux to straighten out affairs in the duchy. He finally arrived on English soil on August 2, 1274.

As king, Edward I continued to support the ideal of the crusade and the cause of **Jerusalem.** In 1287 he entertained at his court in Bourdeaux a **Turkish** Nestorian Christian monk, Rabban Sauma, who had been dispatched to the West by Arghun, the **Mongol** il-khan of Persia. Through this ambassador, who also visited the emperor of **Byzantium,** King **Philip IV** of France, and the pope, Arghun proposed a Mongol-Western alliance against the **Mamluk** empire. Edward was enthusiastic to the point that he once again assumed the **crusader's cross.** However, circumstances in both Persia and Europe prevented the consummation of a Mongol-Christian alliance, and likewise, domestic affairs prevented Edward's ever fulfilling his vow of 1287 and returning to the **Holy Land.** Less than four years after Edward I swore the cross for the second time, Acre was in Muslim hands and the **crusader states** were dead. **Related Entries:** Charles of Anjou; Crusade of 1239–1241.

Suggested Reading

S. D. Lloyd, *English Society and the Crusade, 1216–1307* (1988); Christopher Tyerman,

England and the Crusades, 1095–1588 (1988).

Eighth Crusade (1270–1272)

The last of the classic crusades, its failure mirrored the state of Western Christendom's inability or unwillingness to wage effective **holy war** in the East in the late thirteenth century.

Like its predecessors, the crusade can conveniently be divided into several stages: (1) preparation; (2) the campaign in Tunis; and (3) the campaign in **Syria-Palestine.** One of the singular aspects of this crusade is that two princes who went on crusade returned home as kings: **Philip III** of France (r. 1270–1285) of France and **Edward I** of England (r. 1272–1307).

Preparation

The Eighth Crusade was very much the creation of **Louis IX** of France, who began planning the crusade in 1266, despite the initial coolness of Pope Clement IV to the enterprise. The **crusader states** were in dire straits as **Baybars** systematically captured **Frankish castles** and towns. In 1266 alone the **Mamluk** sultan took the castles of *Saphet, Toron, Chateauneuf,* and *Arqa,* destroyed the army of Cilician **Armenia,** occupied the Armenian capital, Sis, and threatened **Antioch.** Believing it was his Christian duty to go on crusade despite his duties at home, the king assumed the **crusader's cross** on March 25, 1267. On June 24, 1268, Prince Edward of England also took the **crusader's vow.** The following year Louis lent Lord Edward 70,000 *livres* (about 140,000 ounces of silver) to underwrite the English prince's crusade.

The Expedition to Tunis

The initial objective of the crusade was Tunis in North Africa, far from the embat-tled crusader states. Why? Louis apparently believed that his presence there would effect the conversion to Christianity of the local *emir,* Muhammad al-Mustansir. The plan seems to have been that once this piece of **missionary** work was completed, Tunis would serve as the jumping-off point for an expedition farther east, either Egypt or Syria-Palestine. Envoys from the **Mongol** il-khan of Persia had been present at King Louis's formal investiture with the crusader's cross and had probably assured the king that their master, Abaga, would join up with the Christian crusaders to liberate **Jerusalem** and crush the Mamluks.

Louis's party set sail from Aigues Mortes on July 2, 1270, at least a month behind schedule. The delay meant that his army would campaign in the worst possible summer conditions, and the time for moving on to the second phase of the operation, before winter conditions prevented sea travel, was dangerously short. Other portions of his army sailed from several southern French ports on or around the same time. The army, which numbered probably no more than 10,000, assembled on the island of Sardinia, and from there sailed in a body to Tunis, where it landed on July 18.

Louis's dream that the emir would welcome him and convert to Christianity proved erroneous, and fighting ensued. The summer heat and unsanitary conditions brought on inevitable **disease,** and Louis took ill. On August 25 he died. His son and heir, King Philip III, was also sick, so Louis's brother, **Charles of Anjou,** who arrived with reinforcements from Sicily on the same day Louis died, took over effective command of the army.

Charles soon decided that the campaign was a dead end and began negotiations for a peaceful withdrawal. On November 1 a treaty was ratified, and the crusaders began to prepare to quit Tunisian soil just as Prince Edward arrived ready to fight.

The Expedition to Syria-Palestine

Unhappy with the situation, Edward had no choice but to leave with the army and sailed to Sicily, where he survived a storm that destroyed about forty vessels off the Sicilian coast. The French and Sicilians returned home after this disaster, but Edward was determined to press on. He spent the winter in Sicily, where he was joined by crusaders led by his brother Edmund. Despite the reinforcements, when Edward sailed to **Acre** in spring 1271 he had with him an army of slightly less than 1,000.

The size of his army prevented his undertaking any decisive actions against the Mamluks or any other **Muslim** power. After a bit of skirmishing in which he lost many more soldiers from disease and diet than to battle wounds, Edward gave his blessing to a truce between Sultan Baybars and the Franks of **Outremer.** Edward departed the **Holy Land** in September 1272, unaware that his father, Henry III, had died, and he was now a king.

In the final analysis, despite the personal valor and dedication to the crusade ideal shown by King Louis and Lord Edward, as well as by unknown numbers of anonymous crusaders, the Eighth Crusade had no significant achievements and did little or nothing to forestall the disaster for the crusader states that loomed on the horizon. **Related Entries:** Capetians; Gregory X, Pope.

Eleanor of Aquitaine

Born 1122, died 1204. Duchess of Aquitaine (r. 1137–1204), queen of France (1137–1152), queen of England (1154–1189), participant in the **Second Crusade.**

The **Byzantine** historian Nicetas Choniates expressed outrage at the behavior of a number of **women** who accompanied the armies of the Second Crusade. They rode horses, he noted, not sidesaddle but shamelessly astride in the manner of men, carried lances and other weapons, wore male clothing, and presented a totally military appearance. Among them there was one who stood out like the legendary queen of the Amazons, Penthesilea, and because of the gold embroidery that ran along the hem and fringes of her clothing, she was called Goldfoot. Goldfoot was undoubtedly Queen Eleanor of Aquitaine, who accompanied her husband, **Louis VII,** on the Second Crusade.

Latin historians, as well, charged Eleanor and the noble women who accompanied her with scandalous behavior and blamed them for many of the misfortunes of this ill-fated crusade. In what must be a timeless male complaint, the women were accused of slowing down the progress of the army because of their excess baggage. What was worse, the luxuries that they brought with them outraged God, who demanded humility from His penitential **pilgrim** crusaders. Worst of all, the presence of these women encouraged the men to sin, and those sins of the flesh made them unworthy of success. Added to these generalized accusations was the specific charge that the queen was the greatest sinner of all because of her supposed adulterous affair with her uncle, Prince Raymond of **Antioch.** The charge surfaced in the West as early as 1149, and a generation later **William of Tyre** claimed that Eleanor, "being a fatuous woman," not only disregarded her marriage vows but also plotted with Raymond against her husband's life.

William probably heard stories of Queen Eleanor's putative infidelities while he was studying in France. Such stories satisfy prurient interests and tend to grow into mythic proportions. By 1260 the story was circulating in France that the queen tried to elope with **Saladin** at **Tyre**—a rather amazing feat, given that the ten-year-old boy was living in **Damascus** at the time.

The fact is, we know very little about Queen Eleanor's crusade exploits, and the stories regarding her supposed sexual relations with her uncle are uncorroborated but widely circulated rumors. However, William of Tyre's report that Eleanor took the side of her uncle in unsuccessfully urging Louis, who wanted to press on to **Jerusalem,** to remain in the north and wage a campaign against **Aleppo** and other **Muslim** strongholds that were immediate threats to the principality, sounds credible. Credibility is not certainty. All we can say for certain is that during the course of the crusade major rifts in the royal marriage opened up, and Queen Eleanor began proposing that they seek an annulment. Apparently fun-loving, high-spirited Eleanor discovered that she and sober, pious Louis were ill suited for one another.

Their marriage ended in 1152. Eight weeks later Eleanor married Henry, count of Anjou and duke of Normandy, who in 1154 became King Henry II of England. Henry and Eleanor had eight children, one of whom was **Richard the Lionheart,** who would be one of the leaders of the next great crusade. Other major crusade figures descended from Queen Eleanor included her grandson **Henry of Champagne,** her great grandson **Edward I,** and her great granddaughter Queen **Margaret,** wife of **Louis IX.** It is interesting to speculate that Margaret, who exhibited such fortitude and initiative while on the **Seventh Crusade,** inherited those qualities from Queen Eleanor.

Suggested Reading

Marion Meade, *Eleanor of Aquitaine: A Biography* (1977, reissued 1991); Richard D. Scheurman and Arthur K. Ellis, *Eleanor of Aquitaine and the Crusade of the Kings* (2000); Alison Weir, *Eleanor of Aquitaine* (1999); Bonnie Wheeler and John C. Parsons, eds., *Eleanor of Aquitaine, Lord and Lady* (2003).

Eugenius III, Pope

Pope of the Roman Church (r. 1145–1153) who authorized the **Second Crusade.**

News of the fall of **Edessa** reached the West during the summer of 1145. In response, Pope Eugenius III dispatched the letter *Quantum praedecessores* (How greatly our predecessors) to the court of King **Louis VII** of France on December 1 and reissued it in slightly revised form on March 1, 1146. In this second version, addressed to all the French, the pope reminded his audience of Pope **Urban II**'s call to liberate the Eastern Church and of the crusaders' victory in the East. He then mentioned the recent capture and desecration of Edessa by "enemies of the cross," and implored those who heard or read this letter to vigorously defend the Eastern Church, which had been initially freed from tyranny "by the effusive pouring out of your fathers' blood," and to deliver from the hands of the enemy "the many thousands of our captive brothers." Following this impassioned appeal, Eugenius enumerated the **privileges** that he would bestow on each person who heeded the call: the **crusade indulgence;** papal protection of family and possessions; freedom from civil suits regarding property issues while wearing the **crusader's cross;** freedom from payment of interest on debts; and the right to mortgage lands, even **feudal** fiefs, to **finance** the journey. He also instructed all who undertook this armed **pilgrimage** to put aside lavish clothing and other signs of pomp and pride, for such displays did not befit a warrior fighting for the Lord.

Although *Quantum praedecessores* was not the first formal **crusade bull** issued by the **Roman papacy,** it set two important precedents. It unequivocally affirmed that calling a crusade was the *sole* responsibility of the pope, and its careful delineation of crusader privileges set the pattern for all subsequent papal crusade bulls.

Along with the bull, Eugenius dispatched letters that empowered his former abbot, **Bernard of Clairvaux,** to preach the crusade north of the Alps, which Bernard did with his usual fervor and brilliance.

As enthusiasm for the crusade built, Eugenius granted King Alfonso VII of Castile an extension of the crusade against the **Moors** of Spain, and he also authorized, at the behest of Bernard of Clairvaux, a **missionary** crusade against the pagan Wends of the **Baltic.** Eugenius's crusade now had three widely scattered fronts. Of the three fronts, only the Iberian crusade met with any success. **Related Entries:** Christians, Eastern; Cîteaux, Order of.

Eustace III of Boulogne

Count of Boulogne in Flanders and holder of a large **fief** in southeastern England, elder brother of **Godfrey of Bouillon** and **Baldwin of Boulogne,** and participant in the **First Crusade.**

Count Eustace, who led crusaders from Flanders and England, traveled with Counts **Robert of Flanders** and **Robert of Normandy** to **Constantinople,** rather than with his two brothers, and he appears to have served with these two counts throughout most of the crusade's campaigns. He did, however, join his brother Godfrey's forces in the assault on Jerusalem's walls in July 1099. Shortly after the victory at **Ascalon** in August 1099, he returned home. On his deathbed in April 1118, King Baldwin I named Eustace as his heir, and the barons of **Jerusalem** sent word to Eustace of the offer. Eustace traveled only as far as southern Italy when word reached him of the accession of his kinsman, **Baldwin II of Le Bourcq,** to the crown. Reluctant to engage in a civil war, and apparently not too eager to return to the **Levant** anyway, he headed back home.

F

Family Traditions, Crusading

See Capetians; Eleanor of Aquitaine; Hohenstaufens; Montferrat, Family of; Recruitment; Women.

Fatimids

A dynasty of **Shia Muslims** that ruled in Tunisia (909–972) and **Egypt** (969–1171).

The Fatimid family claimed descent from the Prophet Muhammad's daughter Fatima, and by virtue of that lineage also claimed to be the true caliphs, or deputies of the Prophet, as opposed to their **Sunni** rivals, the **Abbasids** of Baghdad. More than that, the founder of the dynasty proclaimed himself to be the *Mahdi*—the returned Hidden Imam, or long-promised deliverer of **Islam** (see Shia). As a consequence, the Fatimids believed they had a divine mandate to rule the world.

At various times the Fatimids held lands from Tunisia to **Syria-Palestine,** as well as Sicily, the Red Sea coast of East Africa, and the western and southern coasts of Arabia. Under the Fatimids Egypt flourished commercially, serving as a major area of transport and exchange for commodities from the Indian Ocean.

The Fatimids were generally noted for their tolerant policies toward their Jewish and Christian subjects, with the exception of Caliph al-Hakim, who embarked on a seven-year persecution of Christians and **Jews** in 1008. In 1009 he ordered the destruction of **Jerusalem's Church of the Holy Sepulcher.** Many contemporaries believed al-Hakim was mad, and following his mysterious disappearance in 1021 most of his Muslim subjects breathed a sigh of relief. The Fatimids were less tolerant toward **Sunni** Muslims, who were the majority in the lands that the Fatimids seized. Because of persecution, quite a few Sunnis embraced Shia. The shallowness of these conversions is demonstrated by the fact that following **Saladin**'s rise to power in Egypt in 1171, the country quickly and easily returned to the fold of Sunnism. **Related Entries:** Almohads; Almoravids; Cairo; Islamic Peoples; Seljuks.

Suggested Reading

Yaacov Lev, *State and Society in Fatimid Egypt* (1991).

Feudalism

Feudalism is a modern term, coined to describe a complex system of lordship, mil-

A sarcophagus of ca. 1100 depicting an act of feudal investiture. The vassal kneels before his lord and receives a lance as a token of his service. Behind him stands an abbot (the head of a monastery), who blesses the act. The rite of feudal homage was thought to be sacred, and the oath of fealty was on a par with all other sacred vows. Strasbourg, France.

itary service, land tenure, and political authority that existed under various guises in portions of Europe between roughly 900 and 1300. From Europe, it was exported in a variety of forms to the **Latin East.**

Historians today hesitate to use the term in reference to medieval Europe, and when they do, they point out that it was never a single, all-embracing or coherent system. That noted, the term has utility, and should not be discarded just because it is imprecise or because Europe's feudal institutions were so variegated.

The best way to define feudalism is to begin with the Latin word from which it is fashioned, *feudum,* which means "fief" or "fee." A fief was something of value, often land, given by a lord to a subordinate, known as a *vassal,* in return for service. Normally,

the service was military service. Usually the vassal was a freeman and professional warrior and not a common laborer or farmer, and his obligations to his lord were honorable in the sense that they did not demean his status as a free warrior. More often than not, a vassal served as an **armored** warrior on horseback, or *knight,* but this was not an absolute rule. Foot soldiers, or **sergeants,** could also be vassals. The vassal's fief supported him so that he could perform his military functions and whatever other services his lord demanded of him.

Another important aspect of feudalism was *subinfeudation,* whereby a vassal became the lord of another man, who then was his vassal. This could happen in many ways and for a variety of reasons, but one common reason was the need to raise additional warriors to meet one's own feudal obligations. A vassal might be obliged to provide a certain number of knights and sergeants in his lord's service. To raise them he might give out portions of his extensive fief to his own vassals, who then become *rear-vassals*—vassals of a vassal. The great vassals of any state tended also to enjoy governmental and juridical powers within their fiefs and to be petty sovereigns, but their degrees of independence depended on many factors. Those who held fiefs directly from a king, who either in theory or reality was the lord to whom they were directly answerable, were known as *tenants-in-chief.* Tenants-in-chief usually regarded themselves as the king's social equals and demanded the right to be consulted and to give their assent whenever the king pondered any weighty matter.

Feudal ties and obligations were much more complicated and varied than this brief overview suggests, but these four elements—lordship, enfeoffment, vassalage, and military service—were the heart and soul of the so-called feudal system, wherever it existed. The French, Provençal, and Italo-**Norman** crusaders and settlers who established the first **crusader states** in the East came from lands that were governed along feudal lines, and they naturally imposed the forms of government and the social structures that they knew back home on the states that they created in **Outremer. Related Entries:** Amalric; Antioch; Cyprus; High Court; Jerusalem, Kingdom of; Transjordan; Tripoli.

Suggested Reading

Primary Sources

Peter Speed, ed., *Those Who Fought: An Anthology of Medieval Sources* (1996).

Historical Studies

John LaMonte, *Feudal Monarchy in the Latin Kingdom of Jerusalem, 1100 to 1291* (1932);

David Nicolle and Christa Hook, *Knight of Outremer: A.D. 1187–1344* (1996); Jonathan Riley-Smith, *The Feudal Nobility and the Kingdom of Jerusalem, 1174–1277* (1973); Joshua Prawer, *Crusader Institutions* (1980); Steven Runciman, *The Families of Outremer: The Feudal Nobility of the Crusader Kingdom of Jerusalem, 1099–1291* (1960); Steven Tibble, *Monarchy and Lordships in the Latin Kingdom of Jerusalem, 1099–1291* (1989).

Fief

See Feudalism.

Field of Blood, Battle of the (June 28, 1119)

The battle at Darb Sarmada in **Syria** in which the **Norman** forces of the principality of **Antioch** were annihilated.

In 1119 the **Turkish** sultan Il-Ghazi ibn Artuk, ruler of **Aleppo,** invaded the lands of Antioch, which was threatening the security of his state. Although reinforcements were on the way from **Jerusalem** and **Tripoli, Roger of Salerno,** regent of Antioch, rushed to meet the invasion with an inadequate force of about 700 **knights** and 3,000 foot soldiers. Camped in an untenable position, his army was taken by surprise by attacks on three sides and cut to pieces. Roger was killed in the battle along with most of his knights and soldiers. Many of those taken **prisoner** were tortured and executed, but some were ransomed.

Due to the annihilation of the cream of Norman knighthood at this battle, Norman power and influence in Syria permanently decreased, and the balance of power in the region shifted to crusader colonists from other areas of France and **Languedoc.** The atmosphere of crisis occasioned by this disaster, which placed both **Edessa** and Antioch in immediate peril, also led King

Baldwin II of Jerusalem to request assistance from Pope Calixtus II and Venice in 1120, which resulted in the pope's planning a new crusade. As far as the Muslims were concerned, the victory showed that local rulers could meet and defeat the Franks without relying on the aid of the Great Seljuk sultan, and it gave impetus and validity to the notion of holy jihad against the invaders from the West. Related Entries: Crusade of 1122–1126; Massacres.

Fifth Crusade (1217–1221)

The Fifth Crusade appeared to be on the brink of victory several times but ended in disaster, the victim of bad strategy, poor battlefield tactics, divided leadership, and a support system that could not supply the troops and resources needed to triumph in a hostile land far from home.

With its divided leadership and manpower shortages, the Fifth Crusade presents some striking, if superficial, similarities with the Third Crusade. There is another similarity. The specter of Frederick II, king of Sicily and Germany and emperor-elect, whose arrival was eagerly awaited, hung heavily over the Fifth Crusade. He never arrived, allowing many to ask bitterly "what if?" Much like his grandfather Emperor Frederick I, who died en route during the Third Crusade, Frederick II possibly could have provided the manpower and leadership necessary for a successful crusade. We shall never know in either case.

What we do know is that this crusade can be divided into six segments: (1) Preparation for crusade, 1213–1216; (2) the diversion to Portugal, 1217–1218; (3) the Hungarian and Austrian Crusade, 1217–1218; and (4) the siege of Damietta, May 1218–November 1219; (5) a period of watching and waiting, 1220–mid-1221; and (6) defeat, July–August 1221.

Preparation for Crusade

The Fifth Crusade must be understood against the background of the so-called Children's Crusade of 1212 and the general atmosphere of religious enthusiasm and frustration at recent crusade failures that it reflected. In April 1213 Pope Innocent III announced his intention to convene a General Council to discuss reform of the Church and a crusade. As far as he was concerned, and the events of the previous year only served to confirm this belief, the two were inextricably intertwined. Reform of Christian morals, especially those of the clergy, was a necessary precondition for a successful crusade. Victory and defeat in the Holy Land were equally direct consequences of the moral state of Christendom. At the same time, the crusade was the perfect instrument for reforming Christian society because of the sacrifices it entailed and the way in which it focused Christian hearts and minds on God.

Innocent's preparations for the Fifth Crusade rested on precedents that he and his predecessors had established for earlier crusades. But he was also an innovator, and cumulatively his innovations were a turning point in crusade history. The pope reinterpreted and restructured the support machinery of crusading so far as recruitment and finance were concerned, and he also broadened the crusade indulgence and redefined the crusade vow. The Fourth Crusade had revealed the inadequacies of traditional recruitment and finance systems, despite his best attempts to widen the base of crusader-enlistment and money-raising for that earlier crusade.

In 1213 Innocent divided Christian Europe into preaching zones and appointed prominent local churchmen to promote the crusade in each region. Only Spain and the Latin empire of Constantinople, which had their own crusade-related concerns, were omitted from this system. He sought special arrangements with secular and ecclesiastical lords, as well as cities and villages, to provide set numbers of soldiers whose expenses they would support for three years. He went so far as to command all churches and monasteries to contribute fighting men, according to their means. Maritime cities were expected to provide ships and sailors. He also temporarily revoked the indulgences granted crusaders who traveled to Spain and **Languedoc** to wage **holy war** against the **Moors** and the **Albigensians,** claiming that recent successes in both theaters had rendered the call for outside help unnecessary. Clearly he did not want people opting to fight on these close-to-home fronts when the overseas crusade to save the **Latin kingdom of Jerusalem** was a more pressing need. Finally, he instructed his regional procurators to enlist everyone who wished to take the vow and not to concern themselves with their suitability to serve the crusade in some useful way. Those who were later judged unfit for service could have their vows commuted by performing appropriate acts of penance or, better, could redeem their vows with money in support of a crusader, the amount depending on their status and means.

To further finance this new crusade, Innocent continued the policies he had instituted for the Fourth Crusade: offering **crusade indulgences** to people who made suitable donations in support of the expedition and setting up chests in each church throughout the West to receive "alms for the aid of the Holy Land."

In November 1215 Innocent presided over the Fourth Lateran Council, which published a formal crusade decree that became the model for the crusade legislation of subsequent councils. Although Innocent had promised in 1199 that the unpopular one-year tax of two and a half percent on clerical income in support of the Fourth Crusade was not a precedent, now, speaking through the council, he imposed a three-year tax of five percent on most clerical incomes and of ten percent on himself and all his cardinals.

Moreover, because Innocent still blamed the Venetians for the two diversions of the Fourth Crusade, the council stipulated that crusaders were to assemble in and sail from southern Italy and Sicily in June 1217, just as the current truce with the **Ayyubid** sultan of Egypt ended. To further ensure that there was no repeat of the events of 1202 and 1203, when, as Innocent believed, the Venetians forced an impoverished army to sail to Zara and **Constantinople,** the pope pledged 30,000 pounds of silver. Finally, the council ordered a four-year moratorium on all seaborne commerce with the **Muslim** East, so that there would be sufficient vessels to transport the army and so that the **Saracens** would no longer benefit from this trade.

Enthusiasm for the crusade swept most of Europe, and tens of thousands enlisted. King **Philip II** of France, who had reluctantly participated in the Third Crusade, was not one of the enthusiasts, but a number of other kings and great lords offered the initial promise of leadership. Among these was the young Frederick II of **Hohenstaufen,** orphaned son of Emperor **Henry VI.** During his coronation as king of Germany in July 1215, Frederick unexpectedly took the cross. A still-smoldering civil war in Germany, however, precluded his immediate departure on crusade. A bit earlier, in March 1215, King John of England took the crusade vow, but a baronial rebellion and his death in 1216 prevented his participation. The only crowned head from the West to leave on this crusade would be King Andrew II of Hungary, who had taken the vow in 1196 but had received a number of postponements over the years. Finally, the pope would allow no further delays, and Andrew promised to depart in 1217. Duke Leopold VI of Austria, who had also taken the cross years earlier, in 1208, now was moved to make good on his vow. In addition, scores of other lords, leading contingents from all over Europe, prepared to move east.

It looked as though a crusade—the best financed, most widely recruited, and most carefully organized one to date—was ready to get under way. Even the death of Innocent III in July 1216 did not seem sufficient reason to worry over the eventual outcome of this great crusade.

The Diversion to Portugal

Few crusaders assembled at the Sicilian and southern Italian ports that the council had designated, choosing rather to sail from ports closer to home. The first to depart were some 300 vessels carrying crusaders from Frisia and the northern Rhineland, which sailed from the Netherlands on May 29, 1217.

After losing about forty vessels to storms at sea, they arrived at Lisbon in late July, where local church leaders attempted to enlist them in the siege of the fortress of al-Qasr. The Rhenish contingent decided to tarry and fight the Moors before proceeding; the Frisians pressed on, wintered in Italy, and arrived in **Acre** in the spring of 1218.

Those who remained in Portugal assisted in the capture of al-Qasr, which capitulated in October 1217. The victory was costly and the crusaders' losses were high. Many of the survivors were no longer able to continue on and were absolved of their vows. The remainder, now a small percentage of those who had stayed to fight, limped on to the **Holy Land,** which they reached in late April/early May 1218.

The Hungarian and Austrian Crusade

The first crusaders to arrive at Acre were Austrians and Hungarians, who departed from Split in Serbia in August and September 1217 and arrived in the **Levant** during late summer and early fall. So large was the Hungarian army that assembled at Split, the ships proved inadequate to transport all of them, and many had to wait until the spring of 1218 before departing. Some simply returned home and stayed there.

The crusaders who assembled in Acre in the autumn of 1217 joined forces with armies led by the prince of **Antioch,** the king of **Cyprus,** and **John of Brienne,** the former king and now regent of Jerusalem. Altogether, it was an army of considerable size, which was cursed by having too many would-be leaders. Unable to reach a consensus, and believing that Frederick II would soon arrive to assume overall command, the leaders decided to engage immediately in a number of small military operations in northern **Palestine** while awaiting Frederick and the other crusade contingents. The plan was not a bad one because they first had to secure the region before engaging in larger campaigns farther from Acre. The most significant battle they fought was a series of two unsuccessful assaults on Muslim fortifications on Mount Tabor in early December. Following that, about 500 crusaders made a sweep into Lebanon, where they were ambushed in the wintry mountain passes and virtually annihilated.

With the failure at Mount Tabor, King Andrew who had absented himself from the mountain assault, declared his crusade vow fulfilled and left for home in early January 1218, taking many of his troops with him. Hugh I, king of Cyprus, and Bohemond IV of Antioch also departed with their forces. The remaining crusaders busied themselves with building fortifications while they awaited reinforcements from the West.

The Siege of Damietta

Reinforcements began to arrive in late April 1218, including the remaining

Rhineland Germans, the Frisian crusaders, and a sizeable Italian contingent. With a reinvigorated army and now a sizeable fleet, the leaders, including John of Brienne, decided it was time to attack their immediate primary objective: Egypt. With Egypt conquered, recovery of all of the captured territories of the kingdom of Jerusalem would be easy. They chose the port city of Damietta as their initial point of invasion, and on May 27 a landing party encamped outside the city, meeting little resistance as it set up a fortified position. This initial success was followed by eighteen bitter months of siege combat, during which crusaders arrived and departed with frequency. Duke Leopold of Austria, for example, left for home in May 1219 accompanied by large numbers of Austrians and Germans.

Perhaps the constant coming and going of crusaders, which had some precedent in all previous crusades in the East but never to this extent, was due, at least in part, to the **Albigensian Crusade.** There crusaders had become accustomed to serving in the field for a set period of time, normally a minimum of forty days. Regardless of the reason, the average length of service during the Fifth Crusade, which lasted four years, was a little over one year for secular lords and a bit less for bishops and abbots. Data do not exist that allow us to determine how long the average **knight, sergeant,** other foot soldier, or priest served. Whatever the length of a tour of duty, the rhythm of constantly changing leaders and fluctuating numbers of soldiers in the field caused considerable problems for the crusade.

Leadership was by committee, but with leaders arriving and leaving, a good deal of authority devolved first upon John of Brienne, who remained with the army for much of its campaign, and then with the **papal legate,** Cardinal **Pelagius,** who arrived in September 1218 with crusaders from Rome

and its environs. The result was a contest for dominance in the councils of the leadership between King John and Cardinal Pelagius.

With this as background, bitter fighting between the crusaders and the Egyptians continued. One of the early crusader successes was their capture on August 25, 1218, of the Chain Tower, a fortification on an island that controlled all river traffic by means of heavy iron chains stretched across the Nile.

On August 31 the aged **al-Adil (Saphadin)** died, and his son **al-Kamil** succeeded him as sultan of Egypt. The new sultan continued to prosecute the war, aided by his brother, al-Muazzam, the sultan of **Syria.** By February 1219, however, both brothers were prepared to negotiate a return of Jerusalem in exchange for the crusaders' withdrawal from Egypt. The terms were generous. Apparently they proposed a thirty-year truce, returning **Jerusalem** to the Christians, and handing over captured crusader **castles** west of the Jordan River, if the crusaders withdrew. When the crusaders insisted that al-Kamil include two key fortresses in **Transjordan,** the brothers balked because the castles threatened the route between **Cairo** and **Damascus,** the nerve center of the Ayyubid sultanate of Syria. Al-Kamil proposed, instead, that he pay an annual tribute of either 15,000 or 30,000 gold *byzants* (sources differ as to the amount) for the right to retain these two captured strongholds. John of Brienne wanted to accept this offer because it promised almost everything that he was fighting to attain, namely restoration of the pre-1187 holdings of the kingdom of Jerusalem. To the contrary, Cardinal Pelagius and the masters of the two major **military orders,** the **Templars** and the **Hospitalers,** thought it a bad deal, and their arguments won the day. The war continued.

On August 29, 1219, an ill-considered crusader attack on the sultan's camp ended in disaster, and this victory gave al-Kamil the opportunity to offer again the terms he had set forth in February. This time he added a promise of funds for the reconstruction of Jerusalem's fortifications, which al-Muazzam had ordered dismantled earlier that year. Once again, John of Brienne and Pelagius divided on the issue, and Pelagius prevailed. His belief in Frederick II's imminent arrival with a massive army of fresh troops might have been the deciding factor in his counseling rejection of the sultan's offer.

Initially it seemed the cardinal was correct, because Damietta fell on November 5, when its remaining defenders could no longer defend a dying city. The crusaders scaled the walls without any serious opposition and moved into a city where they discovered corpses everywhere and huge caches of riches.

Watching and Waiting

The capture of Damietta was not an end unto itself but only the first step in a master plan to capture all of Egypt. Cairo was next. But there was a problem. The army had suffered heavy losses in combat and to **disease**—probably well in excess of one-third of its total strength. It now needed to recuperate and refit. Unfortunately, after the autumn of 1219 the number of replacements from the West fell precipitously and continued to decline for the remainder of the crusade.

The ill feelings between Pelagius and John of Brienne also continued to smolder. John was the commander in the field, or at least the chairman of the board of the council of leaders. Pelagius, as papal legate, represented the interests not only of the pope but also of the absent and expected emperor-elect, Frederick II. As such, he saw himself as a check on John's ambitions. Early in 1220 pressure on Acre from al-Muazzam's Syrian forces forced John to return home,

along with a large number of crusaders. He also left because he wanted to establish his claim to the throne of Cilician **Armenia,** made vacant by the death in 1219 of his father-in-law, Leo II.

Despite the losses and diminishing replacements, Pelagius pressed for action, but intense debate among the leaders led only to continued inactivity, as the army waited and watched for Frederick throughout 1220. Meanwhile, back in Rome, Pope **Honorius III** tried to lure John back to Egypt and to heal his rift with Pelagius, as well as to negotiate Frederick's imperial coronation and his departure date.

Frederick was crowned emperor on November 22, 1220, and he promised to send part of his army in the spring and to arrive with the bulk of it in August 1221. By the spring of 1221, however, Pelagius was desperate, knowing the longer the army tarried, the more its numbers would dwindle. He further believed that the longer the crusaders remained in the fleshpots of Damietta the more sinful they would become and the less worthy they would be of victory. Finally, the promised imperial reinforcements arrived in May with Duke Ludwig of Bavaria. They were substantial but not the massive imperial army that was expected. But action was needed. Even though the annual flooding of the Nile was imminent, Pelagius and the duke of Bavaria thought the time was right to strike.

On July 6 the army was finally ready to depart Damietta, and the following day John of Brienne returned at the head of a large force. John was aghast at the plan and urged caution. His reward for expressing a prudent point of view was to be accused of treason by the papal legate and threatened with excommunication. The decision to force a battle was beyond discussion, as far as Pelagius was concerned. Leaving behind a large part of the army to defend Damietta, the legate led the invasion force south, carrying with him relics of the **True Cross.** Because probably more than half of the crusade army remained in Damietta, it is likely that Pelagius did not envision an all-out offensive against Cairo but rather sought simply to probe at the enemy while awaiting the emperor's arrival.

Defeat

The army first proceeded to a point about three miles out of Damietta, where it organized itself into a coherent force for the march. Before setting out from this mobilization point on July 17, the crusaders received another offer from al-Kamil to exchange Jerusalem for Damietta. Confident in victory, Cardinal Pelagius again refused the bargain.

According to **Oliver of Paderborn,** with 1,200 knights, not counting **Turcopoles** and numerous other mounted warriors, 4,000 archers (of whom almost 2,500 were **mercenaries**), and uncounted large numbers of other **infantry,** the army proceeded along the eastern bank of the Nile. Substantial numbers of **noncombatants,** including **women,** marched along with the army. Some 630 vessels guarded the crusaders' right flank and carried supplies.

Toward the end of July, against the advice of John of Brienne, who urged retreat, the army advanced onto a narrow triangle of land bounded by two branches of the Nile and lying opposite al-Mansurah. Just as they were entering this precarious bottleneck, al-Kamil's two brothers arrived in Egypt, each leading a large army in support of his sibling. The combined Muslim forces and al-Kamil's navy now closed the trap. The crusaders were cut off and their supplies were dwindling. Finally Pelagius, who wanted to await reinforcements, was overruled, and the army began to withdraw on August 26.

It was too late. The Nile was at full flood, and the army was hampered by its sick, wounded, and noncombatants. To make matters worse, al-Kamil opened the dikes, adding water to water. Except for the Templars and Hospitalers, who maintained discipline, the army became a mass of confused and dispirited individuals. Disorganized and fighting to keep their heads above water, the crusaders suffered heavy losses from harassing enemy bands.

At this point, Pelagius asked John of Brienne to negotiate a safe withdrawal. Al-Kamil, who seems always to have preferred a peaceful solution (and who also knew that Damietta was still held by a large force), agreed. On August 29, 1221, the surrounded crusaders surrendered to the sultan and promised to turn over Damietta. In return, food would be supplied to the encircled army and there would be an exchange of **prisoners,** an eight-year truce, and a peaceful withdrawal from Egypt. Both sides scrupulously adhered to the settlement. The Fifth Crusade was over.

Related Entries: Apocalypse and the Crusades; Chivalry; Francis of Assisi; James of Vitry; Seventh Crusade; Sixth Crusade.

Suggested Reading

Primary Sources

Edward Peters, ed., *Christian Society and the Crusades, 1198–1229* (1971).

Historical Study

James M. Powell, *Anatomy of a Crusade, 1213–1221* (1990).

Financing the Crusades

The burden of financing a person's participation in a crusade primarily rested on the individual, even though in the twelfth and thirteenth centuries kings and popes created institutional means for raising funds on a large scale.

Many, probably most, participants in the **People's Crusade** of 1096 set off without a thought of how they would finance their **pilgrimage.** Undoubtedly inspired by **apocalyptic** hopes, at least some of them thought that God would provide, just as the God of Israel sent down manna from Heaven during the Exodus of the Hebrews out of Egypt. When divine aid was not forthcoming, quite a few crusaders turned to **pillaging and plundering** Christian and non-Christian communities as they marched eastward. The more organized **feudal** contingents led by some of the great lords of Europe in the second wave of the **First Crusade** took longer to get under way because they had to deal in a more responsible manner with the issue of finance.

The costs were staggering. A **knight** needed the equivalent of four or five times his total annual income to equip himself with horses and **armor** and to pay for provisions along the way as he traveled through Christian territory. If he was a sincere crusader, as most were, he could not expect to supplement his resources by pillaging until he reached **Muslim** lands. Given Europe's agricultural economy, most crusade funds were raised through land transactions. This usually meant that an entire family sold off or mortgaged major portions of its holdings to underwrite the crusade pilgrimage of a single knight and possibly his few retainers. For the great lords, who had to support large numbers of fighters and **noncombatants,** the financial burden was all the greater and their mortgages often placed their families at risk of ruin. The sheer sacrifice involved in raising sufficient money was tremendous at any time. It was made the sharper in 1096 by drastically falling land values due to an agricultural depression caused by a long series of droughts and a glutted market caused by so many mortgages and sales within such a short period of time. Also, most mortgages stipulated that if the crusader died or otherwise failed to return, the land was forfeited to the creditor. Often the creditor was a church or a monastery, and land that passed from a family into the hands of an ecclesiastical organization was lost to that family forever. All of this suggests strongly that most knights and lords who raised funds on such unfavorable terms to go on crusade, especially the First Crusade, did so for religious reasons and not out of a desire for material gain.

In addition to land transactions, the feudal lords of Europe also attempted to squeeze as much money as possible out of their **vassals** (especially those who were not crusading with them) and other dependents, including churches, monasteries, and local **Jewish** communities. Gifts from pious friends and family members also provided substantial help.

No kings went on the First Crusade, but toward the middle of the twelfth century the kings of France and Germany undertook the **Second Crusade,** and thereafter the monarchs of Europe would play increasingly important roles in the crusades. With royal involvement came royal taxation. In 1146 King **Louis VII** of France attempted to raise funds for his upcoming crusade by extorting money from selected subjects of his realm. The first clear kingdom-wide tax in support of the **Holy Land** took place in 1166 when the same king, in response to papal appeals, levied a small (about 0.4 percent) five-year property and income tax on himself and almost all his subjects, clerics and laity alike, to raise money for the defense of **Jerusalem.** King Henry II of England followed Louis's lead with a similar tax for the same purpose. Although they established precedents, both levies were not technically meant to support crusaders or a crusade. The proceeds were earmarked for the payment of **mercenary** soldiers serving the crusader states and the building and repair of fortifications in **Outremer.**

The loss of Jerusalem to **Saladin** in 1187 led to greater efforts by monarchs and popes alike to create large-scale means for raising crusade funds. In 1188 Henry II of England and **Philip II** of France imposed on all non-crusaders within their lands the *Saladin Tithe* to pay for their projected crusade to reconquer the Holy City. The tithe was an uncustomarily steep, one-time levy of ten percent on all income and nonessential movable goods, and its high rate occasioned loud complaints and resistance. King Philip was forced to promise that never again would he or his successors levy such a tax. Philip kept his promise, but his thirteenth-century successors instituted kingdom-wide crusade taxes. In 1221 Emperor **Frederick II** imposed a tax on his kingdom of Sicily to support his projected crusade, and in 1222 regents for the young Henry III of England authorized a crusade poll, or head, tax on all subjects of the realm. Such poll taxes were unpopular and largely unproductive, even though the thirteenth-century **papacy** encouraged princes and kings to impose them.

On its part, the papacy increasingly used the Church's penitential system to raise crusade funds. In 1198 **Pope Innocent III** offered the full crusade **indulgence** to anyone who supported a qualified crusader for at least two years. Others offering donations would receive indulgences in relation to the size of their subsidies and in proportion to their devotion. On December 31, 1199, he made the deal sweeter by offering a full indulgence to anyone who supported a qualified crusader for at least a year. He also ordered a locked chest to be placed in each church throughout the West for crusade donations offered "for the remission of sins," and he also empowered bishops to commute penances imposed by the Church in return for crusade alms, provided the quality of the person's contrition and the

extent of his or her resources had been taken into account. The crusade-donation chests became a fixture in Europe's churches from that time onward.

In the same general letter of 1199, Innocent built upon Pope Clement III's attempts in 1188 to tax all clergy in support of the recovery of Jerusalem, by imposing a one-year tax of two and a half percent on the annual income of all clergy (with the exception of certain exempted religious orders, such as the **Cistercians**). All clerics who paid the tax faithfully were to be granted remission of one-fourth of all church-imposed penances. Although the pope promised that this extraordinary tax would not be a precedent, it was. In 1215 he imposed another universal clerical tax, this time a three-year tax of five percent (and a ten-percent tax on himself and the cardinals). Due to massive resistance, collections of these clerical taxes were slow, uneven, and uncertain, but they continued. In 1245 the First Council of Lyons imposed a similar three-year tax of five percent on all clerics except members of exempt religious orders and clergy who had sworn the **cross.**

The most successful and heaviest crusade levy was raised by Pope **Gregory X** as he vainly tried to organize yet another crusade to counter **Mamluk** pressure on the crusader states. In 1274 his Second Council of Lyons stipulated a six-year tax of ten percent on all clerics, with no exceptions. After Gregory's death in 1276, however, the money was largely diverted from the Holy Land to other papal programs. Although papal taxes on clerics continued to be a common feature of life in the Church, they largely ceased to support crusades to the Holy Land by the last quarter of the thirteenth century.

Even at their height, the crusade taxes raised by monarchs and popes failed to support fully the heavy expenses incurred by crusaders to the East—expenses made all the worse by a steady rise in prices during the Crusade Era. Despite Innocent III's attempts to create new ways of raising large sums of money for the liberation of Jerusalem, it was the poverty of the army of the **Fourth Crusade** that set in motion the events that led to its diversions to Zara and Constantinople in 1202 and 1203. Ultimately most crusaders had to pay their way, and they found it more difficult to do so as the crusading movement grew older. **Related Entries:** Councils and Synods; Eighth Crusade; Fifth Crusade; Fulk of Neuilly; Louis IX; Military Orders; Privileges, Crusader; Raymond IV of Saint-Gilles; Robert II of Normandy; Seventh Crusade; Templars; Vow, Crusader's.

Suggested Reading

Primary Source

Corliss K. Slack, ed. and trans., *Crusade Charters, 1138–1270* (2001).

First Crusade (1096–1102)

Called in November 1095 by Pope **Urban II** at the **Council of Clermont,** the crusade was waged by three waves of **pilgrim**-warriors during the years 1096–1102: (1) the **People's Crusade** of 1096; (2) the **Crusade of the Great Lords** of 1096–1099; and (3) the **Crusade of 1101,** which actually stretched from 1100 to 1102. Its crowning achievement was the capture of **Jerusalem** on July 15, 1099.

Prelude and Prologue

Evidence strongly suggests that when Pope Urban II called for a **holy war** against the **Turks** in his famous sermon of November 27, 1095, and in his later appeals, he envisioned a war fought by professional soldiers from his own **feudal** class. The fact is, however, his call to arms struck a respondent chord in all levels of Western Christian society.

The walls of Nicaea.

The First Wave: The People's Crusade

Due to the appeals of **preachers,** such as **Peter the Hermit,** large groups of people flowed out of Europe, especially from northern France, the Low Countries, the German Rhineland, Saxony, and Bohemia in the spring of 1096. Altogether, they probably numbered between 20,000 and 30,000. Although these bands probably contained a higher percentage of **noncombatants** and untrained would-be warriors than later crusade armies, they also attracted professional soldiers and some high-ranking nobles. If we can believe the **chronicler** Albert of Aachen, some people in this initial wave, believing that a goose and a goat were inspired by the Holy Spirit, used the two animals as guides along the way. If the story is true, these animal-chasing crusaders were probably few in number, and they played no significant role in the People's Crusade.

The People's Crusade was a confused affair, with groups heading off at various times, but we can identify five major forces that left Europe in the spring. Two, led respectively by **Walter Sansavoir** and Peter the Hermit, reached **Constantinople** in high summer but were destroyed in **Anatolia** in October 1096, and with their destruction the People's Crusade was finished. The three other armies never made it as far as Constantinople. A priest named Volkmar (or Folkmar) led a mass of crusaders from eastern Germany; another priest named Gottschalk was in charge of a group from western and southern Germany; a count named Emicho, possibly from Leiningen in the Rhineland, assembled and led a large, multilingual, fairly well-organized contingent of West German, Flemish, English, and French crusaders. All three armies were routed and dispersed with great losses in Hungary. Those who survived either went home or joined the armies of the princes that followed in their steps and constituted the crusade's second wave.

The reason for Hungarian resistance was simple: Lack of discipline and supplies led to brigandage and worse on the part of many of the crusaders. The five armies had left Europe too hastily and too early to benefit from the harvest of 1096. Also, too many participants were too poor to supply themselves adequately under even the best of circumstances, and too many were subject to no effective controlling authority. Walter Sansavoir's army, the first to pass through Hungary, was fairly well controlled and reached Constantinople without major incident. Peter the Hermit's army, which arrived next, was larger and less disciplined. Just before leaving Hungarian territory, Peter's crusaders sacked a town and killed a large number of its Christian inhab-

itants, despite the king of Hungary's best attempts to provision the crusaders. When the next crusader groups arrived, the Hungarians were wary and ready to resist their coreligionists. After some initial pillaging, Volkmar's and Gottschalk's groups were cut to pieces and the survivors were driven back; when Emicho's army, which had already devastated several **Jewish** communities in the Rhineland, tried to force entry into Hungary, the king's army met and drove it back with great losses. Emicho survived but did not resume his crusade.

The Second Wave: The Crusade of the Great Lords

One of the major factors contributing to the destruction of the armies of the first wave was low supplies, which meant they had to **pillage and plunder** even before leaving Christian territory. As many discovered, this was not a wise strategy. Ironically, Emicho's army was defeated in mid-August 1096, right around the very date, August 15, that the pope had set as the projected departure date for the armies. A realist as well as an idealist, Pope Urban realized that solving the logistical difficulties associated with organizing large contingents of professional soldiers required more than just zeal; it required time and large expenditures of money, which themselves took time to raise.

The second wave, which we can conveniently think of as the pope's official wave, consisted of a number of separate contingents that left Europe at different times and along different routes from August to October. Its leaders were some of Europe's, and especially France's, greatest lords and included Duke **Godfrey of Bouillon,** Count **Hugh of Vermandois,** Count **Raymond of Saint-Gilles,** Count **Stephen of Blois,** Count **Robert of Flanders,** Duke **Robert of Normandy,** Count **Eustace of Boulogne,** and **Bohemond of Taranto.** None was a king, but several were sons and brothers of kings and most were related to royalty.

Constantinople was designated as their initial place of rendezvous, and they arrived there between November 1096 and mid-May 1097. Even before they arrived at the imperial city in late December, the forces of Duke Godfrey pillaged **Byzantine** property in response to a rumor that Count Hugh of Vermandois was a **prisoner** of the emperor. This was not an auspicious start to a holy war that was based on the assumption that the Christians of the West were going to the aid of their Eastern coreligionists, who would cooperate fully with their **Latin** rescuers.

The staggered arrival of tens of thousands of largely unwanted, poorly disciplined, and independent warriors who had no intention whatsoever of enlisting as **mercenaries** in the Byzantine army posed a serious threat to Emperor **Alexius I,** his city, and its empire. Indeed, one of the crusade leaders, Bohemond of Taranto, had invaded and attempted to conquer imperial territory fifteen years earlier. To gain control of the situation, the emperor offered the crusade leaders gifts of money but demanded from them two oaths: to return to him all lands they conquered that were previously part of the empire and to swear fealty to him as their feudal liege.

Some leaders, such as Hugh, the two Roberts, Stephen, and even Bohemond, offered little or no objection to the oaths. Godfrey of Bouillon agreed only after his army had clashed with Byzantine forces outside of the city and had been beaten back. Count Raymond, angry at the Byzantines for losses inflicted on his army as it marched though imperial territory, also initially refused but later took a compromise oath not to attack Alexius and to respect his honor.

With the oaths out of the way and the crusader armies at least nominally absorbed into the service of the Byzantine empire, the crusaders, numbering around 50,000 to 60,000, counting noncombatants, crossed the Bosporus in waves throughout April and May 1097. Their first objective was Nicaea, capital of the **Seljuk** sultanate of Rum, which lead elements reached on May 6. Rather than suffer an attack and **massacre,** the city surrendered to Emperor Alexius on June 19. The crusaders, who had incurred heavy casualties in the short **siege,** were disappointed at being denied the opportunity for glory and plunder.

Between June 26 and 28, the crusaders set out in two divisions on their march south, accompanied by a small imperial **cavalry** detachment of **Turcopoles** under the command of a converted **Turk,** Taticius. On his part, the emperor set off with the bulk of his army into the interior of Anatolia. The plan was that he and the crusaders would reunite for the assault on Jerusalem, but until then the emperor had to reoccupy the ancient heartland of his empire.

Near **Dorylaeum** on July 1 the crusaders won a resounding victory in the field against Seljuk Turkish forces. While the main army moved toward **Antioch, Baldwin of Boulogne,** brother of Duke Godfrey, broke off from the army and entered **Armenian** territory, eventually becoming lord of **Edessa** in March 1098.

The main crusader force reached Antioch on October 21, 1097, and initiated a siege that was to last until June 3, 1098—seven and a half months of misery that witnessed three major battles, numerous skirmishes, epidemics, a bitter winter, and near total starvation for both sides. When the siege began the crusader army numbered somewhere around 40,000 men, **women,** and children, having suffered appalling losses from **disease,** combat, and desertions over the previous four and a half months. Probably fewer than 5,000 **knights** remained fit for service. When the city finally fell, the crusade army's total numbers were likely well below 30,000, including noncombatants. Inasmuch as the army received streams of reinforcements from the West throughout its campaign, it seems likely that in a little over one year, the second wave had suffered a fifty percent or greater casualty rate.

Antioch finally fell, thanks to a traitor who allowed crusader forces to climb the wall at night. Prior to the city's fall several notable defections had taken place, including Taticius, the emperor's military representative, and Count Stephen of Blois. Almost immediately upon capturing the city, the starving crusaders found themselves besieged by a late-arriving Turkish relief force that outnumbered them by a factor of two or three. Thanks to good fortune, desperate bravery, and belief in the miraculous powers of the **Holy Lance** of Antioch, the crusaders broke the siege and drove the enemy from the field on June 28. Amazingly, the crusaders, who had almost no horses left, advanced as **infantry** and routed a numerically superior army that consisted primarily of fast-moving horse-mounted archers.

The crusaders had no desire to continue their march during the hot summer months. Moreover, they needed to rest and refit and to absorb the continuing stream of reinforcements from the West, as well as plot their next move. In July they sent a delegation to Emperor Alexius, inviting him to join them at Antioch to take possession of the city and to lead them to Jerusalem. His reply arrived in April 1099, promising the army that he would arrive in June. The emperor's answer was too late. The army was already well on its way to Jerusalem.

As far as the crusade leaders were concerned, Alexius's tardiness in answering them was final proof of his cowardice and untrustworthiness and justified their no longer honoring their oaths to him. Earlier, during the summer of 1098, he had decided not to reinforce the crusaders at Antioch thanks to the misguided advice of Stephen of Blois, who had abandoned the army out of despair of its surviving the arrival of the Turkish relief force. Based on Stephen's counsel, Alexius had decided that the crusaders were a lost cause, and he would not risk his army in a foolish attempt to relieve them.

With crusader loyalty to the emperor now dead, Bohemond of Taranto seized control of Antioch, turned it into a principality, and settled down to rule it. Unlike Bohemond, the other crusade leaders did not forget their **vow** to liberate Jerusalem, but they would now do so without Alexius. Whatever lands and cities they conquered along the way would not be returned to the empire. During their post-battle, six-month stay in and around Antioch, the crusade leaders began to create the idea and reality of a **Latin East**.

Between mid-January and mid-March 1099 various elements of the army set out for Jerusalem. The leaders were indecisive and unclear as to strategy and tactics, but the rank and file were clear in their goal. They wanted Jerusalem, and nothing else would satisfy them. It was this pressure from below that propelled the crusade's second wave to its denouement.

On June 7 the crusaders arrived before Jerusalem. According to one contemporary source, the army's fighters now included only 1,200 to 1,300 knights and 12,000 other men-at-arms. Its major leaders were reduced to Robert of Normandy and Robert of Flanders, Duke Godfrey, Count Raymond, and **Tancred,** Bohemond's nephew. Such a small force could not surround and wear down the city. Frontal assault was its only hope. On June 13 the crusaders assaulted the city but were beaten back by the **Fatimid** defenders. On July 8, mindful that they were penitent pilgrims, the crusaders marched barefoot around the city's walls and attended a sermon on the Mount of Olives. Convinced they had set themselves right with God, the resumed their attack on July 13 and broke into the city on the 15th.

Jerusalem was now back in Christian hands, and those hands ran red with blood, but not all of Jerusalem's inhabitants and defenders were killed. Some were **enslaved** and some were released for ransom. Following negotiations, the Egyptian defenders of the city's citadel were allowed to leave under safe conduct.

On July 22 Godfrey of Bouillon was chosen to rule over the city and organize its defenses, a situation made difficult not only by the threat of an Egyptian counterattack but also by the desire of a majority of the crusaders to return home immediately, now that they had accomplished their mission.

A Fatimid relief force of around 20,000 arrived in the area too late to save Jerusalem, but it still threatened to retake the city. On August 12, a hastily thrown-together crusader army of about 1,200 knights and 9,000 foot soldiers surprised the Egyptians at **Ascalon** and crushed them. Jerusalem was safe; the second wave of the crusade had won the day and the war.

The Third Wave: The Crusade of 1101

Large numbers of persons who had sworn the **cross** had never embarked for the **Holy Land,** and as the years passed, increased pressure was put upon them to undertake the armed **pilgrimage** to Jerusalem. Realizing the need to reinforce his crusaders, in the spring of 1099, just months before his death, Pope Urban II commissioned a new preaching of the crusade. Already well under way, the movement gathered momentum after news reached the West of the capture of Jerusalem. The stories and war wounds brought back by returning, victorious cru-

saders in 1099–1100 only added to the rising enthusiasm in Europe for another major crusade effort—this time to defend and expand the gains of the second wave.

Pope **Paschal II,** Urban's successor, was no less a supporter of the crusade and used every means of persuasion, including threats of excommunication against reluctant crusaders, to get another expedition under way. The result was a massive outpouring of crusade pilgrims from France, Germany, and northern Italy, whose combined numbers equaled or exceeded those of the second wave at its peak. Its leaders included Dukes William IX of Aquitaine and Welf IV of Bavaria, as well as two veterans of the second wave, Counts Hugh of Vermandois and Stephen of Blois, both of whom were shamed into returning because neither had reached Jerusalem.

Disaster followed upon disaster during this ill-fated third wave. The only crusader force that managed to gain a victory without suffering defeat was a Venetian fleet of more than 200 vessels that arrived in June 1100, captured Haifa in August, and then returned home.

Most third-wave crusaders did not begin to get under way until mid-September 1100 and later. The first to leave were Lombards from northern Italy, who traveled overland to Constantinople, where they encamped outside the city, awaited reinforcements, and pillaged the countryside. Hostilities broke out between the Byzantines and the Lombards, but happily Raymond of Saint-Gilles happened to be in Constantinople at the time. Trusted by both sides, he acted as peace mediator.

In April 1101 the Lombards crossed the Bosporus and camped at Nicomedia. There they were joined by German and French contingents, with the latter led by Stephen, count of Blois, and Stephen, count of Burgundy. At the request of the crusaders,

Emperor Alexius dispatched Raymond of Saint-Gilles, a **Greek** general, and a Turcopole force of around 500 to act as advisors and guides.

In early June the crusaders set out eastward to rescue Bohemond, who was now a prisoner of the Turks. On June 23 they captured Ankara, which they returned to Emperor Alexius in accordance with the oaths of 1097. In early August, as they marched in the direction of the Black Sea, they met a large coalition force of Turks. The result was a battle near a site known as Mersivan that lasted several days. On the evening of the fourth day panic struck the crusader knights, who scattered, leaving behind their infantry, as well as women, children, and other noncombatants. So much for **chivalry.** A general slaughter ensued, although a number of notables, including Count Raymond and the counts of Blois and Burgundy, escaped and made their way to Constantinople.

Other crusading forces fared no better. A second army under Count William II of Nevers initially attempted to catch up with the Lombards but at Ankara turned south. At Heraclea, in the far southeast corner of Anatolia, they were attacked in late August by a large Turkish force and routed. As at Mersivan, the infantry, women, children, and others not fortunate enough to be on horses were abandoned by the cavalry to be killed or captured. The Turkish slave markets were glutted with captured crusaders. William of Nevers, however, made it out alive and free and led a small band to Antioch, where they were well received by Tancred.

At Antioch they were joined by the wretched remnants of a third ill-fated crusader coalition—the Aquitanians and the Bavarians. Duke William IX of Aquitaine, a young and romantic troubadour-warrior, had left home in mid-March 1101 and joined up along the way with the Bavarian army of Duke Welf IV. They reached Constantinople

in early June. Although some Germans decided to sail to the Holy Land from Constantinople, most crossed the Bosporus with William's French forces in mid July.

The combined armies reached the environs of Heraclea in early September, only weeks after the disaster suffered by Count William of Nevers, and they suffered the same fate. Lured into an ambush, they were cut to pieces, with most killed or enslaved. Once again, large numbers of women were carried off into slavery. Also once again, most of the survivors were knights who had fast horses. Count Hugh of Vermandois was mortally wounded, but Dukes William and Welf escaped.

Remnants of the different contingents that had escaped death or capture by flight had another opportunity to redeem themselves, and several did. In February 1102 Raymond of Saint-Gilles captured Tortosa with the help of the counts of Blois and Burgundy, Duke William of Aquitaine, and a Genoese fleet. The city was to become the base for further operations that resulted in the creation of the **county of Tripoli.**

Duke Welf bypassed Tortosa and went on directly to Jerusalem to complete his pilgrimage. On his homeward voyage he died at **Cyprus.** The other crusader leaders left Tortosa and also traveled to Jerusalem to complete their pilgrimage vows. Duke William then left for home, but many of the other survivors joined the small army of King Baldwin I in an ill-considered campaign against the Egyptians that ended in defeat. At Ramla, Count Stephen of Blois redeemed his name by dying in a desperate sally against overwhelming numbers.

The third wave of the First Crusade was now over. Its sole achievements were the capture of Ankara, Haifa, and Tortosa, but the price in human lives was disproportionate to the gains. Contemporaries in the West had an explanation: The destruction of the great armies of 1101 was God's punishment for their sins. More mundane reasons were poor leadership, woeful organization, ignorance of the land and of their enemy, and rotten luck. **Related Entries:** Adhémar of Monteil; Anna Comnena; Apocalypse and the Crusades; Cannibalism; Fulcher of Chartres; *Gesta Francorum;* Kerbogha; Kilij Arslan I; Tafurs.

Suggested Reading

Primary Sources

The "Canso d'Antioca": An Occitan Epic Chronicle of the First Crusade, trans. by Carol Sweetenham and Linda M. Patterson (2003); Fulcher of Chartres, *A History of the Expedition to Jerusalem, 1095–1127,* trans. by Frances Rita Ryan (1969); Gilo of Paris, *The Historia vie [sic] Hierosolimitane (The History of the Journey to Jerusalem),* ed. and trans. by C. W. Grocock and Elizabeth Siberry (1997); Guibert of Nogent, *The Deeds of God through the Franks,* ed. and trans. by Robert Levine (1997); August C. Krey, ed., *The First Crusade: The Accounts of Eye Witnesses and Participants* (1958); Orderic Vitalis, *The Ecclesiastical History of Orderic Vitalis,* 5 vols., ed. and trans. by Marjorie Chibnall (1969–1980), book 9 in vol. 5; Edward Peters, ed. *The First Crusade: The Chronicle of Fulcher of Chartres and Other Source Materials,* 2nd ed. (1998); Raymond of Aguilers, *Historia Francorum qui ceperunt Iherusalem (The History of the Franks Who Captured Jerusalem),* trans. by John H. and Laurita L. Hill (1968); Peter Tudebode, *Historia de Hierosolymitano itinere (History of the Journey to Jerusalem),* trans. by John H. and Laurita L. Hill (1974).

Historical Studies

Marcus Bull, *Knightly Piety and the Lay Response to the First Crusade: The Limousin and Gascony, c. 970–c.1130* (1993); Michael Foss, *People of the First Crusade* (1997); John France, *Victory in the East: A Military History of the First Crusade* (1994); Jonathan Philips, ed., *The First Crusade: Origins and Impact* (1997); Jonathan Riley-Smith, *The First Crusade and the Idea of Crusading* (1986) and *The First Crusaders, 1095–1131* (1997).

Fourth Crusade (1202–1204)

Conducted between October 1202 and April 1204, the Fourth Crusade captured and sacked the Christian cities of Zara and **Constantinople** and established the **Latin empire of Constantinople.**

The crusade had three related but distinctive stages: (1) the expedition to Zara in 1202; (2) the voyage to Constantinople and the first capture of the city in 1203; and (3) the second capture of the city in 1204. Many modern historians, as well as a few thirteenth-century critics, have wrongly blamed the Venetians and their leader, Doge Enrico Dandolo, for perverting the crusade to achieve political and economic gain.

Prologue and Preparation

Pope **Innocent III** proclaimed a new crusade on August 15, 1198, but it was not until November 28, 1199, that a group of French lords assumed the **crusader's cross** at a tournament at Ecry-sur-Aisne. The crusade's initial military leaders, the counts of Champagne, Flanders, and Blois, decided to transport their forces by sea and dispatched six plenipotentiaries to find suitable ships and supplies. The envoys chose Venice and in early 1201 concluded a treaty with the Venetians for the transportation and provisioning of 33,500 warriors and 4,500 horses for up to one year in return for a fee of 85,000 marks (42,500 pounds) of silver. Additionally, Venice would provide fifty war galleys at its own expense and would participate as an equal crusading party. The fleet would be ready to sail on June 29, 1202.

Constantinople's Golden Gate, so called because of its golden façade, which was stripped away centuries ago. The triumphal gate through which emperors entered the city, it served a darker purpose in April 1204 when thousands of refugees fled through its portals as they tried to escape with their lives and some of their fortunes.

Rather than sailing directly to the **Holy Land,** the crusade leaders secretly settled on Alexandria in Egypt as their initial objective. Egypt, weakened by famine and **disease,** appeared ripe for conquest, and from there the crusaders could march triumphantly to **Jerusalem.** That was the plan, but there was a fatal error in their calculations. The estimate of 33,500 crusaders embarking at Venice was unrealistic, and that single miscalculation was *the* factor that prevented the crusaders from ever reaching Egypt or the **Holy Land.** It drove them, instead, to Zara and Constantinople.

When the count of Champagne died in May 1201, the other crusade lords prevailed upon Marquis Boniface of **Montferrat** to join their ranks and accept nominal leadership of the yet-to-be-assembled army. He duly assumed the crusader's cross in late summer 1201.

The following summer it became clear that the fleet, which the Venetians had prepared on schedule and at great expense, would not sail anytime near the planned departure date. By the end of summer only about 11,000 crusaders had arrived in Venice, roughly one-third of the projected army.

Too few crusaders meant too little money, and the army managed to raise only 51,000 marks—forty percent less than the contracted fee. Venice needed to recoup its investment. To make matters worse, the army's campsite became increasingly unlivable as the summer wore on. Deaths

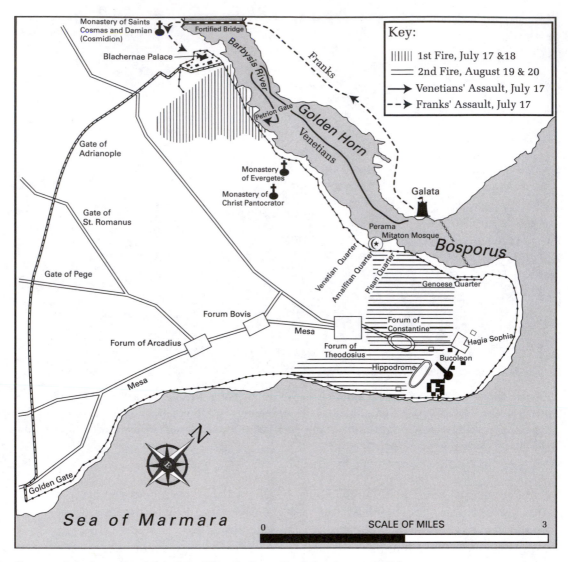

Constantinople at the time of the Fourth Crusade, July–August 1203.

and defections rose alarmingly. If the crusade did not get under way soon, it never would.

The Expedition to Zara

In the midst of this crisis, Doge Dandolo proposed a compromise. Venice would defer payment of the 34,000-mark balance until the army **plundered** the riches of Egypt, if the army would assist Venice in regaining control over Zara, a rebel city on the Croat-

ian coast. There was a problem. Zara's citizens were **Latin** Christians who had placed themselves under the authority of the king of Hungary, himself a sworn crusader. As a crusader, his lands were papally protected. When Innocent III learned of the Venetian proposal, he threatened excommunication should the crusaders attack Zara, but his prohibition was ineffective.

The fleet set sail at the beginning of October 1202 and arrived at Zara on Novem-

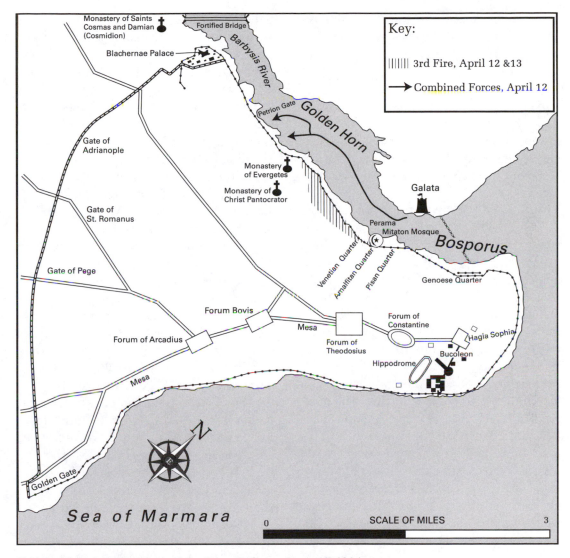

Key:

|||||| 3rd Fire, April 12 & 13

→ Combined Forces, April 12

Monastery of Saints Cosmas and Damian (Cosmidion)

Fortified Bridge

Barbysis River

Blachernae Palace

Petrion Gate

Golden Horn

Gate of Adrianople

Monastery of Evergetes

Monastery of Christ Pantocrator

Galata

Gate of St. Romanus

Perama

Mitaton Mosque

Bosporus

Venetian Quarter

Amalfitan Quarter

Pisan Quarter

Genoese Quarter

Gate of Pege

Forum Bovis

Mesa

Forum of Constantine

Hagia Sophia

Forum of Arcadius

Forum of Theodosius

Bucoleon

Mesa

Hippodrome

N

Golden Gate

Sea of Marmara

0   SCALE OF MILES   3

Constantinople at the time of the Fourth Crusade, April 1204.

ber 10 and 11. Despite the pope's threat, most members of the army joined the Venetians in attacking the city, which capitulated on November 24. After sacking Zara, the crusaders settled down for the winter. During the interlude a number of dissidents left the army. Some returned home; others made their way independently to the Holy Land.

The remaining **Frankish** (non-Venetian) crusaders were eager to be absolved of the ban of excommunication and sent a legation to Rome to beg papal forgiveness. Innocent accepted their plea that they had acted out of necessity and lifted the ban but only with the understanding that the crusade leaders would make full restitution to the king of Hungary. There is no evidence they ever did so, nor is there any evidence that the pope subsequently pressed the point. Another condition that Innocent placed on their absolution was the leaders' formally swearing never again to attack Christians, save in the most exceptional circumstances and then only with the approval of the pope or his **legate.** They did so, but how sincere their oaths were is open to question.

The Venetian crusaders admitted no wrongdoing and remained excommunicated. Although Christians normally were obliged to shun excommunicated persons, Innocent allowed the army to continue to sail with the Venetians. He had no choice.

The Voyage to Constantinople

Meanwhile, the crusaders' provisions were dwindling, and their funds were exhausted. Help was needed, and apparent help arrived when the crusaders at Zara received emissaries from **Philip of Swabia,** claimant to the throne of Germany, begging the army to help his brother-in-law, Alexius, regain his patrimony. Alexius's father, Emperor **Isaac II** of Constantinople, had been deposed, blinded, and incarcerated by his brother, also named Alexius, who now reigned as Alexius III. Prince Alexius had fled to the West in 1201, where he sought aid. During the 1201 Christmas season Alexius the Younger had met Boniface of Montferrat at Philip's court. Boniface supported his cause and even argued Alexius's case before the pope in 1202 but without success.

Through Philip's emissaries, Prince Alexius promised, in return for the crusaders' help in ousting Alexius III, to place the **Greek** Church under the authority of the **Roman papacy,** to support the crusade with 200,000 marks and provisions for a full year, to raise and supply at his own expense 10,000 mounted soldiers for the crusade, and to maintain for the rest of his life 500 soldiers in the Holy Land.

The army's top military leaders decided they could not refuse such an offer. One factor that weighed heavily in the decision was their belief that this would be a short and safe diversion because the citizens of Constan-tinople would depose the unpopular Alexius III when the rightful heir appeared. Despite the leaders' optimism, most crusaders did not initially favor the diversion to Constantinople. The leaders managed, however, largely through public entreaties and by keeping secret the pope's prohibition of this adventure, to convince the majority of the rank and file to go along with the plan—a plan that involved only a brief stay in Constantinople.

The fleet reached the environs of Constantinople on June 24. Much to the crusaders' consternation and confusion, when they sailed up to the city's walls on July 3 and displayed the young prince, they were met with insults and missiles. It was now clear that they had to risk battle.

On July 6 the army attacked and captured the Tower of Galata, located at the entrance to Constantinople's major harbor, the Golden Horn. This, in turn, enabled the Venetians to break the chain that protected the harbor. Once inside and settled across the harbor from the city, the crusaders' next step was to attack the city walls. A two-pronged attack on July 17 against both the harbor and land walls ended in retreat, but not before the Venetians had taken and held for a while some twenty-five towers along the harbor and set a fire that consumed about 125 acres of the city. Despite his apparent victory, Alexius III had enough. That night he stole away and the city threw its gates open to Prince Alexius, but only after Emperor Isaac II had been reinstalled on his throne.

The crusaders made two demands before they allowed Prince Alexius into the city. Isaac II had to confirm the young man's promises to the crusaders, and he had to crown Alexius as co-emperor. Isaac agreed to the terms. The crusaders camped across the harbor and waited for the two emperors to honor their commitment.

An initial down payment large enough to allow the army to retire its debt to the

Venetians exhausted the imperial treasury, and the co-emperors had to confiscate church treasures to continue to pay off the crusaders. Even this source was inadequate. Alexius IV proposed that the army remain in his service until March 1204 and campaign with him so that he could capture his uncle, secure control over the provinces, and replenish his treasury. The plan made sense to the crusade leaders. With most crusaders remaining in Constantinople as a security force, Alexius and some of the crusade army marched northwest, where they won over a few cities but failed to capture Alexius III. Meanwhile, back in Constantinople disaster was the order of the day.

The Second Capture of Constantinople

Around August 18 a riot broke out in which **Byzantines** attacked and slaughtered a number of Western resident aliens and burned and looted their quarters. The riot probably was a reaction to the hatred that the citizens of Constantinople felt for the crusaders across the harbor whose apparent greed was impoverishing the empire and despoiling its churches. Many survivors of the riot fled to the crusader camp. On August 19 a group of armed Latins, probably refugees and crusaders alike, crossed the Golden Horn and attacked a mosque that stood alongside the harbor. The **Muslims,** assisted by their Byzantine Christian neighbors, put up a stiff resistance. As the Western attackers retreated, they set fires that mushroomed into a single great conflagration. When the flames subsided two days later, about 450 acres within the heart of the city lay in ashes, and approximately 100,000 inhabitants were homeless.

Blame fell on Alexius IV, who had brought the crusaders to the city. Following his return from his expedition in November, he began to distance himself from his crusader patrons, although he continued to depend on them for his precarious hold on the crown. This balancing act of trying to consolidate his power by satisfying both the rabidly anti-Western citizens of Constantinople and the crusaders to whom he was deeply in debt proved impossible.

To complicate matters, Isaac II suffered a mental breakdown, and the inexperienced Alexius IV was on his own. Out of this crisis a new player emerged into prominence, Alexius Ducas, nicknamed Mourzouphlous, the leader of the faction opposed to the Latins.

Eventually Alexius IV was forced to suspend payments to the crusaders, and on December 1 armed conflict broke out between the crusaders and the Byzantines, with deaths on both sides. Hostilities now began in earnest, with the crusaders pillaging the countryside around Constantinople. There is, however, no reason to conclude that the crusaders intended at this time to conquer the city. They wanted to force Alexius to honor his contract or plunder wealth equal to what the emperor owed them. On his part, Alexius seems to have harbored hopes of reestablishing friendly relations with the crusaders. Mourzouphlous had other plans, however.

Following two unsuccessful Byzantine attempts to destroy the Venetian fleet with fire ships and the defeat of an imperial land force led by Alexius Ducas, Alexius IV's popularity plummeted. On January 25, 1204, an urban mob declared Alexius IV deposed. In desperation, he turned to the crusaders for assistance, but Mourzouphlous moved faster. Late at night he seized and imprisoned Alexius IV and declared himself Emperor Alexius V. Shortly after hearing of his son's imprisonment, Isaac II died.

Alexius Ducas was crowned on February 5, and two days later he tried to negotiate a peaceful crusader withdrawal from Constantinople. The crusaders refused, neither trusting Alexius V nor wishing to abrogate their treaty with Alexius IV. On the evening of February 8 Alexius V had the young emperor strangled. With his death, the crusaders had no reason to hope for any accommodation with the Byzantines. Their measured war against Alexius IV now metamorphosed into a full-scale war against Alexius V and the imperial city. The clergy traveling with the army assured the crusaders that they were waging a **just war.**

The first assault on the city came on April 8, when the crusaders attacked the same area of harbor walls that the Venetians had taken and held for a while in July 1203. This time they were beaten back with heavy losses. After resting and refitting, they made another assault on April 12. This time they managed to penetrate the harbor defenses. As evening fell, the crusaders established a precarious forward position within the city. The situation was still very much in doubt, and during the night the crusaders set a defensive fire—the third they visited upon Constantinople in nine months. This last conflagration brought the overall destruction by fire to about one-sixth the total area of the city and one-third of its houses.

During the night Alexius V fled the city, and on the morning of April 13 the crusaders unexpectedly found themselves in uncontested possession of Constantinople. They then subjected the city to three days of brutal **pillage,** and during the second week of May elected Count **Baldwin of Flanders** the new emperor of Constantinople. Baldwin was crowned on May 16, thereby inaugurating the Latin empire of Constantinople, which lasted to 1261. **Related Entries:** Christians, Eastern; Frankish Greece; Second Crusade; Third Crusade.

Suggested Reading

Primary Sources

Alfred J. Andrea, ed. and trans., *Contemporary Sources for the Fourth Crusade* (2000); *The Capture of Constantinople: The "Hystoria Constantinopolitana" of Gunther of Pairis,* trans. and ed. by Alfred J. Andrea (1997); Nicetas Choniates, *O City of Byzantium,* trans. by Harry J. Magoulias (1984); Robert of Clari, *The Conquest of Constantinople,* trans. by Edgar H. McNeal (1936); Geoffrey of Villehardouin, *The Conquest of Constantinople,* trans. by M. R. B. Shaw (1963).

Historical Studies

Michael Angold, *The Fall of Constantinople, 1204: Byzantium, the Fourth Crusade and Its Consequences* (2002) and *The Fourth Crusade* (2004); Charles M. Brand, *Byzantium Confronts the West, 1180–1204* (1968); Thomas F. Madden, *Enrico Dandolo and the Rise of Venice* (2003); Donald E. Queller and Thomas F. Madden, *The Fourth Crusade: The Conquest of Constantinople,* 2nd. ed., (1997).

Francis of Assisi (ca. 1182–1226)

Early thirteenth-century founder of the Franciscans, an order of **mendicant friars** who served as crusade **preachers** in Europe and as **missionaries** among **Muslims, Mongols,** and other non-Christian and non-Western peoples. They were also quite active in the religious life of the **Latin East.** Francis himself briefly participated in the **Fifth Crusade** as a preacher and missionary.

Francis was born into a prosperous textile-merchant family in the central Italian town of Assisi. Baptized Giovanni (John), he acquired the nickname *Francesco* (the Little Frenchman) possibly because of his love of French romantic songs and stories, a love he might have acquired from his mother, Giovanna, who was at least partially French in ancestry. The nickname, as well as the romantic streak, stuck throughout his life.

Early in his life, Francis had dreams of **chivalrous** military adventure and glory. In 1205, he went off to join a **political crusade**

A contemporary fresco portrait of Francis of Assisi following his visit to the monastery of Subiaco in Italy. The parchment in his hand reads "Peace to this house."

called by Pope **Innocent III** against Markward of Anweiler, a supporter of the **Hohenstaufen** family's cause in Italy and Sicily. Francis had not traveled very far before he experienced a voice calling him back to Assisi to pursue a more spiritual form of romantic adventure.

A long period of agonizing religious conversion followed in which Francis struggled to find out what God demanded of him. Finally, he discovered his mission while reflecting on a passage in the Gospel of Matthew, where Jesus commanded the apostles to go out, without any money, possessions, or provisions, and preach the Good News fearlessly, despite whatever persecutions they might encounter. As he did so often in his life, Francis took the words lit-

erally and decided that he must live a life of full and uncompromising poverty and must preach the Gospel of contrition, penance, and reconciliation. He and those who followed him in this mission would own nothing. They would earn by their labor only their daily food and no more. When that failed, they would beg.

In 1210 he and eleven followers traveled to Rome, where Innocent III approved their evangelical way of life. Over the next several years, Francis's fame spread. Hundreds and then thousands flocked to join what was becoming a new religious order, the Order of Friars Minor (the Lesser Brothers), popularly known as the Franciscans.

Francis and his followers initially traveled and preached only in Italy, but Francis never forgot his dream of evangelizing the entire world. In 1212 he attempted to sail to **Syria.** According to Francis's biographer and friend, Brother Thomas of Celano, Francis was motivated by "a desire for holy martyrdom [through] preaching the Christian faith to **Saracens** and **infidels.**" Contrary winds, however, forced Francis back to Italy. The following year, he attempted to go to Morocco, again to preach and seek martyrdom, but illness forced him to abandon his trip in Spain.

In 1219 he succeeded in finding transportation to Egypt and the army of the Fifth Crusade. There in late summer, Francis took advantage of a temporary truce to cross into the camp of Sultan **al-Kamil,** where he and a companion, Brother Illuminatus, endeavored to convert the sultan to Christianity. They were captured by Muslim soldiers, who treated them roughly, but were then escorted to the sultan, who received them graciously. A pious Franciscan legend, which has a ring of authenticity, maintains that Francis offered to walk through fire with only a copy of the Gospels to protect him to prove Christianity's superiority. Al-Kamil, himself a man of spiritual sensitivity, perceived that Francis was a holy man, albeit an infidel. Out of concern for him, the sultan declined the offer and offered Francis and Illuminatus rich gifts, which they declined. He then had them escorted back to the crusader camp.

Francis' example, even though it ended in failure, set the tone for Franciscan missionary activities for centuries to come. As early as 1220, while Francis was in Syria following his sojourn in Egypt, five of his followers suffered martyrdom while trying to convert the Muslims of Morocco.

The Franciscans' largest (and safest) thirteenth-century missions across the seas were in the crusader principalities of **Palestine** and Syria, as well as throughout the **Latin empire of Constantinople.** They set up houses in **Acre, Antioch, Constantinople,** and elsewhere, where they attempted to convert Muslims and **Eastern Christians** alike. Indeed, the Franciscans, and a bit later the other major order of mendicant friars, the **Dominicans,** served as the peaceful element in the thirteenth-century **Roman papacy**'s two-pronged assault against **Islam.** While they continued to preach and bless crusades, popes also supported efforts to convert Muslims to Christianity through the efforts of the friars. Despite their often heroic efforts, however, Franciscan (and Dominican) attempts to convert Islamic unbelievers and schismatic Eastern Christians to the faith of Rome bore disappointing results.

Franciscan friars also served as diplomats to the **Byzantine** emperor-in-exile at **Nicaea,** in a vain effort to repair the breach between the Byzantine Orthodox Church and Rome. Beginning in 1245 and extending into the mid–fourteenth century, Franciscans also traveled far into Central and East Asia to the courts of the Mongol khans, where they unsuccessfully attempted to convert the Mongols to Christianity and seal an alliance with them against Islam.

Many historians have argued that the missionary activities of Francis and his followers reveal a basic Franciscan antipathy toward **holy war,** which sprang from the pacifistic temperament of Francis himself. Such a judgment is based more on sentiment than a sober study of available evidence. According to Thomas of Celano, while at **Damietta,** Francis tried unsuccessfully to dissuade the crusaders from launching a disastrous attack on August 29. Thomas, however, is less than clear regarding Francis's reason for the warning. It seems the saint either thought the day was not propitious or that the crusaders were momentarily unworthy of victory because of their sins. Other sources indicate that Francis praised those who fell in battle against Muslims and considered them holy martyrs. It seems that much like the popes who supported the work of friars and crusaders alike, Francis and his followers considered their missionary activities and their courting of martyrdom through preaching as a complement to the armed struggle against Islam and not as an antithetical alternative. What is more, from about 1234 onward, the Franciscans served as enthusiastic propagandists for the crusades and enlisted tens of thousands, probably hundreds of thousands, of crusaders through their efforts. **Related Entries:** Criticism of Crusades; Gregory IX, Pope.

Frankish Greece (Latin Greece)

The regions of mainland Greece and the islands of the Aegean that fell under **Latin** control.

Upon its capture of **Constantinople** in 1204, the army of the **Fourth Crusade** partitioned about a third of the empire's lands into **feudal** principalities. The two major states to emerge from this distribution of **Byzantine** territories were the kingdom of

The lion of Saint Mark: A symbol of Venetian power on the wall of a harbor castle in Crete.

Thessalonica in northeast Greece and the principality of Achaea, which encompassed central and southern Greece (also known as the Morea) and a number of Aegean Islands. The kingdom of Thessalonica was short-lived, and dead by the end of 1224; the principality of Achaea had a long life, with mainland remnants of it extending down to the mid–fifteenth century and some of its islands remaining in Western hands until the end of the seventeenth century.

During their occupation of Greece and its islands the Latins introduced settlers, especially Italians, into the cities; created a Latin church structure that exploited the native Byzantine Church and failed to win over the **Greek** populace to the Roman Church; and gave out lands to the three major **military orders.** The Western lords and their **knights** also constructed a fair number of **castles** and strongholds. Some thirty towers remain standing today, with the best-preserved example at Markopoulo, about fifteen miles from Athens. **Related Entries:** Constantinople, Latin Empire of; Cyprus; Latin East.

Suggested Reading

Primary Sources

Peter W. Topping, ed. and trans., *Feudal Institutions as Revealed in the Assizes of Romania, The Law Code of Frankish Greece* (1949, reissued 1980); Harold E. Lurier, trans., *Crusaders as Conquerors: The Chronicle of Morea* (1964).

Historical Studies

Eric Forbes-Boyd, *In Crusader Greece: A Tour of the Castles of the Morea* (1964); Peter Lock, *The Franks in the Aegean, 1204–1500*

(1995); Peter Lock and G. D. R. Sanders, *The Archeology of Medieval Greece* (1996); William Miller, *The Latins in the Levant: A History of Frankish Greece (1204–1566)* (1908, reissued 1964); Kenneth M. Setton, *The Papacy and the Levant (1204–1571),* 4 vols. (1978–1985).

Franks

The term generally used to designate all Westerners in the Eastern Mediterranean regardless of their country of origin. To the Arabs, the Franks were *al-Faranj.*

The original Franks were a Germanic people who in the fifth century settled in lands that today comprise France, western Germany, and parts of the Low Countries. By the eleventh century, the western portion of the old Frankish kingdom, which had been known as Western *Francia,* had been transformed into the kingdom of France, and the term *Franci* meant all free inhabitants of France.

The First Crusade was overwhelmingly a French enterprise—called by a French pope and executed mainly by Frenchmen or Frankish Italo-**Normans.** Moreover, most of the crusade's noble leaders claimed descent from the greatest of all Frankish heroes, Charlemagne. It was, therefore, only natural that from the beginning crusaders and those who followed them to the East should be known collectively as Franks. We see this documented as early as 1100–1101 in the title of the anonymous and highly influential crusade account the ***Gesta Francorum*** (*The Deeds of the Franks*). Shortly thereafter, Raymond of Aguilers and Guibert of Nogent entitled their respective **histories** of the same crusade *The History of the Franks Who Captured Jerusalem* and *The Deeds of God through the Franks.*

Such terms die hard. During the sixteenth and seventeenth centuries, Portuguese travelers to India were known as *Faringis,* a Persian variation of the Arabic *al-Faranj*. **Related Entries:** Greeks; Latins; Saracens; *Song of Roland, The.*

Frederick I Barbarossa

See Hohenstaufens; Third Crusade.

Friars, Mendicant

The thirteenth-century Roman Church produced four orders of mendicant friars, or begging brothers: The Order of Friars Minor (the Lesser Brothers), more popularly known as the Franciscans; the Order of Preachers, more popularly known as the **Dominicans;** the **Carmelite** Friars; and the Augustinian, or Austin, Friars.

Friars were not cloistered monks. They were religious brothers who lived in the world among the people to whom they ministered, especially urban populations, and, at least in theory, friars lived lives of total poverty, supporting themselves by their labor or by begging. By the mid–thirteenth century, mendicant friars became **Latin** Christendom's most important tool for **preaching** the crusades and for **missionary** work among unbelievers of every sort, including **Muslims** in Spain and overseas, **Mongols** throughout Asia, **Cathars** and other **heretics** in Western Europe, pagans in the **Baltic,** and **Eastern Christians** throughout the **Latin East.** Of the four orders, the Franciscans and the Dominicans dominated this work, even though the Carmelites originated in the **Latin kingdom of Jerusalem. Related Entries:** Cîteaux, Order of; Francis of Assisi.

Suggested Reading

C. H. Lawrence, *The Friars: The Impact of the Early Mendicant Movement on Western Society* (1994).

Fulcher of Chartres (1059–1127?)

An eyewitness **historian** of the **First Crusade** and the early years of the **Latin kingdom of Jerusalem,** whose account spans the period from 1095 to 1127.

Fulcher, a priest of Chartres in the Île de France, probably was present at the **Council of Clermont,** although nowhere does he claim that distinction. What is certain is that he participated in the second wave of the First Crusade. In 1096, he set out for the East in the company of **Stephen, count of Blois and Chartres** and **Robert, duke of Normandy,** and subsequently became the chaplain of **Baldwin of Boulogne,** who seized the principality of **Edessa** in 1098. Fulcher accompanied Baldwin from Edessa to **Jerusalem** in 1100 when his lord became King Baldwin I. Probably a year later, in 1101, Fulcher began to compose the *Historia Hierosolymitana* (*The Jerusalem History*), a history of the crusade and the subsequent fortunes of the Latin kingdom of Jerusalem. He carried his history down to 1127, apparently the year of his death. Because his account of Urban's speech appears at the beginning of his history, we can be reasonably sure that he set it down in or around 1101. Some historians have concluded that Fulcher consulted a now-lost copy of the decrees of the council as he turned to composing his history. **Related Entries:** *Deus Vult; Gesta Francorum;* William of Tyre.

Suggested Reading

Primary Source

Fulcher of Chartres, *A History of the Expedition to Jerusalem, 1095–1127,* trans. by Frances Rita Ryan (1969).

Fulk of Anjou

Count of Anjou, Touraine, and Maine, **king of Jerusalem** (r. 1131–1143) by virtue of his marriage to Queen **Melisende,** father of **Baldwin III** (r. 1143–1163) and **Amalric** (r. 1163–1174), and great-grandfather of **Richard I the Lionheart** through a son by his first marriage, Geoffrey of Anjou.

In 1109 Fulk V assumed authority over Anjou, one of the most powerful and richest counties of France. In 1120 he went on crusade to the **Holy Land,** returning in 1122. Before he left **Outremer,** Fulk provided for the full expenses for one year of 100 knights to serve in defense of the kingdom. This involved a considerable outlay of money and won for Fulk prestige and a reputation for piety. Also while in the East, Fulk became associated with the emerging **Order of the Temple.**

Fulk, therefore, was a mature ruler and someone who already had earned a reputation for being a vigorous defender of the kingdom of Jerusalem when King **Baldwin II** dispatched envoys to him in 1127–1128 proposing that Fulk, a widower, marry Baldwin's eldest daughter and heiress, Melisende, and participate in a planned crusade against **Damascus.** Baldwin, whose wife had recently died and who had no intention of remarrying, had four daughters and no sons and looked to Fulk to continue the royal line of succession.

Fulk accepted both offers. He arrived with a large force in the **Latin East** in late May 1129 and married Melisende that same month. In November he participated in the ill-fated **Damascus Crusade.** For the next three years he loyally assisted his father-in-law, who educated him in the ways of kingship. During this time Fulk also served as lord of **Acre** and **Tyre.**

On his deathbed on August 21, 1131, King Baldwin named Melisende, Fulk, and their infant son Baldwin as his joint successors, meaning that Melisende and Fulk would be co-monarchs until Baldwin III came of age. On September 14, 1131, the feast day of the Exaltation of the Holy Cross, Melisende and Fulk were crowned in the **Church of the Holy Sepulcher** in Jerusalem, a break from the tradition established by **Baldwin I** to have the king crowned in Bethlehem.

Fulk proved to be a strong king who succeeded in extending royal power and prerogatives within and beyond the frontiers of the kingdom. He quashed several internal rebellions by overly ambitious **vassals,** and in 1132 he intervened successfully in a dispute over succession to the principality of **Antioch,** a struggle that resulted in his taking the field and defeating Pons, the count of **Tripoli.** Later that same year, Fulk led an army north to defend both Tripoli and Antioch from a **Muslim** invasion.

Despite all of his strengths, Fulk was defeated in his early attempt to dismiss Melisende's claims to coequal monarchic rights. Supported by a good percentage of the barons of the kingdom, Melisende won the day and succeeded in exerting her authority.

Early on, Fulk faced two major Muslim enemies, **Zangi,** the *atabeg* (governor) of **Mosul** and **Aleppo,** and the city of Damascus. Luckily for the kingdom of Jerusalem, Zangi considered Damascus a rival that he intended to conquer, and his **siege** of the city in 1139 drove the Damascenes into an alliance with Fulk. As a result of the alliance, Damascus and Jerusalem combined forces in 1140 to drive Zangi away from the key town of Banyas, which controlled access to both cities.

Granted breathing room on his northern frontier by this victory and his alliance with Damascus, Fulk was then free to strengthen his southern frontier fortifications.

Fulk died at the age of fifty-three in a hunting accident on November 10 (or 13), 1143. With his death, the kingdom lost an able warrior and diplomat whose reign had made the kingdom more secure and stable.

Because Baldwin III was only thirteen, the equally able and vigorous Melisende took over sole control of the government. **Related Entries:** Crusader States; Second Crusade; William of Tyre.

Fulk of Neuilly

A university-educated priest from Neuilly-sur-Marne, a town near Paris, who became one of the most popular evangelical preachers of late twelfth-century France and the most famous **preacher** of the **Fourth Crusade.**

Born sometime in the 1160s, Fulk was a fellow student of **James of Vitry** at the University of Paris, where he studied theology. While at Paris Fulk began to realize his abilities as a public preacher of moral reform. Moral reform, evangelical piety, and the crusades were inextricably linked themes, and Fulk played all three. From 1195 to his death in May 1202 Fulk wandered through northern France, Flanders, and Champagne attacking a number of perceived vices, especially prostitution, clerical sexual incontinence, and usury. The last of these targets led him into fulminations against the **Jews.**

In 1198, if not before, he began preaching the crusade and collecting funds to **finance** it. In September 1198 Fulk traveled to **Cîteaux** seeking help from the Cistercians, but was rebuffed. Two months later, Pope **Innocent III,** who had heard Fulk preach during his own student days at Paris, gave him permission to enlist monks and other religious in his mission. When Fulk returned to Cîteaux in September 1201 he had both papal support and a record of success, and the Cistercians could no longer deny his request for help. According to contemporary accounts, thousands took the **cross** from Fulk. Most were not **knights** or professional soldiers of other ranks, and how many of them actually undertook the crusade is anyone's guess. In addition to the masses, Fulk's activities also apparently influenced such nobles as Thibault of Champagne to assume the cross, and with their enlistment, the crusade truly got under way.

Fulk's death in May 1202 came as a great shock to the crusaders, but there was now no stopping the momentum of the crusade. At least some of the money that he raised reached the **Holy Land** through the agency of the Cistercians, where it was used to repair fortifications destroyed in an earthquake of 1202. Notwithstanding, a scandal erupted charging that much of this money had been criminally misdirected. **Related Entries:** Oliver of Paderborn; Peter the Hermit.

Suggested Reading

John M. O'Brien, *Fulk of Neuilly* (1969).

G

German Crusade (1197–1198)

The German Crusade of 1197–1198, organized by Emperor **Henry VI,** can be considered the last wave of the **Third Crusade.** Although Henry died in Sicily and never reached the **Holy Land,** substantial numbers of Germans landed at **Acre** between May and late September 1197 and reoccupied the port cities of Sidon and Beirut.

Frederick I had entrusted governance of his vast German-Italian empire to his twenty-three-year-old son Henry, when the aged emperor left on the **Third Crusade.** Upon Frederick's death in **Anatolia** in 1190, Henry succeeded to the throne. In addition to his lands in Central Europe and northern Italy, Henry was married to Constance, heiress of the **Norman** kingdom of Sicily, which included southern Italy, as well as the island of Sicily. Money gained from the ransom of King **Richard I** enabled Henry to secure the crown of Sicily for himself in November 1194.

With the expiration of the three-year, eight-month truce that **Richard I** and **Saladin** had pledged in 1192, Henry began to think of completing the crusade that his father's and brother's deaths had cut short.

Henry also harbored the ambition of extending his imperial influence into the East and possibly even dreamed of conquering the **Byzantine empire.**

If so, this dream was secondary to his first priority—solidifying his hold on the kingdom of Sicily and gaining the **Roman papacy's** acquiescence to his wearing the Sicilian crown. Given its troubled history with Frederick I, the papacy feared Henry's simultaneous control of northern and southern Italy because he surrounded Rome and the papal lands of central Italy. By going on crusade, Henry could possibly allay the papacy's fears of his intentions and gain papal support of his imperial ambitions.

Henry assumed the **crusader's cross** while in southern Italy during Easter Week of 1195 and pledged to support 3,000 mounted **mercenaries** for a full year of crusade campaigning. In June he left for Germany to promote the crusade, and on August 1, 1195, Pope Celestine III authorized the crusade and instructed the clergy of Germany to **preach** it.

The German response was enthusiastic, and thousands flocked to the cross. Meanwhile, in late 1196 Henry's envoys reached the court of **Constantinople,** where they pressured Emperor Alexius III to contribute a large sum of gold toward the costs of the crusade. The financially strapped emperor had to resort to levying a special tax, the *Alamanikon* (the German tax), and to plundering imperial tombs to raise the requisite 1,600 pounds of gold. But even those expedients failed to yield the necessary gold. Luckily for Emperor Alexius, Emperor Henry's ill health soon made moot payment of this extorted protection money.

A large German army arrived in **Syria-Palestine** piecemeal from ports in southern Italy and Sicily between May and late September 1197. Henry's ill health, however, and problems in Sicily prevented his leading the army overseas. On September 28 the emperor died of fever. Unaware of the emperor's death, the army, under the command of the duke of Brabant, occupied the abandoned and destroyed port city of Sidon. From there it marched to Beirut, which it also found abandoned and in ruins.

Before leaving Beirut, the army began to hear rumors of Henry's death, but it still moved on to the city of Toron, which it besieged, beginning on November 28. Before the crusaders could capture the city, news of the approach of an Egyptian army and the mounting fears of the crusade's leaders regarding the state of their holdings and offices back home, now that the emperor was dead, caused the army to break up. Henry had left behind an infant son, **Frederick (II),** and there was sure to be a fight for the imperial crown.

In March 1198 the bulk of the crusaders embarked for Europe, correctly fearful that a raging civil war awaited them at home. It was left to the new **king of Jerusalem, Aimery of Lusignan,** to make peace with **al-Adil (Saphadin).** A truce of five years and eight months, concluded on July 1, ceded Beirut to the kingdom. **Related Entries:** Fourth Crusade; Hohenstaufens.

Gesta Francorum (The Deeds of the Franks)

An anonymous history of the **First Crusade** composed by a **feudal** vassal of **Bohemond of Taranto,** who surveys events from the **Council of Clermont** in November 1095 to the Battle of **Ascalon** in August 1099.

The Deeds of the Franks and the Other Jerusalem Pilgrims (to give it its full title) was completed no later than early 1101 and possibly before 1100, making it the first and, therefore, an especially important eyewitness account of the First Crusade. Contemporaries appreciated its value to the point that it served as a major source for a good number of early twelfth-century histories of the crusade. Three **historians**—Robert of Rheims, Baldric of Dol, and Guibert of Nogent—openly claimed that they recast the *Gesta,* whose style they judged primitive, into a form that was more polished, more intellectually elevated, and more worthy of the crusade's great events.

The *Gesta* is certainly rustic, even artless in style, but that provides much of its charm. Beyond that, its tone and vision remind the reader of *The Song of Roland.* Very much like that epic, the author admires the bravery of his **Muslim** enemies but assumes that they are perfidiously wrong. To his mind, all Muslims are polytheistic pagans and deserve death for their sins, whereas Christians who die in this **holy war** are martyrs.

The *Gesta*'s value lies in the fact that its author, a pious **Norman** warrior from southern Italy, provides a view of the crusade from the ranks of Bohemond's knights. As such, he fought in early key battles and was one of a small band of men chosen to lead the way into **Antioch** in a night assault. He writes partisan history in which Bohemond plays a hero's role, but all of the other noble lords of the crusade are equally heroic (except for the cowardly **Stephen of Blois**), as are the brave Christian **pilgrim**-soldiers who follow them.

The **Byzantine** emperor, **Alexius I,** is another matter. The author shows nothing but contempt for Alexius, whom he characterizes as anti-Western, devious, and deceitful. The Western notion that the **Greeks** were false Christians and enemies of the crusade certainly finds early expression in these pages.

The author's high opinion of Bohemond did not prevent his leaving Bohemond's service at Antioch, marching with the main body of the army to **Jerusalem** (probably in the company of Bohemond's nephew **Tancred**), and participating in all of the army's trials and triumphs along the way. As a result, we have a vivid, compelling picture of the final campaign to win and secure Jerusalem, and it is a picture that is unsurpassed by the more rhetorically artful accounts of the historians who tried to improve upon the *Gesta*'s plain, straightforward style. **Related Entries:** Anna Comnena; Christians, Eastern; Chronicles; Franks; Fulcher of Chartres.

Suggested Reading

Rosalind Hill, ed. and trans., *The Deeds of the Franks and the Other Pilgrims to Jerusalem* (1962).

Godfrey of Bouillon

Duke of Lower Lorraine (r. 1087–1100), a leader of the **First Crusade,** and ruler of **Jerusalem** (r. 1099–1100). In medieval crusade lore, Duke Godfrey was memorialized as the ideal crusader.

Godfrey was about thirty-five years of age when he set off for the East in mid-August 1096 from his duchy of Lower Lorraine (essentially modern southern Belgium

and portions of northeastern France and northwestern Germany) accompanied by his younger brother **Baldwin of Boulogne,** another relative, **Baldwin of Le Bourcq,** and a large army of Lorrainers, French, and Germans. To **finance** his expedition, he mortgaged and sold vast amounts of his lands, including the county and castle of Bouillon, which he used to secure a loan from the bishop of Liége.

Godfrey was a better than average leader. His army, which was the second largest of all the crusade contingents (the largest being that of **Raymond of Saint-Gilles**), set off at the time appointed by Pope **Urban II,** and it passed through Hungary almost without incident, arriving at **Constantinople** on December 23—the first crusader army to reach the city. The march of about 1,500 miles in around 130 days was a remarkable feat.

Godfrey initially refused to take an oath of fealty to Emperor **Alexius I,** which resulted in an armed clash between **Byzantine** forces and Godfrey's crusaders, who came off second best. Consequently, on January 20, 1097, he took the oath. A month later he and his followers were shipped across the Bosporus to **Anatolia.**

On April 30 Godfrey's forces led the way on the march to Nicaea, which they reached on May 6. During the **siege** that ensued, Godfrey performed with conspicuous bravery. After the city's capitulation, Godfrey's forces again led the way, this time toward **Antioch,** setting out from Nicaea on June 26. At the **Battle of Dorylaeum** of July 1, he fought boldly and bravely and was instrumental in helping turn the tide in favor of the crusaders. During the seven-and-a-half-month siege of **Antioch,** which began on October 21, Godfrey's forces occupied one of the key positions, and he fought with his usual élan when the crusaders sallied out of the captured city on June 28, 1098, and routed the besieging **Muslim** army. During the period of rest and refitment that followed, Godfrey led his forces into nearby areas, where he engaged in numerous battles. Godfrey and his followers likewise played a key role in the siege and capture of **Jerusalem.** On July 15, 1099, the Lorrainers were the first to reach the top of the city's north wall and led the assault into the city.

On July 22 the crusade leaders set about choosing a ruler for Jerusalem. Their initial choice was Duke Godfrey's rival, Count Raymond of Saint-Gilles, to whom they offered a royal crown. When he refused it, for reasons that are not clear, their choice fell on Godfrey. The sources are unclear as to Godfrey's title, but he seems to have been given, then or before the year was over, the title "defender of the **Holy Sepulcher**," a title that would not offend the clergy. Whatever his title, Godfrey was virtual king of Jerusalem, and later generations considered him the kingdom's first monarch.

As ruler of the city and its environs, Godfrey marshaled his forces to meet and defeat an Egyptian army at **Ascalon** on August 12, thereby securing the crusaders' hold on the Holy City. For the remainder of the year and for half of the next, Godfrey attempted, with some success, to strengthen and expand the new **crusader state** of Jerusalem, despite the small force left to him after most surviving crusaders returned home. Early in June 1100 Godfrey fell ill, and he died on July 18. He was buried in the Church of the Holy Sepulcher at the foot of the altar of Mount Calvary. He had ruled Jerusalem for one year less four days. In that year he had put a struggling state on its feet and laid the basis for the successive strong rules of his brother Baldwin (I) of Boulogne and his cousin Baldwin (II) of Le Bourcq. **Related Entries:** Eustace III of Boulogne; Jerusalem, Kingdom of; Investiture Controversy.

Suggested Reading

John C. Andressohn, *The Ancestry and Life of Godfrey of Bouillon* (1947).

Great German Pilgrimage of 1064–1065

A **pilgrimage** to the **Holy Land** that foreshadowed the creation of the armed pilgrimage, or crusade, thirty years later.

The Great German Pilgrimage of 1064–1065 probably included more than 7,000 men and **women,** rich and poor, accompanied by their priests and several bishops. Clearly, at least some of the pilgrims were motivated by **apocalyptic** hopes and fears. Believing that the Day of Judgment would occur on Easter, March 27, 1065, they wanted to be in **Jerusalem** to greet the Second Coming of Christ. Given this mind-set and in concert with the most ancient traditions of pilgrimage, the pilgrims were unarmed, having embarked on a journey of inner peace. Moreover, within the Western Christian tradition, pilgrimages were a normal means of atoning for sins of violence, especially murder, and carrying arms was antithetical to that purpose. On March 25, 1065, however, while only miles from Jerusalem, the pilgrim band was set upon by Arab bandits. A large number of pilgrims refused to resist, and quite a few of them were killed. The survivors resorted to defending themselves with stones and captured weapons, until they managed to secure a guarantee of safe conduct from the local emir—in exchange for a hefty sum of gold. With their ranks depleted, on April 12 the pilgrims finally entered Jerusalem, which had not, in the meanwhile, witnessed Christ's Second Coming. There they spent thirteen days in their devotions. Their pilgrimage goal attained, they set out for home. If we can believe the **chroniclers,** fewer than 2,000 made it all the way back to Germany.

The events surrounding the Great German Pilgrimage suggest several conclusions. First, pilgrimages to Jerusalem were growing in size as the eleventh century progressed. Second, even before the Battle of **Manzikert** and the rise of the **Seljuk** empire, pilgrims to **Palestine** could expect harassment and even attack. Third, the fact that some German pilgrims felt justified in abandoning the tradition of nonviolence and nonresistance while on pilgrimage foreshadowed **Urban II**'s creation of a new phenomenon thirty years later at **Clermont**—the armed pilgrimage, or crusade. **Related Entries:** Relics; Santiago de Compostela.

Suggested Reading

J. Wilkinson, *Jerusalem Pilgrims before the Crusades* (1977).

Greeks

What Western Europeans called **Byzantines.**

The Byzantines never called themselves anything but *Romaioi* (Romans) because they considered themselves the true heirs of Roman imperial legitimacy and viewed **Constantinople** as *New Rome*. To Westerners, however, the inhabitants of this empire were Greeks by reason of the fact that the official language of Constantinople was Greek, even though the empire was multilingual—at least until its borders were severely circumscribed after the late eleventh century. **Related Entries:** Christians, Eastern; Franks; Latins.

Gregory VII, Pope (r. 1073–1085)

The pope in whose reign the **Investiture Controversy** began and the first pope to articulate a plan for an armed expedition to the East to save fellow Christians from the onslaught of the **Turks.**

Gregory VII was a militant champion of moral reform and a defender of the **Roman papacy**'s claims to universal jurisdiction over the Church, who did not shrink from threatening and using violence against those whom he judged to be enemies of Righteousness. In 1073, two years after the disaster at **Manzikert,** Emperor Michael VII appealed to Pope Gregory for aid against the **Seljuks.** In February 1074 Gregory sent a letter to Count William of Burgundy urging him to send troops to Italy to defend papal lands against the **Normans.** Gregory went on to note that once the Normans were pacified, he hoped to "cross over to **Constantinople** to aid the Christians who are oppressed by frequent **Saracen** attacks." The following month the pope issued a general summons to all **Latin** Christians to aid their siblings in the East. On December 7, 1074, Pope Gregory informed King Henry IV of Germany that already 50,000 men stood ready, *if they could have Gregory as their leader,* "to take up arms against the enemies of God and push forward *even to the Lord's Sepulcher.*" Gregory further informed Henry that, if God granted him his wish to lead this army to the East, he wanted Henry to remain behind to defend the Church. Nothing immediate came of this plan. By December 1075 Gregory was upbraiding Henry for his unwillingness to support the papal program of reform, and in February 1076 he excommunicated the king. The Investiture Controversy had begun, and it would consume Gregory for the rest of his life.

The idea of armed intervention in aid of **Eastern Christians** was not forgotten by the papacy, however. It remained for Gregory's successor-once-removed, **Urban II,** to transform the idea into a mass movement. **Related Entries:** Clermont, Council of; Great German Pilgrimage of 1064–1065; Peace and Truce of God.

Suggested Reading

Primary Source

The Register of Gregory VII, 1073–1085: An English Translation, trans. by H. E. J. Cowdrey (2002).

Historical Study

H. E. J. Cowdrey, *Pope Gregory VII: 1073–1085* (1998).

Gregory IX, Pope (r. 1227–1241)

A kinsman of Pope **Innocent III,** Gregory is noted for his support of the **mendicant friars,** his use of them as crusade **preachers** and as a special force against **heresy,** his calling of the **Crusade of 1239–1241,** and his struggles with **Frederick II.** Beginning in 1234, Gregory IX transformed the Franciscans and the **Dominicans** into propagandists for all major and most minor crusades—a position they held for the rest of the century and well beyond. **Related Entries:** Hohenstaufens; Political Crusades.

Gregory X, Pope (r. 1271–1276)

Teobaldo Visconti, who assumed the pontifical name Gregory X, focused his pontificate on the spiritual renewal of Christendom, the reunification of all Christians, and the security of the **Holy Land.**

Teobaldo was in **Acre** with Prince **Edward (I)** of England on the **Eighth Crusade,** when word reached him that he had been elected pope. The new pope rushed back to Italy, but not before he dispatched three Venetian merchants, Niccolò, Maffeo, and Marco Polo, and two **Dominican** friars to the court of Kublai, the Great Khan of the **Mongols,** in northern China in the hope of establishing diplomatic contact with the khan and a **mission** church in his lands.

Teobaldo hoped that through these efforts he might also enlist the help of Mongol forces in the **Middle East** against the **Mamluks** of Egypt, who threatened the very existence of the **crusader states.**

In 1274 Pope Gregory presided over the Second Council of Lyons, where he called for a new crusade and mandated the Roman Church's most ambitious and heaviest crusade tax to date: one-tenth of all clerical income for a period of six years was to be set aside for the crusade. The crusade was never realized, and how much money was actually raised is anyone's guess.

Believing, as his predecessors had, that lack of success in the Holy Land was a direct result of **Latin** Christians' sinful unworthiness, the pope also excoriated the assembled church leaders at the **council.** Calling them the bane of Christendom, he threatened that if they did not reform themselves, he would do so. Time ran out before the pope could implement his reforms. Whether or not they would have been effective was another issue, given the deep involvement of church leaders in the political affairs of their day, especially the issue of what was to be done with the remains of the **Hohenstaufen** empire.

Because the emperor of the restored **Byzantine empire,** Michael VIII Palaeologus, feared the Mediterranean ambitions of **Charles of Anjou,** Gregory was able to convince Emperor Michael to send envoys to the council at Lyons to discuss reunion of the **Greek** and Latin Churches. Under pressure from their emperor, the ambassadors agreed to accept the pope's authority. Although the council triumphantly announced an end to the schism in July 1274, the triumph was a mirage. The patriarch of **Constantinople,** who had not attended the council, denounced the emperor's "treason" against the Orthodox faith, as did the vast majority of the clergy and people of the empire. The Greeks could never forget nor forgive the **Fourth Crusade** and its aftermath. Emperor Michael found himself unable to deliver the promised reunion of Churches, despite his best attempts, and for his failure he found himself excommunicated by Pope Martin IV in 1281. Pope Martin, a Frenchman and undisguised supporter of Charles of Anjou, probably welcomed the opportunity. Excommunicated by Rome, Michael was also spurned by Constantinople. When the emperor died in 1282, he was denied Christian burial by the Byzantine Church.

These three failures, which owed much to Pope Gregory X's death in January 1274, could not overshadow his one diplomatic victory. Fearing Charles of Anjou almost as much as Michael VIII did, the pope worked to establish a balance of power in Italy, and to that end he engineered the election of Rudolph of Hapsburg as Western emperor on October 1, 1273. **Related Entries:** Criticism of Crusades; Financing the Crusades; Latin Empire of Constantinople.

Suggested Reading

Deno J. Geanakoplos, *Emperor Michael Palaeologus and the West, 1258–1282: A Study in Byzantine-Latin Relations* (1959).

Guy of Lusignan

King of **Jerusalem** (r. 1186–1190), participant in the **Third Crusade,** and ruler of **Cyprus** (r. 1192–1194).

Guy, a native of Poitou and recent arrival in the **Holy Land,** married **Sibylla,** sister of King **Baldwin IV,** in 1180, with the consent of the king and probably the connivance of **Agnes of Courtenay,** Sibylla's mother. Guy and his brother **Aimery** were favorites of Agnes, the power behind the throne and an accomplished intriguer. In August 1183, the grievously ill Baldwin IV appointed Guy his **bailli,** or regent, to meet a new threat posed by **Saladin.** A few

months later King Baldwin removed Guy from the regency, convinced that he was not suited to rule the kingdom and lead its armies. According to **William of Tyre,** who knew Guy well: "He was unequal in strength and wisdom to the great burden he had taken upon himself." Baldwin was so disappointed with Guy that he contemplated having Guy's marriage with Sibylla annulled to exclude him from the line of royal succession. Because Sibylla refused to cooperate, the marriage remained intact, but King Baldwin excluded Guy from succession to the throne when he crowned his nephew Baldwin, Sibylla's son, as co-monarch in November 1183. On his part, Guy refused to cooperate further with the king and publicly defied his authority. Only the intervention of Patriarch Heraclius and the masters of the **Temple** and the **Hospital** prevented a civil war.

The boy-king succeeded his uncle as sole monarch in 1185, and Guy remained outside the circle of royal power during the brief reign of his stepson. When **Baldwin V** died in 1186, Sibylla was the logical and legal successor. The question was: What about Guy? Because Guy polarized the barons, Sibylla agreed to leave him as a condition for her coronation as queen. The precedent was her father, **Amalric,** who had to consent to the dissolution of his marriage to Agnes of Courtenay before he was crowned king. Sibylla's coronation took place in either August or September 1186. On that day she received the crown and then confounded Guy's detractors by bestowing a second one on him. The annulment of the marriage had never taken place nor would it. Guy was now king, but in less than a year he would be a captive king.

Because King Guy was unable to convince or compel **Reynald of Châtillon** to return plunder that he had acquired in an illegal raid, Saladin declared war on the kingdom. The result was the **Battle of Hattin,** a disaster that owed much to Guy's incompetent generalship, and the king's capture on July 4, 1187. Saladin released Guy in the summer of 1188 upon his oath that he would cross the sea and never again bear arms against him. Guy soon secured release from his oath on the grounds that it had been made under compulsion and to an **infidel.** He and Sibylla then set about trying to restore their royal authority and to regain lost portions of the kingdom.

Conrad of Montferrat, the defender of **Tyre** and Sibylla's brother-in-law by a previous marriage, refused them entry into his city when they appeared there in late 1188. Rebuffed then and again in April 1189, Guy gathered a small army of recently arrived reinforcements from Europe, including his brother Geoffrey, and of barons and **knights** from the kingdom. On August 27, 1189, the king and his outnumbered force took up a position before **Acre,** determined to dig in and await further relief from overseas. Saladin was taken totally by surprise, and by the time he acted it was too late. The **siege** of Acre was under way. By this act of daring, Guy had reasserted his military command and moral authority over the Latin forces of his kingdom. The surrender of Acre on July 13, 1191, and subsequent successes of the armies of the Third Crusade, which rewon and restabilized much of the **Palestinian** coast, owed much to Guy's almost quixotic counterattack at Acre. He might have lacked many qualities of leadership, but he did not lack courage and élan.

During the summer of 1190 Sibylla and their two daughters, Alice and Mary, died, and with their deaths Guy lost clear title to two claims: the crown and a regency in the name of his daughter. The principle of hereditary succession dictated that the person next in line for the throne was Sibylla's half-sister,

Isabella (I). Against her will, Isabella was forced to see her marriage to the handsome but weak Humphrey of Toron annulled and her hand given to Conrad of Montferrat, who now claimed the crown by virtue of his marriage.

Perhaps because of his heroic actions at Acre, Guy enjoyed wide support among the baronage in 1190 and refused to surrender the throne. The matter was referred to the crusader kings, **Philip II** and **Richard I the Lionheart,** who arrived at Acre in the spring of 1191. Philip favored Conrad, a kinsman, and Richard favored Guy, one of his French vassals. A compromise was reached at a meeting of the **High Court** in July 1191, whereby Guy would retain the crown for the rest of his life, and Conrad would be acknowledged as his heir. Meanwhile, Conrad would serve as lord of Tyre, Sidon, and Beirut.

Conrad was not happy with the agreement and worked to woo Guy's baronial supporters to his side. By April 1192, as King Richard was preparing to leave the Holy Land, it was clear that Guy's support had largely vanished. Sensing this, King Richard asked the lords and knights of the High Court to name the leader whom they would follow in a continuing crusade. They unanimously chose Conrad, and Richard assented. Conrad was now king-elect, and Guy was out of luck.

Conrad's assassination on April 28, 1192, did not change Guy's luck. On May 5, 1192, **Henry of Champagne** married the widowed Isabella I and became lord of Jerusalem (even though Jerusalem was in **Muslim** hands). Guy's fortunes did change for the better, however, when the Templars, to whom King Richard had given the island of Cyprus, sold it to Guy in May 1192. Still calling himself king of Jerusalem, Guy repaired to Cyprus with a number of his supporters. Guy served as lord of the island for two years, dying in 1194. He was succeeded as lord and later king of Cyprus by his brother Aimery, who in 1197 was called to Acre to marry the twice-widowed Isabella I and assume the kingship upon the death of Henry of Champagne. The family of Lusignan now had its revenge. **Related Entries:** Prisoners; Women.

Suggested Reading

Robert L. Nicholson, *Joscelyn III and the Fall of the Crusader States, 1134–1199* (1973).

H

Hattin, Battle of (July 4, 1187)

The battle at the Horns of Hattin, a twin-peaked, extinct volcanic cone near the city of Tiberas in the Galilee, where **Saladin** crushed an army led by King **Guy of Lusignan.**

To counter the danger presented by Saladin, who had declared his peace treaty with the **kingdom of Jerusalem** null and void, King Guy assembled the largest force ever put into the field by the **Franks** of **Outremer**—around 20,000 warriors, of whom only ten percent or fewer were heavily

The Horns of Hattin.

armored **knights.** To raise such an army, the lords of Outremer had to enlist the services of most able-bodied men in the **crusader states,** as well as employing the services of about 4,000 **Turcopole** light **cavalry.** Facing them was a **Muslim** army whose horsemen alone numbered around 13,000.

The battle began with skirmishes on July 3 after the Franks abandoned a prime strategic position with plentiful water to aid the **besieged** defenders of Tiberas. Forced to halt for the night after a march that saw them deplete their meager stores of water, the Franks took up positions on the plain. The next day, still without water, they resumed their march toward the springs of Hattin, fighting every foot of the way the enemy that encircled them. Finally the heat, maddening thirst, and an increasing breakdown of discipline forced the crusaders to take up defensive positions on the waterless slopes of the Horns of Hattin, far from the springs they sought. Their position was untenable. The enemy set brush fires to add to the Franks' misery, advanced behind this covering smokescreen, and cut down the **Latins** singly and in isolated groups. Breakout was now the Franks' only hope. Several desperate charges into the ranks of the enemy were beaten back with heavy losses, with only a handful managing to break through to safety. Crusader dead littered the hillside, and the survivors were taken captive.

Saladin treated King Guy and all but one of the other captive lords with courtesy but struck down with his own hand **Reynald of Châtillon,** who had broken the peace accord. Except for the captured Master of the Temple, whose life he spared, Saladin, as was his custom, ordered the beheading of all captive **Templars** and **Hospitalers** because he saw them as fanatical and implacable enemies of **Islam.** The Order of the Temple, alone, lost some 230 knights that day. Captured Turcopoles suffered the same fate of

summary execution because Saladin viewed them as traitors to Islam. The rest of the captives were treated according to rank and wealth. The well-to-do were held for ransom; the poor were **enslaved.** Also captured that day was a large piece of the **True Cross.** It was never recovered, despite subsequent **Latin** attempts to negotiate its return.

The defeat was a catastrophe for the Franks because it denuded the Latin states of most of their fighting men and made possible Saladin's triumphal march through **Syria-Palestine.** Fifty-two cities and castles surrendered to him, including **Acre** on July 10 and **Jerusalem** on October 2. Saladin was now at the apogee of his career and appeared to be on the brink of achieving his dream of rooting out from lands sacred to Islam every last Frankish Christian enclave. In the face of this crisis, the West roused itself to launch a new grand crusade, the **Third Crusade. Related Entries:** Balian II of Ibelin; Chivalry; Massacres; Prisoners.

Suggested Reading

Marshall W. Baldwin, *Raymond III of Tripolis and the Fall of Jerusalem (1140–1187)* (1936); David Nicolle, *Hattin 1187: Saladin's Greatest Victory* (1993).

Henry of Champagne

Count of Champagne and count-palatine of Troyes (r. 1181–1197), husband of Queen **Isabella I,** and lord of **Jerusalem** (r. 1192–1197).

Henry, the most powerful baron of France and nephew of **Richard I the Lion-heart** and **Philip II** of France, arrived with a large force before **Acre** in July 1190 in the early stages of the **Third Crusade.** His arrival forced **Saladin**'s retreat and ensured the eventual success of the **siege.** After King Philip left the crusade army to return to France, Henry stayed on to campaign with

King Richard, whom he served as a trusted and valuable lieutenant.

Following **Conrad of Montferrat**'s assassination in April 1192, the barons of the kingdom implored Henry to marry the widowed queen, and she assented. King Richard I gave his blessing to the union, and the marriage took place almost immediately. Possibly because King **Guy of Lusignan** was still alive and considered himself king-in-exile, Henry refused the title of king, contenting to refer to himself as count-palatine of Troyes. Notwithstanding, he proved to be an effective ruler and skilled diplomat. He reasserted the kingdom's hegemony over the county of **Antioch** and managed to play off against one another the various **Ayyubid** factions. Henry was also a first-rate warrior. Early in the **German Crusade of 1197,** he saved the encircled German crusaders, who had blundered into an impossible situation. Following that he prepared to march to **Jaffa,** which was under attack by the forces of **al-Adil.** Before he could act, Henry accidentally fell out of a tower window in Acre (Jerusalem was now in **Muslim** hands) and died on September 10, 1197. With his death, the kingdom lost a valued leader. On her part, Queen Isabella turned to **Aimery of Lusignan,** whom she married and made king in October. **Related Entry:** Alice of Champagne.

Henry VI

See German Crusade; Hohenstaufens.

Heretics

Persons who profess a deviant form of the official or mainstream faith.

The word *heresy* derives from a Greek word that means "to choose." In theory, heretics have chosen to espouse a *heterodox* (contrary thinking), as opposed to an *orthodox* (correct thinking), version of a particular religion. In brief, heretics are not **infidels** or pagans; they are people who, in the eyes of the leaders of an established religion, believe in a corrupted form of the faith. Heretics are also not *schismatics*. A person in schism is separated from the disciplinary authority of the established church or faith but accepts all of that faith's core doctrines.

When **Urban II** called for the rescue of **Eastern Christians** in 1095, he probably envisioned them as schismatics, but crusaders soon discovered that many Christians of the East held doctrines that were considered heretical in the West. That was not true of the **Greek,** or **Byzantine** Church, in 1095. Although the Churches of Rome and **Constantinople** had two quite different notions of how the Church was governed, they agreed on all major points of doctrine. As time went by, however, they came to see each other as not just schismatics but as heretics. That was partly due to increasing emphasis on papal primacy in the West. An equally if not more significant factor was the growing distrust and animosity between both cultures that the early crusades engendered. By the time of the **Fourth Crusade,** many crusaders were all too willing to believe their clerics who told them that the Greeks were "the enemies of God," as Robert of Clari remembered being so instructed.

The first crusaders thought that **Muslims** were polytheistic, idol-worshipping pagans, and that notion never was fully corrected, as ***The Song of Roland*** bears witness. Yet, as some crusaders and **settlers** in the East came to learn more about **Islam,** many, but still a minority, came to see Muslims more as heretics than as anything else. **Oliver of Paderborn** characterized Islam as "a law written under the dictation of the Devil," but he also understood the affinities between Islamic and Christian doctrine. Consequently, he concluded that "they should be called heretics rather than **Saracens.**"

Heretics were usually perceived as more dangerous than pagans because they were believed to have perverted the true faith and were seen as offering a counterfeited version that might lead orthodox believers astray. For that reason, the battles between Islam's **Sunnis** and **Shias,** between its **Seljuks** and **Fatimids,** were quite bitter. For that reason, also, it was a logical step for the **Latin West** to bring the crusade back home and to employ it as a tool against heretics in Europe, as was done early in the thirteenth century in the **Albigensian Crusade.** In fact, crusading against Western Christians who believed differently became a tradition in Europe. During the fifteenth century the Roman Church crusaded unsuccessfully against Bohemian religious rebels known as the *Hussites.* During the sixteenth and early seventeenth centuries Europe was awash in blood as Protestants and Catholics alike waged **holy wars** against those whom they perceived to be false Christians. Whereas, the **Roman papacy** was still calling for crusades against these home-bred enemies of the faith and granting crusade **indulgences** to all who enrolled in the fight, Protestants did not call their wars crusades. After all, according to the Protestant vision, the crusades and all of their traditions, especially the indulgence, were the devilish inventions of the Antichrist papacy. Regardless, Protestant wars of religion were no less holy and **just** in the eyes of those who fought them. **Related Entries:** Apocalypse and the Crusades; Cathars.

Suggested Reading

Malcolm Barber, *Crusaders and Heretics, 12th–14th Centuries* (1995); Malcolm Lambert, *Medieval Heresy: Popular Movements from the Gregorian Reform to the Reformation,* 3rd. ed. (2002); Gordon Leff, *Heresy in the Later Middle Ages: The Relation of Heterodoxy to Dissent, c. 1250–1450* (1999); Andrew Roach, *Heresy and Medieval Society: 1100–1320* (2002).

High Court (Haute Cour)

A **feudal** court that served as the central organ of government in each **crusader state;** in the **kingdom of Jerusalem,** it was where the king, royal ministers, major church leaders, royal tenants-in-chief and their **vassals,** and notable crusaders who happened to be in the kingdom, such as King **Louis VII** of France in 1148, met to discuss and decide policy and to settle any and all important matters relating to the well-being of the state.

Unlike modern courts, feudal courts exercised plenary powers; that is, they had ultimate judicial, executive, and legislative powers. The theory was that a king or other lord was most powerful and effective when he was in his court, surrounded by his vassals and ministers. A feudal court was to secular government as a church **council** was to ecclesiastical government.

Originally the High Court of the kingdom of Jerusalem was largely advisory and met only when convened by the king, and it discussed only matters put to it by the king or his presiding officer. By the second half of the twelfth century, however, and more so during the thirteenth century, the High Court came to replace the diminishing power of the crown. At first this was due to disputed cases of royal succession in which it often played a decisive role. Later it was due to the absence of any king, good or bad, legitimate or illegitimate. From 1229 to the collapse of the kingdom of Jerusalem in 1291, there was no king-in-residence. Jerusalem's so-called kings resided in either Europe or **Cyprus,** but the High Court continued to meet and exercise authority. Indeed, during these last sixty-two years, the High Court became the de facto governing body of the kingdom.

Another important development occurred in its composition. By the mid–thirteenth century, all important persons in the kingdom were members of the High Court, and all significant constituencies had their representatives. Members of the court included not only all **fief**-holders, no matter how small their holdings, and all church leaders (including the grand masters of all the **military orders**), but also the executive officers (often called *consuls*) of the semi-independent towns, or communes, of the kingdom and representatives from various charitable brotherhoods and guilds. All of the High Court's constituents were **Franks. Eastern Christians** and non-Christians had their own lesser courts, which dealt only with judicial, religious, and financial matters.

By the last days of the kingdom of Jerusalem, its High Court had become a representative parliament, very much like those that were evolving in England and other areas of thirteenth-century Western Europe. **Related Entries:** Conrad of Montferrat; Melisende; Second Crusade; Settlement and Colonization; Sibylla.

Historians and Chroniclers, Islamic

Although most of **Islam**'s successful champions in the fight against the crusaders and the **crusader states** were either **Turks** (the **Seljuks,** the **Zangids,** and the **Mamluks**) or Kurds (the **Ayyubids**), most Islamic historians of the crusades were ethnic Arabs. Those who were not Arabs were Arabicized **Muslims** who wrote history according to Arabic models and in the Arabic language.

Unlike their **Latin** counterparts, Islamic historians of the crusades did not treat the **Frankish** invasions, which is how they viewed the crusades, as an isolated topic, and they almost never composed histories of a specific crusade or countercrusader. Rather, the crusades and the Islamic struggles against them were mainly incorporated into several classical types of Arabic history writing: world histories that began with Creation and extended to the present, thereby underscoring the universalistic nature of Islam; biographies of notable Muslim leaders; dynastic histories; chronicles of specific cities and regions; and memoirs.

The most important Arab historian to incorporate a large volume of crusade-era events into his universal history was Ibn al-Athir (1160–1233) of **Mosul,** who traveled with **Saladin**'s army and lived for a while in both **Aleppo** and **Damascus.** In addition to his universal history, which he entitled *The Perfect History,* he also composed a history of the Zangid dynasty. Because of his Zangid loyalties, he was not always sympathetic with Saladin. He is also an important source for the initial **Mongol** invasion of the Islamic World in the period 1219–1223.

The most significant Arab biographer to deal with the crusades was Imad ad-Din (1125–1201) of Isfahan and Damascus, who served as court biographer for several rulers, most notably Saladin. Imad ad-Din was an exception to the rule that Arab historians rarely wrote histories of a specific crusade or countercrusade. In addition to his life of Saladin, which he entitled *The Lightning of Syria,* he wrote *Ciceronian Eloquence on the Conquest of the Holy City,* a history of Saladin's wars of reconquest, the Holy City being **Jerusalem,** which fell to Saladin in 1187. One of the special strengths of Imad ad-Din's highly stylized and often difficult-to-read histories is that he quoted many of the diplomatic letters that he composed while serving as secretary first to **Nur ad-Din** and then to Saladin.

The most comprehensive biography of Saladin, as well as a vivid account of the **Third Crusade,** is *Sultanly Anecdotes and Josephly Virtues* by Baha ad-Din Ibn Shaddad (also known as Baha al-Din) of Mosul (1145–1234), who entered Saladin's service in 1188 and remained a faithful retainer until the sultan's death in 1197. "Josephly virtues" in this context refers both to Saladin, whose given name was Yusuf (Joseph in English), and the ancient Islamic prophet of the same name. Baha ad-Din's point was that Saladin exhibited all of the virtues that the prophet Yusuf (the Islamic counterpart to the biblical patriarch Joseph) was noted for, such as steadfastness, generosity, and faith. Despite its ornate title, the work, which is based on personal experiences, is easy to read because its author avoided literary affectations. Unlike Imad ad-Din, he avoided obsequious flattery of Saladin, despite his clear admiration for the man.

Ibn al-Qalanisi (1073–1160) was twice mayor of Damascus and the first Arab chronicler to write about the crusades in his *Continuation of the Chronicle of Damascus.* More than two-thirds of his work provides eyewitness accounts of the **First** and **Second Crusades,** as well as the lesser crusades that separated them, and continues the story down to 1154 and Nur ad-Din's entry into Damascus. His style was as dry as dust, but his extensive use of documents and oral testimonies made him an important source for subsequent Arab historians, as well as for modern historians of the crusades.

The most significant memoirist of the Crusade Era was Usamah ibn Munqidh, emir of Shaizar in **Syria** (1095–1188), whose *Book of Instructions with Illustrations* is a fascinating pastiche of anecdotes, self-portraits, and poetry and is our richest Arabic source for twelfth-century **Frankish-Muslim** relations in the East. Although he had a low opinion of Frankish culture and thought that most Franks had but one virtue, courage in battle, his rambling autobiography is a necessary corrective to those who maintain that Muslims and Latins were never able to reach any accommodation or find any common grounds.

In many respects Usamah's work is unique because he alone, of all the Arab writers of the Crusade Era, showed any interest in Frankish customs and ideas. Like their Latin counterparts (the exception being **William of Tyre**), Muslim historians' sense of cultural superiority and their contempt for those who did not share their faith (especially Latin Christians, who seemed to them so much more culturally backward than **Eastern Christians**) led them to a position of deliberate indifference and ignorance regarding the social and cultural ways of life of the **infidel. Related Entries:** Chronicles; Crusade of 1122–1126; Damascus Crusade; Historians and Chroniclers, Latin; Islamic Peoples; Settlement and Colonization.

Suggested Reading

Primary Sources

Baha al-Din Ibn Shaddad, *The Rare and Excellent History of Saladin,* trans. by D. S. Richards (2001); Francesco Gabrieli, ed. and trans., *Arab Historians of the Crusades,* trans. into English by E. J. Costello (1969); Ibn al-Qalanisi, *The Damascus Chronicle of the Crusades,* trans. and ed. by H. A. R. Gibb (1932; reissued 2003); Usamah ibn Munqidh, *An Arab-Syrian Gentleman and Warrior in the Period of the Crusades,* trans. and ed. by Philip K. Hitti, with a new foreword by Richard W. Bulliet (2000).

Historical Studies

Amin Maalouf, *The Crusades through Arab Eyes,* trans. by Jon Rothschild (1984); Chase Robinson, *Islamic Historiography: An Introduction* (2002).

Historians and Chroniclers, Latin

Unlike their **Islamic** counterparts, Latin historians created a new genre of historical writing, the crusade history, and they did so because they believed that this new era of **holy war** was a major turning point in God's providential plan for His Christian Chosen People. As sacred history, the crusade account was expected to strike a balance between the power and will of God and the efforts of the crusaders. Victory is ascribed to the help of the Lord and to the faith, heroism, and skill of those who fought in His Name; defeat is explained as a manifestation of God's displeasure at the sins of His people, a consequence of the crusaders' stupidity and arrogance, and, sometimes also, the enemy's skill or cunning. Two of the most common themes found in Latin crusade histories are that those who had faith and died on crusade were triumphant holy martyrs, and crushing defeats, such as the loss of **Jerusalem** in 1187, were allowed by God "for the cleansing of our sins."

Lacking any Greco-Roman models for the crusades or crusade histories, the earliest crusade historians looked to contemporary oral epics of knightly deeds and to the epic books of the Bible, such as Exodus, Joshua, and Kings, in which, by divine command, the Israelites fought ungodly pagans. The first history of the **First Crusade,** the artless and anonymous *Gesta Francorum* (*The Deeds of the Franks*) of 1100–1101, certainly borrowed heavily from the mood and tone of the **chivalric** stories that were circulating within knightly circles, even as it also displayed a simple piety and trust in Divine Providence. Soon, however, churchmen, such as Guibert of Nogent, took the basic story of the *Gesta* and placed it into a more fully developed theological context. Guibert quite deliberately entitled his reworking and correction of the *Gesta Francorum,* which he composed sometime between 1106 and 1109, *Gesta Dei per Francos* (*The Deeds of God Performed through the Franks*).

These two themes, **Frankish** valor and divine direction, would remain central motifs of Latin crusade historiography almost until the end, but as time went by and as Europe and the crusades changed in complexion, new themes were added and changes in tone and mood appeared.

The disastrous experiences of King **Louis VII** and Emperor **Conrad III** during the **Second Crusade** gave rise to a new notion that became an increasingly important theme in crusade histories for the next sixty years, the faithlessness of the **Greeks** of **Constantinople,** who sabotaged the crusade and proved themselves false Christians. Odo of Deuil, crusade chaplain of King Louis and author of *The Journey of Louis VII to the East,* which he wrote in or around 1148, was especially loud in his condemnation of Greek perfidy. Needless to say, apologists for the **Fourth Crusade,** which captured and sacked Constantinople in 1204, found it an easy chord to strike. Gunther of Pairis, a German **Cistercian** monk, went so far as to argue in his *Hystoria Constantinopolitana* (*A Constantinopolitan History*) of 1205 that God had directed the capture of Constantinople as a means of both bringing the Greeks back from their sinful ways and rewarding and blessing His faithful Latin Church. Indeed, Gunther further argued that this singular event marked a new stage in human history.

By the time of the **Third Crusade,** Europe's emerging monarchic states were becoming a new focal point of Western civilization, and crusade histories reflected this new reality, even as they maintained old themes and notions. The Third Crusade was led by the West's three most powerful monarchs, and it is logical to expect its histories and **chronicles** to focus on the deeds of Emperor **Frederick I** and Kings **Richard I** and **Philip II.** Nevertheless, the fact that all three monarchs appear in histories written by their respective partisans as hero-kings suggests that a new cult of monarchy was emerging in Western Europe. Thus, the anonymous *Journey of the Pilgrims and Deeds of King Richard* presents Richard as stronger than the legendary Roland, and Rigord's *Deeds of Philip Augustus* and Ansbert's *History of the Expedition of Emperor Frederick* present their respective monarchs as the central figures of this crusade.

During the late twelfth century the **Latin East** began producing a few of its own histories. Although the clergy of the **crusader states** generally was not noted for academic or intellectual achievements, one churchman did emerge as an historian of the first rank, Archbishop **William of Tyre.** William's *Jerusalem History* is a monumental achievement that traces the history of the crusades and Latin fortunes in the East from 1095 to 1184. The archbishop exhibited a wide-ranging knowledge of available documentary and oral sources and used them judiciously and critically. Without his work our knowledge of the twelfth-century history of the **kingdom of Jerusalem** would be greatly diminished.

William of Tyre's history was a mine for subsequent crusade historians, who liberally borrowed from it, and it also inspired the work of a large number of continuators in the East and in France, who endeavored to fill the gap between 1184 and their own day. Early in the thirteenth century William's history was translated into French, and a number of the translated manuscripts had continuations tacked on. One, written in **Acre,** took the story to as late as 1277. All of these translations, with their continuations, are known generically as *L'Estoire de Eracles empereur et la conqueste de la Terre d'Outremer* (*The History of the Emperor Heraclius and the Conquest of the Land Beyond the Sea*). This general title derives from the fact that William's work opens with the story of how in the age of Heraclius (Eracles in French), a seventh-century emperor of Constantinople, the "pernicious doctrines of Muhammad had gained a foothold in the East."

In addition, the Latin East produced its own French-language history of the crusades, which had no connection with William of Tyre's work. Entitled *The Chronicle of Ernoul,* it begins with the founding of the crusader states and ends in 1231 (in one of its several versions). Ernoul, who possibly carried the story only down to 1187 in the initial version of his history, was a squire and partisan of **Balian II of Ibelin,** the defender of Jerusalem in 1187.

The appearance of crusade histories in French around the turn of the century points out the growing importance of vernacular literature, especially French Romances, which were tales of **chivalry** and courtly love. The two most important eyewitness histories of the Fourth Crusade, Geoffrey of Ville-hardouin's *The Conquest of Constantinople* and Robert of Clari's account by the same name, were dictated and written down in French and show the influence of Romantic literature in their style and tone. The two works nicely complement each other, inasmuch as Geoffrey was one of the army's second-rank leaders and Robert was a humble knight.

Although lay warriors, such as Ralph of Caen and the anonymous author of the *Gesta Francorum,* had crafted histories of the First Crusade, clerical historians had largely claimed the genre for themselves during the early twelfth century and dominated the field until around 1200. Like Guibert of Nogent who had recrafted the *Gesta Francorum,* these clerical historians had imposed their theological perspectives on crusade historiography. With the appearance of essentially military histories, such as narrated by Geoffrey and Robert, God and Divine Providence were not forgotten, but they became convenient clichés to be plugged in by their pious yet militarily minded authors who focused on logistics, strategy, and tactics.

Clerical crusade histories written in Latin were not a total thing of the past. The **Fifth Crusade** provided the setting for **Oliver of Paderborn**'s first-rate *Damiettan History,* which he composed while participating in the crusade. Master Oliver judged that the main reason for the crusade's failure was that "our pilgrims grew sluggish through idleness and riotous living and, being eager for earthly gain, they provoked the wrath of the Almighty against themselves."

The best history of the later crusades, however, was composed in French by a layman, John, lord of Joinville, whose *Life of Saint Louis* concentrated on the years 1248–1254 and King **Louis IX**'s crusade in Egypt and **Syria-Palestine.** Dictated more than a half century later (1305–1309), the story still sparkles with life as Joinville recounts Louis's and his own trials and triumphs during the **Seventh Crusade.** Although this biography was in many respects a hagiography (the edifying story of a saint's life), miracles played no part in the crusade as narrated by Joinville. Rather, King Louis stands at the center of the action as the model chivalric warrior, the epitome of the pious crusader, and the nearly perfect king. Whatever successes and prestige Louis enjoyed in the **Holy Land** were due to his exceptional virtues and qualities. It is as king of France that Louis dominates the story. At the same time, Joinville judges Louis to have been a martyr for the faith because of his death while on the **Eighth Crusade.**

By 1300 crusade histories as written or narrated by Latin Christians had evolved significantly from those of almost 200 years earlier, even as they retained some of the same qualities. But then, European civilization had

changed over the years, even as it still retained the ideal of the crusade. **Related Entries:** Apocalypse and the Crusades; Criticism of the Crusades; Fulcher of Chartres; Historians and Chroniclers, Islamic; James of Vitry; *Song of Roland, The.*

Suggested Reading

Primary Sources

Consult specific crusade and historian entries.

Historical Study

Christopher Tyerman, *The Invention of the Crusades* (1998).

Hohenstaufens

A royal-imperial family from Swabia in southwestern Germany that played a significant role in the crusades from the mid–twelfth to the mid–thirteenth century.

From first to last, the Hohenstaufens, Western emperors and kings of Germany, Italy, and Sicily, were involved in the crusades and the **Latin East.** Conrad III (r. 1137–1152), the first Hohenstaufen to assume the royal crowns of Germany and Italy, as well as the Western imperial title, was one of the two leaders of the **Second Crusade**'s campaign in the East in 1147–1149. Accompanying him on crusade were his half-brother, Bishop Otto of Freising, and his nephew Frederick. Despite Conrad's best attempts, the crusade in the East was a miserable failure highlighted by a series of disasters for his imperial forces. The vast majority of Conrad's huge heterogeneous army died in the course of this ill-conceived and misfortune-plagued expedition. The only positive result of Conrad's crusade was a closer personal alliance with Emperor **Manuel I** of **Byzantium.**

Frederick succeeded his uncle as king in 1152 and was crowned Western emperor in 1155. History knows him as Frederick I Barbarossa (Red Beard), a man who dominated Central European politics throughout his long reign (r. 1152–1190). Following the capture of **Jerusalem,** Pope Gregory VIII dispatched a **papal legate** to Frederick's court at Mainz, to enlist the emperor in a projected new crusade—the **Third Crusade.** Frederick, who was almost seventy but still vital, swore the **cross** on March 27, 1188. Departure was set for April 23, 1189, the feast of Saint George, and it is a monument to Barbarossa's organizational talents that his massive army, the largest by far of all the contingents of this crusade, assembled on that date and began its march on May 11, 1189.

Because Frederick could not be sure that any Palestinian port would remain in **Latin** hands, he decided on the difficult and dangerous overland route that his uncle had followed with such disastrous results more than forty years earlier. In preparation, Frederick dispatched envoys to **Constantinople** and Iconium (modern Konya), requesting free passage and fair markets from the Byzantine emperor and the **Seljuk** sultan of Rum, respectively. He also sent an ambassador to **Saladin,** threatening war if he did not return the Christian holy places. This last act, which might seem quixotic, was dictated by **chivalric** protocol, which demanded that a true **knight** openly challenge and defy an enemy. Saladin scornfully rejected the emperor's warning, but Emperor **Isaac II** and the sultan of Iconium promised cooperation. Neither kept his word.

Very much like Conrad III's journey across **Anatolia** in 1147, Frederick's army suffered greatly. When the emperor drowned on June 10, 1190, at a point not far from the border of **Syria,** the dispirited and greatly reduced army disintegrated. The dead emperor's son, Duke Frederick of Swabia, attempted to rally the survivors, but only a portion chose to follow him. Their numbers further reduced by enemy attacks, **disease,** and shipwreck, the remnant of a once-huge army finally reached **Acre,** where Duke Frederick succumbed to illness on January 20, 1191. With his death, the imperial army was a negligible factor for the remainder of the crusade.

Duke Frederick's elder brother, Henry, succeeded to Frederick I's three crowns as Henry VI (r. 1190–1197). He added the crown of Sicily by virtue of his marriage to Constance, the heiress to the kingdom, and undertook military operations to secure his wife's inheritance. By 1194 Sicily was pacified, and Henry was ready to embark on the grander project of extending Hohenstaufen authority into the **Levant.** Possibly he envisioned conquering **Byzantium;** at the least, he intended to make his imperial presence felt in **Syria-Palestine.** To that end, he assumed the **crusader's cross** in the spring of 1195 and set in motion the **German Crusade** of 1197–1198. The large German (and Italian and Sicilian) army that Henry sent on before him to the East accomplished little in relation to its size, capturing only the abandoned port cities of Sidon and Beirut. Henry never made it to the East to link up with his forces. On September 28, 1197, he died in Messina, Sicily, and when word reached the East, the leaders of the crusade army rushed back home to prepare for the civil war in Germany that was sure to follow, as the Hohenstaufens battled their dynastic enemies, the Welf family, for the crown of Germany and the imperial title.

The Hohenstaufen-Welf struggle prevented Philip of Swabia (d. 1208), Henry's brother and claimant to the imperial legacy of his father, from ever assuming the crusader's cross. He did, however, play a pivotal role in the **Fourth Crusade** when he supported the overtures of his brother-in-law, Alexius Angelus, to the crusader army. Philip was married to Irene, daughter of the deposed Byzantine emperor, **Isaac II,** and it was through Philip's agency that the crusade leaders accepted the young **Greek** prince's proposal that the crusade army help restore him and his father to the throne of Constantinople. The result was the **Latin empire of Constantinople.**

The assassination of the childless Philip on June 21, 1208, left the fortunes of the family in the hands of Henry VI's son and heir, Frederick, the boy-king of Sicily. Henry had secured the German princes' promise in 1196 to elect his then two-year-old son as king, but the infant's claim had been passed over after his father's death. Pope **Innocent III** had crowned the Welf candidate, Otto IV, emperor in October 1209 but in November 1210 excommunicated him, and soon turned to the cause of the young Frederick. In 1212 the young man was crowned Frederick II, king of Germany and emperor-elect (r. 1212–1250), and three years later, on July 15, 1215, he was solemnly recrowned, to mark his full and final triumph over Otto IV. On this occasion, he surprised everyone by **vowing** to go on crusade. That vow would come back to haunt him.

Circumstances at home prevented Frederick from participating in the **Fifth Crusade,** even though the crusaders in Egypt eagerly awaited his arrival. All that Frederick could do was to dispatch some money, troops, and orders that were largely unrealistic and unheeded. The crusade's dismal end and the emperor's failure to aid the crusade in any substantive way brought him both public recriminations and papal anger.

Frederick, who had been crowned emperor on November 22, 1220, wanted to go to the East, especially in light of his marriage in 1225 to **Isabella (Yolanda),** heiress of the **kingdom of Jerusalem.** Fate kept imposing barriers, however, including the emperor's illness. Pope **Gregory IX,** however, had enough, and excommunicated Frederick as a perjurer on September 29, 1227. Despite his excommunication, Frederick set sail for the East in June 1228, initiating the most curious of all thirteenth-century Western expeditions to Palestine, the **Sixth Crusade.** The result was something that Frederick's grandfather and father never achieved, recovery of Jerusalem, but recovery through treaty, not war. On March 18, 1229, Frederick crowned himself king of Jerusalem in the Holy City.

Pope Gregory's anger expressed itself in a war against Frederick at home in Sicily, but on September 1, 1230, the pope and this eccentric crusader made their peace. The peace did not last long. In 1239 the struggle between Frederick and the papacy broke out again, this time due to Frederick's attempts to dominate northern Italy. The emperor was excommunicated in March 1239, and in early 1240 Pope Gregory called for a crusade against Frederick. In February 1241 the pope went so far as to allow crusaders to commute their vows to a crusade in the **Holy Land** to a crusade against Frederick. This **holy war** outlived both Gregory and Frederick and continued down to 1268.

Meanwhile, the Hohenstaufens continued to claim the crown of Jerusalem. When Queen Isabella died in 1228, Frederick's legitimate claim to the monarchy ended, even though he crowned himself in 1229. Legally the crown passed to their son, Conrad, known in the West as Conrad IV, king of Germany, Italy, and Sicily (r. 1250–1254) and the uncrowned Western emperor. In the Latin East he was known as Conrad II (1228–1254); the first King Conrad was the uncrowned **Conrad of Montferrat.** On April 25, 1244, Conrad became fifteen, the age of legal majority, and his father's regency was over. Because both Frederick and Conrad resided in the West, their rule was more theoretical than real, although they were represented in the East by **baillis** (administrative deputies). When Conrad died in 1254, the pope recognized his two-year-old son Conrad (better known as Conradin) as King Conrad III (r. 1254–1268). On October 31, 1268, the teenaged Conrad/Conradin was publicly beheaded in Naples after an abortive attempt to wrest ancestral Sicily from **Charles of Anjou,** who had won it in battle two and a half years earlier from Manfred, Frederick II's illegitimate son. To counter Conradin's threat to the papacy's champion, Pope Clement IV preached a crusade against the young Hohenstaufen and later did nothing to prevent his execution. With Conradin's death the "viper breed of Hohenstaufen," as one pope characterized it, came to an end, and the title of king of Jerusalem passed to the king of **Cyprus,** Hugh III. **Related Entries:** Adrianople; Capetians; Montferrat, Family of; Political Crusades; Saints, Warrior.

Suggested Reading

David Abulafia, *Frederick II: A Medieval Emperor* (1988); Ernst Kantorowicz, *Frederick II* (1957); Peter Munz, *Frederick Barbarossa: A Study in Medieval Politics* (1969); Thomas C. Van Cleve, *The Emperor Frederick II of Hohenstaufen, Immutator Mundi* (1972).

Holy Land

The land of **Palestine** made holy by its association with the events of the Old and New Testaments, and especially the life, death, and resurrection of Jesus.

Christians accept the books of the Jewish Bible as divinely inspired and see the events related in those books as necessary prologue to the Christian dispensation. For this reason Christians view such biblical figures as Abraham, Joshua, and David as holy people whose histories are as relevant to sacred history as those of any Christian saint. Likewise, their **relics** and places associated with them are worthy of **pilgrimage** and veneration. The holy people of ancient Israel were offered by their God a special place—a Promised Land—which was roughly the land of Palestine, and for that reason Palestine became a holy land.

The primitive Christian Church also was associated with that land. The Church's first teachers, first leaders, and first martyrs lived, ministered, and died in Palestine, and for that reason also it was a holy land.

As far as Christians were (and are) concerned, however, the saints of ancient Israel and of the Early Church would have no relevance whatsoever were it not for Jesus Christ, God made man, who lived, taught, died, and was resurrected in this land. Through those events he transformed history by securing salvation for humanity, and because of him Palestine truly became the Holy Land.

From earliest days Christians traveled to the Holy Land to worship at the hundreds of shrines that dot the landscape. Holiest among them is the **Holy Sepulcher** in **Jerusalem,** the empty tomb of Christ that stands as a token of Jesus' victory over sin and death. Next to it is Golgotha, or Mount Calvary, the site of Jesus' crucifixion. Bethlehem, the place of his birth, and Nazareth, the village in which he was raised, have also been prime sites of Christian pilgrimage since the first century. Sites associated with Mary, the mother of Jesus, were just as avidly visited. Within the walls of Jerusalem crusaders in the twelfth century raised the Church of Saint Anne, the most perfect of all crusader churches in the Holy Land, on a site that they identified as the home of Anne and Joachim, the parents of the Virgin Mary. During the twelfth century Latin clerics also discovered what they believed to be the relics of the Jewish Patriarchs Abraham, Isaac, and Jacob at Hebron, and they transformed the tomb into a major site of pilgrimage.

Because of these religious associations, medieval Christians looked upon the Holy Land as *their* land. Complicating the issue was the fact that **Muslims** and **Jews** also considered Palestine to be holy land. Hebron is a fine example of a site that is sacred to all three faiths. As far as Muslims are concerned, Abraham, Isaac, and Jacob were early prophets of **Islam.** During the age of the crusades, Jewish claims on the Holy Land did not cause much in the way of conflict, but competing Christian and Islamic claims contributed to seas of blood being spilled over this land called holy. **Related Entries:** Apocalypse and the Crusades; Cross, True; Preaching.

Suggested Reading

Primary Source

"Letters of the Crusaders Written from the Holy Land" in *University of Pennsylvania Translations and Reprints from the Original Sources of European History,* Vol. I, No. 4, edited by Dana C. Munro (1902).

Historical Studies

Steven Brooke, *Views of Jerusalem and the Holy Land* (1998); Jerome Murphy-O'Connor, *The Holy Land: An Archeological Guide from Earliest Times to 1700,* 3rd ed. (1992); R. N. Swanson, ed., *The Holy Land, Holy Lands, and Christian History* (2000).

Holy Sepulcher, Church of the

The chief Christian church of **Jerusalem,** which covers the sites of Golgotha, or Mount Calvary, where Jesus was crucified, and his empty tomb, or sepulcher, from which Christians believe he arose from the dead. **Greek** Christians know it as the Church of the *Anastasis* (the Resurrection).

From the Church's earliest days, Christians worshiped at the places of Jesus' cruci-

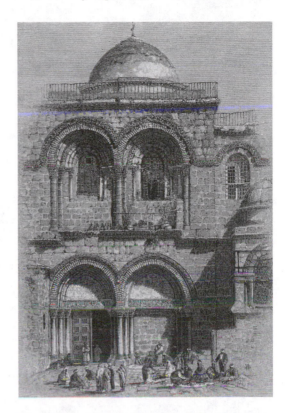

The entrance to the Church of the Holy Sepulcher. Charles W. Wilson, *Picturesque Palestine, Sinai and Egypt,* 2 vols. (New York: D. Appleton & Co., 1881), 1:16.

fixion and nearby burial, both of which originally lay outside the walls of Jerusalem until around 41–43 C.E. In 326 Emperor Constantine, the first Christian Roman emperor, began construction of a great church over both sites and dedicated the completed project in 335. The church was a complex of four connected elements from east to west: (1) an *atrium,* or open forecourt; (2) a *basilica,* or long, rectangular church; (3) a second open courtyard, in which was located the stone tip of Golgotha, or Mount Calvary, and other sites associated with Jesus' suffering and death; and (4) a separate domed structure, or *rotunda,* which sheltered the *Edicule* (little house) that was built around the Holy Sepulcher, or tomb of Jesus. As time went on, Christians also began to identify Golgotha as the spot where Adam, the first human, was created and died, and the entire holy site as the center of the universe.

In 614 the complex was set on fire by invading Persians and badly damaged, but it was restored after the city was recaptured by imperial forces. A few years later, in 638, the **Muslim** army of Caliph Umar captured Jerusalem, but the caliph allowed the Christians to retain the Church of the Holy Sepulcher. In 1009 the **Fatimid** caliph of Egypt, al-Hakim, ordered the destruction of the church and demolition of the tomb. Although the church was reduced to ruins, the tomb escaped total destruction, perhaps protected by the rubble that fell on it. Reconstruction began in 1012 and was completed around 1040, with much of the work funded by the emperor of **Constantinople,** Michael IV. The result was a smaller church built in the **Byzantine** style, which now housed within a single structure the rotunda over the tomb and all other sites of worship, including Mount Calvary.

After the **Latins** captured Jerusalem, they set about expanding and refashioning the church in a contemporary European style known as *Romanesque*. Work continued into the late 1160s. An inscription commemorating the consecration on July 15, 1149, of the church's two chapels at Mount Calvary has misled most modern historians into concluding that the entire church was completed and consecrated fifty years to the day of the crusaders' capture of the city.

About twenty years after reconstruction was completed, the church fell into **Islamic** hands when **Saladin** captured Jerusalem in 1187. Rather than destroying the church or converting it into a mosque, he handed it over to the care of **Eastern Christian** clerics.

Although lost to the West, the Church of the Holy Sepulcher was never forgotten. Wishing to bring a bit of Jerusalem back home, church architects of the twelfth and thirteenth centuries created in Europe a distinctive style of crusader architecture in imitation of the rotunda of the Holy Sepulcher—the round church. The **Templars** were particularly active in this regard, and one of the best surviving examples is Temple Church in London. **Related Entries:** Holy Land; Pilgrimage; Relics.

Suggested Reading

Martin Biddle, et al., *The Church of the Holy Sepulchre* (2000) and *The Tomb of Christ* (1999); Jaroslav Folda, *The Art of the Crusaders in the Holy Land, 1098–1187* (1995); A. Parrot, *Golgotha and the Church of the Holy Sepulcher,* trans. by E. Hudson (1957).

Holy War / Just War

The classic distinction is that a holy war is accepted on faith as divinely mandated, with a God-directed purpose and the promise of sanctifying its agents, whereas a just war is secular, is based on law and reason, and is fought in righteous defense of peace and good order. In the medieval Christian West this distinction was so blurred that crusades were seen as both holy and just.

Christianity, a religion based on the principle of love, invented neither the just war nor the holy war. Roman theorists had developed a notion of the secular just war, and the Old Testament was filled with examples of God commanding the Israelites to fight holy wars against heathens as a means of furthering the Divine Plan and binding this Chosen People more closely to Him. On their part, Western Christians embraced and reinvented both the Roman just war and the biblical holy war to justify violence in the name of Christian charity.

Saint Augustine of Hippo (354–420) provided Western Christendom with its classic concept of the just war when he defined it as warfare against sin. Augustine saw war as both a consequence of sin and a cure for it. Love of neighbor legitimated struggle against a sinful neighbor. When waged by a proper authority for moral reasons and with due restraint, a just war was not simply an acceptable defensive action but a positive moral act. To Augustine's mind, the just warrior restrains the sinner from evil; while killing the body, he saves the soul, but like a surgeon cutting out a malignant tumor, he must act benevolently and never out of hatred or with murderous passion. Thus the Christian just warrior fights sin in both himself and in others.

According to medieval theologians and church lawyers in the age of the crusades, just wars fell into two categories: wars fought for secular just causes, such as defensive action against an unjust aggressor; and wars for a sacred cause called by a spiritual authority. Wars that fell into the latter category were not only just, they were holy. Being holy, such wars had the potential to sanctify their participants. Like soldiers in a just war, soldiers in a holy war were guiltless of the sin of murder (provided their motives were proper), but more than that, holy warriors could earn salvation by their actions.

Given this definition, clearly the crusades were seen as both just and holy. They were just because the Christian West assumed it was fighting to regain lands from which Christendom had been unjustly dispossessed and to rescue Christians who were being persecuted. They were holy because God commanded them and offered them as a special means of sanctification for those who fought them. But they were holy wars of a special kind because of their particular attributes. First, church lawyers generally agreed that only a pope could call a crusade. Second, crusaders were set apart from other holy warriors by the **vow** they took, the insignia of the **crusader's cross** that they wore, the **indulgence** granted them, and the various other **crusader privileges** offered them. **Related Entries:** Bernard of Clairvaux; Bull, Papal; Criticism of Crusades; Deus vult; Innocent III; Jihad; Pilgrimage; Saints, Warrior; *Song of Roland, The;* Truce and Peace of God; Urban II.

Suggested Reading

David S. Bachrach, *Religion and the Conduct of War, c. 300–1215* (2003); Norman Housley, *Religious Warfare in Europe, 1400–1536* (2002); Tomaž Mastnak, *Crusading Peace: Christendom, the Muslim World, and Western Political Order* (2002); Thomas P. Murphy, ed., *The Holy War* (1976); Peter Partner, *God of Battles: Holy Wars of Christianity and Islam* (1997); Jonathan Riley-Smith, "Crusading as an Act of Love," *History,* 65 (1980): 177–92; Frederick H. Russell, *The Just War in the Middle Ages* (1975).

Honorius III, Pope (r. 1216–1227)

Honorius inherited three crusades from his predecessor **Innocent III:** the crusade in the **Baltic,** the **Albigensian Crusade,** and the **Fifth Crusade.**

Crusades in Europe and **Outremer** occupied much of Pope Honorius's attention and energy. From 1217 to 1223 he attempted to organize an army that would be strong enough to crush the pagan Prussians in northeastern Europe, but his efforts proved futile. One consequence of this failure was the Golden Bull of Rimini of 1226, by which Emperor **Frederick II** granted considerable independence and powers to the **Teutonic Knights** to assure their participation in the Prussian theater of operations. With this grant, the Teutonic Knights began conquering and colonizing the lands of Prussia and carving out for themselves an independent state in Eastern Europe.

As far as the Albigensian Crusade was concerned, Honorius desperately but futilely tried to rally support for Simon of Montfort, whose brutal tactics against **Cathars** and Catholics alike had lost him much support and the key city of Toulouse. With Simon's death in 1218, crusader fortunes went swiftly downhill in **Languedoc,** and Honorius's pleas that King **Philip II** intervene in the south went unheeded, although Philip's son, Louis, did a limited amount of campaigning against the count of Toulouse. With Prince Louis's accession to the throne of **France** in 1223, as **Louis VIII,** a new era of royal-papal cooperation began that led to the successful conclusion of the Albigensian Crusade. The pope approved a heavy crusade tax on the clergy of France to **finance** renewed crusade efforts, and he authorized clergy to travel throughout the kingdom as crusade **preachers.** To define more clearly the enemy, he excommunicated Count Raymond VII through the agency of his **legate** to France. On his part, King Louis set off on crusade in June 1226. Even King Louis's death later that year could not fully stop the momentum, although it gave Raymond a respite and a few minor gains. When Honorius III died on March 18, 1227, the war was not quite over, but victory was no longer in doubt.

Despite his interest in the Baltic and Albigensian crusades, Honorius, like Innocent III before him, believed the major focus of crusading had to be on the recovery of **Jerusalem,** and it was there that he concentrated most of his attention.

One of the major crusade problems that Honorius grappled with was bringing pressure on Frederick II of **Hohenstaufen** to join the army of the Fifth Crusade, as he had **vowed** to do in 1215. As far as the pope was concerned, Frederick was the logical choice to serve as the crusade's supreme military commander. By way of inducement, Honorius crowned Frederick emperor in 1220, but

still Frederick delayed. Finally in exasperation, in 1225 Honorius threatened Frederick with excommunication if he did not sail for the East before mid-1227. Honorius died before he was forced to deliver on his threat, and it was left to his successor, **Gregory IX,** to excommunicate Frederick.

While Frederick delayed in Europe, the first element of the Fifth Crusade departed on May 29, 1217, less than eleven months after Innocent III's death. Pope Innocent had set down the basic outlines of this crusade at the Fourth Lateran Council of 1215, and Honorius was determined to bring the plans to fruition by following the lead of his predecessor, but he never did so slavishly.

Honorius continued to employ the services of Cardinal **Pelagius.** In 1214 Innocent had appointed Pelagius as **papal legate** to the East, and in June 1218, Honorius named him crusade legate. When, in July 1220, Honorius centralized the collection of crusade subsidies in the hands of papal collectors and remitted the money directly to Pelagius, who was with the crusaders in Egypt, the pope greatly strengthened the authority of this controversial crusade leader, who was involved in a power struggle with **John of Brienne.** Just as significant, Honorius achieved his primary goal of improving the collection and disbursement of crusade funds, thereby laying the basis for further papal centralization of crusade taxation by his successors, Gregory IX and Innocent IV.

Honorius was separated by the Mediterranean Sea from a crusade that dragged on into the late summer of 1221. What is more, this span of more than four years witnessed a seemingly endless stream of crusader departures and returns. Space, time, and the crusade's own rhythms combined to make Honorius more of a crusade coordinator, counselor, and cheerleader than commander in chief. Neither the crusade's near success nor dismal failure could be laid at his door.

Hospitalers

The *Order of the Hospital of Saint John of Jerusalem,* crusader Europe's second greatest **military order** and the ancestor of today's *Knights of Malta* and England's *Most Venerable Order of Saint John.*

The Hospital of Saint John was founded in **Jerusalem** in the eleventh century, well before the **First Crusade,** as a charitable institution to minister to the **Holy Land**'s ill and needy, especially its **pilgrims.** Even after the Order of Saint John became a military order, its brothers maintained their commitment to serving "the holy poor," motivated by the principle that they should treat all who came into their care, including **Jews** and **Muslims,** as honored guests.

Sometime in the 1130s the Hospitalers of Saint John began to assume military functions in the **Latin East.** In 1148 several Hospitaler brothers were engaged in the **siege** of Tortosa in Spain, and the following year the order received a frontier **castle** to defend along the Christian-**Moorish** border of Spain. The Hospitalers now had a second front—the **Reconquista.**

Managing to survive the collapse of the last **crusader state** in **Syria-Palestine** in 1291, the order retreated to **Cyprus** and then to the island of Rhodes in 1309, where it managed to escape the **Templars'** fate by establishing a sovereign state. The hospital on the island of Rhodes, which still stands, is testimony to the continuing charitable work of the order, even as it carved out a state and carried on offensive military operations against **Islam.** From Rhodes the Hospitalers took part in various minor crusades and fought Muslim pirates, while engaging in their own piratical activities. In addition to serving as a forward base for military operations, Hospitaler-controlled Rhodes was an important center for commerce between Europe and the eastern Mediterranean. When Rhodes fell to the **Ottoman Turks** in 1522, the Hospitalers moved westward. In 1530 they took up residence in Tripoli in North Africa (not to be confused with **Tripoli** in Syria) and on the Mediterranean islands of Gozo and Malta, which lie south of Sicily. In 1551 the Ottomans captured Tripoli and devastated Gozo, leaving Malta as the Hospitalers' sole possession. There the Hospitalers beat back a massive Turkish invasion in 1565 and established themselves as a significant outpost of militant **Latin** Christianity in the Central Mediterranean. In 1798, however, the **knights** surrendered Malta almost without a fight to the forces of Napoleon. They had lost their military edge and religious fervor.

Remnants of the order, already long known as the Knights of Malta, took themselves to papal Rome. There in the 1850s, the order, which legally was and remains a sovereign state, returned exclusively to its original humanitarian mission and transformed itself into one of the Catholic Church's preeminent charitable institutions. In England a parallel development took place. During the 1860s the non-Catholic *Order of Saint John,* which traced itself back to French Knights of Malta, assumed a medical mission that continues to the present (the St. John Ambulance Service). Additionally, three other non-Catholic orders of **chivalry** claiming descent from the Order of Saint John exist in Germany, Sweden, and the Netherlands. **Related Entries:** Disease; Holy War/Just War; Lazarus, Order of Saint; Military Orders of Iberia; Teutonic Knights; Turcopoles.

Suggested Reading

Primary Sources

The Rule, Statutes and Customs of the Hospitallers, 1099–1310, trans. by Edwin J. King (1934).

Historical Studies

Helen Nicholson, *The Knights Hospitaller* (2001); Jonathan Riley-Smith, *Hospitallers: The History of the Order of St. John* (1999) and *The Knights of St. John in Jerusalem and Cyprus, c. 1050–1310* (1967); H. J. A. Sire, *The Knights of Malta* (1994).

Hugh of Vermandois

Brother of King Philip I (r. 1060–1108), Hugh, count of Vermandois, sometimes called "the Great," was one of the highest ranking leaders of the **First Crusade.**

Hugh led a large contingent of soldiers out of France in 1096, but few of them reached **Constantinople,** much less **Jerusalem.** According to **Anna Comnena,** Hugh carried the golden banner of Saint Peter, a sign of papal favor bestowed upon him in Rome, and in a series of letters announcing that he would soon arrive by sea in **Byzantine** territory, Hugh proclaimed himself "king of kings, superior to all under the sky" and "the highest leader of all the armies of France" and demanded an appropriate reception. Much to his embarrassment, a storm in the Adriatic destroyed a large part of his force and cast him up as a bedraggled refugee on the Albanian coast, where he was rescued by the local authorities and escorted to Constantinople. There he swore an oath of fealty to Emperor **Alexius I,** who treated him generously.

Hugh crossed into **Anatolia** with the other crusader forces of the second wave and served honorably as a leader down through the victory over **Kerbogha**'s army at **Antioch** on June 28, 1098. Shortly thereafter, Hugh, who seems to have wished to return home, was commissioned to find Emperor Alexius and invite him to come to Antioch and take charge of the city and the army. Hugh traveled all the way to Constantinople, barely escaping death in an ambush along the way, before he found the emperor, who was unable or unwilling to accept the crusaders' offer immediately.

His mission completed, Hugh reached France, where he found a good deal of indignation over his premature departure from the army and his unfulfilled **pilgrimage vow.** Faced with public charges of cowardice and impiety, Hugh joined the army of Duke William IX of Aquitaine, one of several contingents that set out on the so-called **Crusade of 1101,** the third wave of the First Crusade. In early September 1101, the army was ambushed and cut to pieces in Anatolia. Hugh, badly wounded by an arrow, was carried to Tarsus, where he died on October 18. His vow to reach Jerusalem remained unfulfilled. **Related Entries:** Capetians; Stephen of Blois and Chartres.

I

Iberia

See Reconquista.

Indulgence, Crusade

Remission of the penalties due for sins that was granted to crusaders.

The crusade indulgence was the most significant and popular of the crusade **privileges** granted anyone who swore and fulfilled the **crusade vow** or died in the attempt. Although many people joined crusades for a wide variety of worldly reasons, spiritual and religious considerations were the primary factors that motivated people to undertake such hazardous and costly ventures. Most crusaders probably expected to return home, if they survived, quite a bit poorer in the goods of this world but enriched spiritually.

It took several centuries for the **Latin** Church to evolve a full theological understanding and legal definition of indulgences, and the crusades provided the primary context in which that dual development took place.

The earliest known papal grant of an indulgence is when Alexander II promised in a letter of 1063 that any soldier who enlisted in a campaign to liberate Barbastro from the Spanish **Moors** would not have to perform any church-imposed penance that he might owe for his sins. Since earliest times, the clergy had laid penances, such as penitential **pilgrimages,** on persons who had confessed grave sins and sought reconciliation with the Church. Such imposed penances were an attempt to help the penitent satisfy Divine Justice, but no one claimed to know whether or not they did, and they were also intended to set the person right with the community that he had injured. By this letter, Pope Alexander acknowledged that the expedition in Spain was sufficiently harrowing and meritorious as to equal the penance for any and all confessed sins—no matter how horrendous.

It was in this context that **Pope Urban II** likewise promised in 1095 at **Clermont** that anyone who undertook the expedition to liberate **Jerusalem** could substitute that pilgrimage for all imposed penances—as long as the person journeyed out of a sense of devotion and not for glory or money. From this point onward the indulgence was a permanent fixture of the crusades, but the indulgence was understood in different ways by different people right from its inception. What is more, as crusading became an integral part of the Western Church's vision of and response to the world, the Church expanded the ways in which a person could earn a crusade indulgence, and it also broadened considerably its understanding of what was remitted in an indulgence.

Twelfth-century **historians** of the First Crusade unanimously described the indulgence promised by Pope Urban as "remission of sins"—a vague term that reflected an already widespread misunderstanding of the crusade indulgence. In the popular mind, right from the start, this meant a total wiping away of all sins and a free pass into Heaven. This simplistic and incorrect understanding of the original crusade indulgence continued to be the majority view, even as popes, theologians, and church lawyers expanded and refined the Church's official teachings regarding this spiritual privilege.

Papal bulls calling for crusades in the twelfth and early thirteenth centuries invariably offered crusade indulgences, and as crusading became more sweeping in scope and a more complex and difficult undertaking to launch, popes became increasingly generous in identifying the parties who merited indulgences. As early as 1098 indulgences granted to persons involved in the Spanish **Reconquista** were equated with those offered to crusaders to Jerusalem. Later the crusade indulgence was granted to those who participated in the **Baltic crusades** against pagans in the North, to those who fought in the **Albigensian Crusade** and in similar crusades against **heretics** at home, and even to those who joined papal **political crusades.** Beginning late in the twelfth century, crusade indulgences were increasingly granted to those who simply assisted a crusade without enlisting in it. Contributing funds to support a crusade could earn someone this privilege, as well as **preaching** a crusade, or collecting money for one, or serving as a missionary along the borderlands of Europe, or settling as a colonist in the **Holy Land.** In 1252 the wives of crusaders were granted the same indulgence as that given their crusading husbands, in recognition of the **women**'s sacrifice. All of this could be and was justified on two planes: It allowed all Western Christians to share in the spiritual benefits of crusading, despite their circumstances; and it broadened and deepened support for the crusades in an age in which crusading was becoming more costly and less popular.

At the same time the Church's theologians and lawyers were redefining the indulgence. By the mid–thirteenth century an indulgence was understood to be not simply the commutation of a specific penance imposed on a contrite sinner but, more significantly, a wiping away, in part or entirely, of the *temporal punishment* that Divine Justice demands for all sins already confessed and forgiven. Such punishment is known as temporal (lasting for a time) because through confession and absolution the penitent has escaped the eternal torments of Hell. Nevertheless, because all sin violates God's Right Order, forgiven sinners must still undergo punishment either on Earth or in Purgatory, a place of purification in the afterlife, where souls settle in full all divinely mandated penalties prior to admission to Heaven.

A crusade indulgence was now seen as a *plenary* (full) remission of all temporal punishment. The Church had, therefore, readjusted its definition of crusade indulgence so that it was closer to the popular notion that it was the wiping clean of a person's slate in the eyes of God. At the same time, the Church's theologians insisted that indulgences were earned only by truly contrite penitents. **Related Entries:** Councils and Synods; Fifth Crusade; Financing the Crusades; Innocent III, Pope.

Infantry

Foot soldiers, or infantry, were differently valued and used by the **Franks** and their **Muslim** enemies.

It is a myth that **knights** were the dominant force in **Latin** crusade armies. Rather, foot soldiers bore the brunt of combat and often proved the decisive factor. **Islamic** armies, to the contrary, were dominated numerically and tactically by their light **cavalry,** and Muslim infantry played a far less significant role than their crusader counterparts.

Whether in Europe or **Outremer,** Western foot soldiers, armed with spears, bows, and crossbows, greatly outnumbered knights and mounted **sergeants,** usually by a factor of at least four or five to one. Much like modern tanks, Western knights were vulnerable without the protection of large numbers of disciplined foot soldiers. One of the most famous instances of infantry acting as a defensive screening force for mounted knights occurred on September 7, 1191, when the army of **Richard I of England** confronted **Saladin**'s forces at Arsuf as the crusaders marched along the coast from **Acre** to **Jaffa.** The infantry, which numbered around 10,000, as opposed to about 1,200 knights, was able to blunt an attack by a Muslim cavalry force that possibly was more than twice as large as the entire crusader army, thereby allowing the knights to launch an effective counterattack. On that day Frankish crossbowmen played a key role by keeping the enemy's mounted archers at a distance thanks to the superior killing range of their crossbow bolts.

If crusader horse soldiers needed the support of foot soldiers, it was equally true that crusader foot soldiers needed the support of horse soldiers. More often than not, infantry units could not hold off Muslim cavalry attacks indefinitely without breaking in the face of barrages of arrows and terror tactics. Just as Frankish soldiers on foot bought their mounted comrades-in-arms time to mass and pick the optimum moment for their charge, Frankish horse warriors protected their comrades on foot by blocking and counterattacking the enemy.

Regular foot soldiers were commoners, but combat on foot was not confined to this class. Circumstances often forced Western knights to dismount, as at the Battle of **Hattin,** and to fight as infantry. The same was not true of Muslim cavalry, who tended to remain in their saddles. **Related Entries:** Armor; Dorylaeum, Battle of; Siege Warfare; Sergeant; Tafurs; Weapons, Hand.

Suggested Reading

John France, *Western Warfare in the Age of the Crusades, 1000–1300* (1999).

Infidel

A term meaning "unbeliever" that was used freely by both **Muslims** and Christians to signify anyone who did not share their faith.

The term was sometimes used in the heat of controversy to describe a **heretic,** or someone who confessed a variant and presumably misguided form of the faith, such as a **Shia** Muslim in the eyes of a **Sunni** or a Nestorian Christian in the eyes of a **Byzantine.** Strictly speaking, however, an infidel, unlike a heretic, does not ascribe to any of the most basic doctrines of a particular religion. **Related Entry:** Christians, Eastern.

Innocent III, Pope (r. 1198–1216)

The crusader pope without peer whose pontificate was a watershed in the history of the crusades.

Innocent III's crusade activities were as diverse as his age and as complex as the man himself. He summoned and set in motion the **Fourth Crusade** and laid the groundwork for the **Fifth Crusade.** He anticipated and set a precedent for the thirteenth-century papacy's **political crusades** with a short-lived war

A Western view of two antithetical types of worship—that of a faithful Christian and that of an infidel. On the left a royal or noble pilgrim (Godfrey of Bouillon?) prays before the *edicule* that houses the Holy Sepulcher; on the right, three male Muslims worship the idol *Mahomet* (Muhammad) in Jerusalem, while a man and a woman look on. Despite abundant evidence to the contrary, throughout the Age of the Crusades and following, many Westerners continued to believe that Muslims were idol-worshipping polytheists. From a manuscript copy of the *Estoire d'Eracles*, a continuation of William of Tyre's history to 1229. Late thirteenth century (1295?), Paris or northern France. The Walters Art Museum, Baltimore.

against Markward of Anweiler (1199–1202). He launched the **Roman papacy**'s first crusade against **heretics,** the **Albigensian Crusade.** He promoted the **Baltic Crusades** and the establishment of the first **Baltic military order,** the Sword Brothers. He encouraged the armies of the **Reconquista** and was rewarded with the great Spanish victory at **Las Navas de Tolosa.** Sensitive to the spiritual currents of his day, Innocent apparently gave his blessing to the piety and zeal of the participants of the so-called **Children's Crusade,** even as he urged them to return home. More significantly, he welcomed and patronized the new orders of **mendicant friars,** which became the thirteenth-century papacy's new crusade weapon. As a self-conscious lawyer-pope, he established a wide variety of legal precedents regarding crusade activities, including restricting the rights of wives to prevent their husbands' swearing **crusade vows.**

He redefined who might take a crusade vow, opening it to all, no matter their physical abilities, and put in place new procedures for the commutation and redemption of those vows. He pioneered and experimented with new methods for **recruiting** crusaders, including establishing specific **preaching** zones throughout Europe. Wishing to make the spiritual benefits of the crusade available to all, Innocent offered the opportunity to participate in the **crusade indulgence** to every **Latin** Christian, not just those traveling on crusade, and by liberalizing access to this indulgence, he unwittingly set the Church on a course that would bring down on it widespread **criticism** for abuse of its spiritual treasures. In like manner, he created new methods for **financing** crusades, which ultimately made it possible for the Church to establish a highly organized system for collecting taxes, but this tax-collecting would also earn the

A contemporary portrait of Pope Innocent III at the monastery of Subiaco in Italy.

Church a good deal of hostile criticism in future years. In short, Innocent, more than any other individual, was responsible for transforming the crusade into a tool of papal policy and defining it as a regular institution of the Roman Church, but he also set in motion forces that would contribute to the Church's troubles in the fourteenth, fifteenth, and sixteenth centuries. **Related Entries:** Apocalypse and the Crusades; Bull, Papal; Councils and Synods; Fulk of Neuilly; Honorius III, Pope; Legates, Papal; Women.

Suggested Reading

Primary Source

"The Registers of Innocent III," in *Alfred J. Andrea,* ed. and trans., *Contemporary Sources for the Fourth Crusade* (2000), pp. 7–176.

Historical Studies

John C. Moore, *Pope Innocent III (1160/61–1216): To Root Up and To Plant* (2003); Jane E. Sayers, *Innocent III: Leader of Europe, 1198–1216* (1994); Helene Tillmann, *Pope Innocent III* (1980).

Investiture Controversy

A conflict between the **Roman papacy** and a number of secular lords, principally Emperor Henry IV, that lasted from 1076 to 1122 and served as background to the **First Crusade.**

The Investiture Controversy ostensibly centered on the issue of whether or not lay rulers, especially emperors and kings, could legitimately install churchmen in their ecclesiastical offices and invest them with the symbols of those offices. In fact, however, it revolved around a more basic issue: Who is the God-ordained head of the Christian people on Earth, the pope or various emperors and kings in their respective realms? Begun in the pontificate of Pope **Gregory VII,** the controversy pitted Gregory and five of his successors against two Western emperors, Henry IV and Henry V.

Early in the conflict, Emperor Henry enthroned an imperial antipope, Clement III, who claimed to be the rightful holder of the papal office, as opposed to Pope Gregory and his successors, Victor III and **Urban II.** When Victor III died in 1088, Odo, cardinal-bishop of Ostia, was elected to succeed him and chose the name *Urban,* probably to signify his determination to rule Christendom from the city (*urbs* in Latin) of Rome. At the time, Clement III controlled most of Rome. It was not until 1094 that Pope Urban was able to become undisputed master of the city. Following this papal victory, Clement III returned to his home in northern Italy and no longer challenged Urban's authority. With this turn of events, Urban increased the tempo of church reform. One tactic he employed was to preside over reform **councils** in France and Italy. One such council was held at **Clermont** in November 1095, and at that council the pope set in motion a new movement that, at least in his mind, was an integral part of his overall program of a papally directed, moral reformation of Christendom—the First Crusade.

Because of the still-raging Investiture Controversy, almost all of Henry IV's high-ranking imperial nobles chose not to participate in the crusade, the only notable exception being **Godfrey of Boullion,** the duke of Lower Lorraine. **Related Entries:** Holy War/Just War; Truce and Peace of God.

Suggested Reading

Uta-Renata Blumenthal, *The Investiture Controversy* (1988).

Isaac II Angelus

Emperor of **Constantinople** (r. 1185–1195 and 1203), whose life and career touched the **Third** and **Fourth Crusades.**

Isaac II ascended the imperial throne in 1185 by accident when his foiling of a plot hatched by the bloodthirsty and probably mad Emperor Andronicus I to murder him sparked an urban riot and the crowd demanded his installation as emperor. The unpopular Andronicus I fled the city but was captured, brought back in chains, and publicly executed.

Isaac's reign was troubled from the start. **Norman** invaders from the kingdom of Sicily were devastating **Byzantine** lands in the Balkans, having invaded the region three months before Isaac's palace coup. By the end of the year, the invaders had been largely beaten back with heavy losses, but King William II of Sicily continued the fight, begun a century earlier by Robert Guiscard and his

son **Bohemond of Taranto,** with piratical attacks on Byzantium's islands and seacoast. In this effort, William was allied with the rebel Isaac Comnenus, who held the island of **Cyprus** and claimed the imperial title as his due. One result of the attacks was the permanent loss of various western islands to the Sicilians.

It was not until 1187 that peace was finally concluded between William II and Isaac. **Saladin**'s conquests in the **Holy Land** that year played a major role in convincing King William to agree to a treaty because as soon as he heard of the fall of **Jerusalem,** he focused all of his energies on sending aid to the embattled **crusader states.**

The Norman invasion, one of the most serious attacks that Byzantium had experienced in recent memory, a raised **Greek** fears of Western aggression to a high level. It was within this context that Isaac heard of the coming of Emperor **Frederick I Barbarossa,** who proposed to march his forces, which constituted the single largest contingent of the armies of the Third Crusade, across Byzantine soil. Isaac was aghast and prepared a hostile welcome.

Frederick, who was eager to reach **Syria-Palestine,** had no intention of conquering Byzantium, but Isaac did not know that. Although a Byzantine ambassador had assured Frederick that his forces could pass safely through Byzantine lands and food would be provided at reasonable prices, Isaac was not about to grant Barbarossa an easy passage. In his fear, he turned to Saladin and reached an understanding whereby he would delay and destroy Frederick's army in the Balkans, in return for some concessions in the Holy Land. Ironically, in this same year, 1188, Frederick renewed a pact with the **Seljuk** sultan of Iconium to secure his army's unhindered passage across the desolate wastes of south-central **Anatolia** (a pact that the sultan later broke).

As Frederick's army marched through the Balkans, it initially encountered hostile attacks by peasant guerrillas acting on Isaac's orders and no markets in which to purchase food. Later it encountered regular Byzantine forces, which, however, fled when confronted by the German **cavalry**. The way to Constantinople now lay open to Barbarossa, but he initially favored pin-prick raids and foraging expeditions, to strengthen his hand in negotiations, rather than an all-out assault on the Byzantine capital. In mid-November 1189, he concluded that this strategy was not working and decided to attack the capital city. By December, Isaac realized that continuing the war was not a good idea, and he yielded on all points in a treaty that was concluded on February 14, 1190. As one of his concessions, Isaac agreed to release numerous Westerners whom he had held captive for years.

Having gained everything he desired, Frederick crossed the Dardanelles into Anatolia, where he met his death on June 10, 1190. His son and successor, **Henry VI,** who also gained the crown of Sicily in 1194, saw the Byzantine empire as a tempting target, whose weaknesses had been revealed by his father's exploits. Carrying on the tradition of Italo-Norman ambitions in the Balkans, Henry demanded in early 1195 that Isaac cede him lands that William II had momentarily conquered ten years earlier.

An exhausted Isaac was spared further humiliation at the hands of a **Hohenstaufen** Western emperor when his brother Alexius deposed and blinded him in April 1195. Eight years of comfortable house arrest followed. If we can believe the Byzantine **historian** Nicetas Choniates, the deposed emperor freely received guests and was able to send letters to the West, requesting that his daughter Irene, who was married to **Philip of Swabia,** Henry VI's younger brother, avenge her father against the new emperor, Alexius III.

In 1201 Isaac's young son, also named Alexius, escaped his uncle's not-very-careful supervision and fled to his sister in Germany. There he encountered crusaders preparing to attack Egypt by way of the port city of Alexandria. After a long period of negotiation and with some incredible luck, he was able, in January 1203, to convince the crusade's leadership to transport him in the coming sailing season to Constantinople to free his father and to rewin his patrimony. Thanks to crusader intervention, Alexius III fled the city in mid-July, and Isaac was released and reinstalled as emperor, with his son crowned as co-emperor, Alexius IV.

Isaac apparently never recovered from his years of captivity, and his physical and mental health rapidly declined in the half year that followed. Following his son's deposition and imprisonment in a palace coup early in January 1204, the demented Isaac died in unclear circumstances. His death spared him the horrors that befell Constantinople three months later when the city was captured and sacked by the same crusader army that had won Isaac's release. **Related Entries:** Adrianople; Conrad of Montferrat.

Suggested Reading

Primary Source

Nicetas Choniates, *O City of Byzantium,* trans. by Harry J. Margoulias (1984).

Historical Study

Charles M. Brand, *Byzantium Confronts the West, 1180–1204* (1968).

Isabella I

Heiress and queen of **Jerusalem** (r. 1190–1205). Three of her four husbands acquired claims to the crown by virtue of marriage to her.

Isabella, the younger daughter of King **Amalric,** married Humphrey IV of Toron in 1183 at the age of eleven. By all accounts, it was a love-filled marriage. At the time, she had no reason to hope that the crown would ever pass to her because King **Baldwin IV,** her older half-sister **Sibylla,** and Sibylla's son, the future **Baldwin V,** all stood between her and the throne. By 1190 they were all dead, as well as Sibylla's two young daughters, Alice and Maria. Against heavy odds, Isabella was now heiress to the throne. In that same year she married **Conrad of Montferrat,** after her marriage to Humphrey was annulled—despite her and Humphrey's heated protests. Conrad was elected but never crowned king, falling to an **Assassin**'s dagger in 1192. Isabella's next husband, **Henry of Champagne** (r. 1192–1197), exercised regal powers but never claimed a royal title. Like Conrad, he met a tragic death, falling backward out of a window. Her fourth husband, King **Aimery of Lusignan** (r. 1197–1205), died after overindulging in a feast of fish. When Aimery died Isabella was only thirty-three, but she died soon after, passing her inheritance to her daughter **Maria of Montferrat. Related Entry:** Guy of Lusignan.

Isabella (Yolanda) II

Princess and heiress of **Jerusalem** (1212–1225); queen of Jerusalem (r. 1225–1228), wife of Emperor **Frederick II,** and mother of **Conrad IV** of **Hohenstaufen** (King Conrad II of Jerusalem).

Born to Queen **Maria of Montferrat** and King **John of Brienne,** the infant Isabella (also known as Yolanda) became heiress to the kingdom when Maria died in 1212, although John continued to rule as king. Her marriage, at age fourteen, to Frederick II on November 9, 1225, resulted in John's being outmaneuvered by Frederick,

who informed John that he, Frederick, was now king of Jerusalem. Upon her death in childbirth on May 8, 1228, the crown passed to her infant son, Conrad, even though Frederick crowned himself king of Jerusalem in 1229. **Related Entries:** Montferrat, Family of; Sixth Crusade.

Islam

Islam, a religion of Arabic origin, was the enemy against which Christian Europe launched crusades in **Anatolia, Syria-Palestine,** Egypt, other portions of North Africa, and the Iberian Peninsula.

Islam means "submission" in Arabic, and a **Muslim** is anyone who submits to God's Will by following His teachings as transmitted through the Prophet Muhammad (ca. 571–632) and set down in the Koran (*al-Qur'an*). Around 610, Muhammad ibn Abdullah, a prosperous merchant of Mecca, began to receive visions in which he was called to be the Messenger of Allah, a divinity whose Arabic name (*al-Llah*) means "*the God.*" Muhammad's mission was to preach the Oneness of God ("There is no god but the God."), the imminence of the Resurrection of the dead, the coming of a divine Day of Judgment, and the existence of an all-consuming hell fire for the unjust and unbelievers and a paradise of bliss for the faithful. Muhammad believed that, just as Jews and Christians had their divine revelations from God, now the Arabs were receiving the full and final word of God through him, the last and greatest of the prophets but still only a man. Abraham, Moses, Jesus, and the other prophets had been earlier messengers of God, but Muhammad was the *Seal of the Prophets.*

Most Meccans were initially unmoved by Muhammad's message, so in 622 Muhammad and the majority of his small band of converts journeyed over 200 miles

Islam's connection with Judaism: The Dome of the Rock, Jerusalem. A seventh-century Islamic shrine on Jerusalem's Temple Mount, it covers Mount Moriah, the rock on which Muslims believe Abraham, the father of all Muslims, was prepared to sacrifice his elder son, Ishmael, to God, and also the spot from which Muhammad made his mystical Night Journey to Heaven. Known to the Latins as the *Templum Domini* (The Lord's Temple), because it was probably the site of the inner sanctuary (Holy of Holies) of the Temple, it was converted by the crusaders into a Christian church. It returned to its original Islamic use when Saladin recovered the city in 1187.

to an oasis settlement that would become known as *Medinat al-Nabi* (City of the Prophet) or, more simply, Medina. By this act, known as the *hijra* (breaking of ties), these first Muslims abandoned their tribal bonds and opted for membership in an Islamic community, or *umma,* that was defined by a shared faith and not blood kinship. This migration was so pivotal in the history of Islam that Muslims later designated it the beginning of the Era of Islam—the Year 1 of the Islamic calendar.

It was at Medina that circumstances forced Muhammad to add the duties of statesman and warrior to that of prophet. After more than seven years of holy **jihad,**

Muhammad and a reputed 10,000 followers were able to enter Mecca in triumph in 630. The Messenger of Allah was now the most powerful chieftain in Arabia, and most of the tribes of the peninsula soon were united under his leadership. Muhammad died in 632, but Islam continued to grow under his successors, the *caliphs* (deputies of the Prophet), who claimed leadership over the family of Islam. This new community of faith was so strong that under the second caliph, Umar, Islam exploded out of the Arabian Peninsula in a series of raids that soon turned into wars of conquest.

Before Umar's death in 644 the **Byzantine empire** had lost all of Syria-Palestine

Islam's connection with Christianity: The Shrine of the Ascension on the Mount of Olives outside Jerusalem, believed by Christians and Muslims to be the site of Jesus' Ascension into Heaven. Reconstructed during the Crusader Era, today it is a Muslim shrine where Christians also worship.

and Egypt to Islam, and the Arab conquest of the Persian empire was virtually completed. By 750 lands under Islamic domination reached from the Pyrenees and Atlantic coast in Spain to the Indus Valley of South Asia (modern Pakistan) and China's western borders in Central Asia.

Originally the Arabs considered Islam their special revelation and had little or no intention of sharing the faith with their non-Arab subjects, but several factors combined to attract large numbers of non-Arabic converts. These included Islam's uncompromising monotheism and the straightforwardness of its other central doctrines; the psychic and social security offered by membership in a totally integrated Muslim community, where one's entire life is subject to God's Word; and the desire to escape the second-class status of Islam's non-Muslim subjects. When the

Abbasid caliphs established their court at Baghdad on the Tigris in 762, they claimed dominion over a multiethnic empire bound together by one of the most attractive and fastest growing religions in human history.

Later other peoples, especially the **Turks,** converted to Islam and carried it farther afield, especially into the heart of India and deeply into Central Asia. Arab and East African merchants transported the faith across the Indian Ocean to the ports of Southeast Asia, and Berbers from North Africa introduced Islam into western sub-Saharan Africa. **Related Entries:** Almohads; Almoravids; Assassins; Fatimids; Islamic Peoples; Shia; Sunnism.

Suggested Reading

Jonathan P. Berkey, *The Formation of Islam: Religion and Society in the Near East, 600–1800* (2002); John Esposito, ed. *The Oxford History of Islam* (1999); Bernard Lewis, *The Middle East: A Brief History of the Last 2,000 Years* (1995); Francis Robinson, ed., *The Cambridge Illustrated History of the Islamic World* (1996).

Islamic Peoples

Islam in the Age of the Crusades was a religion that encompassed a wide variety of ethnic groups within the Afro-Eurasian World.

Although Islam had its origins in Arabia and was centered on a sacred book, the Koran, which was written in Arabic and was memorized and recited by Muslims whoever they were and wherever they lived, the majority of Muslims by 1100 were not Arabs. A common Islamic religion, in which belief and lifestyle are inextricably intertwined, gave life and reality to an entity that Muslims call *Dar al-Islam* (the House of Islam), an international family of Muslims that stretched from the Atlantic to the Indian Ocean, from sub-Saharan West African kingdoms to outposts in China during the Crusade Era. As this geographic sweep suggests, within the family of Islam many different ethnic groups existed side by side.

So far as the crusades were concerned, a few of the more important Islamic groups were: (1) The Arabs, who inhabited Arabia and Iraq and were the major ethnic group in Syria-Palestine. They could also be found in Egypt and in portions of North Africa, but there they were mixed with other ethnic groups, mainly the native Copts of Egypt and the Berbers of central and western North Africa. (2) The major folk of North Africa west of Egypt were the various Berber tribes, who also resided in Iberia, where they were known as **Moors.** (3) Various **Turkic** tribes out of Central Asia, most notably the **Seljuks,** settled in **Anatolia** and bordering areas and were in the process of transforming much of Anatolia into a new homeland. (4) In the mountains of eastern Anatolia and western Iraq dwelled a people known as the Kurds; the most famous Kurd of this era was **Saladin.** (5) Iran was home to the Iranian, or Persian, people who differed radically in culture and language from the Arabs but who, in concert with the Arabs, provided the Islamic world with its second major cultural matrix. Indeed, it is quite correct to speak of the Irano-Arabic, or Persian-Arabic, high culture of the portion of the Islamic World that centered on Baghdad in Iraq and stretched east into northern India and west into **Syria-Palestine.** Mastery of both Persian and Arabic literature was the hallmark of an educated Muslim in this broad region regardless of ethnic identity. **Related Entries:** Almohads; Almoravids; Ayyubids; Historians and Chroniclers, Islamic; Khorezmians; Ottomans; Zangids.

Suggested Reading

Richard Bulliet, *Conversion to Islam in the Middle Ages* (1979); Carole Hillenbrand, *The Crusades: Islamic Perspectives* (2000).

J

Jaffa

The closest harbor to **Jerusalem,** the natural port of entry for **pilgrims** from the West, and the center of an important **feudal** county within the **kingdom of Jerusalem.**

A squadron of six Genoese and English ships sailed into Jaffa on June 17, 1099, to discover the city abandoned. The food and supplies that they unloaded and carried to the crusaders besieging Jerusalem proved essential to the crusaders' successful attack on the city the following month. Until other ports along the Palestinian coast were captured, such as Caesarea (1101), **Acre** (1104), Sidon (1110), **Tyre** (1124), and **Ascalon** (1153), Jaffa was the kingdom of Jerusalem's sole lifeline to the West. Even after the kingdom acquired additional port cities, Jaffa remained an important element in the kingdom's commercial and military infrastructure.

Jaffa passed back into Muslim hands in July 1187, when **Saladin** captured it by storm and **massacred** or **enslaved** all of its **Frankish** inhabitants. He then ordered its fortifications destroyed. **Richard I** retook the city on September 9, 1191, and partially restored its walls and towers. On July 27, 1192, Saladin attacked Jaffa and took the entire city on July 30, except for the citadel, where the last of the garrison held out. Richard, upon hearing of the attack, immediately sailed from Acre with a small force and arrived on August 1, just as the defenders in the citadel were about to surrender. His quick reaction saved the day and resulted in the enemy's headlong retreat with heavy losses. Richard then set about repairing the city's walls. While this work

Richard the Lion-Heart delivering Jaffa. Dover Pictorial Archives.

was going on, Saladin realized that he greatly outnumbered Richard's army and decided to take the crusaders with a surprise envelopment. Saladin's maneuvers, which began the night of August 4, failed to surprise Richard, and the following day witnessed another crusader victory and Muslim rout—the last battle of the **Third Crusade.**

In the peace treaty that followed, Richard handed Ascalon and several other fortified sites back to Muslim control but held firmly on to Jaffa, fully aware of its strategic importance.

In September 1197 Sultan **al-Adil (Saphadin)** retook Jaffa, but he found it expedient to return it as part of a peace settlement in September 1204. It remained in Frankish hands for almost sixty-four more years, during which time both **Frederick II** and **Louis IX** funded reconstruction of portions of its defenses during their stays in the **Holy Land.** These defenses, however, could not prevent its capture by **Baybars** on March 7, 1268. Determined that crusaders would never again use it as a stronghold, he destroyed its citadel and ordered its stones and timbers transported to **Cairo,** where they were used to build the sultan's grand mosque. Today, almost nothing remains of Jaffa's crusader structures.

Suggested Reading

S. Tolkowsky, *The Gateway of Palestine: A History of Jaffa* (1925).

James of Vitry

Born in Champagne around 1170; died in Rome 1240. Crusade **preacher,** bishop of **Acre** (r. 1216–1228), **missionary, historian,** participant in the **Fifth Crusade,** church reformer, cardinal bishop of Tusculum (1228–1240).

James preached the **Albigensian Crusade** in 1211–1212 and, several years later, the Fifth Crusade. A number of his crusade

sermons still exist and show us a preacher who dwelt on the theme of the **cross** as the altar on which Christ sacrificed Himself for humanity's sins and the emblem of the Christian's commitment to his Savior.

In 1216 he was elected bishop of Acre and arrived at his post probably in October. There, and in other coastal cities in the **kingdom of Jerusalem,** he continued to preach the upcoming crusade. There he also tried to reform a city that had a reputation for moral laxity. In letters to the West he described in detail his duties and trials in the "sin city" of the **Latin East.** His description of what he perceived to be the effeminate, gone-native ways of the *poulain* inhabitants of **Syria-Palestine** reveals as much, if not more, about the cultural divide that separated native-born **Franks** and newcomers from the West than it does about the moral quality of life in **Outremer.**

As bishop of Acre, James was a pioneer missionary among the **Muslims** of the region, but his attempts to convert by persuasion in no way contradicted his fervent support of crusading. In 1217 he joined the forces of the Fifth Crusade, sailed with the army to Egypt in 1218, and remained with it to the end. His seven extant letters to the West that cover the period 1216–1221 constitute one of the most important eyewitness accounts of the crusade.

In addition to his letters, James also composed a history of the East entitled *The Jerusalem History,* which borrowed heavily from **William of Tyre,** including his now-lost *The Deeds of the Eastern Princes.* James was back in Europe by 1225, and in 1228 he was raised to the cardinalate by Pope **Gregory IX. Related Entry:** Oliver of Paderborn.

Jerusalem, City of

The principal city of **Palestine,** Jerusalem is sacred to three monotheistic faiths, Judaism,

Christianity, and **Islam,** and served as the focal point of the crusades.

According to biblical accounts, Jerusalem became the capital of the kingdom of Israel under King David around 1000 B.C.E., and it was there that David's son and successor, Solomon, raised the First Temple to the God of Israel around 960 B.C.E. The Temple served as the religious center for the Israelites until the invading army of King Nebuchadnezzar destroyed it in 586 B.C.E., but the **Jews** rebuilt it upon their release from captivity in Babylon after 538 B.C.E. During the first century B.C.E. King Herod substantially enlarged and beautified the Temple. This Second Temple, in which Jesus of Nazareth worshiped, was destroyed in 70 C.E. by Roman armies that razed the city while suppressing a general rebellion in the province of Judea. The city was rebuilt and reconfigured many times over in the following centuries, but the Temple never again rose. All that remained of it was a retaining wall constructed by Herod's engineers. Known formally as the *Western Wall,* it became known popularly as the *Wailing Wall,* for it was there that pious Jews lamented the destruction of the Temple and their general exclusion from the City of David, which remained in the hands of various gentile peoples until the mid–twentieth century.

The Golden Gate, Jerusalem. Large numbers of crusader dead were buried outside this gate after the city's capture on July 15, 1099, in expectation of the Last Judgment. It was believed that Jesus would gather up the souls of the dead at this spot at his Second Coming. Muslims also believe this is the place where Jesus the Messiah will usher in the Last Judgment. The graves in the foreground are Muslim and date from the post-crusade period.

The Christian Church was born in Jerusalem around 30 C.E., but the city became a major center of Christian worship and administration only in the early fourth century when Emperor Constantine the Great adopted Christianity as his favored religion. Constantine, his mother, Helena, and Constantine's imperial successors transformed the pagan city of *Aelia Capitolina* (as Jerusalem was then known) back into the holy city of Jerusalem, but now it was a Christian holy city and center of pious **pilgrimage.** The city and its environs were filled with monasteries, churches, and shrines, all of which commemorated moments in the ministry of Jesus or in the history of the early Christian Church. Chief among them was the **Church of the Holy Sepulcher** that Emperor Constantine built at state expense in 335.

Despite vicissitudes, such as the Persian sack of the city in 614, Jerusalem remained an important center of Christianity until its capture by the Islamic armies of Caliph Umar in 638. The **Muslims** treated Jerusalem with great respect because in Islamic eyes it is exceeded in sanctity only by the cities of Mecca and Medina in Arabia. Known in Arabic as *al-Quds* (The Holy Place), Jerusalem enjoys this place of honor for several reasons. First, it is a city made sacred by Abraham, whom the Koran, the holy book of **Islam,** identifies as a true Muslim (and not a Jew) and the father of all Arabs. Second, tradition identifies Jerusalem as the place from which the Prophet Muhammad made his mystical Night Journey to Heaven. Because Islam views Jews and Christians as *Peoples of the Book,* that is, people who received a portion of God's revelation and enshrined it in sacred books (the Torah and the Gospels), the Muslim victors accepted them as *dhimmis,* or tolerated non-Muslim subjects. Jews were allowed to return to Arab-controlled Jerusalem, and the

supreme religious authority of Judaism, the *Gaonim,* moved its seat from Tiberias in the north back to the holy city, where it remained until expelled by crusaders at the end of the eleventh century.

At the same time, the new conquerors of Jerusalem were eager to assert their religious superiority over their Jewish and Christian subjects. The Temple Mount, the broad, elevated plaza on which the destroyed Second Temple had stood, was transformed into a Muslim holy place, the *al-Harem as-Sharif* (The Noble Sanctuary). Over Mount Moriah, presumed location of the Temple's sanctuary, Caliph 'Abd al-Malik constructed late in the seventh century a small, exquisitely beautiful octagonal shrine known as the *Dome of the Rock.* The dimensions of the shrine's golden dome exactly match that of the rotunda that then covered the Holy Sepulcher, but its magnificence far surpassed that of the Christian shrine, thereby proclaiming to all who saw it that Islam is God's full and final truth. Nearby stands the early eighth-century *Al-Aksa* Mosque, which commemorates Muhammad's Night Journey to Paradise. Constructed in imitation of the Constantinian church of the Holy Sepulcher but on a much grander scale, it also serves as a statement in stone of Islam's supremacy.

Between 661 and 750 mainstream, or **Sunni,** Islam was ruled by caliphs from the Umayyad dynasty, who established their capital at **Damascus** in **Syria.** Their proximity to Jerusalem assured the holy city close supervision and generous care. In 750 the Umayyads were overthrown and supplanted by the **Abbasid** dynasty, who in 762 moved the capital farther east to Baghdad in Iraq. Conditions in now-neglected Palestine degenerated, especially as the Abbasids slipped into a state of powerlessness in the tenth century.

In 969 the **Fatimids,** adherents of the rival **Shia** branch of Islam, added Jerusalem and all of **Palestine** to their empire, which was centered in Egypt. Although the Fatimids normally were tolerant of Jews and Christians, Caliph al-Hakim ordered the destruction of the Church of the Holy Sepulcher in September 1009 as part of a program of repression of non-Muslims. Al-Hakim's persecution of Christians and Jews left the city a shambles, which was exacerbated by an earthquake in 1016.

In 1071, the same year as the **Battle of Manzikert,** a **Turkish** adventurer captured Jerusalem. When the city rebelled, he retook it in a bloodbath in which Sunni Turkish Muslims slaughtered large numbers of Shia Muslims on the Temple Mount, thereby strangely presaging the crusader capture of Jerusalem several decades later. In 1079 the city was incorporated into the empire of the Great **Seljuk,** but in 1098 the rival Fatimids regained control of the city, just as the armies of the **First Crusade** were marching toward it.

The crusaders captured Jerusalem on July 15, 1099. Contemporary **historians and chroniclers** describe the capture as a frenzied slaughter in which no one was spared, and undoubtedly there was a **massacre** in which many unresisting Muslims and Jews were killed, especially on the Temple Mount. According to one crusader eyewitness:

Some of the pagans were mercifully beheaded; others, pierced by arrows, plunged from towers; yet others, tortured for a long time, were burned to death in searing flames. Piles of heads, hands, and feet lay about in the houses and on the streets.

At the same time, evidence suggests that the killing was not as all-embracing as the **chronicles** suggest. Many non-Christians were taken alive, either for ransom or **slavery.**

A little over a year later, the Latin **kingdom of Jerusalem** was established, and its monarchs held the holy city until October 2, 1187, when the forces of **Saladin** retook it. During the eighty-eight years of **Frankish** occupation, non-Christians were generally not permitted to establish permanent residence in Jerusalem, but Muslims and Jews were allowed into the city for business and even for prayers. With Saladin's capture of Jerusalem the situation was reversed. Western Christians either left the city, having been granted their liberty by Saladin, or were sold into slavery. Only **Eastern Christians** remained to maintain worship at the few churches that Saladin allowed them to keep—the major one being the Church of the Holy Sepulcher.

In March 1219 the **Ayyubid** ruler of Syria-Palestine, al-Muazzam, fearing crusader attacks in the course of the **Fifth Crusade,** ordered the destruction of Jerusalem's walls and many of its buildings. Ten years later his brother **al-Kamil** ceded the unfortified city of Jerusalem to Emperor **Frederick II** as part of a ten-year truce. The Temple Mount, however, remained in Muslim hands, and Muslims residing in Jerusalem were to be governed by Islamic law and subject to their own judge. Although Frederick was accorded the right to refortify Jerusalem, little was done to rebuild the walls. On December 7, 1239, the Muslim lord of **Transjordan** recaptured a nearly defenseless Jerusalem. In 1241 the Franks recovered Jerusalem through an alliance with the sultan of Egypt but lost the city for good in July 1244 when **Khorezmians** swept through the region and massacred the Christians whom they encountered.

Jerusalem's capture inspired **Louis IX** to take the **crusader's cross,** but his efforts to recover the city ended in disaster. The city remained in Egyptian hands until the **Ottomans** conquered Palestine in

1516–1517. It was not until December 9, 1917, that a Western army was able to wrest the Holy City from Ottoman control when the Allied forces of General Allenby entered Jerusalem in triumph. **Related Entries:** Balian II of Ibelin; Crusade of 1239–1241; Holy Land; Jerusalem, Kingdom of; Jerusalem, Latin Patriarchate of; Montjoie; Pillage and Plunder; Relics.

Suggested Reading

Primary Source

Francis E. Peters, *Jerusalem: The Holy City in the Eyes of Chroniclers, Visitors, Pilgrims, and Prophets from the Days of Abraham to the Beginning of Modern Times* (1985).

Historical Studies

Amikan Elad, *Medieval Jerusalem and Islamic Worship: Holy Places, Ceremony, Pilgrimage* (1995); Kamil Jamil Ascali, ed., *Jerusalem in History* (2000); Dan Bahat, *The Illustrated Atlas of Jerusalem* (1990); Adrian J. Boas, *Jerusalem in the Time of the Crusades* (2001); Martin Gilbert, *Jerusalem: Illustrated Atlas,* 3rd. ed. (1994); Joshua Prawer and Haggai Ben-Shammai, eds., *The History of Jerusalem: The Early Muslim Period, 638–1099* (1996); Andrew Sinclair, *Jerusalem: The Endless Crusade* (1995).

Jerusalem, Kingdom of (1099–1291)

The largest, most important of the four **crusader states** carved out of lands conquered during the **First Crusade** and its aftermath.

On July 22, 1099, seven days after the conquest of **Jerusalem,** the lords of the army elected **Godfrey of Bouillon** ruler of the city and defender of its churches, ignoring the demand of many clerics that they choose a "spiritual deputy" (presumably of the pope) rather than a lay lord. The second **Latin patriarch of Jerusalem,** Daimbert of Pisa,

who was elected to the office on December 25, 1099, attempted to change in his favor the balance of power between secular and ecclesiastical authority in this new **Latin** state. Godfrey's defense of his powers and prerogatives prevailed, however, and when Godfrey died on July 18, 1100, he left behind a secular state for his brother and successor, **Baldwin of Boulogne.**

Baldwin I also brushed aside the patriarch's claims to supremacy and went beyond his brother by claiming the title "king" and being crowned in Bethlehem on Christmas Day 1100. By this act, King Baldwin linked his crown with the biblical House of King David and with Jesus; his position as king was now unassailable.

Baldwin I was a strong monarch who set the kingdom on a solid base by pursuing a vigorous policy of expansionism in all possible directions, In 1104, for example, he captured **Acre** with Genoese help, and by this conquest gave the kingdom a superior harbor, which soon became the economic center of the kingdom. In 1118 King Baldwin died on campaign, but before his death he had conquered most of the Palestinian coast, had halted Egyptian and **Seljuk** aggression against his kingdom, had established an understanding of mutual nonaggression with **Damascus,** and had added **Transjordan** and territories in the south to his realm. In short, he had created a true kingdom and had established himself as the leading Latin statesman in **Outremer.** Because of his accomplishments, future kings of Jerusalem would be able to claim the status of first among equals in the hierarchy of prestige and authority among the four crusader states.

Baldwin I was succeeded by his cousin, **Baldwin II of Le Bourcq,** and by this act the family of Godfrey of Bouillon was established as the hereditary royal dynasty of Jerusalem. Thereafter, succession to the crown was by inheritance, although at times the **High Court** of the kingdom had to decide between competing claims. Baldwin I and his immediate successors created a strong **feudal** monarchy, dividing the kingdom into two types of lands: crown lands and lordships.

Crown lands, also known as royal domain lands, consisted of three strategically important blocks of territory: in the heart of the kingdom a large region centered on the cities of Jerusalem and Nablus; along the northern coast lands that surrounded the key ports of Acre and **Tyre;** in the far south a piece of territory along the Gaza Strip. The king ruled and exploited crown lands directly. His control over the kingdom's heartland around Jerusalem gave him the Holy City as his capital and also ready access to the rest of his kingdom. Control over Acre and Tyre allowed him to tap into the riches of the two most important commercial centers in his kingdom. Control over the Gaza Strip gave him a launching area for raids and campaigns into Egypt.

The lordships were huge contiguous areas that the king gave out in feudal tenure to a number of important **vassals** known as tenants-in-chief. Tenants-in-chief, who included the prince of Galilee and the lords of Caesarea, Ascalon, and Hebron, to name but a few, governed their lands pretty much without royal interference, conducted their own foreign relations with their Christian and **Muslim** neighbors, and exercised jurisdiction over their own vassals to whom they gave **fiefs.** From 1163, however, these so-called rear vassals were obliged to render homage directly to the king, as well as to their immediate lords.

In return for their baronies, the king's tenants-in-chief were responsible for providing a set number of **knights** and **sergeants** for the royal army. For example, the prince

of Galilee, was required to supply 100 knights whenever the king needed to muster an army.

During the thirteenth century the monarchy, which had been powerful prior to 1187, lost power to the great noble families and the High Court of the kingdom, especially after 1229 when the kingdom's monarchs resided elsewhere, in Europe or **Cyprus.**

Despite losing Jerusalem and most of its other territories to **Saladin** in 1187, the kingdom survived for another century. Subsequent crusades, especially the **Third Crusade,** enabled the kingdom to recover the Palestinian coast and, most important of all, to recapture Acre, which served as the kingdom's new capital from 1191 to 1291. Treaties with the **Ayyubids** of Egypt and **Syria** in 1229 and 1241 restored the city of Jerusalem and additional lands to the kingdom. The second and final Muslim reconquest of the kingdom began in 1244, with the recapture of Jerusalem, and ended in 1291 with the fall of Acre and the total collapse of the kingdom. **Related Entries:** Aimery of Lusignan; Baldwin III; Baldwin IV; Baldwin V; Conrad of Montferrat; Fulk of Anjou; Henry of Champagne; Hohenstaufens; Isabella I; Isabella (Yolanda) II; John of Brienne; Maria of Montferrat; Melisende; Sibylla; Women.

Suggested Reading

Peter W. Edbury, *John of Ibelin and the Kingdom of Jerusalem* (1997); Alan V. Murray, *The Crusader Kingdom of Jerusalem: A Dynastic History, 1099–1125* (2000); Jean Richard, *The Latin Kingdom of Jerusalem,* 2 vols., trans. by Janet Shirley (1979); Jonathan Riley-Smith, *The Feudal Nobility and the Kingdom of Jerusalem, 1174–1277* (1973); Sivia Rozenberg, ed., *Knights of the Holy Land: The Crusader Kingdom of Jerusalem* (1999); Steven Tibble, *Monarchy and Lordships in the Latin Kingdom of Jerusalem, 1099–1291* (1989).

Jerusalem, Latin Patriarchate of

The patriarch (ruling father) of **Jerusalem** was the chief ecclesiastical authority not only in the **kingdom of Jerusalem** but throughout the entire region of the **Latin East** that encompassed the four **crusader states.**

Circumstances conspired against the Latin patriarch of **Antioch** and prevented his making counterclaims to those of the patriarch of Jerusalem, even though his patriarchate was older and **Eastern Christians** considered it superior in dignity and authority.

Ever since being accorded patriarchal status in the mid–fifth century, the head of the Church of Jerusalem had been a member of the **Greek,** or **Byzantine,** branch of Christianity. When, however, the crusaders captured Jerusalem on July 15, 1099, they discovered a vacant patriarchate because Symeon II, its Byzantine patriarch, had earlier departed for **Constantinople,** where he died. On August 1 the crusaders elected Arnulf of Chocques, the chaplain of **Robert of Normandy,** to lead the Jerusalem Church. Arnulf was unpopular and his election contained irregularities. In December 1099 the **papal legate,** Archbishop Daimbert of Pisa, deposed Arnulf and got himself elected as patriarch, a position he held until 1102, when he was deposed for numerous sins and crimes, including alleged treason against King **Baldwin I.**

The Latin patriarchs of Jerusalem were a mixed lot. Some were learned; a few were ill educated. Some were noted for their piety; a few led scandalous lives. Several were noted for both their lack of learning and irregular lives. On balance, they were no better or worse than any other cohort of high-ranking churchmen in the East or the West, although several certainly brought no honor to their office. For example, Arnulf of Chocques got himself reelected patriarch in 1112 and managed to hang onto his office until his death in 1118, despite his condemnation for corruption and immorality in 1115. Patriarch Heraclius (r. 1180–1191) was described by one contemporary as "a worldly and rather ignorant cleric who openly paraded his mistress, known as the Patriarchess, around Jerusalem." When he vacated Jerusalem in 1187 following **Saladin**'s conquest of the city, Heraclius was rumored to have carted away a fortune in church property, which he refused to use to ransom the city's poorest Latin citizens from certain **slavery.**

On the other side of the ledger, Patriarchs Gormand (r. 1118–1128), William (r. 1130–1145), and Fulcher (r. 1146–1157) were all praised by **William of Tyre** for their piety. Even Heraclius, for all of the rumors regarding his private life and values, was well educated and an able diplomat. It was rare, however, for spirituality and administrative ability to be found in the same patriarch, although Patriarch Gormand managed to combine both qualities. The same was true of Albert of Vercelli (r. 1206–1214), whom the Roman Church canonized as a saint.

From about 1220 to 1291 the papacy usually designated the patriarch of Jerusalem as its permanent legate-in-residence for the kingdom of Jerusalem, thereby strengthening the patriarch's position as spiritual head of the entire Latin East. Special papal legates, however, continued to accompany various crusade armies to the East.

After 1118 all of the patriarchs of Jerusalem were appointees of the king. Whenever the patriarchate fell vacant, the canons of the **church of the Holy Sepulcher,** that is the clerics who served that church's various offices and subordinate churches, selected two nominees, whose names were forwarded to the king. He then chose one of them. In 1180 King **Baldwin**

IV's choices were Archbishop William of Tyre and Archbishop Heraclius of Caesarea. He delegated the task of selection to his mother, **Agnes of Courtenay,** who chose Heraclius.

Heraclius was the last in the line of twelfth-century Latin patriarchs to reside in Jerusalem. In 1191 the seat of the patriarchate was moved to **Acre.** One of the holders of this see-in-exile, James Pantaléon (r. 1255–1261), was elected pope and assumed the papal throne as Urban IV (r. 1261–1264). The last patriarch of Jerusalem to reside at Acre, Nicholas of Hanapes (r. 1288–1291), played a heroic role in the defense of the city. When the city was overrun on May 18, 1291, and only a small force of **Templars** and **Hospitalers** stood between the refugees fleeing to ships in the harbor and the **Mamluks** who pursued them, the aged patriarch allowed himself to be rowed out to an awaiting ship. But he permitted so many others to crowd into his vessel that it sank and he was drowned. **Related Entries:** Balian II of Iberlin; Carmelites; Sixth Crusade.

Suggested Reading

Bernard Hamilton, *The Latin Church in the Crusader States: The Secular Church* (1980); Denys Pringle, *The Churches of the Crusader Kingdom of Jerusalem: A Corpus,* 3 vols. (2 published to date: 1993 and 1998).

Jews and the Crusades

For the various Jewish communities of Europe and **Syria-Palestine,** the Crusade Era was at best troublesome and at worst a disaster.

In the spring and early summer of 1096 armies of German, Flemish, English, and French crusaders attacked a number of Jewish communities, with the most destructive attacks falling on the cities of Mainz, Worms, and Cologne. These were the first of many assaults on Jewish communities during the Age of the Crusades. Contrary to what is often written, as terrible as they were, the attacks of 1096 did not constitute a demographic, economic, or cultural point of decline in the history of medieval European Jewry nor did they presage the coming of an era dedicated to the physical eradication of Jews by Church or state. Indeed, the **Roman papacy** took pains when calling for future crusades to repudiate the notion that Jews were legitimate targets of attack, and a number of secular lords and kings aggressively placed Jews under their protection. At the same time, the anti-Judaic attacks of 1096 were symbolic of changes in **Latin** Christendom's vision of its place in the world whereby it was defining more clearly than ever before itself and the "other." Be the "other" **Muslim** or Jew, that person was increasingly viewed as an enemy of Christianity. This view bred England's expulsion of Jews in 1290, France's several expulsions (and readmissions) of them, and Spain's expulsion of them in 1492.

The fact that medieval Jewish **chroniclers** of the crusades referred to **Clermont,** where Pope **Urban II** called for the First Crusade, as *Har Afel,* "the Mount of Gloom," speaks eloquently of how they perceived this movement, and with reason. Despite the attempts of most local authorities to protect their Jewish residents, the Jewish communities of several cities suffered attack, attempts at forced conversion, and murder as elements of the first wave of the First Crusade passed through the Rhineland and beyond in the spring and early summer of 1096. In response, Jews met these assaults in several ways: Some fought back; some quietly accepted martyrdom; many killed their loved ones and themselves as an act of pious devotion—a radically new expression of the *Kiddush ha-Shem,* or martyrdom for the glory of God.

The army of Count Emicho of Leiningen gained much-deserved infamy for its assaults on the Jews of the Rhineland. At Speyer on May 3 the crusaders tried to storm the synagogue. Frustrated in their efforts, they killed eleven Jews who fell into their hands, but the city's bishop was able to rescue the vast majority of his city's flourishing Jewish community. Worms was next on the route of march, and reportedly 800 Jews died there, many by their own hands or by those of their loved ones. Late in the month Emicho's army reached Mainz.

According to Solomon bar Simson, a Jewish **historian** writing in the 1140s, Duke **Godfrey of Bouillon** had extorted protection money from the Jewish communities of Mainz and Cologne. Bar Simson's testimony on this point has been questioned on several levels, but whatever the truth, Duke Godfrey's forces never molested the Jews of Mainz or Cologne. The same was not true for Count Emicho's crusaders. Try as he did, the archbishop of Mainz could not save his city's Jewish inhabitants. Despite resistance by some Jews, the community was overwhelmed, and a reported 1,000 died, many by self-sacrifice. The Jews of Cologne fared no better. The archbishop dispersed and hid them in seven nearby towns, but late in June Emicho's crusaders systematically sought and wiped out most of them. Other Jewish communities farther east suffered attacks from various first-wave bands of crusaders, but none seems as destructive as those of the Rhineland.

Even Christians were sickened by the **massacres.** The German churchman, Albert of Aachen, reported with glee the destruction of Count Emicho's army in Hungary, and remarked that "the hand of the Lord is believed to have been against the **pilgrims** . . . who had slaughtered the exiled Jews through greed for money." He went on to note that the Lord orders no one to be compelled to become a Christian.

Hebrew sources for the attacks indicate that the primary goal of many of these crusaders was, indeed, the forced conversion and not the death of the Jews whom they attacked. Thus, when the Jews of Regensburg accepted a mass baptism in the waters of the Danube River they were not otherwise molested. After the crusaders left, the community did penance for its forced apostasy and continued to live and worship as Jews. At the same time, a desire to wreak vengeance on Jews whom Christians blamed for the crucifixion of Jesus was another motive that drove some soldiers of the **cross,** and this motive led them to kill, rather than baptize, Jews.

When the second wave of the First Crusade captured **Jerusalem** on July 15, 1099, the crusaders burned down a synagogue, with its congregation trapped inside. The Jewish survivors in the city were **enslaved,** and a number of them were later redeemed by Jewish communities abroad, including the Jews of **Cairo.** Between 1099 and the city's recapture by Muslim forces in 1187, most Jews and Muslims were barred from residing in Jerusalem, lest they defile its holiness, but they were allowed to visit the city for business or pilgrimage. In a few rare cases, some Jews (and Muslims) were given special license to live in Jerusalem because of vital business interests, but they had to pay a special tax for the privilege.

The initial massacre and enslavement of Jews in Jerusalem was probably the norm throughout Syria-Palestine for the first several years' of conquest, as great slaughter often attended the capture of cities and towns. But the crusaders soon learned they needed Jews and Muslims to fuel the economies of their states. Consequently, Jews (and Muslims) were welcomed back into urban areas, where they were accorded special legal status—the status of protected, second-class subjects—and allowed to live and work in peace. Like tolerated non-Muslims in **Islamic** states, every urban Jewish and Muslim male age fifteen or older paid a special tax as a token of his protected but subservient status. Outside of the cities and towns, all Jews fell into the category of serfs—semi-free agricultural workers who were bound to a particular estate or village.

Meanwhile, back in Europe, calls for subsequent crusades were often accompanied by local anti-Jewish activities in one region or another. During the summer of 1146 a **Cistercian** monk named Ralph fomented violence against the Jews of the Rhineland while **preaching** the **Second Crusade,** until **Bernard of Clairvaux** pointed out the error of his ways and sent him packing back to his monastery. Bohemia, Austria, and France also saw a few isolated attacks on Jews.

As soon as word reached Germany of the fall of Jerusalem to **Saladin,** Emperor **Frederick I,** anticipating trouble, placed all Jews in the empire under his protection and forbade all anti-Judaic sermons. In return, he received a large sum of money for his services. The bishops of the empire echoed Frederick's protection by threatening excommunication of anyone who attacked a Jew. This protection might have cost a lot of silver, but it secured the lives and property of the empire's Jews. The Rhineland saw no repeat of 1096 or 1146 as forces mustered for the **Third Crusade.**

The situation was different in England, where attacks on Jewish communities occurred in several locales, the most serious taking place in March 1190 in the city of York, where a sizeable group of Jews met death in horrible ways. Evidence strongly indicates that many of the murderers were motivated as much by their desire to destroy the business records of Jews to whom they were indebted and to rob their victims as by religious fervor.

During the thirteenth century crusade-related attacks on Jews in Europe declined in number and ferocity, although central France seems to have had a fairly vicious massacre in 1236, which Pope **Gregory IX** condemned. Two popular, unofficial crusades, one of 1251 and the other of 1320, each known as a **Shepherds' Crusade,** also provided opportunities in France for attacks on Jewish communities. The assaults of 1320 were the more violent and destructive of the two. Despite Pope John XXII's attempt to halt the movement by excommunicating all participants, in a spring and summer of mayhem, tens of thousands marched from Paris to northern Spain, attacking Jewish communities along the way and killing hundreds, perhaps thousands of Jews, as well as forcing others to be baptized. The violence of the so-called shepherds forced secular authorities to react vigorously. Finally, in July the crusade was crushed in Spain by the son of King James II of Aragon.

The Shepherds' Crusade of 1320 underscored a reality that had become apparent as early as 1096. Although the official church hierarchy, as a matter of doctrine and practice, consistently condemned violence against Jews who were living in peace with their Christian neighbors and likewise forbade all attempts at forced conversions, its efforts at raising the level of religious zeal in **Latin** Christendom as it promoted **holy war** against Islam resulted in some very unpleasant consequences for the Jews of Europe and the **Middle East. Related Entries:** Crusade of 1239–1241; Peter the Hermit; Settlement and Colonization.

Suggested Reading

Primary Source

Shlomo Eidelberg, ed. and trans., *The Jews and the Crusaders: The Hebrew Chronicles of the First and Second Crusades* (1996).

Historical Studies

Robert Chazam, *European Jewry and the First Crusade* (1987), *God, Humanity and History: The Hebrew First Crusade Narratives* (2000), *In the Year 1096: The First Crusade and the Jews* (1996), and *Medieval Stereotypes and Modern Antisemitism* (1997); Mark R. Cohen, *Under Crescent and Cross: The Jews in the Middle Ages* (1994); Joshua Prawer, *The History of the Jews in the Latin Kingdom of Jerusalem* (1988); Michael A. Signer and John Van Egen, eds., *Jews and Christians in Twelfth-century Europe* (2001).

Jihad

Jihad means "striving" in Arabic, and today it is understood by non-Muslims to mean a **holy war** against forces perceived to be hostile to **Islam.** The word has meant that, and it continues to have that connotation, but the fullness of its meaning transcends simple armed struggle against **infidels.**

Islamic jurists who interpret *Shari'a,* or Islamic Sacred Law, have historically identified four forms of jihad that God demands of **Muslims:** *jihad of the hand* (doing good deeds, especially acts of charity); *jihad of the mouth* (proclaiming the faith); *jihad of the heart* (the inner transformation of one's personality to the point of becoming God-centered); and *jihad of the sword* (defending Islam as a *mujahid,* or warrior of God). *Sufis,* the mystics of Islam, add a fifth: *jihad of the soul,* or the struggle to reach God through a mystical experience. An early Islamic tradition also records the story that following a successful military campaign against enemies from Mecca, the Prophet Muhammad informed his followers: "We have now returned from the lesser jihad to the greater jihad." That greater jihad is a moral struggle against evil. In this sense all true Muslims are *mujahidin,* who carry on a lifelong struggle in the way of God by praying, fasting, making **pilgrimage** to Mecca, studying and

teaching the Koran, performing acts of charity, and generally fighting against their lower selves.

These aspects of jihad in no way negate the fact that Muhammad and his Companions, the first Muslims, were warriors, and almost from the beginning Islam has accepted the notion that holy war in defense of the true faith is an obligation to be borne by all able-bodied men. What is more, those who die in defense of Islam are martyrs and are assured Paradise.

In their early struggles for survival during the 620s and early 630s, the first Muslims generally tried to convert by force only Arabia's pagans; they largely were content to enter into alliances with Arab Jews and Christians, whereby these "Peoples of the Book" acknowledged the supremacy of Islam and accepted the subordinate status of *dhimmis,* or people who had accepted a treaty of peace and toleration. When the Muslims of Arabia exploded out of their homeland in the 630s, they did so largely driven by the warrior traditions of their culture and the simple desire for conquest, rather than out of a desire to convert unbelievers through the sword. As they carved out an empire that stretched from Central Asia to the Atlantic, Muslim conquerors were normally quite happy to accept the people whom they overran as *dhimmis,* as long as the conquered people accepted their second-class status. Conversion to Islam in Muslim lands outside of Arabia was a long, slow process and rarely was accomplished by armed threats.

According to traditional Islamic thought, people who embrace the Faith enjoy God's peace, because of their submission to His Will, and reside in *Dar al-Islam,* the House of Submission (or Peace). Conversely, unbelievers reside in *Dar al-Harb,* the House of Chaos (or War), because they lack God's guidance. Needless to say, the two

Houses are mutually hostile. By the late eighth century, most Islamic jurists agreed that while there might be momentary truces between Muslims and residents of the House of Chaos, the two Houses could never be permanently at peace. Indeed, for the True Believers of Dar al-Islam, holy war is inevitable, necessary, and an act of piety. Consequently, Islamic legal theorists crafted treatises on the law of jihad, in which they set out rules governing the calling and prosecution of a jihad of the sword.

Despite the theory of perpetual jihad, after about 750 most Muslim states learned to live in a state of equilibrium with their non-Muslim neighbors. To be sure, wars continued to be fought between Islamic and non-Islamic states (as well as between Islamic states), and often Muslims called these wars jihads. Regardless, holy jihad was not a constant preoccupation in the Islamic World—until the coming of the crusaders. The capture of **Jerusalem** and the establishment of several **crusader states** in the East, as well as the **Reconquista** in Iberia, spurred the rise of a number of individuals and dynasties, such as **Saladin** in **Egypt** and **Syria,** and the **Almohads** in North Africa and Spain, who declared holy jihad against the crusader menace. In **Syria-Palestine** jihads succeeded in driving the crusaders back into the sea; in Iberia they failed. **Related Entries:** Ayyubids; Almoravids; Assassins; Baybars; Field of Blood; Mamluks; Nur ad-Din; Ottomans; Seljuks; Shia; Zangi; Zangids.

Suggested Reading

Primary Source

Rudolph Peters, ed., *Jihad in Classical and Modern Islam: A Reader* (1996).

Historical Studies

Peter Partner, *God of Battles: Holy Wars of Christianity and Islam* (1997); Hadia Dajani-Shakeel and Ronald A. Messier, eds., *The Jihad and Its Times* (1991).

John of Brienne

King of **Jerusalem** (r. 1210–1212), **bailli** (regent) for his daughter **Isabella II** (1212–1225), military leader of the **Fifth Crusade** (1218–1221), unsuccessful claimant to the crown of Cilician **Armenia** (1220), leader of a papal war against **Frederick II** (1228–1230), and co-emperor of the **Latin empire of Constantinople** (r. 1231–1237). An able and brave warrior, John is remarkable for his continued attempts to secure one crown after another, despite setbacks.

Born around 1170, John, a younger son of the count of Brienne, was invited to come East in 1210 to marry **Maria of Montferrat,** heiress of the kingdom of Jerusalem. By this act, John became co-monarch of the kingdom. When Maria died in 1212, John's claim to the crown became tenuous. Although he continued to act as king and claim the title, legally he was only regent for his infant daughter Isabella II. Perhaps because of the precarious nature of his hold on the throne of Jerusalem, in 1214 he married Rita, daughter of King Leo II of Lesser Armenia, and after Leo died in 1219, John unsuccessfully laid claim to that kingdom, in the midst of the Fifth Crusade. Although John took temporary leave of the crusade in Egypt to pursue his claim (and also out of a sense of frustration with the course of the crusade), he served the crusade faithfully and well. Its disastrous outcome was not due to his leadership.

The crusade left John bankrupt, and in 1222 he was forced to travel to the West to beg for funds. In October he was in Italy, where he initiated negotiations for his daughter's marriage with Frederick II, in the hope of securing help for the kingdom of Jerusalem. Despite her projected marriage, John planned on retaining the throne for the rest of his life. It was not to be. When Isabella married Frederick in November 1225, Frederick immediately shunted John aside, claiming the regency and the crown for himself. The barons of **Outremer** had no problem with this, stipulating only that Frederick had to appear in the East within a year and a day to make good on his claim.

In 1228, John, still smarting from having lost the crown of Jerusalem, took on the role of papal champion by invading the Sicilian lands of the excommunicated Frederick II, who was currently in the East on an unauthorized crusade. By the autumn of 1229 John's armies were in retreat, having been routed by the forces of Frederick who had hastened back from the **Levant.** In May 1230, Pope **Gregory IX** was forced to make peace with the emperor, and once more John of Brienne had been outmaneuvered.

In the midst of this most recent setback, the barons of the Latin empire of Constantinople, whose military situation was steadily worsening, invited John to come East and assume the coemperorship of Constantinople. The plan was for Mary, John's daughter by his most-recent wife, Berengaria of Castile, to wed the teenaged Emperor Baldwin II. John would be crowned senior coemperor and serve for life. John and Pope Gregory IX agreed to the pact in April 1229, and John was invested as a crusader to wage **holy war** in defense of the Latin empire against **Eastern Christians.** He and an army of about 5,500 other crusaders arrived in Constantinople in the summer of 1231, where he was duly crowned.

In 1235 and again in 1236 John heroically threw back a numerically superior coalition of **Greek** and Bulgarian forces beneath the walls of Constantinople. Despite these victories, the situation was desperate. The nineteen-year-old Baldwin II left for Italy in 1236 to seek Western help. During his absence John died on March 23, 1237, leaving an empire that extended little beyond its capital city. **Related Entries:** Crusade of 1239–1241; Pelagius; Political Crusades.

Just War

See Holy War / Just War.

K

Al-Kamil Muhammad, Nasir ad-Din

Ayyubid sultan of Egypt (r. 1218–1238), foe of the **Fifth Crusade,** and one of **Islam**'s premier diplomats.

The eldest son of **al-Adil (Saphadin)** and nephew of **Saladin,** al-Kamil participated in his father's usurpation of the sultanate of Egypt in 1200 from Saladin's grandson. Al-Adil's death in August 1218 came at a critical moment, inasmuch as the army of the Fifth Crusade had commenced a full-scale assault on Egypt in May of that year. Upon his father's death, al-Kamil secured the throne of Egypt and began jockeying with his two siblings for supremacy over the fragmented Ayyubid empire. It was against this background of intrafamily struggle that al-Kamil faced the formidable task of fending off a large crusader army on his home ground.

A bloody but indecisive battlefield victory over the crusaders on August 29, 1219, offered al-Kamil an opportunity to resume truce negotiations to end the **siege** of **Damietta,** talks that he had initially begun in February. The new negotiations in turn offered a newcomer to the crusade camp, **Francis of Assisi,** the opportunity to visit the sultan's camp, where he tried to convert al-Kamil to Christianity. The sultan declined Francis's offer, offered him gifts and food, and sent him safely back across the lines.

Negotiations continued as the situations in the **Muslim** and crusader camps grew more miserable and desperate. Given the plight of his army and the horrendous losses in besieged Damietta, where tens of thousands had already died, al-Kamil offered generous terms. As he had done earlier that year, he proposed returning the holy city and much of the pre-1187 holdings of the **kingdom of Jerusalem** if the crusaders withdrew from Egypt. The crusaders refused his offer, and fighting resumed in late September.

On the night of November 5, 1219, the crusaders walked into Damietta, a city unable to defend itself anymore. After much delay, the crusaders prepared to launch an offensive in July 1221. Once again, al-Kamil proposed a truce and the exchange of **Jerusalem** for Damietta, and once again his offer was rejected. The crusader offensive soon bogged down when the army's leaders marched their forces into the rising waters of the Nile's annual flood. Instead of destroying the cut-off crusader army, al-Kamil again favored negotiations because he did not want to try to recapture by siege and battle a well-fortified Damietta. This time his proposals were accepted. On August 29, the crusader army surrendered to the sultan after agreeing to hand back Damietta and to evacuate all their forces from Egypt. The treaty also provided for the full exchange of **prisoners** and an eight-year truce. Al-Kamil treated his captives well and honorably, even arranging for the delivery of food to them as they marched back to Damietta, from where they set sail for **Acre.**

The eight-year truce did not bind Emperor **Frederick II,** whose arrival in the East had been expected for years. With this in mind, in 1227 al-Kamil exchanged embassies with Frederick in an effort to secure a treaty that would free the Sultan to concentrate his energies on achieving dominance over his brother al-Muazzam, the sultan of Syria. Al-Muazzam died in November 1227, but al-Kamil remained eager to reach some accommodation with Frederick, who arrived in Acre on September 7, 1228. Although desirous of a truce, al-Kamil was not initially prepared to offer the same generous terms that he had proposed in 1219. When, however, Frederick's army threatened to move on Jerusalem, al-Kamil had to choose between defending Jerusalem or continuing his plans to seize Syria. He chose the latter, and in February 1229 he concluded a ten-year treaty with Frederick that included handing over Jerusalem, Bethlehem, and some other sites that enabled the crusaders to have a narrow corridor connecting the holy city with the coast.

This tactic of strategic negotiation with the crusaders rather than all-out war paid large dividends. Before 1229 had ended, al-Kamil and his brother al-Ashraf gained joint supremacy over all of the Ayyubid lands, and this partnership lasted, with some strain, until al-Ashraf's death in 1237. The death of al-Kamil the following year removed one of Islam's most skilled diplomats from the scene and ushered in a new age of Ayyubid family strife. **Related Entry:** Sixth Crusade.

Kerbogha (Karbuqa; Kerbuqa)

Turkish *atabeg* (governor) of **Mosul** and leader of the relief force that attempted to save **Antioch** in 1098 from the army of the **First Crusade.**

Kerbogha was a **mamluk,** or former **slave,** who rose to power by virtue of his military abilities and had ambitions to widen Mosul's influence in the **Islamic** World. Consequently, the crusader presence at Antioch must have seemed to him to be a gift.

In late April 1098 he led an allied force of **Muslim** warriors out of northern Iraq in an effort to catch the crusaders while they still were encamped outside Antioch, which they had been besieging since late October 1097. His army, which gathered strength as various allies joined it along its march, stopped at **Edessa** around May 4, where it initiated an unsuccessful three-week **siege** of the city, which was securely in the hands of **Baldwin of Boulogne.** This delay probably contributed to the eventual defeat of Kerbogha's army at Antioch.

The crusaders at Antioch, who were in communication with Edessa, which was 160 miles away (about ten days' march), heard of his approach and realized they had to take the city immediately or be crushed between it and the relief army. Luckily for them, they captured the city by stealth on the night of June 2–3. On June 4 the lead elements of Kerbogha's forces reached the outskirts of the fallen city.

The crusader army within the city walls was almost without food, **disease**-ridden, battle-weary, greatly outnumbered, and desperate. Because of the size of his army, Kerbogha was able to set up a rigorous siege of the city, even though its walls extended for miles. What is more, a Turkish garrison still held out in the city's citadel, which was perched on a hill high above the city proper. Every factor seemed to favor Kerbogha.

Fighting along the high ground near and around the citadel was fierce, and before a week had passed the crusaders were experiencing starvation, high casualties, desertions, and even the treachery of some who went over to the enemy. It was at this point that crusader morale, which had hit a new low, was raised to the level of religious exaltation by Peter Bartholomew's unearthing of what was believed to be the **Holy Lance** on June 14.

Even with that discovery and its resultant morale boost, the crusade leaders were ready to negotiate with Kerbogha, apparently offering to surrender the city under favorable terms. To that end, they sent a two-person embassy, consisting of **Peter the Hermit** and a translator, to Kerbogha. Whatever they offered was not acceptable to him.

With the embassy a failure, the crusaders saw no alternative but to risk battle outside the city walls. On June 28 they sallied forth against an enemy that probably outnumbered them by three to one. Kerbogha did not immediately attack the crusaders as they came out of the city on foot. Perhaps his massive army was too spread out along the city's extensive walls to allow a quick reaction. Whatever the case, he allowed them to exit unmolested and to align themselves in tactical formations. It was a mistake.

The result of the battle that ensued, as improbable as it must have seemed to many, was a rout and general slaughter of the allied Muslim forces. Ethnic divisions and political jealousies within Kerbogha's army made this huge alliance far less of an effective fighting machine than hoped for. This, combined with what appear to have been a number of poor military decisions and a lack of leadership skills on Kerbogha's part, made defeat almost a foregone conclusion.

Kerbogha managed to escape with the bloodied remnants of his army, but his plans of greater power died that day on the plains before Antioch. Four years later he also was dead. **Related Entries:** Bohemond I of Taranto: Seljuks.

Khorezmians (Khwarazmians; Khwarismians)

A confederation of scattered **Turkic** horsemen from Central Asia who around 1220 fled west to escape the **Mongols** and entered into the service of the **Ayyubid** sultan of Egypt, who was struggling against the Ayyubids of **Syria** and the **Franks.**

In 1244 bands of Khorezmians invaded and ravaged Syria and then swept into Frankish territories. Before the Franks realized it, they were before **Jerusalem,** which the **Latin kingdom of Jerusalem** had recovered four years earlier. On July 11 the Khorezmians burst into the city and sacked it, burning and desecrating the **Church of the Holy Sepulcher** in the process and killing large numbers of Western and **Eastern Christians.** In all, only about 300 survivors reached the safety of **Jaffa.** Jerusalem once again passed into **Muslim** hands and would never be regained by the **Latins.**

On October 17, 1244, at **La Forbie** the Khorezmians, in concert with Egyptian forces, inflicted a crushing defeat on a coalition army consisting of troops provided by both the Franks and the Ayyubids of **Damascus.** In the end, the ferocity of the Khorezmians proved too much for even their Egyptian paymasters, and in 1246 they were crushed by the Syrian Ayyubids with the encouragement of their Egyptian cousins. **Related Entries:** Cavalry; Crusade of 1239–1241; Al-Kamil Muhammad, Nasir ad-Din; Massacres; Mercenaries.

Kilij Arslan I

Seljuk sultan of Rum (r. 1092–1107) and foe of the armies of the **First Crusade.**

In 1092 Kilij Arslan restored the sultanate of Rum with its capital at the ancient **Byzantine** city of Nicaea. Four years later the first wave of the **First Crusade** entered his lands. In two separate engagements in October 1096 his troops easily disposed of the forces of the so-called People's Crusade, **massacring** most and **enslaving** the rest. The second wave proved tougher, as the sultan learned to his dismay.

His easy victory in 1096 lulled the sultan into a false sense of security that led him to march east in a border dispute with a rival **Turkish** lord, leaving his wife, family, and most of his treasury in his capital. While he was away, combined crusader and Byzantine forces be**sieged** Nicaea. When word reached him, he rushed back and attacked the besieging army on May 21, 1097, only to be beaten back with heavy losses. Defeated, he was forced to retreat and leave the city to its fate. On the night of June 18, Nicaea capitulated to Emperor **Alexius I.** After a delay of several months, Alexius returned the sultan's wife and family without ransom. Today's enemy might be tomorrow's ally.

On July 1 Kilij Arslan's army attacked the crusaders in force as they marched into the interior of **Anatolia.** The battle was close, but when it was over the sultan's army was routed and most of his remaining treasure fell into crusader hands. The dispirited sultan issued orders that cities along the crusaders' projected route of march should be abandoned. From this point on, he ceased to effectively resist the armies of the second wave.

The third wave, the so-called Crusade of 1101, was another matter. His soldiers destroyed two of the crusader armies that invaded Anatolia and played a key role in the defeat of the third. These successes led Kilij

The crusaders take Nicaea and capture the wife and sons of Kilij Arslan I. From a manuscript copy of the *Estoire d'Eracles*, a continuation of William of Tyre's history to 1261. Paris ca. 1300. The Walters Art Museum, Baltimore.

Arslan to embark on a campaign of new expansionism at the expense of rival Turkish powers. In 1107, while fighting the sultanate of the Great Seljuk, Kilij Arslan was killed. **Related Entry:** Dorylaeum, Battle of.

Knights

See Cavalry; Chivalry; Feudalism.

L

La Forbie, Battle of (October 17, 1244)

One of the most catastrophic defeats ever suffered by **Frankish** forces in **Outremer.**

A combined **Khorezmian**-Egyptian army destroyed an allied army of Franks and Syrian **Muslims** at La Forbie, a site not far from Gaza. One contemporary estimate put Frankish losses at 16,000, if one counted auxiliary **Turcopoles.** Out of 348 **Templars,** 312 were killed or captured; likewise, the **Hospitalers** lost 325 out of 351, and the **Teutonic Knights** 397 out of 400. The severed heads of the dead Christians were brought to **Cairo,** where they were displayed on the city walls.

With this defeat, only a few hundred men-at-arms remained in service to defend the **crusader states** of **Syria-Palestine.** The question was: Could the Franks resist successfully the next major Muslim offensive push? **Related Entries:** Baybars; Lazarus, Order of Saint; Louis IX; Mamluks; Seventh Crusade.

Lance, Holy

A supposed **relic** discovered at **Antioch** during the **First Crusade** that provided a necessary boost to crusader morale. The story of the Holy Lance of Antioch reveals a lot about popular religiosity in the Age of the Crusades, especially regarding the power of visions and relics.

The Holy Lance is believed to be the spearhead that pierced Jesus' side during his

The ancient Church of Saint Peter in Antioch, where the supposed Holy Lance was unearthed.

crucifixion. According to one tradition, it was discovered in **Jerusalem** in the early fourth century. The point of the lance was broken off and sent to **Constantinople** in 614; later the lance's shaft was dispatched to the imperial city to join the point. There the Holy Lance remained, escaping even the **pillage** of the **Fourth Crusade.** In 1238–1239 Baldwin II, ruler of the **Latin empire of Constantinople,** sold what appears to have been the broken-off tip of the Holy Lance to King **Louis IX** of France, along with the Crown of Thorns and other relics associated with Jesus' crucifixion. The shaft of the lance apparently remained in Constantinople until 1492, when Sultan Bayazid II sent it to Pope Innocent VIII in Rome, where it resides today.

That is one Holy Lance. There were others. One, of unknown provenance, had been secured in 926 by Emperor Henry I of Germany, and subsequently it became part of the coronation insignia of the German emperors. A third Holy Lance emerged in the course of the First Crusade.

Following the **Franks'** capture of Antioch on June 3, 1098, the army found itself enclosed within the **disease**-ridden, food-depleted city by a **Turkish** relief army that threatened to annihilate the crusaders, if they did not starve to death first. In the face of this crisis significant numbers of crusaders deserted. The crusade army needed a miracle, and that miracle was produced by a peasant from Provence, Peter Bartholomew. Peter approached Count **Raymond of Saint-Gilles** and Bishop **Adhémar of Monteil** on June 10, informing them that Saint Andrew had appeared to him in four **visions** and told him that the Holy Lance lay buried within the city's church of Saint Peter. Bishop Adhémar had his deep doubts, but Count Raymond, a man of simpler piety, believed Peter. A few days later excavations were conducted in the church, and Peter dug up a lance on the evening of June 14.

If anyone doubted the lance's authenticity, those doubts were put aside, at least for the moment, because of grim reality. Following an unsuccessful attempt to negotiate their peaceful withdrawal from the city, the crusaders realized that their only hope was a frontal assault against a larger, healthier, and far better fed enemy force. The idea seemed mad, but they had no choice. Needing a sign of divine favor, they turned to the lance. On June 28 they sallied out, attacked, and defeated their besiegers.

One tradition maintains that the formerly skeptical Bishop Adhémar bore the Holy Lance into the battle, but Raymond of Aguilers, chaplain of Count Raymond, claimed in his eyewitness history of the crusade that he, Raymond of Aguilers, was privileged to carry the Holy Lance on that day. The identity of the person who carried the relic into battle is not important; what is significant is the effect that it had on the army that routed and cut to pieces its besiegers.

Soon after this victory the **Norman** forces of **Bohemond,** who claimed Antioch as his own principality, and the Provençal forces of Raymond of Saint-Gilles had a bitter falling out that reflected the animosity between their two leaders. One manifestation of this hostility was a growing tendency on the part of the Normans to reject the authenticity of the Holy Lance and to treat Peter Bartholomew, who continued to have and report visions, as a charlatan. Crusaders allied with Bohemond, who only a short time earlier had looked upon the Holy Lance's discovery as a miracle, could no longer accept as genuine a relic and a visionary who were so closely allied with the count of Toulouse.

The controversy came to a head on April 8, 1099. To prove the validity of his visions and of the relic, Peter Bartholomew underwent a trial by ordeal in which he walked between two closely placed burning pyres while carrying the Holy Lance. The results of trials by ordeal were often ambiguous, and this was no exception. The Norman **historian** Ralph of Caen, who characterized Peter as a fraud with an unsavory reputation, reported that he was badly burned and died the next day, and his death proved that he was an evil magician. Raymond d'Aguilers saw and reported the incident differently. According to this partisan of Count Raymond of Toulouse, Peter emerged with minor burns but was crushed by a crowd of frenzied crusaders who mobbed him in a frantic rush to grab pieces of his clothing and hair as holy relics. Although the authenticity of the Holy Lance was proved by Peter's successful ordeal, as well as by a vision of the now-dead Bishop Adhémar that one of the army's priests experienced, Peter Bartholomew subsequently died from the wounds he received from the crowd.

If Peter's death caused Count Raymond to harbor doubts about the authenticity of his relic, he kept them to himself and continued to venerate the Holy Lance of Antioch, but what next happened to the relic is unclear. One story, told by **Anna Comnena,** is that the count gave the relic as a gift to **Alexius I;** if true, this must have been something of an embarrassment for the emperor. We can only guess at how Alexius disposed of this gift of doubtful worth. Another story is that the count held the relic until he lost it in battle in eastern **Anatolia** in the course of the **Crusade of 1101.** Shortly thereafter a presumed relic of the Holy Lance appeared in Christian **Armenia. Related Entries:** Kerbogha; Siege Warfare.

Languedoc

The region of southeastern and south central France that was home for a major **First Crusade** contingent and the site of the **Albigensian Crusade.**

Languedoc was the cultural region in which *langue d'oc,* or the Romance language of those who say "oc" (yes), was spoken. Today this language is known as *Occitan.* The language and culture of the people of Languedoc differed substantially from those who lived in northern France, looked to the area around Paris (the *Île de France*) for cultural leadership, and spoke *langue d'oil,* or Old French, a language in which *oil* (today *oui*) was used to signify "yes." The southeastern portion of Languedoc that borders the Mediterranean is also known as *Provence,* and its people are referred to as *Provençals.*

Languedoc was a hodgepodge of political entities, but its most powerful lords were the counts of Toulouse. **Raymond IV of Saint-Gilles,** count of Toulouse, played a major role in the First Crusade, and his descendants, Raymond VI (r. 1194–1222) and Raymond VII (r. 1222–1249), were major players in the Albigensian Crusade, which devastated the people, land, and culture of Languedoc. **Related Entry:** Cathars.

Las Navas de Tolosa, Battle of (July 16, 1212)

A major turning point in the Spanish **Reconquista** when the allied armies of Alfonso VIII of Castile, Peter II of Aragon, and Sancho VII of Navarre, in concert with significant contingents from Portugal, León, and various **military orders,** crushed the **Almohads.**

The almost immediate effects of this victory were the expulsion of the Almohads from Iberia and the disintegration of **Muslim** power in **al-Andalus** into competing petty principalities. A slightly more remote consequence was the almost total reconquest of Iberia by 1248, except for the emirate of Granada in the extreme south.

The Christian army that fought on the plains (*navas*) of Tolosa was the largest force assembled to that date by the crusaders of the Reconquista. The army of Caliph Muhammad an-Nasir was even larger but, despite fierce fighting, could not prevent defeat and the slaughter that followed upon its rout. In his report to Pope **Innocent III,** an exultant King Alfonso VIII claimed, with obvious exaggeration, that 100,000 or more **Saracens** were killed that day, while the Christian forces lost only twenty-five or thirty. Hyperbole aside, the victory was one-sided and Muslim losses were staggering. **Related Entries:** Military Orders of Iberia; Moors.

Latin East

Any area in the eastern Mediterranean ruled by **Latin** Christians. The **crusader states** of **Syria-Palestine,** the **Latin empire of Constantinople,** and **Frankish Greece** were all parts of the Latin East. **Related Entries:** Outremer; *Poulain;* Settlement and Colonization; William of Tyre.

Suggested Reading

Jonathan Phillips, *Defenders of the Holy Land: Relations between the Latin East and the West* (1996).

Latins

Western European Christians, whose culture emerged out of the western, Latin-speaking regions of the late Roman empire, as opposed to **Greek,** or **Byzantine,** Christians, whose culture evolved out of the eastern Greek-speaking regions of the late Roman empire. Latin was the language of the Church of Rome and the basis for the Romance languages, such as French, that most of the **Frankish** conquerors and colonizers of the **Latin East** spoke.

Lazarus, Order of Saint

A minor **military order** that arose in the **Latin East** and recruited many of its brethren from the ranks of **knights** and others afflicted with **leprosy.**

Like the Order of the Hospital of Saint John of Jerusalem, the Order of Saint Lazarus began as a religious congregation of hospital attendants and assumed military obligations many years after its foundation. Despite their hospital functions, however, the knights of Saint Lazarus had far closer ties with the **Templars** than with the **Hospitalers.**

Records indicate that by 1142 the brothers of Saint Lazarus ran a leper hospital in **Jerusalem,** but the earliest firm date for their participation in a battle is at **La Forbie** in 1244, where every member of the order who fought there was killed. A few years later members of the order campaigned with **Louis IX** in Egypt. Notwithstanding its new military duties, as long as the order remained in the **Holy Land,** it continued to maintain leper hospitals.

Until 1253 all of the order's masters were lepers, but membership in its ranks was also open to the healthy. Following the deaths of all of its leper knights in battle in 1252, the custom of choosing only lepers as their leaders was dropped with papal approval.

From the mid–thirteenth century onward, the order's history becomes progressively murky. We know that following the fall of Jerusalem in 1187, the order moved its headquarters to **Acre,** and its members participated in the city's defense in 1291. After the fall of Acre, the order transferred its base of operations to **Cyprus.** From there its headquarters moved to France, possibly as late as 1307. By 1572 only the French and Italian branches of the order remained. Both maintained tenuous holds on life until swept away in the late eighteenth century. In the twentieth century the Order of Saint Lazarus reemerged as a world-wide charitable order of chivalry dedicated to relieving human suffering. **Related Entries:** Baldwin IV; Disease; Teutonic Knights.

Suggested Reading

David Marcombe, *Leper Knights: The Order of Saint Lazarus of Jerusalem in England, c. 1150–1544* (2003).

Legates, Papal

Representatives of the pope who had authority to speak and act on his behalf within the limits of their assigned missions. Because crusades were papally blessed expeditions, legates were assigned to all official crusades.

Bishop **Adhémar of Monteil** was the first person to **swear the cross** at **Clermont,** thereby becoming the first crusader in history; he was also the first papal legate to accompany a crusade. Adhémar proved to be an effective religious leader, as well as a fighting-bishop who took up arms and commanded troops at several critical junctures during the **First Crusade,** but he did not lack detractors because of his close association with **Raymond of Saint-Gilles.**

Some legates who accompanied subsequent crusades were also centers of controversy, and much of this controversy resulted from their ambiguous roles. Were they solely spiritual leaders and moral authorities, or were they authorized to take active military roles? This conundrum was a result of the dichotomous nature of the crusades themselves, which were **holy wars** authorized by popes but organized and led by lay warriors.

In 1202 Cardinal Peter Capuano, legate to the **Fourth Crusade,** was informed by the Venetians that he could accompany the crusader army and fleet as a chaplain but not in his official capacity as a papal legate. Apparently, the Venetians feared he would try to prevent the crusade's diversion to Zara. Consequently, Cardinal Peter, who could not tolerate this insult to the pope and himself by accepting his reduced status, was forced to exercise his duties from afar and communicated with the army through envoys. He rejoined the army only after the capture of **Constantinople** in 1204.

Rightly or wrongly, papal crusade legates were sometimes faulted for what appeared to be their wrongheaded decisions. Thus, Pope **Innocent III** excoriated Cardinal Peter for having dispensed from their **crusade vows** all members of the army and fleet of the Fourth Crusade who promised to remain in the **Byzantine** East until March 1205 to defend the new **Latin empire of Constantinople.**

Some crusade legates also left themselves open to charges of disastrous meddling in matters beyond their competence. Thirteenth-century critics, as well as many modern historians, have judged Cardinal **Pelagius,** legate to the **Fifth Crusade,** responsible for the defeat of the crusade army in Egypt because of his interference in military decisions. A forceful personality by any standard of evaluation, Pelagius did not hesitate to disagree with **John of Brienne** over strategic and tactical decisions, because of his desire to maintain the momentum of the campaign, to keep the army together, and to raise morale. Certainly a case can be made that the debacle of August 1221, which brought the crusade to a disastrous finish, was a consequence of the legate's obstinacy and poor judgment.

Levant

A term that means the region of the eastern Mediterranean stretching from Greece to Egypt. **Related Entries:** Anatolia; Crusader States; Latin East; Outremer; Syria-Palestine.

Suggested Reading

William Harris, *The Levant: A Fractured Mosaic* (2003).

Louis VII

See Capetians; Second Crusade.

Louis VIII

See Albigensian Crusade; Capetians.

Louis IX

King of France (r. 1226–1270), leader of the **Seventh** and **Eighth Crusades,** and saint of the Roman Church.

Louis took the **crusader's vow** in December 1244 during a serious bout of illness. **Jerusalem** had fallen once again to **Islam** on August 23, 1244; apparently word had reached him and played a part in his decision. On October 9, 1245, Louis received his barons' approval to go on crusade, and a significant number of them also assumed the **crusader's cross.** Louis then spent almost three years preparing for his crusade, not leaving France until August 25, 1248.

Louis, Queen **Margaret of Provence,** and the royal party arrived in **Cyprus** on September 17, 1248, where they reprovisioned and met up with the rest of the army that dribbled in. The fleet finally set sail for Egypt on May 30, 1249, arrived on June 4, landed its forces on June 5, and captured **Damietta** the following day. Following that, Louis settled down to await reinforcements.

On November 20 his army began its march through the swampy terrain of the Nile Delta to **Cairo** but by December 19 was cut off by the enemy. Sick with dysentery, Louis was captured on April 6, 1250; his army was cut to pieces and forced to surrender shortly thereafter. Ransom for the defeated monarch and his army was set at 400,000 *livres* and the return of Damietta.

Upon the crusaders' abandonment of Damietta and a down payment of 200,000 *livres,* Louis was released after a month of captivity and traveled to **Acre** in May 1250. Rather than returning home, Louis decided to stay in the **Holy Land,** until all captured crusaders had been released and the defenses of the **kingdom of Jerusalem** shored up. In the four years that followed he negotiated the release of the **prisoners** who had been left behind in Egypt, purchased the freedom of other Christian **slaves** held in Egypt, rebuilt key coastal fortifications, negotiated with the **Assassins** and **Mongols,** and generally stabilized the **crusader states.** In April 1254 he finally departed for France.

His departure did not signal the end of his concern for the **Latin East.** He left behind at Acre 100 **knights** commanded by one of France's best warriors and paid for by the French royal treasury. This contingent was at the disposal of the leaders of the kingdom of Jerusalem and served as a permanent crusade-in-place.

Despite the best attempts of these French warriors and of the **military orders,** the fortunes of the Latin East continued to decline. Because of the onslaught of **Mamluk** attacks against **Frankish** castles and towns that threatened the very existence of the severely reduced crusader states, Louis took up the crusader's cross again on March 25, 1267, despite the initial opposition of Pope Clement IV. The pope, a Frenchman and friend of the king, was aware of how much Louis was needed at home and how fragile his health was, but Louis was adamant. Louis decided to sail initially to Tunis in North Africa, which he reached on July 18. Within two weeks Louis was ill with dysentery and died on August 25.

Because so many contemporaries considered Louis to be the epitome of the true crusader-king and Christian knight, as well as a martyr for the faith, in 1272 the papacy began an investigation of his life and the posthumous miracles ascribed to him to ascertain if he was worthy of canonization as a saint. On August 9, 1297, Pope Boniface VIII solemnly placed Louis's name in the list of saints officially recognized by the Church. **Related Entries:** Capetians; Disease; Lance, Holy.

Suggested Reading

Primary Source

John of Joinville, *The Life of Saint Louis,* trans. by M. R. B. Shaw (1967).

Historical Studies

William C. Jordan, *Louis IX and the Challenge of the Crusade* (1979); Jacques Le Goff, *Saint Louis* (1996); Jean Richard, *Saint Louis, Crusader King of France* (1983).

Lusignans

See Aimery of Lusignan; Cyprus; Guy of Lusignan.

M

Ma'arra (Ma'arrat an-Nu'man)

See Cannibalism.

Mamluks (Mameluks)

A line of sultans that originated as a caste of slave-soldiers (mamluks), they came to power in Egypt in 1250 and conducted the final, successful offensive against the remaining vestiges of **Frankish** power in **Outremer.**

Mamluk slave-soldiers comprised the heart of the armies of the **Abbasids, Fatimids, Seljuks,** and **Ayyubids.** Slaves who were not **Muslims** were purchased for their potential military abilities; the majority were **Turks** from Central Asia, and a minority were Circassians from north of the Caucasus Mountains. Trained as **cavalry,** they were also converted to **Islam** and upon conversion were given their freedom and provided with pay, but they remained obligated to live in garrisons as members of a professional warrior force.

Cadres of elite warriors can turn an army into a formidable fighting force, but they also can be a menace to those whom they serve when they turn their loyalties primarily to their comrades, their commanders, their unit, and their traditions, rather than to the heads of state. The mamluks added another element to this mix: They usually were blindly loyal to the masters who freed them but were not necessarily committed to their successors. In 1249 the Ayyubid sultan of Egypt, al-Malik al-Salih, died in the midst of a life-and-death struggle with the crusader forces of **Louis IX.** A group of Turkish mamluks known as the *Bahris* had served al-Malik with fierce loyalty but feared his son and successor, Turan Shah, who favored his own mamluks, whom he brought in from Iraq. Fearing for themselves and al-Malik's widow, Shajar al-Durr, and led by an officer known as **Baybars,** they murdered Turan Shah in May 1250 and declared Shajar al-Durr the new sultan. There followed an extraordinary three-month reign by Shajar al-Durr, who styled herself "queen of the Muslims." Despite her political astuteness, widespread opposition because of her sex forced Shajar al-Durr's abdication in favor of a mamluk general, Aybeg, who assumed the title of sultan and married his former queen. In 1257 Shajar al-Durr arranged Aybeg's murder but was herself assassinated three days later. Into this void stepped a new mamluk general, Qutuz, who was proclaimed sultan in 1259.

As this drama unfolded, the Islamic World was facing a new crisis—the

The ruins of the Templar castle of *Athlit*, better known as *Chastel Perlerin* (Pilgrim's Castle). Built in 1218, it was never taken by assault but was abandoned after the fall of Acre 1291. Charles W. Wilson, *Picturesque Palestine, Sinai and Egypt*, 2 vols. (New York: D. Appleton & Co., 1881), 2:101.

onslaught of the **Mongols,** who captured and destroyed Baghdad in 1258, thereby ending the Abbasid caliphate. In January 1260 the Mongols destroyed **Aleppo,** and **Damascus** surrendered in March to avoid a similar fate. With the capture of these two cities, Ayyubid rule in Syria was effectively over.

Egypt was next on the Mongols' list. To reach Egypt, they had to pass through the **kingdom of Jerusalem.** Choosing to try diplomacy first, the Mongols proposed to the crusader kingdom's **High Court** at **Acre** protection and a favorable alliance in return for unhindered passage. The **Frankish** barons rejected the offer.

Meanwhile, Qutuz was determined to meet the Mongols head-on and convinced the Franks to allow his army safe passage and the right to purchase supplies on its northward march to meet the Mongol menace. On September 3, 1260, Mamluk forces defeated the Mongols at **Ayn Jalut.** Following that victory, Qutuz launched a counterattack that enabled his army to occupy most of Syria, which now

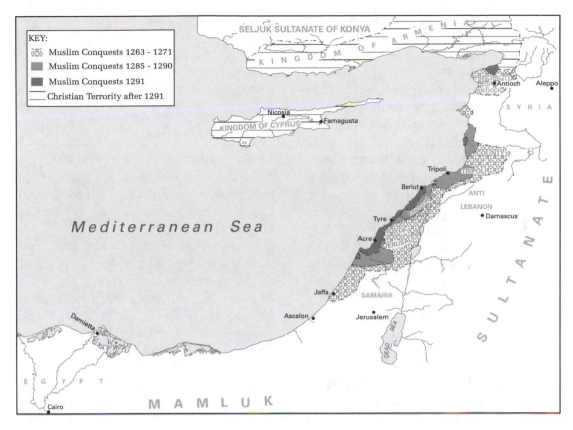

Mamluk Conquests, 1263–1291.

passed under Mamluk control. Qutuz, however, did not live long to enjoy his triumph. In October he was assassinated at the instigation the hero of Ayn Jalut, his general Baybars, who then usurped the sultanate.

Baybars soon became the **crusader states'** implacable enemy. Between 1263 and 1271 he **besieged,** captured, and destroyed crusader **castles** and towns in a series of almost annual campaigns. His strategy was simple: Deny crusaders from overseas bases from which they could launch attacks and at the same time systematically drive the Frankish colonists out of **Syria-Palestine.** In 1265 the coastal towns of Caesarea, Haifa, and Arsuf fell to his forces, and in 1268 **Jaffa** was captured and demolished. The crowning achievement of 1268 was the capture of **Antioch,** which had been in the continuous possession of the successors of **Bohemond of Taranto** for 171 years. The fall of Antioch essentially finished off the principality.

In 1271 Baybars conducted his last great campaign against the Franks, capturing the **Hospitaler** fortress of *Krak des Chevaliers* on April 8. One month and a day later Prince Edward of England arrived in **Acre** at the head of a small crusader force. Edward convinced the Franks to conclude a truce with Baybars. On his part, the sultan desired a temporary truce to concentrate his energies against the Mongols of Persia. In May 1272 a truce of ten years, ten months, ten days, and ten hours was signed. Before it ended

Baybars was dead, dying in 1277 following an unsuccessful campaign against the Mongols in **Anatolia.**

Baybars had attempted to turn the sultanate into a family possession, but in 1279 his son was deposed by another mamluk Turk, Kalavun, who assumed the throne himself. Even before the peace accord had run its course, the new sultan decided to attack those Frankish territories not covered by the truce, especially the holdings of the Hospitalers, who were in alliance with the Mongols. Once the truce was over, he launched all-out **jihad. Tripoli** fell to him in April 1289. Of the five cities that had served as capitals of crusader states—**Edessa,** Antioch, **Jerusalem,** Tripoli, and Acre—only Acre remained in Frankish hands. It was next on Kalavun's list, but he died in November 1290 before he could achieve total victory.

Kalavun's son and successor, al-Ashraf Khalil, had the honor of ending the Frankish presence in Outremer. In May 1291 Acre fell in a bloodbath; in an anticlimactic series of retreats, **Tyre,** Sidon, Beirut, and several remaining **Templar** castles were soon surrendered without a fight or abandoned. By mid-August the Franks were gone, except for an inconsequential Templar presence in Cilician **Armenia.** All that remained was for the sultan to systematically destroy every coastal fortification so that the Western **infidels** would never again establish a foothold on this soil. And they did not—until the twentieth century.

Suggested Reading

Primary Sources

Ibn al-Furat, *Ayyubids, Mamluks and Crusaders: Selections from the "Tarik al-Duwal wa'l-Muluk" of Ibn al-Furat,* trans. by Ursula and Malcolm C. Lyons, 2 vols. (1971); P. M. Holt, ed. and trans., *Early Mamluk Diplomacy (1260–1290): Treaties of Baybars and Qalawun with Christian Rulers* (1995).

Historical Studies

Robert Irwin, *The Middle East in the Middle Ages: The Early Mamluk Sultanate, 1250–1382* (1986); David Nicolle, *The Mamluks, 1250–1517* (1993).

Manuel I Comnenus

Emperor of **Byzantium** (r. 1143–1180), who had a deserved reputation for pro-Western sentiments but might have worked to sabotage the French army during the **Second Crusade.**

Manuel undoubtedly liked **Latin** Christians. His mother was a Hungarian princess, and he married two Latins: in 1146, Bertha of Sulzbach, who was related to Emperor **Conrad III** of Germany; in 1161, Maria, daughter of **Constance of Antioch.** Throughout his reign Western merchants, adventurers, and relatives were warmly welcomed in the empire in large numbers. He also made unsuccessful but apparently sincere overtures to Pope Alexander III (r. 1159–1181) to reunite the Churches of Byzantium and Rome and in 1167 entered into an alliance with King **Amalric** of **Jerusalem** for combined operations against Egypt. At the same time, geopolitical realities forced him into actions that were neither understood nor appreciated in some quarters of the West.

Throughout the Second Crusade, Manuel maintained good relations with Conrad III, but his relations with the French degenerated into a situation that engendered a good deal of animosity. Positioned as his empire was, Emperor Manuel had to perform a difficult balancing act as the year 1147 bore witness. In that year he concluded a much-needed peace treaty with the **Turkish sultan of Rum;** he suffered attacks on Corfu and Greece by Roger II, the king of Sicily; and he unwillingly received the armies of Conrad III and Louis VII in Constantinople, despite his best attempts to convince them to bypass the city. Their arrival meant that Manuel could not concentrate his forces in a counterattack against Roger. It would be two years before he could drive Roger out of imperial territory.

Manuel had earlier promised the crusaders fair markets throughout his lands and assured them that his treaty with the **Seljuk** sultan of Rum would not hamper his aiding the crusade, but their encampment outside the imperial capital was proving too much. Manuel finally was happy to see the Germans cross into **Anatolia,** but then the French arrived, procrastinated when it came to leaving, and proved more than just vexatious. When certain factions in the French army accused him of treason because of his treaty with the Turks and called for an alliance with King Roger and an attack on Constantinople, Manuel decided that the French were an unstable ally.

He refused the French any guides or supplies until Louis swore an oath to return all captured lands to the empire. Upon receiving that oath, Manuel commenced to offer only half-hearted help—at best. The subsequent disasters experienced by the French in Anatolia convinced them, perhaps correctly, that Manuel was willing to throw them to the dubious mercy of his Turkish neighbors.

In the aftermath of the crusade, Conrad III did not hesitate to renew with Manuel a pre-crusade alliance that they had entered into against Roger II. Louis, to the contrary, visited Roger on his way back home and strengthened his ties with Sicily's king. Nothing substantial came of either alliance. Conrad was prevented from invading Sicily by rebellion at home, and Louis did not undertake an anti-**Greek** crusade as Roger advocated, even though a number of influential French churchmen, including **Bernard of Clairvaux,** advocated such a crusade. **Related Entries:** Christians, Eastern; Montferrat, Family of.

Suggested Reading

Primary Sources

John Kinnamos, *The Deeds of John and Manuel Comnenus,* trans. by Charles M. Brand (1976); Niketas Choniates, *O City of Byzantium, Annals of Niketas Choniates,* trans. by Harry J. Magoulias (1984).

Historical Study

Paul Magdalino, *The Empire of Manuel I Komnenos, 1143–1180* (1993).

Manzikert, Battle of (August 26, 1071)

A turning point in the history of the **Byzantine empire.** In response to **Seljuk Turkish** forays into eastern **Anatolia,** Emperor Romanus IV Diogenes led a large army into **Armenia,** where his forces were destroyed and he was captured by Sultan Alp Arslan.

Alp Arslan was primarily focused on advancing into **Syria-Palestine** and Egypt and desired an alliance with **Constantinople** against the **Fatimids.** Therefore, he released Romanus under generous peace terms and with an understanding that he and the emperor would cooperate in the future. Romanus, however, was deposed in a palace coup before he could return to Constantinople. Romanus's deposition and subsequent death at the hands of his enemies ended any chance of a Seljuk-Byzantine alliance. With the annihilation of the imperial army at Manzikert, Anatolia now lay open to invasion and settlement by Turkish nomads seeking new pasture lands and Turkish *gazis* (warriors of the faith), who lived on booty acquired from raids on **infidel** border lands. The situation soon was desperate enough to occasion Emperor Michael VII to request help from **Pope Gregory VII.**

The Battle of Manzikert was the first step in the centuries-long process in which Byzantine Anatolia was transformed into Turkey, and it also precipitated the sense of crisis in Christendom that led to the **First Crusade. Related Entry:** Alexius I Comnenus.

Suggested Reading

Alfred Friendly, *The Dreadful Day: The Battle of Manzikert, 1071* (1981).

Margaret of Provence

Queen of France, wife of King **Louis IX,** and a participant in the **Seventh Crusade.**

Margaret might hold the record for childbearing while on a crusade, giving birth to three children during this six-year crusade: John-Tristan (1250); Peter (1251); and Blanche (1253). More than that, her wise and courageous actions at **Damietta** in 1250 probably helped avoid a greater disaster than that already suffered by the crusaders.

Louis's marriage at age twenty-one to the thirteen-year-old Margaret in 1234 signaled his coming of age, and he could not have chosen a wife better suited to match his own abilities, piety, and courage.

Queen Margaret accompanied her husband to Egypt in 1249 and stayed behind in Damietta while Louis led his forces to defeat in the delta. Three days before she was to give birth to a son, word reached her of her husband's capture. Determined not to fall into enemy hands, she commanded a knight in her retinue to kill her should she be in danger of being taken **prisoner.** On the very day that she gave birth, she learned that the Italian merchants, who controlled the fleet, were planning to abandon the city, thereby severely weakening its defenses and probably precipitating a panic. The next day she summoned the merchants to her bedchamber, where she reminded them that Damietta was a valuable bargaining chip that could not be lost prematurely. To counter their excuse that famine was driving them out, she bought up all of the food within the

town at a cost of 360,000 *livres* and took it upon herself to provision the town's inhabitants. She also won over the merchants by employing them at royal expense. The city was saved for the moment. Without it, King Louis might never have been released.

Margaret, and all Christians who were not immobilized by ill health, prudently abandoned Damietta before the **Muslims** retook control of it, thereby avoiding the general **massacre** of the sick and wounded that ensued, despite promises of mercy. The queen then sailed to **Acre,** where she awaited her husband.

Four years later, she and Louis and their expanded family were sailing back to France when the flame of a candle caused an onboard fire in her bedchamber. The queen awoke to find her room in flames; not panicking, she quickly extinguished the fire and averted a disaster.

Queen Margaret did not accompany Louis on the **Eighth Crusade.** Following Louis's death in 1270, she lived another twenty-six years, passing on in 1296. **Related Entries:** Disease; Eleanor of Aquitaine; Noncombatants; Women.

Maria of Montferrat (1191–1212)

Queen of **Jerusalem** (r. 1210–1212). This daughter of Queen **Isabella I** and **Conrad of Montferrat** is also known as Maria la Marquise because her father was marquis of **Montferrat.**

In 1205 Maria became heiress to the crown when her stepfather, King **Aimery of Lusignan,** mother, and stepbrother all died within a short time of one another. After almost five years under the regency of her uncle, she married **John of Brienne** in 1210, thereby making him king. She gave birth to a daughter, **Isabella (II),** the future wife of Emperor **Frederick II.** Maria's death in

1212 reduced John of Brienne from king to regent (**bailli**) for his infant daughter. **Related Entry:** Women.

Massacres

The wholesale slaughter of captured soldiers and **noncombatants**—men, **women,** and children—was common enough in an age when war was fought under the shared assumption that defeated enemies had no inherent rights. Religious zeal, as well as the usual hatreds and desires for revenge engendered by years of war and bursts of violent combat, made massacre even more likely. Other reasons for killing captives included operational necessity (an army on the move considered captives a hindrance), giving the enemy a lesson he would not forget, and ensuring that the enemy would never return to fight again. Also, according to contemporary customs of war, when resisting towns, cities, and **castles** were taken by bloody assault, vengeful massacre was the expected norm, but this did not necessarily mean everyone was killed. When the **Mamluk** sultan Kalavun captured **Tripoli** in 1289 all of the city's men were summarily killed but surviving women and children were **enslaved.**

Acre stands as a symbol of some of the whys and ways of massacres in the land called "holy." The city had escaped massacre through negotiation and surrender when first captured by crusaders in 1104, and its Christian occupiers negotiated a similar peaceful capitulation to **Saladin** in 1189. The subsequent two captures of the city were not so bloodless.

In July 1191 the city surrendered to the combined armies of the **Third Crusade** with the understanding that the garrison would be spared in exchange for **Saladin**'s paying a huge sum of money, his returning the **relic** of the **True Cross** captured at **Hattin,** and his freeing about 1,500 Christian captives. Delays postponed payment of the ransom, delivery of the True Cross, and the exchange of **prisoners.** As King **Richard the Lionheart** later wrote: "When the time limit expired, the pact that he had agreed to was totally voided, and so we quite properly had the **Saracens** whom we held in custody—about 2,600 of them—put to death." However, as Richard also wrote: "A few of the more noble were spared, and we hope to recover the Holy Cross and certain Christian captives in exchange for them." The cross was never recovered. As for the Christian captives, Saladin responded in kind, executing all **Franks** whom he captured during the campaign of 1191–1192.

A number of explanations have been put forward to explain Richard's motives: anger at a perceived deception; pathological bloodlust; a desire to avenge the massacre of **Templar** and **Hospitaler** captives at **Hattin;** the decision that the prisoners were a brake on his mobility. We shall never know, but this mass killing impressed both his enemies and friends. It also was not Acre's last.

The recapture of Acre by Kalavun in June 1291 was described as follows by Ismail Abu'l-Fida, a young officer who participated in the **siege:**

Inside the town were a number of towers holding out like citadels. A great mass of Franks entered them and fortified themselves. . . . Then the sultan demanded the surrender of all who were holding out in the towers, and not one held back [from surrendering]. The sultan gave the command and they were beheaded around Acre to the last man.

Regardless of these massacres, we should not be misled by the many modern historians who tend to exaggerate the number of incidents of indiscriminate slaughter that took place during the Age of the Crusades. Captives were the spoils of war and an economic resource, and for that reason captured enemy were often spared. Even the crusaders' bloody capture of **Jerusalem** in July 1099 witnessed the sparing of large numbers of the city's population. **Related Entries:** Baybars; Castles, Crusader; Cannibalism; Pillage and Plunder; Siege Warfare.

Suggested Reading

Michael Gervers and James M. Powell, eds. *Tolerance and Intolerance: Social Conflict in the Age of the Crusades* (2001).

Melisende

Queen of **Jerusalem** (r. 1131–1152), daughter of King **Baldwin II,** wife of King **Fulk of Anjou,** and mother of Kings **Baldwin III** and **Amalric,** Melisende is regarded as one of the most vigorous rulers the kingdom of Jerusalem ever enjoyed.

Melisende's insistence on her right to rule alongside her husband established the principle that hereditary succession to the crown could pass to and through a woman. Although the royal heiress would need a co-ruling husband who would lead armies (the major duty of any ruler in the **crusader states**), her husband would hold his office only by virtue of his marriage. Her continued insistence on her right to rule once her elder son reached his majority resulted in a civil war and her fall from power.

Melisende was the eldest daughter of Baldwin II, who chose Count Fulk of Anjou as her husband and the future king of Jerusalem. The marriage took place in May 1129, and three years later, as King Baldwin lay dying, he designated Fulk and Melisende as co-rulers, who would hold power jointly

The Church of the Tomb of the Virgin outside the walls of Jerusalem. Rebuilt from 1112 onward by Benedictine monks in the Romanesque style. In 1161 Queen Melisende, a patroness of the church, was buried in one of its small chapels.

during the minority of their son, Baldwin III, who was born in 1130. Fulk and Melisende were crowned as king and queen on September 14, 1131. Although they were theoretically equals, Fulk initially had other plans.

Melisende frustrated Fulk's early attempt to rule by himself and through her tenacity became an equal in royal dignity and the counselor to whom Fulk constantly turned. It was said of Fulk during his latter years as king that even in trivial matters he did nothing without his wife's consent.

When Fulk was killed in an accident in November 1143, Baldwin was only thirteen, two years short of legal majority. A month later, Melisende and Baldwin were crowned as co-monarchs on Christmas Day. In fact, however, Melisende took over sole control of the government. As Baldwin grew older, he became increasingly dissatisfied with the arrangement. On her part, Melisende had no intention of letting go of royal power, even when Baldwin reached legal adulthood. Her argument from the beginning was that she was more than just a regent governing in the name of a not-yet-mature boy king; she was the rightful heiress of her father and queen in her own right.

From 1149 onward relations between the queen and her son grew bitter. Whereas most barons had earlier supported her claims against Fulk's pretensions to sole authority, many now were sympathetic to Baldwin. Melisende, however, had the support of men whom she had placed in key positions, especially in the Church. Despite his mother's power, the twenty-year-old Baldwin proved to be an able tactician in this contest for supremacy, and Melisende made several blunders that alienated many barons.

By early 1152 opposition to Melisende was strong enough for Baldwin to make his move. The **High Court** of the kingdom tried to avert a confrontation by dividing the kingdom between the two monarchs. The compromise lasted three weeks before open war broke out. Baldwin besieged **Jerusalem,** the center of his mother's power, and forced her capitulation.

Stripped of her authority over the government, Melisende was allowed to retire to Nablus, where she lived well and continued to exercise rights over a few crown lands and over appointments to some church offices. She died in 1161. **William of Tyre,** writing more than twenty years after her death, best summed up her personality: "It was her ambition to emulate the magnificence of the greatest and noblest princes and to show herself in no way inferior to them." **Related Entries:** Alice of Antioch; Bailli; Second Crusade; Sibylla; Women.

Mercenaries

Professional soldiers hired to fight for a paymaster whose major hold on their loyalty is money, as opposed to: (1) soldiers raised through **feudal** levies or other means of conscription; (2) those whose primary motive for fighting is not pay but religion or a similar ideal; and (3) persons who fight in self-defense. **Islamic, Byzantine,** and **Frankish** armies all employed mercenaries but in differing degrees.

From the mid–ninth century on, **Muslim** rulers in the **Middle East** came to depend increasingly on paid professional soldiers to staff their armies. Many of these, however, were *mamluks,* the so-called **slave**-soldiers, who had been purchased as slaves, converted to Islam, and freed but were obligated to serve as soldiers. Freed mamluks, although paid, cannot be properly termed mercenaries because they had been conscripted into military service. In addition to the slave-soldiers, many true mercenaries also served in these armies, especially from tribes with long warrior traditions. They included **Turks** of various Central Asian tribes, Kurds from the eastern mountains of **Anatolia,** Bedouins from Arabia, Egypt, and **Syria,** Berbers from North Africa, and Arabs from throughout the Middle East. The **Fatimid** army employed thousands of Sudanese foot soldiers, drawn from the region south of Egypt. Reportedly, **Saladin** inherited 30,000 Sudanese mercenaries when he took over the Fatimid army, but he drove them out of his army and Egypt, preferring to rely on the loyalties of Turkish and Kurdish mounted soldiers.

Byzantium was *the* major employer of mercenaries in this region of the world, and it had always hired the best soldiers it could attract, including pagans, Muslims, and **Latin** Christians. The famed Varangian Guard, which protected the emperor, was composed almost exclusively of ax-wielding Scandinavians and English. When the army of the **Fourth Crusade** captured **Constantinople**'s Tower of Galata in 1203 it discovered the tower's defenders were English, Pisan, Genoese, and Danish. In fact, in **Anna Comnena**'s view, the great lords and their retinues who embarked on the second wave of the **First Crusade** and entered into bonds of dependence with her father, **Alexius I,** were mercenaries. After all, that was what Alexius had wanted and expected from the West, not free-roaming religious fanatics. But, of course, the crusaders saw things differently and thought of themselves as in the exclusive pay of their Lord and Savior, Jesus.

Idealism might have been the primary force driving the first crusaders, but even some of them became mercenaries. In 1199 Count **Raymond of Saint-Gilles,** in an attempt to gain leadership over the army as it prepared to march on **Jerusalem,** offered money-**fiefs** to a number of crusader leaders. Apparently **Tancred** and **Robert of Normandy** accepted the money and entered his service. Once

Jerusalem was captured and most surviving crusaders had left for home, their **vows** fulfilled, the need for soldiers rose appreciably as the new lords of **Outremer** struggled to expand, consolidate, and defend their states.

The **crusader states** never had sufficient trained manpower to meet all of their military needs, and for that reason Frankish rulers employed large numbers of mercenary soldiers, as well as using the services of the **military orders.** Indeed, the military orders themselves became increasingly dependent on mercenaries as their duties expanded but their numbers of sworn brothers in the **Holy Land** remained constant and small. For that reason, the majority of the troops garrisoning their **castles** were paid professionals.

As helpful as the military orders were in shoring up the defenses of the crusader states, they were independent of any direct control by the lords and kings whom they assisted, and for that reason alone these same lords needed to create armies that they, and they alone, controlled. Increasingly, that meant armies with substantial numbers of mercenaries, especially once the Muslim counterattack led by **Zangi** and his successors got under way and large tracts of land that supported feudal **vassals** were lost.

William of Tyre notes on several occasions the use of paid **knights** and foot soldiers in the service of the twelfth-century crusader **kingdom of Jerusalem.** During this same century, when the kings of France and England found themselves unable to lead crusader contingents to the Holy Land, they sent money for the hiring of troops. During the **siege** of Jerusalem in 1187, **Balian of Ibelin,** commander of the city's defenses, found it necessary to strip gold and silver from the city's churches, which was then melted down into coins to pay the native **Eastern Christian** troops, who constituted a major portion of the small force resisting **Saladin**'s advance. During the thirteenth century, as the crusader states went from crisis to crisis and all crusade efforts from the West failed, the **papacy** on many occasions dispatched funds to the East for the purpose of hiring soldiers.

In the end, there were nowhere near enough soldiers, mercenaries and non-mercenaries alike, to stem the overwhelming tide of advance by the **Mamluks** of Egypt. **Related Entries:** Cavalry; Infantry; Khorezmians; Sergeant; Turcopoles.

Middle East

A modern, somewhat vague geographic-cultural term coined by the British in 1902 to distinguish the **Islamic** lands stretching from Egypt to Iraq (or Iran) from the Near East (western and central North Africa, **Anatolia,** and the Balkans) and the Far East (China, Korea, and Japan). The term is imprecise and anachronistic, and its meaning is rooted in early twentieth-century British and French imperialism. It is employed here, however, because it is an integral part of contemporary vocabulary.

Military Orders

Religious congregations of **knights, sergeants,** and clergy that arose in the twelfth century as a means of maintaining control over the **crusader states** in **Syria-Palestine** but became offensive instruments for Catholic

Two functions in one: The Hospitaler fortress-church of Saint John, Portomarín, Spain. Last half of the twelfth century.

Europe's expansion in all regions touched by the crusades.

The military orders were the result of crusader Christendom's attempt to combine two of the highest ideals of its age: **chivalry** and the religious life. Unlike the monastic orders, however, the military orders were dominated by laymen, who held most offices. The lay brothers often, but not always, were divided into knights and mounted sergeants-at-arms, and a separate class of clerical brothers, or priests, served the religious needs of the warriors but generally provided no direct military service. Additionally, several military orders created an underclass of brothers-at-service, who performed only menial tasks, relieving the military brothers of these burdens.

All of the military orders also engaged in charitable functions, such as the maintenance of hospitals and almshouses and the ransoming of Christian captives. To further their spiritual and charitable missions, several military orders had separate but affiliated houses of religious **women.** In fact, a number of early **Hospitaler** houses, including its first headquarters in **Jerusalem,** were "double convents," in which brothers and nuns resided but in separate areas, each sex under the supervision of its own superior. A growing general notion from the mid–twelfth century that such mixed convents were not a good idea led to their disappearance.

The two earliest and greatest of the orders, the **Templars** and the Hospitalers, drew members from all over Europe. Their energies were primarily devoted to the crusader states of **Syria-Palestine** and secondarily to Spain and other areas along Europe's frontiers, where they occupied strategic strongholds and carried on military operations in the field. Although each order was capable of putting only about 300 brothers into the field at any one time in the **Mid-**

dle East, their presence was critical to the survival of the crusader states, whose armies were chronically undermanned. The Templars and Hospitalers provided fairly constant numbers of dedicated, elite troops who pledged lifelong service to the **holy war** against **Islam.** Given their training, commitment, and esprit, these two military orders were normally assigned the most important and precarious frontier fortresses and were placed in key positions on the battlefield. What is more, they used their vast resources to employ large numbers of **mercenaries,** including native **Turcopole** light **cavalry,** who proved quite effective in battle.

As was true of the Hospitalers, a number of military orders began as charitable orders devoted to maintaining hospitals in the **Holy Land** and only gradually assumed military roles. The powerful Teutonic Order, better known as the **Teutonic Knights,** fell into this category, as did the much smaller and fairly poor orders of Saint Thomas of **Acre** and **Saint Lazarus.**

Because of their success, perceived arrogance, and setbacks in the Holy Land, the military orders came under increasing criticism in the late twelfth and thirteenth centuries. The orders, especially the Templars and Hospitalers, were widely accused of putting their own interests before those of Christendom and allying with the enemy against Christians when it served their selfish needs. Critics, such as **William of Tyre,** pointed out that the military orders' bitter rivalries even led them to turn their arms on one another on occasion. These criticisms represented a minority view and were often exaggerated, but they contained a kernel of truth. By the end of the thirteenth century the military orders were thought by some to be in need of major reform, maybe amalgamation into a single order, but this suggestion to create a super military order, possibly under the rule of one of Europe's kings, was never implemented.

The loss of Acre and the remaining crusader settlements in Syria-Palestine in 1291, as well as the halt to the tempo of the **Reconquista** by the mid–thirteenth century, forced many of the military orders, such as the Hospitalers and the Teutonic Knights, to redefine themselves and their missions. The Templars, however, failed to do so in time and were dissolved in 1312 after a messy and, at times, brutal inquisition. Although many military orders still had centuries of history before them, the Templars, the first and greatest of the orders, had officially existed for a scant 183 years. **Related Entries:** Bernard of Clairvaux; Castles, Crusader; Criticism of the Crusades; La Forbie, Battle of; Military Orders of Iberia; Military Orders of the Baltic; Philip IV; Slavery.

Suggested Reading

Alan J. Forey, *The Military Orders: From the Twelfth to the Early Fourteenth Centuries* (1992); Zsolt Hunyadi and József Laszlovszky, eds., *The Crusades and the Military Orders: Expanding the Frontiers of Medieval Latin Christianity* (2001); Helen Nicholson, *Love, War and the Grail: Templars, Hospitallers and Teutonic Knights in Medieval Epic and Romance, 1150–1500 (2001)* and *Templars, Hospitalers and Teutonic Knights: Images of the Military Orders, 1128–1291* (1993); Dominic Selwood, *Knights of the Cloister: Templars and Hospitallers in Central-Southern Occitania, 1100–1300* (1999).

Military Orders of Iberia

Influenced by the **Templars** and **Hospitalers,** the Christian kingdoms of Iberia created a number of homebred **military orders,** whose primary function, from the beginning, was to further the **Reconquista.**

In 1122 King Alfonso I of León-Castile, who led a successful crusade against Saragossa in 1118, established a quasi-military order, the Confraternity of Belchite,

but this loose organization of soldiers, who apparently consecrated their swords to fighting **Muslims,** seems to have had no formal rule or official status within the Church and was later absorbed by the Templars.

By the mid–twelfth century the Iberian Reconquista had attracted the Templars and Hospitalers, particularly to the kingdom of Aragon. In time, their presence and example helped spawn a large number of native military orders, most of which modeled themselves on the rule of the Templars. The three giants of Spain were the *Order of Calatrava,* founded in Castile in 1158, and the orders of *Santiago* and *Alcántara,* founded in León in 1170 and around 1176 respectively. In the kingdom of Aragon the *Order of Montjoie* appeared in 1173. The *Order of Aviz,* originally known as the *Order of Evora* (c. 1146?), was Portugal's sole home-grown military order prior to the fourteenth century. Like the Templars and Hospitalers, the Iberian military orders commanded frontier fortresses from which they defended potential invasion routes and launched attacks against neighboring Muslim states, but unlike the Hospitalers and the **Teutonic Knights,** and several smaller military orders in the Holy Land, all of the Iberian military orders were created from the beginning to serve a military purpose. They were envisioned as the cutting edge of the Reconquista. As such, they provided the backbone of the army that won the decisive victory at **Las Navas de Tolosa** in 1212, which led to the reconquest of all of Iberia by 1248, except for the **Islamic** emirate of Granada in the extreme south. Granada's eventual fall in 1492 to the armies of Ferdinand and Isabella was facilitated by the orders of Santiago, Calatrava, and Alcántara, whose border castles combined to strangle the last **Moorish** outpost in Iberia.

Following the dissolution of the Knights of the Temple, Templar estates and castles in Valencia passed to the new order of the

Knights of Montesa (1317), and in Portugal they passed to the *Order of Christ* (1319). Beginning in the fifteenth century the grand mastership of the Order of Christ was reserved for princes of the royal family, the most famous of whom was Henry the Navigator. Prince Henry reformed the order, used its resources to help finance Portuguese oceanic exploration, and secured for it spiritual jurisdiction over the Atlantic and African lands that his sailors explored and colonized. **Related Entries:** Almohads; Almoravids; Cid, El; Santiago de Compostela.

Suggested Reading

D. W. Lomax, *Another Sword for St. James* (1974); Joseph F. O'Callaghan, *The Spanish Military Order of Calatrava and Its Affiliates* (1975).

Military Orders of the Baltic

The **Baltic Crusades** produced two **military orders:** the *Brothers of the Knighthood of Christ of Livonia,* more popularly known as the *Sword Brothers,* because of their badge, a red sword surmounted by a small cross; and the *Brothers of the Knighthood of Christ of Livonia against the Prussians,* who wore a red sword surmounted by a star and were better known as the *Knights of Dobrin* (or Dobrzýn).

The Sword Brothers, who were founded around 1202 by Albert of Buxtehunde, the German **missionary**-bishop of Riga in Livonia (Latvia), fought during the early stages of the crusade against the pagan Livs in the eastern Baltic. To the west of Livonia lay East Prussia (modern western Poland), where in or before 1228 the **Cistercian** missionary-bishop of Dobrin, Christian, established an order modeled on the Sword Brothers and aimed at the prosecution of

holy war against the pagan Prussians. Neither order was very large. The Sword Brothers never exceeded 120 professed brothers; the Knights of Dobrin were much smaller. Reportedly in 1235 the order had only fifteen members. Both orders differed from the military orders of the East and of **Iberia** in four significant ways: (1) Their **knights** were men of mixed social background; (2) they were not autonomous but were subject to the jurisdiction of a bishop; (3) they were unendowed with lands, had no rich or influential patrons back in the West, and had to seize whatever lands they could; and (4) their mission was to assist in the conversion of pagans.

Both orders were unsuccessful as independent entities, although the Sword Brothers lasted long enough to earn a reputation for rapacity. In 1235 the Knights of Dobrin were amalgamated into the **Teutonic Knights,** and in 1237 the Sword Brothers went the same way. The previous year they had invaded Lithuania, where they suffered virtual annihilation. According to one report they lost fifty knights. With the absorption of the Sword Brothers, the Teutonic Knights extended their interests into Livonia and lands to its east, including Estonia and Russia. **Related Entry:** Military Orders of Iberia.

Missionaries

The crusades did not begin as a missionary effort. Rather than seeking the conversion of **Muslims,** the first crusaders who went east sought simply to fight a war in defense of Christendom and its holy sites. **Papal crusade bulls,** which summoned **Latin** Christians to **holy war,** also failed to include conversion of **infidels** as an objective. Despite these traditions, toward the middle of the twelfth century the idea of converting nonbelievers began to become associated with the crusading movement. Over the course of the next century and a half it developed into a secondary but significant crusade element.

Actually, the conversion of Spanish Muslims had been an avowed aim of several prominent supporters of the **Reconquista,** such as Popes **Gregory VII** and **Urban II,** even before the **First Crusade,** and the idea could not be confined indefinitely to the Iberian wars of reconquest. On the eve of the **Second Crusade, Bernard of Clairvaux** called for the annihilation *or conversion* of the pagan Wends along Germany's northeastern border, and the conversion of pagans and even **Eastern Christian** peoples remained a constant feature of the **Baltic Crusades** throughout their long and torturous history. There is also evidence that in the midst of the **Second Crusade** certain French crusaders articulated the unofficial goal of either killing or converting their Muslim foes.

More significant were the often unrecorded attempts to convert Muslims during the early years of the **crusader states.** Evidence suggests, for example, that a substantial percentage of **Turcopoles** serving in the armies of the crusader states were converts from **Islam.** Evidence also points to a number of Muslim **slaves** who chose Christianity, often out of a desire to gain their freedom. Still, the numbers of converts were not large relative to the population, and early attempts at missionary work among the Muslims of the **Middle East** were isolated and unsustained episodes.

This changed early in the thirteenth century with the rise of the **mendicant friars,** specifically the Franciscans and the **Dominicans,** who established convents in Spain, North Africa, and the **Latin East** that had the specific purpose of being centers of missionary activity, particularly for the conversion of Muslims but also for the **Latinization** of Eastern Christians. At the very moment that many mendicants were employing their energies and skills in **preaching** to Muslims, many others were preaching crusades against them, as thirteenth-century popes increasingly depended on the friars to publicize their holy wars. Indeed, a number of friars participated in both missionary work and crusade promotion. The irony was lost on most Western contemporaries, who saw the two phenomena, mission and crusade, as related elements of a single struggle against evil and unbelief. As far as the friars were concerned, both also offered the opportunity for holy martyrdom.

The friars' efforts at converting Muslims bore little fruit. Their greatest successes came in Spain; elsewhere results were meager. The overall failure to convert Muslims led many to conclude that a crusade was the only way in which to combat Islam, but even as disillusionment over more peaceful means of fighting Islam emerged, the crusade itself was losing its viability.

The search for new crusade allies and new converts to Christianity led the friars, especially the Franciscans, deep into Central Asia and beyond to China during the last half of the thirteenth century. Seeking to convert and ally with the **Mongols,** popes dispatched friars to the courts of the khans. The result was that in 1294 or 1295 the Franciscan John of Monte Corvino arrived in Khanbaliq (Beijing), the capital of the Great Khan. Here he was allowed to establish a church, where he labored to convert Mongols, Chinese, and Nestorian Christians (largely **Turks** and Alans) and kept in touch with the West through several letters transmitted by Italian merchants. His results were modest, and he never managed to convert the khan or many Mongols. Nevertheless, John was appointed archbishop of Khanbaliq and patriarch of the East 1307 by Pope Clement V. When John died in 1328 the mission to China continued under several successors, until it died out in the late fourteenth or early fifteenth century following the expulsion of the Mongols from China in 1368. Western Christian missionaries would not return to China until the sixteenth century. **Related Entries:** Criticism of the Crusades; Francis of Assisi; Gregory X, Pope; James of Vitry; Military Orders of the Baltic.

Suggested Reading

Primary Source

Christopher Dawson, ed., *Mission to Asia: Narratives and Letters of the Franciscan Missionaries in Mongolia and China in the Thirteenth and Fourteenth Centuries* (1966) [originally printed as *The Mongol Mission* (1955)].

Historical Studies

Benjamin Z. Kedar, *Crusade and Mission: European Approaches toward the Muslims* (1989); James Muldoon, *Popes, Lawyers, and Infidels: The Church and the Non-Christian World, 1250–1550* (1979).

Mongols

A group of nomadic, horse-riding pastoral peoples speaking related Mongolian languages who inhabit the high plateau region to the northwest of the Chinese heartland.

During the latter half of the thirteenth century, several popes and King **Louis IX** of France unsuccessfully sought to convert the Mongols, whom they mistakenly called the *Tartars,* to **Latin** Christianity and to enlist them as allies in the struggle against **Islam.** Likewise, during the late thirteenth century, several Mongol leaders sought military alliances with various Western leaders against the **Mamluks,** but all proposals failed.

Between 1206 and 1279, under the leadership of Chinggis (Ghengis) Khan (1167?–1227) and his successors, the Mongols carved out the largest land empire Eurasia had ever seen. At its fullest extent, it stretched from China to Poland, from the southern borders of Siberia to the northern frontiers of Southeast Asia, from lands north of the Black Sea to lands bordering the Arabian Sea.

When the Mongols overran large portions of Eastern Europe in a two-pronged campaign that lasted from 1236 to 1242, the Latin West was forced to confront this new menace from the East. Fortunately for the West, the Mongols withdrew back to the Volga in 1242 due to the death of the Great Khan and the succession struggle that followed. This withdrawal took place, however, only after the Battle of Liegnitz in western Poland on April 9, 1241, where one Mongol army destroyed a combined Polish and German army that contained a large contingent of **Templars, Hospitalers,** and **Teutonic Knights.** Reportedly the victorious Mongols collected nine sacks of ears from the European **knights**. One day later, a second Mongol force wiped out a massive Hungarian army at the Sajo River, where the Mongols' use of exploding shells, which they had learned from the Chinese, foreshadowed a new era of European warfare.

The West's initial reaction was fear. Tales of horrendous atrocities committed against any people who resisted them convinced Western Europeans that these "Devil's horsemen" were demonic forces of the Antichrist who presaged the Final Days as foretold in the Bible. **Frederick II** wrote to the kings of England and France proposing a common front against this menace and complaining that Pope **Gregory IX** should have called a crusade against the Tartars rather than against himself, the emperor. The

The Mongols passed this way. Remains of the once-great city of Harran in northern Syria (today southeastern Turkey) destroyed by the Mongols and never rebuilt.

pope did call a crusade against the Mongols in 1241, and his successor, Innocent IV (r. 1243–1254), renewed it in 1243, but in both cases, like Frederick II's call for concerted action, they were empty gestures. Western Europe was too caught up in the struggle between Emperor Frederick II and the papacy to rouse itself too much against a foe that had retreated mysteriously in 1242.

Fearing, however, that the Mongols would return, Pope Innocent IV and King Louis IX of France tried diplomacy, dispatching a series of legations aimed at discovering Mongol intentions and converting these "enemies of God and friends of the Devil" to Christianity. These initial missions, which began in 1245 and lasted down to 1255, were conducted by **mendicant friars,** mainly Franciscans, and were met with Mongol indifference. To the Mongol mind, the West had only one option: submission. Two of the embassies, those of Friar John of Plano Carpini (1245–1247) and Friar William of Rubruck (1253–1255), did bear some fruit. They not only reached the court of the Great Khan in Mongolia but produced highly detailed written accounts of the Mongols and their culture—the West's first authoritative descriptions of this people.

After the Mongols captured Baghdad in 1258 and then reached a level of stalemate in the **Middle East** following their setback at the **Battle of Ayn Jalut** in 1260, their leaders in the western regions of the Mongol empire, the il-khans (subordinate rulers) of Persia, were finally willing to discuss an alliance with the Christian West against the Mamluks. Because these same Mamluks were pressing hard against the rapidly weak-ening crusader states of **Syria-Palestine,** the West was willing to negotiate. Indeed, the dream of converting the Mongols and mak-ing common cause with them had never dis-appeared. It was for that reason that Pope **Gregory X** had commissioned Niccolò and Maffeo Polo (and Maffeo's seventeen-year-old son, Marco) to serve as papal envoys on their second trip to China and the court of the Great Khan in 1271. A bit earlier, King Louis IX had set off on the **Eighth Crusade** confident that he would eventually link up with Arbaga, the il-khan of Persia, and lib-erate **Jerusalem.**

In 1287 Arghun, il-khan of Persia, dis-patched a **Turkish** Nestorian monk, Rabban Sauma, to the West, entrusting him with the task of proposing an alliance. Sauma trav-eled to Constantinople, where he met the emperor. He then traveled to Italy, where he discovered a vacant papal throne. From there he traveled to Paris, where he met King **Philip IV,** and then on to Bordeaux, where he was received by King **Edward I.** Upon hearing of Pope Nicholas IV's elec-tion, he hurried to Rome. Everywhere he went he was treated with respect, and Arghun's proposal was met with enthusi-asm. When Sauma left Rome in April 1288, he carried with him several warm papal let-ters for the il-khan. Shortly thereafter, in 1289, the pope sent Friar John of Mon-tecorvino to the il-khan's court. Before any-thing could come of these negotiations, Arghun died, and his successor embraced Islam in 1295. All hopes for a Mongol-Latin crusade were dashed.

Never defeated by circumstances, Friar John set off for China in 1291, arriving there, by way of India, in 1294 or 1295. Although he was too late to meet Kublai Khan, who died in 1294, the Franciscan friar set up a mission church in Khanbaliq (Bei-jing), which enjoyed Mongol protection until the Mongols were evicted from China in 1368. Although the Ming dynasty, which reasserted native Chinese rule, was hostile to all foreign elements that had any association with the hated Mongols, this mission church probably continued to exist until the late fourteenth or early fifteenth century.

After 1294 the Mongol empire under-went substantial changes, and before the next century was over, the empire was dead. The il-khanate of Persia, now quite Islami-cized, was destroyed by Timur i-Leng (Tamerlane) in 1393; the Chinese realm of the Great Khan collapsed earlier, in 1368; the khanate of the Golden Horde that ruled Russia, Ukraine, and contiguous lands sur-vived until 1502, but long before then it had become a shadow of its former self. **Related Entries:** Abbasids; Aleppo; Apocalypse and the Crusades; Assassins; Ayyubids; Canni-balism; Damascus; Khorezmians; Mission-aries; Political Crusades.

Suggested Reading
Primary Source
Christopher Dawson, ed., *Mission to Asia: Nar-ratives and Letters of the Franciscan Mission-aries in Mongolia and China in the Thirteenth and Fourteenth Centuries* (1966) [originally printed as *The Mongol Mission* (1955)].

Historical Studies
Paul D. Buell, *Historical Dictionary of the Mongol World Empire* (2003); James Cham-bers, *The Devil's Horsemen: The Mongol Invasion of Europe* (1985); Robert Marshall, *Storm from the East: From Genghis Khan to Khubilai Khan* (1993); David O. Morgan, *The Mongols* (1986); Morris Rossabi, *Voyager from Xanadu: Rabban Sauma and the First Journey from China to the West* (1992); Antti Ruotsala, *Europeans and Mongols in the Mid-dle Thirteenth Century: Encountering the Other* (2001); Jean-Paul Roux, *Ghenghis*

Khan and the Mongol Empire (2003); J. J. Saunders, *The History of the Mongol Conquests* (1971).

Montferrat, Family of

The family of the marquises of Montferrat in north central Italy, whose service and fortunes in the East point out the role that family traditions played in attracting crusade **recruits** and the rewards and dangers that awaited those who went to **Outremer.**

Marquis William III (r. 1135–1188), known as the Elder, served in the **Second Crusade.** In 1185 he returned to the **Holy Land,** where apparently he was determined to live out his remaining years. Despite his age, William fought at the Battle of **Hattin** and was captured. He was freed in a **prisoner** exchange around May 1188 and died soon after. Earlier, his eldest son and namesake, William Longsword, was called to the East in 1176 to marry **Sibylla,** sister of the sickly **Baldwin IV.** William became an instantaneous power behind the throne but died of **disease** six months after his marriage. His posthumous son later became the boy king, **Baldwin V,** and it was probably this young grandson's inheritance of the throne that drew William III back to the East.

William the Elder's youngest son, Renier, married Maria, the daughter of the **Byzantine** emperor **Manuel,** in 1180. He rose to the high position of *caesar* and was awarded rule over the city of Thessalonica, but he died under mysterious circumstances in 1182 while caught up in court intrigues. Reportedly, he was poisoned.

A third son and a successor to the marquisate, **Conrad of Montferrat,** also married a Byzantine princess, Theodora, sister of Emperor **Isaac II,** whom he wed in 1185. In 1187 Conrad abandoned **Constantinople** (and his wife) and traveled to **Syria,** just in time to become the heroic defender of **Tyre.** Subsequently he married **Isabella I,** heiress of the **kingdom of Jerusalem,** despite the fact that he and she were still legitimately married to other people. Indeed, the rumor was that Conrad also had a wife back home in Italy. His new marriage in 1190 gave him a claim to the kingship, which he maintained until he was cut down by an **Assassin** on April 28, 1192.

A fourth son and second successor to the marquisate, **Boniface of Montferrat** (r. 1192–1207), was named leader of the **Fourth Crusade** in 1201. Following the capture of Constantinople and establishment of the **Latin empire of Constantinople** in 1204, Boniface became lord of Thessalonica, which he won by conquest. Following his death in battle in 1207, he was succeeded as marquis by his son William IV (r. 1207–1225), who initially preferred to stay in Italy and refused to go to Thessalonica to claim his father's **Greek** lands. Even the promise of the imperial crown of Constantinople could not initially lure William to the East. Apart from his attachment to his native Italy, William's reluctance might have been influenced by the fact that there was another claimant to the crown of Thessalonica already in the East, Demetrius of Montferrat, the infant son of Marquis Boniface and his wife, Maria-Margaret of Hungary, the widow of Emperor Isaac II.

Finally Marquis William accepted the title of king of Thessalonica in 1217 and was duly invested in Rome. It was not until 1224, however, that William roused himself to go east to defend his kingdom, which was threatened by Byzantine forces. His delay was due in part to the huge cost of **financing** this expedition. Although Pope **Honorius III** gave the crusade legitimacy by granting **indulgences** to all who participated, William had to bear the major burden of cost himself. He finally secured a loan from

Emperor **Frederick II** of 9,000 marks (4,500 pounds) of silver by mortgaging all of his lands. But it was too late. Even before William set sail from Italy, Thessalonica fell to the Byzantines. William of Montferrat arrived in Thessaly and almost immediately died. With his death, his crusade to liberate Thessalonica ended and his forces dispersed. **Related Entries:** Capetians; Hohenstaufens; Maria of Montferrat.

Montjoie

It was a medieval French tradition to bestow the name "Mount Joy" on any elevated natural point from which a **pilgrim** first glimpsed the sanctuary to which he or she was traveling. Hence, hills outside **Santiago de Compostela** and Rome received this appellation. But the most important and celebrated *Montjoie* was the hill, also known as *Nabi Samwil* (The Prophet Samuel's Hill), from which the army of the **First Crusade** got its initial view of **Jerusalem** on July 7, 1099.

It was (and is) customary for pilgrims traveling to Jerusalem to stop at Montjoie for prayer before proceeding into the holy city. Tradition identifies it as the site of the prophet Samuel's tomb, and it is the farthest point from which to view the **Church of the Holy Sepulcher** and the Temple Mount. King **Richard I the Lionheart** is reported to have gotten this far but no farther in his frustrated attempt to capture Jerusalem during the **Third Crusade.**

So central was the hill to the ideology of the crusade as pilgrimage, *The Song of Roland* claimed that "Montjoie" was Charlemagne's battle cry in his **holy war** against the **Muslims** of Spain, and the ship that carried King **Louis IX** of France on the **Eighth Crusade** in 1270 bore the name *Montjoie.* What is more, a religious order founded in Spain in 1180 and dedicated to the liberation of Christians captured in the wars of the **Reconquista** called itself the Order of Montjoie. The order was merged into the **Order of Calatrava** in 1221.

Acre also had a hill named Montjoie that divided the Venetian and Genoese colonies and became the center of a bitter civil war in the mid–thirteenth century when the two merchant communities fought over control of the monastery of Saint Sabas, which was located on the summit. The three major **military orders** headquartered in Acre became involved in the hostilities, with the **Hospitalers** supporting the Genoese and the **Templars** and **Teutonic Knights** taking up the Venetian cause. **Related Entries:** Settlement and Colonization; Slavery.

Moors

The **Muslim** people of mixed Berber and Arabic descent who invaded Iberia in 711 and established the **Islamic** culture of **al-Andalus,** which periodically renewed its close relations with western North Africa and persisted down to the end of the fifteenth century. **Related Entries:** Almohads; Almoravids; Cid, El; Islamic Peoples; Las Navas de Tolosa, Battle of; Reconquista.

Mosul

A city on the Tigris in northern Iraq that served as the Great **Seljuk** empire's only effective center of resistance to the **crusader states** and was a major center of **Islamic** commerce, learning, and power throughout most of the Age of the Crusades.

Zangi became *atabeg* (governor) of Mosul in 1127 and used it as a launching pad for his occupation of **Aleppo** the following year and his conquest of **Edessa** in 1144. The **Zangids** ruled Mosul and Upper Mesopotamia continuously down to 1234, and for much of the twelfth century they were an independent power to be reckoned with. In March 1186, however, Izz ad-Din entered into a treaty with **Saladin** whereby he acknowledged the Kurdish sultan's overlordship, while retaining possession of the city and its environs. With this treaty Saladin's hegemony over the Islamic **Middle East** was complete. In 1234 the office of atabeg of Mosul passed to a former slave-soldier, or **mamluk,** Badr ad-Din Lu'lu, who held onto power until 1259, when the **Mongols** captured the city. **Related Entries:** Damascus; Islamic Peoples.

Muslims

See Islamic Peoples.

N

Noncombatants

Nonwarriors traveling with crusade armies fell into two groups: (1) those attached to the warriors, who usually performed necessary tasks; and (2) uninvited hangers-on, who usually were poor, disorganized, and often an unwanted burden. Attached noncombatants accompanied every crusade army; the unattached were far less evident in the armies that traveled by ship because of the cost of transportation and limited space.

Crusade noncombatants came in every form, in all ages, and in both sexes, and depending on the circumstances, their numbers could equal or exceed those of the warriors. They were priests who served as chaplains; they were wives and children who accompanied husbands and parents; they were servants, merchants, money changers, prostitutes, cooks, washerwomen, unarmed pilgrims, and every other imaginable camp follower.

When circumstances dictated it, many so-called noncombatants placed themselves in harm's way as combat support personnel and even auxiliary troops, and quite a few were killed or wounded in the process. The story is told of one woman who assisted in the construction of an assault ditch in the **siege** of **Acre** during the **Third Crusade.**

When she was mortally wounded, she asked that her body be buried where she fell so that it could take the place of a load of earth. Some clerics even went on crusade as soldiers. The priest Aleaumes of Clari particularly distinguished himself in the fighting at **Constantinople** during the **Fourth Crusade.**

Evidence indicates that Pope **Urban II** strongly discouraged the old, the feeble, and all others unfit for military service from joining the **First Crusade.** The pope also seems to have declared that no woman could set out on this armed **pilgrimage** unless she was accompanied by a husband, brother, or legal guardian. He also clearly forbade cloistered monks from joining the expedition and stipulated that no priest or other cleric could go without the consent of his bishop. Many either did not hear or did not heed the papal directives. The large numbers of unattached noncombatants who flocked to the crusade suggest the gulf that existed between papal policy and popular religiosity.

During the long march from Constantinople to **Jerusalem** in 1097–1099, noncombatants were a severe drain on the crusaders' resources. The poorest and weakest suffered terribly, and their numbers were dramatically reduced by **disease,** war wounds, and starvation. By 1099 all but a handful of clerics, **women,** and children were forced to take up arms as **infantry** due to the army's heavy losses and constant attacks by the enemy.

Noncombatants during the **Second Crusade** included **Eleanor of Aquitaine,** queen of France, and a large entourage of noble ladies, many of whom, like Queen Eleanor, were accompanying their husbands. After the crusade's dismal outcome the women were accused of having seriously impeded the French army's progress with all of their baggage and attendants. (Some stereotypes are timeless.) What was worse, the women were said to have presented the men with terrible temptations to sin. The resultant adulteries supposedly brought down the wrath of God, who turned away from the crusaders and allowed them to meet with the failure they deserved. Moral quotients are impossible to weigh, but the armies of the Second Crusade were probably no more lustful and sinful than any other crusade contingents, and their noncombatants were probably no more or less a burden than those of the First and Third Crusades.

Once crusade armies began traveling exclusively by ship, the costs and logistics of transportation dramatically reduced but did not eliminate the numbers of noncombatants. In 1202, for example, Cardinal Peter Capuano, **papal legate** to the **Fourth Crusade,** dispensed from their crusade vows "the sick, paupers, women, and all feeble persons," while the army awaited embarkation at Venice. Presumably some healthy, well-to-do, and virile noncombatants managed to embark with the crusaders. Certainly, a number of clerical noncombatants attached themselves to this army, as they did to every crusader force.

Odo of Deuil, King **Louis VII**'s chaplain during the Second Crusade, complained that "the weak and unarmed are always a burden to their comrades and a source of prey to their enemies." Undoubtedly Odo, an unwar-

like monk, did not place himself in the category of the weak and unarmed. To his mind, they were the unattached rabble not men such as he who provided valuable services to the king and the army. Odo had a point. At their best, clerical noncombatants provided important support at key moments. On April 11, 1204, the bishops and other prominent clergy traveling with the army of the Fourth Crusade raised the rock-bottom morale of an army that had suffered a devastating defeat at the walls of Constantinople by publicly assuring the soldiers that their cause was righteous. Thus inspired, the crusaders renewed their assault on April 12 and carried the day.

During the **Albigensian Crusade** a group of lower-class, largely unarmed camp followers, known disparagingly as the *ribauds* (the licentious masses), were accused of precipitating the attack on the city of Béziers and the **massacre** that followed on July 22, 1209. Crusade noncombatants certainly were a two-edged sword. **Related Entries:** Adhémar of Monteil; Children's Crusade; Cîteaux, Order of; Francis of Assisi; James of Vitry; Legates, Papal; Oliver of Paderborn; Shepherds' Crusade; Tafurs; Vow, Crusader's; Women.

Normans

Inhabitants of the French duchy of Normandy who were descended from tenth-century Norse invaders and settlers (the Old French word *Normant* means "Northman"). During the eleventh century the Normans became one of Western Europe's most dynamic driving forces.

In 1066 William, duke of Normandy, conquered England, becoming King William I the Conqueror. Because of this conquest subsequent kings of England held French **fiefs,** such as the duchy of Normandy. England's kings from William I through

Richard I the Lionheart were French in culture and speech. The same was true for the vast majority of the **feudal** lords of England until the early thirteenth century. This Anglo-French connection meant that England's crusade armies contained French warriors, and western French crusade contingents had English participants.

During the last half of the eleventh century, the Norman family of Hauteville, led by Robert Guiscard and his brother Roger, conquered **Byzantine** southern Italy and **Muslim** Sicily. In 1071 (the same year as the disaster at **Manzikert**) Robert and his Norman forces captured Bari, the last Byzantine stronghold in southern Italy. Ten years earlier Roger, accompanied by a few thousand Norman warriors, had entered Sicily as an ally of a Muslim emir who requested his help as the island sank into factional chaos. Roger soon turned to carving out his own principality, and in 1091 he was master of the entire island. Under Roger and his successors Sicily was a land in which **Latin** and **Greek** Christians and Muslims largely lived in peace with one another. In 1130 southern Italy was united with Sicily to form the kingdom of Sicily, and it remained in Norman hands until 1194. Even then the Norman element did not disappear. Sicily's greatest thirteenth-century king, **Frederick II,** was half Norman.

The contingents of both Duke **Robert II of Normandy** and **Bohemond of Taranto** were major contributors to the **First Crusade,** and Count **Robert II of Flanders,** another leader of that crusade, was half Norman. Just as significant, the Normans and Italo-Normans remained important factors in the crusades and the **Latin East** for generations to come.

Additionally, the Italo-Normans, from Robert Guiscard to William II (r. 1166–1189), pursued a policy of aggression against the Byzantine empire, in an attempt to conquer lands in the Balkans and farther east. These hostilities played a role in the unfolding of the crusades. Close ties between King Roger II of Sicily and **Louis VII** of France probably helped fuel Emperor **Manuel I**'s antipathy toward the French during the **Second Crusade. Related Entries:** Antioch; Bohemond II; Bohemond III; Field of Blood, Battle of the; *Gesta Francorum;* Hohenstaufens; Lance, Holy; Roger of Salerno; Tancred; Third Crusade.

Suggested Reading

R. Allen Brown, *The Normans* (1984); Marjorie Chibnall, *The Normans* (2000); David C. Douglas, *The Normans* (2002).

Nur ad-Din Mahmud (Nur ed-Din; Nur al-Din)

Turkish ruler of **Syria** (1146–1174) and originator of **Islam**'s anti-**Frankish jihad.**

A sincerely pious and humble man, he often chose not to use his honorific title, Nur ad-Din, which means "light of religion." At the same time, he understood better than most the power of propaganda. His employment of **Sunni** poets, **preachers,** and essayists who publicized his twin programs of religious reformation and **holy war,** as well as his construction and patronage of madrasas (religious schools), convents of Sufi mystics, and mosques, created a sense of religious unity and purpose within the Sunni majority of Syria's **Muslim** population. As part of his program to purify Islam, however, Nur ad-Din instituted repressive measures against his **Shia** subjects.

Zangi's murder in 1146 led to the division of his lands between his two sons. Saif-ad-Din Ghazi received the eastern, or Mesopotamian, portion, with **Mosul** as his capital; Nur ad-Din received **Aleppo** and the western territories, essentially northern Syria and **Edessa.** Although Nur ad-Din's lands were poorer than those of his elder brother, their strategic location gave him an advantageous starting point in his rise to become Islam's leading champion against the **crusader states.**

Northern Syria allowed Nur ad-Din to threaten **Antioch** and **Tripoli,** and in 1149 he was able to destroy an army led by Raymond of Poitiers, prince of Antioch, in which Raymond was killed. If, however, Nur ad-Din wished to strike at the heart of the crusader states—the **kingdom of Jerusalem**—he would have to control **Damascus** in southern Syria. On April 25, 1154, he occupied the city. The entire eastern flank of the crusader states now faced a single, determined enemy.

In his drive to unite all of Islam in his jihad, Nur ad-Din employed many non-Turkish soldiers, including large numbers of Kurds. Three Kurdish officers who attained high rank under him were the brothers Ayyub and Shirkuh and Ayyub's son, **Saladin.** In 1164, 1167, and 1168 Shirkuh traveled to Egypt, with Nur ad-Din's blessing, to intervene in the faltering **Fatimid** state, which seemed ready to be dominated by King **Amalric** of Jerusalem. In January 1169 Shirkuh became vizier, or prime minister, of Egypt, and when he died eight weeks later, he was succeeded by his nephew, Saladin.

In 1171 Saladin suppressed the Fatimid caliphate of Egypt and now governed Egypt as the deputy of Nur ad-Din. Saladin and Nur ad-Din cooperated in a joint invasion of **Transjordan,** but soon the ambitious Saladin realized that it was in his best interest to maintain distance from his overlord in Syria. As Saladin drew away and sent his lord far less from his Egyptian riches than Nur ad-Din thought proper, the senior sultan began to muster his troops for an invasion of Egypt to bring his overly independent subordinate to heel. A clash was avoided by Nur ad-Din's death in Damascus on May 15, 1174.

Although Saladin would soon overshadow his former lord in every way, arguably Saladin would never have become the great hero of the Islamic counter crusade were it not for Nur ad-Din's example and achievements. **Related Entries:** Historians and Chroniclers, Islamic; Second Crusade; Zangids.

O

Oliver of Paderborn

Schoolmaster at the cathedral school of Cologne; **preacher** of the **Albigensian, Fifth,** and **Sixth Crusades;** participant and **historian** of the **Fifth Crusade;** bishop of Paderborn (1224–1225); and cardinal bishop of Santa Sabina (1225–1227). Died 1227.

Master Oliver began his crusade activities in 1208 when he was commissioned to preach against the **Cathars** of **Languedoc.** In 1213 Pope **Innocent III** appointed him regional procurator, or commissioner, in charge of promoting the upcoming Fifth Crusade in northwest Germany, Flanders, and the Netherlands. Oliver and others reported that on several occasions when he was delivering crusade sermons, luminous crosses appeared in the sky, thereby inciting large numbers to take the **crusader's cross.**

Contemporary sources refer to the tens of thousands whom he enlisted. In addition, he raised enough funds to outfit 300 vessels to transport the first wave of the Hollanders, Flemings, Frisians, and Germans whom he had recruited. Oliver joined this contingent, the first to leave Europe on the Fifth Crusade, and served as one of its leaders. Oliver's sizeable force embarked on May 29, 1217, and arrived at **Acre** in late April/early May 1218, its numbers significantly reduced by storms, warfare in Portugal, and **disease.**

We know little about his activities on the crusade except for the important role he played in the capture of **Damietta**'s Chain Tower. The tower, which commanded entry to the Nile, resisted every effort to take it until Oliver designed and built a floating wooden assault tower mounted on two ships that he lashed together. The tower was funded by contributions from Oliver's Frisian crusaders, who collected a total of 1,000 pounds of silver for the enterprise. Once the Chain Tower fell on August 25, 1218, to an assault force composed totally of Oliver's Frisian and German crusaders, the total encirclement of Damietta began.

We know that Oliver was the moving force behind the mobile tower thanks to the testimony of another eyewitness, **James of Vitry.** In his own history of the Fifth Crusade, which he entitled *Historia Damiatina (The Damiettan History),* Oliver modestly ascribed this success to: "The Lord's showing us how and providing an architect and the Frisians' providing supplies and labor."

Oliver's history of the Fifth Crusade, which he probably began crafting while on crusade and completed upon his return to Cologne in 1222, is one of our most important sources for crusade events for the period

1217–1222. Following his return to Europe, Oliver resumed crusade preaching and was involved in promoting **Frederick II**'s Sixth Crusade when death ended his crusade work in 1227. **Related Entries:** Chivalry; Noncombatants.

Suggested Reading

Oliver of Paderborn, *The Capture of Damietta*, trans. by Joseph J. Gavigan in Edward Peters, ed., *Christian Society and the Crusades, 1198–1229* (1971), pp. 48–139.

Ottomans

An **Islamic Turkic** people that around the year 1300 began to expand out of its corner of northwestern **Anatolia** under the leadership of the tribal chieftain *Osman* (hence, the name Ottoman). By 1400 the Ottomans had conquered the entire Anatolian Peninsula and much of the Balkans, isolating **Constantinople,** which was now a small **Byzantine** outpost in a **Muslim** sea. On May 29, 1453, the Sultan Mehmed II captured **Constantinople,** which he rebuilt and converted into the capital of his rapidly expanding empire.

Almost as soon as the Ottomans appeared in southeast Europe, the West began to launch crusades in its defense, many of which were quite ineffective. With the Ottoman conquest of **Adrianople** in 1369, the heartland of Central Europe lay open to Turkish advance. For the next several centuries, the Ottoman menace would be the focus of Europe's latter-day crusades. Despite some successes, such as the naval

Rumeli Castle, **also known as** *Boghaz-Kesen* **(Channel Cutter), constructed in 1451–1452 on the northern end of the Bosporus by Sultan Mehmed II to choke off Constantinople's access to the Black Sea. Anatolia lies across the water.**

victory at Lepanto in 1571, Christian Europe looked on with largely impotent dismay as the Ottoman empire advanced up the Balkans. The high-water point of Ottoman advance into Europe came in 1683, when an allied **Latin** Christian force broke the Turks' three-month **siege** of Vienna. **Related Entry:** Hospitalers.

Suggested Reading

Primary Source

Norman Housley, ed., *Documents on the Later Crusades, 1274–1580* (1996).

Historical Studies

Colin Imber, *The Ottoman Empire: 1300–1481* (1990); Norman Housley, *The Later Crusades, 1274–1580: From Lyons to Alcazar* (1992); Halil Inalcik, *The Ottoman Empire: The Classical Age, 1300–1600* (1973).

Outremer

An Old French term meaning "across the sea," Outremer was used in the age of the crusades to refer to any and all of the trans-Mediterranean lands to which crusaders crossed, but especially the **crusader states.**

P

Palestine

See Syria-Palestine.

Papacy, Roman

The office of the popes of Rome, who claimed spiritual authority over all Christendom. As holders of this office, popes launched and legitimated crusades.

The term *pope* comes from the Latin *papa,* which means "father." The bishops of Rome adopted the title because they claimed that their bishopric had been founded by St. Peter, prince of the apostles and the first bishop of Rome, and as his successors, they had inherited his powers. The chief scriptural source for the belief that Christ had chosen Peter as the head of the Church on Earth is the Gospel of Matthew, 16:17–19, where Jesus tells the Apostle Simon, whom he has just renamed "Peter," that upon this Rock (*Petros* in Greek, the language of the New Testament) he will build his Church, and he will give Peter the keys to the kingdom of Heaven.

This view of the Roman papacy's special place within the Church was largely accepted by the Western peoples who converted to Christianity, but it was not until the eleventh century that reform popes, espe-

cially **Gregory VII,** began to articulate the extreme implications of their office, such as the notion that popes could depose other bishops and even emperors. Such claims were looked upon as radical innovations by many Western churchmen and princes, and the result was the bitter **Investiture Controversy.** Even after the Investiture Controversy was settled, popes and secular rulers, as well as popes and other Western church leaders, continued to argue over the limits and nature of their respective powers.

Eastern Christians, especially the **Byzantines,** were even less willing to accept the Roman papacy's vision of the Church. Byzantine Christians saw the Church as an earthly entity united under the combined leadership of a God-anointed emperor and orthodox, or right thinking, bishops, of whom the pope of Rome was only one. Consequently, to the Byzantine mind, the eleventh-century papacy's agenda of transforming Christian society under papal leadership contravened tradition and dogma. Around 1137 **Anna Comnena** sarcastically characterized Pope Gregory VII as a "barbarian . . . who claimed to be president of the whole world."

By the reign of Pope **Urban II** the differences between the Churches of Rome and **Constantinople** were apparent to many churchmen in East and West. It is likely that one of Urban's motives for setting in motion the **First Crusade** was to bring Eastern Christendom under papal leadership through military intervention in aid of sibling Christians who had wandered away from their papal father. Urban's dream was never realized. Instead of ushering in a new age of Christian harmony, the crusades helped to sever Christendom in ways the pope could never have imagined. **Related Entries:** Bull, Papal; Clermont, Council of; Councils and Synods; Legates, Papal; Individual Popes by Name.

Suggested Reading

Geoffrey Barraclough, *The Medieval Papacy* (1968); Norman Housley, *The Avignon Papacy and the Crusades, 1305–1378* (1986); Maureen Purcell, *Papal Crusading Policy, 1244–1291* (1975); Sylvia Schein, *Fideles Crucis: The Papacy, The West, and The Recovery of the Holy Land, 1274–1314* (1991).

Paschal II, Pope (r. 1099–1118)

The pope who presided over the so-called **Crusade of 1101** (the third wave of the **First Crusade**) and who authorized **Bohemond of Taranto**'s Crusade of 1107.

A monk like his predecessor, **Urban II,** Rainerus of Blera, a cardinal of the Roman Church and former **legate** to Spain, was possibly Urban's handpicked successor and certainly was an uncompromising supporter of the crusade ideal.

Early in his pontificate, he wrote the clergy of France commissioning them to preach a new crusade. Not only were they to enlist new soldiers, offering them the same **crusade privileges** already dispensed to the original crusaders, but they were also to pressure all who had previously taken the **crusade vow** but had not yet departed to do

so immediately, under threat of excommunication if they failed to fulfill their vows. He also wanted pressure put on deserters, who had gone east but fled home before reaching **Jerusalem,** to be likewise threatened with church sanctions if they did not return to the crusade. Following receipt of the news in late 1099 of the capture of Jerusalem, Paschal wrote the crusaders urging them to stay in the East until they completed their task.

At the same time, as a person who knew firsthand the Spanish **Reconquista,** Paschal, like Urban before him, dissuaded the **knights** of Iberia from undertaking the arduous journey to Jerusalem, and in 1101 he dispensed from their vows all those knights from Castile and León who had taken the Jerusalem **crusader's cross.** As he noted, the Spaniards would accomplish their penance in combat at home against the **Moors.** The Spanish Reconquista was, in other words, a valid crusade unto itself.

Paschal's efforts in the rest of Europe, especially in France, Germany, and northern Italy, resulted in huge numbers of new recruits for the defense of Jerusalem, but he provided this new mass movement with no overall strategy, leaving it to the great lay lords who enlisted to work out their individual plans. The result was a series of disconnected expeditions to the East in the period 1100–1102, all of which ended disastrously.

Not easily defeated, Paschal allowed himself in 1105 to be convinced by Bohemond of Taranto that Emperor **Alexius I** was an enemy of the **crusader states,** and in response he authorized the preaching of a new crusade. Although the crusade, which Bohemond launched in 1107, was officially aimed at relieving pressure on Jerusalem, it was actually aimed at the conquest of the **Byzantine empire.** Apparently the pope had allowed himself to be swept up in the anti-

Byzantine sentiment that Bohemond was fomenting in the West. Like the ill-fated third wave of the First Crusade, Bohemond's crusade failed miserably. **Related Entries:** Calixtus II, Pope; Gregory VII, Pope; Normans.

Pastoureaux

See Shepherds' Crusade.

Peace and Truce of God

Two movements that originated in local church **councils** in southern France and later elsewhere in Western Europe during the late tenth and early eleventh centuries as efforts to reduce the level of violence in society.

The Peace of God invested certain places, such as churches, and certain types of people, such as **pilgrims** and clerics, with a special peace, or immunity from attack. Anyone who violated this peace was subject to excommunication. The Truce of God prohibited warfare, except under exceptional circumstances, on certain days and during special times of the year. The earliest extant Truce of God decree, which dates from the period 1035–1041, proscribed fighting from Wednesday evening to Monday morning. Anyone who killed another during this time would be obligated to make a pilgrimage to **Jerusalem.**

In November 1095 a French pope, **Urban II,** universalized the Peace of God movement for the entire **Latin** Church at the **Council of Clermont,** and shortly thereafter he delivered the sermon that launched the **First Crusade.** Accounts of that council and of his crusade sermon clearly connect his call for an armed expedition to the East with his effort at establishing peace in Christian Europe. In essence, the pope called for the West's warriors to turn away from fratricidal warfare and to sanctify their weapons by turning them against **infidels** who were disturbing the peace of Christendom. **Related Entries:** Gregory VII, Pope; Holy War/Just War.

Suggested Reading

Thomas Head and Richard Landes, eds., *The Peace of God: Social Violence and Religious Response in France around the Year 1000* (1992).

Pelagius

Cardinal bishop of Albano (1213–1230) and **papal legate** to the **Fifth Crusade.**

Named legate to the Fifth Crusade by Pope **Honorius III,** Pelagius arrived in Egypt in September 1218, where he became a controversial figure. His commission was to maintain peace and unity among the diverse Christian forces then besieging **Damietta.** Because the crusade was composed of a variety of ethnic groups and lacked a clear, unified command, this was a tall order. Pelagius tried his best, and there is clear evidence that his sermons and exhortations in certain times of crisis raised crusader morale to the point that they bent themselves to a common effort, but that was not the whole story. Pelagius's arrogant personality, his attempt to keep the crusaders always mindful of the crusade's religious principles, and his determination to be faithful to papal policies, at times resulted in his coming into conflict with some of the army's military commanders. The first recorded instance of such tension occurred in September 1219, a full year after his arrival, when Pelagius successfully argued against a truce with **al-Kamil,** despite the sultan's offer of **Jerusalem** for peace.

The capture of Damietta provided another setting for conflict, as Pelagius resisted King **John of Brienne**'s claim to the city. In his attempt to preserve the rights of the absent Emperor **Frederick II** over the city, Pelagius managed to alienate not just King John but most of the army, which saw itself being deprived of its rightful portion of the city's spoils. Pelagius, who up to that point had been popular, now became widely unpopular. In the face of threats against his life by disgruntled crusaders, Pelagius proposed a compromise that was accepted, and the crisis passed.

Early in 1220 King John departed Egypt, along with his army, ostensibly to counter a threat against **Acre** but possibly also due to frustration and anger over the legate's challenges to his authority. With John's departure, Pelagius's influence over the army rose, even though the pope never envisioned his legate as a military leader. Pelagius favored action, even though the crusade army was greatly weakened by battlefield casualties, **disease,** and defections. To raise morale and incite action from an army that was mired at Damietta, Pelagius ordered read aloud to the army a supposed book of prophecies ascribed to Saint Peter that seemed to promise victory in Egypt and **Syria** in the near future.

Pelagius continued to press for action, even though Pope Honorius cautioned him by letter to avoid major confrontations with the enemy until Emperor Frederick arrived and even to explore the possibility of a temporary truce with al-Kamil. Pelagius apparently was not in a mood to wait any longer. In his desire for the army to take the field before it totally disintegrated, Pelagius even convinced King John to return to Egypt for one last push. The campaign season was late when the army prepared to move out in July 1221. Less than a month remained before the Nile would flood, and for this reason, the army that set out probably was only probing and not prepared to engage in an all-out

offensive. Even limited actions, however, can lead to total disaster.

Despite news that al-Kamil's brothers were coming to his aid, the army moved forward, but by July 24 King John was advocating an immediate withdrawal back to Damietta. Pelagius opposed retreat, and the mass of the army backed him. Rejecting the sound tactical advice of King John and opting for Pelagius's overly optimistic reading of the situation, the army marched into an untenable position, whereby they were surrounded and cut off from Damietta. With the crusade army facing annihilation, Pelagius turned now to King John and requested that he negotiate with the enemy. The crusaders were fortunate that al-Kamil favored offering generous terms of surrender.

The crusade was now over. Damietta was exchanged for the captive army, which went home in defeat. Back in the West, Pelagius came under criticism for his mishandling of his leadership role, but to what extent, if any, Pelagius was responsible for this disaster remains an open question. **Related Entry:** Apocalypse and the Crusades.

Suggested Reading

Joseph Donovan, *Pelagius and the Fifth Crusade* (1950).

People's Crusade

See First Crusade.

Peter the Hermit

A popular **preacher** who served as one of the principle leaders of the first wave of the **First Crusade,** the so-called **People's Crusade** of 1096.

About all we can say with a fair degree of certainty about Peter prior to 1096 is that he came from the area around Amiens in northern France, lived as a hermit, or religious recluse, and engaged in evangelical preaching to urban crowds in his neighborhood.

One tradition, which was reported in various versions by **Anna Comnena** and several other twelfth-century **historians,** ascribed to Peter credit for initiating the call for the liberation of **Jerusalem.** According to Albert of Aachen, who completed his history of the First Crusade sometime between 1120 and midcentury, Peter had traveled on **pilgrimage** to Jerusalem, where Jesus appeared to him in a **vision** in the **Church of the Holy Sepulcher.** He commanded Peter to request a letter from the **Greek patriarch of Jerusalem** authorizing him to report back home the oppression suffered by **Eastern Christians** in the Holy Land and to rouse **Latin** Christians to rescue them and the holy places. Peter secured the letter and sailed to Italy, where he visited Pope **Urban II** and delivered his message. The pope promised to obey the command and, with this in mind, crossed the Alps, where he delivered his call for a crusade at **Clermont.** Most historians today reject this and similar stories as twelfth-century fabrications and conclude that Peter played no role whatsoever prior to November 1095 in setting in motion the First Crusade. A few scholars are less certain. The fact is, unless new and compelling evidence comes to light, we shall never know whether or not Peter helped originate the crusade.

What is certain is that Peter became an active preacher and organizer of the crusade in northern France and western Germany following the **council** of Clermont. In his preaching, Peter, as well as a number of other popular preachers, went well beyond the vision that Urban II had articulated at Clermont by introducing two new elements into the ideology of the First Crusade: an anti-Judaic overtone and an appeal to all classes of people, not just able-bodied warriors. Several sources state that he carried with him a letter that he claimed was sent to him from Heaven ordering all Christians to march toward the liberation of Jerusalem.

Whatever his means, Peter aroused large numbers of people to join his ranks, including **Walter Sansavoir,** who set off in April 1096 with a large French detachment while Peter momentarily tarried in Cologne, Germany enlisting more recruits. On August 1, 1096, Peter and his contingent arrived at **Constantinople,** having marched through Hungary and the Balkans, where its lack of discipline and adequate supplies resulted in several bloody clashes with the native Christians.

After crossing the Bosporus with his and Walter Sansavoir's forces, Peter's lack of military skills resulted in his losing control of his forces. Early in October he returned to Constantinople to enlist **Byzantine** help. In his absence, his and Walter's crusaders were almost wiped out in an ambush on October 21, thus ending the People's Crusade.

Thereafter Peter played a more modest role after linking up with elements of the crusade's second wave, the crusading princes. During the crusader siege of **Antioch,** Peter deserted the army and was brought back in disgrace by **Tancred.** He redeemed himself by delivering a message of defiance from the princes to the **Turkish** leader **Kerbogha** when the crusaders found themselves besieged within Antioch in June 1098. Soon after the fall of Jerusalem, Peter returned to France, where he established several monasteries. **Related Entries:** Apocalypse and the Crusades; Jews and the Crusades; Tafurs.

Philip II

See Capetians; Third Crusade.

Philip III

See Capetians.

Philip IV

King of France (r. 1285–1314) and known as "the Fair" (as in handsome), Philip is one of the most controversial crusader kings of France. His most singular act in relation to the crusades was to order the arrest and interrogation of a number of French **Templars** in 1307, which led to the order's suppression in 1312.

Above all else, King Philip believed that the kingdom of France was a sacred political entity that the God-anointed king and his ministers must defend from all enemies, foreign and domestic, **infidel** and Christian. Although he was conventionally pious, Philip believed that his first duty to God lay in his uncompromising efforts to protect and further the well being of the kingdom and the French Church, even if he had to fight the **papacy** or other institutions of the Roman Church.

Philip's relationship to the crusades is easily divided into three periods of his reign: 1285–1301, 1301–1305, and 1305–1314. Prior to 1301 the crusade did not figure significantly in Philip's public pronouncements. In December 1301 a major battle of wills and worldviews broke out between King Philip and Pope Boniface VIII, each of whom had an exalted vision of his own authority and of the entity over which he ruled. This struggle with the pope pushed Philip and his court to use the crusade as a propaganda weapon against a pope who was widely seen as misusing the crusade for selfish family ends. In fact, strained relations between Philip and Boniface had begun in 1296, but in 1297 the pope was forced by circumstances to give way on the immediate issue, taxation of clergy, over which they quarreled. The canonization as a saint of Philip's grandfather, **Louis IX,** in 1297 was partially a gesture of goodwill by the pope. By 1302, however, the pope and the king of France were involved in a no-holds-barred war of charges and countercharges regarding their respective areas of authority. In charges that continued well past Boniface's death, the French royal court characterized this pope as a Satan who was not concerned with the **Holy Land** and who persecuted the French more than he did **Muslims.** In 1305 a Frenchman assumed the papal throne as Clement V, and from that point on Philip seems to have become an active champion of the crusade.

Inasmuch as the last **crusader states** in **Syria-Palestine** had been lost in 1291, Pope Clement V made recovery of the Holy Land a major theme of his pontificate, and he wanted the king of France to take the lead in that enterprise. Between December 29, 1305, when the pope and Philip initially met, and June 5, 1313, when he finally assumed the **crusader's cross,** Philip raised money for his projected crusade through a tax on French clerics and supported the idea of crusade in numerous pronouncements. Less than a year and a half after he formally became a crusader, Philip died with his crusade unrealized.

Despite nine years of activity in support of a crusade, evidence strongly suggests that Philip viewed the crusade as an extension of the authority, power, and prestige of the French royal family and the French state. One indication is that his strategy for the recovery of the Holy Land was linked to his brother Charles of Valois's plan to conquer the **Byzantine empire.** Another indication is his role in the suppression of the Knights of the Temple, the most visible presence in Europe of **Latin** Christendom's commitment to the crusades and **Outremer.**

On October 13, 1307, the Templars in France were unexpectedly arrested on orders from the king and charged with **heresy,** idol worship, blasphemy, and gross sexual misconduct. In spite of Clement V's early attempts to halt the process, between 1307 and 1311 numerous interrogations in France and elsewhere, most under torture or the threat of torture, produced testimony that supported these allegations, although many Templars refused to admit guilt or the truth of any of the charges and many others later retracted their confessions. Faced with this evidence, such as it was, Clement V suppressed the order on March 22, 1312, at the Council of Vienne in France.

Modern historians still debate the question of the guilt or innocence of the Templars. An equally vexing question is: What motivated King Philip? Greed is one possibility and a motive that many fourteenth-century persons accepted: Philip wanted Templar possessions and revenues. Another possible motive was that the Templars resisted Philip's proposal of 1307 to amalgamate all **military orders** into a single entity under his command. A less obvious but equally likely motive is that Philip, who late in life became increasingly preoccupied with religion, actually believed the rumors that circulated about Templar heresy and sacrilegious activities and acted accordingly to save his realm from corruption. **Related Entries:** Capetians; Criticism of the Crusades; Political Crusades.

Suggested Reading

Malcolm Barber, *The Trial of the Templars* (1978); Sylvia Schein, *Fideles Crucis: The Papacy, the West, and the Recovery of the Holy Land, 1274–1314* (1998); Joseph Strayer, *The Reign of Philip the Fair* (1980).

Philip of Swabia

See Hohenstaufens.

Piacenza, Council of

See Clermont, Council of.

Pilgrimage

A journey to a holy place in search of communion with the Sacred.

Pilgrimage is a universal religious practice. Within the monotheistic traditions of Judaism, Christianity, and **Islam** pilgrimages serve several functions. First, a pilgrimage brings the worshiper closer to God by transporting the devotee to a place that is sacred to his or her religious tradition, be that place Judaism's Western Wall in **Jerusalem,** the Christian shrine of **Santiago de Compostela** in Spain, or Islam's holy *Ka'ba* in Mecca. Second, not only does a pilgrimage establish a closer personal tie between the pilgrim and God, but it also affirms and strengthens that person's place within a community of faith because most pilgrimages are undertaken in the company of other believers. Third, most pilgrimages are long, fatiguing, costly, and even dangerous; illness is common, and deaths are not unusual. For these reasons pilgrimages serve a penitential purpose, the reasoning being that such hardships and suffering are expiation for sins.

Because Pope **Urban II** linked his **holy war** to liberate Jerusalem with the ancient practice of penitential pilgrimage, from the start crusaders were considered to be pilgrims. Indeed, for almost the entire first century of crusading, crusaders were normally called "pilgrims." Even after the term *crucesignati* (those signed with the cross) began to be used somewhat frequently in the late twelfth century, the term *pilgrims* continued to be applied to crusaders who went to **Syria-Palestine,** and the **privileges** accorded them were derived from church laws governing pilgrims.

From earliest days Christians have held the **Holy Land,** and especially Jerusalem, in special reverence because of their desire to see the places made sacred by Jesus of Nazareth. Chief among the places in the

Medieval pilgrims carved thousands of crosses and names into the stone of the Church of the Holy Sepulcher.

Holy Land at which Christians worshiped (and continue to do so) is Jerusalem's **Church of the Holy Sepulcher.** Returned pilgrims from Jerusalem, who were known *palmers* because they carried blessed palm branches as a token of having completed the sacred journey, enjoyed special prestige in Europe.

Western Europe experienced a dramatic economic upswing and significant population growth in the eleventh century, and one manifestation of this boom was the growing number of large-scale pilgrimages to Jerusalem and holy sites in **Palestine,** such as the **Great German Pilgrimage of 1064–1065.** Indeed, many popular stories arose in the eleventh century linking Europe's legendary heroes, such as Charlemagne and King Arthur, with the Jerusalem pilgrimage. Even though the historical Charlemagne never traveled to the Holy Land and King Arthur was a mythic figure, the fact that these revered warrior heroes from the past were tied to the pilgrimage to Jerusalem suggests that Europe was ready by century's end for the first armed pilgrimage to the East, better known as the **First Crusade. Related Entries:** Cross, Crusader's; Indulgence, Crusade; Montjoie; Peter the Hermit; Relics.

Suggested Reading

Primary Sources

John Wilkinson et al., ed. and trans., *Jerusalem Pilgrimage, 1099–1185* (1988) and *Jerusalem Pilgrims before the Crusades* (1977).

Historical Studies

Janin Hunt, *Four Paths to Jerusalem: Jewish, Christian, Muslim, and Secular Pilgrimages,*

1000 BCE to 2001 CE (2002); Stewart Perowne, *The Holy Places of Christendom* (1976); Diana West, *Pilgrims and Pilgrimage in the Medieval West* (1999).

Pillage and Plunder

A normal and necessary means of provisioning and rewarding soldiers of all armies, Christian and **Muslim,** in the Age of the Crusades.

Modern rules of war severely limit and often prohibit plundering, especially of civilian goods. In the era of the crusades, however, when the distinction between **noncombatant** and combatant was not so neatly drawn and when armies often depended on living off the land through which they passed, plundering was a reality that few questioned. When questions were raised, they normally revolved around two issues: The wrong people were plundered (for example, the **Latin** Christians of Zara, whose city was sacked in 1202/1203 by the army of the **Fourth Crusade**), or the wrong places were pillaged (for example, the Christian churches of **Constantinople,** which were robbed in April 1204 by the same army of the Fourth Crusade).

Beyond necessity, pillaging was also an essential way of rewarding soldiers. More than a bonus, the booty that a soldier grabbed constituted the bulk of his pay. Indeed, the opportunity for plunder was one of the basic reasons people went to war (self-identity as a soldier, glory, adventure, loyalty, **mercenary** pay, and a sense of purpose were the other main reasons), and a good

The *Horses of the Hippodrome,* late antique gilded-bronze sculptures from the hippodrome, or chariot-racing stadium, of Constantinople, pillaged by the Venetians in 1204–1205 in the wake of the Fourth Crusade. For centuries these tokens of Venetian triumph graced the facade of the basilica of San Marco. Urban pollution forced their removal to a museum in the church.

leader provided his troops with frequent and rich sources of plunder. **Roger of Salerno**'s victory at Danith in September 1115 resulted in his troops' capturing large numbers of Muslim **women** whom they **enslaved,** a significant number of enemy warriors whom they held for ransom (after killing a large number of less valuable **prisoners**), and goods that one **chronicler** computed to be worth 300,000 **Byzantine** gold coins. Even allowing for exaggeration, it is safe to say that the booty was enormous. It took the army two or three days to divide the spoils, and Roger earned the reputation of being a great military leader by virtue of the way that he had enriched his soldiers.

Plundering was so ingrained in the spirit of medieval warfare that military leaders in Europe had to establish protocols for its safe and equitable operation. First, they had to ensure that in the midst of combat soldiers did not turn their hands to pillaging prematurely, thereby placing themselves and their comrades in danger and compromising the army's chances for victory. Often the threat of summary execution and dishonor served as a deterrent. Following victory, the leader would also normally try to organize an orderly collection of pillaged goods and their distribution by rank and merit, with the largest shares going to the lords and **knights,** especially those who had distinguished themselves in battle.

Although there were instances of organized collection and distribution of spoils during the **First Crusade,** the fact that its armies were volatile and fluid assemblies of many competing elements made systematic divisions of plundered goods a near impossibility. As a result, the custom of free seizure became the norm; every person kept what he or she managed to grab. At the same time, there were attempts to distribute captured food on an equitable basis, and even, on occasion, to assess a contribution of a

tenth of all spoils for distribution among the clergy and the poor. Later crusades saw more successful attempts at following the European practice of booty distribution, but free seizure continued as a custom within the **crusader states** of **Syria-Palestine** whenever a town or city was captured by storm.

Pillage and plunder also served as a release from the horrors and terrors of combat. Much of the wanton murder, rape, and mindless destruction that accompanied the sack of a town or city might well be attributed to the soldiers' seeking an outlet for their rage and fear and a way of affirming their escape from death. It also was a means of showing their utter contempt for a defeated enemy, very much like the mutilation of enemy corpses (after they were robbed).

It was common practice by armies of all sides to allow soldiers three days of uninhibited pillaging in any captured city or town that had put up resistance, which served as an incentive for inhabitants to surrender to an advancing enemy. But even surrender without any resistance brought with it no guarantee that soldiers would stay their hand from plundering a now-defenseless and inviting enemy stronghold.

A strong leader could reduce the level of violence associated with plundering if the circumstances were favorable and he was so inclined. When **Saladin** captured **Jerusalem** on October 2, 1187, after it had put up a short but spirited resistance, he took possession of the city under negotiated terms in which he guaranteed the safe conduct out of the city of all who could pay a stipulated ransom. Because Jerusalem was (and is) a city holy to **Islam** and also because Saladin wanted to avoid disrupting the economic and social infrastructures of his newly conquered regions, he stationed troops on every street to keep disorder to a minimum. Nevertheless the churches and other religious structures of the Latin Christians were pillaged, and apparently little or no effort was made to prevent their being looted. Custom, necessity, the acknowledged rules of war, and almost a century of enmity combined to make such plundering a foregone conclusion. What was extraordinary was the fact that Saladin chose to soften the blow and was able to.

One of the most brutal and ironic pillagings of a city during the Crusade Era was the sack of Constantinople by the army of the Fourth Crusade, April 13–15, 1204. Innumerable masterpieces of ancient Greek and Roman art were destroyed, and churches were stripped of their **relics** and sacramental vessels. Unknown numbers of citizens of the city met death at the hands of the crusaders, and even nuns were raped in the streets. According to the estimate of Geoffrey of Villehardouin, an informed and perceptive participant in the crusade, the total take of booty at Constantinople equaled the value of 400,000 pounds of silver. An early thirteenth-century European urban family could live well for a year on the equivalent of two pounds of silver.

Despite attempts to prohibit private hoarding and thievery (several soldiers who tried unsuccessfully to hide some spoils were publicly hanged), most of the booty seized at Constantinople was secretly withheld by individual crusaders. Villehardouin estimated that over sixty percent of the total plunder passed illegitimately into private hands, and he blamed the **Latin empire of Constantinople**'s subsequent misfortunes on the sins of these thieves.

Some of the fruits of the crusaders' plundering can be viewed today in Venice, where the ancient **Greek** horses of Constantinople's Hippodrome now grace the city of canals and many treasures of Byzantine ecclesiastical art fill the church of San Marco. Whatever else they were, the Venetians were connoisseurs when it came to choosing their portion of the city's spoils. **Related Entries:** Balian II of Ibelin; Cannibalism; Massacres; Siege Warfare.

Political Crusades

Crusades inaugurated by the thirteenth-century **Roman papacy** against political enemies in Europe, especially Italy. These crusades largely grew out of the papacy's desire to maintain the integrity of the Papal States, lands held directly by the papacy in central Italy and threatened by enemies in northern Italy and the kingdom of Sicily, which comprised southern Italy and the island of Sicily.

In late 1199, when the **Fourth Crusade** was still in the planning stages, Pope **Innocent III** threatened to divert the crusade to Sicily to counter the actions of a political enemy, Markward of Anweiler, whom the pope characterized as "another **Saladin**," whose actions in the kingdom of Sicily hindered the liberation of **Jerusalem.** Presumably Markward's espousal of the cause of Innocent's **Hohenstaufen** opponent, Philip of Swabia, constituted anti-crusade activity in the pope's eyes. The threatened crusade against Markward was never formally called, but the pope allowed sworn crusaders from Champagne to campaign against Hohenstaufen supporters in the kingdom of Sicily. The quasi-crusade ended with Markward's death in 1202. With this modest half-action, the Roman papacy began its long involvement in the business of political crusades.

The full-fledged political crusade became a reality under Pope **Gregory IX,** who launched several **holy wars** against Emperor **Frederick II.** Gregory began his campaigns against Frederick cautiously, because he was initially reluctant to launch a crusade against a Christian, even an excommunicated one. From 1228 to 1230 papal

The mythic story of how the first Christian Roman emperor, Constantine, surrendered an imperial crown and the city of Rome to Pope Sylvester I. *The Donation of Constantine Fresco Cycle*, the Chapel of San Silvestro, Church of Quattro Coronati, Rome. Dedicated in 1246, the chapel's frescoes display the Roman papacy's view of the proper relationship between pope and emperor in the midst of its struggles with Frederick II.

armies under the command of **John of Brienne** waged war against the southern Italian possessions of the emperor in defense of the lands and rights of the Roman Church. Although John's soldiers were granted an indulgence for their service, the indulgence was not a full **crusade indulgence** and they were not accorded other **crusade privileges.** They also did not wear the **crusader's cross.** Rather, their badge was the papal insignia, the keys of Saint Peter. Peace was made between Frederick and Gregory in 1230, but war broke out again in 1239 over Frederick's attempts to dominate Italy, and in 1240 Gregory brought the full weight of a crusade to bear on his opponent. Because the crusade went so badly for Gregory's army, in Febru-

ary 1241 he permitted Hungarian crusaders who had **vowed** to go to the East to fulfill their obligation by fighting the emperor in Italy. The crusade ended temporarily with Gregory's death in August 1241, but it was renewed by Pope Innocent IV in 1245 at the Council of Lyons. Even Frederick's death in 1250 did not end papal crusades against the Hohenstaufen family, as the papacy launched a series of holy wars against Frederick's descendants, which ended only when the last Hohenstaufen garrison surrendered in 1269.

With such a tradition, it was fairly easy for a French pope, Martin IV, to declare a holy crusade against King Peter III of Aragon in defense of a papal vassal, **Charles of Anjou,** in 1283. The sticking point was the island of Sicily, whose subjects had thrown Charles out as king and offered the crown to King Peter. King **Philip III** of France took up the crusader's cross in defense of his uncle and the papacy and invaded Aragon. The invasion was a disaster, and King Philip died from **disease** in 1285 while withdrawing his army. With his death, the last of the great political crusades was over.

The political crusades were costly for everyone, including the papacy. In addition to losing a fair amount of prestige and moral authority because of its use of a spiritual weapon for secular ends, the papacy saw its strategy for defending the fragile security of the Papal States backfire. With no strong emperor to act as defender of papal interests in Central Italy, the Papal States fell into anarchy—an anarchy that necessitated the papacy's residence outside of Italy from 1305 to 1376.

Prior to this period of self-imposed exile, Pope Boniface VIII (r. 1294–1303) unleashed another, quite minor but symbolically significant political crusade, which illustrates how far the crusade ideal had fallen in a century. In 1297 he declared a holy war against personal enemies, the powerful Colonna family of Rome. Two of its members, both cardinals of the Church, had opposed his election to the papacy and continued to declare him an illegitimate pope. Boniface succeeded in capturing their castles and driving them into exile in France, where they allied with King **Philip IV** against the pope and his policies. **Related Entries:** Capetians; Criticism of Crusades; Councils and Synods; Sixth Crusade.

Suggested Reading

Norman Housley, *The Italian Crusades: The Papal-Angevin Alliance and the Crusades against Christian Lay Powers, 1254–1343* (1982).

Popes

See Papacy, Roman. *See also* popes by name.

Poulain

A term derived from the medieval Latin *polana* (pointed shoe) that became an Old French slang expression meaning "a colt"— a stylish kid with an attitude. It was later applied to any native-born **Frank** of **Syria-Palestine.**

Poulains were often of mixed heritage, having a parent or at least one grandparent who was an **Eastern Christian** or even a converted **Muslim.** Although their education, religion, and general culture largely reflected that of Western Europe, more often than not that of France, they were not wholly European in their tastes, attitudes, and speech. Their dress, diet, and many day-to-day activities were often indistinguishable from that of their non-**Latin** neighbors, servants, and relatives, and the vast majority fluently spoke at least two languages, a Western European tongue and one from the **Levant.** In addition to their suspicious practice of frequent bathing, which drew criticism from less culturally acclimated observers, many *Poulains* were quite willing to tolerate the religious practices of their non-Latin and even non-Christian neighbors.

As early as 1127, **Fulcher of Chartres** remarked on this new multicultural culture in the East:

Consider . . . how in our time God has transferred the West to the East. For we who were Occidentals have now been made Orientals. . . . We have already forgotten our birthplaces. . . . One who was a citizen of Rheims or Chartres now has been made a citizen of **Tyre** or **Antioch** . . . . Some have taken wives not merely from among their own people but from among Syrians, **Armenians,** or even **Saracens** who have received the grace of baptism. . . . Here also are grandchildren and great-grandchildren. . . . [who] use the speech and ways of discourse of different languages.

As attractive as this society of the **crusader states** might seem to us, many newly arrived crusaders from the West looked upon *Poulains* with great distrust and contempt and used the term in a derogatory manner. John of Joinville, **Louis IX**'s friend and biographer, tells how when, as a young man, he dared to advise the king openly in 1250 to remain on crusade in the **Holy Land,** rather than returning to France, as most of the king's great lords wished to do, he was called behind his back a *Poulain,* as though this upstart kid put the concerns of the **Latin East** ahead of those of France.

Conversely, the twelfth-century Syrian-Muslim writer Usamah ibn Munqidh noted that: "Everyone who is a fresh emigrant from the Frankish lands is ruder in character than those who have become acclimatized and have held long association with the Muslims." **Related Entries:** Settlement and Colonization; William of Tyre.

Preaching

Preaching was the main means of publicizing and raising enthusiasm for crusades and **jihads.**

The **First Crusade** was launched with a sermon—Pope **Urban II**'s public address at **Clermont**—and was publicized throughout Europe by preachers, both clerics who were part of the Church's hierarchy and popular evangelists, such as **Peter the Hermit,** who had no official status but were able to reach and move large numbers of people. This remained the paradigm for the remainder of the Age of the Crusades, although as time went on the **Roman papacy** increasingly established procedures to regularize and control preaching.

In anticipation of the **Second Crusade,** the papacy turned to **Bernard of Clairvaux** as its chief public preacher, and his success at **recruitment** established the **Order of Cîteaux** as a major source of crusade preachers for the remainder of the century and a bit beyond. During the early decades of the thirteenth century the **mendicant friars,** primarily Franciscans and **Dominicans,** replaced the **Cistercians** as the Church's main mouthpieces for the crusades.

In 1213 Pope **Innocent III** divided a good portion of Europe into preaching zones, each with its assigned procurators, or agents-in-charge, to spread the word effectively for the upcoming **Fifth Crusade.** This system remained in effect for the remainder of the century and well beyond, and it was nicely suited to the Franciscan and Dominicans Orders, each of which was divided into regional provinces. Their highly structured but flexible organizations, as well as their large numbers of trained preachers, enabled the mendicant friars to serve as the Church's single most effective body of crusade propagandists, recruiters, and collectors of funds to **finance** these **holy wars.**

The friars even developed preaching aids, such as model sermons and collections of *exempla,* or edifying stories, that a preacher could interject into a sermon to make a point. The appearance of such preaching aids actually dated back to slightly before the rise of the mendicant orders—to the late twelfth century when Western Europe witnessed a dramatic new emphasis on the clergy's pastoral mission. In the hands of the friars, however, these preaching aids became an art form in which their creators labored to craft sermons suited to specific audiences and circumstances. Above all else, the friar-preachers were expected to be master psychologists and to have a sure control over all relevant information and theological issues.

The spoken word was also important in summoning **Muslim** opposition to the crusades, especially the words spoken by **Islam**'s imams, or religious teachers, at Friday community prayer services. If an imam appeared to be failing in his duties to summon the faithful to holy struggle against the **infidels,** other Muslims seem to have been willing to call him to account. Ibn al-Qalanisi, the earliest Arab **historian** to write about the crusades, tells the story of how in 1110 a Hashimite sharif (a member of the tribe of Muhammad) from **Aleppo** appeared at the **Seljuk** sultan's mosque in Baghdad on Friday, accompanied by a retinue of Sufi mystics, religious lawyers, and merchants. Shouting down the preacher, they made him descend from the pulpit while they beseeched the worshippers to aid **Syria,** which was then beset by the **Franks.** To underscore their anguish and the gravity of the situation, they smashed the pulpit to pieces. They repeated the performance the following week at the caliph's mosque, and finally caught the attention of the sultan, who pardoned them for their actions and ordered his commanders to prepare for a holy war against the Frankish infidels.

Mindful of the power of such public calls to action, **Nur ad-Din, Saladin,** and all successful holy warriors in the fight against crusaders and the **crusader states** carefully nurtured and used to effect the sermons of imams, Sufi ascetics, and every other religious authority whom they could enlist. **Related Entries:** Bull, Papal; Francis of Assisi; Fulk of Neuilly; James of Vitry; Missionaries; Oliver of Paderborn.

Suggested Reading

Penny J. Cole, *The Preaching of the Crusades to the Holy Land, 1095–1270* (1991); Christoph T. Maier, *Crusade Propaganda and Ideology: Model Sermons for the Preaching of the Cross* (2000) and *Preaching the Cru-* *sades: Mendicant Friars and the Cross in the Thirteenth Century* (1994).

Prester John

John the Priest, a mythic Christian priest-king who ruled a vast empire somewhere beyond the **Muslim** domains and whom the **Latin** West anticipated as an ally in a final, victorious crusade. Although John and his empire were myths, the legend contained threads of truth, inasmuch as there were faraway Christian cultures in Ethiopia and Nubia, along the west coast of India, and in Central and East Asia.

The first known reference to Prester John comes from the **historian** Otto of Freising, who records that in November 1145 Bishop Hugh of Jabla in Lebanon visited Pope **Eugenius III,** in the wake of the capture of **Edessa.** According to Bishop Otto, Hugh informed the pope that Prester John, a Nestorian Christian king and priest and descendant of the Three Magi who lived in the Far East, wished to come to the aid of the beleaguered **Holy Land** but was held back by the Tigris River. After years of waiting for the river to freeze over and after having lost a good portion of his army, he was forced to return home. This story suggests that the legend of Prester John was already circulating in Europe before Bishop Hugh tried to convince the pope that if the **Latin East** were to receive any help it would have to come from the West. Shortly thereafter, the pope launched the **Second Crusade.**

Around 1165 a spurious letter from Prester John began to circulate in Europe, supposedly addressed to Emperor **Manuel I Comnenus.** In the letter, which probably was written by a Latin Christian, Prester John makes extravagant claims regarding his empire that extended over "the three Indies" and was filled with every sort of marvel and riches.

During the **Fifth Crusade** a number of prophetic books circulated within the crusader camp, which promised the imminent collapse of **Islam** due to the simultaneous assault on it by crusaders from the West and allies from the East. **Oliver of Paderborn** informs us that in 1221 the crusaders were heartened to hear rumors of "King David, who they say is the son of Prester John," who had recently defeated the king of the Persians. In fact, King David was none other than the **Mongol** leader Chinggis Khan, whose armies were devastating Central Asia, Iran, and Afghanistan in 1219–1223 and driving the **Khorezmians** west. The West soon learned who the Mongols were.

The Mongols were largely shamanists, although a few were Nestorian Christians, and Chinggis Khan was certainly not Prester John, but once again the West was excited by the idea that somewhere out there was a potential ally who would help Latin Christendom crush Islam. As Latin **missionaries** and diplomats traveled east to see if they could convert the Mongols into Christian allies, they also had one eye open for Prester John. Indeed, several late medieval writers and travelers, such as Marco Polo, claimed to have unimpeachable information as to his whereabouts and status. Although Polo reported around 1300 that Prester John had been killed in battle in 1200 by Chinggis Khan, the search went on well beyond the classic Age of the Crusades. As late as the sixteenth century Portuguese ambassadors to Ethiopia sought out this legendary king. Like the ideology of crusade itself, the myth of Prester John lived on and proved to be a driving force in Western adventurism well into early modern times. **Related Entries:** Apocalypse and the Crusades; Christians, Eastern.

Suggested Reading

Charles F. Beckingham and Bernard Hamilton, eds., *Prester John, the Mongols, and the Ten Lost Tribes* (1996).

Prisoners

Christian and **Muslim** warriors usually killed without compunction all prisoners whom they deemed worthless. In April 1250, for example, victorious Egyptian forces systematically killed the sick and wounded crusaders of King **Louis IX**'s defeated army.

Some prisoners were spared on occasion because of bargains struck or out of a sense of mercy and even grudging respect. At times the defenders of a **castle** or town negotiated their release and safe passage in return for capitulation, and generous victors sometimes allowed a defeated enemy to retire unharmed because of valor shown in battle. Nevertheless, as a general rule prisoners were kept alive only when they seemed capable of being ransomed or when they could be profitably enslaved. A victorious warrior had to consider it worth the time, effort, and even danger for him to spare the life of a captive enemy. Because ransom was a major consideration, captives of high rank could expect much better and more merciful treatment than those of low rank. Also because of the profit factor, raids aimed specifically at capturing redeemable hostages and **slaves** were a fact of life along the frontiers of **Syria-Palestine** and Spain.

At times, condemned prisoners were tortured to death for the sheer fun of it, and there is at least one recorded instance during the **First Crusade** when captive infants were killed and eaten. The rape of female captives was taken for granted, whether they were to be enslaved or killed after the troops had tired of them. Undoubtedly **Fulcher of Chartres** had this in mind when he wrote regarding certain **Turkish women** who were discovered in tents of the enemy at **Antioch:** "The **Franks** did them no evil but drove lances into their bellies."

Captives who were enslaved were sometimes forced (or persuaded) to convert to the faith of their captors, and conversion

An illustration from Gratian's *Decretum*, the Latin Church's standard text-book of church law, completed around 1140. The issue under consideration: Word comes back that a husband has died in captivity, and his wife remarries. Then he returns home (on the left, dressed as a pilgrim). Gratian asks: What is the wife's status, and what is she to do? Surely this was more than an academic question for some women during the crusades. From a late thirteenth- or fourteenth-century southern French manuscript of Gratian's *Concordance of Discordant Canons,* or *Decretum.* The Walters Art Museum, Baltimore.

could bring freedom, although this was not an invariable rule. Because apostasy, or renunciation of the true faith, was considered to be so heinous and soul-damning, Muslims, Christians, and **Jews** alike considered the ransom of captive coreligionists a meritorious act of charity. **Related Entries:** Cannibalism; Massacres; Pillage and Plunder.

Suggested Reading

James Brodman, *Ransoming Captives in Crusader Spain: The Order of Merced on the Christian-Islamic Frontier* (1986); Yvonne Friedman, *Encounter between Enemies: Captivity and Ransom in the Latin Kingdom of Jerusalem* (2002).

Privileges, Crusader

The **crusade vow** placed a man or woman into a special, quasi-ecclesiastical class, and brought with that status specific spiritual rewards and material benefits.

The privileges accorded crusaders took shape over the course of the first century and a half of crusading as various **popes** enumerated and added to them; by the mid–thirteenth century they were fairly well defined.

The greatest and most avidly sought-after reward for crusade service—the **indulgence**—traced its origins to the **First Crusade** and the promises of Pope **Urban II,** but its definition underwent significant modifications as the crusades evolved. Additional spiritual privileges included: (1) release from excommunication (being excluded from the Church's grace and community), which was added to the list by Pope **Gregory IX** in the thirteenth century; (2) license to deal with excommunicates while on crusade without incurring any penalty (a privilege that came out of the **Fourth Crusade**);

(3) the right to have a personal confessor who could grant pardon for sins that normally could be absolved only by the pope; and (4) the right to substitute the crusade vow for another vow that had been taken but not yet fulfilled. Additionally, the crusader shared in the benefit of prayers offered by the Church for the well-being of the **Holy Land** and all who struggled in its defense.

Many of the temporal, or material, benefits that crusaders enjoyed were extensions of the safeguards that the Church had created to protect **pilgrims.** These privileges included: (1) the placing of the crusader and the crusader's family, lands, and possessions under the special protection of the **papacy;** (2) the right of hospitality by the Church; (3) exemption from tolls and taxes; (4) a moratorium on all debt payments and exemption from all interest for any loans; (5) the right to mortgage **feudal** fiefs and family lands to underwrite a crusade, even if the lord or family disagreed; (6) immunity from arrest under limited but significant circumstances; (7) exemption from the authority of secular courts and protection under the authority of church courts in most non-capital criminal cases; (8) suspension of many types of pending criminal and civil cases until the crusader's safe return; (9) in the case of thievery, the crusade was accepted as fitting and full restitution; and (10) the right to share in any crusade subsidies that might be available.

Needless to say, privileges were abused, and protections could fail. Some creditors were defrauded by crusaders who never intended to repay their loans, and before the thirteenth-century papacy limited the extent to which crusaders were immune from the jurisdiction of secular courts, many used their special status to avoid prosecution for such crimes as murder and rape. Some crusaders were gouged by creditors, and some

saw their persons, families, lands, and possessions violated. It was an imperfect world.
Related Entries: Bull, Papal; Financing the Crusades; Women.

Suggested Reading

James A. Brundage, *Medieval Canon Law and the Crusader* (1969); Jonathan Riley-Smith, *What Were the Crusades?* (1977).

R

Raymond IV of Saint-Gilles

Count of Toulouse (r. 1088?–1105) and marquis of Provence, the oldest and wealthiest leader of the **First Crusade,** and titular count of **Tripoli** (1102–1105).

On November 28, 1095, one day after Pope **Urban II**'s historic sermon that set in motion the First Crusade, envoys from Count Raymond appeared at **Clermont** and pledged the count's participation. Raymond, who was then around the age of fifty-five, certainly had foreknowledge of the pope's intentions and had probably been hand-picked by Urban to lead the expedition's military forces. Prior to arriving at Clermont, the pope had visited Raymond's lands and probably discussed his plans with the count. Raymond was lord of thirteen counties and one of the richest rulers in Europe. Consequently he assembled the largest, best-**financed,** and best-equipped crusade army to leave Europe in 1096. Joining his army of Provençals and Burgundians was **Adhémar of Monteil,** bishop of Le Puy and **papal legate** to the crusade. As one contemporary **Latin historian** commented, the count and the bishop were Christian counterparts of Moses and Aaron, who jointly led the Children of Israel toward the Promised Land. As Count Raymond would learn, however, the other great lords, who assembled and led their own forces, were not about to accept his leadership.

It is possible, and certain contemporary **chroniclers** reported it as fact, that Count Raymond swore to end his days in the **Holy Land.** What we know is that he handed over to his son, Bertrand, governance of all his lands, and he was joined by his wife, Elvira, when he departed southern France sometime in October 1096.

Raymond's army marched through the Balkans, and late in the journey he hurried on ahead of his forces to Constantinople, which he reached on April 27, 1097. His army arrived six days later. Of all of the crusade leaders, Raymond was most hostile to the idea of swearing fealty to Emperor **Alexius I,** probably because he saw such an oath as compromising his presumed position as leader of all **pilgrim** forces and as an insult to his maturity, experience, and rank. Finally, Raymond was convinced to take a compromise oath in which he swore to respect the person and possessions of the emperor. Raymond scrupulously honored the oath and enjoyed warm relations with Alexius ever after.

Anna Comnena reports that before Raymond left the imperial city, her father warned the count, for whom he now had deep affection, of **Bohemond of Taranto**'s untrustworthiness. If not then distrustful of Bohemond, Raymond would grow hostile toward him as the crusaders made their way across **Anatolia.** The flashpoint came when Bohemond claimed possession of **Antioch** during the summer of 1098, in violation of the crusaders' oaths to Alexius. The hostility extended down into the ranks of their respective armies, so that the **Normans** and Provençals became mutually antagonistic elements within the grand crusade army, which now hunkered down in northern **Syria.**

As Raymond's troops ranged throughout the countryside capturing and sacking **Muslim** strongholds, he earned a reputation as a ruthless and brutal enemy who, however, kept his word when towns negotiated surrender.

Sound tactical reasons dictated that the army stay, at least for a while, in the environs of Antioch. But loss of momentum could be dangerous, especially as the rank and file of the army became anxious to press on to **Jerusalem.** Aware of this pressure from below, in early January 1099 Count Raymond offered to pay for the services of **Godfrey of Bouillon, Robert of Normandy, Robert of Flanders,** and **Tancred** to assert his overall command of the army. He hoped to win their support away from Bohemond, who was determined to hold on to Antioch, and to spur them to follow him to Jerusalem. Tancred and Robert of Normandy took his money; Godfrey and Robert of Flanders declined. Raymond had one more card to play. On January 13, the count left the burning ruins of **Ma'arra** (Ma'arrat an-Numan) and began a symbolic, barefoot trek toward Jerusalem. By this gesture, he hoped to recall back to their **vows** to liberate Jerusalem all of the remaining crusade leaders who had not pledged to march with him. After Raymond's forces won some victories

along the Syrian coast, Robert of Flanders and Godfrey rushed to join him. Bohemond elected to remain in Antioch.

In the victorious assault on Jerusalem of July 15, 1099, Raymond's Provençals were unsuccessfully attacking the south wall when Godfrey of Boullion's Lorrainers carried the north wall and penetrated the city. Reacting quickly, Raymond then negotiated the surrender of the city's citadel, known as the Tower of David, and entered the city by this route. Seven days later the crusade leaders set about to elect a ruler for the city. Their choice fell on Raymond, who declined for reasons we can only guess at. After Raymond declined the kingship, reportedly stating that he would not wear a royal crown in the city where Jesus wore a crown of thorns, the leaders chose Godfrey. Raymond's refusal of a royal title effectively forced Godfrey to accept the more humble title "Defender of the Holy Sepulcher."

After reluctantly surrendering the Tower of David to Godfrey, Raymond participated in the victory at **Ascalon** on August 12. Thereafter, he began to look for a principality to conquer, and he turned his gaze toward Tripoli on the Syrian coast. In the summer of 1100 he sailed to Constantinople, to gain the emperor's consent and aid for his attempt to capture Tripoli.

Early in 1101 masses of crusaders, the third wave of the First Crusade (the so-called **Crusade of 1101**), arrived in the imperial city, and Alexius turned to Raymond for help in controlling them. Raymond agreed to act as their guide, despite his better judgment. The army was destroyed on August 5, but Raymond escaped.

In 1102 be began styling himself count of Tripoli, even though the city remained unconquered, and continued to lay the groundwork for carving out his new state. Key to his strategy was construction of the **castle** *Mount Pilgrim* on a hill just outside

Tripoli, which he completed in 1103. Before he could realize his conquest, death intervened on February 28, 1105. Tripoli would fall in 1109 to his son and heir, Bertrand. **Related Entries:** Hugh of Vermandois; Lance, Holy; Stephen of Blois and Chartres.

Suggested Reading

John H. Hill and Laurita L. Hill, *Raymond IV, Count of Toulouse* (1962; reissued 1980).

Reconquista

Literally "Reconquest," this struggle in the Iberian Peninsula between Christians and **Moors** lasted from the eighth to the late fifteenth century and ended with the triumph of Christian forces.

Not a continuous war, its battles and campaigns were fought intermittently, with long periods of peace and exchange. Not always a clear-cut conflict between **Muslims** and Christians, Moorish and Christian forces occasionally allied with each other, especially before 1100, in fighting common enemies of either faith. It is useful to divide this almost eight-hundred-year-old struggle into eight segments: (1) The arrival of Islam and the Christian reaction; (2) the age of the caliphate of Córdoba; (3) eleventh-century Christian expansion; (4) the age of the **Almoravids;** (5) early twelfth-century Christian crusades; (6) the coming of the **Almohads;** (7) thirteenth-century Christian victories; and (8) Islam's last days in **al-Andalus.**

The Arrival of Islam and the Christian Reaction

In April 711 Tariq ibn Ziyad, governor of Tangiers, led an expeditionary force across the narrow strait that separates Africa and Spain, landing at a promontory that now bears his name, *Jabal Tariq* (Tariq's Mountain) or Gibraltar. In July 711 Tariq's forces defeated and killed Roderick, last Christian Visigothic king of Spain, and by 715 most of the peninsula was in Muslim hands, except for the far northern regions. Christian resistance initially coalesced in Asturias, located in the northwest, where a small kingdom emerged around 750. During the reign of Alfonso II (r. 791–842), Asturias, which had expanded to encompass the entire northwestern corner of Iberia, had to endure three Muslim invasions, but it held. In the far northeastern corner of the peninsula, Alfonso II's ally and nominal overlord, the Frankish king, Charles the Great (Charlemagne), carved out by 810 a so-called Spanish March (Spanish Frontier) that encompassed Barcelona and extended as far south as the Ebro River. Other Christian centers of power emerged in the northern center—in the Basque region of Pamplona and in Aragon.

Except for Charles the Great's Spanish March, most Christian advances to the south in the ninth century were the work of the lords of Asturias. Under King Alfonso III (r. 866–909), the kingdom retook and repopulated a frontier region that extended across the northern regions of modern Portugal, León, and Castile.

The Age of the Caliphate of Córdoba

While Christian powers were asserting and extending their footholds in the north, Muslim Iberia, which included more than three quarters of the peninsula, was emerging as a culturally vigorous and powerful entity.

In 750 the **Abbasids** captured the caliphate of **Islam** and systematically set about killing all princes of the Umayyad dynasty. One escaped to al-Andalus: Abd al-Rahman, who defeated the resident emir (governor) of Córdoba and established an independent Umayyad state in 756 that refused to recognize the authority of the Abbasids. This state ruled Muslim Spain

The Templar Church of the True Cross, Segovia, Spain. Constructed in the Romanesque style and in imitation of the rotunda of the Church of the Holy Sepulcher in Jerusalem, the church was dedicated in 1208. Originally known as the Church of the Holy Sepulcher, its name was changed when it received a relic of the True Cross from Pope Honorius III in 1226. At the center of the church is an altar within an edicule, reminiscent of the Sepulcher and the little house that covers it in Jerusalem.

until 1031, although it began to lose its grip in 1009.

The ablest of the Umayyad rulers of al-Andalus was Abd al-Rahman III (r. 912–961), who in 929 put aside the title of emir and styled himself "caliph," thereby claiming to be Muhammad's deputy and the ruler of all Islam. Although most of the Islamic World did not recognize his authority, after 950 his power was so great throughout the Iberian Peninsula that he was able to extend his influence into the internal affairs of his northern Christian neighbors, turning them into virtual dependencies. For example, he managed to secure the crown of León for Sancho I. This Muslim influence over the affairs of the Christian states continued after the first caliph's death. In 997 Muslim raiders destroyed the shrine of **Santiago** to punish King Vermudo II of León for breaking his word.

Just at the point that the Christian kingdoms seemed destined to remain forever in the shadow of Islamic power, the caliphate began breaking down due to internal disorders, and in 1031 it ended. The result was division of al-

Andalus into more than twenty petty states known as *taifa* (factional) kingdoms.

Eleventh-Century Christian Expansion

In the midst of this breakdown of Umayyad central authority, al-Andalus experienced a foreshadowing of the crusades in 1064 when a sizeable army of Spaniards and French captured and **plundered** the stronghold of Barbastro, with the support of Pope Alexander II. Evidence suggests that he offered the soldiers a plenary **indulgence** for their efforts.

Spain narrowly missed another crusade dress rehearsal nine years later. In 1073 Count Ebles II of Roucy was planning, with the blessing of Pope **Gregory VII,** to lead an expedition into Iberia "to rescue it from the hands of the pagans." The expedition never came about, but it is worth noting that the pope, anticipating victory, wrote to the barons of France cautioning them that anyone who took part in this campaign must honor the papacy's claim to sovereignty over the entire peninsula.

As significant as these two papal interventions were when considered in the light of later events, in the 1070s and 1080s the weak *taifa* states had more immediate problems. King Alfonso VI (r. 1065–1109), who held the crowns of Castile and León and grandly styled himself "emperor of all Spain," captured the city of Toledo in 1085, with help from **Norman** and Burgundian adventurers. Toledo, the ancient capital of the Visigoths, was both a symbolic and strategic prize of the first order. By its conquest, Alfonso VI extended Castile's borders deep into the heart of the peninsula. Following that success, he pressed forward along several fronts simultaneously and seemed ready to conquer all of al-Andalus.

In fear for their existence, Spain's petty Muslim princes turned to the **Almoravids** of North Africa for help. It was a desperate gamble because the Berber Almoravids and the native-born Moors of Spain differed radically in their religious views and social values, but as the *taifa* ruler of Seville noted, he would rather herd camels for the Almoravids than guard the pigsty of King Alfonso.

The Age of the Almoravids

Intent on the reconquest of Toledo, an enormous Berber army landed in the south and marched to meet King Alfonso. On October 23, 1086, the armies clashed at Sagrajas, far to the southwest of Toledo, and Alfonso was soundly beaten but escaped. He also held on to Toledo and all his other territories. Following this victory, the Almoravids returned home, possibly because of their heavy losses.

Once the Almoravids left Iberia, the Christians went on the offensive again, launching raids from several key sites. Again, the *taifa* princes called in the Almoravids, who returned in June 1089. This time they arrived as conquerors of the *taifa* states. By 1094 they had conquered almost all of Islamic al-Andalus and presented the Christians with an aggressive empire that straddled the Straits of Gibraltar. The Iberian Peninsula was now roughly divided between Christian and Muslim states, yet it seemed that this balance would soon be upset by the advances of victorious Almoravid forces.

The myth of Almoravid invincibility was broken when, in October 1094, Rodrigo Díaz de Vivar, known as **El Cid,** defeated a Berber army that was advancing against the Islamic state of Valencia. The Almoravids eventually took Valencia in 1102, but it was the high-water mark of their fortunes in Spain. They would expend their energy trying to take Toledo and its surrounding frontier lands, which Alfonso VI held onto tenaciously, and in the end they exhausted themselves. By their intervention, however, they blunted Alfonso VI's advance and forced the Christian states into a momentary defensive stance. Meanwhile, back in North Africa, the Almoravids were displaced by a new group of Berber religious reformers and expansionists, the **Almohads** (see below).

Early Twelfth-Century Christian Crusades

As Almoravid power waned in the early twelfth century, the Christians again went on the offensive, but this time as crusaders. King Alfonso I of Aragon and Navarre (r. 1104–1134) prevailed upon a number of French veterans of the First Crusade to join in his expedition against Muslim Saragossa, an enterprise granted crusade status by Pope Gelasius II. The city fell on December 18, 1118, and with its capture, Christian forces and settlers could now advance south of the Ebro River in northeastern Spain.

King Alfonso VII of León-Castile (r. 1126–1157), who had himself crowned emperor of Spain in 1135 (a claim that other Spanish rulers did not recognize), also went on the offensive, capturing Almería, an important port on the southeastern coast on October 17, 1147. Seven days later King Afonso I Henriques of Portugal (r. 1128–1185), with the aid of Northern Europeans who had embarked on the **Second Crusade,** captured an equally important port on the southwestern coast, Lisbon. Aided by a crusading indulgence granted by Pope **Eugenius III,** King Alfonso VII captured the entire Ebro River Valley by the end of 1149, allowing for further Christian expansion and settlements along the eastern flank of Iberia.

By midcentury it seemed as though the total destruction of Muslim power in Spain was imminent, but a new element, the Almohads, soon destroyed that hope.

The Coming of the Almohads

The Almohads arose in Morocco in 1121 under the leadership of Ibn Tumart, who declared himself the *mahdi,* a messianic being who would usher in the final triumph of Islam. By 1147 the Almohads had snuffed out Almoravid power in North Africa; a year earlier they had invaded southern Spain. Even before their arrival, Islamic al-Andalus was in turmoil, as a new generation of *taifa* rulers arose to challenge Almoravid authority. It took over twenty-five years for the Almohads to subjugate all of Muslim Spain, but by 1172 the task was completed. Now the Almohads could concentrate on the five Christian kingdoms that faced them (roughly from east to west: Aragon, Navarre, Castile, León, and Portugal). For the remainder of the century, the Christians would be once again on the defensive.

In response to the Almohad offensive, Pope Alexander III offered crusade indulgences to all who resisted them and excommunicated all Christian collaborators. Despite papal attempts to rally support for an effective counterattack, the Christians of Spain were unable to present a united front against the Almohads. Fearful of the power of Castile, the kings of the four other Christian states warred against King Alfonso VIII (r. 1158–1214) in an effort to cut him down to size. Despite continuing bad feelings, peace was made in 1194. Peace among the Christians, however, did not ensure their success against their Muslim enemies. One year later Alfonso VIII suffered a devastating defeat at the hands of the Almohads.

The Battle of Alarcos of July 19, 1195, could have been a major turning point in the history of the peninsula, had the Almohad caliph, al-Mansur, followed up his victory by seizing Toledo while Alfonso's forces were in disarray. He failed to do so, and that failure marked the apogee of Almohad fortunes in Iberia. Indeed, Alarcos would be the last significant victory for Muslim forces in Iberia.

Thirteenth-Century Christian Victories

The papacy was scandalized by the wars among the Christians of Iberia and took vigorous and fairly effective measures to compel a united front against Islam. Pope Celestine III went so far as to excommunicate the king of León in 1196 and offer indulgences to those who took up arms against him. By 1209 all of the Christian kingdoms were at peace with one another and ready to fight a common Islamic enemy.

The result was the gathering in late spring 1212 of a huge crusade army composed of contingents from all five kingdoms, forces from the major **military orders,** and a large number of French warriors. Leading this multiethnic army were Kings Peter II of Aragon, Sancho VII of Navarre, and Alfonso VIII of Castile. After capturing and sacking a castle (and slaughtering its inhabitants) along the way, the French crusaders left the march and returned home. The Spaniards soldiered on. On July 16 they met and destroyed a much larger Almohad army at **Las Navas de Tolosa.** The victory ended forever the Almohad threat and hastened the Almohads' speedy demise in Iberia and North Africa, as their empire fell apart amid civil war.

Soon after 1212, Islamic al-Andalus was again divided into competing *taifa* states, and they proved singularly incapable of resisting most Christian advances. The victory on the plains of Tolosa had secured three-quarters of the peninsula for the Christian states, and the Christian advance was still picking up momentum. In 1236 Fernando III (r. 1217–1252) of the recently reunited kingdom of León-Castile conquered Córdoba, and in 1248 he took Seville.

At the same time, Aragon was moving aggressively into the Mediterranean, laying the bases for two future empires: the great Aragonese late medieval empire in the Mediterranean and the Spanish overseas world empire of post-1492. Fortified with crusade indulgences, a flotilla and army led by King James I the Conqueror (r. 1213–1276), captured the island of Majorca in 1230, and in 1232 the Muslims of Minorca bowed to the inevitable and recognized James as their sovereign.

By 1275 the four Christian kingdoms (León-Castile, Aragon, Navarre, and Portugal) combined to dominate 90 percent of the peninsula. All that was left to Islam was the far-south emirate of Granada, whose ruler, Ibn al-Ahmar, was forced in 1246 to recognize King Fernando III of León-Castile as his **feudal** overlord.

Islam's Last Days in al-Andalus

Granada remained a Muslim enclave for two and a half more centuries because of several factors. It had a large Muslim population that gave it vitality, and its mountain strongholds were easily defended. Its rulers were masters of diplomacy, and the only bordering Christian kingdom that could conceivably wage war against Granada, León-Castile, largely abandoned crusading for quite a while. Finally, Granada was shored up by a third group of zealous religious reformers from Morocco, the Marinids, who had conquered the Almohad empire in North Africa in 1269.

In 1275 Emir Abu Yusuf launched a **jihad** against Christian Spain and in support of Granada. The invasion was a shock for the Castilians, who suffered several serious losses, but by late 1279 the Marinids were forced to retire to North Africa without having regained any territory for Islam. The Marinids remained a factor to be reckoned with until a combined crusader army of

Spaniards, Portuguese, French, and other northern Europeans decisively defeated an invasion force at the Battle of Saludo on October 30, 1340. Never again would the Marinids mount a major offensive in Spain. The war against Granada and its Marinid allies was favorably concluded in 1344 after several more Christian victories, including the capture of the key port city of Algeciras. Although Granada continued to exist, it did so once again as a vassal state of León-Castile. For their part, the Marinids retained Gibraltar, but little else.

Despite occasional small campaigns against the Moors by the kings of Castile (such as the capture of Gibraltar in 1462), the **Reconquista** was in abeyance until *los reyes católicos* (the Catholic Monarchs), Isabella of León-Castile (r. 1474–1504) and Ferdinand II of Aragon (r. 1479–1518), whose marriage united most of Spain, declared their intention to expel all invaders from Iberia. Supported by crusade indulgences and other benefits accorded them by the papacy, the two monarchs launched their war in 1482. Ten years later, on January 2, 1492, their combined forces captured Granada, the last Moorish stronghold on the peninsula.

One of the witnesses of the Catholic Monarchs' triumphal entry into the city on January 6 was a Genoese sea captain who understood that now, with the dream of the reconquest of Spain realized, the Catholic Monarchs might well fund his enterprise to reach the court of the **Mongol** Great Khan by sailing west. He believed that reestablishing direct contact with the Great Khan would be a positive step toward the recovery of **Jerusalem.**

The fall of Granada presented Spain with the problem of assimilating a large mass of Muslims into its population. In their drive to create a unified community of Spaniards (where none had truly existed before), the Catholic Monarchs decided that a policy of religious uniformity was necessary. Although the Muslims of Granada had been guaranteed freedom of religion, the Catholic Monarchs attempted to convert them through aggressive **missionary** activities. When these activities became too aggressive, such as burning Korans and other religious texts, the Muslims revolted. All revolts were put down severely, and on February 11, 1502, the king and queen published an edict requiring all Muslims to accept Catholic Christianity immediately or leave the kingdom. Most chose baptism, but the depth of these conversions was shallow. Never trusted and often discriminated against, these converted Moors, known as *Moriscos,* revolted in 1569, and the revolt was put down with great severity in 1571. In 1609 the Moriscos were expelled from Spain. **Related Entries:** Calixtus II, Pope; Fatimids; Military Orders of Iberia; Second Crusade; *Song of Roland, The.*

Suggested Reading

Primary Sources

Abd Allah, *The Tibyan: Memoirs of Abd Allah b. Buluggin, Last Zirid Amir of Granada,* trans. by A. T. Tibi (1986); Simon Barton and Richard Fletcher, eds., *The World of El Cid: Chronicles of the Spanish Reconquest* (2000); *The Book of Deeds of James I of Aragon: A Translation of the Medieval Catalan "Libre dels Fets,"* trans. Damian Smith and Helena Buffery (2003); *The Chronicle of James I of Aragon,* trans. by John Foster, 2 vols. (1883); *De expugnatione Lyxbonensi (The Capture of Lisbon),* trans. by Charles W. David and others (1936; reissued 2000); Olivia Remie Constable, ed., *Medieval Iberia: Readings from Christian, Muslim, and Jewish Sources* (1997); Norman Housley, ed., *Documents on the Later Crusades, 1274–1580* (1996).

Historical Studies

Robert I. Burns, *Muslims, Christians, and Jews in the Crusader Kingdom of Valencia* (1984);

Gabriel Jackson, *The Making of Medieval Spain* (1972); Derek W. Lomax, *The Reconquest of Spain* (1978); Joseph F. O'Callaghan, *Reconquest and Crusade in Medieval Spain* (2003); Bernard F. Reilly, *The Contest of Christian and Muslim Spain, 1031–1157* (1992).

Recruitment

As the crusade became a recognizable institution during the twelfth century, so crusade recruitment procedures became fairly standardized.

The Church's recruitment efforts involved the issuance of **papal bulls,** conciliar decrees, and encyclicals (letters intended for widespread dissemination), papal authorization of **crusade indulgences** and other **privileges,** and the appointment of **preachers.** In 1215 and again in 1245, Church **councils** ordered secular lords, cities, towns, and villages to send on crusade "an appropriate number of fighting men together with their necessary expenses for three years," and in 1215 maritime cities were instructed to supply ships and sailors. Earlier, in 1198 and again in 1213, Pope **Innocent III** went so far as to command all churches and monasteries to provide warriors according to their means. Apparently churchmen so resisted this obligation that the **papacy** subsequently abandoned it as a means of recruitment.

In addition to these efforts by the Church's leadership, some clerics and lay people adopted other means to raise the numbers of crusaders. Both secular and ecclesiastical judges offered certain categories of criminals and penitents the opportunity to undertake the penance of a crusade in place of other punishments. Some crusade **historians** also seem to have been motivated to write their accounts, at least in part, out of a desire to attract soldiers to the defense of the **crusader states.** Certainly, **Fulcher of Chartres** and **William of Tyre** fell into that category.

Recruiting people to take the **cross** was one half of the battle; getting them to fulfill the **crusade vow** was the other. Reluctant crusaders were a perennial problem, and threats of excommunication against those who failed to set off for **Outremer** in a timely fashion were a constant refrain.

Peer pressure and family connections were also powerful factors in driving people to undertake a crusade. **Feudal** lords expected their vassals to accompany them on crusade, and one great lord's taking the cross could and often did inspire other lords to join him. Often the lords who joined him were his cousins. Indeed, familial ties and **family crusading traditions** were decisive factors in attracting many recruits. Fathers and sons, older and younger brothers often went off on crusade together, as did the grandsons and great grandsons of earlier crusaders.

Then there was money. Some professional soldiers signed up as **mercenaries** in the employ of various lords.

All of this recruitment resulted in well over a million **Latins** participating in the crusades between 1096 and 1272. Despite these numbers, recruitments never managed to meet the full needs of crusade armies, given the high percentage of losses due to combat, **disease,** and defection. **Related Entries:** Acre; Bernard of Clairvaux; Financing the Crusades; Friars, Mendicant; Fulk of Neuilly; Oliver of Paderborn; Peter the Hermit; Women. *See also* individual crusades.

Relics

Material remains of holy people, which carry supernatural powers because of that association.

Relics, a word that derives from the Latin *reliquae* (things left behind), can be the bod-

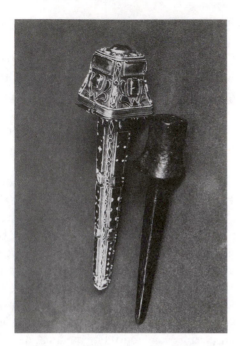

A reliquary, or relic container, and its relic, a supposed nail from the crucifixion of Jesus, Trier Cathedral, Germany.

ies or bodily parts of saints or anything connected with their earthly ministries. Because medieval Christians believed Jesus and Mary, his mother, ascended in body to Heaven, they claimed to possess few corporeal relics of either person, apart from such disposable items as baby teeth, hair and nail clippings, traces of Jesus' blood shed at his crucifixion, and milk from the Virgin's breast. At the same time, they claimed to possess many items from their lives, such as Jesus' sandals and Mary's birthing gown. Of all the items associated with Jesus, the two most sacred and powerful, so far as crusaders were concerned, were pieces of the **True Cross,** on which Jesus was executed, and the **Holy Sepulcher,** the tomb from which Jesus arose on Easter Sunday morning. Arguably, without these two relics there would have been no crusades—at least as we understand them. The first gave the crusaders their special name and status—

crucesignati—"those signed with the cross." The second provided the crusades with their special goal and rationale for being.

Relics were (and are) believed to carry with them supernatural powers, and they invested those who held them with special authority. The theory was that the power of the holy person resided in the relic. To possess or venerate a relic was to enlist the help of the saint associated with it. Needless to say, relics linked with Jesus and Mary were most avidly sought after because of their extraordinary power. Regardless of the primacy of Jesus and Mary relics, it was not enough to have and venerate only them. Pious Christians believed they could never have enough relics. The more relics a devout Christian possessed or venerated, the greater the power waiting to be tapped. Praying before relics brought spiritual benefits, such as the promise of **indulgences** for sins. Veneration of relics also carried the promise of corporeal benefits. In an age in which medical science could do little to cure most serious ailments, relics were often used as a means of seeking heavenly aid for bodily infirmities.

On one level the crusades were an attempt to liberate and then protect **Jerusalem,** the site of Jesus' death, resurrection, and ascension to Heaven. Jerusalem might be (and was) considered to be one large relic. Indeed, the entire **Holy Land** was a holy relic. But some sites within Jerusalem and the Holy Land were holier than others. Among them all, none could compare with the Holy Sepulcher, which, as far as Christians were concerned, proved Jesus' divinity and sealed the promise of salvation for all believers.

Medieval Christians further believed that holy people watched over their relics and protected them (as well as the people who possessed them in devotion). This meant the saints and Jesus assisted the truly pious in securing them and worked to frustrate the designs of the impious who held them or wished to take possession of them. When, however, unbelievers captured a relic from a Christian, such as **Saladin**'s taking of both the True Cross and Jerusalem in 1187, God or the saint allowed it because the Christian or Christians holding the relic were unworthy by virtue of sin. This unworthiness needed to be expiated by acts of penance and renewed efforts to recover the sacred relic.

Such reasoning justified **holy wars** to liberate, defend, and then to rewin Jerusalem. This reasoning also explains why crusaders sent and brought so many relics back to Europe from the Holy Land, and it also helps to explain the **pillage** of **Constantinople** in 1204. There is no evidence to support the theory that the army of the **Fourth Crusade** went to Constantinople in the hope of securing the city's impressive store of sacred relics. However, once the **Byzantines** had, in the eyes of the crusaders, proved themselves to be false Christians, the army and its clerics believed they were justified in seizing and transporting back home large numbers of the city's most important relics. Indeed, to leave them in the hands of such unworthy Christians would be tantamount to insulting Christ and the saints whose relics would never have been liberated without heavenly assistance. **Related Entries:** Lance, Holy; Pilgrimage; Pillage and Plunder; Robert II of Flanders; Santiago de Compostela.

Suggested Reading

Patrick J. Geary, *Sacra Furta: Thefts of Relics in the Central Middle Ages, 800–1100,* rev. ed. (1990); H. W. van Os and others, *The Way to Heaven: Relic Veneration in the Middle Ages* (2000).

Reynald of Châtillon

Also referred to as Rainald, Renaud, and Reginald in modern histories of the crusades, Reynald was prince of **Antioch** (r.

1153–1161) and lord of **Transjordan** (r. ca. 1177–1187). He was and remains one of the most controversial figures of the twelfth-century **crusader states.**

Born around 1125 into one of the great families of Burgundy but dispossessed of his lands by enemies, Reynald accompanied **Louis VII** on the **Second Crusade** and remained in the **Holy Land,** where he entered into the service of King **Baldwin III** of **Jerusalem.** In 1153 he married **Constance,** heiress of Antioch, and assumed control over the principality.

As prince, Reynald displayed high degrees of recklessness, intemperance, greed, and political ineptness. When the **Byzantine** emperor **Manuel** failed to pay Reynald for his services in suppressing a rebellion in Cilician **Armenia,** Reynald shifted sides, allied with the Armenian prince, and in 1156 invaded and brutally **pillaged** the Christian island of **Cyprus,** a possession of his **feudal** overlord, the emperor. With the acquiescence of King Baldwin, an outraged Manuel marched against Reynald and forced his submission in 1159.

In 1161 Reynald was taken **prisoner** by the forces of **Nur ad-Din** and held in **Aleppo** for fifteen years. During his captivity Constance died, and his stepson Bohemond III (r. 1163–1201) became prince of Antioch, making Reynald once again a landless man, should he ever secure his release.

Release came in 1176 thanks to the intervention of his stepson and payment of a huge ransom. Around 1177 Reynald married Stephanie of Milly, lady of Transjordan. Through this marriage Reynald was once again one of the great lords of the **Latin East.** The new lord of Transjordan, ever the brash and rash adventurer, became an increasingly troublesome neighbor of **Saladin,** the new champion of **Islam.**

In 1183 Reynald launched a squadron on the Red Sea to **plunder** the rich merchant

Crusaders captured at the Battle of Hattin are brought before Saladin, who then beheads Reynald. From a manuscript copy of the *Estoire d'Eracles*, a continuation of William of Tyre's history to 1261. Paris ca. 1300. The Walters Art Museum, Baltimore.

ships that plied its waters and to attack the ports that dotted its African and Arabian coastlines. While engaged in this enterprise, his fleet sank a vessel filled with Muslim **pilgrims** headed toward the holy city of Mecca. The Islamic World was horrified. Although the **Frankish** ships were sunk by an Egyptian fleet dispatched by Saladin's brother **al-Adil** and the captured sailors executed as pirates, Saladin could not have been satisfied. Reynald had escaped.

One of Saladin's chief targets now became Reynald's **castle** of *Kerak*. In 1183 and again in 1184 Saladin undertook **siege** operations against the fortress but was forced to abandon both efforts. When King **Baldwin IV** died in March 1185, the exhausted and dispirited barons of the kingdom of Jerusalem decided to seek a four-year truce with Saladin. Because of struggles within his family that needed immediate attention, Saladin agreed. It might seem at that point that *Kerak* and its lord would never fall into his hands. Reynald's recklessness, however, soon provided the Muslim sultan with another opportunity.

In late 1186 or early 1187 Reynald broke the truce by attacking a caravan that was traveling from **Cairo** to **Damascus.** Contrary to popular legend, Saladin's sister was not among the caravan members, but the group contained plenty of rich merchants, whom Reynald robbed, took captive, and held for ransom at *Kerak*. Reynald refused to receive envoys from Saladin demanding their release and compensation, and he equally spurned the request of King **Guy of Lusignan** that he render satisfaction for this outrage. War was now inevitable, and the kingdom of Jerusalem was ill prepared for it.

The result was disaster for the kingdom and its forces. On July 4, 1187, Saladin's troops annihilated a large crusader army at **Hattin.** Among those captured was Reynald, who had fought bravely, as always. Reynald was among the number of high-ranking prisoners whom Saladin received in his tent. The sultan treated King Guy courteously but refused to offer hospitality to Reynald. On his part, Reynald acted haughtily and with intemperate courage, refusing to beg for mercy. After exchanging angry words with Reynald, Saladin struck him down with a sword and his bodyguards rushed in to finish off the murder. Reynald's severed head was sent to Damascus in triumph.

The subsequent siege of *Kerak* lasted over a year, but its fate was inevitable. In November 1188 its starving defenders surrendered, and a few months later Reynald's other great fortress, *Montréal,* also capitulated. Reynald of Châtillon's second and last principality had gone the way of its lord—destroyed by Saladin. **Related Entries:** Chivalry; Settlement and Colonization; William of Tyre; Women.

Ribauds

This Old French term, which meant "people who pursue licentious pleasures"—was applied to the masses of low-born camp followers who accompanied the armies of the **Albigensian Crusade.**

One source credits the *ribauds* with having their own leader, or "king," very much like the **Tafurs** of the **First Crusade,** and our four main sources credit them with initiating the attack on the city of Béziers and the **massacre** that ensued on July 22, 1209. According to one report, the *ribauds* picked up cudgels and stormed the city out of frustration, and the army followed. Once inside the city, they began looting and killing. When the army's barons and other soldiers began to dispossess them of their loot, the *ribauds* set fire to the city and its cathedral, which housed a large number of refugees. This same source places the *ribauds'* numbers at 15,000, and another claims that almost 20,000 inhabitants of the city died that day. Neither figure can be verified. **Related Entries:** Children's Crusade; Noncombatants; Shepherds' Crusade.

Richard I the Lionheart

King of **England** (r. 1189–1199), duke of Aquitaine (r. 1072–1099) and **Normandy** (r. 1189–1199), holder of other French **feudal** lordships, and the major leader of the **Third Crusade.**

Richard, the earliest recorded nobleman north of the Alps to respond to the news of the disaster at **Hattin,** swore the **crusader's**

vow at the French city of Tours in November 1187. Known as *Coeur de Lion* because of his courage and military prowess, he was the eldest surviving son of King Henry II of England and Queen **Eleanor of Aquitaine.** Richard's act, which had been performed spontaneously and without his father's permission, was followed by Henry's assumption of the **crusader's cross** on January 22, 1188, as Henry met in **France** with King **Philip II,** his nominal feudal overlord for lands held in western France. Philip also accepted the **cross** at this time, and together the two monarchs planned a joint crusade, despite a history of mutual animosity and conflict. Quite simply, King Philip wanted to strip Henry of his multiple French lordships, such as the duchy of Normandy.

The planned Anglo-French crusade was almost immediately put on hold due to a renewed outbreak of hostilities between Henry and Philip. To make matters worse, Richard rose in rebellion against his father in the late spring of 1189. Shortly thereafter Henry II died, and the thirty-two-year-old Richard succeeded him as king of England and as feudal lord of most of western France. On December 30, 1189, Richard and Philip met to arrange a compact whereby they pledged mutual friendship and promised to campaign together in the **Holy Land.**

On July 4, 1190, three years to the day since the disaster at Hattin, the two royal armies marched out of the town of Vézelay in Burgundy. Both monarchs had decided to make their way to the Holy Land by sea. The armies parted soon after leaving Vézelay and made their way independently to separate ports, with plans to meet in Messina, Sicily.

The two contingents arrived in Sicily in mid-September, and the lateness of the season forced them to winter over. There Richard clashed with Tancred of Lecce, who had recently seized the throne of Sicily following the death of King William II, who

The reconquest of Jaffa by King Richard. Richard is drawing his sword in the upper-left corner. From a manuscript copy of the *Estoire d'Eracles,* a continuation of William of Tyre's history to 1261. Paris ca. 1300. The Walters Art Museum, Baltimore.

had been married to Richard's sister Joan. To help **finance** his crusade, Richard was determined to collect his sister's dowry, as well as a sizeable amount of wealth that William had bequeathed to Henry II. Richard's high-handed tactics soon led to severe tensions between the Sicilians and his forces, which in turn led to his capturing and **plundering** the city of Messina. This forced Tancred to quickly agree to Richard's terms.

During their Sicilian stopover, Philip and Richard, who had been good friends up to that point, began to fall out over several issues, including Richard's reluctance to ful-

fill his promise to marry Philip's sister Alice. Although Philip was persuaded to release Richard from his promise, seeds of distrust had been laid.

On April 10, 1191, Richard's fleet set sail from Messina. Several of his ships were driven by a storm to **Cyprus,** where his stranded men were robbed and imprisoned by the island's ruler, a **Byzantine** rebel named Isaac Comnenus. On May 6, Richard arrived to rescue his men, as well as his widowed sister, Joan, and his bride-to-be, Berengaria of Navarre, whose ship lay just outside the harbor. Richard conquered the island, dispatched Isaac to **Tripoli** in fetters, and set sail for the Holy Land on June 5.

The next day he arrived before **Tyre** but was refused entry into the city by **Conrad of Montferrat.** A few days later he reached **Acre,** where King Philip had landed on April 2. Soon the two men took to quarreling, although their growing animosity did not preclude joint operations against the enemy.

On July 12 the **Muslim** garrison at Acre surrendered under the condition that their lives would be spared in return for ransom and the return of Christian **prisoners.** On the last day of July, Philip set sail for Tyre as the first stage of his homeward journey, after swearing not to attack Richard's lands in France while the Lionheart remained a crusader—an oath Philip later violated.

Philip's departure left Richard as the highest-ranking crusader in the Holy Land, and one of Richard's first acts as unchallenged commander of the crusade army was to order the beheading of approximately 2,600 Muslim hostages when the time limit expired for Saladin's delivering the relic of the **True Cross** lost at Hattin and 1,500 Christian prisoners.

Brilliantly coordinating his **infantry, cavalry,** and support vessels, Richard then carefully marched his army down the coast toward **Jaffa.** On September 6, Richard's tactics were rewarded when his army repulsed an ambush at Arsuf and won a resounding victory. It would be the last time Saladin dared face Richard in open battle in the field.

Richard's army took Jaffa without a struggle—a major step toward recovery of Jerusalem. By early January 1192, however, Richard realized, much to his disappointment, that recapturing and holding Jerusalem was beyond his resources. As a result, he concentrated on securing the coastal region south of Jaffa, and the key to this was the port of **Ascalon.** Once refortified,

Ascalon would serve as a strong point from which Richard could disrupt communications between Egypt and **Syria.** What is more, from it Richard could launch a campaign against Egypt, the heart of the **Ayyubid** empire, or threaten such a move.

The very threat of an attack on Egypt was a powerful bargaining token, and Richard was ready to bargain with Saladin. In the late months of 1191, Richard had opened treaty negotiations with Saladin through the sultan's brother **al-Adil** Abu Bakr Saif-ad-Din, whom the West knew as **Saphadin.** Both Richard and Saladin needed peace that would allow each the opportunity to return to domestic affairs, which desperately needed attention, but negotiations were not easy.

As negotiations dragged on through the spring and summer of 1192, Saladin looked for his own advantageous positions from which to negotiate. When Richard led his army northward to Acre in July, Saladin struck at Jaffa, which he besieged and largely captured, except for some defenders who held out in the town's citadel. Upon receipt of the news, Richard reacted quickly and decisively by sailing south with a small relief force. In one of the most celebrated moments in crusade history, Richard and his men entered the water from their vessels and waded to shore, where they engaged the enemy on the beach. When the defenders in the citadel saw this, they attacked the Muslims from the rear, thereby enveloping the enemy. The slaughter that followed was massive, and the crusader victory was resounding.

Soon thereafter, Richard fell critically ill—his second major illness since arriving in the Holy Land. In addition to his illness, three other factors impelled him to seek a quick treaty. He realized fully, after two unsuccessful marches on the city, that Jerusalem was beyond recovery, even though he had on one occasion advanced as far as the hill of **Montjoie,** from which he beheld the city in sorrow. It was similarly clear that his plans to invade Egypt were not practical—at least for the moment—given his resources and the temperament of his army, which still saw Jerusalem as the sole goal. Finally, news that Philip II was attacking his French possessions convinced Richard that he must return to France (and he was, first and foremost, a Frenchman who happened to be king of England) as soon as possible.

On September 2, 1192, a formal three-year, eight-month truce was concluded. Saladin guaranteed the security of the Christian coastal possessions from Tyre to Jaffa, and Christian **pilgrims** were allowed unhampered travel to all holy sites, including Jerusalem, where two Latin priests were allowed residence. On his part, Richard surrendered Ascalon, after his forces destroyed its fortifications, and other key sites south of Jaffa.

On October 9, 1192, Richard the Lionheart set sail for Europe. His crusade in the Holy Land had lasted sixteen months, but his trials had not ended.

Despite his **crusader privileges,** which theoretically made his person and lands sacrosanct, Richard suffered attacks on both from fellow Christians. His brother John and King Philip had already conspired to try to rob the absent Richard of his continental possessions. As Richard hurried home to protect his lands, he was taken prisoner by a fellow crusader who hated him. While crossing Austrian lands, Richard was captured on December 21, 1192, by Duke Leopold V of Austria, who bore several grudges against the king. Richard had insulted Leopold by tearing his banner down from the walls of Acre following the city's capture, despite the fact that the duke had spent a bit more time at the **siege** of the city than had the recently arrived king of England. Leopold later sold his royal prisoner to Emperor **Henry VI.**

Both men were cousins of the assassinated Conrad of Montferrat and, probably wrongly, blamed Richard for the marquis's death.

Henry, who imprisoned Richard on the pretext that he was guilty of "treason, treachery, and mischief in the Holy Land," held Richard for a king's ransom. Many of the charges that Henry laid against Richard were products of a propaganda war that King Philip II had initiated against Richard as soon as the French king reached the West. Due to the heavy ransom demanded and John's delaying tactics in raising the funds, Richard did not reach England until March 1194. **Related Entries:** Guy of Lusignan; Massacres.

Suggested Reading

Primary Sources

See the primary sources for the Third Crusade.

Historical Studies

James A. Brundage, *Richard Lion Heart* (1974); John B. Gillingham, *Richard I* (1999).

Robert II of Flanders

Count of Flanders (r. 1093–1111), known as the "Jerusalemite" in recognition of his crusade exploits and one of the leaders of the **First Crusade.**

Count Robert had an interest in the East well before **Urban II**'s call for a **holy war.** His father, Count Robert I, had earlier made a penitential **pilgrimage** to **Jerusalem** and struck up a friendship with Emperor **Alexius I.** Probably with this connection in mind, the pope sent a letter to Flanders in December 1095 informing the Flemings of his desire to "liberate the Eastern Churches," as articulated at the recent **Council of Clermont,** and inviting participation in the enterprise. The pious Robert did not disappoint the pope.

Robert was wealthy enough to **finance** his crusade from personal resources, unlike

The chapel of the counts of Flanders, Ghent (built in 1180). The cruciform window might commemorate the crusade participation of Count Robert II a century earlier.

his impecunious cousin, Duke **Robert II of Normandy.** Count Robert set off with his contingent in the autumn of 1096. From southern Italy, he sailed across the Adriatic to the lower Balkans during winter, a hazardous journey at that time of year, and arrived in **Constantinople** in good order at an unknown date. On April 26, 1097, Robert played the part of a peacemaker by convincing **Raymond of Saint-Gilles** to offer a modified oath of allegiance to Alexius I.

Robert served ably and bravely from the **siege** of Nicaea to the Battle of **Ascalon**—a campaign that included six major battles in the field and three successful sieges. During the seven-and-a-half-month siege of **Antioch** he distinguished himself on numerous occasions, earning a reputation as a bold warrior. He was also an able conciliator, as he showed following the capture of Jerusalem, when he and Robert of Normandy intervened to persuade the disgruntled Raymond of Saint-Gilles to surrender the city's citadel to **Godfrey of Bouillon,** thereby acknowledging him as ruler of the city.

Following the victory at Ascalon, Robert set out for home, first sailing to Constantinople and then following in reverse the route he had taken in 1096–1097. He arrived home in the spring of 1100 with a treasury of **relics** acquired along the way, including the putative arm of Saint George. **Related Entries:** Eustace III of Boulogne; Saints, Warrior.

Robert II of Normandy

Duke of Normandy (r. 1087–1106) and one of the leaders of the **First Crusade.**

Known as "Curthose" because of his short stature, Robert was the eldest son of William I the Conqueror. Upon his death,

William reluctantly bequeathed the duchy of Normandy to Robert, who had been more or less in constant rebellion against William since 1078. The crown of England went to William's next eldest son, William (II).

When Robert decided to take up the **crusader's cross** in 1096, he was forced to mortgage his duchy for 10,000 marks (5,000 pounds of silver) to his brother William to **finance** his expedition. William raised the money by laying a special assessment on his realm, thereby instituting the first kingdom-wide crusade tax. Because both men were childless, the brothers agreed that should either one predecease the other without an heir, the survivor would inherit the other's lands and title.

Robert's entourage included his chaplain Arnulf of Chocques, a future **patriarch of Jerusalem,** and a substantial body of **Normans,** Bretons, and other French, as well as some English. This multiethnic force marched into southern Italy in the autumn of 1096 with the armies of **Stephen of Blois** and **Robert II of Flanders** and accompanied by **Eustace III of Boulogne.** Upon arriving there, Count Robert's Flemish crusaders immediately set sail for the East, but Duke Robert and Count Stephen decided to enjoy the subtropical pleasures of southern Italy, where they spent the winter. Both armies embarked on April 5, 1097, for a voyage across the Adriatic to the Balkans. From there they marched overland, arriving in **Constantinople** around May 14—the last two contingents of the second wave to arrive at the imperial capital.

Duke Robert participated in all of the major battles from Nicaea to **Ascalon** and acquitted himself bravely. During the summer of 1098, however, as an epidemic ravaged **Antioch,** he left the **disease**-ridden city and traveled to Latakia on the **Syrian** coast, which he governed for a few weeks. The fun-loving Robert, whom contempo-raries called "the soft duke" because of his easygoing ways, had been a poor governor of Normandy and was no better in the **Levant.** His rule in Latakia was so unpopular that it might well have been a relief for him when, in accordance with his oath to Emperor **Alexius I,** he handed over the city to a **Byzantine** administrator. In September, when the epidemic abated, he and the other princes who had sought refuge away from Antioch returned to the city. One wonders what the rank-and-file crusaders, who had to endure the dangers of a pestilential summer in Antioch, thought of their leaders' leadership.

Shortly after the victory at Ascalon, Robert embarked with his surviving troops on Byzantine vessels and sailed to Constantinople, where he was received with honor. From there he headed home, arriving in Normandy in September 1100. Unfortunately, his brother, King William II, had been killed on August 2, and a younger brother, Henry, immediately seized the throne of England and claimed the duchy of Normandy. Robert managed to hold onto Normandy—for a while—but fruitlessly claimed the crown of England for himself.

On September 28, 1106, King Henry I defeated and captured Robert. He confiscated Normandy, adding it to his possessions, and imprisoned Robert. Robert never was released, dying in prison in 1134.

Henry I went down in history as one of England's greatest medieval kings; Robert, who was never a competent ruler, became a Norman crusade legend. As the years passed, mythic heroic deeds became associated with his name. **Related Entry:** Godfrey of Bouillon.

Suggested Reading

Primary Source

Orderic Vitalis, *The Ecclesiastical History of Orderic Vitalis,* 5 vols., ed. and trans. by Marjorie Chibnall (1969–1980), books 8–10 in vols. 4 and 5.

Historical Study

Charles W. David, *Robert Curthose, Duke of Normandy* (1920, reissued 1982).

Roger of Salerno

Regent of the principality of **Antioch** (r. 1112–1119).

When **Tancred** died in December 1112, the regency of Antioch fell to his nephew Roger, who governed the principality in the name of the future **Bohemond II.** Bohemond was still a minor and resided in the **Norman** lands of southern Italy. Thanks to Tancred's leadership, Antioch had become a powerful state, and early in his career Roger seemed to be capable of building on that strength. On September 14, 1115, Roger, in alliance with certain **Turkish** rebels, defeated an army of the Great **Seljuk** at Tell Danith, and followed up his victory with a slaughter of several thousand **prisoners,** including children and old people. The defeat made a great impression on the **Muslims** of **Syria,** who now regarded Roger as a larger-than-life foe. Ironically, one of Roger's Turkish allies at that moment was Il-Ghazi ibn Artuk, who less than four years later would defeat and kill Roger at the battle known as **The Field of Blood,** thereby forever weakening Norman power in **Syria. Related Entries:** Massacres; Pillage and Plunder.

Rum, Sultanate of

See Seljuks.

S

Saints, Warrior

Warrior saints, many of whose cults stretched back into Christianity's early centuries, became quite popular in the West in the age of the crusades.

All Christian saints—persons whose lives of heroic sanctity earned them Heaven and veneration as special friends of God and protectors of those who pray for their help—are metaphorically *milites Christi* (soldiers of Christ), inasmuch as they successfully battled the forces of Evil and their own sinful appetites while on Earth. A few saints, however, had served as soldiers while alive and retained their martial qualities while serving as heavenly helpers.

One such soldier-saint was George. **Eastern Christians** had a long, strong, and widespread devotion to Saint George, whom they venerated as an early fourth-century martyr from **Anatolia.** Although the cult of Saint George had found its way to the West by the sixth century, the saint became widely popular in Europe during the age of the crusades, as he and similar warrior saints became identified with the **holy war** against **Islam.** The *Golden Legend,* a mid–thirteenth-century collection of saints' stories, recounts the tale of a handsome young man who appeared to a crusader priest and identified himself as George, captain of the Christian host. He promised to accompany the army to **Jerusalem** if they would carry his **relics** there. Later during the assault on the city, as the crusaders hesitated to climb their scaling ladders, George appeared in white armor marked with a red cross and led them safely over the walls to victory.

By the late Middle Ages, George was the patron of such kingdoms as Aragon, England, Germany, Hungary, Lithuania, and Portugal. Additionally, a large number of principalities and cities throughout Europe adopted George as their heavenly protector. Italy alone had one hundred and eighteen communes, or independent cities, that carried George's name.

Joining George in this heavenly army were such early soldier-martyrs as Demetrius, Maurice, Mercurius, Sebastian, Theodore, and Victor. Of these, Theodore, Sebastian, and Maurice were the most popular, although none probably reached the level of George's popularity.

At least two other heavenly warriors—Saint James the Greater and Saint Michael the Archangel—had never been warriors on Earth but assumed in legend and cult the status of saints who assured victory in holy war and protected those who waged these wars.

Saint James, an apostle, was metamorphosed into *Santiago Matamoros* (Saint

Saint George in early thirteenth-century armor. Chartres Cathedral, France, ca. 1200–1225.

James the Moor-Slayer), the patron saint of the **Reconquista.** Saint Michael the Archangel had never been a human being, but a pious legend had grown up in the West that Michael was the head of the angelic heavenly army that drove Satan out of Heaven. Consequently, he emerged as the patron of soldiers as early as the eighth century. As with George, his cult continued to grow during the Crusade Era. **Related Entries:** Antioch; Lance, Holy; Santiago de Compostela; Relics.

Suggested Reading

Samantha Riches, *St George: Hero, Martyr and Myth* (2000); Christopher Walter, *The Warrior Saints in Byzantine Art and Tradition* (2002).

Saladin (al-Malik al-Nasir Salah ad-Din Yusuf Ibn Ayyub) (1138–1193)

Sultan of **Egypt** and **Syria** (r. 1174–1193), conqueror of **Jerusalem** in 1187, and defender of **Islam** against the armies of the **Third Crusade.**

Born the son of Ayyub, a Kurdish soldier who rose to high rank in the service of the **Seljuk Turks,** Saladin benefited greatly from the accomplishments of his father and his uncle, Shirkuh. Beyond that, his own piety, moral authority, abilities, and deeds combined to transform Saladin into a figure revered by **Muslims** of every ethnic background and respected by his Christian foes.

While his father and uncle served **Nur ad-Din** in Syria, Saladin devoted himself to military and classical Islamic studies in **Damascus,** where he became devoted to the idea that holy **jihad** against the enemies of Islam is a Muslim's primary duty. In 1152 Saladin entered Nur ad-Din's service and soon became a trusted aide. In 1164 Nur ad-Din dispatched Shirkuh to Egypt to intervene in a civil conflict that threatened to tear apart the faltering **Fatimid** state and lay Egypt open to conquest by King **Amalric** of Jerusalem. Accompanying Shirkuh was his twenty-five-year-old nephew, Saladin, on an adventure that would launch the young man's career to unforeseen heights.

In three expeditions Saladin proved his military abilities time and again against Egyptian and **Frankish** enemies alike. Largely due to his nephew's exploits, by late January 1169 Shirkuh controlled Egypt, holding the dual offices of *vizier,* or prime minister, to the Fatimid caliph and commander of Nur ad-Din's expeditionary army in Egypt. His victory was shortlived, for he died two months later from an overdose of rich food. On March 26, 1169, the Syrian army chose Saladin as its new commander,

The siege and surrender of Jerusalem to Saladin. From a manuscript copy of the *Estoire d'Eracles*, a continuation of William of Tyre's history to 1261. Paris ca. 1300. The Walters Art Museum, Baltimore.

and he succeeded to the vizierate soon thereafter.

As a devout **Sunni** Muslim and as the deputy of an equally pious Sunni, Nur ad-Din, Saladin found that holding the office of vizier to a **Shia** Fatimid caliph presented a certain embarrassment—an embarrassment that Nur ad-Din wished removed immediately. Saladin, however, waited more than two years, patiently building up his power, before he moved. As his Fatimid master, al-Adid, lay dying in September 1171, Saladin acted and publicly recognized the authority of al-Mustadi, the **Abbasid** caliph of Baghdad. Egypt's Fatimid Era had ended.

In 1169 Saladin beat back a combined **Byzantine**-Frankish attack on the Egyptian port city of **Damietta,** and in December 1170 he undertook a brief offensive along the frontier separating Egypt and the crusader **kingdom of Jerusalem,** capturing the Red Sea port of Eilat in the process. Both successes added significantly to his growing reputation within the Islamic World. From the Frankish perspective, Saladin's ascendancy meant that they now faced two committed *mujahidin,* or holy warriors, Nur ad-Din to the northeast and his nominal subordinate to the southwest.

A rift between Nur ad-Din and Saladin was almost inevitable, but despite increasingly strained relations, for the longest time neither man was willing to allow the situation to degenerate into open conflict. That apparently changed in 1174 when Nur ad-Din began mustering troops for a campaign, presumably against the upstart Saladin. Whatever he had in mind was made moot when Nur ad-Din suddenly took sick and died on May 15.

The year 1174 was a watershed in the history of the **Latin** crusader states. Not only did Nur ad-Din's death open the way for Saladin's consolidation of power, but King Amalric, a vigorous expansionist who was determined to establish Frankish hegemony over Egypt, also died during that year. On October 28 Saladin occupied Damascus by means of liberal bribery and the force of his personality and religious vision. No blood was spilled in the effort. Southern Syria was now under his control; the next step was to take **Aleppo** and **Mosul,** twin northern centers of Muslim opposition to Saladin's drive for leadership in the jihad against the Franks.

For the next several years Saladin fought the Frankish armies and his Muslim enemies. His battles with Muslim opponents were generally marked with restraint and by a policy of shedding as little blood as possible. Toward the Franks he was far less merciful, often ordering the death of especially hated **prisoners,** such as **Templars, Hospitalers,** and crossbowmen. When Aleppo submitted in June 1183 and Mosul joined forces with him in March 1186, Saladin had succeeded in uniting Syria and Egypt under his uncontested authority. The only obstacle to his immediately putting all of his energies and resources into a grand jihad was a four-year truce that he had concluded with the kingdom of Jerusalem in 1185.

In late 1186 or early 1187, however, the impulsive **Reynald of Châtillon** broke the truce by attacking a Muslim caravan; when reparations were not forthcoming, Saladin went to war. The result was victory at the **Battle of Hattin** on July 4, 1187, the reconquest of **Jerusalem** on October 2, and the recapture of almost every crusader town and fortification, with the exception of **Antioch, Tripoli,** and **Tyre.** Failure to take these three key cities, as well as his overly generous parole of King **Guy of Lusignan,** who had been captured at Hattin, doomed Saladin's grand plan of driving the Westerners completely out of **Outremer.**

In August 1189 King Guy launched a counterattack on **Acre** from Tyre, thereby setting the stage for the **Third Crusade.** The fall of Acre on July 12, 1191, to the combined armies of Kings Guy, **Richard I** of England, and **Philip II** of France signaled a turning point in Saladin's fortunes. Now he was on the defensive. With his resources strained beyond a tolerable level and after a number of military setbacks at the hands of Richard the Lionheart, Saladin was ready to sign a three-year, eight-month truce on September 2, 1192. That truce guaranteed the continued life of a truncated but resurrected crusader kingdom. Jerusalem remained in Islamic hands, but the kingdom reestablished itself at Acre, where it remained for another century. Shortly after concluding the truce, Saladin died on March 4, 1193. Although he had failed to drive the crusaders into the sea, his successes and reputation for bold leadership and generosity of spirit ensured his admiration within the Islamic World, respect by his crusader enemies, and an honored place in history. **Related Entries:** Al-Adil; Assassins; Ayyubids; Chivalry; Conrad of Montferrat; Massacres; Pillage and Plunder.

Suggested Reading

Primary Source

Baha al-Din Yusuf ibn Rafi Ibn Shaddad, *The Rare and Excellent History of Saladin,* trans. by D. S. Richards (2002).

Historical Studies

H. A. R. Gibb, *The Life of Saladin from the Works of Imad ad-Din and Baha ad-Din* (1973); Yaacov Lev, *Saladin in Egypt* (1999); Michael C. Lyons and D. E. P. Jackson, *Saladin: The Politics of the Holy War* (1982); Robert L. Nicholson, *Joscelyn III and the Fall of the Crusader States, 1134–1199* (1973); Geoffrey Regan, *Saladin and the Fall of Jerusalem* (1987).

Santiago, Order of

See Military Orders of Iberia.

Santiago de Compostela

The shrine of Saint James the Greater in the far northwestern corner of the Iberian Peninsula, which became a center of **pilgrimage** and an inspiration to Christian forces involved in the **Reconquista.**

Saint James the Greater is listed in the Gospels as one of Jesus' twelve apostles, or closest followers. Along with his brother John, and Peter, James was part of a three-man inner circle of Jesus' confidants. According to the *Acts of the Apostles,* a New Testament history of the early Church, James was beheaded by order of King Herod Agrippa I in **Jerusalem** sometime between 41 and 44. During the seventh and eighth centuries, the pious myth arose that James the Greater had introduced Christianity to Spain and then returned to Jerusalem, where he was martyred. Various Western church authorities added another layer to this story by popularizing the tradition that following his death James's body was carried back to

An ancient cross along the pilgrimage track known as the French Road, a major route from the Pyrenees to Compostela.

Spain. Around 810 Bishop Theodomir claimed discovery of the long-lost **relics** of Saint James (*Santiago* in Spanish) buried in the abandoned field of Compostela in the region of Galicia in northwestern Spain.

This putative discovery was quite significant for Galicia, a desolate and sparsely populated outpost of Christianity in a peninsula that was largely in **Islamic** hands. Tiny Compostela now rivaled Rome as one of only two places in the entire West to claim the body of an apostle, Rome having the bodies of Peter and Paul. The heavenly patronage of Santiago was also important for Alfonso II, king of Asturias and Galicia, who needed all the help he could find holding his small, fragile kingdom together and carrying on his program of waging a series of vigorous defensive battles and offensive campaigns against the **Moors** to his south.

As the Reconquista heated up, the cult of Santiago became quite important. Despite its isolation and the difficulty of trekking to it, Compostela became one of the West's most popular sites of pilgrimage, and Santiago was transformed into a **warrior saint,** *Santiago Matamoros* (Saint James the Moor-Slayer), who, it was claimed, could be seen in the heavens at crucial moments in battle sitting astride a white horse, carrying a flowing banner and drawn sword, and leading Christian armies to victory over **Muslim** enemies. Tradition records that this transformed saint first appeared in 844 at the Battle of Clavijo, where he killed thousands of the enemy, but most significantly he was credited with the Christian success at the decisive **Battle of Las Navas de Tolosa** of 1212.

Despite this bellicose aspect of his personality, a quality that was largely unknown and uncelebrated outside of Spain, Santiago also retained the unwarlike dress and demeanor of the peaceful pilgrim. Medieval representations of *Santiago Peregrino* abound showing the saint wearing a short pilgrim's cloak and broad-brimmed hat, carrying his pilgrim's water gourd and staff, and displaying somewhere on his person the scallop shell emblem of the pilgrim to Santiago. Arguably, this dual personality of Saint James of Compostela reflects the inherent contradictions within the crusades. **Related Entries:** Cid, El; Holy War; Military Orders of Iberia.

Suggested Reading

Primary Sources

The Miracles of Saint James: Translations from the "Liber Sancti Jacobi," trans. by Thomas F. Coffey, Linda Kay Davidson, and Maryjane Dunn (1996); *The Pilgrim's Guide to Santiago,* trans. by William Melczer (1993).

Historical Studies

Richard A. Fletcher, *Saint James's Catapult: The Life and Times of Diego Gelmirez of Santiago de Compostela* (1984); Vera and Hellmut Hell, *The Great Pilgrimage of the Middle Ages: The Road to St. James of Compostela* (1964); Thomas Kendrick, *St. James in Spain* (1960); Annie Shaver-Crandell and Paula Gerson, *The Pilgrim's Guide to Santiago de Compostela: A Gazeteer with 580 Illustrations* (1995).

Saphadin

See Al-Adil.

Saracens

A **Latin** term used by the Romans originally to denote a specific people of Arabia; later it came to mean all Arabs. As far as the medieval West was concerned, the word was often used as a synonym for all **Muslims,** regardless of ethnic identity. **Related Entries:** Islamic Peoples; Moors.

Suggested Reading

John V. Tolan, *Saracens: Islam in the Medieval European Imagination* (2002).

Second Crusade (1147–1149)

A crusade fought in three theaters of operation, the **Eastern Mediterranean, Iberia,** and the **Baltic,** it is most noted for the involvement of **Bernard of Clairvaux,** who **preached** it, and for the participation of King **Louis VII** of France and Emperor **Conrad III** of Germany, who campaigned in the East with disastrous results.

The Second Crusade achieved gains in Iberia, but its failure on the **Syrian** front caught most of the attention of Western Europe. The Baltic expedition was also a fiasco, despite its apparent conversion of the pagan enemy. Its true significance is that it set a precedent for centuries of crusading against the pagans on Europe's northeastern frontier.

Prelude and Preparation

Zangi's capture of **Edessa** on December 26, 1144, impelled Pope **Eugenius III** to dispatch a letter on December 1, 1145, to the king and nobles of France, in which he called for a new crusade and enumerated the **privileges** to be accorded each **pilgrim**-warrior. Although King Louis VII had decided to take the **crusader's cross** even before receiving the pope's letter, most of his barons and advisors were less than enthusiastic. On March 1, 1146, the pope reissued the letter as a **bull** to all the French and authorized Bernard of Clairvaux to preach the cross. It was a brilliant move; Bernard's oratory and charisma guaranteed a flood of recruits.

Bernard preached his initial crusade sermon at Vézelay in Burgundy on March 31, with the king by his side wearing a cross sent him by the pope. The response was so overwhelming that Bernard ran out of cloth crosses and had to tear up bits of his own clothing to satisfy the demand. Following this triumph, he continued to promote the crusade in letters intended for wide circulation and sermons.

In November Bernard preached the crusade in Frankfurt, Germany, at the court of Emperor Conrad III, but without success. The emperor was pious, yet he had several good reasons to remain in Europe. Pope Eugenius wanted Conrad's help in regaining Rome, from which he had been driven by a popular uprising, and Conrad had his problems in Germany, which was only beginning to recover from a civil war. Independent of Emperor Conrad, however, enthusiasm for the crusade was already sweeping imperial lands in Germany and Italy, and Bernard was not one to ignore what he believed to be a divine sign. At Christmastime he tried again,

and this time he succeeded in convincing Conrad to take the cross. In fact, German support for the crusade was so widespread that Conrad's chief opponent, Duke Welf VI of Bavaria, was forced to rally to the emperor's side and join forces with him.

Even as the two most powerful monarchs of Europe, Louis and Conrad, were preparing to lead large, fairly well-organized armies to the East, the scope of the crusade was widening. Sometime after Bernard's triumph at Vézelay, King Alfonso VII of Castile requested that the pope extend the **crusade indulgence** to those fighting the **Moors** in Spain, and the pope complied. The pope went so far as to permit forces from Genoa, Pisa, and southern France to join in the Spanish crusade. In March 1147 a group of crusaders from Saxony in northern Germany approached Bernard in Frankfurt, as final plans were being set for the imminent departure to the **Holy Land** of Emperor Conrad's army, and informed him they preferred to fight their crusade against the pagan Wends, a Slavic people to their east. This was a radical departure from crusade policies up to that time, but Bernard agreed with their proposal. On April 13 the pope issued the bull *Divini dispensatione* (*By divine dispensation*), which placed the Wendish Crusade on a par with the **Jerusalem** and Spanish Crusades.

The Eastern Theater

Following the precedent of the **First Crusade,** Louis and Conrad agreed to march their armies separately overland and meet in **Constantinople.** Also like the armies of the First Crusade, both armies contained large numbers of **noncombatants,** including King Louis's wife, **Eleanor of Aquitaine,** and her court ladies.

Conrad's huge, heterogeneous army, which mirrored the multiethnic composition of the Western empire, set off in mid-May

1147 and passed through Hungary peace- fully. Discipline began to break down when it entered **Byzantine** territory in the Balkans, and an ugly conflict broke out in the city of **Adrianople,** but soon hurt feel- ings were soothed. By early September the imperial army was encamped outside Con- stantinople. After waiting for Louis's army for several weeks, Conrad decided to press on and cross the Bosporus to **Anatolia** in late September.

Meanwhile, in June the French army, which also contained Italians and other non- French crusaders, departed as a body from Metz in eastern France. It passed through Hungary peacefully and avoided conflicts with the Byzantines on its way to Constan- tinople, which the main body reached on October 4. While encamped outside the city, the army was regaled by the rhetoric of Bishop Godfrey of Langres, who urged the crusaders to attack and capture the Byzan- tine capital city before proceeding against the **Turks.** The majority of the crusaders refused to listen to this advice to sidetrack the expedition, and the small anti-Byzantine faction of hotheads that Bishop Godfrey rep- resented lost the argument.

After waiting two weeks at Constantino- ple and upon hearing rumors of a great vic- tory by Conrad's imperial army, the French army became restless and crossed into Ana- tolia, despite the fact that some forces sailing from southern Italy had not yet arrived. The rumors of an imperial victory that impelled the French forward were totally wrong. Con- rad's main force had been ambushed and cut to pieces near **Dorylaeum,** the site of a major crusader victory in 1097. A secondary impe- rial contingent, composed largely of non- combatant pilgrims and under the command of Bishop Otto of Freising, had earlier split off from the emperor's troops, was making its painful way south, and incurring heavy losses as it marched toward the sea and ships that would transport it to the Holy Land.

The retreat back to Nicaea by Conrad's shattered force became a rout, and it was a dispirited mass of crusaders who straggled into the city in early November. Most of the survivors decided to return home, and Con- rad was left with a shadow of his once-great army when he sent messengers to Louis beg- ging for help.

Conrad and his battered remnant finally linked up with Louis, and the combined forces reached Ephesus near the coast in mid-December 1147, where Conrad took sick and was forced to sail back to Constan- tinople to recuperate. Louis, leading what remained of the imperial crusade army, as well as his own army, continued stubbornly on his way, despite warnings that large Turk- ish forces awaited them on the road ahead and despite the miserable winter weather that now enveloped the region.

While traversing a mountain pass, Louis's army became divided, and the ever- watchful Turks struck. Although the king prevented a **massacre** by his quick and courageous action, his force suffered exten- sive casualties and lost a fair amount of its supplies. For the next twelve days the ill- provisioned army fought off harassing Turkish attacks as it marched to the sea over land that their enemies had systematically stripped of all food. Finally, the crusaders reached the port of Adalia on January 20, 1148.

Too few ships were available to transport more than a fraction of the survivors to **Anti- och.** Louis was forced to take his best remaining soldiers, which he understood to be largely his **knights,** and to leave behind most noncombatants and foot soldiers, after providing for them as best he could. Most of those left behind soon died in battle or of **disease** or were captured and **enslaved.** Very few of them managed to continue their way to the **crusader states.**

Because Louis's army had passed largely through Byzantine-held territory ever since it crossed the Bosporus and had received precious little in the way of support from the **Greeks,** what had once been the minority opinion of the bishop of Langres was now becoming the generally accepted notion of the French survivors: The Byzantines were false Christians and in league with the Turks. Indeed, it is possible they were correct. Emperor **Manuel I Comnenus** might well have conspired to destroy the French out of fear of them. Whatever the case, when veterans of the march across Anatolia returned home, they brought back with them tales and attitudes that helped to poison **Latin** Christian minds regarding their Byzantine coreligionists.

Louis's army, now ten percent or less of its initial strength, reached Antioch on March 19, where he was warmly received by his wife's uncle, Raymond of Poitiers, prince of Antioch. Soon, however, their relations soured when Raymond learned that Louis had no intention of campaigning with him in the north. Louis was determined to press on to Jerusalem, which the German survivors of Bishop Otto of Freising's detachment had reached on April 4 and a recovered Emperor Conrad a few weeks later.

Since arriving in the Holy Land, Conrad had been mustering troops as best he could, enlisting crusaders as they sailed in from the West and hiring **mercenaries.** It was at this time that his attention was turned by King **Baldwin III** and his barons away from Edessa and toward a campaign against **Damascus,** which, although an ally of the **kingdom of Jerusalem** since 1139, was a tempting target. It was only a matter of time before **Nur ad-Din** would occupy it and unite Muslim Syria against the kingdom.

Additionally, if King Baldwin could capture the city, the resultant prestige might enable him to declare his total independence from his mother, Queen **Melisende.**

After King Louis arrived in Jerusalem and performed his pilgrimage devotions, he traveled to Palmarea near **Acre,** where the three kings and Queen Melisende, along with the great lords and leading churchmen of the crusade and of the kingdom, held a meeting of the **High Court** on June 24. The decision, after some debate, was to march against Damascus.

In mid-July a large army assembled at Tiberias under the joint command of the three kings. As the crusaders advanced on the city, the Damascenes sent calls to Nur ad-Din for help. Already the crusaders' strategy was proving counterproductive. The **siege** of the city began on July 24 and ended in failure three days later, thanks to the crusaders' having put themselves in an untenable position in their rush to take the city before Nur ad-Din arrived. An inglorious retreat from Damascus was their only option.

Conrad III left the Holy Land in frustration on September 8; King Louis remained until Easter 1149 but accomplished nothing by his extended stay.

Postscript

Tremendous anger and charges of treason greeted the news in the West over word of the French and imperial fiasco in the East. Bernard of Clairvaux came in for a good deal of recrimination, as did the Greeks. Indeed, several voices in the West openly advocated a new crusade, one aimed not against the Muslims but against the Byzantine empire. Cooler voices prevailed, however. Also cooled was the West's ardor for another crusade. It would be another four decades before Christian Europe roused itself to launch a major crusade effort in the **Levant.**

The only winner in the Eastern theater of the war was Nur ad-Din. In 1154 Damascus opened its gates to him, and Muslim Syria was now united against the crusader states.

The Iberian Theater

The first theater of operations to witness activity was Iberia. On June 16, 1147, a party of seafaring crusaders from the Low Countries, England, Scotland, Normandy, and the Rhineland arrived by ship at Oporto in Portugal on their way to the East. News of their arrival led King Afonso I of Portugal to conclude that with their help he could successfully besiege Lisbon, which lay far to the south. Convinced that this war was included in their **crusade vow,** the crusaders agreed to assist, as long as they were allowed the right of **plunder** once the city fell. The siege began on July 1, and the city fell on October 24. The crusaders got their booty, and Afonso added the city to his realm. Although some of the surviving crusaders decided to settle down in the area, most continued their voyage to the Holy Land in February 1148. Along the way they captured Faro, along Iberia's southwestern Atlantic coast.

A week before Lisbon fell, across the peninsula along Spain's southeastern Mediterranean coast, the city of Almeira fell to King Alfonso VII of Castile on October 17, 1147, in a campaign in which he received naval support from Genoa, Pisa, Aragon, and the ports of **Languedoc,** as well as land forces from Aragon and France. Between July and December 1148, these same forces, aided by a few of the sailors from northeast Europe who had assisted in the capture of Lisbon, besieged and finally took Tortosa, another key Mediterranean port. Late in 1149 the crusaders consolidated their victory in eastern Spain by capturing Fraga and Lerida, the last two Moorish strongholds in Catalonia.

By any standard of evaluation, the separate campaigns along the Atlantic and Mediterranean coasts had been resoundingly successful.

The Baltic Theater

The crusade against the Wends was as ill planned and poorly executed as the crusade of Louis and Conrad, but it eked out a face-saving, nominal victory. As authorized, the crusade had a **missionary** component to it. Despite its dubious theology, the ostensible aim was to force the pagan Slavs of the Baltic into the bosom of the Church. In the end, the Wends agreed to a peace treaty whereby they renounced their idolatry and accepted Christian baptism.

The Baltic Crusade began in a typically confused manner when the Wendish prince, Niklot, a former ally of the Saxon crusader Count Adolf II of Holstein, launched a preemptive strike against the frontier port city of Lübeck on June 26, 1147, three days before the planned start of the crusade. The crusaders, about 40,000 strong, finally got under way in July, anxious to punish Niklot.

Assisted by a large Danish fleet and land force, the main body of crusaders, which consisted of two large Saxon armies (with some Polish allies), besieged the Wendish stronghold of Dobin. The Danes were there to avenge previous sea raids that the Wends had made upon their land, but instead of teaching the Wends a lesson, they learned one. In a surprise attack, the Wends and their allies mauled the Danes and sent them scurrying back home.

Finally the Saxons, who had no desire to devastate a land and a people that they thought of as their own, made peace with Niklot. Danish prisoners were repatriated, Niklot was once again to become an ally of Count Adolf, and the Wends were to receive baptism. This last provision was a dead letter. Pagan idols, sanctuaries, and practices remained an integral part of Wendish culture for quite a while beyond 1147. Not a square foot of territory had been added to Christendom.

In an interesting sideshow, a third Saxon army, totaling maybe 80,000, marched east beyond Dobin, laying the land waste as it advanced. A portion of the army besieged Demmin in August 1147, discovered it could not take the stronghold, and returned home emptyhanded. The other part of the army went even farther east to Stettin. As the army began siege operations, it was surprised to see crosses appear on the walls. Oops! Stettin was a Christian outpost deep in pagan territory. The crusaders grumbled and went back home—as emptyhanded as their colleagues. The first act in the centuries-long Baltic Crusade had ended more like a comic opera than like a tragic holy war. **Related Entries:** Calixtus II, Pope; Capetians; Criticism of the Crusades; Historians and Chroniclers, Latin; Hohenstaufens; Jews and the Crusades; Missionaries.

Suggested Reading

Primary Sources

The Chronicle of the Slavs, trans. by Joseph Tschan (1935); De expugnatione Lyxbonensi (The Capture of Lisbon), trans. by Charles W. David and others (1936; reissued 2000); Odo of Deuil, De profectione Ludovici VII in orientem (Louis VII's Expedition to the East), trans. by Virginia G. Berry (1948).

Historical Studies

Michael Gervers, ed., The Second Crusade and the Cistercians (1992); Jonathan Phillips and Martin Hoch, eds., The Second Crusade: Scope and Consequences (2001).

Seljuks (Selchüks, Seljukids, Selchükids)

Turkish Muslims who dominated much of the **Middle East** in the last half of the eleventh and first half of the twelfth century, representing to the West an immediate threat to Christendom.

In 1055 Tughrul Beg, head of the Seljuk family of Oghuz Turks, a pastoral people whose origins lay in the steppes of Central Asia, entered Baghdad, where the **Abbasid** caliph bestowed on him the title *sultan* (holder of power). The Seljuks, recent converts to the **Sunni** branch of **Islam,** were officially recognized as the defenders of an otherwise impotent caliphate. Unofficially, they were its masters.

Under Tughrul Beg and his immediate successors, Alp Arslan (r. 1063–1072) and Malik-Shah (r. 1072–1092), the Seljuks created the Great Seljuk sultanate, an empire that encompassed Iran and Iraq and stretched into **Syria-Palestine,** where it confronted in a protracted struggle the **Fatimid** caliphate of Egypt. Because the Fatimids were **Shias,** conquering them was an obsession for the Great Seljuks.

Meanwhile, as independent bands of Turkish invaders and settlers moved into **Anatolia** in the wake of the **Battle of Manzikert,** a kinsman and enemy of Sultan Malik-Shah by the name of Suleiman gained ascendancy over many of the scattered groups and consolidated them. Around 1077 he established a rival Seljuk power, the sultanate of Rum, with its capital at Nicaea (modern Iznik) in the far northwest corner of the peninsula, not far from **Constantinople.** By styling his sultanate *Rum,* which is Turkish for "Rome," Suleiman proclaimed himself the conqueror of the lands of the Roman (**Byzantine**) empire. When **Emperor Alexius I** recovered Nicaea and the coastlands of western Anatolia in 1097, Suleiman's son and successor, Sultan **Kilij Arslan I,** transferred the capital of the sultanate of Rum to Iconium (modern Konya) deep in the interior of Anatolia.

Pressure on Constantinople by the Seljuks of Rum and incursions into the **Holy**

A twelfth-century Seljuk *caravanserai* (place of refuge for caravans). Protection of Anatolia's vital caravan routes was a Seljuk priority.

Land by other Turks who were at least nominally subservient to the Great Seljuk (**Jerusalem** was in Seljuk hands from 1071 to 1098) combined to create an image in the West of the Turk as the new enemy of Christendom who had to be stopped and rolled back. Such was the message of Pope **Urban II** at **Clermont.**

Despite crusader military victories over the Seljuks of Rum, such as at the **Battle of Dorylaeum,** by the end of the reign of Sultan Masud I (r. 1116–1155) the Seljuk sultanate of Rum was the dominant power in Anatolia. Its rival, the Great Seljuk sultanate, had broken up into a number of small, competing successor states ruled by *atabegs* (regents), such as **Zangi,** by the mid–twelfth century.

In the mid–thirteenth century the sultanate of Rum became a **Mongol** protectorate until it faded out of history around 1308 and its lands passed under the direct rule of Mongol lords. With the collapse of Mongol power in Persia shortly after 1335, the way was open for a new Turkish people, the **Ottomans,** to become the dominant force in Anatolia. **Related Entries:** Assassins; Field of Blood, Battle of the; First Crusade; Islamic Peoples; Kerbogha; Nur ad-Din Mahmud; Zangids.

Suggested Reading

Claude Cahen, *Pre-Ottoman Turkey* (1968); Taef Kamel El-Azhari, *The Saljuqs of Syria: During the Crusades, 463–549 A.H./1070–1154 A.D.* (1997).

Sergeant

The Old French term *sergen* derived from the Late **Latin** word for "servant" (*serviens*) and was used to designate a common soldier, as opposed to a noble **knight** who owed military service to some lord because of **feudal** obligations. Although not a **knight,** the sergeant was often a professional or semi-professional soldier.

Sergeants fought on both foot and horse, and the mounted sergeant was more highly valued than his counterpart on foot but was deemed of lesser worth than the knight. When computing knight-service owed to a lord or king, two mounted sergeants usually were considered equal to one knight. At the division of booty following the capture of **Constantinople** by the army of the **Fourth Crusade,** each knight was awarded twenty marks' worth of **plunder,** each mounted sergeant received ten marks' worth, and each foot soldier only five.

The **military orders** also distinguished between their brother knights, who had to be high born, and their warrior brothers of humble origin who served as mounted sergeants. The **Knights of the Temple** even prescribed different battle dress for their sergeants, who wore black surcoats over their **armor,** while Templar knights wore white.

Whether a member of a military order or not, mounted sergeants tended to have lighter and far less expensive armor and equipment than the knights. Sergeants on foot were even less well equipped.

Notwithstanding social distinctions and equipment disadvantages, sergeants were the backbone of every crusader army. The laws of the **kingdom of Jerusalem** mandated not only the number of knights owed the king's army by his tenants-in-chief and lesser **vassals** but also the far larger number of sergeants owed by the kingdom's cities and religious communities. John of Ibelin, writing in 1265 but basing his information on excellent sources, calculated that a total of 5,025 sergeants were owed for emergency service in the king of Jerusalem's army in the period preceding the disasters of 1187. John

also counted but 675 knights due the same army by virtue of feudal tenure. **Related Entries:** Cavalry; Infantry; Mercenary; Weapons, Hand; Siege Warfare.

Suggested Reading

Peter W. Edbury, *John of Ibelin and the Kingdom of Jerusalem* (1997).

Settlement and Colonization

Frankish settlements in the **Levant** were influenced by the conditions that the settlers discovered there. This meant that although the Franks brought with them ways of life that differed from those of the East and wished to retain their cultural identity, the colonial society that they created in **Syria-Palestine** was not an exact replica of what they knew back home. In a real sense, they created a Franco-Levantine culture that retained its essential Western European and **Latin** Christian features but adopted many Levantine ways of life and evolved by responding to forces that were unique to the region.

Another important aspect of this colonial experience was that these Frankish colonies differed substantially from those of antiquity and modern times, inasmuch as not a single one was carved out by a faraway state that desired to extend its influence far beyond its frontiers. Consequently, no Latin colony of Syria-Palestine had any direct political links to an overseas mother country. This, in turn, meant that these Western settler-colonists were largely on their own, despite occasional gifts from the West to finance certain military operations and to rebuild defenses and despite the influx of **pilgrims,** crusaders, and new settlers from Europe. At the same time, although dependent on their own resources, these settlers were not immune to general developments that were taking place within Western

The Church of St. Anne, constructed in Jerusalem on the site believed to have been the childhood home of the Virgin Mary and her parents, Anne and Joachim. It served as the center of worship for a convent of Latin nuns. Completed in the 1140s, it is the most striking extant example of crusader Romanesque architecture. Saladin transformed the church into a *madrasa* (koranic school) in 1192 and put the *qadi* (Islamic jurist) and historian Baha ad-Din Ibn Shaddad in charge. In the nineteenth century the Ottomans handed the building over to the French in gratitude for support in the Crimean War.

Europe, such as the growing tendency in the thirteenth century for Western monarchs to concern themselves more with affairs of state and less with the liberation of **Jerusalem.**

Far removed from but still connected to Western Europe in some important ways, Frankish settlers in the **crusader states** created a frontier society with all of the distinctiveness that the term implies. What is more, many of the settlers, probably a majority by the early twelfth century, were not crusaders who decided to stay on once they had fulfilled their **vows.** Rather, they were immigrants, largely from Mediterranean France and Italy, who sought out the Levant as a place of new economic and social opportunity.

Those opportunities became less attractive and real, however, toward the end of the twelfth century when **Muslim** countercrusades began rolling back the Frankish frontier. As a result, both the number of new immigrants and of native-born Latin colonists declined steeply and remained in decline for the remainder of the life span of the crusader states.

Historical population estimates are difficult to arrive at and questionable at best. That noted, it still seems reasonable to conclude that around the year 1187, just before the disaster of the **Battle of Hattin,** the crusader states had reached the high point of Latin settlement. Anywhere from about 100,000 to as many as 120,000 Franks lived in the **kingdom of Jerusalem**, and about the same number or fewer inhabited the combined northern states of **Antioch** and **Tripoli.**

Many of the immigrants, especially the Italians, settled in urban centers, particularly coastal cities and towns; many other immigrants, especially the southern French, settled in rural villages. Whereas Italians tended to be merchants, many of the other settlers were artisans. Among the artisans, a higher than normal percentage practiced such critical crafts as blacksmithing, carpentry, and masonry. Because their skills were so highly valued for building and maintaining a vital infrastructure, as a group they earned far higher wages and fared far better in the East than they could at home. A significant number of free peasants also migrated to the **Holy Land,** where they farmed and also practiced such specialized agrarian skills as pig farming and vine cultivation—two occupations usually not practiced by Muslims because of dietary restrictions. Some even learned and practiced new agricultural occupations, such as camel breeding and goat herding. As was true of artisans from the West, peasant colonists probably saw their standards of living rise as a consequence of their eastward migration, provided they survived the land's endemic **diseases** and wars. As was later true in the American Wild West, the crusader Wild East attracted more than its share of miscreants, grifters, misfits, and outlaws.

Whether warrior, artisan, farmer, or ne'er-do-well adventurer, the Western colonist found him- or herself surrounded by a non-Latin majority of subject peoples. At the height of their numbers around 1187, fewer than a quarter-million European newcomers and native-born Frankish colonists controlled over a million Muslim and **Eastern Christian** subjects, with a scattering of **Jewish** inhabitants here and there. An esti-mate of Muslim and Eastern Christian urban dwellers in the kingdom of Jerusalem places their numbers at between 300,000 and 360,000, with an additional 250,000 living in the countryside. It seems reasonable to assume that the combined states of Antioch and Tripoli had similar total figures of non-Latin subjects.

Whereas Antioch's non-Western population was predominantly Christian—Jacobite and **Byzantine Greek** being the dominant religious cultures—it is impossible to say which religion, Islam or Christianity, was practiced by the majority of Tripoli's and the kingdom of Jerusalem's subject populations. They probably were about evenly divided, each with its enclaves where it was the majority culture. The county of **Edessa,** which was a crusader state for a fairly short period of time, 1097–1150, and was never widely settled by colonists from the West, was predominantly **Armenian** Christian.

Once the Franks settled the lands they captured, their subject populations, whose view of life was formed by many centuries of rule by various conquerors, remained fairly docile, except on occasion when invading Muslim forces appeared as their liberators. Docility, however, did not mean they were happy.

Life and circumstances for the non-Latin natives of the crusader lands of the Levant differed from place to place and time to time, but certain general patterns emerged.

The Western settlers tended to displace high-ranking Eastern Christian religious leaders, such as the Byzantine patriarch of Antioch, and replace them with Latin churchmen. They also converted many mosques and Islamic shrines into Latin Christian churches and took over control of certain Eastern Christian churches. Thus, Jerusalem's Dome of the Rock became the Christian church of the Temple of the Lord, and the Byzantine **Church of the Holy Sepulcher** was taken over in 1099, rebuilt, and rededicated as a Latin church.

Notwithstanding this policy of converting physical places of worship, by and large the Latin settlers did not attempt to forcibly convert their subjects to the faith and practices of the Roman Church. Rather, they allowed both their Christian and Islamic subjects to worship as they wished and even allowed Muslims to retain some mosques and to pray at shrines that were sacred not only to Muslims but to Christians or Christians and Jews, as well. The Tomb of the Patriarchs at Hebron, for example, welcomed Christian, Jewish, and Muslim worshippers alike. Although force was rarely used to convert Muslims to Christianity, the Roman Church did dispatch **missionaries,** especially mendicant friars, to the crusader states, and they were mildly successful in converting members of the lower strata of Islamic society during the latter half of the thirteenth century.

This toleration, whereby each ethnic and religious group was allowed to retain its customs and laws, was necessitated by the reality of sheer numbers. It certainly was not motivated by any notion of cultural relativity. Frankish settlers treated Eastern Christians as inferior to Latin Christians and treated Muslims as inferior to Eastern Christians. In 1120 a church **council** at Nablus decreed that all Muslims were forbidden to dress like Franks, presumably to discourage intimacy between members of these two separate and unequal cultures. The same rule of separate garments governed *dhimmis,* or tolerated non-Muslims, in Islamic lands.

Even though evidence is scanty and ambiguous, it seems reasonable to infer that the subject populations of cities and towns tended to feel more heavily the impact of crusader colonization, whereas inhabitants of rural areas experienced far less disruption in their traditional ways.

In fact, the average Muslim villager probably found his Frankish lord less oppressive than the Muslim lords who had preceded him. A Spanish Muslim traveler, Ibn Jubair, on his way home from pilgrimage to Mecca, crossed from **Damascus** to **Acre** in 1184, a journey that allowed him to spend thirty-two days in crusader territory. In his journal, which contains a number of insightful and unflattering observations of the Franks, he has this to say about coreligionists through whose lands he passed:

A road went through contiguous farms, all inhabited by Muslims who live in great prosperity under the Franks (God preserve us from temptation!). Their obligations are payment of half the crop . . . and payment of a poll-tax. . . . The Christians do not demand anything more, except for a light tax on fruit. But the Muslims are masters of their habitations and rule themselves as they see fit. . . . The Muslims are chagrined seeing the state of their coreligionists in the provinces ruled by Muslims, as their situation is precisely the opposite of security and happiness.

Although this is hearsay testimony based on a quick journey through the land, other evidence supports his observation. In the kingdom of Jerusalem, for example, the Muslim population of the countryside was largely governed in matters touching religion and custom by their *qadis,* or Islamic jurists, who settled matters of religious law, and by councils of elders. When the local Frankish lord had not appointed a steward to oversee a village in his name and to collect its taxes, the *rais,* or patriarchal head of the council of elders, would serve in this capacity. This high level of Muslim rural autonomy probably owed much to the fact that Frankish agricultural colonists tended to avoid settling in regions whose populations were wholly or largely Muslim, restricting their settlements to areas where local Christians dominated.

Of course, not every indigenous custom and institution was scrupulously preserved by the Franks and not every Latin lord ruled the local populace benignly. Nevertheless, as a general rule, life in the villages went on very much as it already had for thousands of years, despite the fact that new masters had taken over. **Related Entries:** Jerusalem, Latin Patriarchate of; *Poulains;* Slavery; William of Tyre.

Suggested Reading

Aharon Ben-Ami, *Social Change in a Hostile Environment: The Crusaders' Kingdom of Jerusalem* (1969); Philippe Aziz, S. Van Vliet White, and L. Van Vliet White, *The Palestine of the Crusaders* (1979); Meron Benvenisti, *The Crusaders in the Holy Land* (1972); Adrian J. Boas, *Crusader Archeology: The Material Culture of the Latin East* (1999); T. S. R. Boase, *Castles and Churches of the Crusading Kingdom* (1967); Ronnie Ellenblum, *Frankish Rural Settlement in the Latin Kingdom of Jerusalem* (1998); James M. Powell, ed., *Muslims under Latin Rule* (1990); Joshua Prawer, *The History of the Jews in the Latin Kingdom of Jerusalem* (1988), *The Latin Kingdom of Jerusalem: European Colonialism in the Middle Ages* (1972), and *The World of the Crusaders* (1972); Denys Pringle, *Fortification and Settlement in Crusader Palestine* (2000) and *The Churches of the Crusader Kingdom of Jerusalem: A Corpus,* 2 vols. (1993 and 1998; a third volume is forthcoming); R. C. Smail, *The Crusaders in Syria and the Holy Land* (1974).

Seventh Crusade (1248–1254)

Conducted by King **Louis IX** of France, the crusade is best understood if divided into three parts: (1) the preparatory stages, 1244–1249; (2) the Egyptian campaign, 1249–1250; and (3) the years spent in support of the **kingdom of Jerusalem,** 1250–1254.

Stage One

King Louis swore the **crusader's vow** in December 1244, but did not embark for **Outremer** until almost four years later. The intervening period was spent in preparation, including receiving authorization from Pope **Innocent IV,** whose First Council of Lyons of 1245 commissioned all clerics in Western Christendom to **preach** a crusade and imposed a three-year tax of a twentieth on all clerical income to help **finance** the expedition. The resulting crusade was the last major **holy war** launched by a medieval pope against **Islam.**

The bitter experience of the first three major crusades showed that the long, perilous trek across **Anatolia** to reach **Syria-Palestine** was to be avoided at all cost. As was the case for all crusades since 1197, Louis's army would travel by sea, and the fleet would sail from Aigues-Mortes, a port town that Louis had begun constructing in the 1240s on newly acquired royal land on the Mediterranean coast.

As Louis's agents began to arrange for the acquisition and provisioning of vessels, it became clear that the income at the king's disposal, from which he had to support the normal activities of the royal court, was not sufficient. His average annual income was around 250,000 *livres* (a *livre* was about two ounces of silver); the crusade would ultimately cost him about 1,537,570 *livres,* according to fourteenth-century royal treasury estimates. To finance the crusade he turned mainly to extorting "loans" from the towns of northern France and taxing clerical incomes. About 950,000 *livres* were raised as a result of the clerical tax, and municipal grants accounted for about another 274,000 *livres.*

Frankish warriors at the time of the Seventh Crusade. Stained-glass window of Louis IX's royal chapel of Sainte Chapelle in Paris, constructed between 1239 and 1248 to house his collection of the relics of the Passion (suffering) of Jesus.

On August 25, 1248, accompanied by Queen **Margaret,** Louis set sail for **Cyprus,** where the royal party converged with an army that ultimately numbered around 25,000, including between 2,500 and 2,800 **knights.** Although largely recruited from northern France, the force included small contingents from Italy, Scotland, and England. Cyprus was key to a successful campaign, serving as a site of rendezvous, a depot for supplies and war materials already dispatched there, and a supplier of fresh food. It was, in other words, the crusade's forward base and, once the army was in **Muslim** territory, its rear echelon.

Because the army could not afford to be cut off from Cyprus by foul winter weather, the crusaders planned to delay departure until February 1249, but unforeseen circumstances forced a May departure. Louis's leadership of the Seventh Crusade was characterized by meticulous planning and careful, deliberate actions, but too much deliberation possibly cost him victory in Egypt. The longer-than-anticipated sojourn on Cyprus had cost the army dearly; at least ten percent of the army died there of **disease.** Further delays in Egypt would be even more costly.

Stage Two

The fleet finally got under way on May 30 and landed troops on June 5 in an assault aimed at **Damietta.** The inhabitants of the city, mindful of the bitter year-and-a-half **siege** thirty years earlier during the **Fifth Crusade,** panicked and fled. At the cost of very few casualties, Louis marched triumphantly into the city on the morning of June 6. Rather than pursuing and destroying the retreating Egyptian army and heading straight for **Cairo,** Louis settled down to await reinforcements, especially those led by his brother, Alphonse of Poitiers, who belatedly arrived on October 24.

With these reinforcements, Louis set off on November 20 for Cairo. While his army marched south along the Nile's right bank, ships bearing supplies and siege weapons covered his left flank. Progress was slow, as the army continually had to stop to fill in intersecting canals. Moreover, the Egyptian army harried them. On December 19 the crusaders reached the fortress of al-Mansurah, close to where the army of the Fifth Crusade had been cut off and defeated twenty-eight years earlier. Al-Mansurah was protected by an arm of the river that separated it from the crusaders. The Egyptian army was also encamped across that body of water, directly in front of the fortress, and an Egyptian fleet barred the further passage of the crusaders' vessels.

For over a month there was a stalemate, as the two armies skirmished and exchanged constant barrages of missile fire without either side gaining an advantage. Casualties mounted. On February 8, in an effort at a breakthrough, a detachment led by the king's brother, Robert of Artois, forced a crossing at a ford downstream, overran an Egyptian camp, and **massacred** everyone within reach. It made its way all the way into the fortress, where Muslim defenders cut down the attackers, including Count Robert and 280 knights. The main body of the crusade army marched toward the enemy camp that Robert's force had overrun only to discover that the enemy had regrouped. The Egyptian counterattack stopped all further advance. Although they were now across the river and had technically won the field, the crusaders were in a precarious position.

Mamluks, led by their commander **Baybars,** reengaged the crusaders on both banks on February 11 and began the process of systematically wearing the enemy down. Additionally, the Egyptian fleet gained full mastery of the Nile, blocking attempts to reprovision and reinforce the crusaders by water and to withdraw their sick and wounded by boat. Finding themselves in an impossible position, the crusaders began a strategic retreat on the night of April 5, hoping to regain the safety of Damietta.

Pursuit by the Egyptian army was relentless, and King Louis was deathly ill. On April 6 the king, too sick to travel, was captured along with his two surviving brothers and a number of close friends. The rest of the soldiers and accompanying boats continued their retreat until they arrived at Fariskur, where they were surrounded and crushed. The victorious Egyptians immediately massacred the sick and wounded and captured about 12,000 others. A significant number of these were also killed when they either proved too inconvenient to their captors or refused the offer to convert or die. Perhaps as many as 10,000 were not given that option and survived to be marched off to captivity in al-Mansurah. How many crusaders saved themselves by accepting **Islam** is unknown.

Two issues remained to be resolved: to negotiate the ransom and release of Louis and his army and to force the surrender of Damietta. Louis offered the city and 500,000 *livres* for the release of all prisoners. Sultan Turan Shah, whose treatment of the king swung between the extremes of threatening execution and torture and solicitous concern for Louis's physical and spiritual health, decided to be no less magnanimous and reduced the sum to 400,000 *livres.* The king understood that prisoners taken in earlier defeats, such as at **La Forbie,** would be included in the deal, bringing the total Christian **prisoners** to be released to about 12,000.

The agreement, which included a ten-year truce, was ratified on May 1; the next day mamluks led by Baybars assassinated Turan Shah, and on May 3 the agreement was reconfirmed by the new masters of Egypt. Queen Margaret and the French garrison evacuated Damietta, and the victors marched in and immediately broke their word by killing the sick who had been left behind in the city. On May 6 half the ransom was paid, and Louis and his chief barons were released and set sail for **Acre,** arriving there around May 13. Much to Louis's horror, the majority of the crusaders captured at Fariskur remained captives, awaiting payment of the balance of the ransom.

Stage Three

As far as King Louis was concerned, the crusade was not over until all captives were freed and the **Holy Land** was made secure from Muslim threats. Although many of his barons, including his brothers, Alphonse of Poitiers and **Charles of Anjou,** left for home in the weeks following their arrival at Acre, the king remained behind, asking that new crusaders be dispatched to join him in 1251.

The kingdom of Jerusalem was a checkerboard of competing principalities and **military orders** with no effective central authority. Its nominal monarch, Conrad of **Hohenstaufen,** was in Europe and not especially interested in Eastern affairs. When it came to prestige and resources, no individual in the **crusader states** could match King Louis. As a result, for almost four full years Louis functioned as the unofficial king of Jerusalem.

In 1252 Louis negotiated the release of all remaining Christian captives in Egypt, as well as the remains of those who had perished. The Mamluk sultan even waived payment of the remaining 200,000 *livres* as a gesture of good will because he wanted Louis's help in his struggles with the **Ayyubids** of **Damascus.** When Cairo made its peace with Damascus in 1253, the alliance with Louis was allowed to lapse, but Louis still had his diplomatic victory. In February 1254 Louis completed his diplomatic activities by concluding a two-year, six-month, forty-day truce with the Ayyubids of Syria.

In addition to diplomacy, Louis rebuilt the fortifications of Acre, Caesarea, **Jaffa,** and Sidon—four key coastal towns. The total cost, which he paid out of his own purse, came to over 100,000 *livres.*

When Louis departed for home on April 25, 1254, the kingdom of Jerusalem was far more stable than it had been for decades. **Related Entries:** Bull, Papal; Capetians; Councils and Synods; Eighth Crusade; Legates, Papal; Mongols.

Suggested Reading

Primary Sources

Janet Shirley, trans. *Crusader Syria in the Thirteenth Century: The "Rothelin" Continuation of the "History" of William of Tyre with part of the "Eracles" or "Acre" Text* (1999); John of Joinville, *The Life of Saint Louis,* trans. by M. R. B. Shaw (1967).

Historical Study

William C. Jordan, *Louis IX and the Challenge of the Crusade* (1979).

Shepherds' Crusade (Crusade of the Pastoureaux of 1251)

A popular movement that began in reaction to news of King **Louis IX**'s defeat in Egypt, the Shepherds' Crusade was an **apocalyptic** event, very much like the so-called **Children's Crusade** of 1212, that grew out of a deepening sense of frustration over the inability of the **Latin** West to liberate **Jerusalem** and crush **Islam.**

A shadowy figure named Jacob, who styled himself the Master of Hungary, appeared in Flanders in 1251, proclaiming that he carried a letter from the Blessed Virgin Mary. Its message was simple: The sinful pride of nobles and high churchmen doomed the crusades to failure, but just as simple shepherds had been worthy to be the first to view the Christ Child, so shepherds and other humble folk would lead the way in the redemption of Jerusalem. A ragtag army of largely young people, most of them herders and farmers, collected around Master Jacob and created its own military standard, a flag with a lamb bearing a banner on which was displayed a cross.

Church leaders certainly did not regard these shepherds, or *pastoureaux,* as crusaders. By the mid–thirteenth century, the crusade had become a defined institution of the Church with established protocols, including a specific papal mandate and a **vow** taken before a priest. In their own eyes, however, all who joined this movement saw themselves as legitimate **pilgrim** crusaders.

The army of poor moved south to Paris, where Louis's mother, Queen Blanche, received Master Jacob courteously. Despite this reception, the Master of Hungary's followers became violent, attacking and killing a number of Parisian clerics. From there the so-called crusade headed south, becoming more unruly and fragmented as it traveled. At Orléans the group led by Master Jacob sparked a riot that resulted in the deaths of about twenty-five university students and teachers. The shepherds' increasing anticlerical violence, especially against **mendicant friars,** whom they characterized as worldly hypocrites, occasioned resistance by local authorities. The Master of Hungary was killed at Bourges in June 1251 and his followers scattered, with many of them cut down as they dispersed. Some survivors begged forgiveness, assumed the **crusader's cross** as penance, and set out for the **Holy Land.**

In 1309 and 1320 France witnessed two additional popular crusade movements, both of which were stimulated by renewed public **preaching** for recovery of the Holy Land. The second of these is also known as a Shepherds' Crusade. Like the original Shepherds' Crusade, both began in the north around Easter time, moved south with increasing waves of violence, and were repressed by late summer. Elements of the Shepherds' Crusade of 1251 had attacked the **Jews** of Bourges but apparently only after they ran out of Catholic clerics to attack. Both fourteenth-century movements, however, were characterized by numerous deliberate and vicious attacks on Jewish communities throughout France. **Related Entries:** Criticism of the Crusades; Fulk of Neuilly; Peter the Hermit.

Shia

The smaller of the two major branches of **Islam;** its adherents believe that **Sunni** Muslims follow false leaders.

The Shia break with Sunni Muslims dates back to the mid–seventh century. Partisans of Ali, the Prophet Muhammad's cousin and son-in-law, who composed a faction known as the *Shi'atu Ali* (Party of Ali), managed to have him installed as fourth caliph (r. 656–661) following the murder of Caliph Uthman. Many of Uthman's followers did not recognize Ali, and civil war ensued. The result was Ali's assassination in 661, establishment of the rival Umayyad dynasty in the caliphate (r. 661–750), and the martyrdom in 680 of Ali's son, Husayn, Muhammad's sole surviving grandson, and most of Husayn's family. Supporters of the family of Ali refused to accept the

Umayyads as rightful successors of the Prophet, claiming that only a member of Muhammad's family could succeed him as *imam,* or religious leader, of Islam. The result was a schism in Islam.

Often persecuted as religious dissidents and at times driven underground, many Shia groups evolved a vision of reality that emphasized their role as a righteous remnant that needed to struggle against all the forces of Evil, including the **heretical** Sunnis.

Shias not only traced the rightful succession of leadership over the community of Islam from Muhammad and Ali through a number of subsequent imams who claimed descent from Ali but whom the Sunnis did not accept as legitimate, but they also developed the notion of a messianic Hidden Imam, or *Mahdi* (the Guided One). According to this theological vision, the imams who followed Muhammad were infallible teachers, divinely appointed at birth, who spoke with the same authority as the Prophet. However, because of devilish enemies, who martyred each imam in turn, this line of earthly imams ended at an early point in time (here the various Shia sects disagree as to who was the last imam). The imamate, however, was not destroyed. Rather, the last visible imam had, through the power and mercy of God, withdrawn from human sight into a state of spiritual concealment, as protection against his enemies. There he would remain until some future time when he would reappear as the Mahdi to gather his faithful, persecuted followers around him, usher in an Islamic holy age, and herald the Last Judgment.

So far as the crusades are concerned, the most important Shia group was the *Ismailis,* also known as *Seveners,* because they accepted Ismail as the seventh and last historical imam, rather than his younger brother Musa, whom *Twelver* Shias revere as true imam in a line that stretched through twelve imams. The Ismaili sect had many subdivisions, including the **Fatimids** and **Assassins. Related Entries:** Abbasids; Apocalypse and the Crusades; Heretics; Islamic Peoples.

Suggested Reading

Heinz Halm, *Shiism,* trans. by J. Watson (1991); Moojan Momen, *An Introduction to Shi'i Islam* (1985).

Sibylla (Sibyl; Sybil)

Queen of **Jerusalem** (r. 1186–1190), wife of King **Guy of Lusignan,** and the last queen to reign with any authority in Jerusalem.

Born around 1158 to **Agnes of Courtney** and the future King **Amalric** of Jerusalem, Sibylla was the elder sister of King **Baldwin IV,** the so-called leper king.

In 1169, when Sibylla was about eleven, she was promised in marriage to Count Stephen of Sancerre, who traveled from France to Jerusalem in 1171 to meet his bride-to-be. Undoubtedly King Amalric, mindful that he had only two young children (at the time) and no close male heirs, wanted to ensure a smooth transition of power should he die prematurely. Baldwin was only eight when his sister's marriage was arranged. Because the age of majority in the kingdom of Jerusalem was fifteen, Baldwin would need a regent (**bailli**) to govern in his name should Amalric die before 1176, and Sibylla's intended husband would serve that role nicely. In 1171 or shortly thereafter, the first symptoms of Baldwin's leprosy began to appear. Because it was an incurable and fatal **disease,** Sibylla's marriage became all the more important, even though diagnosis of Baldwin's ailment was not yet certain.

Although this marriage potentially carried with it the crown of Jerusalem, for unknown reasons Stephen refused to wed Sibylla and returned to France. When Amalric unexpectedly died in 1174, his daughter was still unwed. Baldwin was still suffering from what many suspected was incipient leprosy, and he was still a minor. The kingdom now needed Sibylla married more than ever before. The **High Court** of the kingdom selected William Longsword, eldest son of William III, marquis of **Montferrat** in northern Italy. Because it was wrongly believed that leprosy was a sexually transmitted disease that forced sexual continence on its suffers, Baldwin IV would never marry, if an official diagnosis of leprosy was made. William, therefore, was potentially a future king of Jerusalem, provided he did not follow Stephen's example.

William arrived in the **Holy Land** in October 1176, and the marriage took place in November. Six months later William was dead, probably of disease, and Sibylla was pregnant with the future **Baldwin V.**

As symptoms of Baldwin IV's leprosy became increasingly undeniable, it became increasingly clear that Sibylla would not remain a widow too long. In 1180 she married Guy of Lusignan, who had recently arrived from France. King Baldwin probably chose Guy because he saw him as the best available candidate to act as regent, if needed, and to be heir apparent to the throne. There is reason to believe Sibylla also importuned her brother to approve the marriage because she was smitten with the young Frenchman.

In 1183, a very sick Baldwin IV named Guy regent of the kingdom, an office that brought with it command of the army. The choice was not a good one. Before the year was over, Baldwin removed Guy from the regency, excluded him from succession to the crown, and sought to have the marriage annulled. Sibylla, who was genuinely devoted to her husband, would not hear of annulment. Without her consent, the attempt to dissolve her marriage went nowhere.

Baldwin IV died in 1185 and was succeeded by his nephew Baldwin V, Sibylla's eight-year-old son, who had been crowned co-reigning king in 1183, following Guy's removal from the regency. When the sickly boy-king died the following year, most nobles wanted Sibylla as their next monarch, but sentiment ran strongly against Guy. Sibylla was forced to promise to divorce Guy, and she agreed on the condition that she, and she alone, could choose her next husband and co-monarch. She also demanded that the daughters she had borne to Guy be declared legitimate and that Guy retain his **feudal** counties. Lulled by these demands, to which they acceded, the nobles of the realm proceeded with Sibylla's coronation. Once crowned, she then chose Guy as her co-king.

Sibylla was a loving wife but a poor judge of royal competence. Guy led the kingdom's army to a crushing defeat at **Hattin** on July 4, 1187, and was captured by **Saladin,** who now threatened to roll up the entire **Latin East.** With characteristic sensitivity, however, Saladin did not move against Jerusalem until he had made it possible for the queen to leave the city safely and join her imprisoned husband.

Released from captivity in the spring of 1188, Guy undertook an offensive operation to recover **Acre** in late August 1189. Queen Sibylla, faithful to the end, accompanied Guy to the **siege.** There she and her two daughters died of disease in 1190. With her death, Guy's claim to the crown became precarious. Soon thereafter he was ex-king of Jerusalem. **Related Entries:** Aimery of Lusignan; Conrad of Montferrat; Isabella I; Melisende; Prisoners; Women.

Siege Warfare

From the Old French *sege* (seat). To assume a static, blockading position in order to force a fortified position into submission.

**In the foreground we see a catapult known as a *mangonel,*
which used torsion to drive its missile. This weapon dated
from Roman times. The three massive artillery pieces with
slings are *trebuchets.* The one in the center appears to be
the more primitive traction trebuchet, which employed
men pulling on ropes to provide the force to launch the missile. Later, counterweight trebuchets, developed shortly
before 1200, used heavy containers of rocks or dirt to provide greater force. The sling greatly added to the missile's
velocity and destructive power. Dover Pictorial Archives.**

By the late eleventh century, most European warfare consisted not of clashes
between armies in open fields but of sieges
of **castles** and cities. Wars in the **Islamic**
World prior to the Age of the Crusades were
predominantly decided by light **cavalry**
maneuvering in open areas, but this did not
inhibit **Muslim** military engineers from
developing superior artillery and sapping

techniques prior to the **First Crusade.** Once
the crusaders arrived in the Eastern Mediterranean, warfare rapidly came to be dominated by the European model—sieges of
fortresses by crusader and Muslim armies
alike.

The fastest way to take a fortification
was by frontal assault using ladders and
wheeled wooden towers. It was also the most

costly, carried with it great risk of failure, and was often a tactic of desperation. Other options left to the besieging army were: (1) to knock down a wall using stone-hurling artillery and other machines of war or to undermine it using the services of sappers, and then to attack through the breach; (2) to starve out the enemy; (3) to secure the services of a traitor within who would secretly allow the besiegers to enter; and (4) to trick or terrorize the defenders into capitulating.

Frontal assault with little artillery support won the day at **Jerusalem** on July 15, 1099, and at **Constantinople** on April 12–13, 1204, in the course of the First and **Fourth Crusades.** In the first instance, the besieging crusaders constructed two siege towers at the site. One siege tower was set on fire by the enemy and knocked out of action; the other, although less well constructed, survived and allowed the attackers to cover the point of attack with suppressive hand-launched missiles shot from the heights of the tower, thereby enabling crusaders on the ground to scale the walls with ladders. At Constantinople the crusaders made an amphibious assault along the city's harbor walls. Venetian sailors and marines, as well as some **Frankish** soldiers, leaped onto the walls from flying bridges constructed on the ships' masts, while another group of Franks landed along the beach that ran beneath the walls and forced their way into a poorly defended gate.

At both Jerusalem and Constantinople frontal assault without adequate artillery support was a grim decision forced on the crusaders by circumstances. The Europeans who marched on the First Crusade were far behind their Muslim enemies in the development and employment of missile-launching machines and mining techniques and possessed only the most rudimentary stone-hurling devices. At the siege of Jerusalem the entire army could muster only fourteen not terribly effective stone-launching machines. In the course of the twelfth century, however, the Franks learned how to construct better engines of war from their Muslim enemies and also learned how to undermine walls. The soldiers and sailors of the Fourth Crusade had better heavy weapons but were severely limited in the number of artillery pieces they could employ on the narrow beach and from the decks of their ships as they made their assault on Constantinople's harbor walls.

The capture of these two cities was due equally to the audacity of the attackers and the inadequacies of the defenders. The latter factor could not be counted on with regularity. Moreover, soldiers with scaling ladders unsupported by covering fire could hardly hope to succeed against any well-defended fortification, and siege towers were cumbersome, easily frustrated by ditches and other obstacles, and vulnerable to incendiaries. When facing a determined, well-armed enemy in a well-fortified position, besiegers intent on an assault favored using artillery and sappers to weaken the defenses.

Armies of all sides used a variety of missile-hurling weapons, the most lethal being the *trebuchet,* a counterweighted device that enabled trained soldiers to hurl with great force a carved stone ball weighing as much as 300 pounds over 150 yards. Larger balls, some up to 600 pounds, could be thrown shorter distances. The size of the ball dictated not only distance but also trajectory, the force of impact, the weight of the counterweight, and the size of the crew. Modern experiments show that a three-hundred-pound ball is best launched with a crew of fifty and a counterweight of ten tons. According to one twelfth-century account, a single stone hurled against the city of **Acre** in 1191 killed twelve Muslim defenders.

Invented by the Chinese several centuries before the Christian Era and known to

Islamic forces in the seventh century, the trebuchet became a regular part of the European arsenal only after the First Crusade. By the end of the twelfth century it was being employed in Europe as well as by crusaders in the **Holy Land.** The force of its projectiles could knock holes in walls and also destroy the wooden fences that shielded the defenders on the walls. Stones that fell within the fortification could cause casualties, as well as forcing defenders to take cover. Decapitated enemy heads and other body parts, as well as rotting animal carcasses, were routinely hurled inside fortifications to destroy enemy morale and to spread contagion. The dominant medical theory shared by all cultures was that epidemics were a result of *miasma,* the putrid fumes given off by decaying organic matter.

Muslim armies used trebuchets with great effect to hurl jars of *naft,* an incendiary material that they had learned of from the **Byzantines.** Of all forces engaged in crusade warfare, the **Mamluks** used trebuchets most effectively and fully. Sultan **Baybars** had them constructed in prefabricated sections so that they could be easily transported and assembled in the field. His conquest of the **Templar** castle of *Beaufort* in 1268 was aided by twenty-six of these weapons. In 1291 ninety-two trebuchets kept up a constant bombardment of Acre and played a major role in the fall of this last significant crusader stronghold in **Syria-Palestine.**

Because of their deadly effectiveness and accuracy, trebuchets were equally employed by defenders and attackers. Often a siege became an exchange of barrages between the artillery of besiegers and besieged. At Acre during the **Third Crusade** a French stone thrower called "Bad Neighbor" (*Malvoisine*) was repeatedly knocked out of action by a Muslim trebuchet nicknamed "Bad Cousin" (*Mal Cousine*). On

each occasion it was repaired and returned to action, eventually destroying a portion of the main city wall and shattering a key fortification known as the Cursed Tower.

Western crusaders also had torsion-driven catapult devices, inherited from Roman antiquity, such as *mangonols* and *petraries,* which propelled missiles from the energy of coiled animal sinews. These tossed substantially smaller stones with far less force than trebuchets and were far less effective against masonry walls. They were, however, effective anti-personnel weapons and could also be used to hurl firebombs, assorted corpses, and any other light items that could cause confusion, such as beehives.

Armies on both sides also used the *ballista,* a giant crossbow that required the combined labor of several men and projected large missiles in a flat trajectory against fortifications and human targets.

There was also the battering ram, which the crusaders favored but which Islamic armies seem not to have used. Battering rams had one major drawback; they had to be brought up to a wall or a door, which made them vulnerable to enemy missiles, especially jars of naft. For protection, battering rams were covered by wooden structures, and wet hides were laid over the wood as a fire suppressant. When mounted on wheels, the protective shelters were often known as "sows" or "cows." Sheltered rams were, nevertheless, not invincible. During the siege of Acre by the armies of the Third Crusade, the city's Muslim garrison managed to burn a great ram, despite its hide-covered sow.

Machines of war could bring down walls, but so could men tunneling under them. The work was dangerous, necessitated large numbers of laborers, demanded the direction of highly skilled engineers, and could be done only when the fortress's soil and location allowed mining. Sappers could not undermine castles built on rocks. Yet, when circumstances were favorable, sappers could be the decisive factor that brought victory to the besiegers. On balance, Muslim forces had superior sappers, and even **Richard I the Lionheart** is said to have employed Muslims for this purpose in 1191.

Sappers normally dug a tunnel under a wall, often at a point where there was a tower, filled the tunnel with wood that they set on fire, and waited for the fire to take effect. Even if the wall collapsed (and not all did), the besiegers still often had to fight their way into the castle or city. But that was not always the case. The **Hospitaler** castle of *Krak des Chevaliers* fell to Baybars in 1271 because sappers collapsed a huge tower on the castle's outer defensive wall, allowing Mamluk forces to enter the area between the inner and outer lines of defense. Once that happened the defenders surrendered.

In the thirteenth century countermining became a normal defense against sappers. Defenders would dig one or more tunnels that were intended to intersect or meet head-on the enemy's tunnel. When that happened, a fierce fight would ensue underground.

Most sieges resulted in a good deal of combat. In addition to barrages and counter-barrages of missiles, short but brutal hand-to-hand fighting in tunnels, and assaults through breaches or over walls, there were also sorties from the besieged fortifications aimed at disrupting and harrying the enemy. Besieged defenders rarely sat still, passively awaiting the enemy's assault or retreat, and besieging armies never just settled down and quietly awaited an enemy's surrender.

Starving out a fortress rarely worked and was rarely tried as a sole or even main tactic. Besieging armies normally campaigned during the spring and summer because feeding it over the winter was a formidable task. Besieging armies normally had far fewer supplies of food and water than those whom they besieged. Castles and towns had many months' worth of food and almost unlimited water. Armies far from home had to forage from the countryside, and any army that set up camp in one place for a prolonged period was an army that would inevitably suffer great privations, if not outright famine. The hunger of the crusaders at the siege of **Antioch** during the winter of 1097–1098 became so great that some were driven to **cannibalism.** Camp **disease** was another reality. Epidemics often raged through armies whose sanitary conditions invited disease. Maintaining morale was also a problem for a besieging army. Inactive soldiers became unhappy soldiers, especially when there seemed to be little chance for immediate **plunder.**

For all of these reasons, the Mamluks emphasized short sieges based on massive use of artillery and sappers. As Baybars and his successors swept the crusaders out of Syria-Palestine during the late thirteenth century, they needed no more than six weeks, and often far less, to capture any crusader stronghold.

Traitors who would open gates, leave strong points unguarded, or lure their comrades into surrendering were always welcome and sometimes found. **Bohemond** used a Christian traitor's assistance to capture Antioch in June 1098, and there is evidence that some Frankish inhabitants of **Jaffa** proposed treason and might even have helped Baybars's army capture the city in 1268. Two years earlier Baybars used a Templar **sergeant** named Leo to trick the garrison holding the castle of *Saphet* into surrendering. Sent as an envoy to the sultan's camp to negotiate terms of surrender, Leo understood that Baybars would never allow the defenders to leave alive. He reported, however, to his fellow Templars that the sultan would guarantee them safe passage to Acre if they immediately gave up the struggle. They agreed. Once they marched out they were cut down. Leo was spared and converted to Islam. According to Western sources the murdered included 150 Templars, 767 other men-at-arms, and two **friars.**

The Templars of *Saphet* capitulated because they knew well the primary rule of siege warfare: "He who holds out and is conquered dies." Believing their situation was ultimately untenable, they wagered their lives on Leo's judgment and Baybars's word and lost the gamble. Indeed, because prolonged resistance usually meant **massacre** by an enraged foe, the defenders of many towns and castles decided that prudence was a greater virtue than valor and surrendered with little or no resistance and often were more fortunate than the defenders of *Saphet.* Many castles and towns opened their gates to **Saladin** following his victory at **Hattin** in 1187. To be sure, his reputation as a man of his word helped, but undoubtedly fear of the consequences if they resisted also played a role. Terror did have its uses.

During the two centuries that comprised the classical Age of the Crusades there was a constant race between castle builders and besiegers. Whereas castle builders developed stronger walls and more sophisticated forms of construction to withstand sieges, besieging armies developed better artillery and tactics in their attempt to counter new forms of castle construction. In the end the besiegers won, as the Mamluks captured the last remaining crusader strongholds in Syria-Palestine and drove the Franks into the sea. **Related Entries:** Armor; Damascus; Damietta; Jaffa; Tyre; Weapons, Hand.

Suggested Reading

Jim Bradbury, *The Medieval Siege* (1992); Christopher Gravett and others, *Medieval Siege Warfare* (2002); Christopher Marshall, *Warfare in the Latin East, 1192–1291* (1992); David Nicolle and Gerry Embleton, *Medieval Siege Weapons: 1. Western Europe, A.D. 585–1385* (2002); David Nicolle and Sam Thompson, *Medieval Siege Weapons: 2. Byzantium, the Islamic World and India* (2003); Randall Rogers, *Latin Siege Warfare in the Twelfth Century* (1997); R. C. Smail, *Crusading Warfare, 1097–1193,* 2nd. ed. (1995).

Sixth Crusade (1227–1229)

Some historians prefer to see this crusade of Emperor **Frederick II** as the last wave of the **Fifth Crusade** and not a separate crusade unto itself. Others choose not to consider it an official crusade because Frederick lay under the ban of papal excommunication when he embarked on it. Some are willing to call it a crusade but are uncomfortable with assigning it a number, which would imply it was a major crusade, and so they simply refer to it as the "Crusade of Frederick II." Still others view it as a series of polite negotiations backed up by the threat of armed force and not a true **holy war.** Whatever it was, it was extraordinary.

The Sixth Crusade can be conveniently divided into three segments: (1) negotiations and diplomatic skirmishes in Europe; (2) negotiations and diplomatic skirmishes in the **Holy Land;** and (3) war and negotiations in Europe.

Negotiations and Diplomatic Skirmishes in Europe

Frederick of **Hohenstaufen,** king of Sicily since his father's death in 1197, spontaneously and unexpectedly **vowed** to go on crusade at his coronation as king of Germany on July 15, 1215. For the moment, Pope **Innocent III** chose to overlook Frederick's vow because of the unsettled state of affairs in Germany. It was not until late 1218 that the next pope, **Honorius III,** began to put pressure on Frederick to participate in the Fifth Crusade, which was under way in the **Levant.** In the negotiations that ensued, Frederick requested postponements first until late September 1219 and then until March 1220. Honorius agreed to both. In February 1220 Frederick again instructed the pope that he needed another postponement. Again Honorius agreed, this time setting the departure date at May 1, 1221, and warning Frederick that further delays would result in excommunication.

On November 22, 1220, Honorius crowned Frederick emperor, and Frederick again took up the **crusader's cross** at this coronation, receiving it from the hands of Cardinal Ugolino, the future Pope **Gregory IX.** The string of delays had obviously not destroyed the relationship between pope and emperor, even though the situation in Egypt was growing critical.

In April 1221 Frederick dispatched an advance party of crusaders to Egypt under the command of Duke Ludwig VI of Bavaria, with instructions not to undertake any new operations until Frederick arrived later in the year. May 1 came and went, and still Frederick had not departed, largely due to problems facing him in Sicily, where anarchy reigned.

While Frederick was restoring order in Sicily, the Fifth Crusade met its defeat. Although the eight-year truce that the crusaders had entered into with **al-Kamil** specifically excluded Frederick, who retained the right to crusade in person despite the truce, Frederick was too busy with Sicily to worry about the East.

The surprising defeat of the Fifth Crusade, when victory seemed so near, stunned the West, and quite a bit of the anger and disappointment was directed at the emperor, whose arrival in Egypt had been so long anticipated. In November 1221, Pope Honorius, who up to that point had been patient with Frederick, roundly excoriated Frederick and himself for the postponements of the past five years.

For the second time, Frederick renewed his crusade vow and set a new date for departure: June 24, 1225. At the same time, because he was a widower, Frederick arranged to marry **Isabella,** daughter of **John of Brienne** and heiress to the **kingdom of Jerusalem,** giving Frederick a vested interest in a successful crusade. However, the disappointment engendered by the failure of the Fifth Crusade, which had enrolled so many tens of thousands of Germans and Italians, now was translated in Frederick's lands of Germany, Italy, and Sicily to a lukewarm response to this new crusade initiative.

In July 1225, the pope granted Frederick another postponement till August 15, 1227, but with the understanding that should Frederick fail to leave on the appointed date, he would be excommunicated. The emperor agreed.

On November 9, 1225, Frederick married Isabella, who had been crowned queen of Jerusalem earlier that year. On the same day as his wedding, Frederick added "king of Jerusalem" to his already long list of titles. John of Brienne, who had expected to be allowed to continue as regent of the kingdom for the rest of his life, now became Frederick's implacable enemy. On his part, Frederick shifted his crusade focus away from Egypt and toward **Syria-Palestine,** and especially the recovery of Jerusalem.

On March 18, 1227, Honorius III died, and the following day the aged but energetic Cardinal Ugolino was elected as Gregory IX. Gregory was determined not to be played with by Frederick.

By midsummer 1227 a large crusade force had mustered in southern Italy. Despite heavy losses to camp **diseases,** by mid-August the expedition was under sail for **Outremer.** On September 8 an already-sick emperor set out but soon had to put into port because of his grave condition. He sent word to Rome to explain, but Gregory refused to listen and declared Frederick excommunicated on September 29. Meanwhile, the emperor's fleet continued on to the East, reaching **Acre** in October. While awaiting Frederick, most of them engaged in rebuilding fortifications along the coast—a clear violation of the eight-year truce because Frederick was not there in person.

Negotiations and Diplomatic Skirmishes in the Holy Land

The excommunicated emperor recovered, set sail for Palestine on June 28, 1228, and reached Acre on September 7. From there Frederick sent word back to Rome requesting absolution—to no avail. Gregory had already instructed the **Latin patriarch of Jerusalem** and the masters of the **military orders** to have nothing to do with Frederick.

Frederick's army was too small to achieve anything significant, and the emperor had already decided that he would rather negotiate than fight, especially inasmuch as some of his crusaders were reluctant to serve an excommunicated lord. Since 1226 he had already been in diplomatic contact with al-Kamil, the sultan of Egypt, who had requested Frederick's help against his brother and rival, al-Muazzam, the sultan of Syria. Al-Muazzam's recent death now made Frederick's presence an embarrassment for al-Kamil. Moreover, the sultan also did not want war and had to find some way of buying Frederick off. Jerusalem, which al-Kamil had recently occupied after his brother's death, was a likely bargaining chip.

Exchanges of emissaries and rich gifts ensued, with Frederick greatly impressing his **Muslim** counterparts with his intellect and learning, especially his knowledge of Islam. One Arab author, Ibn Wasil, even described Frederick as "a friend of Muslims." Another, Ibn al-Jauzi, was less generous when he noted disapprovingly, "It was clear . . . that he was a materialist and that his Christianity was simply a game to him."

When negotiations bogged down Frederick put on a show of force, marching his troops in November 1228 from Acre to **Jaffa.** In January 1229 word came from the West that John of Brienne was invading Frederick's southern Italian lands as a papal champion. He needed a quick resolution of affairs in the Holy Land. Happily, al-Kamil had his own problems, as he was currently besieging **Damascus,** which was held by al-Muazzam's son.

Renewal of negotiations led to an act that shocked the Islamic and Christian worlds equally: a truce signed on February 18, 1229, which was to last ten years, five months, and forty days, and the surrender of Jerusalem and a number of other sites to Frederick. Frederick pledged to support the sultan against all enemies, including Christians, for the duration of the truce. Muslims were shocked that any **infidel** should be given this sacred city; many Christians were appalled that the holy city had been rewon by negotiations between an infidel and an excommunicated emperor of doubtful orthodoxy. What made the treaty even more unacceptable to Christians was that the Temple Mount, known to Islam as *al-Harem as-Sharif* (The Noble Sanctuary), was to remain in Muslim hands, and Muslims would be allowed full freedom to worship there.

Gerald, the Latin patriarch of Jerusalem and a virulent hater of Muslims, was rabid in his denunciation of the concordat. The **Templars** were equally irate at Frederick and certain concessions he had made that weakened their position in the Holy Land.

On his part, Frederick entered Jerusalem in triumph on March 17, 1229, and on the following day he crowned himself king of Jerusalem in the **Church of the Holy Sepulcher.**

John of Brienne's attacks on his lands back home now forced Frederick to beat a hasty retreat, but first he had to protect himself from his enemies in Palestine. He helped the **Teutonic Knights** establish themselves in their headquarters of *Montfort,* which commanded the heights above Acre, thereby creating a counterbalance to the Templars. He also destroyed or carried away all surplus weapons and war machines, thereby denying them to Patriarch Gerald and the Templars. Finally, he left behind a strong garrison in Acre.

On May 1, 1229, Frederick tried to sneak out of Acre in the early morning hours, but as he hurried through the street of the butchers he was pelted with rotting meat and animal entrails. The patriarch's propaganda against this presumed "disciple of Muhammad" had struck a nerve.

War and Negotiations in Europe

Frederick secretly arrived in southern Italy on June 10, taking the pope and John of Brienne unaware. Frederick's Sicilian and German subjects rallied to him, and by August he had routed John of Brienne's forces. All he had to do was now make his peace with the pope.

Through the intervention of Hermann of Salsa, the grand master of the Teutonic Knights, an armistice was agreed upon between Frederick and the papacy. In May 1230 Gregory agreed to formal peace terms, and on September 1, 1230, he lifted the ban of excommunication. Frederick had prevailed in his contest with Gregory IX, but it was only the first battle in a long campaign. **Related Entries:** Criticism of the Crusades; Political Crusades.

Suggested Reading

Primary Sources

Edward Peters, ed., *Christian Society and the Crusades, 1198–1229* (1971); Philip of Novara, *The Wars of Frederick II against the Ibelins in Syria and Cyprus,* trans. by John L. LaMonte and Merton J. Hubert (1936).

Historical Study

Thomas C. Van Cleve, *The Emperor Frederick II of Hohenstaufen, Immutator Mundi* (1972).

Slavery

The **Muslim** and **Frankish** inhabitants of the **Levant** equally considered slavery a normal, even necessary institution that was vital to their economies and a merciful alternative to killing **prisoners.** In addition, slavery played a key role in the recruitment of professional soldiers for **Islamic** armies.

Islamic and Christian law generally forbade the enslavement of free-born coreligionists, but both cultures accepted slavery as a station in life that had divine approval and willingly enslaved those whom they deemed to be **infidels.**

In addition to the children born into slavery by virtue of their parents' servile status, slaves were acquired either by purchase or war. The Islamic World of Spain, North Africa, and the **Middle East** was deeply tied into the slave trade that emanated from such distant markets as sub-Saharan West Africa, the Swahili Coast of East Africa, Central Asia, and Circassia, a region north of the Caucasus Mountains between the Black and Caspian Seas. Central Asia and, to a lesser extent, Circassia provided young men who were trained to serve as **mamluks,** or slave-soldiers, the backbone of many Muslim armies.

War was also a rich source of slaves. According to the Arab **historian** Imad ad-Din, when **Saladin** captured **Jerusalem** on

October 2, 1187, he liberated 5,000 Muslim slaves and enslaved about 15,000 Christians—7,000 men and 8,000 **women** and children—who could not pay the negotiated ransom. Most of the women and girls became concubines; most of the men and boys were required to perform menial functions considered essential to the overall economy of the **Ayyubid** empire.

Slavery played an equally vital role in the economy of the **Latin East.** A high proportion of slaves held by the Franks were artisans, and their skilled work brought great rewards to their masters. Two of the largest holders of artisan-slaves were the **Templars** and the **Hospitalers.** So profitable were these slaves that neither **military order** would accept an exchange of Christian and Muslim slaves proposed by **Baybars** in 1267—a refusal that brought down on them the scorn of Christians and Muslims alike.

The Roman Church taught that the liberation of Christian slaves was a meritorious act of mercy, and toward the end of the twelfth century several religious orders arose with the primary mission of purchasing the freedom of Christians held by Muslims. The largest and most successful was the Order of the Most Holy Trinity for the Redemption of Captives, popularly known as the Trinitarians, which Pope **Innocent III** approved in 1198. The Trinitarians, whom King **Louis IX** favored as chaplains, pledged one-third of their wealth toward the redemption of Christian slaves and concentrated their energies in North Africa and Spain but were also active in the Middle East.

In like manner, Islamic tradition held that liberation of Muslim slaves from bondage to infidels was an act that merited God's favor, and brotherhoods of pious Muslims sought to ransom their fellow True Believers from Christian masters, lest they deny the faith and convert to Christianity.

Until 1237, Muslim slaves who converted to Christianity had to be freed. That provision played such havoc with the economy of Europe and the Latin East that Pope **Gregory IX** stipulated that converted slaves would remain in a servile status. Even so, many Frankish masters tried to prevent their Muslim slaves from hearing Christian sermons, lest by their conversion the slaves put their masters in an embarrassing, even impossible position because keeping Christian slaves was still frowned on by **Latin** society. Indeed, some captured Muslims escaped slavery by experiencing a sudden desire to accept the teachings of the Roman Church. Likewise, many captured Christians avoided enslavement by embracing Islam or, once enslaved, were freed by virtue of their conversion. It is anyone's guess how numerous and sincere these conversions were.

Professing the same religion as that of a would-be master was not a perfect safeguard against enslavement because the institution was also employed as an extreme form of punishment against coreligionists. The Roman Church's Third Lateran Council of 1179 mandated that Christians who sold war materials to Muslims or served as captains or pilots in Muslim war galleys or pirate vessels should become the slaves of the Christians who captured them. Church **councils** in 1215, 1245, and 1274 reaffirmed and reissued that decree.

In summary, slavery was common to Islamic and Christian societies during the Age of the Crusades and was justified on religious, military, economic, and penal grounds. **Related Entries:** Massacres; Missionaries; Montjoie; Pillage and Plunder.

Song of Roland, The

A French epic composed around 1100, ascribed to the poet Turoldus and permeated with early crusade ideals.

In 778 a **Frankish** army under the command of King Charles (r. 768–814) was crossing the Pyrenees from Spain when its rear guard was ambushed by bandits near the village of Roncevaux. The skirmish was an embarrassing setback, but little else. One of the three officers killed in the battle was Hruodlandus, who was in charge of key lands in Brittany. Other than that, we know very little about him. Over time, however, legend and oral poetry transformed the shadowy Hruodlandus into the vivid Count Roland, Charlemagne's nephew and France's greatest **feudal** warrior. Of course, there was no France in 778 and eighth-century Franks were not French, feudalism was in its infancy, and King Charles was still many years away from becoming the emperor whom Europe would remember as Charles the Great, or Charlemagne. The muses of folk memory, oral tradition, and poetry are not fettered by prosaic historical facts.

By the time that *The Song of Roland* was crafted into the epic that we know today, the **First Crusade** was already a reality, and the epic portrays that world, although it never mentions the crusade. The closest it comes to a crusade reference is making **"Montjoie"** Charlemagne's battle cry. The bandits who had ambushed Charles's army were probably Christian Basques, possibly seeking revenge for Charles's recent razing of the Christian city of Pamplona; the enemy facing Roland in the epic are **Muslims.** Charles in 778 was a thirty-seven-year-old king; Charlemagne in the poem is a two-hundred-year-old patriarchal figure right out of the Old Testament who ceaselessly fights God's **holy wars,** performs a battlefield miracle, and receives divine instructions from the Angel Gabriel. The historic Charles had waged an unsuccessful short campaign in northern Spain in 778 in alliance with several Muslim rebels; as the poem opens, Charlemagne's army is completing a seven-year campaign aimed at the total conquest of Spain, and by the end of the poem it will conquer all of the peninsula from **Islam.** The epic's image of Islam is quite distorted, but it is unclear whether this was deliberate or done out of ignorance. Muslims are portrayed as polytheistic, idol-worshipping pagans; they are brave warriors but otherwise are minions of the Devil.

Roland and the 20,000 warriors who accompany him in the army's exposed rear guard are treacherously ambushed and wiped out but not without first acquitting themselves bravely and killing untold thousands of the enemy, thereby crippling them as an effective fighting force. The poet makes clear that all of these fallen heroes are martyrs, whose certain reward is Paradise. Indeed, the very blows that they lay on the enemy are penance for their sins. Charles and his remaining forces exact a terrible revenge on the Muslims and on Roland's stepfather, who together had plotted the count's death. Charles's total victory results in his conquest of all Spain and the forced conversion of more than 100,000 Muslims in the stronghold of Saragossa, a city that had successfully resisted Charles in 778. **Related Entries:** Chivalry; Cid, El; Reconquista; Santiago de Compostela.

Suggested Reading

Patricia Terry, trans. and ed., *The Song of Roland,* 2nd ed. (1992).

Spain

See Reconquista.

Stephen of Blois and Chartres

The count of Chartres and Blois and one of the leaders of the second and third waves of the **First Crusade.**

In September 1096 Stephen departed in the company of **Robert of Normandy,** whose sister Adela was Stephen's wife. In northern Italy the crusade leaders met with **Urban II,** who gave them his blessing. Stephen and Robert then spent the winter in southern Italy and set sail for the Balkan coast on April 5, 1097. From there they marched overland to **Constantinople,** which they reached around May 14. The first of Stephen's two extant letters to Adela, whom he addressed as "my beloved," shows us a man who was utterly enchanted with Constantinople, the **Byzantine empire,** and Emperor **Alexius I.**

In the course of the nine-month journey to Byzantium, Stephen and Robert's forces lost large numbers of crusaders to desertion, **disease,** and accident. Stephen's much-reduced contingent crossed the Bosporus at the end of May and joined in the **siege** of Nicaea. Following the city's capitulation, Stephen marched south with the **Norman** element of the crusade army and participated in the so-called **Battle of Dorylaeum,** where he was reported to have comported himself bravely. At **Antioch,** or shortly before the army's arrival there on October 20, 1097, Stephen was chosen to act as leader of the entire crusade army. The honor did not make him the unquestioned commander in chief of this heterogeneous mass of crusaders; rather, his duty was to act as the expedition's chief quartermaster and the presiding officer over the council of crusade leaders. The leaders were a fractious group, and Stephen was probably chosen for his diplomatic skills and reputation as a good administrator.

After he was there six months, Stephen wrote his wife again, boasting that he had already fought in seven engagements and had not lost one soldier. Over the winter and spring, conditions became miserable, and by late March Stephen had enough, but he delayed leaving for another two months.

Finally, on June 2, 1098, the day before the city's capture, he left the army. Arguably, he departed only after he was reasonably sure that the city would be taken by **Bohemond of Taranto**'s stratagem that very night. When the crusade army found itself besieged by **Kerbogha**'s huge relief force, it sent emissaries to Stephen, who was about forty miles away, to come to its assistance. Stephen came, surveyed the situation from a distance, decided that the situation was hopeless, and departed for Constantinople.

While en route, he sought out Alexius I and informed the emperor that Antioch and the crusader army were lost causes. Alexius, who was on his way to join the crusaders at Antioch, heeded the words and retreated back to his capital city, accompanied by Stephen. Alexius's decision to abandon the crusaders at Antioch was to have both immediate and far-reaching effects. The myth of **Greek** cowardice and treachery would forever after poison **Latin**-Greek relations.

From Constantinople, Stephen returned home, where he was reviled as a coward and a perjurer who had broken his sacred **vow** and where he found himself under the ban of excommunication for having left the crusade prematurely. Adela, whom Stephen loved deeply, joined the chorus of angry voices raised against him.

Faced with this hostility, Stephen decided to return to the East to complete his **pilgrimage** and to assist in securing the newly captured city of **Jerusalem.** By late spring 1101 he was back in Constantinople, where he and **Raymond of Saint-Gilles** agreed, much against their better judgment, to lead a large contingent of new crusaders across **Anatolia** in an ill-considered attempt to rescue Bohemond of Taranto, who had been taken **prisoner.** Following its capture of Ankara on June 23, the army wandered aimlessly into the wilds of eastern Anatolia and was cut to pieces in early August by a huge **Turkish** army, but Stephen, who managed to escape, fought well and courageously. Late in September, Stephen sailed to Antioch with a mixed crusader force. From there his group marched south to Tortosa, which it besieged and captured. Finally, on March 30, Palm Sunday, Stephen reached Jerusalem and completed his pilgrimage during Easter week.

Stephen was now ready to return home. Contrary winds, however, drove his ship back to **Jaffa.** While he awaited favorable sailing conditions, he was convinced by King **Baldwin I** to join his army, which was marching to head off an Egyptian advance, even though Stephen had grave misgivings about the wisdom of Baldwin's hastily thrown-together counterstroke. On May 17, 1102, Baldwin's much smaller army was destroyed outside Ramala. The king and Stephen survived, however, and took refuge within the city. Baldwin managed to escape, but Stephen remained behind. He was either killed on May 18 in battle or, more probably, captured that day and executed on the 19th.

The charge of cowardice had so stung Stephen that on two occasions during the so-called **Crusade of 1101** he allowed himself to be talked into participating in almost-suicidal missions. This desire to clear his name, as well as bad luck, cost him his life. **Related Entries:** Robert II of Flanders; Women.

Sunnism

The majority branch of **Islam,** whose adherents, known as Sunni **Muslims,** claim to follow the correct, well-beaten path (*sunna*) of tradition as it evolved from the days of the Prophet Muhammad.

Underlying the Sunni self-image is the belief that God's community is infallible, which means that it can never err. Consequently, the practices and institutions of mainstream Islam are always correct. This meant that most medieval Sunnis acknowledged at least the theoretical authority of first the caliphs of **Damascus,** the Umayyad dynasty (r. 661–750), and then their successors, the caliphs of the **Abbasid** dynasty, who resided in Baghdad from 762 until the conquest of that city by the **Mongols** in 1258. Adherents of **Shia** Islam, Sunnism's major rival, did not accept these caliphs as valid successors of Muhammad.

Most of the great heroes of the Islamic countercrusades, such as **Nur-ad-Din, Saladin,** and **Baybars,** were Sunni Muslims. **Related Entries:** Almohads; Almoravids; Ottomans; Reconquista; Seljuks.

Suggested Reading

Hugh N. Kennedy, *The Prophet and the Age of the Caliphates: The Islamic Near East from the Sixth to the Eleventh Century* (1986).

Sword Brothers

See Military Orders of the Baltic.

Syria-Palestine

The region of the **Middle East** south of **Anatolia** that encompassed three of the four major crusader states and several of the **Islamic** powers that opposed them.

Syria and Palestine were two separate but connected areas along the eastern coast of the Mediterranean. Historians often use the term *Syria-Palestine* to refer to the entire region of the eastern Mediterranean from **Antioch** in the north to the Gaza Strip in the south and including **Transjordan.**

Historical Palestine, whose name derives from the Philistines who invaded and settled the coastal areas of Israel and Gaza around 1200 B.C.E., was much larger in crusader times than the narrow coastal strip inhabited by its ancient namesakes. It was also considerably larger than the small state of Palestine that is currently taking shape in lands occupied by Israel since 1967. Although the term was and is imprecise, Palestine in the Age of the Crusades was essentially the **Holy Land** and was roughly coterminous with the **Latin kingdom of Jerusalem.** That is, it encompassed the lands of the modern nation of Israel, as well as portions of western Jordan, southern Syria, southern Lebanon, **Egypt**'s Gaza Strip, and the territory of the proposed Palestinian state.

To the north lay Syria, which consisted of lands that today comprise most of the nations of Syria and Lebanon and small portions of southern Turkey. Syria's chief cities included the Islamic strongholds of **Damascus** and **Aleppo,** as well as Antioch, **Tripoli,** and **Tyre.** Two major crusader states, the principality of Antioch and the county of Tripoli, lay largely in lands that can be termed Syrian. Except for its coastal regions, Syria was never captured and held by the crusaders. Along with Egypt, it was a major center of Islamic opposition to the crusaders and their states. **Related Entries:** Acre; Ascalon; Jaffa; Jerusalem, City of; Outremer; Settlement and Colonization.

Suggested Reading

P. M. Holt, *East Mediterranean Lands in the Period of the Crusades* (1977).

T

Tafurs

Infantry elements of the **First Crusade** largely drawn from the poorest classes of Flanders and northern France.

The term *Tafur* is of uncertain origin and meaning. One theory is that it derived from the large wooden shield, the *talevart* (pronounced *tafar* in the dialect of Flanders) that many of them carried. Another theory is that it derived from the Arabic *tâfoûr*, meaning "miserable."

Whatever its origin, Tafur entered the vocabulary of the crusades as a term that designated the poorest and most unruly of all the foot soldiers who participated in the First Crusade's second wave. Some were probably survivors of the **People's Crusade** of 1096; others had surely marched along with the various contingents that the great lords led from Europe in 1097, especially the force led by Count **Robert II of Flanders.** Although they might have attached themselves to armies led by **feudal** lords, the Tafurs apparently fought under their own leaders, and several sources refer to a "king of the Tafurs." One source even claims he was a former knight from Normandy. There is, however, debate over the historicity of this so-called Tafur king. Conceivably he was, like Robin Hood, the legendary creation of a later time. However they were led, the Tafurs had a reputation for being undisciplined, and they fought and behaved with a ferocity that repelled foe and friend alike. It was the Tafurs, for example, who committed acts of **cannibalism** at **Antioch** and Ma'arra in 1098. **Related Entries:** Jews and the Crusades; Peter the Hermit; *Ribauds;* Walter Sansavoir.

Tancred (1075/76–1112)

Second-in-command of the Italo-**Norman** contingent of the **First Crusade,** hero of Ralph of Caen's history, *The Deeds of Tancred on the Expedition to Jerusalem* (ca. 1113), lord of Galilee, and regent of the principalities of **Antioch** and **Edessa.**

Tancred took the **crusader's cross** in 1096 at the urging of his uncle **Bohemond I of Taranto.** Although only around twenty-one when he embarked on the crusade, Tancred was already a veteran soldier and commander. Tancred's actions during and following the crusade suggest that his primary motives for joining the expedition were a desire for winning a princely estate in the East and the promise of adventure and glory.

Tancred displayed his independence and ambition on numerous occasions in the course of the crusade. In late April 1097 Tancred passed secretly through **Constantino-ple** in the disguise of a common soldier rather than render an oath of fidelity to Emperor **Alexius I.** Bohemond had already taken the oath in an attempt to mollify his former **Byzantine** enemy; Tancred had a different viewpoint and objectives. Some evidence suggests that Tancred finally swore an oath to the emperor in June, but if he did, he did so under protest. A few days later on July 1, Tancred was wounded at the Battle of **Dorylaeum** when he rashly led a small contingent of **cavalry** away from the main force, despite Bohemond's heated objections.

As the main body of the army resumed its march in mid-September, two contingents, one led by Tancred and the other by **Baldwin of Boulogne,** split off to invade Cilicia, a region of southeastern **Anatolia** inhabited largely by Christian **Armenians.** There Tancred captured the **Seljuk**-held city of Tarsus but was forced to cede it to Baldwin's larger army. Tancred then turned east, where the Armenian city of Mamistra welcomed him as its lord. Once again Baldwin's forces appeared, threatening to wrest this prize from Tancred. Baldwin's soldiers were admitted into the city, but soon hostilities broke out between Tancred's Normans and Baldwin's Lorrainers. With neither commander eager to earn the odium that would follow upon a wholesale shedding of crusader blood, they managed to keep conflicts to a low level and eventually reconciled. After laying down a set of laws for his new Armenian subjects, Tancred headed toward **Syria.** Along the way he captured the port of Alexandretta and then rejoined the main army around mid-October 1097.

Tancred arrived in time to participate in the **siege** and then defense of Antioch, continually distinguishing himself in the field. With Antioch secured, Tancred revisited the Cilician cities that he had conquered, including Tarsus, which Baldwin had abandoned,

and secured them with garrisons. Following his return to Antioch, Tancred participated in the siege of **Ma'arra.**

Meanwhile, Bohemond and **Raymond of Saint-Gilles** bickered with increasing frequency and bitterness; one of the main issues dividing them was when to resume the march to **Jerusalem.** Raymond, convinced that the army should leave sooner rather than later, set out on January 13, 1099, with Tancred in his retinue. Bohemond stayed behind in Antioch but probably gave his blessing to his nephew to accompany Raymond. In the midst of the march, Tancred shifted his loyalties to **Godfrey of Bouillon.** Twelfth-century **historians** ascribed the falling out to Tancred's dissatisfaction with the amount of money Raymond had paid him for his services, but the long-simmering animosity between the Normans and Count Raymond's Provençals probably was a major factor, for it was during this time that the heated controversy over the authenticity of the **Holy Lance** of Antioch came to a head.

Duke Godfrey dispatched Tancred to capture Bethlehem, which he did on June 7. A week later, on July 15, the troops of Tancred and Godfrey fought their way into Jerusalem in the vanguard of the crusader army. Hearing of the treasures of the Temple Mount, Tancred hastened there and **plundered** the Islamic shrines of their rich decorations. With his booty, which he shared with Godfrey, he was able to pay off his followers and to attract new recruits. In an attempt to gain additional wealth from ransom, Tancred offered his protection to a number of **Muslims** who took refuge on the roof of *Al-Aksa* Mosque on the Temple Mount. Other crusaders, however, ignored his tokens of security and slaughtered the **prisoners.**

Tancred's last action on the First Crusade occurred at the Battle of **Ascalon** on August 12, when the crusaders crushed an Egyptian relief force. Thereafter Tancred played the role of a prince in the newly formed crusader states of the **Latin East.**

In the months that followed, Tancred served as Godfrey of Bouillon's second in command—Godfrey having been named ruler of Jerusalem. The young Norman captured several northern towns, including Tiberias, which Duke Godfrey gave to Tancred as a **feudal** fief, thereby making him lord of Galilee. When Godfrey died suddenly, Tancred attempted to seize control of Jerusalem, rather than allow Godfrey's brother, Baldwin of Boulogne, to claim the city. Tancred failed to win sufficient support but resisted Baldwin's election until March 1101, when he was called to serve as regent of Antioch in the wake of Bohemond's capture and imprisonment. Tancred surrendered his possessions in the Galilee to Baldwin and moved to Antioch.

As regent, Tancred did nothing to secure his uncle's release from captivity. Bohemond's ransom of 100,000 gold coins was paid by others, and when he returned to Antioch in May 1103, he stripped his nephew of lands and power, leaving him only two small **castles.** When **Baldwin of Le Bourcq,** prince of Edessa, was taken prisoner in May 1104, Tancred was named regent of Edessa, which he ably defended. Once again, Tancred did nothing to secure the release of the prince whose principality he temporarily occupied.

When Bohemond decided to travel to the West in late 1104 to secure help for beleaguered Antioch, he named his reconciled nephew as regent. Antioch at the moment was in dire straits, squeezed by pressures from the Seljuks, Raymond of Saint-Gilles, and Emperor Alexius I—all of whom desired to conquer it. Bohemond never returned to the East, and Tancred was left with a free hand to display his military and diplomatic genius, and to give free rein to his ambitions.

Between autumn 1104 and spring 1108, Tancred's successes brilliantly reversed Antioch's fortunes and placed it on a secure foundation. Edessa, however, remained a troubled state. In 1108 Baldwin of Le Bourcq was released, but Tancred initially refused to return his principality; the result was a short but bitter and bloody war, which resulted in Tancred's surrender of Edessa to Baldwin in September 1108.

Despite this setback, Tancred and Antioch continued to prosper. When he died in December 1212 at a still-young age, Tancred was a major force in Syria and northern **Palestine,** and his successes helped ensure for decades to come a powerful Latin presence in that region.

Suggested Reading

Robert L. Nicholson, *Tancred* (1978).

Templars

The Poor Fellow-Soldiers of Christ and the Temple of Solomon, more commonly known as the *Templars,* the first and greatest of Catholic Europe's **military orders** until its dissolution in 1312.

Around 1119/1120 a small group of Western **knights** under the leadership of Hugh of Payns, a native of Champagne, formed a religious community in Jerusalem. Although they took the usual monastic **vows** of poverty, chastity, and obedience, they remained laymen and devoted themselves to policing the **pilgrimage** routes of the **Holy Land,** especially the vital but dangerous road from the port of **Jaffa** to **Jerusalem.** The new order was probably first recognized in January 1120 at the **Council** of Nablus, one of the most important assemblies of the **Latin** Church in the **Levant.** In that same year, King **Baldwin II** donated part of his royal residence, the former *Al-Aksa* Mosque, to them as quarters and a few years later

Al-Aksa **Mosque on the Temple Mount, headquarters of the Templars until Saladin recaptured the city in 1187.**

handed over the entire building to them. Because Westerners called *al-Aksa* "the Temple of Solomon," the new inhabitants became known as the *Knights of the Temple.* In 1139 Pope Innocent II recognized the Templars as an official religious order.

Within a few years of its foundation, the community expanded its military role to include joining various Christian armies to fight in the field against **Muslim** enemies and maintaining key fortifications throughout **Syria-Palestine.** Templar detachments also assumed military duties in the Iberian Peninsula. As early as 1128 the Templars were given a **castle** along the Portuguese frontier, and three years later they took over a stronghold in eastern Spain. From these humble beginnings the Templars became a significant force in the **Reconquista,** and they also inspired the development of native **Iberian military orders.** By 1129, the year in which the Council of Troyes in France confirmed the Templars and accepted their

rule, these knights were already recognized as Western Christendom's newest force in the ongoing war with **Islam.**

Originally there were no distinctions of rank within the Order of the Temple, but as its numbers grew two distinctive ranks of warriors emerged: knights and mounted sergeants-at-arms. By the thirteenth century, Templar knights were expected to be born into that class, whereas sergeants only had to be freemen. In addition, the order had a rank of chaplains—nonfighting priests who ministered to the spiritual needs of the brothers.

Just as there were three ranks, there were also three levels of authority within the order, and these positions were largely in the hands of the knights. At the bottom was the individual *convent* headed by a *preceptor.* Whether it was a fighting castle on a frontier or a comfortable house in France that supported the order's military mission, the Templar convent normally housed only a handful of sworn brothers, but many other persons resided there, serving the order in a variety of ways. In Syria-Palestine and Iberia these hangers-on included large numbers of **mercenary** soldiers, some of whom might be **Muslims.** Groups of convents were joined into a geographic *province* headed by a *provincial master.* At the top stood the *grand master,* the order's commander in chief, who resided in Jerusalem and later, when Jerusalem was no longer in Christian hands, in **Acre.** When Acre fell in 1291, headquarters moved to **Cyprus,** but its days on Cyprus were brief, as enemies were now looking to disband the order and confiscate its property.

From the start the Templars excited the imaginations of many European Christians who sought either to join the order's ranks or support its operations through generous donations. As a result, the Order of the Temple became the largest and richest of the military orders. With its success came deep involvement in long-distance banking, as the order passed large sums of money from its European sources of income to its military outposts in the **crusader states** and Iberia. The order also became involved in moneylending, often drawing upon its rich resources to loan large sums to the kings of Europe. Indeed, the Temple of Paris became something of a regular bank for the kings of France.

Rich bankers can be easy targets for those who are envious, avaricious, or easily outraged. This is especially true when the rich bankers claim to serve a higher purpose but are perceived, rightly or wrongly, as hypocritical, corrupt, and arrogant. In October 1307 the Templars of France were suddenly arrested on the initiative of King **Philip IV.** Royal lawyers drew up a long list of charges against the Templars, accusing them of heresy, blasphemy, idolatry, and a variety of sexual sins. Pope Clement V protested, but when a number of Templars confessed under torture, he relented and ordered all Christian rulers to arrest the Templars and seize their holdings. Some Templars resisted and held out for years, especially in Aragon; most did not resist, but only a minority confessed to any of the charges. On March 22, 1312, the pope declared the order dissolved. A few Templars were executed for having confessed and then recanted their presumed crimes, but most were quietly sent off to other religious houses. Most of the order's possessions were awarded to the second largest military order, the **Hospitalers,** and although the Order of the Hospital was unable to secure everything awarded it, it was enriched greatly by what it did get. There is, however, no evidence to support any theory that might implicate the Hospitalers in a conspiracy to crush the Templars.

The dissolution of the Templars was complete. The myth that connects modern Freemasonry with the Templars was a German invention of the mid–eighteenth century and has no basis in historical fact. **Related Entries:** Bernard of Clairvaux; Castles, Crusader; Criticism of Crusades; Damascus Crusade; Hattin, Battle of; Holy War/Just War; La Forbie, Battle of; Seige Warfare; Turcopoles.

Suggested Reading

Primary Sources

Malcolm Barber and Keith Bate, eds. and trans., *The Templars* (2002); J. Upton-Ward, trans., *The Rule of the Templars: The French Text of the Rule of the Order of the Knights Templar* (1992).

Historical Studies

Malcolm Barber, *The New Knighthood: A History of the Order of the Temple* (1994) and *The Trial of the Templars* (1978); Anne Gilmour-Bryson, *The Trial of the Templars in Cyprus* (1998); Helen Nicholson, *The Knights Templar: A New History* (2001).

Teutonic Knights

The *Military Order of the House of St. Mary of the Germans in Jerusalem,* better known as the *Teutonic Order* or the *Teutonic Knights,* was Germany's greatest **military order,** most noted for its work of conquest, colonization, and conversion in the **Baltic.**

The Teutonic Order originated at the **siege** of **Acre** in 1190 during the **Third Crusade** as a group of hospital attendants sworn to aid sick and indigent German crusaders in the **Holy Land.** In 1198 its members assumed military duties and adopted a rule modeled on that of the **Templars.**

Their primary responsibilities up to 1291 were in the eastern Mediterranean, but as early as 1211 the king of Hungary assigned the Teutonic Knights the defense of a frontier region in Transylvania. When the **knights** introduced German colonists and seemed to be on the verge of creating an autonomous state, the king expelled them. In that same year, 1226, Conrad of Mazovia invited the Teutonic Knights to defend his Polish duchy against the pagan Prussians to his east, and Emperor **Frederick II** granted the order's grand master the status of imperial prince with the right of governance over all conquered lands. The conquests began in 1229, with the order using Prussia as a testing ground for knights scheduled to be shipped to the Holy Land. In 1245 the papacy recognized the Prussian campaign as a perpetual crusade, and by midcentury the Teutonic Knights had carved out an independent state along the eastern littoral of the Baltic Sea, from which they continued to push eastward. To stabilize their recently conquered lands, the knights invited in large

The ruins of Montfort near Acre, headquarters of the Teutonic Knights from the 1230s or 1240s until captured by Baybars in 1271.

numbers of German merchants and farmers, and hundreds of German villages, towns, and cities arose, protected by the order's fortresses. Following their expulsion from the Holy Land in 1291, the Teutonic Knights moved their headquarters to **Venice** and from there, in 1309, to Marienburg in Prussia. The knights' involvement in the trading activities of the Hanseatic League, as well as the fertile farms of Prussia, brought great prosperity to the Teutonic Order in the fourteenth century. Between 1309 and 1410 the order waged a century-long crusade against pagan Lithuania, Orthodox Russia, and even Catholic Poland. Lithuania's conversion to Roman Catholicism and its union with Poland in 1385–1386 led to the order's crushing defeat at the hands of united Polish, Lithuanian, Russian, and **Mongol** forces at Tannenberg in 1410. This defeat and the huge indemnity the knights were forced to pay began the order's rapid fall from power. In 1457 Marienburg was abandoned, and the most of the order was converted to Lutheranism and secularized in the sixteenth-century Protestant Reformation. A small remnant remained loyal to the Church of Rome in southern Germany and played a minor role in the Hapsburg emperors' wars against Protestants and the **Ottoman Turks.**

Today two small branches of the Teutonic Order continue its original charitable mission: a Catholic group, consisting solely of priests since 1923, has its headquarters in Vienna, and a Protestant group survives as the *Bailiwick of Utrecht of the Teutonic Order* in the Netherlands. **Related Entries:** Baltic Crusades; Castles, Crusader; Holy War; Hospitalers; Military Orders of the Baltic; Sixth Crusade.

Suggested Reading

William Urban, *The Teutonic Knights: A Military History* (2003) and *The Prussian Crusade,* 2nd ed. (2002).

Third Crusade (1188–1192)

The so-called Crusade of Kings because it involved Emperor **Frederick I Barbarossa,** King **Richard I the Lionheart** of England, and King **Philip II** of France.

Called by Pope Gregory VIII in October 1187 in response to news of the catastrophe at **Hattin,** the crusade had four stages: (1) the response of King William II of Sicily, 1188–1189; (2) the travels of Europe's three great monarchs to the East, 1189–1191; (3) the **siege** and capture of **Acre,** August 27, 1189–July 12, 1191; and (4) the campaign of King Richard, September 1191–October 1192. The major achievements of the crusade were rewinning key coastal areas from **Saladin,** especially Acre and **Jaffa,** and stabilizing the position of the **crusader states.** Although **Jerusalem** was still in Muslim hands and the **Latin East** was confined to a narrow coastal strip, the crusader states were given another century of life. An additional consequence was that the troubles that occurred in both the Balkans and **Cyprus** between **Latin** crusader forces and the **Greeks** went a long way toward deepening hostility and distrust between these two Christian cultures and served as background to the events of the **Fourth Crusade.**

The Crusade of William II

As news of Saladin's victorious march through crusader lands filtered into the West, it became clear that immediate help was needed to assist the three **Frankish** strongholds that were still holding out, **Tyre, Tripoli,** and **Antioch.** The first monarch to respond was King William II of Sicily, who immediately ended a war with the **Byzantine empire** and in March 1188 dispatched a small fleet of fifty or sixty vessels and several hundred **knights** to Tyre. When the fleet arrived in the summer of 1188, **Conrad of Montferrat** sent it north to Tripoli to bolster

The River Saleph, where Emperor Frederick I died on June 10, 1190. The Armenian castle of Silifke dominates the hill in the background.

the city's defenses and to discourage any siege, which it did. In August 1188 King William sent an additional 300 knights. Through the summer of 1189, the Sicilian fleet continued to patrol the waters of the **Levant,** harassing the enemy and keeping the sea lanes open for crusaders from all over Europe who were already sailing to the East. All the while, King William was preparing a larger expedition, which he planned to lead himself. Death, however, intervened on November 19, 1189, and prevented any further Sicilian contribution to the crusade. The fleet already in the East was recalled by Tancred of Lecce, who had seized the throne on William's death. Tancred needed it at home to bolster his hold on the kingship.

Three Kings Go to War

Before he died, William bequeathed a large legacy to King Henry II of England to support his crusade. On January 21, 1188, Henry and King Philip II met and together assumed the **crusader's cross,** along with the count of Flanders and other French lords. Earlier, in November 1187, Henry's eldest surviving son, Richard, had taken the **crusader's vow.** In late March 1188 Emperor Frederick I pledged the cross, along with large numbers of his German and Italian barons.

Just when it seemed all of Western Europe was ready to go on crusade, war broke out between Richard and the count of Toulouse and soon escalated into a war between Philip and Henry (with Richard shifting to Philip's side). Scarcely had Henry and Philip made peace when Henry died on July 6, 1189, and Richard succeeded him as king. After setting his affairs and new kingdom in order, Richard met King Philip (who was Richard's **feudal** lord for all of Richard's

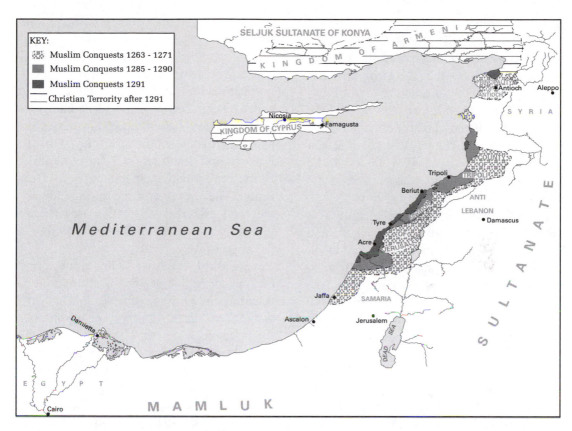

KEY:
- Muslim Conquests 1263 - 1271
- Muslim Conquests 1285 - 1290
- Muslim Conquests 1291
- Christian Terrirory after 1291

The Middle East after the Third Crusade, 1192.

extensive French possessions) at Vézelay on July 4, 1190, and together they began leading their armies toward the Mediterranean. At Lyons they separated. Philip marched to Genoa, where his troops set sail in hired Genoese ships; Richard marched to Marseilles, where his troops embarked on hired French vessels. In September the two armies met at Messina in Sicily, where they established winter quarters.

Meanwhile, Emperor Frederick, who had set out overland with a huge army on May 11, 1189, was well into the Balkans. Here he encountered trouble with the Byzantine armies of Emperor **Isaac II.** Fearful of Frederick's intentions and of all crusaders, Isaac had negotiated an understanding with Saladin to delay and destroy Frederick's army in return for the **relic** of the **True Cross** captured at Hattin and the sultan's installing Byzantine clerics in all the Christian sanctuaries in the **Holy Land.** The result was open warfare between the two imperial forces, in which the Byzantines came out second best. On February 14, 1190, the two sides concluded a peace treaty, and in March Frederick's army was ferried across the Dardanelles at Gallipoli by Byzantine ships.

During the march though **Anatolia** tragedy struck when Frederick drowned in the River Saleph on June 10, 1190. With his death, the crusade lost its most prestigious and probably most able leader. His son Frederick, duke of Swabia, took command and led the army to Antioch, which it reached on June 20. There the imperial army largely fell apart. Many died of an epidemic that broke out in the city; many others went home.

Those who remained struggled on their way south, dogged by **disease.** A small band of survivors, which included only 300 knights, reached Acre on October 7, 1190; on January 20, 1191, Duke Frederick died of disease. By the time spring arrived, most of the imperial crusaders who still remained alive had left for home. The few who continued on crusade placed themselves under Duke Leopold V of Austria, who arrived in the spring.

While Frederick Barbarossa's army was disintegrating, the armies of Richard and Philip were wintering in Sicily. Richard took the opportunity to demand back from Tancred of Lecce the dowry of his sister Joan, the widow of King William II, as well as the legacy bequeathed Henry II by King William but never delivered. When Tancred hesitated, Richard, never noted for patience, struck, capturing the southern Italian city of Bagnara and sacking the Sicilian city of Messina. The sack of Messina hastened Tancred's coming to terms with Richard in October 1190.

On March 30, 1191, Philip set sail for the East, arriving at Acre on April 20. Richard did not depart until April 10. Along the way he stopped at **Cyprus** on May 6.

Several vessels from his fleet, including at least one treasure ship, had been driven to Cyprus by a storm and wrecked offshore. The survivors were badly treated by the island's Greek ruler, Isaac Comnenus, who had successfully rebelled against Byzantine authority in 1184. The ship carrying Richard's sister, Queen Joan, and Richard's fiancée, Berengaria, had survived but was moored offshore, its crew and passengers wisely refusing to land. Richard demanded total return of his men and treasure, and when Isaac refused he attacked. The result was Richard's conquest of the entire island, which began nearly four continuous centuries of Latin rule. On June 5, eager to reach the Holy Land and new opportunities for

battle, Richard left Cyprus, arriving at Acre on June 8, 1191.

The Siege and Capture of Acre

Before the three great kings even got under way, independent crusader contingents from England, Scandinavia, northern Germany, the Low Countries, Brittany, northern France, and Italy set sail from Atlantic, Baltic, and Mediterranean ports to **Outremer.** They began arriving during the summer and fall of 1189, and most of them joined forces with King **Guy of Lusignan** at the siege of Acre.

Saladin had released Guy in the spring of 1188 in exchange for the stronghold of **Ascalon** and Guy's oath never to bear arms against him again. After keeping his promise for better than a year, Guy decided in the summer of 1189 that it was time to strike back and save his rapidly diminishing kingdom. After being turned away at Tyre by **Conrad of Montferrat,** Guy marched to Acre and began siege operations on land in late August 1189, while a Pisan fleet blockaded the port.

Forces from the West continued to arrive during the sailing seasons of 1190 and 1191, including an advance party from England led by the archbishop of Canterbury. On June 7 Richard's fleet sank a large vessel carrying Muslim reinforcements for the besieged city, and the next day he landed at Acre. With Philip's and Richard's armies in place, the crusaders were finally strong enough to force the issue. Despite deteriorating relations between Philip and Richard, their two armies worked in concert. French siege machines battered the walls, while Richard's forces kept Saladin's forces from relieving the city. On July 11 or 12 the defenders negotiated capitulation after a heroic defense that lasted almost twenty-three months.

Much to Richard's disgust, King Philip, who had suffered several illnesses while on crusade, took this opportunity to declare his crusade complete and departed for France on July 31. A large body of his French crusaders remained behind, now under the command of the duke of Burgundy. As duke of Normandy, count of Anjou, count of Poitou, and duke of Aquitaine—that is, lord of most of western France—Richard also had large numbers of Frenchmen in his so-called English army. That army, reinforced by a number of splinter contingents from all over Europe, was now ready to try to rewin Jerusalem.

The Campaign of Richard the Lionheart

On August 22, 1191, Richard marched his forces south from Acre along the coast toward Jaffa, with his fleet protecting and supplying his right flank. He could not hope to take Jerusalem until first he recovered that key port city. On September 7 at Arsuf (Asur), a few days' march north of Jaffa, the crusaders came under heavy attack but won the day, thanks to Richard's superior generalship. This defeat, as well as the loss of Acre, combined to destroy the myth of Saladin's invincibility. After Arsuf, never again would he attempt to destroy Richard in an open pitched battle.

Three days later the crusaders reached Jaffa and began rebuilding its fortifications. In October Richard began a cautious advance toward Jerusalem. On January 3, 1192, he reached a point only twelve miles from Jerusalem, but knew he could not go farther. Reluctantly he withdrew to Ascalon. In June he tried for Jerusalem again, but once again halted short of the city, knowing his supplies and manpower were insufficient to take and hold the city. On July 26 he returned to Acre.

Before and during his advances toward Jerusalem, Richard carried on negotiations with Saladin and his brother **al-Adil**

(**Saphadin**) for return of **Palestine** to the Christians. If the testimony of the Arab **historian** Baha ad-Din can be trusted, Richard went so far as to propose the marriage of his sister Queen Joan and Saphadin, who jointly would rule all Palestine. Additionally, prisoners would be exchanged and the True Cross returned. According to Baha ad-Din, Saladin readily agreed, knowing the proposal was simply Richard's idea of a joke. Whatever was the case, nothing came of this extraordinary offer.

By mid-August Richard was quite ill, his crusade had lost momentum, and news arrived of Philip's plotting against him back home in France. These factors combined to convince him to hurry along peace negotiations. Since Saladin also had problems that needed immediate attention, the two adversaries, who never met face-to-face, decided on a three-year, eight-month truce, which they concluded on September 2. By terms of the truce the coast from Tyre to Jaffa was to remain in Latin hands. Jerusalem remained in Muslim hands, but Christian **pilgrims** could freely visit it. Perhaps because he never could take the city by storm, Richard did not take advantage of the opportunity to visit the holy city.

On October 9, 1192, Richard left the Holy Land. One of the several legacies that he left behind was the English hospital at Acre dedicated to Saint Thomas of Canterbury. About forty years later the hospital's brethren became a minor **military order,** the Order of Saint Thomas of Acre. **Related Entries:** Adrianople; Bull, Papal; Capetians; Christians, Eastern; Financing the Crusades; German Crusade; Hohenstaufens; Infantry; Massacres.

Suggested Reading

Primary Sources

Marianne Ailes and Malcolm Barber, eds. and trans., *The History of the Holy War: Ambroise's*

"Estoire de la guerre sainte" (2003); Thomas A. Archer, ed. and trans., *The Crusade of Richard I, 1189–92* (1889); Baha al-Din Yusuf ibn Rafi Ibn Shaddad, *The Rare and Excellent History of Saladin,* trans. by Donald S. Richards (2002); *Chronicles of the Crusades, Being Contemporary Narratives of the Crusade of Richard Coeur de Lion,* trans. by John A. Giles (1848); Peter W. Edbury, ed. and trans., *The Conquest of Jerusalem and the Third Crusade: Sources in Translation* (1996); Keneth Fenwick, ed. and trans., *The Third Crusade: An Eyewitness Account of the Campaigns of Richard Coeur-de-Lion in Cyprus and the Holy Land* (1958); Helen J. Nicholson, ed. and trans., *Chronicle of the Third Crusade: A Translation of the "Itinerarium Peregrinorum et Gesta Regis Ricardi" (The Journey of the Pilgrims and the Deeds of King Richard)* (1997); Richard of Devizes, *The Chronicle of Richard of Devizes of the Time of King Richard the First,* ed. and trans. by J. Appleby (1963).

Transjordan

Known to the crusaders as *Oultrejordain,* it was the region east of the Jordan River and the Dead Sea (essentially the modern nation of Jordan).

King **Baldwin I** pursued an aggressive expansionistic policy into this area, despite its remoteness, because he wished to control the caravan routes that connected **Syria** with Egypt and the Red Sea. **Muslim** merchant and **pilgrim** traffic between **Damascus** and the cities of eastern Arabia passed through the area and offered rich opportunities for taxation. Possession of the region also meant that the **kingdom of Jerusalem** had a strategic salient that could effectively interrupt **Islamic** military movement between Egypt and Syria. The southern tip of Transjordan also gave the **crusader state** access to the waters of the Red Sea and the rich markets of Arabia and the Indian Ocean through the fortress of *Eilat* on the Gulf of Aqaba, which was in **Frankish** hands until **Saladin** captured it in late 1170.

Transjordan remained part of the royal *demesne,* or lands, under Baldwin I and **Baldwin II,** but in the reign of **Fulk,** third king of Jerusalem, the land was given out as a **feudal** lordship. Records of around 1180 show that the lord of Transjordan owed the king the services of sixty knights. In 1188 the forces of Saladin swept through and conquered Transjordan, and the **Franks** never recovered it. **Related Entries:** Castles, Crusader; Fifth Crusade; Reynald of Châtillon.

Tripoli

A port city on the northern Lebanese coast and the **crusader state** (1109–1289) to which it gave its name.

Count **Raymond IV of Saint-Gilles** died in 1105 before completing his conquest of Tripoli and its environs. His elder son, Bertrand, who was experiencing difficulties back home, arrived in 1108 to carry on his father's work, and on July 12, 1109, completed the capture of Tripoli, with help from Genoese and Provençal fleets. Bertrand accepted the **feudal** overlordship of King **Baldwin I** of **Jerusalem,** and Tripoli became the fourth, last, and smallest crusader state to be carved out in the **Middle East.** It was a bitter commercial blow for **Damascus,** which had used Tripoli as its port up to that point.

When Bertrand died in 1112, he was succeeded by his son Pons (r. 1112–1137), and under Pons the county's anti-**Norman** policies, which had begun with the clash between Raymond of Saint-Gilles and **Bohemond of Taranto** during the **First Crusade,** were put to rest. **Antioch** and Tripoli were now allied.

The county of Tripoli anchored the **kingdom of Jerusalem**'s northern frontier and proved resilient during **Saladin**'s invasion in 1188, despite having lost most of its army at the **Battle of Hattin** the previous

The castle of Tripoli. Charles W. Wilson, *Picturesque Palestine, Sinai and Egypt*, 2 vols. (New York: D. Appleton & Co., 1881), 2:9.

year. In July the timely arrival of a Sicilian fleet deterred Saladin from attacking the capital city, and although the port city of Tortosa fell to the sultan, its citadel held out. Three **Hospitaler castles** also withstood his assault, including the massive fortress of *Krak des Chavaliers,* which defended the county's eastern border. With these successes, the county became the base for **Frankish** resistance and recovery even before the **Third Crusade.** It was from here that King **Guy of Lusignan** launched his counterattack against **Acre.**

Tripoli remained a bulwark in the **Latin East**'s defenses until the **Mamluk** invasion in 1288, which found the county vulnerable due to an internal conflict. Although forces rushed to the city of Tripoli from **Cyprus** and Hospitaler and **Templar** contingents also went to its aid, they could not prevent its capture on April 26, 1289. A general **massacre** followed the city's fall. Already almost all of the rest of the county had been overrun and its castles systematically destroyed. All that remained in Frankish hands was the fortified town of Jubail (Gibelet), whose lord was allowed to reside there for another eight or nine years, but under close Mamluk control. **Related Entries:** Edessa; Settlement and Colonization.

Turcopoles

Literally "sons of **Turks**," they were native **mercenary** troops employed by the armies of the **crusader states** and the **military orders.** Some were **Muslims;** some were converts from **Islam;** many more were **Eastern Christians;** even more seem to have been *Poulains,* or the offspring of parents of mixed unions, either **Latin** and Eastern Christian or Christian and Muslim. By the late twelfth century the term was also applied to **Franks** who fought in the Turkish manner.

On its march from **Nicaea** to **Antioch,** the army of the second wave of the **First Crusade** was accompanied by a Turcopole detachment headed by a converted Turk, Taticius, who acted as the personal military representative of Emperor **Alexius I** and the crusaders' guide over treacherous terrain.

Given the extensive duties of the military orders, especially during the thirteenth century, and the low number of sworn brothers in the **Holy Land,** it made sense to hire Turcopoles to fill out their armies and **castle** garrisons. Both the **Templars** and **Hospitalers** commissioned a brother, who bore the title *Turcopolier,* to command their Turcopole troops, who made up a significant portion of their armies.

William of Tyre wrote that most Turcopoles were lightly equipped horsemen. Whether or not they were primarily horse-archers is debated by historians. Some used the Turkish compound bow while mounted; others, possibly the majority, fought with swords, lances, and maces but lacked the **armor** of fully equipped **knights** and rode the small, agile ponies bred by the Turks. Other Turcopoles served as foot soldiers, possibly primarily as archers. **Related Entries:** Cavalry; Weapons, Hand.

Turks

Various peoples who originated as nomadic pastoralists in Central Asia and spoke a variety of languages that belong to the Turkic subfamily of languages.

The Turks entered the **Islamic** World as **infidel** slaves and **mercenary cavalry** in the ninth and tenth centuries, converted to Islam, and became the driving force of militant Islam after the year 1000 and for centuries thereafter. **Muslim** Turks also were important carriers of Islam into their ancestral lands, a process that led to the gradual conversion of most of Central Asia to Islam from the eleventh century onward. **Related Entries:** Islamic Peoples; Khorezmians; Ottomans; Seljuks; Turcopoles.

Tyre

A port city in the most northerly reaches of the **kingdom of Jerusalem,** it was captured by the **Franks** on July 7, 1124, and continuously held by them until retaken by **Muslim** forces on May 19, 1291.

Tyre's most important moment in the history of the **Latin East** was its successful resistance against the advances of **Saladin** between November 13, 1187, and January 1, 1188. Its heroic defense proved to be a vital element in frustrating Saladin's plan to sweep the **Latins** out of the **Holy Land.**

Situated on a peninsula, Tyre has always been difficult to conquer. Because of that fact, it was the last Muslim city along the northern coast of **Syria-Palestine** to fall to Frankish forces and one of the very last to capitulate to the **Mamluks** 167 years later.

It was less resistant to **disease** and earthquakes. As a commercial center that welcomed visitors from near and far, it experienced periodic epidemics, and because of its location near a fault line, it was subject to frequent earth tremors, both small and great. A massive earthquake in 1202 destroyed large portions of its walls, which were then rebuilt thanks in great part to money raised in the West to support the **Fourth Crusade.**

The Venetians were the first European merchants to establish themselves in Latin-held Tyre and to take advantage of its commercial opportunities. They were followed by the Genoese and the Pisans. Although an important center of trade, crusader Tyre never reached the size or importance of **Acre,** but it was substantial enough that the city was required to send a total of twenty-eight **knights** and 150 **sergeants** to the king's army in times of crisis. Ibn Jubair, returning from Mecca to his home in Muslim Spain, visited Tyre in 1184 and reported that it was cleaner than Acre and its citizens were kinder to Muslims. Although the city was smaller than Acre, its harbor was deeper and able to accommodate larger vessels, and its port was livelier. **Related Entries:** Conrad of Montferrat; Crusade of 1122–1126; Mamluks; Third Crusade; William of Tyre.

U

Urban II, Pope (r. 1088–1099)

The pope who set in motion the **First Crusade.**

In response to overtures from Emperor **Alexius I** for help against the **Seljuk Turks** and inspired by the success of Christian warriors in the Spanish **Reconquista,** Pope Urban II joined two traditions of Western Christianity—the **just war** and the penitential **pilgrimage**—to create a new tradition: a **holy war** against **Islam** that became the First Crusade. On November 27, 1095, the pope delivered a public sermon at **Clermont** in southern France, where he had just presided over a church **council** that made the establishment of peace throughout Western Christendom a priority. In that spirit, Pope Urban called upon the warriors of the West to turn their arms to a just cause: the defense of all Christendom and the relief of **Eastern Christians** who were suffering grievously at the hands of the Turks, as well as the liberation of the **Holy Land**—especially the **Holy Sepulcher** in **Jerusalem**—from the hands of **infidels.** Those who undertook this dangerous task were assured that they would merit a plenary, or full, **indulgence,** provided they truly repented and confessed their sins—the normal reward for anyone who undertook a pilgrimage to the tomb of Christ in expiation for sins. By granting this indulgence, Urban transformed warriors into armed pilgrims.

The pope's appeal fell on ready ears. The audience at Clermont was probably large but certainly numbered only in the thousands. In the weeks that followed Urban renewed his appeal as he traveled across southern and western France, and he sent letters with this same message throughout the West, three of which survive to this day. At the same time, he tried to dissuade Spanish lords in Catalonia from joining this expedition because they were needed at home, fighting the **Almoravids.**

The pope's message was also spread by **preachers**—both commissioned members of the clergy and self-appointed popular evangelists, such as **Peter the Hermit.** Many of these unofficial preachers went far beyond the pope's original vision as they stirred up masses of people who were ill-suited for the war in the East and were probably precisely the sort of people Urban did not want taking up his challenge. Some, perhaps many, of these same popular preachers also introduced elements into their preaching that were far removed and even antithetical to the pope's message—such as strong anti-Judaic and **apocalyptic** notes. Thus was born the **People's Crusade,** as opposed to the more organized and more official second wave of the First Crusade.

Urban II had no way of anticipating the magnitude of the centuries-long movement that his words inspired. He also never learned of the success enjoyed by his crusade's second wave. The pope died on July 29, 1099, fourteen days after the crusaders' capture of Jerusalem and months before word of that deed reached the West. **Related**

Entries: Adhémar of Monteil; Cross, Crusader's; *Deus Vult;* Gregory VII; Jews and the Crusades; Noncombatants; Privileges, Crusader; Raymond IV of Saint-Gilles; Truce and Peace of God.

Suggested Reading

Carl Erdmann, *Origins of the Idea of the Crusade* (1935).

V

Vassal

See Feudalism.

Venetian Crusade

See Crusade of 1122–1126.

Visions

See Adhémar of Monteil; Antioch; Children's Crusade; Lance, Holy; Oliver of Paderborn; Peter the Hermit; Saints, Warrior; Santiago de Compostela; Shepherds' Crusade.

Vow, Crusader's

The solemn, binding promise made to God, and normally in the presence of a priest or other cleric, to participate in a crusade.

Monks and nuns swear permanent vows to live lives of poverty, chastity, and obedience to their religious superiors. Lay men and women take temporary vows for a variety of reasons, including the undertaking of a **pilgrimage,** and it was the pilgrim's vow that provided the initial context for the crusaders' vow. Indeed, it was not until around 1200 that church lawyers began to distinguish the crusade vow from the pilgrimage vow. In 1095 Pope **Urban II** joined the expedition to rescue the **Holy Land** to the penitential pilgrimage, and by that act he transformed the warriors whom he was unleashing into pilgrims bound by sacred vows to perform specific tasks: namely, to struggle for the liberation of **Jerusalem** and to crown their victory with devotions before the **Holy Sepulcher.** Failure to *attempt* to achieve these goals would bring with it excommunication from the Church and the risk of eternal damnation. Long after Jerusalem ceased to be the sole crusade objective, the crusader remained a person on a holy mission who was bound to that task by a sacred vow, and that vow was sufficiently solemn to impel some dying crusaders who had not had the opportunity to embark on the journey to designate surrogates to whom they bequeathed their crusade funds and obligations.

Before 1095 the Western Church lacked a well-defined theory of the vow and its obligations and sanctions. With tens of thousands of lay people now assuming the crusade vow, church lawyers and theologians were impelled to define more precisely the nature of a vow over the course of the twelfth and thirteenth centuries, and crusade circumstances helped drive that definition.

A noblewoman damned to hell, Chartres Cathedral, France, 1200–1225. The hope of gaining sufficient merit to avoid eternal damnation and to gain Heaven was a major factor in the decision of hundreds of thousands of Latin Christians, women as well as men, to vow to go on crusade.

Because of the hardships associated with a crusade, clerics were initially instructed by the papacy to accept crusade vows only from people who appeared able to undertake the expedition and to contribute to its success, and because of its binding force, a person was released from his or her crusade vow only in the most exceptional circumstances. All of this changed in the reign of Pope **Innocent III.** While establishing the groundwork for the **Fifth Crusade,** the pope decreed in 1213 that his preachers were to accept the vow from each and every willing lay person, regardless of sex, age, or other circumstances. Those who proved unfit for the expedition could then have their vows commuted (by performing a substitute penitential act), deferred to a later time (when the person would be able to carry out the crusade), or redeemed by a money payment (proportional to one's means but ideally a sum that would support one crusader for several years).

Innocent made this ruling out of a desire to offer all Western Christians the opportunity to share in the spiritual benefits of the crusade, especially its **indulgence,** and also to raise substantially the number of people involved in contributing to the success of the crusade, by their participation, by their prayers, and by their money. Although cash redemption of vows addressed an immediate problem, raising funds for the crusades, in the long term it proved unhealthy for Western Christendom because of the abuses it spawned. It was only several short steps from vow redemption to the outright buying and selling of indulgences—one of the many issues that contributed to the sixteenth-century Protestant Reformation. **Related Entries:** Albigensian Crusade; Criticism of the Crusades; Financing the Crusades; Privileges, Crusader; Recruitment; Women.

W

Walter Sansavoir

Often mistakenly referred to as "Walter the Penniless," Walter was one of the abler leaders of the **People's Crusade.**

The mistranslation of Walter's surname has led to the mistaken impression that he was a poverty-stricken knight; in fact, his family were the lords of Poissy-sans-Avoir. Along with four kinsmen, Walter joined the ranks of the **First Crusade** in early 1096, probably in response to the **preaching** of **Peter the Hermit.**

In the company of only seven other knights, Walter led the first large party of crusaders to arrive at **Constantinople,** reaching the city in mid-July 1096. Walter's military skills enabled him to maintain fairly good order among his followers as they marched through southern Germany, Hungary, and the Balkans. After about two weeks, his forces were joined by those of Peter the Hermit; together the two armies, along with some Italian crusaders, encamped outside Constantinople's walls.

Due to the restlessness of their people, Walter and Peter accepted transportation by the **Byzantines** across the Bosporus to the shores of **Anatolia** on August 6. From there they marched inland to Civetot, an abandoned frontier fort. When a German-Italian force that had foolishly gone off in search of **plunder** was besieged and captured at Xerigordon, the French crusaders at Civetot rushed to their aid and right into an ambush. Despite Walter's misgivings and his pleas for caution, he accompanied the relief force and was killed in the disaster on October 21.

Weapons, Hand

Muslim and **Frankish** warriors largely carried the same hand weapons, but some of the ways they employed them differed. The three most significant differences were the **Islamic cavalry**'s reliance on the compound bow, a similar reliance on the crossbow by Western **infantry,** and the **Frankish knights'** use of the couched lance.

The double-curved compound bow was known to the Franks as the "**Turkish** bow," a reasonably correct attribution, given that it originated with the nomadic horse archers of Central Asia. Made from layers of horn and sinew on a wooden frame, the strung bow had a double curve with the center bending toward the archer and both ends bending away. The bow's composite construction and double-curved shape demanded a pull of between 100 to 160 pounds, but it provided an effective killing range of over 200 yards. Some historians claim its killing range exceeded 350 yards, but that does not seem likely, given the lightness of the bow's arrows.

The compound bow was known in the West, thanks to invasions of Europe by various steppe peoples in the centuries preceding the crusades. Nevertheless, so far as the crusades in the **Middle East** were concerned, the Turkish bow remained largely the exclusive weapon of Islamic mounted soldiers and the native **Turcopole mercenaries** who served the Frankish armies as light cavalry and foot soldiers. Other than Turcopoles, the only crusader forces that used the compound bow in any significant numbers were the Christian archers of **Iberia** during the **Reconquista.** Indeed, the Spaniards had units of mounted archers who fired the compound bow in the manner of their **Moorish** enemies.

As far as conventional bows made from a single wooden stave were concerned, originally Western archers used a short bow, and in the course of the thirteenth century began to lengthen it, thereby giving it more power and range. The virtue of these bows was that they were inexpensive and when put into sufficient hands could deliver a deadly mass of arrows on the enemy at short range. If the archers had any training whatsoever, they could repeat their volleys at a fairly rapid rate until they exhausted their arrows.

The Franks' premier handheld missile-launching weapon was the crossbow—a triggered, mechanical device that delivered a short, iron-tipped bolt with devastating force, accuracy, and range. It was an ancient weapon, initially developed by the Chinese during the fifth century B.C.E. and introduced to the Romans probably in the first century C.E. The crossbow was used by Western armies off and on in the centuries that followed, but it did not become popular in Europe until the eleventh century, perhaps because of its cost of production, the relative

slowness with which it was loaded, and the special training and abilities required for those who used it. During the Age of the Crusades, however, the crossbow became a favored infantry weapon and underwent a number of technical improvements, including the introduction of a more flexible composite crossbow made of horn, sinew, and glue. Because of its superior lethal qualities, the Franks used it as an offensive and defensive weapon, but those same qualities impelled the Roman Church to condemn it as a devilish weapon that could not be used against Christians. The condemnation, however, had little or no effect on the West's pious soldiery. **Richard I,** who championed its use, was killed by a crossbow bolt shot by French soldier.

Anna Comnena, writing during the first half of the twelfth century, characterized the crossbow as a barbarian weapon unknown to the **Byzantines** until they witnessed crusaders using this "truly diabolical machine." Evidence suggests that she was wrong, and Byzantine armies employed crossbowmen well before the Era of the Crusades. At the same time, the weapon never became a key element in the Byzantine military arsenal. The same was true of the Muslims, who knew and used a handheld crossbow well before the **First Crusade,** yet never during the classical Age of the Crusades did Islamic armies in the Eastern Mediterranean use the weapon as extensively as did their crusader opponents.

If the compound bow was the weapon that distinguished the Muslim cavalryman, the couched lance was the weapon that distinguished the Frankish knight. Both sides employed spears and lances. Muslim foot soldiers and horsemen alike used lances as hand missiles and thrusting weapons, and Frankish infantrymen used thrusting spears for impaling enemies in close combat. The knight on horseback, however, became noted for couching his lance, that is, tucking it under his right arm and close against his side, while holding the shaft just in front of his shoulder and using his horse's weight and momentum to drive the lance into his enemy's body.

The other weapon of choice of the knight was the sword, and swords of many types were used by Franks and Muslims alike, as were axes, slings, maces, and knives, all of which had the sole purpose of maiming, mutilating, incapacitating, and killing the enemy. **Related Entries:** Armor; Siege Warfare.

Suggested Reading

Kelly DeVries, *Medieval Military Technology* (1992); Robert Elgood, *Islamic Arms and Armour* (1979); David Nicolle, *Arms & Armour of the Crusading Era, 1050–1350* (1999); R. Ewart Oakeshott, *A Knight and His Weapons* (1997).

William of Tyre

Native-born archbishop of **Tyre** (r. 1175–1185 or 1186) and author of the *Jerusalem History,* also known as *A History of Deeds Done beyond the Sea.*

William of Tyre's history spans the years 1095 to 1184 and is the only contemporary or near-contemporary account of the **Latin East** recorded by a Western resident for the period from the late 1120s to 1184. It is especially important for the years 1165–1184 because during that era William played increasingly important roles in the Church and the **kingdom of Jerusalem.** In addition to being an eyewitness for much of what he reported in the latter parts of his history, William judiciously examined and critically used a wide variety of documentary evidence and oral testimony throughout his work.

William was unique among **Latin historians** of the crusades inasmuch as he learned Arabic, used **Islamic** sources, and was deeply interested in the history of the Islamic faith and its people, although he looked upon Muhammad as "the first-born son of Satan" and a false prophet. In fact, William composed a history of Islam, *The Deeds of the Eastern Princes.* Begun at the behest of King **Amalric,** the work covered the period from the time of Muhammad to 1184. Unfortunately, that history is now lost.

William was born in Jerusalem around 1130, departed for Europe around 1146, where he studied the liberal arts, theology, and law in Orleans, Paris, and Bologna, and returned home in 1165. Upon his return he entered into the service of the bishop of **Acre** and later of the archbishop of Tyre. He also served as tutor to the future King **Baldwin IV.** In 1174 he was named chancellor of the kingdom, the official in charge of the secretariat that drafted and recorded all royal documents. The following year he was elected archbishop of Tyre, a position that ranked second only to the **patriarch of Jerusalem** in the Latin Church of the East. William continued to hold both offices until his death, which occurred on September 29 in either 1185 or (less likely) 1186.

A modern edition of William's richly detailed *Jerusalem History* fills just under 1,000 pages, and inevitably such a massive work, written and revised serially over a long period, contains narrative lapses, clumsy insertions, inconsistencies, anachronisms, and chronological errors. Regardless, when checked against other evidence, the work stands up very well as a major source for a pivotal period in the life of the crusader kingdom of Jerusalem. **Related Entries:** Agnes of Courtenay; James of Vitry; *Poulain.*

Suggested Reading

Primary Source

Emily Atwater Babcock and A. C. Krey, eds. and trans., *A History of Deeds Done beyond the Sea by William, Archbishop of Tyre,* 2 vols. (1976).

Historical Study

Peter W. Edbury and John Gordon Rowe, *William of Tyre: Historian of the Latin East* (1988).

Women

Whether they crusaded or stayed at home, women played a variety of important roles in the crusades.

During the summer of 1202 Pope **Innocent III** instructed his **papal legate** to the **Fourth Crusade** army to absolve or commute the **crusade vows** of all persons whose presence he judged would be a detriment to the upcoming expedition: the poor, the weak, and women unaccompanied by husbands, *except for women leading groups of soldiers!* Extant Western sources do not provide any further evidence of involvement by women in positions of crusade leadership, and the issue remains murky, although the Arab **historian** Imad ad-Din claimed that one rich queen arrived at the **siege** of **Acre** (1188–1191) leading 500 knights, whom she maintained at her own expense. Unsupported by Western sources, this story cannot be verified. Regardless of whether they led troops or not, women played important roles in the crusades, both in the field and at home.

Some wives accompanied their husbands on crusade, but the women accompanying crusader forces included more than just wives. It is impossible to say what percentage of any crusade force was female, but we know something about the motives that impelled women to undertake these dangerous expeditions. Many were crusaders and **pilgrims;** that is, they had sworn public vows and wore the **crusader's cross.** Others, who had chosen not to wear the cross, performed a variety of functions in support of the armies with which they traveled. Some were merchants; others were washerwomen. And then there were the prostitutes, both male and female. **Holy war** did not inhibit sexual drive. Imad ad-Din reported that 300 lovely Frankish women, each a "licentious harlot," arrived by sea to give support to the soldiers besieging Acre during the **Third**

After his victory at Hattin, Saladin receives the surrender of nearby Tiberias from Eschiva, the countess of Tripoli. On occasion, wives of nobles and kings were called upon to lead the defense of besieged castles and towns when their husbands were on campaign or otherwise unavailable. From a manuscript copy of the *Estoire d'Eracles,* a continuation of William of Tyre's history to 1261. Paris ca. 1300. The Walters Art Museum, Baltimore.

Crusade, maintaining, as he sarcastically noted, that they were performing meritorious acts of piety by plying their trade.

Women who accompanied crusade armies shared the dangers with their male companions. Death could and did come in many ways, including summary execution at the hands of the victorious enemy, if they were not **enslaved** when taken **prisoner.** Combat also took its toll. On occasion, women accompanying crusader armies participated in the fighting and in other military activities. The Arab historian Ibn al-Athir reported that a number of Frankish women donned **armor** and took part in the fighting at Acre during its siege by the armies of the Third Crusade. During the siege of **Damietta** by the army of the **Fifth Crusade** in 1219, crusader camp women killed a number of fleeing Muslims whose attack on the crusader lines had been repulsed. Shortly thereafter, army leaders sought to bolster the crusaders' diminishing strength by dividing everyone, women included, into camp security groups. Severe penalties, including loss of a hand, were established for anyone, including a woman, who deserted a post. Any woman or man found without weapons after having been assigned guard duty would be excommunicated.

Despite their many contributions to various crusades, sexual stereotypes and prejudices turned women into convenient targets of blame when situations turned sour. **Fulcher of Chartres** reported that during the bitter siege of **Antioch** in 1097–1098 the army suffered terribly because of its sins. After deliberating on the matter, the army drove all women, both married and unmarried, out of the camp, "lest they, stained by the defilement of dissipation, displease the Lord." The women found places to live in neighboring camps.

Many women who remained back home in Europe were also touched by and had an influence on the crusades. Within a number of noble families crusading became a multigenerational tradition, and women often carried these traditions to the families into which they married. Wives, mothers, sisters, and aunts also helped **finance** the crusades of their male relatives. They financed crusades in other ways, as well. A fair portion of the money contributed to support the **Fifth Crusade** came from women who had taken the crusade vow but then were permitted (and encouraged) to redeem the vow for cash solely on the grounds of their sex. Wives left behind by crusaders were often called upon to perform their absent husbands' duties. For noblewomen, this meant managing estates; for wives of every station, it meant being exposed to an uncertainty as to their husbands' fate that lasted for years, and for some, a lifetime. For many women, it also meant being exposed to exploitation on numerous fronts.

At the same time, popular lore tended to look upon women as inhibitors rather than facilitators of crusading. Churchmen and troubadours alike often portrayed wives, female lovers, and mothers as weeping frail vessels who tried to dissuade their menfolk from leaving home. Such a characterization must have amused Adela, wife of Count **Stephen of Blois,** who shamed her husband into returning to the crusade (and his death) after his flight from Antioch during the **First Crusade.** Evidence does not exist to allow us to say anything with certainty regarding relative numbers, but it seems likely that for every woman who fired her husband and sons with ardor for crusading, there were probably at least several who tried to disabuse them of such notions.

Certainly church leaders thought so. The Church considered the marriage bond so sacred that twelfth-century canon, or church, law stipulated that a husband needed his wife's consent before he could licitly swear a crusade vow. This changed early in the reign of Pope Innocent III. So eager was Innocent to enlist crusaders for the **Fourth Crusade,** he ruled that husbands did not need their wives' permission to assume and execute a crusade vow. The status of the crusade wife was altered forever.

Women also played significant roles as **settlers and colonists** in the **crusader states** of the **Latin East,** where they functioned as artisans, entrepreneurs, mothers, wives, nuns, and rulers. By tradition, if there was no male heir, the crown of the **kingdom of Jerusalem** passed from a king *or a queen* to the eldest daughter and her husband. The husband would be crowned co-monarch but retained his right to rule only as long as his wife, the queen, lived. By virtue of this tradition, a number of strong women, such as Queen **Melisende,** exercised considerable authority as co-monarch in their own right and also as regents for their underage, fatherless children. The same rule held for **feudal** baronies in the crusader states, which allowed adventurers from the West, such as **Reynald of Châtillon,** to become great lords, as long as their heiress-wives lived. **Related Rntries:** Agnes of Courtenay; Alice of Antioch; Alice of Champagne; Bailli; Constance of Antioch; Dorylaeum, Battle of; Eleanor of Aquitaine; Isabella I; Isabella (Yolanda) II; Margaret of Provence; Maria of Montferrat; Noncombatants; Prisoners; Sibylla.

Suggested Reading

Derek Baker, ed., *Medieval Women* (1978); Susan B. Edgington and Sarah Lambert, eds., *Gendering the Crusades* (2002); Graham McLennan, *Women Crusaders: Women and the Holy Land, 1095–1195* (1997).

Z

Zangi (Zengi), Imad ad-Din

Turkish *atabeg* (governor) of **Mosul** and **Aleppo** (r. 1127–1146), conqueror of **Edessa,** and one of the first important leaders in the **Islamic** counter-crusade.

In 1127, Zangi rose to power as the *atabeg* of Mosul, a city in northern Iraq that, at the time, was the only portion of the once great but now fragmented Great **Seljuk** empire capable of offering effective resistance to the **crusader states.** As *atabeg,* Zangi nominally served as the appointee and subordinate of the Great Seljuk sultan; in fact, he ruled independently, free of any effective control from above.

The following year, 1128, Zangi was able, in a bloodless coup, to add Aleppo in northern **Syria** to his domain. This step led him to concentrate on bringing **Damascus,** the major Islamic stronghold of southern Syria, under his control. His efforts only resulted in driving Damascus into an alliance with the crusader **kingdom of Jerusalem** in 1139.

Frustrated in the south, Zangi turned his attention to the north and succeeded in capturing the crusader city of Edessa in December 1144. Edessa, the first state established by the crusaders in the East, was now the first to fall to an Islamic counteroffensive. News of this disaster spurred Pope **Eugenius III** to call for a new crusade—the so-called **Second Crusade** of 1147–1149.

Despite his own lukewarm piety, Zangi's success at Edessa transformed him into Islam's most visible champion of resistance to the crusader states, and he exploited that image by presenting himself as the leader of a pan-Islamic **jihad** against the **infidels** from the West. He prosecuted his wars with such ferocity that the **Franks** called him *Sanguin* (blood).

Zangi's ambitions were cut short on September 14, 1146, when he was murdered by a Frankish slave as he lay drunk. With his death, Mosul passed to his eldest son, Saif ed-Din Ghazi, and his second son, **Nur ad-Din,** took control of Aleppo. It would be Nur ad-Din who would lead the fight against the Franks and who would profit the most from the ill-conceived strategy and tactics of the armies of the Second Crusade. **Related Entries:** Baldwin I; Fulk of Anjou; Zangids.

Zangids

A **Turkish** family that derives its name from **Zangi,** who initiated the first major **jihad** against the **crusader states.**

The Zangids remained in the forefront of the countercrusade until the death in 1176 of their greatest member, **Nur ad-Din,** who united **Muslim Syria** in 1154. After Nur ad-Din's death leadership in the struggle against the **Latin East** passed to **Saladin** and his family, the **Ayyubids.**

Important Crusade Dates and Events

This chronological chart focuses almost exclusively on the classic Age of the Crusades (1095–1291) and with the crusades in the Levant, although a few important events are noted relating to the *Reconquista,* the Baltic crusades, and several crusades and quasi-crusades in Europe. The papacy's political crusades against the Hohenstaufens do not appear here.

August 26, 1071—Battle of Manzikert

May 25, 1085—Alfonso VI of Castile and León Captures Toledo

June 1089–1094—Almoravids Conquer Most of Moorish Spain

November 27, 1095—Pope Urban II's Sermon at Clermont

1096–1102—**First Crusade**

October 21, 1096—First Wave Wiped Out Near Nicaea

March 9, 1098—Baldwin of Boulogne Seizes Power in Edessa

June 3, 1098—Crusaders Capture Antioch

July 15, 1099—Crusaders Capture Jerusalem

July 22, 1099—Godfrey of Bouillon Elected Defender of the Holy Sepulcher

December 25, 1100—Baldwin I of Boulogne Crowned King of Jerusalem

August–September 1101—Third-Wave Crusaders Suffer Three Major Defeats

May 1104—Crusaders Capture Acre

July 12, 1109—Crusaders Capture Tripoli

December 18, 1118—Saragossa Falls to King Alfonso I of Aragon and Navarre

June 28, 1119—Muslim Victory at the Battle of the Field of Blood

1119/1120—Templars Are Founded

1122–1126—**Crusade of 1122–1126**

July 7, 1124—Crusaders Capture Tyre

June 18, 1128—Zangi Enters Aleppo

1129—**Damascus Crusade**

1132/1133—Assassins Move into Syria

December 24–26, 1144—Zangi Captures Edessa

December 1, 1145—Pope Eugenius III Issues *Quantum praedecessores,* Proclaiming a New Crusade

March 31, 1146—King Louis VII Assumes the Crusader's Cross

September 14, 1146—Zangi Killed; Nur ad-Din Succeeds Him at Aleppo

November 3, 1146—Nur ad-Din Captures and Sacks Edessa

Christmas 1146—Conrad III Vows to Crusade

1147–1149—**Second Crusade**

October 1147—Conrad III and Imperial Forces Defeated Near Dorylaeum

October 24, 1147—Crusaders Capture Lisbon

January 1148—Louis VII and French Forces Defeated Near Cadmus

July 24–28, 1148—Crusaders' Failed Siege of Damascus

September 8, 1148—Conrad III Leaves for Home

Easter 1149—Louis VII Departs for Home

August 22, 1153—King Baldwin III Captures Ascalon

April 25, 1154—Nur ad-Din Occupies Damascus

September 1163–December 1169—King Amalric's Five Campaigns in Egypt

March 1169—Saladin Becomes Vizier of Egypt

September 13, 1171—Last Fatimid Caliph of Egypt Dies

1172—Almohads Complete the Conquest of Muslim Spain

May 15, 1174—Death of Nur ad-Din

July 11, 1174—Death of King Amalric

October 28, 1174—Saladin Occupies Damascus

May 1175—Abbasid Caliph Invests Saladin with Authority over Egypt and Syria

March 3, 1186—Saladin Recognized as Lord of Mosul

1186–early 1187—Reynald of Châtillon Breaks Truce with Saladin

July 4, 1187—Saladin's Victory at Hattin

October 2, 1187—Jerusalem Surrenders to Saladin

Late October 1187—Pope Gregory VIII Proclaims a New Crusade

November 13, 1187–January 1, 1188—Tyre Resists Saladin's Siege

1187–1188—Saladin Conquers Almost All of the Latin East, Except for Tyre, Tripoli, and Antioch

1188–1192—**Third Crusade**

Summer 1188—Sicilian Fleet Arrives in the Levant

August 27, 1189—Guy of Lusignan Begins the Siege of Acre

June 10, 1190—Emperor Frederick I Dies in Cilicia

May 6–June 5, 1191—Richard the Lionheart Conquers Cyprus

July 12, 1191—Acre Surrenders to Crusaders

July 31, 1191—King Philip II Leaves for Home

September 7, 1191—King Richard's Victory at Arsuf

August 1–5, 1192—King Richard's Victories at Jaffa

September 2, 1192—Truce Concluded

March 4, 1193—Death of Saladin

July 19, 1195—Almohads Victorious at the Battle of Alarcos

1197–1198—**German Crusade**

September 28, 1197—Emperor Henry VI Dies

August 15, 1198—Pope Innocent III Proclaims a New Crusade

1202–1204—**Fourth Crusade**

November 24, 1202—Crusaders Capture Zara

July 17, 1203—Crusaders Assault Constantinople

July 18, 1203—Alexius the Younger and the Crusaders Invited into the City

August 18–19, 1204—Anti-Latin Riot and the Great Fire in Constantinople

February 8, 1204—Murder of Emperor Alexius IV

April 12–13, 1204—Crusaders Assault, Capture, and Pillage Constantinople

May 16, 1204—Baldwin of Flanders Crowned Emperor

1204–1261—Latin Empire of Constantinople

January 14, 1208—Murder of Peter of Castelnau in Languedoc

1209–1229—**Albigensian Crusade**

July 22, 1209—Capture of Béziers

August 1209—Simon of Montfort Elected Leader of the Albigensian Crusade

Spring–Summer 1212—**Children's Crusade**

July 16, 1212—Moors Defeated at the Battle of Las Navas de Tolosa in Spain

September 12, 1212—Montfort's Victory at Muret

April 1213—Innocent III Begins Preparations for the Fifth Crusade

July 15, 1215—Frederick II Vows to Crusade

November 30, 1215—Fourth Lateran Council Issues a Decree for the Fifth Crusade

1217–1221—**Fifth Crusade**

Fall 1217–January 1218—Hungarian-Austrian Segment of the Fifth Crusade

May 27, 1218—Siege of Damietta Begins

June 25, 1218—Montfort Killed at Toulouse

November 5, 1219—Damietta Falls to the Crusaders

November 22, 1220—Frederick II Crowned Emperor and Again Vows to Crusade

July 1221—Crusade Army Marches out of Damietta

August 29, 1221—Army of the Fifth Crusade Surrenders to al-Kamil

Early June 1226—King Louis VIII Leads a Crusade against the Cathars

November 8, 1226—King Louis Dies on Campaign

1227–1229—**Sixth Crusade**

September 29, 1227—Frederick II Excommunicated

February 18, 1229—Frederick Gains Jerusalem through a Truce with al-Kamil

March 18, 1229—Frederick Crowns Himself King of Jerusalem

April 12, 1229—Peace of Paris Ends the Albigensian Crusade

May 1, 1229—Frederick Sets Sail for the West

September 1234—Pope Gregory IX Begins to Plan a New Crusade

1239–1241—**Crusade of 1239–1241**

September 1, 1239—French Crusaders Arrive at Acre

December 7, 1239—Muslims Reoccupy Jerusalem

Spring–Summer 1240—Thibault of Champagne Concludes Favorable Treaties with the Sultans of Damascus and Cairo

September 1240—Thibault Departs for Home

October 8, 1240—English Crusaders Arrive at Acre

April 13, 1241—Richard of Cornwall Secures the Return of Jerusalem

May 3, 1241—English Crusaders Depart for Home

April 5, 1242—Alexander Nevsky Defeats the Teutonic Knights

August 23, 1244—Khorezmians Capture and Pillage Jerusalem

December 1244—Louis IX Vows to Crusade

1248–1254—**Seventh Crusade**

August 25, 1248—Louis Sails for the East

June 6, 1249—Crusaders Occupy Damietta

April 6, 1250—Louis and His Crusaders Surrender

May 2, 1250—Mamluks Depose and Murder the Ayyubid Sultan of Egypt

May 6, 1250—Damietta Is Surrendered and Louis Ransomed

Spring–Summer 1251—**Shepherds' Crusade**

1252—Louis Allies with the Mamluks of Egypt

February 1254—Louis Concludes a Truce with the Ayyubids of Syria

April 24, 1254—Louis Sails for Home

February 1258—Mongols Destroy Baghdad and the Abbasid Dynasty

September 3, 1260—Mamluks Defeat the Mongols at Ayn Jalut

October 23, 1260—Baybars Usurps the Mamluk Throne

July 25, 1261—Greeks Regain Constantinople

March 25, 1267—Louis IX Vows Another Crusade

March 7, 1268—Baybars Captures Jaffa

May 18, 1268—Mamluks Capture and Destroy Antioch

June 24, 1268—Prince Edward Vows to Crusade

1270–1272—**Eighth Crusade**

July 18, 1270—French Crusaders Land at Tunis

August 25, 1270—Louis IX Dies of Disease

November 1, 1270—Charles of Anjou Concludes a Truce

April 8, 1271—Baybars Captures *Krak des Chevaliers*

Spring 1271—Prince Edward Arrives in Acre

September 1272—Edward (Now King of England as Edward I) Departs

July 9, 1273—Last Assassin Stronghold in Syria Falls to the Mamluks

July 1, 1277—Baybars Dies

April 26, 1289—Mamluks Capture and Sack Tripoli

May 28, 1291—Acre Falls to the Mamluks

May–mid-August 1291—Remaining Frankish Strongholds in Syria-Palestine Surrender to the Mamluks

1309—Teutonic Knights Establish New Headquarters in Prussia

March 12, 1312—Templars Dissolved

July 15, 1410—Teutonic Knights Crushed at Tannenberg

May 29, 1453—Constantinople Falls to the Ottoman Turks

January 2, 1492—Catholic Monarchs of Spain Capture Granada

A Basic Crusade Library

In addition to the books on special crusade topics that are listed in the **Suggested Reading** lists that follow many of the entries in this encyclopedia, there are a number of general books that any serious student of the crusades should consult. Each of the books recommended below deserves consultation by anyone who wishes to have a solid understanding of the crusades in their many forms.

Atlases

The only atlas worth considering, and it is an invaluable research tool, is *The Atlas of the Crusades* (1991), edited by Jonathan Riley-Smith. This collection of maps, illustrations, and short essays covers the crusades from 1095 to the eighteenth century and is a first-rate example of the pluralist approach to crusade studies. The atlas is enriched with excellent chronological tables and a short but useful glossary of important terms. Reflecting the notion that crusade history must deal with common individuals, as well as the high and mighty, the atlas contains sections devoted to such topics as **settler** villages in the **Latin East,** the European home front, and shipping and trade.

General Histories

Ten excellent crusade histories are available in paperback editions and should be considered for purchase.

Although its scholarship is considerably out of date, Steven Runciman's three-volume *A History of the Crusades* (1951–1954) should be read because it is a pioneering classic, it looks at the crusades with an Eastern slant, and it is beautifully written. It is also an excellent example of the traditionalist approach to the crusades. Many people have devoted their lives to crusade studies because they were introduced to these holy wars by Runciman.

Hans Eberhard Meyer, *The Crusades,* 2nd ed., translated by John Gillingham (1988), is a weighty and important book by Germany's leading crusade specialist. Like Runciman, Meyer presents a traditionalist view of the crusades and the crusader states, focusing exclusively on the Eastern Mediterranean in the period 1095–1291.

Jean Richard, the dean of French crusade historians, is sympathetic to the pluralist position, but his *The Crusades, c. 1071–c. 1291,* translated by Jean Birrell (1999), presents essentially a view of the crusades within a traditionalist framework. Written by a historian who has devoted a long life to mastering the crusades in all of their intricacies, this book is filled with important information and wise insights.

The leading pluralist among today's crusade historians is Jonathan Riley-Smith of the University of Cambridge in England. His *The Crusades: A Short History* (1987) covers all of the theaters of crusade war and takes the story down to 1798. A favorite textbook for professors offering survey courses on the crusades, the book is reader-friendly and presents the mature insights of one of the world's foremost experts on the crusades.

Another book that appeals to students and teachers alike is Thomas F. Madden, *A Concise History of the Crusades* (1999). Madden, a young scholar who has already established himself as a leading interpreter of the crusades, wrote this book primarily for American collegiate students, and he succeeded in reaching his audience. Madden is a pluralist and touches on crusades outside of the East and beyond 1291, but most of the book's focus is on the traditional crusades to the Levant.

Malcolm Billings, *The Crusades: Five Centuries of Holy Wars* (1996), is out of print but well worth securing if possible. The book, which Billings initially produced under the title *The Cross and the Crescent* (1987) to accompany a BBC radio series of the same name, is richly illustrated and reflects the pluralist vision of the crusades.

Norman Housley's most recent contribution to crusade scholarship is *The Crusaders* (2002). Although he presents a thumb-nail sketch of crusading from the First Crusade to the early fifteenth century, he does not aim to give his reader a detailed crusade narrative. Rather, through his analysis of crusade accounts that span the period from 1095 to 1409, Housley presents us with a study of the crusaders' psychological makeup. He asks and answers such questions as: Who were these men and women who took up the cross? What motivated them, and how did they see themselves and their enemies?

The Oxford Illustrated History of the Crusades, edited by Jonathan Riley-Smith (1995), is a lavishly illustrated compendium of articles by a number of specialists on various thematic aspects of the crusades. Mirroring the pluralist viewpoint of its editor, the book traces the crusades and crusade institutions into the eighteenth century.

One of the more interesting one-volume surveys of the crusades from a pluralist perspective is Elizabeth Hallam, ed., *Chronicles of the Crusades: Eye-witness Accounts of the Wars between Christianity and Islam* (1989; paperback ed., 2000). The book begins with a survey of the Islamic

World before 1096 and then traces the crusading tradition down to the sixteenth-century conquistadors in the New World. It does so by offering a pastiche of short excerpts from primary sources interspersed with sidebar essays on a wide variety of interesting and important topics (for example, "Muslim fortifications" and "The Kurds") and numerous illustrations, many from medieval manuscripts. Adding to its value are an appendix of short biographies of notable crusaders and countercrusaders and a short glossary of terms.

Hallam quotes from Islamic, as well as Western, sources, but for a fully satisfying view of the crusades from a Muslim viewpoint, one must turn to Carole Hillenbrand, *The Crusades: Islamic Perspectives* (2000). This is an important contribution to crusade historiography, and its numerous illustrations, which appear on almost every page, add to its value.

In addition to these readily available and fairly inexpensive general histories, there is a hard-bound, six-volume *A History of the Crusades,* 2nd ed. (1969–1989), edited by Kenneth Setton and others. This collaborative effort of many authors contains articles of uneven quality, as is inevitable in a work of this magnitude. Some are cutting-edge and well written; others are out of date or poorly styled. Its strength lies in the fact that it covers so much ground and presents a pluralist vision of the crusades. Whatever its shortcomings, it is an important reference work that belongs in every school and public library.

The recent appearance of *The New Cambridge Medieval History,* *Volume 5: c. 1198–1300* (1999), edited by David Abulafia, presents the student of the crusades with a number of important articles on thirteenth-century crusade topics by some of the leading scholars in the field and should not be overlooked. Volume 6, which covers the period ca. 1300–1415 and is edited by Michael Jones (2000), and Volume 7, which covers the period ca. 1415–ca. 1500 and is edited by Christopher Allmand (1998), have less crusade coverage but do contain several important articles on the Later Crusades and associated topics. Volume 4, which will center on the period ca. 1024–1198 and, therefore, the first century of crusading, is scheduled to appear in January 2004. Because Jonathan Riley-Smith is one of its two editors, we can expect this volume to pay special attention to the crusades.

General Collections of Primary Sources

An important collection of primary sources, but now unfortunately out of print, is Louise and Jonathan Riley-Smith, eds., *The Crusades: Idea and Reality, 1095–1274* (1981). An older but still valuable collection is James A. Brundage, *The Crusades: A Documentary Survey* (1962). Chapter 11, "The Crusades: Expanding Europe's Horizons," in Alfred J. Andrea, ed., *The Medieval Record: Sources of Medieval History* (1997), also has some crusade sources worth consulting. For Islamic sources, the standard collection is Francesco Gabrieli, *Arab Historians of the Crusades,* translated from Italian by E. J. Costello (1969).

Collections of Crusade Studies

Collections of specialized articles devoted to the crusades are legion. Most are by specialists for specialists, but Thomas F. Madden has drawn together an interesting set of articles that can be read and appreciated by the general reader. *The Crusades: The Essential Readings* (2002) contains twelve studies that center on three questions: What were the crusades? Who were the crusaders? What was the impact of the crusades on the East?

The Crusades in Modern History

One of the most important books produced in the last several years is Elizabeth Siberry, *The New Crusaders: Images of the Crusades in the Nineteenth and Early Twentieth Centuries* (2000), which traces the continuation of crusade ideology and imagery, largely in England, from the nineteenth century down to around the end of World War I.

Index

Primary entries are in **bold;** illustrations and maps in *italics*.

Abbasids (dynasty), **1,** 105, 174, 180, 203, 255, 275, 283, 307

Achaea, principality of, 131

Acre, port city of, **1–3,** *2,* 85–86, 100, 112, 130, 133, 177, 200, 222, 292, 299; capital of the Latin kingdom of Jerusalem, 3, 89, 149, 183, 185, 276, 303, 313; compared with Tyre, 323; described, 2, 178; massacres at, 3, 209, 267; Order of Saint Thomas of Acre, 214; siege and capture (1104), 2, 33, 182; siege and capture (1189–1191), 2–3, 37, 68, 144, 148, 183, 225, 267, 276, 295, 297, 298, 314, 315, 318, 321, 332–33; siege and capture (1291), 3, 198, 206, 298

Adela, 306, 333

Adhémar of Monteil (Adhémar of Le Puy), bishop and papal legate, **3–4,** 72, 196, 199, 253

Al-Adil (Saphadin), Ayyubid sultan, **4,** 30, 65, 111, 138, 178, 190, 264, 267, 319

Adrianople, city of, **4–5,** 36, 83, 230, 280

Agnes of Courtenay, **5,** 14, 143, 185, 294

Aigues Mortes, town of, 101, 289

Aimery of Lusignan, king of Jerusalem and Cyprus, **5–6,** 89, 138, 143, 144, 149, 172, 208

Al-Aksa Mosque, 180, 310, 311, *312*

Alamut, castle of, 28, 29

Alarcos, Battle of (1195), 258–59

Alberic of Trois-Fontaines, historian, 68

Albert of Aachen, historian, 97, 116, 186, 237

Albert of Vercelli, patriarch of Jerusalem, 55, 184

Albigensian Crusade, **6–10,** 63–64, 81, 111, 150, 162, 166, 226, 229. *See also* Ribauds

Albigensians. *See* Cathars

Aleppo, city of, **10,** 30, 43, 103, 107, 204, 222, 228, 276, 308, 335

Alexander II, Pope, 165, 257

Alexander III, Pope, 38, 206, 258

Alexandria, city of, *14,* 49, 90, 123

Alexius I Comnenus, emperor of Constantinople, **10–12;** and the First Crusade, 11–12, 18, 118, 119, 121, 139, 164, 306; and the Normans, 11, 16, 18–19, 42, 43, 44, 118, 310; and Raymond of Saint-Gilles, 197, 253–54, 269; and Robert II of Flanders, 268, 269; and the Seljuks, 11, 283; and Stephen of Blois, 119, 306; and Urban II, 45–46, 325. *See also* Anna Comnena; Crusade of 1107

Alexius III Angelus, emperor of Constantinople, 77, 126, 127, 137–38, 171

Alexius IV Angelus, emperor of Constantinople, 126–28, 156–57, 171

Alexius V Ducas, emperor of Constantinople, 127, 128

Alfonso I, king of Aragon, 84, 258

Alfonso II, king of Asturias-Galicia, 277–78

Alfonso VI, king of León-Castile, 69–70, 257–58

Alfonso VII, king of León-Castile, 104, 258, 279, 282

Alfonso VIII, king of Castile, 197, 198, 258, 259

Alfonso I Henriques, king of Portugal, 258, 282

Alice of Antioch, regent, **12,** 74–75

Alice of Champagne, queen of Cyprus, **12–13,** 44

Almohads (dynasty), **13,** *13, 189,* 197–198, 258–59

Almoravids (dynasty), 13, *13,* **14,** 69–70, 257–58, 325

Alphonse of Poitiers, Capetian prince, 53, 54, 291, 292

Amalric, king of Jerusalem, **14–16,** *14,* 49, 94, 172, 206, 210, 228, 274, 276, 294

Anatolia, 21, 45, *284;* definition of, **16**

Al-Andalus, 13, 14, **16,** 224. *See also* Almohads; Almoravids; Cid, El; Moors; Portugal; Reconquista; Spain

Andrew II, king of Hungary, 109, 110

Anna Comnena, historian, **16–17,** 96, 164, 197, 212, 233, 237, 253–54, 330

Ansbert, historian, 154

Antichrist, 19–21

Antioch, city of, **17–19,** 40, 101, 130, 205, 276, 280, 281, 307, 315, 317; and the First Crusade, 11–12, *17,* 18, *27,* 43, 51–52, 95, 118–19, 139–40, 192–93, 248, 254, 270, 306, 309. *See also* Lance, Holy; Siege Warfare

Antioch, principality of, 19, 33, 44, 88, 103, 205, 229, 308, 309, 311, 320; disaster at the Field of Blood, 107–8; estimated Latin population, 288–89; non-Frankish subjects, 287–89. *See also* Alice of Antioch; Bohemond of Taranto; Bohemond II; Constance of Antioch; Crusader states; Reynald of Châtillon; Roger of Salerno; Siege Warfare; Tancred

Apocalypse, **19–21,** *20,* 63, 114, 140, 218, 292, 325

Aragon, kingdom of, 8, 51, 54, 62, 215, 313. *See also kings by name;* Reconquista

Armaments. *See* Artillery; Siege warfare; Weapons, hand

Armenia/Armenians, **21–22,** *22,* 31–32, *56, 57,* 66, 88, 90, 99–100, 101, 112, 189, 197, 206, 207, 245, 263, 287, 310

Armor, **22–26,** *23, 24, 27,* 60–61, *60, 274,* 285, *290*

Arnold Amalric, papal legate, 7, 71

Arnulf of Chocques, patriarch of Jerusalem, 184, 270

Arqa, castle of, 101

Arsuf, Battle of (1191), 167, 267, 329

Artillery, 291, *296,* 297–98

Ascalon, Battle of (1099), 26, 120, 140, 254, 310; Battle of (1123), 50, 84

Ascalon, port city of, **26–27,** 267; captured by Baldwin III (1153), 15, 26, 177; occupied by Richard I (1192), 26; recovered by Ayyubids (1247), 26–27; recovered by crusaders (1239), 26, 84, 85–86; recovered by Saladin (1187), 26, 318; recovered by Saladin (1192), 26, 178, 268

Al-Ashraf, Mamluk sultan, 206

Assassins, **27–29,** *27,* 40, 74, 100, 200, 294

Athlit, castle of. *See Chastel Perlerin*

Audita tremendi, papal crusade bull, 44–45

Austrian Crusade, 110, 111

Ayn Jalut, Battle of (1260), **29,** 204, 219

Ayyubids (dynasty), 4, **29–30,** 49, 86, 93, 193, 204, 205, 292; Ayyub, 228, 274, 336. *See also* Al-Adil; Al-Kamil; Al-Muazzam; Saladin; Turan Shah

Baghras, castle of, *57*

Baha ad-Din Ibn Shaddad, historian and jurist, 151–52, *286,* 319

Bailli (regent), definition of, **31**

Baldric of Dol, historian, 138

Baldwin I (of Boulogne), king of Jerusalem, **31–33;** and the First Crusade, 31–32, 99, 104, 118, 133, 139, 310; as king of Jerusalem, 32–33, 56, 88, 99, 104, 121, 133, 140, 182, 184, 307, 311, 320

Baldwin II, Latin emperor of Constantinople, 85, 190, 196

Baldwin II (of Le Bourcq), king of Jerusalem, 12, 32, **33,** 50, 74, 84, 93–94, 99, 104, 133, 139, 140, 182, 210, 311

Baldwin III, king of Jerusalem, 26, **33–34,** 133, 134, 211, 263, 281

Baldwin IV, king of Jerusalem, 5, **34–35,** *34,* 143, 221, 294, 295, 331

Baldwin V, king of Jerusalem, 31, **35,** 143, 221, 295

Baldwin IX of Flanders and I of Constantinople, count and Latin emperor, 5, **35–36,** 78, 83, 122, 128, 320

Baldwin of Ford, archbishop of Canterbury and crusader, 71, 320

Balian II of Ibelin, lord of Nablus, **36–38,** 154, 212

Balkans, 3, 4–5, 11, 42–43, 44, 45, 52, 78, 84–85, 164, 170, 171, 227, 230–31, 237, 253, 269, 270, 280, 306, 315, 317, 329. *See also* Crusade of 1239–1241

Baltic Crusades, **38–39,** 42, 161, 166, 217. *See also* Military orders of the Baltic; Second Crusade; Teutonic Knights; Wendish Crusade

Barbastro, town of, 165, 257

Barons' Crusade. *See* Crusade of 1239–1241

Baybars, Mamluk sultan, 19, 27, 29, **39–41,** 58, 59, 100, 101, 102, 178, 205–6, 291, 292, 228, 299, 304, *314*

Beaufort, castle of, 299

Beirut, port city of, 137, 138, 156, 206

Belvoir, castle of, 57, *58*

Bernard of Clairvaux, Cistercian monk and crusade preacher, 21, **41–42,** *41,* 70, 81, 104, 187, 207, 217, 246, 279, 281

Bertrand, count of Tripoli, 253, 255, 320

Bethlehem, town of, 32, *66*, 84, 134, 158, 182, 191, 310

Béziers, city of, 7, 265

Blanche of Castile, queen of France, 9, 293

Bohemond I of Taranto, crusader and prince of Antioch, **42–44;** and the Byzantine empire, 11–12, 16, 170, 234–35, 253–54, 310; and the First Crusade, 11–12, 18–19, 119, 138–39, 196, 227, 253–54, 299, 306, 309, 310; as prince of Antioch, 19, 88, 121, 234–35, 311

Bohemond II, prince of Antioch, 12, **44**

Boniface of Montferrat, crusader and lord of Thessalonica, 123, 126, 221

Boniface VIII, Pope, 199, 238, 245

Bull, papal, 6, 20–21, **44–45,** 51, 80, 84, 166, 261. *See also Audita tremendi; Divini dispensatione; Quantum praedecessores; Zelus fidei*

Byzantine empire, 10–12, **45–47,** 62, 67, 88–89, 137, 173–74, 212, 227. *See also* Alexius I; Alexius III Angelus; Alexius IV Angelus; Anna Comnena; Bohemond of Taranto; Charles of Anjou; Charles of Valois; Constantinople, city of; Constantinople, Latin empire of; Crusade of 1107; Fourth Crusade; Isaac II Angelus; John II Comnenus; Manuel I Comnenus; Michael VIII Palaeologus; Robert Guiscard

Cairo, city of, 15, 30, **49–50,** *50,* 86, 94, 195, 200. *See also* Fifth Crusade; Seventh Crusade

Calatrava, Order of, 215, 222

Caliphate, 1, 40, 173–74, 283, 293–94, 307. *See also* Abbasids; Almohads; Fatimids; Umayyads

Calixtus II, Pope, 33, **50–51,** 79–80, 83–84, 108

Cannibalism, **51–52,** 250, 299, 309

Capetians (dynasty), 9, **52–55.** *See also* Alphonse of Poitiers; Charles of Anjou; Charles of Valois; Louis VII; Louis VIII; Louis IX; Philip II; Philip III; Philip IV

Capuano, Peter, cardinal and papal legate, 199, 226, 332

Carmelites (religious order), **55**

Castile, kingdom of, 51, 69–70, 215, 234. *See also kings by name; Reconquista*

Castles and fortifications, Armenian, *22,* 55–56, *55, 316*

Castles and fortifications, Byzantine, *17, 22,* 55, *56, 76, 76, 116*

Castles and fortifications, Crusader, **55–59,** 111, 131. *See also Arqa; Baghras; Beaufort; Belvoir; Chastel Perlerin; Chateauneuf; Kerak; Krak des Chevaliers; Montfort; Montréal; Le Roche de Guillaume; Saphet; Le Toron des Chevaliers*

Castles and fortifications, Muslim, *27,* 28, 29, 55, *116*

Cathars (religious sect), 6–10, **59–60,** 96

Cavalry, 23–26, **60–61,** 147–48, 167, 203, 296, 299–30. *See also* Armor; Infantry; Weapons, hand

Celestine III, Pope, 38, 137, 259

Charles of Anjou, king of Sicily, Naples, and Jerusalem, **61–62;** and the Byzantine empire, 46, 77, 142–43; and the Eighth Crusade, 54, 61–62, 101–2; and the kingdom of Jerusalem, 54, 62; and the Seventh Crusade, 53, 61, 292; and the Sicilian Crown, 54, 62, 158, 244–45

Charles of Valois, Capetian prince, 54, 62, 238

Chastel Perlerin, castle of, *204*

Chateauneuf, castle of, 101

Children's Crusade, 45, *63–64,* 108, 168, 292

Chivalry, xix, 34, 35, 37, 41, 54, **64–65,** 69, 121, 128–29, 153, 154, 155, 156, 163, 198, 214

Christians, Eastern, 3, 18, 39, 59–60, **65–68,** 88, 90, 99, 100, 141, 149, 151, 152, 181, 220, 227, 233; conversion missions to, 90, 130, 217, 245; crusades and wars against, 4–5, 38–39, 85, 126–28, 190, 221–22, 226, 234–35; an impetus for the First Crusade, 32, 67, 72, 103, 237, 325; under Latin domination, 287–88; relative population numbers, 287. *See also* Armenia/Armenians; Byzantine empire; Constantinople, Latin empire of; Frankish Greece; Prester John; Schism between the Churches of Rome and Constantinople

Chronicle of Ernoul (history), 36

Chronicles, definition of, **68**

Cid, El, **68–70,** 257

Cistercians. *See* Cîteaux, Order of

Cîteaux, Order of, 6, 38, 41–42, 68, **70–71,** 81, 115, 134, 216, 246

Clement III, Pope, 115

Clement IV, Pope, 101, 158, 200

Clement V, Pope, 54, 218, 238–39, 313

Clermont, Council of (1095), **72–73,** 79, 82, 95, 133, 165, 170, 235, 253, 325

Cologne, city of, 185, 186

Commerce, crusader, 2, 61–62, 78, 80, 84, 90, 109, 163, 208, 222, 332

Commerce, Islamic, 10, 49, 222

Conradin/Conrad III, king of Jerusalem, 90, 158

Conrad (I) of Montferrat, king-elect of Jerusalem, 37, **73–74,** 144, 172, 208, 221, 267, 268, 315, 318

Conrad III of Hohenstaufen, Western emperor, 42, 155, 206–7, 279–80, 281

Conrad II (IV) of Hohenstaufen, king of Jerusalem and uncrowned Western emperor, 13, 157–58, 172, 222

Constance of Antioch, regent, 12, 44, **74–75,** 206, 263

Constantinople, city of, 5, 36, 45–47, 66, **75–77,** *76, 85,* 109, *123, 124, 125,* 130, 171; capture in 1204, 77, 127–28, *241,* 243, 285, 297; capture in 1453, 77, 231; maps of, *124, 125. See also* Fourth Crusade; Siege Warfare

Constantinople, Latin empire of, 35–36, 46, 62, 77, **77–79,** 128, 130, 130–31, 157, 199, 221; crusades in defense of, 84, 85, 190, 221–22

Conversion, 248–50; to Christianity, 20, 185–86, 217, 260, 282–83, 288, 304, 314, 322; of Eastern Christians, 38–39, 90; to Islam, 174, 203, 220, 283, 291, 300, 304. *See also* Missionaries

Councils and synods, 44, 66, **79–80,** 150, 170, 235, 261, 304. *See also* Clermont, Council of; Lyons, First Council of; Lyons, Second Council of; Nablus, Council of; Piacenza, Council of; Troyes, Council of; Fourth Lateran Council

Criticism of the crusades, 21, 42, **80–81,** 168–69, 238, 281. *See also* Children's Crusade; Shepherds' Crusade

Cross, crusader's, xxii–xxiii, **81–82,** 93–94, 161, *269, 279*

Cross, True, *20,* 64, *82,* **83,** 113, 148, 209, *256,* 262, 267, 317, 319

Crossbow, 276, 329, 330

Crucesignati. See Crusade/crusader as terms

Crusade/crusader as terms, xxii–xiii, 82, 239

Crusade historiography, xix–xxiv, 151–55

Crusade of 1101, 51, 234, 254, 306–7. *See also* First Crusade

Crusade of 1107, 44, 235–36

Crusade of 1122–1126, 33, 50–51, **83–84,** 108

Crusade of 1239–1241, 26, **84–86,** 142

Crusader states, 39–40, **86–89,** *87,* 107, 150, 154, 200, 212, 231; Jews in, 187, 206, 238, 245–46; king of Jerusalem as first among equals, 88, 182. *See also* Antioch, principality of; Edessa, county of; Jerusalem, kingdom of; Settlement and colonization; Tripoli, county of

Cyprus, kingdom of, 5–6, **89–91,** 95, 144–45, 150, 183, 200, 263, 290; captured by Richard I, 89, 266–67; and the military orders, 89, 90, 163, 198, 313; Symeon, Greek patriarch in exile, 3. *See also* Lusignans

Daimbert, patriarch of Jerusalem, 32, 182, 184

Damascus, city of, 30, 86, **93,** 152, 182, 193, 204, 274, 302, 308, 320, 335; and the Second Crusade, 93, 152, 281; occupied by Nur ad-Din, 228, 282; occupied by Saladin, 276. *See also* Damascus Crusade

Damascus Crusade, 45, **93–94,** 133

Damietta, port city of, 15, 49, **94–95,** 130, 190–91, 200, 208, 235, 236, 275. *See also* Fifth Crusade; Seventh Crusade; Siege warfare

Dandolo, Enrico, doge of Venice, *78,* 124

Deus Vult (God wills it!), 95

Disease, 94, **95–96,** 101, 102, 112, 118, 123, 124, 192, 198, 200, 226, 229, 236, 270, 287, 290, 299, 301–2, 318, 322; theory of, 298. *See also* Leprosy

Divini dispensatione, papal crusade bull, 279

Dome of the Rock, Shrine of the, *173,* 180

Dominicans (religious order), 9, **96,** 130, 217, 246

Doré, Gustave, illustrations by, xix, *xx, 63, 177, 296, 296*

Dorylaeum, Battle of (1097), 3, **96–97,** 118, 139, 284, 306, 310

Edessa, city of, 32, **99–100,** 118, 192, 230; conquest by Zangi, 32, 34, 99, 103, 222, 279, 335

Edessa, county of, 32, 44, 88, **99–100,** 287, 309, 311; Armenian majority, 287. *See also* Crusader states

Edward I, king of England, **100–101,** 101–2, 103, 205, 220

Egypt, 15, 34, 64, 105, 121, 123, 124, 129, 183, 202, 206, 228, 235–36, 267. *See also* Al-Adil; Alexandria; Al-Kamil; Ayyubids; Cairo; Damietta; Fatimids; Fifth Crusade; Mamluks (dynasty); Seventh Crusade; Saladin

Eighth Crusade, 61–62, 100–101, **101–2,** 155, 200

Eleanor of Aquitaine, queen of France, **102–3,** 226, 279

Emicho of Leiningen, crusader, 117, 186

Epic literature, 52, 64, 69

Eracles L'Estoire de Eracles (history), *14, 27, 34, 41, 60,* 154, *168, 194, 264, 266, 275, 332*

Ernoul, The Chronicle of (history), 36, 154

Eschiva, countess of Tripoli, *332*

Eugenius III, Pope, 41, 45, 70, 99, **103–4,** 258, 279, 335

Eustace III of Boulogne, crusader, **104,** 270

Family crusading traditions, 261. *See also* Capetians; Eleanor of Aquitaine; Hohenstaufens; Lusignans; Montferrat, family of; Women

Fatimids (dynasty), 28, 49, **105,** 119, 120, 160, 180–81, 203, 207, 212, 228, 283, 294; and Saladin, 105, 274–75

Fernando III, king of León-Castile, 259

Feudalism: the Byzantine emperor's feudal claims, 44; definition of, **105–7;** feudal investiture, *106;* in Frankish Greece, 130–31; in the kingdom of Cyprus, 89; in the kingdom of Jerusalem,

14–15, 32–33, 56, 183, 320, 311, 334; king of Jerusalem's feudal preeminence, 34, 320; in the Latin empire of Constantinople, 78; obligations of vassals, 7, 106–7, 114, 183; throughout the crusader states, 88, 107. *See also* Chivalry; *Bailli*; Cid, El; High Court; Knights; Sergeants; *The Song of Roland*

Field of Blood, Battle of the (1119), 17, 33, 84, **107–8,** 271

Fifth Crusade, **108–13;** al-Kamil's generosity of spirit, 65, 129–30; Cairo the goal, 49; capture of the Chain Tower, 111, 229; eyewitnesses to the crusade, 155, 178, 229–30, 248; financing the crusade, 335; Francis of Assisi, 129–30; Frederick II, 157, 162; Fourth Lateran Council, 80, 109; prophecy, 21; siege of Damietta, 94. *See also* Al-Kamil; Honorius III; John of Brienne; Pelagius

Financing the Crusades, 80, 81, **113–16,** 142, 166, 221–22, 238, 246; Albigensian Crusade, 162; First Crusade, 114, 139, 268, 270; Second Crusade, 103, 114; Third Crusade, 115, 266; Fourth Crusade, 45, 115, 116, 122–23, 134–35, 328; Fifth Crusade, 108–9, 115, 333; Sixth Crusade, 115; Seventh Crusade, 289; Eighth Crusade, 101; Innocent III's innovations, 45, 115, 116, 168–69, 328

First Crusade, 42–43, 114, **116–22,** 225–26; background to, 68–70, 72–73, 140–41, 141, 169–70, 207, 233–34, 235, 237, 240, 257–58; and the Byzantine empire, 11–12, 16–17, 76–77, 212; and the Jews, 185–86, 237, 325. *See also* Adhémar of Monteil; Alexius I; Baldwin I (of Boulogne); Bohemond of Taranto; Clermont, Council of; Dorylaeum, Battle of; Eustace of Boulogne; Godfrey of Bouillon; Hugh of Vermandois; Lance, Holy; People's Crusade; Peter the Hermit; Raymond IV of Saint-Gilles; Robert of Flanders; Robert of Normandy; Stephen of Blois and Chartres; Tancred; Urban II; Walter Sansavoir

Fourth Crusade, 20, 45, 49, 95, 108, 116, **122–28,** 156–57, 212, 225; capture and pillage of Constantinople, 46, 67, 77, 79, 83, 153, *241,* 263, 285. *See also* Alexius III; Alexius IV; Alexius V; Baldwin IX of Flanders and I of Constantinople; Boniface of Montferrat; Capuano, Peter; Constantinople, City of, capture in 1204; Dandolo, Enrico; Fulk of Neuilly; Innocent III; Zara

Fourth Lateran Council (1215), 80, 108–9, 162

Franciscans (religious order), 9, 96, 128–30, 217–18, 219, 246

Francis of Assisi, **128–30,** *129,* 190

Frankish Greece, 46, 62, 96, **130–32,** *131*

Franks, definition of, **132**

Frederick I Barbarossa, Western emperor, 155–56, 187; and the Third Crusade, 4–5, 153–54, 156, 170–71, 315, 316, *316,* 317

Frederick II, Western emperor and king of Jerusalem, 80, 85, 115, 138, 157–58, 161, 162, 172, 178, 218–19, 222, 227, 236, *244;* and the Fifth Crusade, 108, 109, 110, 112, 236, 300–301; and political crusades, 142, 189, 190, 243–44, *244;* and the Sixth Crusade, 191, 300–303; and the Teutonic Knights, 303, 314

Friars, mendicant, 55, 71, 89, 96, **132,** 142, 168, 199, 293; as missionaries, 130, 217, 289; as preachers, 246. *See also* Carmelites; Dominicans; Francis of Assisi; Franciscans

Fulcher of Chartres, crusader and historian, 76, 95, **133,** 245–46, 298, 261, 333

Fulk of Anjou, king of Jerusalem, 12, 33, 34, 75, 94, **133–34,** 210–11, 320

Fulk of Neuilly, crusade preacher, 71, **134–35**

Gelasius II, Pope, 258

Genoa, port city of, 2, 10, 18, 54, 64, 78, 121, 177, 182, 212, 222, 279, 282, 317, 320, 323

Geoffrey of Villehardouin, crusader and historian, 154, 243

George, Saint, 18, 156, 269, 273, *274. See also* Saints, Warrior

Gerald, Latin patriarch of Jerusalem, 302, 303

German Crusade, **137–38,** 149, 156

Gesta Francorum (The Deeds of the Franks) (history), 132, **138–39,** 153, 154

Godfrey of Bouillon, crusader and defender of the Holy Sepulcher, 31–32, 104, 118, 119, 120, **139–40,** *168,* 182, 186, 254, 310, 311

Godfrey of Langres, crusader bishop, 70, 282, 283

Granada, emirate of, 199, 215, 259–60

Great German Pilgrimage of 1064–1065, **140–41,** 240

Great Seljuk, sultanate of the, 181, 194, 222–23, 271, 283–84, 335. *See also* Rum, sultanate of; Seljuks

Greeks, 139, **141,** 153. *See also* Byzantine empire; Christians, Eastern; Schism between the Churches of Rome and Constantinople

Gregory VII, Pope, 32, **141–42,** 207, 217, 233, 257. *See also* Investiture Controversy

Gregory VIII, Pope, 44–45, 156, 315

Gregory IX, Pope, 39, 85, 90, 96, **142,** 187, 199, 250, 304; apparent portrait of, *244;* and Frederick II, 157, 162, 190, 218–19, 243–44, *244,* 301, 302, 303

Gregory X, Pope, 115, **142–43,** 220

Guibert of Nogent, historian, 19–20, 132, 138, 153, 154

Gunther of Pairis, historian, 71, 153

Guy of Lusignan, king of Jerusalem, 5–6, **143–45,** 149, 266; lord of Cyprus, 89; marriage to Sibylla, 35, 37, 295; struggle with Conrad of Montferrat, 74; struggles with Saladin, 2, 147–48, 276, 318, 321

Hadrian IV, Pope, 53

Hagia Sophia, Church of, *46, 78*

Al-Hakim, Fatimid caliph, 105, 160, 181

Hasan-i Sabbah, Assassin leader, 28

Hattin, Battle of (1187), 36, 45, 56–57, 83, 144, **147–48,** *147,* 167, 209, 264, *264,* 276, 286, 295

Haute Cour. See High Court

Hebron, town of, 158–59

Henry II, king of England, 103, 114, 115, 265, 266, 316

Henry IV, Western emperor, 72, 141. *See also* Investiture Controversy

Henry VI, Western emperor, 6, 89, 137, 138, 156, 171, 268

Henry of Champagne, lord of Jerusalem, *27,* 28, 37–38, 103, 144, **148–49,** 172

Heraclius, patriarch of Jerusalem, 37, 143, 184, 185

Heretics, 66–67, 90, **149–50;** Armenian Church, 21–22, 90; Cathars, 6–10, 59–60; crusades against, 6–10, 80, 81, 150, 168; missions to, 96; within Islam *13,* 27–29. *See also* Infidel; Schism between the Churches of Rome and Constantinople; Templars

High Court (*Haute Cour*), 14, 31, 35, 74, 144, **150–51,** 183, 204, 211, 281, 295

Historians and chroniclers, Byzantine. *See* Anna Comnena; Nicetas Choniates

Historians and chroniclers, Islamic, **151–52.** *See also* Baha ad-Din Ibn Shaddad; Ibn al-Athir; Ibn al-Jauzi; Ibn al-Qalanisi; Ibn Jubair; Ibn Wasil; Imad ad-Din; Usamah ibn Munqidh

Historians and chroniclers, Jewish, 185. *See also* Solomon bar Simson

Historians and chroniclers, Latin, 18, 19–20, 36, 72, 102, **152–55;** and Pope Urban's sermon at Clermont, 72, 166. *See also* Alberic of Trois-Fontaines; Albert of Aachen; Ansbert; *Eracles; Ernoul, Chronicle of;* Fulcher of Chartres; *Gesta Francorum;* Geoffrey of Villehardouin; Guibert of Nogent; Gunther of Pairis; James of Vitry; Odo of Deuil; Oliver of Paderborn; Otto of Freising; Peter of Vaux-de-Cernay; Ralph of Caen; Ralph of Coggeshall; Raymond of Aguilers; Rigord; Robert of Clari; Robert (the Monk)

of Rheims; Roger of Hoveden; Thomas of Celano; William of Tyre

Hohenstaufens (dynasty), 31, 62, 129, **155–58.** *See also* Conrad II (IV); Conrad III; Conrad III/Conradin; Frederick I Barbarossa; Frederick II; German Crusade; Henry VI; Philip of Swabia; Political Crusades; Second Crusade; Sixth Crusade; Third Crusade

Holy Land, 20, 239–40; description and definition, **158–59.** *See also* Bethlehem; Great German Pilgrimage of 1064–1065; Hebron; Holy Sepulcher, Church of the; Jerusalem, city of; Pilgrims and pilgrimages; Relics; Saint Mary, Church of

Holy Sepulcher, Church of the, 35, 83, 134, 140, 141, 158, **159–60,** *159, 168,* 180, 181, 184, 222, 237, 240, *240, 256,* 262, 288, 303, 327; destruction or sacking of, 105, 160, 193

Holy War, 80–81, 138, 150, **160–61;** associated concepts, 153, 199, 214, 263; and Bernard of Clairvaux, 41–42, 70; and Calixtus II, 51; and the Franciscans, 130; and Urban II, 72, 325. *See also* Jihad; Just War; Saints, warrior

Honorius III, Pope, 9, 112, **161–62,** 221–22, 235, *256,* 300–301

Hospitalers (military order), 29, 90, 111, **163–64,** 198, 206, 214, 215, 304, 313; castles and churches, of, 57–59, *58,* 163, 205, *213,* 299, 321; female Hospitalers, 214; influence on Iberian military orders, 215; prisoners killed by Saladin, 148, 209, 276; *Turcopolier,* 322

Hugh of Payns, Templar founder, 94, 311

Hugh of Vermandois, crusader, 52, 120, 121, **164**

Hugh I of Lusignan, king of Cyprus, 6, 13

Hugh III of Lusignan, king of Cyprus and Jerusalem, 90, 158

Humbert of Beaujeu, crusader, 85

Hungarian crusades, 110, 218, 244

Hungary, 31, 124, 125, 139, 237, 280, 314, 299; Master of Hungary, 293

Iberia. *See* Portugal; Spain

Ibn al-Athir, historian, 36, 68, 73, 151, 333

Ibn al-Jauzi, historian, 302

Ibn al-Qalanisi, historian, 68, 152, 247

Ibn Jubair, historian, 289, 323

Ibn Wasil, historian, 302

Imad ad-Din, historian, 151, 152, 303, 332, 332–33

Indulgence, crusade, 6, 39, 45, 51, 72, 80, 84, 103, 108–9, 115, 150, 161, **165–66,** 168, 250, 325, 328; other indulgences, 165, 244, 257, 262

Infantry, 25, 61, **166–67.** *See also* Armor; Cavalry; Tafurs; Weapons, hand

Infidel, definition of, **167;** representation of, *168. See also* Heretics

Innocent II, Pope, 312

Innocent III, Pope, 110, 157, 161, 162, **167–69,** 300, 304; and the Albigensian crusade, 6–7; and the Baltic crusades, 38; and the Children's Crusade, 64; and crusade finances, 45, 115, 116, 328; and crusade recruitment, 134, 246, 261, 333–34; and the crusade vow, 328, 333–34; and the Fifth Crusade, 20–21, 80, 108–9, 328; and the Fourth Crusade, 20, 122, 124, 125–26, 199, 332, 334; and the Franciscans, 96, 129; crusade watershed, xxii–xxiii, 108, 167–69, 333–34; and political crusades, 128–29, 243; portrait of, *169*

Innocent IV, Pope, 80, 162, 219, 244, 289

Inquisition, 9–10, 96

Investiture Controversy (1076–1122), 72, 79, 141, **169–70,** 233

Isaac Comnenus, despot of Cyprus, 89, 266, 267, 318

Isaac II Angelus, emperor of Constantinople, 4–5, 73, 126, 127, 156, 157, **170–71,** 221, 317

Isabella I, queen of Jerusalem, 6, 37–38, 74, 89, 144, 148, 149, **171–72,** 208, 221

Isabella (Yolanda) II, queen of Jerusalem, 157, **172,** 189–90, 208–9, 301

Islam, 105, **172–74,** 180; in Christian perspective, 19–21, 149, *168, 305,* 333; holy sites, *13, 173, 174, 179,* 180, 242, 287–88, 302, 310, 311, *312. See also* Muslims

Islamic Peoples, 174, **174–75,** 212. *See also* Khorezmians; Kurds; Mamluks; Moors; Saracens; Turks

Jaffa, Battle of (1192), 177, *177, 266, 267*

Jaffa, city of, 57, 65, **177–78,** 292, 299, 315, 319

James of Vitry, archbishop of Acre and historian, 134, **178,** 329

James I, king of Aragon, 259

Jerusalem, churches and mosques of, *173, 174, 210,* 242–43, *286,* 287–88, 310, 311, *312. See also* Al-Aksa Mosque; Dome of the Rock; Holy Sepulcher, Church of the; Relics; Tomb of the Virgin, Church of the

Jerusalem, city of, 112, *173, 174,* **178–82,** *179, 286;* captured in 1099, 119–20, 140, *179,* 181, 254, 297, 310; captured in 1187, 36–37, 148, 151, 153, 160, 181, 183, 210, 242–43, 263, *275,* 276, 304; captured in 1239, 84, 86, 181; captured in 1244, 181, 183, 194, 200; focus of the crusades, 72–73, 80, 111, 162, 319, 325, 327; Jews in Jerusalem, 180, 181, 186; recovered in 1229, 157, 181, 183, 191, 302; recovered in 1241, 84,

86, 181, 183. *See also* Holy Land; Holy Sepulcher, Church of the; Pilgrimage

Jerusalem, kingdom of, 40, 85, 88, 93, 140, 181, **182–83,** 200; estimated Latin population, 286–87; extent of, 308; non-Frankish subjects, 287–89; and Louis IX, 200, 292; women in, 334. *See also* Acre; Agnes of Courtenay; Aimery of Lusignan; Alice of Champagne; Amalric; Baldwin I (of Boulogne); Baldwin II (of Le Bourcq); Baldwin III; Baldwin IV; Baldwin V; Balian II of Ibelin; Charles of Anjou; Conrad of Montferrat; Crusader states; Frederick II; Fulk of Anjou; Guy of Lusignan; Henry of Champagne; High Court; Isabella I; Isabella (Yolanda) II; Melisende; Sibylla; William of Tyre

Jerusalem, Latin patriarchate of, 32, *34,* 55, **184–85,** 331; appointees of the crown, 184–85; papal legates-in-residence, 184. *See also* Albert of Vercelli; Arnulf of Chocques; Daimbert; Gerald; Heraclius; William of Tyre

Jews, 42, 114, 134, 159, 180, 181, **185–88,** 237, 293, 325

Jihad, 13, 34, 108, 173, **188–89,** 259; and Baybars, 39, 40; and Kalavun, 206; and Nur ad-Din, 227, 275–76, 335; preaching jihad, 247; and Saladin, 189, 274, 275–76; and Zangi, 335. *See also* Holy War; Just War

Joan, queen of Sicily, 266, 318, 319

John of Brienne, king of Jerusalem and Latin emperor of Constantinople, 172, **189–90,** 208–9, 244, 301, 302, 303; and the Fifth Crusade, 110, 111–13, 162, 189, 199, 236

John of Ibelin, 285

John of Joinville, crusader and historian, 155, 246

John of Monte Corvino, Franciscan missionary, 217–18, 220

John II Comnenus, emperor of Constantinople, *46,* 84

John XXII, Pope, 187

Joscelin II, count of Edessa, 99

Just War, 128, 150, **160–61.** *See also* Holy War; Jihad

Al-Kahf, castle of, *27*

Kalavun, Mamluk sultan, 206, 209

Kalojan, Vlacho-Bulgarian king, 5, 36

Al-Kamil, Ayyubid sultan, 4, 30, 65, 111, 112, 113, 129–30, 181, **191–92,** 235, 236, 302

Kerak, castle of, 56, 264

Kerbogha, governor of Mosul, 43, **192–943,** 237, 306

Khorezmians, 181, **193,** 195, 248

Kilij Arslan I, Seljuk sultan of Rum, *60,* **193–94,** *194,* 283

Knights, *14, 23, 24, 27, 60,* 61, 64–65, 88, 95, 106, *106,* 114, 121, 167, *194,* 213–14, 242, 280, 285, 312; owed knight service, 323. *See also* Armor; Cavalry; Chivalry; Feudalism; Military orders; Weapons, hand

Knights of Dobrin (military order), 216

Korykos, port town of, *22, 56*

Koutoubia Mosque, *13*

Krak des Chevaliers, castle of, 58–59, 205, 299, 321

Kurds, 151, 175, 229. *See also* Ayyubids; Saladin

La Forbie, Battle of (1244), 193, **195,** 198, 292

Lance, Holy, 18, 119, 193, **195–97,** 309

Languedoc, 6–10, 60, 88, 96, 107, 196, 229; definition of, **197.** *See also* Albigensian Crusade; Raymond IV of Saint-Gilles; Raymond VI of Saint-Gilles; Raymond VII of Saint-Gilles

Las Navas de Tolosa, Battle of (1212), 13, 168, **197–98,** 215, 259, 278

Latin East, 70–71, 119, 130, 154; definition of, **198.** *See also* Antioch, principality of; Constantinople, Crusader states; Cyprus; Edessa, county of; Frankish Greece; Jerusalem, kingdom of; Latin empire of; *Outremer; Poulain;* Settlement and colonization; Tripoli, county of; William of Tyre

Latins, definition of, **198**

Lazarus, Order of Saint (military order), **198–99,** 214

Legates, papal, 3–4, 6–7, 32, 44, 126, **199,** 234. *See also* Adhémar of Monteil, Arnold Amalric; Daimbert; Pelagius; Peter of Castelnau

León, kingdom of, 69, *82,* 197, 215, 234. *See also kings by name;* Reconquista

Leopold V, duke of Austria, 268, 318

Leprosy, 34–35, 198, 294, 295

Levant, definition of, **199**

Liegnitz, Battle of (1241), 218

Lisbon, port city of, 110, 258, 286

Lombards, 120–21

Louis VII, king of France, 42, 52–53, 102–3, *103,* 114, 150, 153, 206–7, 227, 279, 280–81

Louis VIII, king of France, 8–9, 53, 162

Louis IX, king of France, 81, 196, **200–201,** 218, 219; canonization of, 200–201, 238; and the kingdom of Jerusalem, 178, 200, 292; and the Seventh Crusade *xxii,* 53, 155, 200, 289–92; and the Eighth Crusade, 53–54, 100, 101, 200, 220. *See also* Blanche of Castile; Margaret of Provence

Lusignans (dynasty), 5–6, 89. *See also* Aimery of Lusignan; Alice of Champagne; Cyprus; Guy of Lusignan; Hugh I of Lusignan; Hugh III of Lusignan; Peter I of Lusignan

Lyons, First Council of (1245), 115, 244, 289

Lyons, Second Council of (1274), 46, 115, 142

Ma'arra, town of, 51–52, 254, 309, 310

Mainz, city of, 185, 186

Al-Malik, Ayyubid sultan, 203

Malta, Knights of (military order), 163. *See also* Hospitalers

Mamluks (dynasty), 49, 50, 90, 200, **203–6,** 219–20; capture Acre (1291), 3, 198, 206, 298; conquests from 1263 through 1291, *205;* gain control of Syria, 10, 19, 29, 30, 93, 204; 321; seize the sultanate of Egypt, 30, 50, 203, 292; siege tactics of, 298, 299. *See also* Ayn Jalut; Baybars

Mamluks (slave soldiers), 192, 203, 211, 291, 303, 322

Manfred of Hohenstaufen, 54

Al-Mansurah, fortress of, 113, 291

Manuel I Comnenus, emperor of Constantinople, 12, 15, 16, 34, 75, **206–7,** 221, 247, 263; and the Second Crusade, 155, 206–7, 227, 281

Manzikert, Battle of (1071), 45, 141, **207–8,** 283

Margaret of Provence, queen of France, 103, 200, **208,** 290, 292

Maria Comnena, wife of Amalric and Balian II, 14, 36

Maria of Montferrat, queen of Jerusalem, 6, 74, 172, 189, **208–9**

Marinids (dynasty), 259–60

Markward of Anweiler, 128–29, 167–68, 243

Martin IV, Pope, 54, 62, 143, 244

Massacres, **209–10,** 248, 300; by crusaders, 7, 18, 43, 65, 120, 181, 186, 209, 226, 242, 248, 259, 265, 267, 271, 291, 310; instances of mercy, 37, 40, 65, 191, 242; by Muslims, 40, 99, 107, 121, 148, 177, 181, 192, 206, 208, 209, 271, 276, 291, 292, 299–300, 321. *See also* Chivalry; Prisoners; Ransom; Slavery

Mehmed II, Ottoman sultan, 47, 77, 230, *230*

Melisende, queen of Jerusalem, 12, 33, 34, 94, 133–34, **210–11,** *210,* 281, 334

Mercenaries, 8, 11, 46, 68–70, 72, 73, 113, 114, 118, 137, **211–13,** 214, 241, 261, 281, 313, 322

Michael VII, emperor of Constantinople, 141, 207

Michael VIII Palaeologus, emperor of Constantinople, 46, 62, 77, 79, 142–43

Middle East, definition of, **213;** maps of, *87, 205, 317*

Military orders, 1, 57–59, 70, 131, 151, 212, **213–15,** 285; plans to amalgamate, 214, 239. *See also* Hospitalers; Lazarus, Order of Saint; Military orders of Iberia; Military orders of the Baltic;

Templars; Teutonic Knights; Saint Thomas of Acre, Order of

Military orders of Iberia, **215–16**. *See also* Reconquista

Military orders of the Baltic, 168, **216**. *See also* Baltic crusades; Teutonic Knights

Missionaries, 101, 166, **216–18;** in the Baltic, 38–39, 42, 104, 216, 217, 282; to the Cathars, 96; to Eastern Christians, 67, 96, 130, 217; to the Mongols, 128, 130, 142, 217–18, 219–20, 248; to Muslims, 128, 129–30, 216–17, 260, 288. *See also* Conversion; Friars, Mendicant; James of Vitry

Mongols, 30, 151, 193, **218–20**, *219,* 223, 248, 260, 315; defeat at Ayn Jalut, 29, 219; menace the Mamluks, 40, 50, 93, 204, 205, 206, 284; negotiations with the crusader West, 100, 101, 130, 142, 200, 217, 219–20; reputation, 51, 218. *See also* Missionaries, to the Mongols

Montferrat, family of, **221–22**. *See also* Boniface of Montferrat; Conrad of Montferrat; Maria of Montferrat; William III (the Elder) of Montferrat; William IV of Montferrat; William Longsword

Montfort, castle of, 58, 303, *314*

Montjoie, **222**, 268, 305

Montjoie, Order of (military order), 215, 222

Montréal, castle of, 56, 265

Moors, definition of, **222**

Mosul, city of, 192, **222–23**, 227–28, 276, 335

Mount Pilgrim, castle of, 254–55

Al-Muazzam, Ayyubid sultan of Syria, 111, 112, 113, 181, 191, 302

Muhammad, the Prophet of Islam, 19, 21, *168,* 172–73, 188, 293, 307, 331

Muret, Battle of (1213), 8

Muslims: connections with Christians and Jews, 159, 172, *173, 174,* 178–79, 180, *179;* definition of, 172; diversity of, 174–75; under Frankish domination, 287–89; perceived as Christian heretics, 149; perceived as idol worshipers and polytheists, *168;* Sunni-Shia struggles, 28–29, 181, 283, 293–94, 307. *See also* Islam; Islamic peoples; Moors; Saracens; Shia/Shias; Sunnism

Nablus, Council of (1120), 289, 311

Nicaea, city of, 11, *60,* 77, 78–79, *116,* 118, 130, 192, 283. *See also* Rum, sultanate of

Nicetas Choniates, historian, 102, 171

Nicholas IV, Pope, 220

Noncombatants, 113, 114, 116, 121, 140, **225–26**, 279, 280

Normans, 11, 16, 42–44, 88, 107, 138, 170, 198–99, **226–27**, 257. *See also* Bohemond of Taranto; Bohemond II; Robert II of Normandy; Roger of Salerno; Tancred

Nur ad-Din Mahmud, sultan of Syria, 15, 75, 151, 152, **227–28**, 263, 335; occupies Damascus, 93, 228, 281, *282,* 336; recaptures Edessa, 99; relations with Saladin, 228, 274, 275, 276. *See also* Jihad

Odo of Deuil, crusader and historian, 153, 226

Old Man of the Mountain, *27,* 28, 29. *See also* Sinan ibn Salman

Oliver of Paderborn, crusader and historian, 65, 67, 113, 149, 155, **229–30**, 248

Ottomans (dynasty), 10, 47, 50, 75, 76, 77, 79, 90–91, 163, 181–82, **230–31**, *230,* 284, *286,* 315

Otto of Freising, crusader bishop and historian, 155, 247, 280, 281

Outremer, definition of, **231**

Palestine. *See* Syria-Palestine

Papacy, Roman, 67, 79–80, 104, 141, 169–70, **233–34**, *244;* and the Jews, 185, 238; and political crusades, 243–45. *See also* popes by name

Paschal II, Pope, 44, 120, **234–35**

Pastoureaux. *See* Shepherds' Crusade

Peace and Truce of God, 235

Peace of Paris (1229), 9, 53

Pelagius, cardinal and papal legate, 21, 162, 201, **235–36**. *See also* Fifth Crusade

Penance, xxi–xxii, 42, 51, 115, 119–10, 129, 140, 165–66, 186, 235, 239, 261, 262, 293, 305, 327

People's Crusade (1096), 114, 116–17, 192, 236–37, 309, 325, 329

Peter Bartholomew, crusader, 18, 191, 196–97

Peter I of Lusignan, king of Cyprus, 90

Peter II, king of Aragon, 8, 197, 259

Peter III, king of Aragon, 54, 62, 244–45

Peter of Castelnau, papal legate, 7

Peter of Vaux-de-Cernay, crusader and historian, 71

Peter the Hermit, preacher and crusader, 52, 116, 117, 192, **236–37**, 246, 325, 329

Philip II, king of France, 6, 74, 109, 115, 144, 265, 268, 319; and the Third Crusade, 53, 74, 153–54, 266, 267, 276, 315, 316–17, 318, 319

Philip III, king of France, 54, 61, 62, 101, 245

Philip IV, king of France, 54, 100, 220, **238–39**, 245, 313

Philip of Swabia, king of Germany, 126, 156–57, 243

Piacenza, Council of (1095), 72

Pilgrims and pilgrimage, 3, 83, 84, 102, 165, *168,* 237, **239–41,** *240, 250, 277,* 289, 311, 332; crusaders as pilgrims, xxi–xxii, 72–73, 103, 120, 239, *249;* crusader's cross as pilgrim badge, 81–82; the *hajj* (pilgrimage to Mecca), 188, 239, 264; pilgrim's vow, 327; protections for, 235, 250. *See also* Great German Pilgrimage of 1064–1065; Holy Land; Islam, holy sites; Jerusalem, churches and mosques of; Montjoie; Penance; Relics; Santiago de Compostela

Pillage and plunder, 75, 81, 84, 90, 114, 117, 124, 127, 128, 236, **241–43,** 266, 282, 285, 299, 310, 329

Pisa, port city of, 2, 212, 282, 318, 323

Political crusades, 62, 81, 128, 157–58, 166, 190, 218–19, **243–45,** *244,* 302, 303

Polos, 142, 220, 248

Portugal, 110, 197, 215, 216, 282. *See also* Reconquista

Poulain, 178; definition of, **245–46,** 322

Preaching, *41,* 42, 44, 63, 72–73, 85, 108, 132, 162, 166, 168, 217, **246–47,** 289, 293, 325. *See also* Bernard of Clairvaux; Dominicans; Franciscans; Francis of Assisi; Fulk of Neuilly; James of Vitry; Oliver of Paderborn; Peter the Hermit; Urban II

Prester John, **247–48**

Prisoners, 33, 43, 75, 99, 113, 191, 200, 208, 242, **248–50,** *249,* 291–92, 310, 333

Privileges, crusader, 7, 38–39, 44–45, 62, 80, 103–4, 161, 234, 239, **250–51.** *See also* Indulgence, crusade; *Quantum praedecessores*

Prophecy, 20–21, 236, 248, 293. *See also* Apocalypse; Visions

Quantum praedecessores, crusade bull, 45, 103–4, 279

Qutuz, Mamluk sultan, 29, 50, 203–4

Radulph, patriarch of Antioch, 12

Ralph of Caen, historian, 52, 154, 197, 309

Ralph of Coggeshall, historian, 68

Ransom, 37, 43, 53, 65, 120, 137, 148, 181, 200, 209, 214, 242, 248, 250, 263, 268, 291–92, 311

Raymond of Aguilers, historian, 132, 198, 199

Raymond of Poitiers, prince of Antioch, 102, 281

Raymond IV of Saint-Gilles, crusader, 16, 43, 88, 118, 119, 120–21, 140, 196–97, 199, 212, **253–55,** 269, 306, 310, 320

Raymond-Roger Trencavel, viscount of Béziers, 7, 9

Raymond VI of Saint-Gilles, count of Toulouse, 7–9

Raymond VII of Saint-Gilles, count of Toulouse, 8–9, 53, 162

Reconquista, 13, 51, *82,* 84, 104, 163, 166, 217, **255–61,** 312, 330; a full-fledged crusade, 234, 279. *See also* Al-Andalus; Almohads; Almoravids; Cid, El; Las Navas de Tolosa, Battle of; Military orders of Iberia; Moors; Santiago de Compostela; Second Crusade, *Song of Roland*

Recruitment, 80, 93–94, 108–9, 134–35, 168, 221–22, **261,** 328. *See also* Preaching

Relics, 83, 158–59, 243, *256,* **261–63,** *262,* 269, 273. *See also* Cross, True; Holy Sepulcher, Church of the; Lance, Holy; Santiago de Compostela

Religious orders. *See* Carmelites; Calatrava, Order of; Cîteaux, Order of; Dominicans; Francis of Assisi; Franciscans; Friars, mendicant; Hospitalers; Lazarus, Order of Saint; Military orders; Military orders of Iberia; Military orders of the Baltic; Montjoie, Order of; Templars; Teutonic Knights; Trinitarians

Reynald of Châtillon, prince of Antioch and lord of Transjordan, 75, 143, 148, **263–65,** *264,* 276, 334

Rhodes, 163

Ribauds, 226, 265

Richard I the Lionheart, king of England, 103, 144, 148, 149, 227, **265–68,** 330; captures Cyprus, 89, 266–67, 276, 318; and the Third Crusade, 26, 65, 65, 74, 153–54, 177–78, 209, 222, 265–69, *266,* 276, 299, 315, 316–17, 318, 319

Richard of Cornwall, crusader, 86

Rigord, historian, 154

Robert Guiscard, duke of Apulia and Calabria, 42–43, 170, 227

Robert of Artois, Capetian prince, 53, 291

Robert of Clari, crusader and historian, 76, 149, 154

Robert II of Flanders, crusader, 104, 119, 227, 254, **268–69,** *269,* 270, 309

Robert II of Normandy, crusader, 104, 119, 212, 227, 254, 269, **269–70,** 306

Robert (the Monk) of Rheims, historian, 82, 95, 138

Le Roche de Guillaume, castle of, 59

Roger II, king of Sicily, 206, 207, 227

Roger of Hoveden, historian, 68

Roger of Salerno, regent of Antioch, 107, 242, **271**

Rum, sultanate of, 156, 170, 192, 206, 207, 283–84

Saint Anne, Church of, 158, *286*

Saint George. *See* George, Saint

Saint John, Order of. *See* Hospitalers

Saint Lazarus, Order of. *See* Lazarus, Order of Saint

Saints, warrior, 18, *23,* **273–74,** *274. See also* George, Saint; Holy War; Santiago de Compostela

Saint Thomas of Acre, Order of (military order), 214, 319

Saladin, Ayyubid sultan of Egypt and Syria, 49, 102–3, 156 170, **274–77,** 317, 336; and the Assassins, 28–29; biographies of, 151–52; campaign of 1187–1188, 26, 36–38, 73–74, 143–44, 147–48, 170, 264–65, 276, *286,* 295, 300, 320; compared with Baybars, 39–40; generosity and mercy of, 37, 65, 152, 242–43, 295; massacres prisoners, 65, 264, *264,* 276, 322; rise to power, 15–16, 94, 105, 212, 228, 274–76, 320; and the Third Crusade, 177–78, 209, 267, 268, 276, 319; unites Egypt and Syria, 30, 93, 223, 276. *See also* Jihad; Truces

Saladin Tithe, 115

Saludo, Battle of (1340), 259–60

Sancho II, king of Castile, 69

Sancho VII, king of Navarre, 197, 259

Santiago, Order of (military order), 215

Santiago de Compostela, Shrine of, 69, 81–82, 222, 239, 256, 273–74, **277–78,** *277*

Saphadin. See Al-Adil

Saphet, castle of, 58, 101, 299–301

Saracens, definition of, **278**

Saragossa, city of, 51, 258, 305

Sauma, Rabban (Master Sauma), Nestorian Christian monk, 100, 220

Schism between the Churches of Rome and Constantinople, 3, 67, 79, 89–90, 96, 126, 130, 131, 142–43, 149, 153, 190, 206, 233–34, 263, 281, 315. *See also* Byzantine empire; Christians, Eastern; Constantinople, city of; Constantinople, Latin empire of; Councils and Synods; Fourth Crusade; Frankish Greece; Investiture Controversy; Missionaries; Papacy, Roman

Second Crusade, 21, 41–42, 70–71, 81, 93, 99, 102–3, 103–4, 153, 217, **278–83;** and Emperor Manuel I, 155, 206–7; and the Jews, 42, 187; and the Reconquista, 104, 258, 279, 282. *See also* Conrad III; Louis VII; Manuel I; Wendish Crusade

Seljuks, 1, 11–12, 28, 93, 96–97, 118, 156, 181, 203, **283–84,** *284,* 325. *See also* Great Seljuk, sultanate of the; Kilij Arslan; Manzikert, Battle of; Rum, sultanate of

Sergeants, 61, 106, 213, 214, **284–85,** 312, 323

Settlement and colonization, 1–3, 38–39, 86–89, 131, 152, 166, **285–89,** 334. *See also* Crusader states; Poulain

Seventh Crusade, 49, 80, 94–95, 95–96, 155, 200, **289–92,** *290;* cost of, 289

Shajar al-Durr, queen of Egypt, 203

Shepherds' Crusade, 45, 70, 187, **292–93**

Shia/Shias (Islamic branch), 150, 180–81, 227, 275, 283, **293–94.** *See also* Assassins; Fatimids

Shirkuh, uncle of Saladin, 228, 274

Sibylla, queen of Jerusalem, 35, 37, 74, 143–44, 172, 221, **294–95**

Sicily, 54, 61–62, 67, 101–2, 105, 115, 137, 138, 156, 157, 170, 190, 206–7, 227, 243, 245; Crusade of William II, 315–16; Richard I in Sicily, 265–66, 318. *See also* Charles of Anjou; William II

Sidon, port city of, 137, 138, 156, 206, 292

Siege warfare, 5, *14,* 26, 69, 70, **295–300;** at Antioch, 3, 11, 18, *27,* 43, 118–19, 191–92, 196, 229, 310, 333; at Constantinople, 6, 76, 77, 126, 127–28; at Damascus, 281; at Damietta, 15, 94, 95, 111–12, 333; at Edessa, 99, 192; at Jerusalem, 37, 119–20, *275;* at Lisbon, 282; at Nicaea, 118, 193, *193;* at Tyre, 36, 73. *See also* Acre

Simon of Montfort, crusader, 7–9, 162

Sinan ibn Salman, Assassin leader, 28

Sixth Crusade, 157, 191, 230, **300–303**

Slavery, 37, 97, 118, 119, 146, 175, 179, 182, 184, 192, 200, 209, 217, 242, 248, 280, **303–4,** 322, 333. *See also* Mamluks (slave soldiers); Prisoners

Solomon bar Simson, historian, 186

Song of Roland, The, 52, 64, 138, 149, 222, **304–5**

Spain, 13, 14, 16, 51, 68–70, 72–73, 84, *213.* See *also* Al-Andalus; Aragon; Castile; Cid, El; León; Military orders of Iberia; Moors; Reconquista; Santiago de Compostela; *Song of Roland*

Speyer, city of, 186

Stephen of Blois and Chartres, crusader, 18, 118, 120, 121, 138, 270, **305–7,** 333

Stephen of Burgundy, crusader, 120, 121

Sunnism/Sunnis (Islamic branch), 28, 105, 150, 180–81, 227, 275, 283, 293, 294, **307**

Sword Brothers (military order), 216

Syria-Palestine, definition of **307–8**

Tafurs, 52, 265, **309**

Tancred, crusader, 19, 31–32, 44, 88, 99, 119, 121, 212, 237, 254, **309–11**

Tancred of Lecce, claimant to Sicily, 265–66, 318

Taticius, Byzantine cavalry commander, 11, 18, 118, 119, 322. *See also* Turcopoles

Templars (military order), 29, 33, 41, 57–58, 81, 89, 90, 111, 133, 160, 198, *204,* 206, 214, 215, *256,* 285, 302, 303, 304, **311–13,** *312;* castles and churches of, 57, 58, 59, 101, 160, 215, 229–300, *256, 312,* 312, 313; influence on Iberian military orders, 215, 312; model for Teutonic Knights,

314; prisoners killed by Baybars, 300; prisoners killed by Saladin, 148, 209, 276; suppression of, 238–39, 313; *Turcopolier,* 322

Teutonic Knights (military order), 38–39, 57–58, 161, 214, 215, 216, 303, **314–15,** *314*

Thessalonica, kingdom of, 130–31, 221–22

Thibault IV, count of Champagne, 85–86

Third Crusade, 148, 153–54, 183, 209, 276, **315–20;** and the Jews, 187. *See also* Arsuf, Battle of; Jaffa, Battle of; Frederick I Barbarossa; Philip II; Richard I the Lionheart; Saladin

Thomas of Celano, biographer, 129, 130

Tiberias, city of, 148, 180, *332*

Toledo, city of, 257, 258

Tolerance and intolerance, 6–10, 27–29, 59–60, 96, 167, 168, 227, 245–46, 260, 288

Tomb of the Virgin, Church of the, *210*

Le Toron des Chevaliers, castle of, 57, 101

Tortosa, port city of, 121, 320

Toulouse, county of, 6–10

Transjordan, lordship of, 56, 86, 111, 182, 228, 263–65, 307, **320**

Trebuchet. *See* Artillery

Trinitarians (religious order), 304

Tripoli, city of, 121, 206, 209, 254–55, 276, 308, 315–16, **320–21,** *321*

Tripoli, county of, 88, 121, 228, 254, 308, **320–21,** *332;* estimated Latin population, 286–87; non-Frankish subjects, 287–89; resists Saladin, 320–21. *See also* Bertrand; Crusader states; Raymond IV of Saint-Gilles

Troyes, Council of (1129), 41, 94, 312

Truces, 58, 94, 109, 129, 235, 236; al-Adil and Aimery (1198), 138; al-Kamil and the Fifth Crusade (1221), 111, 113, 191, 236, 301, 302; al-Kamil and Frederick II (1229), 80, 85, 181, 191, 302; Baybars and the kingdom of Jerusalem (1272), 40, 100, 102, 205, 206; Charles of Anjou and the emir of Tunis (1270), 61–2, 102; Islamic theory, 189; Louis IX and Turan Shah (1250), 95, 292; Louis IX and Ayyubids of Syria (1254), 292; Richard I and Saladin (1192), 26, 38, 137, 178, 267–68, 274, 319; Saladin and the kingdom of Jerusalem (1185), 264, 276. *See also* Peace and Truce of God

Tunis, city of, 61–62, 64, 101–2, 105, 200

Turan Shah, Ayyubid sultan of Egypt, 203, 291, 292

Turcopoles, 58, 61, 118, 121, 148, 212, 214, 217, **322,** 330. *See also* Cavalry; Mercenaries; Taticius

Turks, 72, 141, 174, 207, 212, **322.** *See also* Khorezmians; Mamluks; Ottomans; Seljuks

Tyre, port city of, 36, 50, 73–74, 84, 133, 177, 183, 206, 276, 308, 315, **322–23.** *See also* Conrad of Montferrat; William of Tyre

Umayyads (dynasty), 1, 180, 293–94, 307; caliphate of Córdoba, 255–56

Urban II, Pope, 32, 43, 46, 72–73, 82, 95, 116, 117, 120, 141, 165, 169–70, 217, **325–26;** crusade motives and plans, 67, 103, 225, 233–34, 235, 237, 239, 253, 268–69, 284, 325, 327

Urban, IV, Pope, 185

Usamah ibn Munqidh, historian, 65, 152, 246

Venetian Crusade, 50, 84, 108

Venetians, 2, 5, 36, 62, 77–79, 83–84, 90, 109, 120, *124, 131,* 199, 222, *241,* 243, 297, 315, 323. *See also* Dandolo, Enrico; Fourth Crusade

Visions, 4, 18, 64, 229, 237, 293. *See also* Lance, Holy; Prophecy

Vow, crusader's, 45, 51, 80, 82, 93, 108–9, 161, 164, 168, 234, 250, **327–28;** vow redemption, 81, 109, 168, 199, 328, 333

Walter Sansavoir, crusader, 117, 237, **329**

Weapons, hand, 60–61, **329–31**

Welf IV, duke of Bavaria, 120, 121, 279

Wendish Crusade, 38, 42, 104, 217, 279, 282–83

William, marquis IV of Montferrat, 221–22

William II, king of Sicily, 170, 171, 227, 265–66, 315–16, 318

William III (the Elder) of Montferrat, crusader, 73, 221, 295

William IX of Aquitaine, crusader, 120, 121, 164

William Longsword of Montferrat, 35, 221, 295

William of Tyre, archbishop and historian, 5, 34, 94, 102, 143, 152, 154, 178, 184, 185, 211, 212, 261, 322, **331–32;** critic of the military orders, 214

Women, 65, 102, **332–34,** *332;* active in crusade finance and recruitment, 333; in battle 96, 113, 225, 333; as queens, 334; rape of, 242, 248; rights of wives, 166, 168, 203, 214, *248,* 333–34; as settlers and colonists, 334; as slaves, 121, 242, 248; stereotypical images of, 102, 225, *328,* 333. *See also notable women by name*

Worms, city of, 185, 186

Xerigordon, fortified town of, 329

York, city of, 187

Zangi, Imad ad-Din, governor of Mosul and Aleppo, 93, 99, 222, 227, 279, 284, **335**

Zangids (dynasty), 151, 222–23

Zara, port city of, 84, 109, 116, 122, 124–26, 199, 241

Zelus fidei, crusade bull, 80

About the Author

ALFRED J. ANDREA (Ph.D., Cornell University) is Professor Emeritus of Medieval History at The University of Vermont. Additionally, he has served as Eli Lilly Visiting Professor at the University of Puget Sound (1978–1979) and Distinguished Scholar-in-Residence in Liberal Studies at the University of Louisville (2001). His research and publications center on the Fourth Crusade, the schism between Eastern and Western Christianity, and global history before 1500. His most recent books include *Contemporary Sources for the Fourth Crusade* (2000) and *The Human Record: Sources of Global History,* Vol. I, 5th ed. (2004).